E-LEARNING, EXPERIENCES AND FUTURE

Edited by
SAFEEULLAH SOOMRO

E-Learning, Experiences and Future

Edited by Safeeullah Soomro

Republished by InTech

Janeza Trdine 9, 51000 Rijeka, Croatia

Technical Editor Maja Jakobovic

Cover Designer Dino Smrekar

Additional hard copies can be obtained from orders@intechopen.com

E-learning, experiences and future,
Edited by Safeeullah Soomro
p. cm.
ISBN 978-953-307-092-6

For EU product safety concerns:
IN TECH d.o.o., Prolaz Marije Krucifikse Kozulić 3, 51000 Rijeka, Croatia,
info@intechopen.com or visit our website at intechopen.com.

Meet the editor

Dr. Safeeullah Soomro received B.Sc (Hons) computer Science (1996) and M.Sc in Computer Science (1997) from University of Sindh, Jamshoro (www.usindh.edu.pk) Pakistan. He defended his PhD in 2007 from Graz University of Technology, Austria. He carried out research at Graz University of Technology (www.tugraz.at), Austria during 2003 - 2007. He has been involved in research and teaching since 1998. He has taught in different institutes of Pakistan. His research interest revolves around software debugging, formal verification and software testing. In particular, He is interested in applying model-based diagnosis and reasoning techniques to the field of automated software debugging of java programs. Furthermore, He is interested to carry out research in the formal methods. He is author of several national and international publications in conference proceedings, books and journals. He is a reviewer and committee member of different international and national conferences. He has more than 12 years of experience in teaching and research. He is an approved supervisor of Higher Education Commission (HEC) Pakistan and can supervise PhD Students. He is a member of IEEE, IEEE Computer Society, ISOC and SUCSA. Previously He supervised MS students from top ranking university in Pakistan. He is editor of three books and these are recognized internationally.

Preface

Basically e-learning is new way of providing knowledge to peoples to interact with web based systems which is need of current world. E-learning based systems received tremendous popularity in the world since this decade. Currently most of the universities are using e-bases systems to provide interactive systems to students which can make communication fast to grow up the knowledge in every field of study. Many advantages comes to adopt e-learning systems like paper less environment, pay less to instructors, students can access systems from any part of world, advanced computer trainings provided at homes and access any material using web. In advanced countries e-learning systems play major role in an economy to produce productive output in the industries without having paid huge amount for personal staff that are locating physically and also provide big advantage to peoples of developed countries who can not attend physically courses neither afford experts in a professional fields. This is big achievement of e-learning bases systems to promote education online.

This book is consisting of 24 chapters which are focusing on the basic and applied research regarding elearning systems. Authors made efforts to provide theoretical as well as practical approaches to solve open problems through their elite research work. This book increases knowledge in the following topics such as e-learning, e-Government, Data mining in e-learning based systems, LMS systems, security in elearning based systems, surveys regarding teachers to use e-learning systems, analysis of intelligent agents using e-learning, assessment methods for e-learning and barriers to use of effective e-learning systems in education.

Basically this book is an open platform for creative discussion for future e-learning based systems which are essential to understand for the students, researchers, academic personals and industry related people to enhance their capabilities to capture new ideas and provides valuable solution to an international community.

The editor and authors of this book hope that this book will provide valuable platform for the new researchers and students who are interested to carry research in the e-learning based systems. Finally we are thankful to I-Tech Education and publishing organization which provides the best platform to integrate researchers of whole world though this published book.

Dr. Safeeullah Soomro

Yanbu University College,

Kingdom of Saudi Arabia

Contents

Preface VII

1. E-Learning Indicators: A Multidimensional Model For Planning Developing And Evaluating E-Learning Software Solutions 001
Bekim Fetaji and Majlinda Fetaji

2. Barriers to Effective use of Information Technology in Science Education at Yanbu Kingdom of Saudi Arabia 035
Abdulkarem Eid S. Al-Alwani and Safeeullah Soomro

3. The Use of Multi-Agents' Systems in e-Learning Platforms 047
Tomasz Marcin Orzechowski

4. Quality Metrics of an Integrated E-Learning System – students' perspective 071
Ksenija Klasnić, Jadranka Lasić-Lazić and Sanja Seljan

5. Intelligent Interaction Support for e-Learning 095
Takashi Yukawa and Yoshimi Fukumura

6. Supporting Technologies for Synchronous E-learning 111
Juan C. Granda, Christian Uría, Francisco J. Suárez and Daniel F. García

7. Bayesian Agent in e-Learning 129
Maomi Ueno

8. Data Mining for Instructional Design, Learning and Assessment 147
Lluís Vicent and Xavier Gumara

9. A learning style – driven architecture build on open source LMS's infrastructure for creation of psycho-pedagogically – 'savvy' personalized learning paths 163
Kerkiri Al. Tania , Paleologou Angela-M.,
Konetas Dimitris and Chatzinikolaou Kostantinos

10. E-learning in information accessibility of disabled assistanttechnology 189
Chunlian Li Yusun

11. Application of Data-Mining Technology on E-Learning Material Recommendation 213
Feng-Jung Liu and Bai-Jiun Shih

12. Loosely-Tied Distributed Architecture for Highly Scalable E-Learning System 229
Gierłowski and Nowicki

13. Evolution of Collaborative Learning Environments based on Desktop Computer to Mobile Computing: A Model-Based Approach 261
Ana I. Molina, William J. Giraldo, Francisco Jurado, Miguel A. Redondo and Manuel Ortega

14. From the discovery of students access patterns in e-learning including web 2.0 resources to the prediction and enhancement of students outcome 275
Raquel Hijón-Neira and Ángel Velázquez-Iturbide

15. Dependable e-learning systems 295
Ali Al-Dahoud, Marek Woda and Tomasz Walkowiak

16. Ontology-driven Annotation and Access of Educational Video Data in E-learning 305
Aijuan Dong, Honglin Li and Baoying Wang

17. When a robot turns into a totem: The RoboBeggar case 327
Gaetano La Russa, Erkki Sutinen and Johannes C. Cronje

18. Virtual patients as a practical realisation of the e-learning idea in medicine 345
Andrzej A. Kononowicz and Inga Hege

19. Data Warehouse Technology and Application in Data Centre Design for E-government 371
Xuanzi Hu

20. The Emergence of the Intelligent Government in the Second Society 385
Dennis de Kool and Johan van Wamelen

21. A Lightweight SOA-based Collaboration Framework for European Public Sector 397
Adomas Svirskas, Jelena Isačenkova and Refik Molva

22. Spatial Aided Decision-making System for E-Government 413
Liang WANG, Rong ZHAO, Bin LI, Jiping LIU and Qingpu ZHANG

23. Evaluating Local E-Government: A Comparative Study of Greek Prefecture Websites 441
Prodromos Yannas and Georgios Lappas

E-Learning Indicators: A Multidimensional Model For Planning Developing And Evaluating E-Learning Software Solutions

[1]Bekim Fetaji and [2]Majlinda Fetaji
[1, 2] South East European University, (Computer Sciences Faculty) Macedonia

1. Introduction

Many current e-learning initiatives follow the "one-size-fits-all" approach just offering some type of Learning Management System (LMS) to learners or Learning Content Management System (LCMS). Typically, this approach is related to lack of knowledge of the learner audience or factors influencing that audience and e-learning project overall and therefore fail to provide satisfactory support in the decision making process (Fetaji, 2007a).

In order to address this issue, an approach dealing with e-learning indicators is proposed, assessed, measured and evaluated. The proposed E-learning Indicators Methodology enables successful planning, comparison and evaluation of different e-learning projects. It represents an empirical methodology that gives concrete results expressed through numbers that could be analysed and later used to compare and conclude its e-learning efficiency. With the application of this methodology in e-learning projects it is more likely to achieve better results and higher efficiency as well as higher Return on Investment ROI.

The purpose of e-learning indicators was to raise the awareness of the factors influencing e-learning project in order to identify the nature of obstacles being faced by e-learners. This research argues that if such obstacles could be recognized early in the process of planning and development of e-learning initiatives then the actions that remedy the obstacles can be taken on time. We believe that the absence of appropriate on-time actions is one of the main reasons for the current unsatisfactory results in many e-learning projects.

The e-learning indicators approach is a multidimensional model used in planning, developing, evaluating, and improving an e-learning initiative. Thus, the model comprises e-learning projects as iterative development processes where at each iteration step appropriate actions to improve the initiative outcomes can be taken. The iteration steps of this development process include:

- Planning phase with the initial measurement of e-learning indicators. The obtained results influence all the other phases.
- Design phase where (group or so called "collective") personalisation issues and pedagogical and instructional techniques and aspects are addressed.

- Implementation phase where a number of e-learning experiments are conducted based on the results from the previous phases.
- Evaluation phase to obtain precise results of the initiative outcomes.
- Analysis phase where guidelines and recommendations are written down.

The proposed model defines 18 indicators that were practically applied in a number of case studies including their application with Angel LMS and a number of self developed and implemented e-learning interactive tools.

E-learning indicators have been defined with help of different focus groups, realised literature review and a web based survey of academic staff and students in the framework of South East European University. In addition, the approach was revised closely with experts in the field during participation in several research projects (mentioned in acknowledgement).

The experiences from these projects show that a more successful e-learning is not possible only if a generic approach or generic guidelines for the learners are applied. Rather, individual learning services are needed in supporting learners according to their personal preference profile.

However, although not the focus of the research because of the interconnection with the above identified issues several projects and research initiatives that deal with personalization have been shortly reviewed. The reviewed projects are the OPen Adaptive Learning Environment (OPAL), (Dagger, et al 2002) and ADELE-Adaptive e-Learning with Eye Tracking (Mödritscher, et al 2006). The OPAL research shows personalization as difficult to achieve and "… are often expensive, both from a time and financial perspective, to develop and maintain." (Dagger, et al 2002). Therefore, a conclusion is drown that learner personalisation should not bee addressed at to finely grained level. Typically, personalisation at that starting level is not practical based on the findings of OPAL project (Dagger, et al 2002) and since it has too include all of those learners preferences that change each time the learner uses the system clearly does not represent a constant factor that can be addressed (Fetaji, 2007g). Instead, a recommendation is to use the defined approach with e-learning indicators as starting point when developing an e-learning initiative. Then after the measurements the learners are divided into groups so called "collectives" (in Universities these are the departmental levels) were personalisation is offered to the specifics of the collectives majority primarily based on learning style categorization and type of learner they are (indicator 4, 4). We have adopted the Felder-Silverman model for learning style categorization (Felder, 1993). After that learner personalisation can be designed and offered tailored to each collective (Fetaji, 2007g). Furthermore, based on the measurements of these e-learning indicators a design of a sustainable e-learning initiative can be supported. Each e-learning initiative is unique and involves specifics that can not be taken under consideration in the form of "one-size-fits-all" solution.

However evaluating e-learning indicators in the planning phase is only the first step in more successful e-learning. E-learning indicators can be used in other phases as well in particular in evaluating different e-learning initiatives in conjunction with ELUAT methodology to assess e-learning effectiveness. Comparison of different projects can be realised comparing e-learning indicators measurements in conjunction with the evaluated e-learning effectiveness (how effective they have shown measured using the ELUAT methodology) (Fetaji, 2007g).

2. E-Learning Indicators Methodology

E-learning indicators are defined as the important concepts and factors that are used to communicate information about the level of e-learning and used to make management decisions when planning an e-learning strategy for an institution or University according to the study of (Fetaji et al 2007a). The purpose was to raise the awareness of the factors and concepts influencing e-learning in order to enhance learning and identify the nature of obstacles being faced by e-learners and therefore proposed is a methodological approach in developing any e-learning initiative. Because there are too many factors, personalization and specifics related to each situation and circumstances it is considered that would be wrong offering one size solution for all.

It is of great importance to have standardised guide of e-learning indicators accepted by scientific community to be able to compare and to evaluate the different initiatives regarding e-learning in a standardised manner.

In order to define and assess the e-learning indicators the data have been gathered from interviews with e-learning specialists, 2 focus groups (one student and one instructors), web based survey of academic staff and students and literature review of similar previous research work found at (Bonk, 2004). The web based survey was realised through questionnaire that was developed in three cycles. In the first cycle the questions were developed based on the e-learning indicators. For most of the e-learning indicators there was just one question to cover it, while for some 2 (two) or more questions. At the beginning developed were more questions but after thorough consultations with survey experts shortened and come up with 23 questions. In the second cycle the developed survey questionnaire was tested on a 2 different focus groups. One group consisting of students and the other group from instructors. After analyses of the survey data they were presented to the focus groups and confronted to them how much do they agree and consider this results as realistic and accurate. The initial response was that although the survey captures in substantial level the real situation there were a lot of discussions especially on the student focus group regarding the appropriateness of the survey questions. In discussion with both of the focus groups most of the questions have changed according to the discussions and proposals of the group. In the third cycle both of the focus group were filled the new survey and after the survey data were given to them both of the focus groups agreed that it really gives an accurate clear picture of the participants.

The survey was designed following the rule of thumb for all communications: Audience + Purpose = Design. This survey was divided into 18 (eighteen) sections to cover al the e-learning indicators previously defined and had 23 (twenty three) questions in total. It was communicated to the participants and provided as link in the message board of the eservice system of the University.

As e-learning indicators defined are: (1) learner education background; (2) computing skills level (3) type of learners they are, (4) their learning style and multiple intelligence, (5) obstacles they face in e-learning (e-learning barriers), (6) attention, (7) content (suitability, format preferences), (8) instructional design, (9) organizational specifics, (10) preferences of e-learning logistics; (11) preferences of e-learning design; (12) technical capabilities available to respondents; (13) collaboration; (14) accessibility available to respondents; (15) motivation, (16) attitudes and interest; and (17) performance-self-efficacy (the learner sense their effectiveness in e-learning environment); (18) learning outcomes. Recommendation is to use the defined e-learning indicators as starting point when developing e-learning initiative and based on the measurements of these e-learning indicators to tailor the specifics of e-learning. Each e-learning initiative should measure the provided indicators and based on them to design and build their e-learning sustainability.

3. Research Methodology

The research methodology used was a combination of qualitative and quantitative research as well as comparative analyses of factors influencing e-learning. Background research consisted of an in depth literature review of e-learning. The background research consisted of analyses of e-learning trends, e-learning technologies and solutions, e-learning standards, learning theories, concepts and factors that influence e-learning. Then grounded theory research was realised through exploratory research to determine the best research design and then constructive research was undertaken to build the software solution followed by empirical research to describe accurately the interaction between the learners and the system being observed. The data for this research was gathered from research interviews with e-learning specialists and participants, focus group and a web based survey as well as printed hard copy survey of academic staff and students.

In order to develop a systematic methodology, either substantive or formal, about improving and enhancing e-learning by addressing the deficiencies from the findings and in this manner to contribute in enhancing e-learning effectiveness. In order to achieve this, the following research objectives have been tried to be addressed:

- Review key authoritative literature on e-learning trends, e-learning standards, technologies and e-learning systems provided as e-learning solutions, and evaluation of e-learning effectiveness in order to provide a thorough understanding of e-learning in general and associated knowledge dissemination.
- Discuss the advantages and disadvantages of different approaches to e-learning solutions.
- Analyses of different e-learning environments and solutions
- Asses, measure and evaluate concepts and factors influencing e-learning defined as e-learning indicators
- Design, develop and conduct experiments in order to asses the best modelling approach to developing e-learning software solutions
- Connect e-learning indicators with each e-learning software solution approach and learning theory and design
- Analyse and discuss the data gathered from the experiments
- Conclude and deliver recommendations for enhanced learning and future improvements.

Key variables and themes that have been studied are: students needs analyses, usage environment feasibility analyses, e-learning indicators, e-content and learning processes issues, feasibility analyses of authoring issues, assessment of e-learning effectiveness, and discussion of the purpose and evaluation of results of the research and proposed recommendations for e-content and e-learning processes issues, applications specifics and requirements in correlation with the environment and situation of the Communication Sciences and Technologies Faculty at south East European University, accessibility and learning specifics based on learners needs, deployment, testing and evaluation of the solution.

Interviewed and realised direct observation of students as program implementation case study for the three subjects: Advanced Elective course "Object Oriented Programming in Java" and the two core courses "Software Engineering" and "Algorithms and Data Structures". There implemented the solutions proposed under the part of the research study on e-content issues and e-learning processes.
Developed is a novel e-learning indicators-(ELI) model to be used for developing information retrieval courseware's by concentrating on previously assessed e-learning indicators. Secondly, the research is conveying the need for close correlation of software development and e-learning pedagogy. Recommend that technology should adapt to theories of learning and e-learning indicators assessed earlier. This process modelling based on e-learning indicators should be used as guidelines in similar developments.
A pilot study was conducted on e-learning interactive courseware applying network analyses method in order to find the critical activities and assess the risks. The main focus and aim of research was set on software development proposed and based upon the e-learning indicators and the design of the courseware in compliance with theories of learning and didactical pedagogical approach. For the assessment of e-learning effectiveness proposed a methodology, called ELUAT (E-learning Usability Attributes Testing), for which developed an inspection technique the Predefined Evaluation Tasks (PET), which describe the activities to be performed during inspection in the form of a predefined tasks, measuring previously assessed usability attributes.

4. The Experiments

In order to investigate the implementation strategy and try to address the above identified issues 7 (seven) experimental case studies were developed and evaluated.
The experiments have been separated in 3 (three) groups based on their research nature and investigation focus. The first 2 (two) experiments concentrate on e-learning indicators and their usage in planning as well as evaluating e-learning projects. In the next 4 (four) experiments various e-learning software solutions as interactive tools are designed and developed in order to test several hypotheses as well as to investigate the new e-learning indicators methodology approach in developing e-learning software solutions and at the same time to investigate instructional strategies discussed and reviewed earlier. The final experiment is devised in order to investigate and analyse the e-content and attention correlation and conjunction in the e-learning process. Each case study experiment is tailored based on the information collected in the first step, evaluated e-learning indicators.
The technological part of the research involved analyses of software engineering issues in designing e-learning environments. Proposed is ELI (E-Learning Indicators) model - as methodology for developing e-learning software solutions (Fetaji, 2007e).
Further, the experiments also investigated applications of different instructional techniques and pedagogical learning models and how they are reflected in the software development process according to different devised scenarios in supporting instructional strategy. An analysis of Project, Problem, Inquiry-based and Task based learning instructional techniques and their appropriateness for different scenarios was realized. In the final step, each experiment and its underlying pedagogical model was once more evaluated using the evaluation methodology developed for this purpose. The developed methodology is called ELUAT (E-Learning Usability Attributes Testing) through the PET (Predefined Evaluation

Tasks) inspection technique (Fetaji, 2007c). The developed 4 (four) e-learning software solutions as case study experiments were created under two research projects realised in a time framework of more than two years and later evaluated:

- Intranet Gateway research project and
- E-Learning Framework research project,

The e-learning software solutions developed for the needs of the experiments are:

- XHTML and XML e-learning Interactive tool,
- E-learning interactive mathematical tool,
- Information Retrieval Courseware system-Intranet Gateway.
- Online Dictionary of Computer Science terms and nomenclatures.

The results of this research show that e-learning indicators approach is of primary importance (Fetaji, 2007e). Having a standardised set of e-learning indicators accepted by scientific community enables comparison and evaluation of different e-learning initiatives and their e-learning projects in a systematic manner. Moreover this approach combined with experimental approach to e-learning brings new insights into the specifics of e-learning that might help in increasing the learning outcomes, especially knowledge transfer. Therefore, conclusion is that no new systems are needed but a series of experiments has to be conducted to see what does and does not work in a particular situation and to provide guidelines and recommendations for that situation.

Furthermore, an investigation of issues in authoring e-learning content (e-content) was realised. The main purpose was to effectively identify the vehicles into increased knowledge dissemination and efficient knowledge transfer and thus improve the overall e-learning process. Preparing quality e-content delivered digitally is probably the major aspect for long term success of any e-learning endeavour. It is the content, however, that learners care for and judge how much they learn from it. Therefore we have identified and addressed most important authoring issues by analyzing different courses using an Learning Management System.

5. Data Collection and Analysis

Depending from the Software Lifecycle used for each e-learning software solutions developed in particular for the given experiment used is the ELUAT methodology and PET testing as described thoroughly at (Fetaji et al 2007a). Questionnaires, surveys, focus groups, usability testing and other software testing groups were used. Groups of students filled out different surveys discussing e-learning indicators, barriers to distance education and usability surveys of e-learning software solutions modelled and developed. The return rate for the surveys for each experiment was different and the highest was for distance education with 64.89 %, (The distance education program at the moment has 81undergraduate full time students, and 13 part time students, or in totals 94 students) while for the e-learning indicators the response rate was 9.7 % (There were in total 701 student surveys filled. The University at the moment of the research survey has 6.386 undergraduate and 188 postgraduate full time students, and 643 part time students, or in total 7217 students). The majority of the participants (63.8%) have used the e-learning software solutions discussed. Ten percent of the participants took fewer than all of the courses mentioned previously since Object Oriented Programming in Java was an elective subject. Large amount of data was collected and used from the literature reviews and inputs from other related projects.

Several statistical procedures were conduct for data analysis. First, the zero-order correlations were computed among all variables. The aim of this operation is to have an initial test of whether there were relationships among the variables. The interaction of technology with teaching or social presence was considered if including those items would increase the power of the regression model substantially. The standard multiprogression procedures were conducted with course subjective satisfaction through the perceived learning outcome, learning engagement assessed through time to learn and time of performance as dependent variables. All assumptions of normality, usability, of residuals were checked in those regression analyses. In order to handle those data the triangulation technique from Dumas and Redish (1999) was used, were we look at all data at the same time to see how the different data supports each other.

6. E-Learning Indicators Specification and Analyses

(1) Learner education background together with his cultural background is set as indicator since it is a direct factor that is associated and impacts e-learning. According to Gatling et al, (2005), students today come from a variety of cultural backgrounds and educational experiences outside of the traditional classroom. How do students construct meaning from prior knowledge and connect it with the new experiences? Based on this facts and interviews with e-learning specialist It was set it as important indicator.
(2) Computing skills level of the learner is set as indicator since it directly influences the way e-learning is conducted with the use of Information and communication technologies (ICT) and use of computers and the computing skills requirements are essential in learning. "As we move toward the 21st century, anyone who is not "computer literate" will find themselves at a disadvantage when competing in the job market." (Johnson, Gatling, Hill, 1997).
The indicator (3) type of learners they are depends primarily on the balance in the two dimensions of the Learning Style scale model formulated by Richard M. Felder and Linda K. Silverman of North Carolina State University according to Felder & Soloman (n.d) based on four dimensions (active/reflective, sensing/intuitive, visual/verbal, and sequential/global). According to Felder & Soloman (n.d) "students preferentially take in and process information in different ways: by seeing and hearing, reflecting and acting, reasoning logically and intuitively, analyzing and visualizing, steadily and in fits and starts. Teaching methods also vary. Some instructors lecture, others demonstrate or lead students to self-discovery; some focus on principles and others on applications; some emphasize memory and others understanding. Active learners tend to retain and understand information best by doing something active with it, discussing or applying it or explaining it to others. Reflective learners prefer to think about it quietly first. Sensing learners tend to like learning facts; intuitive learners often prefer discovering possibilities and relationships. Visual learners remember best what they see: pictures, diagrams, flow charts, time lines, films, and demonstrations. Verbal learners get more out of word, written and spoken explanations. Sequential learners tend to gain understanding in linear steps, with each step following logically from the previous one. Global learners tend to learn in large jumps, absorbing material almost randomly without seeing connections, and then suddenly getting it". Therefore assessing and knowing the learning audience is crucial in order to know whom to support and there is an extensive need for this input data in order for the e-learning initiative to be successful and effective. Then after the measurements the learners

are divided into groups so called"collectives" were personalisation is offered to the specifics of the collective majority (in Universities these are the departmental levels) primarily based on learning style categorization and type of learner they are according Felder-Silverman model for learning style categorization (Felder, 1993).

The importance of the type of learner and (4) their learning style and multiple intelligence is for the both sides: instructor and student. For instructors it is of importance since it reflects the preferences of Learning style in their teaching and delivery style to students. We advise to tend to use each learning style to teach also in a delivery type suited to other types of learners and truing to bring it closer and generalize to include all the types using visualization and verbal communications, as well as other communication tools. According to Tomas Armstrong (n.d.) Multiple Intelligences are eight different ways to demonstrate intellectual ability. 1) Linguistic intelligence ("word smart"), 2) Logical-mathematical intelligence ("number/reasoning smart"); 3) Spatial intelligence ("picture smart"); 4) Bodily-Kinesthetic intelligence ("body smart"); 5) Musical intelligence ("music smart"); 6) Interpersonal intelligence ("people smart"); 7) Intrapersonal intelligence ("self smart"); 8) Naturalist intelligence ("nature smart"). Again assessing the audience and having this input data is very important e-learning indicator in planning and developing e-learning initiative.

The indicator (5) obstacles they face in e-learning (e-learning barriers) is set as important based on interviews and speaking with e-learning specialists. Each e-learning project has different barriers and they are specified as learner input and depend from a situation.

Assessing what the learner audience faces as barrier is crucial in achieving effective e-learning. Indicator (6) attention is set as very important. Attention cues when the learners begin to feel some mental workload, Ueno, M. (2004).

(7) e-content (suitability, format preferences), e-learning content (e-content) considered as vehicle of the e-learning process and knowledge construction. The quality of the virtual learning environment is mainly depending on the quality of the presented e-learning content. Fetaji, B. (2006).

Indicator (8) Instructional design has gained significant prominence in e-learning for a number of compelling reasons. One of them is the possibility for instructional design to systematically address the need for creating and evaluating students' learning experience as well as learning outcome. The other is instructional design can help faculty to focus on using the appropriate format and tools for the appropriate learning objectives. Fetaji, B. (2006).

Indicator (9) organizational specifics - every instituion has its specific business processes that influences and impacts e-learning, Galotta et. al. (2004)

(10) preferences of e-learning logistics - targeted at learners of different experience levels and organizational background/hierarchy, based on the ELA model-the European Logistics Association (ELA), (Zsifkovits, 2003). The following 7 (seven) variables have been set as priority in determining viable learning environment and its e-learning logistics: 1) Interoperability; 2) Pricing; 3) Performance; 4) Content development; 5) Communication tools; 6) Student Involvement Tools; 7) Evolving technology.

(11) indicator preferences of e-learning design; designing instruction that acknowledges that students differ in their learning preferences and abilities and that instruction needs to be flexible to address these differences, (Kumar 2006).

The next indicators (12) technical capabilities available to respondents (13) collaboration; (14) accessibility available to respondents, ares defined as important indicators in discussions with e-learning specialist and experts. They represent the essential influencing

factors on e-learning mentioned in different studies such as (Coleman, B., Neuhauser, J. & Fisher, M. 2004).
(15) Motivation is essential to learning and performances, particularly in e-learning environments where learners must take an active role in their learning by being self directed (Lee, 2000).
(16) Attitudes and interest. A review of studies on attitudes toward learning and using information technology in education has revealed that most studies have shown that students' attitudes toward technology are critical, (Liu, et. al. 2004);
(17) performance: self-efficacy (the learner sense their effectiveness in e-learning environment); Self-efficacy refers to people beliefs about their capabilities to perform a task successfully at designated levels, (Bandura, 1997).
(18) According to Jenkins, A. and (Unwin, 1996) learning outcomes are defined as statements of what is expected that a student will be able to do as a result of a learning activity. Learning outcomes are usually expressed as knowledge transfer, skills, or attitudes (Unwin, 1996). Therefore, it is a very important indicator in planning, designing and evaluating e-learning.

7. E-Learning Indicators Assessment, Measurement and Evaluation

7.1 Definition

E-learning indicators have been defined with help of different focus groups, realised literature review and a web based survey of academic staff and students in the framework of South East European University as well as revised closely with experts in the field during participation in several research projects. In order to investigate e-learning indicators in planning phase of e-learning projects a case study was initiated in order to asses, measure and evaluate e-learning indicators a web based survey has been used. The survey was designed following the rule of thumb for all communications: Audience + Purpose = Design. The survey was divided into 18 (eighteen) sections to cover al the e-learning indicators previously defined. It was communicated to the participants and provided as survey in Angel LMS. It was offered to two different department from two different Universities. One using angel LMs as e-learning platform and the other using Moodle as learning platform. There were in total 701 student surveys filled. The answer rate was 30.48%. There were 701 filled survey, and the total number of students in using Angel platform was 2300. The data was collected using Angel Learning Management System and further analyzed in Excel. The second e-learning project that is using Moodle as e-learning platform was focused on computer Science Faculty and in total 44 surveys were filled and the answer rate was 9.78%.

7.2 Analyses of indicator: Self efficacy in e-learning

Please rate your self efficacy in e-learning. How effective and efficient you are?

Bad	Not so good	OK	Good	Very good
□ 1	□ 2	□ 3	□ 4	□ 5

7.2.1 ANGEL LMS - Findings for indicator: Self efficacy in e-learning

Most of the respondents, 43.7% have rated them self's as good their efficacy in e-learning. While 24.1 % have rated them self's as very good.

On the other hand 1% of them were not satisfied with the e-learning environment and their efficacy and have rated them self's as bad, 4.7 % not so good, and 26.5% rated them self's as OK, meaning they are partially satisfied with the e-learning system and their effectiveness in it.

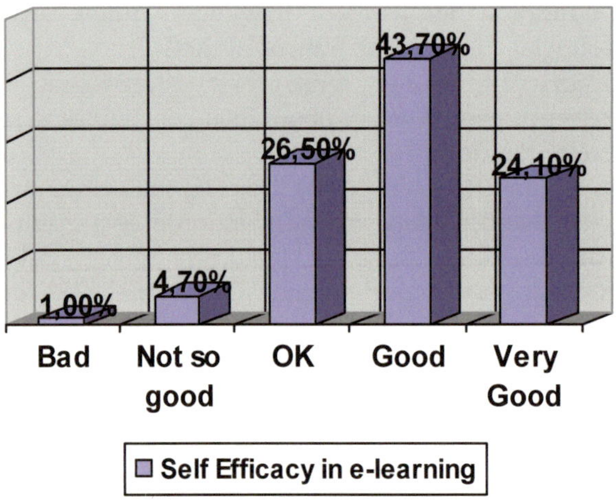

Fig. 1. ANGEL LMS - Findings for indicator

7.2.2 Moodle LMS- Findings for indicator: Self efficacy in e-learning

Most of the respondents, 33.17%, have rated them self's as good their efficacy in e-learning. While 26.54 % have rated them self's as very good.

On the other hand 1.12% of them were not satisfied with the e-learning environment and their efficacy and have rated them self's as bad, 9.7 % not so good, and 29.47% rated them self's as OK, meaning they are partially satisfied with the e-learning system and their effectiveness in it.

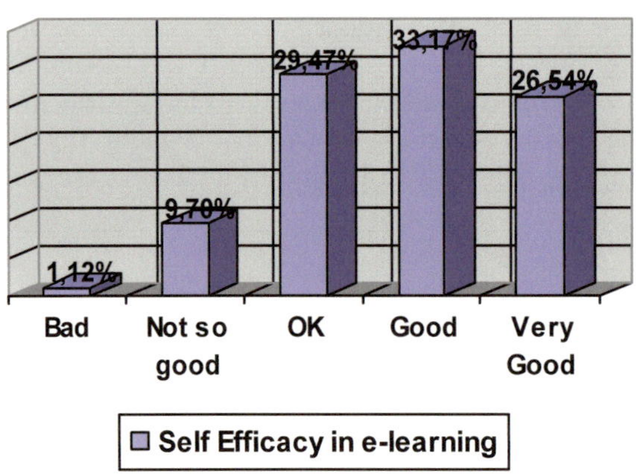

Fig. 2. Moodle LMS - Findings for indicator

7.2.3 Discussion of the Findings for Indicator: Self Efficacy in E-learning

As Bandura (1997) defined it, self-efficacy refers to people beliefs about their capabilities whether or not they can perform successfully at designated levels using the e-learning environment. From the analyses of the findings it indicates that there is an increase in student's achievement after their engagement in an e-learning environment. Overall 94.3% of the students in Angel and 89.18 % of students in MOODLE are satisfied with their self-efficacy and have shown progress moving in the new e-learning environment from the traditional classroom. However there are 5.7 % of the students (ANGEL) and 10.82 % (MOODLE) that are not satisfied with their achievement. The main reason among others for this result is identified in the usability issues of the two offered e-learning systems. Other reasons will be discussed in conclusions. However in general students rated their self efficacy as better in using ANGEL compared to MOODLE.

7.3 Analyses of Indicator: Type of Learner

What type of learner you are? (Please Circle one option: a) or b) for each row)

a) ACTIVE or **b)** REFLECTIVE Learner

(Explanations: Active learners tend to retain and understand information best by doing something active with it--discussing or applying it or explaining it to others. Reflective learners prefer to think about it quietly first.)

7.3.1 ANGEL LMS - Findings for Indicator: Type of Learner

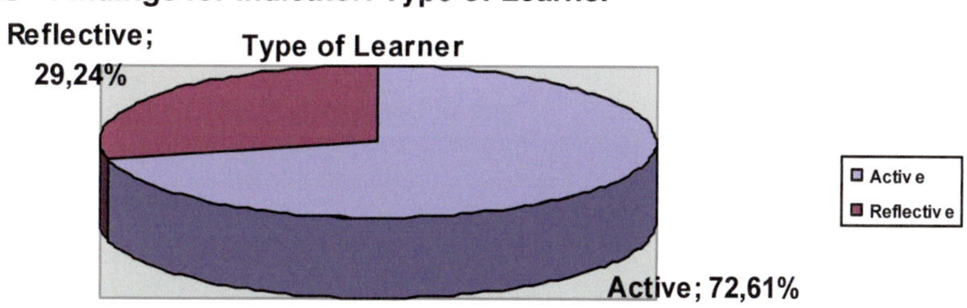

Fig. 3. ANGEL LMS - Findings for indicator

On the whole, 72.61 % of respondents rated them self's as Active learners while the others 29.24 % as Reflective learners.

7.3.2 MOODLE - Findings for indicator: Type of Learner

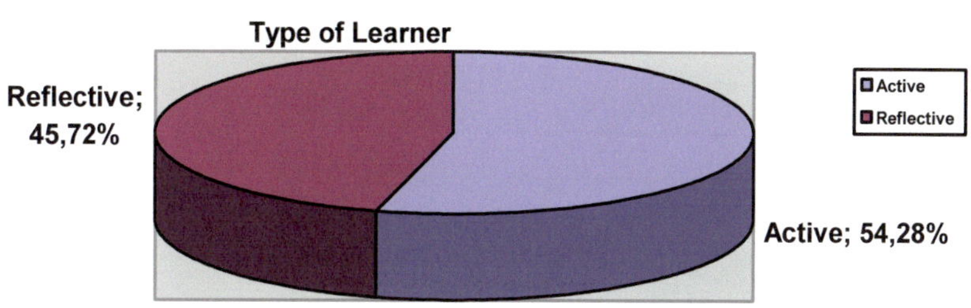

Fig. 4. Moodle LMS - Findings for indicator

On the whole, 54.28 % of respondents rated them self's as Active learners while the others 45.72 % as Reflective learners.

7.3.3 Discussion of the findings for indicator: Type of Learner

The indicator (3) type of learners they are depends primarily on the balance in the two dimensions of the Learning Style scale model formulated by Richard M. Felder and Linda K. Silverman according to Felder & Soloman (n.d). The findings indicate that students in using ANGEL are primarily of the Active type of learner 72.61% in comparison to 29.24% Reflective type of a learner. The students in using MOODLE are primarily of type reflective learners 54.28% in comparison to 45.72 %. These findings indicate that the structure and curriculum of the studies should change and embrace this type of learner more by preferring and choosing a hands on approach in comparison to the theoretical approach for the learners using ANGEL and the opposite for the learners using MOODLE were learners should be provided more reading materials and solved examples so they can reflect this and learn by doing this.

7.4.3 Analyses of indicator: Type of Learner

a) SENSING or b) INTUITIVE Learner

(Explanations: Sensing learners tend to like learning facts; intuitive learners often prefer discovering possibilities and relationships.)

7.4.3.1 ANGEL LMS - Findings for indicator: Type of Learner

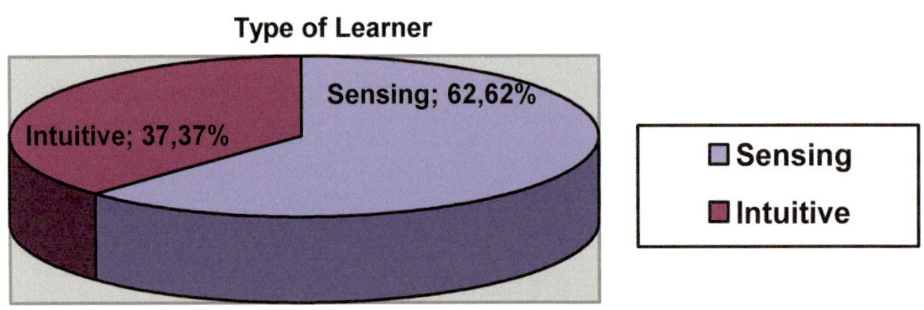

Fig. 5. ANGEL LMS - Findings for indicator

On the whole, 62.62 % of respondents rated them self's as Sensing learners while the others 37.37% as Intuitive learners.

7.4.3.2 MOODLE - Findings for indicator: Type of Learner

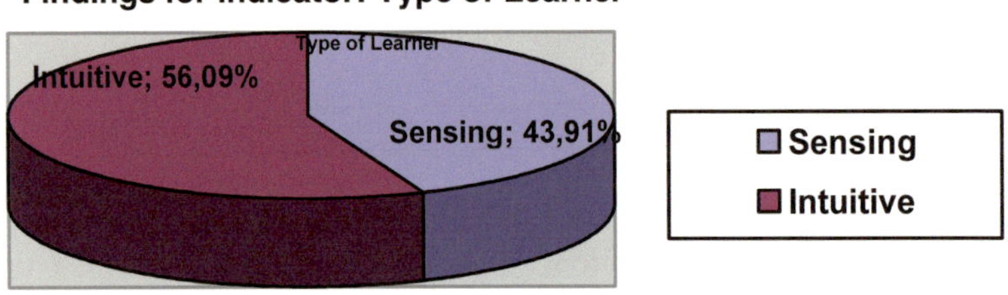

Fig. 6. Moodle LMS - Findings for indicator

On the whole, 43.91 % of respondents rated them self's as Sensing learners while the others 56.09% as Intuitive learners.

7.4.3.3 Discussion of the findings for indicator: Type of Learner

The findings indicate that ANGEL LMS students are primarily of type sensing and they tend to learn by learning facts 62.62%. The minority group of the students are of type intuitive learners 37.37% and they prefer discovering possibilities and relationships for them self's. These finding suggests that the content created and used in the e-learning environment should be concentrated around facts and detailed descriptions rather then on living this to students to discover for them self's. MOODLE students are primarily of type Intuitive 56.09% compared to the sensing group with 56.09%. For the students of this type the recommendations are to provide more information and case studies for students in order to intuitively learn and find the answers.

7.4.4 Analyses of Indicator: Type of Learner

a) VISUAL or b) VERBAL LEARNER

(Explanations: Visual learners remember best what they see--pictures, diagrams, flow charts, time lines, films, and demonstrations. Verbal learners get more out of words-written and spoken explanations.)

7.4.4.1 ANGEL LMS - Findings for indicator: Type of Learner

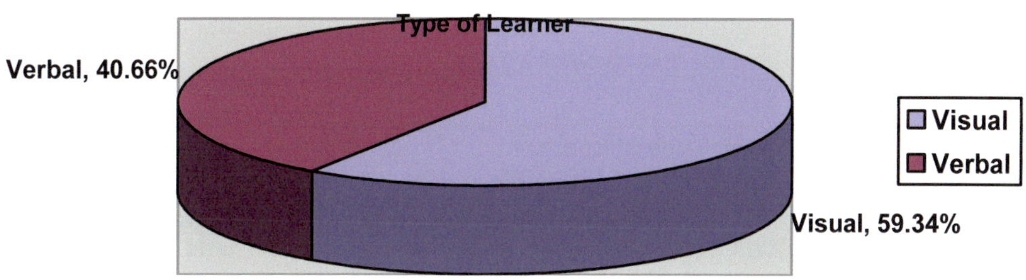

Fig. 7. ANGEL LMS - Findings for indicator

On the whole, 59.34 % of respondents rated them self's as Visual learners while the others 40.66% as Verbal learners.

7.4.4.2 MOODLE - Findings for indicator: Type of Learner

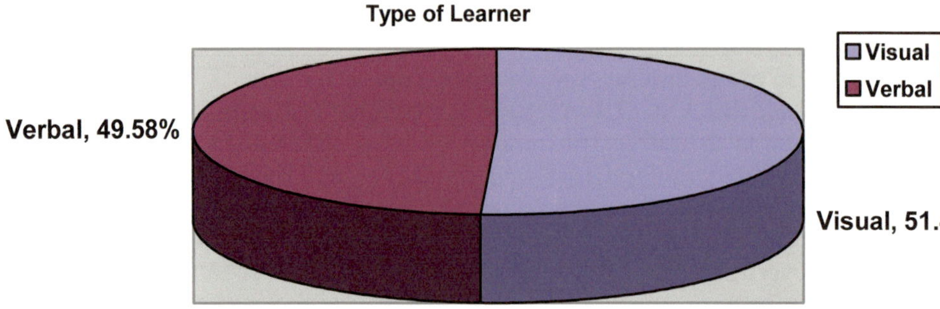

Fig. 8. Moodle LMS - Findings for indicator

On the whole, 51.42 % of respondents rated them self's as Visual learners while the others 49.58% as Verbal learners.

7.4.4.3 Discussion of the findings for indicator: Type of Learner

The findings indicate that ANGEL students are 59.34% while MOODLE 51.42% primarily of type Visual learners and they tend to learn by pictures, diagrams, flow charts, time lines, films, and demonstrations. The other group of the students is of type verbal learners Angel 40.66% and MOODLE 49.58% and they prefer to learn out of words, written and spoken. This findings suggests that the e-content created and used in the e-learning environment should contain more multimedia elements like pictures, diagrams, flow charts and demonstrations rather then just text explanations.

7.4.5 Analyses of indicator: Type of Learner

a) SEQUENTIAL or b) GLOBAL LEARNER

(Explanations: Sequential learners tend to gain understanding in linear steps, with each step following logically from the previous one. Global learners tend to learn in large jumps, absorbing material almost randomly without seeing connections, and then suddenly "getting it.")

7.4.5.1 ANGEL LMS - Findings for indicator

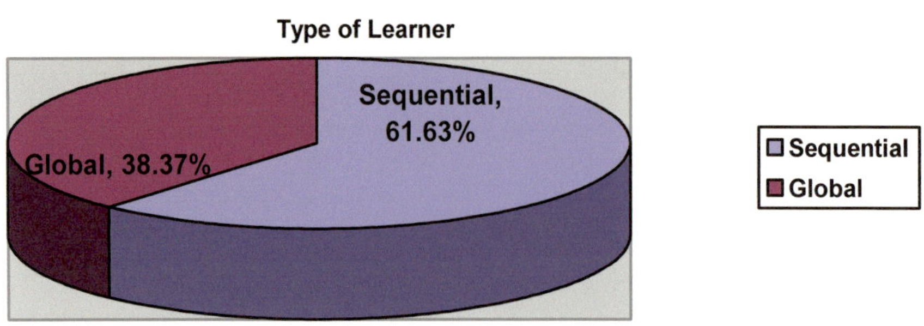

Fig. 9. ANGEL LMS - Findings for indicator

On the whole, 61.63 % of respondents rated them self's as Sequential learners while the others 38.37% as Global learners.

7.4.5.2 MOODLE - Findings for indicator

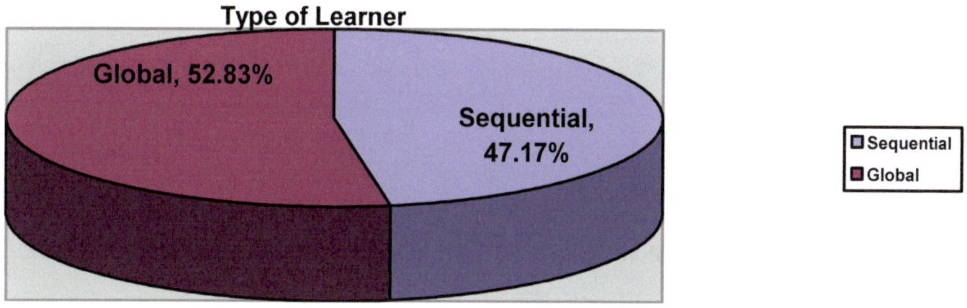

Fig. 10. Moodle LMS - Findings for indicator

On the whole, 52.83 % of respondents rated them self's as Sequential learners while the others 47.17% as Global learners.

7.4.5.3 Discussion of the findings

The findings indicate that 61.63 % Angel students and 47.17% Moodle students are primarily of type Sequential learners and they tend to learn in linear steps, with each step following logically from the previous one. The other group of the students are of type Global learners 38.37% Angel students and 52.83% Moodle students and they prefer to learn in large jumps, absorbing material almost randomly without seeing connections, and then suddenly "getting it.". This findings suggests that the e-content created and used in the e-learning environment should present the subject sequentially and then progressing step by step to the global and general issues for Angel environment students while for the Moodle environment students the content provided should contain information that provides global picture of the content.

7.4.6 Analyses of indicator: Learning Style and intelligence

1) Linguistic ("word smart", sensitivity and ability to spoken and written language):
2) Logical-mathematical ("number/reasoning smart", analyze problems logically, investigate issues scientifically)
3) Spatial ("picture smart", potential to recognize and use the patterns of wide space)
4) Bodily-Kinesthetic ("body smart", mental abilities to coordinate bodily movements)
5) Musical ("music smart", skill in the performance, composition, and appreciation of musical patterns)
6) Interpersonal ("people smart", capacity to understand the intentions, motivations and desires of other people)
7) Intrapersonal ("self smart", capacity to understand oneself, to appreciate one's feelings, fears and motivations)
8) Naturalist ("nature smart", recognize, categorize certain features of the environment)

7.4.6.1 ANGEL LMS - Findings for indicator

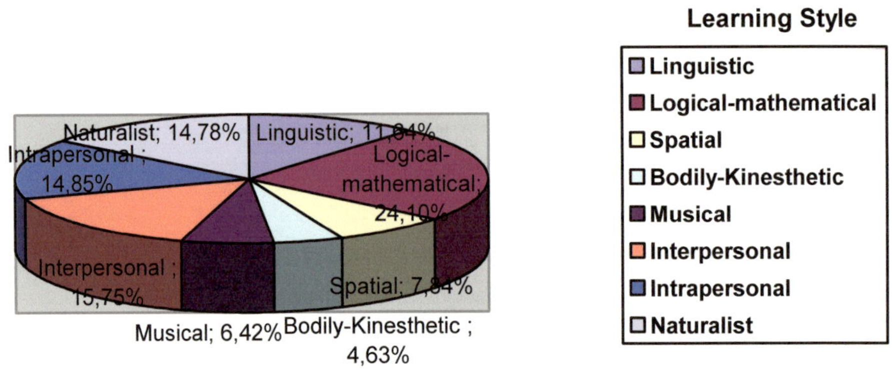

Fig. 11. ANGEL LMS - Findings for indicator

7.4.6.2 MOODLE - Findings for indicator

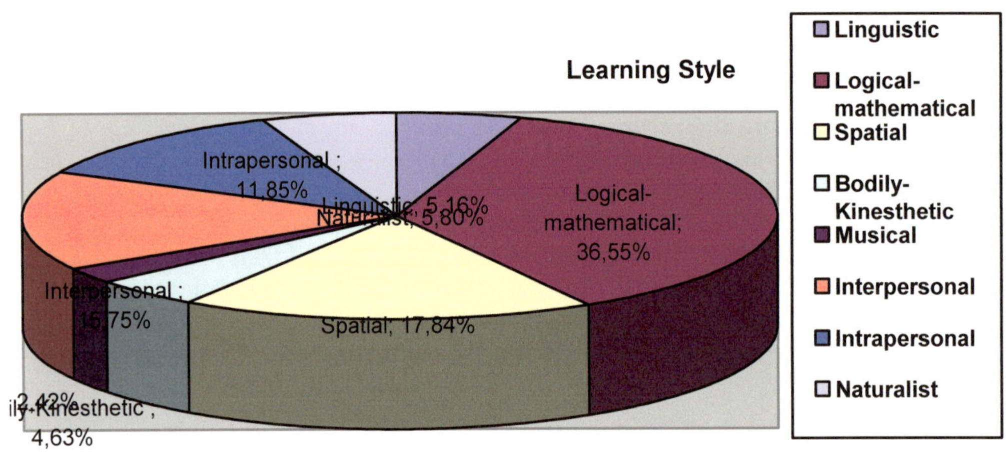

Fig. 12. Moodle LMS - Findings for indicator

7.4.6.3 Discussion of the Findings

The findings indicate that Angel and Moodle students are more or less with a balanced and similar learning style and intelligence were slightly prevails the Logical-mathematical, and linguistic style and intelligence preferences.

7.4.7 Analyses of indicator: Obstacles - Borders

Please define the obstacles you face in e-learning?

7.4.7.1 ANGEL LMS - Findings for indicator

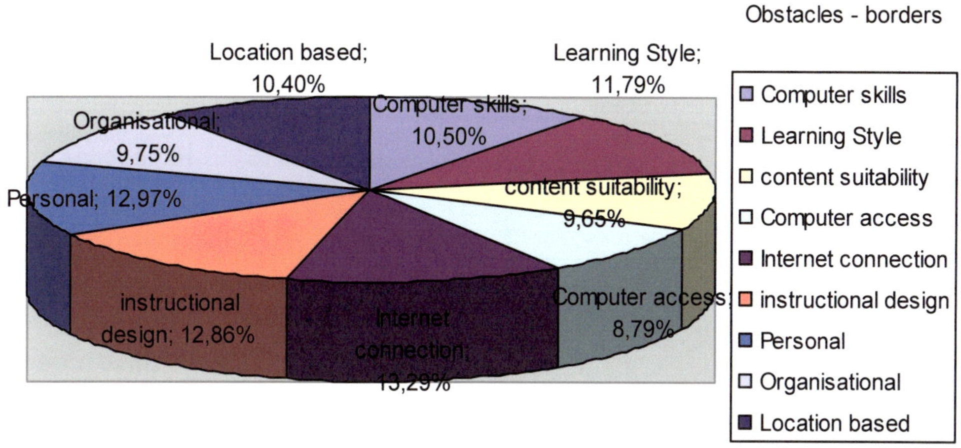

Fig. 13. ANGEL LMS - Findings for indicator

7.4.7.2 MOODLE - Findings for Indicator

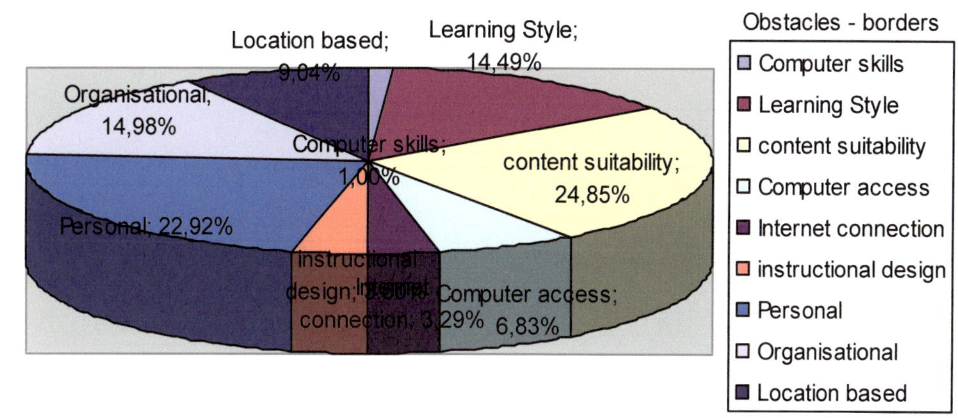

Fig. 14. Moodle LMS - Findings for indicator

7.4.7.3 Discussion of the Findings

The findings indicate that there are a lot of obstacles and barriers to e-learning and they are rated as follows in percentage: Angel: Based on these findings the internet connection and e-content not suited to learners learning style are rated as the biggest obstacles and barriers to enhanced learning. Moodle: Based on the findings content suitability, personal issues and learning style are rated as the biggest obstacles to enhanced learning.

7.4.8 Analyses of indicator: Attention

What captures best your attention in ANGEL that helps you learn best?

7.4.8.1 ANGEL LMS - Findings for indicator

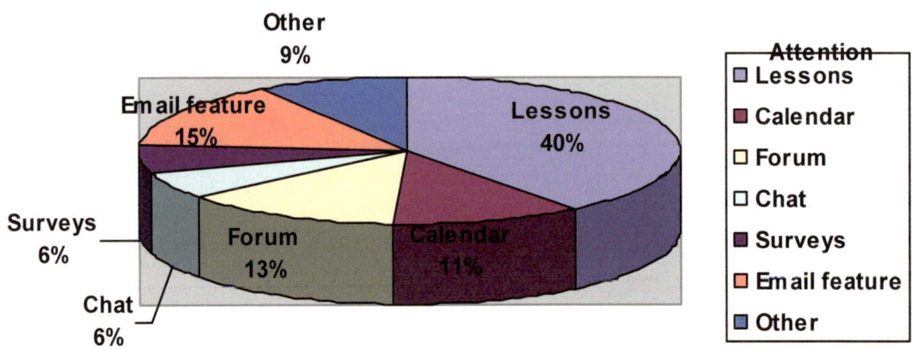

Fig. 15. ANGEL LMS - Findings for indicator

The findings indicate that e-learning attention is based on different factors and they are rated as follows in percentage: 39.31% rated that their attention on Lessons; 11.40% rated that their attention on Calendar; 13.43% rated that their attention on Forum; 5.85% rated that their attention on Chat; 6.00% rated that their attention on Surveys; 14.70% rated that their attention on email feature; 9.30% rated that their attention on other factors.

7.4.8.2 MOODLE - Findings for Indicator

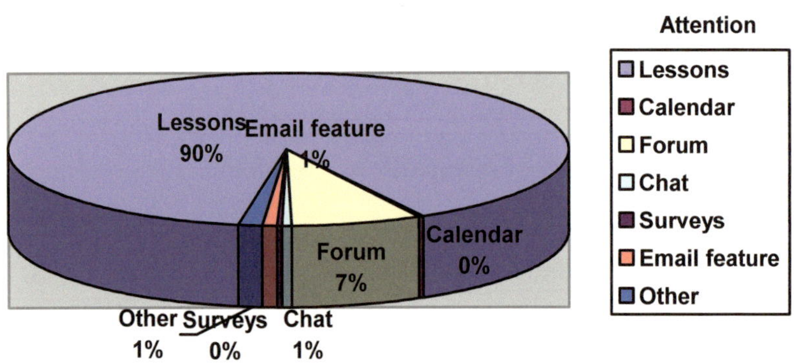

Fig. 16. Moodle LMS - Findings for indicator

The findings indicate that e-learning attention is based on different factors and they are rated as follows in percentage: 89.31% rated that their attention on Lessons; 0.14% rated that their attention on Calendar7.37% rated that their attention on Forum; 0.62% rated that their attention on Chat; 0.23% rated that their attention on Surveys; 1.03% rated that their attention on email feature; 1.30% rated that their attention on other factors.

7.4.9 Analyses of indicator: Content format

If you could choose different formats for the same content which one do you think is best to convey knowledge and to learn from?

7.4.9.1 ANGEL LMS - Findings for indicator

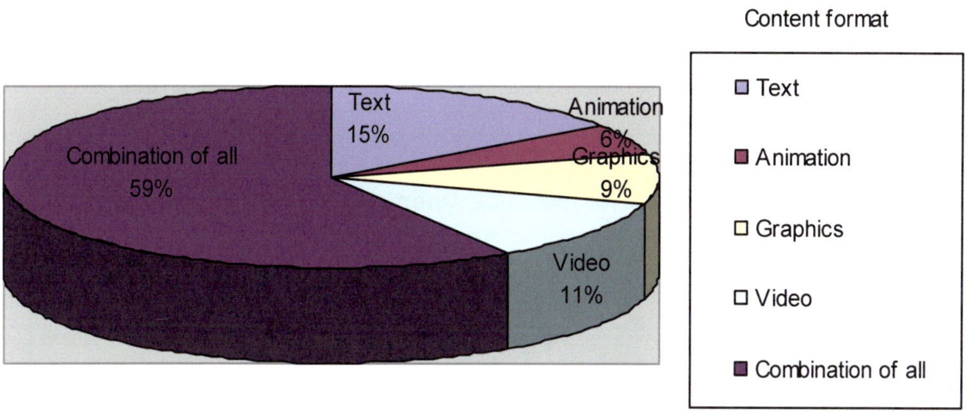

Fig. 17. ANGEL LMS - Findings for indicator

7.4.9.2 MOODLE - Findings for indicator

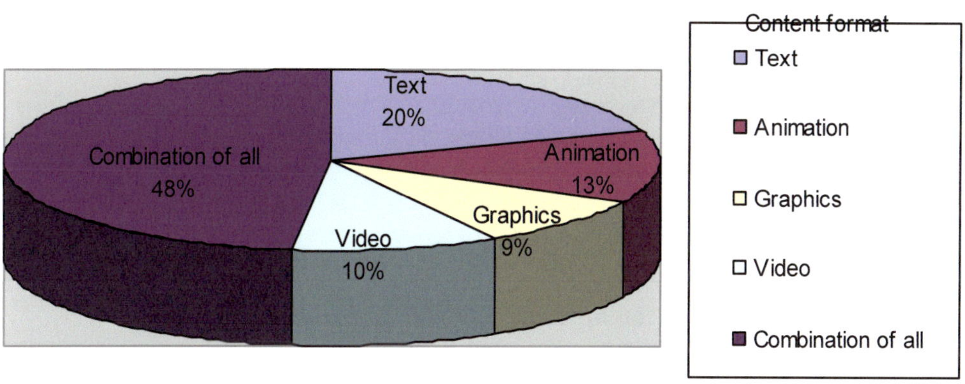

Fig. 18. Moodle LMS - Findings for indicator

7.4.9.3 Discussion of the findings

Most of the respondents, in both of the environments prefer mostly a combination of all media in representing the course e-content. Then the preferences are for Text as their representation of learning e-content, then respondents prefer Video as their e-content, Graphics and animation representation of their learning e-content. This data highlights the importance of the e-learning content and its format of representation which should be provided in different formats and most desirably as combination of all the media. The structure and interactivity should also be embedded in the content as well and provide clear summary and outcomes for the e-content.

7.4.10 Analyses of indicator: Optimal Course to Learn

When is your optimal time to learn, what do you prefer?

- a self-paced e-learning course completed independently
- an e-learning course facilitated by an instructor who requires completed assignments and discussions with peers
- a real-time e-learning course conducted online with a facilitator and participants in different locations

7.4.10.1 ANGEL LMS - Findings for indicator: Optimal Course to Learn

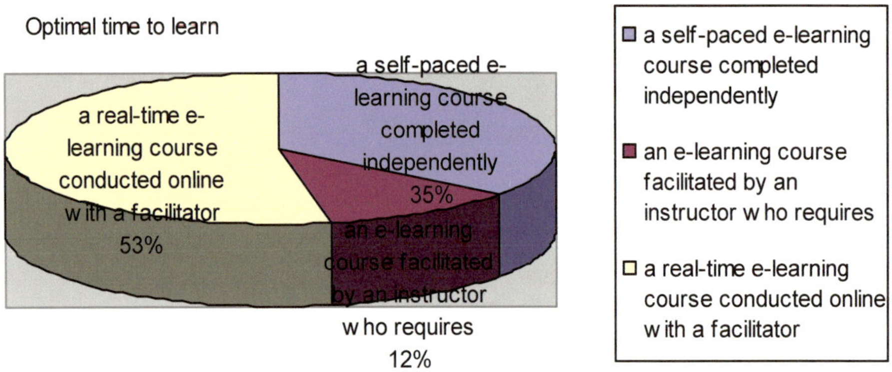

Fig. 19. ANGEL LMS - Findings for indicator

Most of the respondents, 53% prefer a real-time (synchronous) class conducted by a facilitator and participants in different locations. 12%, prefer an asynchronous e-learning course facilitated by an instructor who requires completed work and participation in discussions. Only 35% prefer a self-paced course. This data highlights the importance of a facilitator who can structure interaction and provide assistance and accountability.

7.4.10.2 MOODLE - Findings for Indicator: Optimal Course to Learn

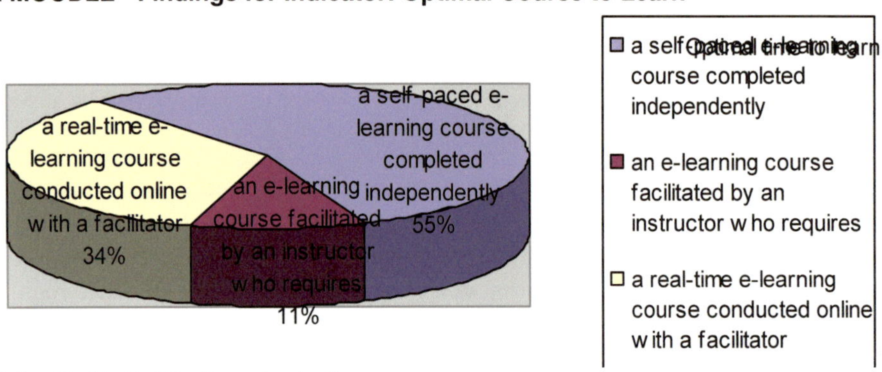

Fig. 20. Moodle LMS - Findings for indicator

Most of the respondents 55% prefer a self-paced course. Then, 34% prefer a real-time (synchronous) class conducted by a facilitator and participants in different locations. 11%, prefer an asynchronous e-learning course facilitated by an instructor who requires completed work and participation in discussions. This data highlights the importance of having a self paced course were the focus will be in the e-content since the content is the main vehicle into learning.

7.4.11 Analyses of indicator: Optimal time to learn

When is the best time for you for a real-time online classes or online discussion with your instructor or colleague student?

7.4.11.1 ANGEL LMS - Findings for indicator

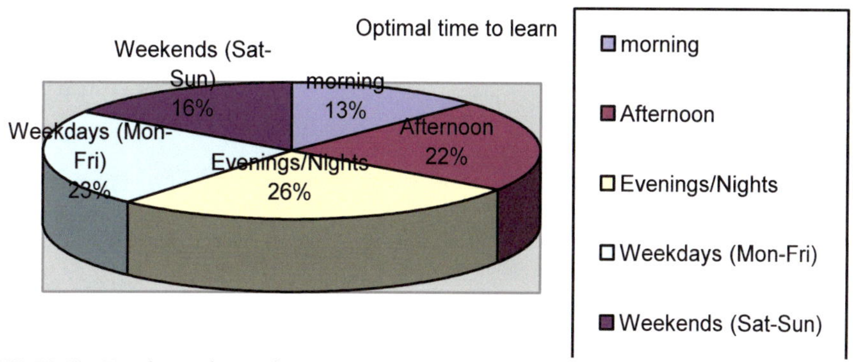

Fig. 21. ANGEL LMS - Findings for indicator

7.4.11.2 MOODLE - Findings for indicator

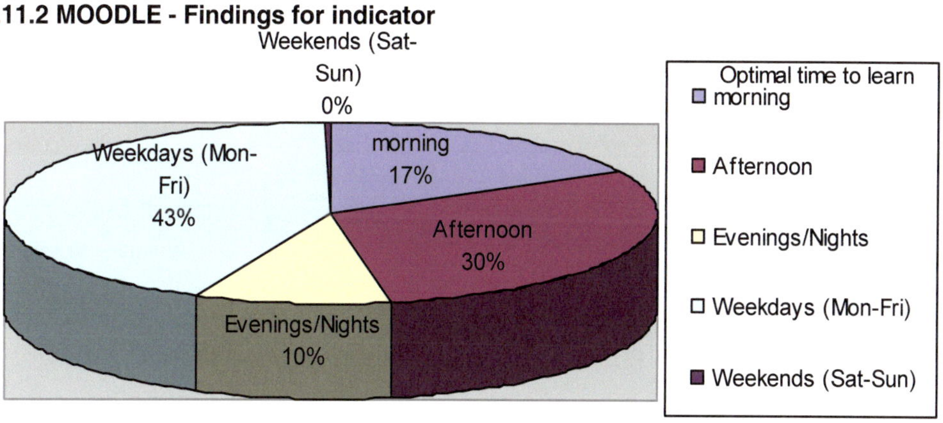

Fig. 22. Moodle LMS - Findings for indicator

In Angel: Most of the respondents, 26%, prefer Evenings/nights for online classes or online discussion. 23% prefer Weekdays Monday to Friday, 22% prefer afternoons, 16% prefer Weekends Saturday and Sunday, and 13% prefer morning for online classes and online discussions. This data suggests that e-learning most preferred efficient time is during evenings in the weekdays, second option is at least to be in the afternoon and very few learners desire to learn during weekdays. In Moodle: Most of the students 43% prefer weekdays as optimal time to learn. Then afternoon is the second choice with 30% and morning with 17% while evenings/nights with 10%.

7.4.12 Analyses of indicator: Online positives

If you study at home or workplace, how much do you agree with the following statements?

7.4.12.1 ANGEL LMS - Findings for indicator

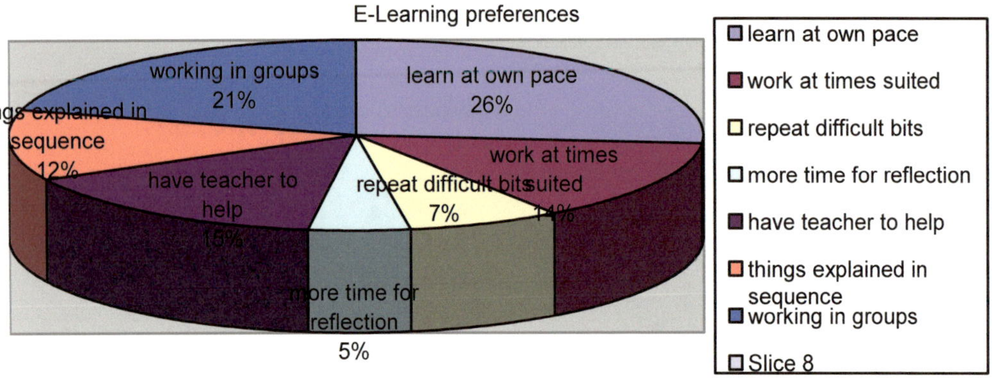

Fig. 23. ANGEL LMS - Findings for indicator

7.4.12.2 MOODLE - Findings for indicator

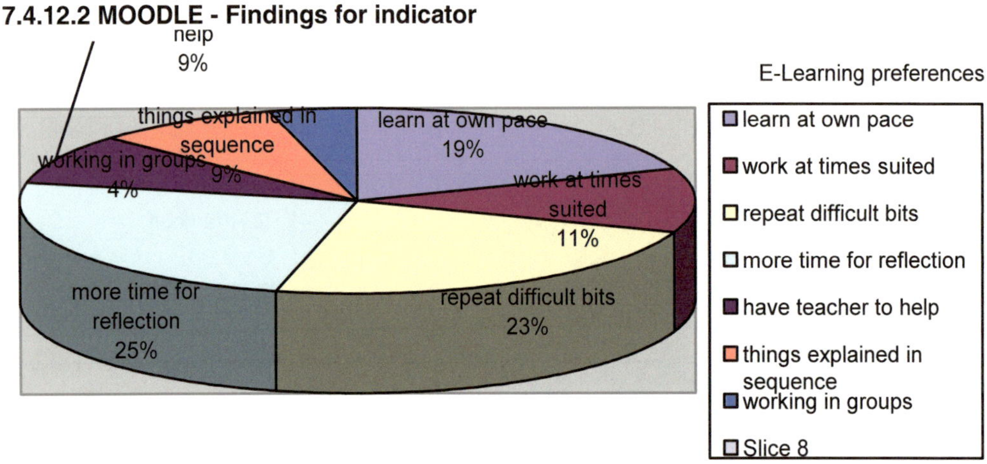

Fig. 24. Moodle LMS - Findings for indicator

7.4.12.3 Discussion of the findings

Angel: Most of the respondents, 26% prefer online learning because they can learn at their own peace. 21% prefer online working in groups, 15 % need teachers/instructors to help,

14% prefer online because they can work at times suited to their schedule, 12% prefer things explained in sequence, 7% prefer online because they can repeat difficult bits, 5 % prefer online because they have more time for reflection.

Moodle: Most of the respondents, 25% prefer online learning because they have more time for reflection. 23% because they can repeat difficult bias, 19 % prefer learning in their own pace, 11% prefer working at times suited to their schedule, 09% prefer things explained in sequence, 4% prefer working in groups.

This data highlights the importance of the factors that drove the learners decision for choosing e-learning compared to traditional classroom. The most preferred positive option of e-learning for student learners are the facts that they can learn on their own peace, at times suited to their schedule, they can repeat difficult bias and they have more time for reflection.

7.4.13 Analyses of indicator: Learning preferences

Do you prefer to study ALONE or as part of a TEAM?

7.4.13.1 ANGEL LMS - Findings for indicator:

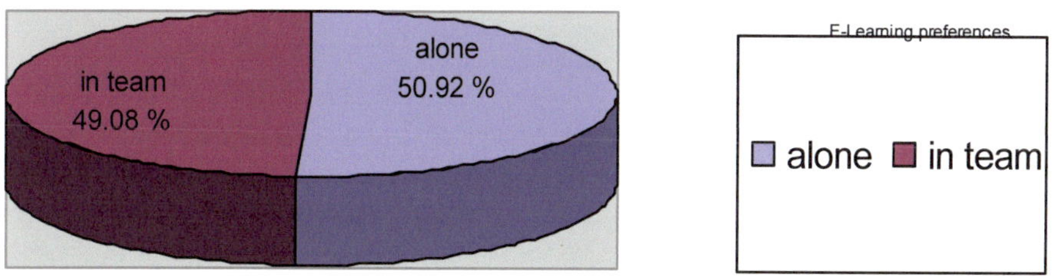

Fig. 25. ANGEL LMS - Findings for indicator

7.4.13.2 MOODLE - Findings for indicator:

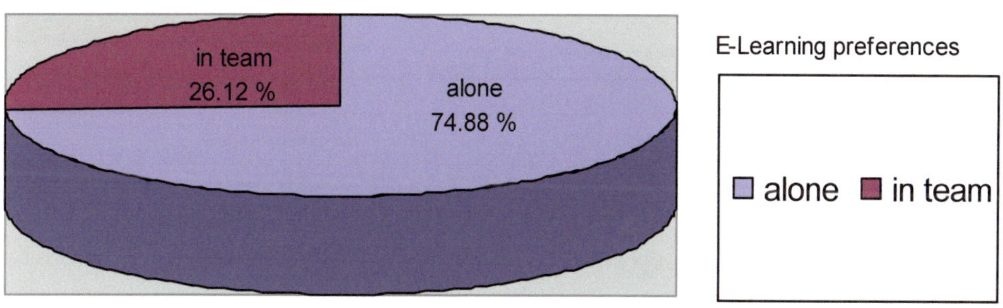

Fig. 26. Moodle LMS - Findings for indicator

7.4.13.3 Discussion of the findings

In Angel: Most of the respondents, 50.92 % prefer working alone and learn at their own peace. 49.08 % prefer team work. The preferences of the student learners are almost divided the same in favor of working alone or in team. In Moodle: Most of the respondents 74.92% prefer working alone, while 26.08% prefer working in team.

Based on the findings we concluded that this is not such an issue for them and it is not influencing the learning process substantially.

7.4.14 Analyses of indicator: Communication preferences

As Learner how do you usually work with fellow students on your course and share ideas with him/her? 1) Face to Face; 2) Telephone; 3) Email 4) chat room; 5) Moderated discussion forum

7.4.14.1 ANGEL LMS - Findings for indicator

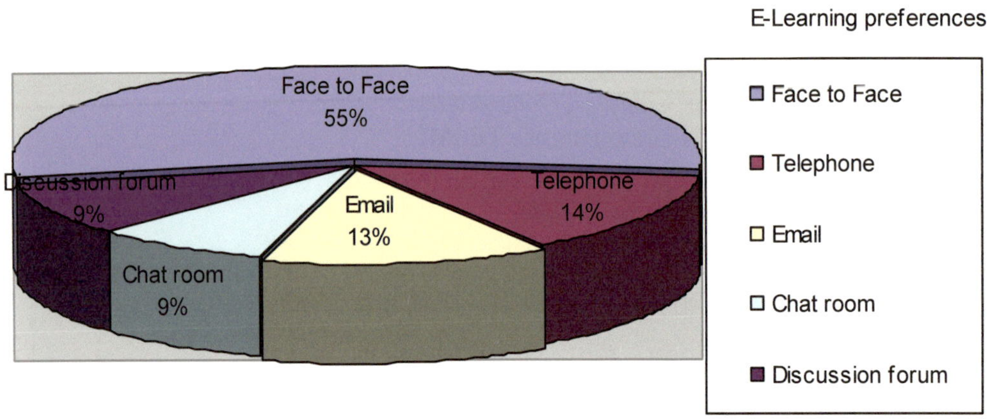

Fig. 27. ANGEL LMS - Findings for indicator

7.4.14.2 MOODLE - Findings for indicator

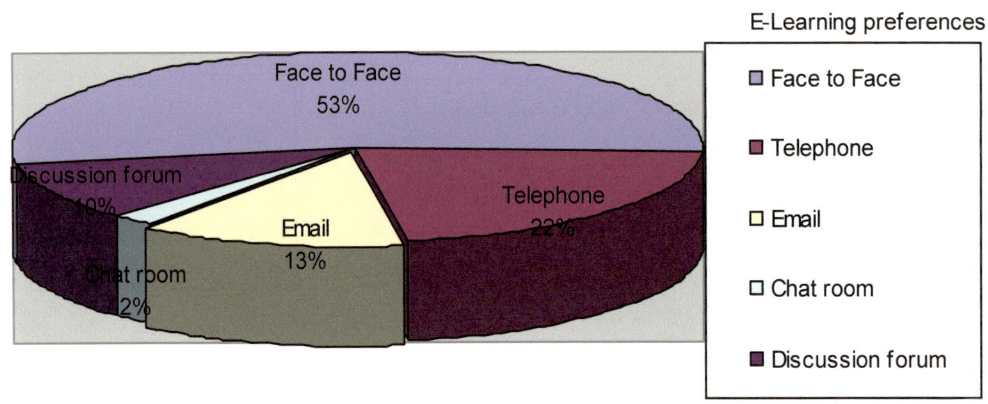

Fig. 28. Moodle LMS - Findings for indicator

7.4.14.3 Discussion of the findings

Most of the respondents, similarly in both cases angel and Moodle prefer Face to Face communication with their colleges. Then they prefer telephone communication to exchange ideas with their colleges, and then prefer email communication, afterwards prefer Discussion forum to communicate with their colleges, and at the end prefer chat rooms for communication.

7.4.15 Analyses of indicator: Technology usage extending learning

To what extent have your skills and learning improved by your personal use of technology outside the University?

7.4.15.1 ANGEL LMS - Findings for indicator:

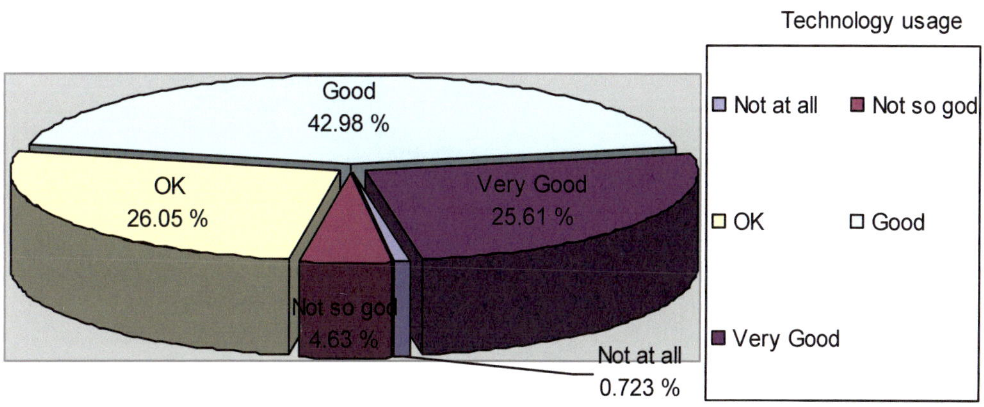

Fig. 29. ANGEL LMS - Findings for indicator

7.4.15.2 MOODLE - Findings for indicator:

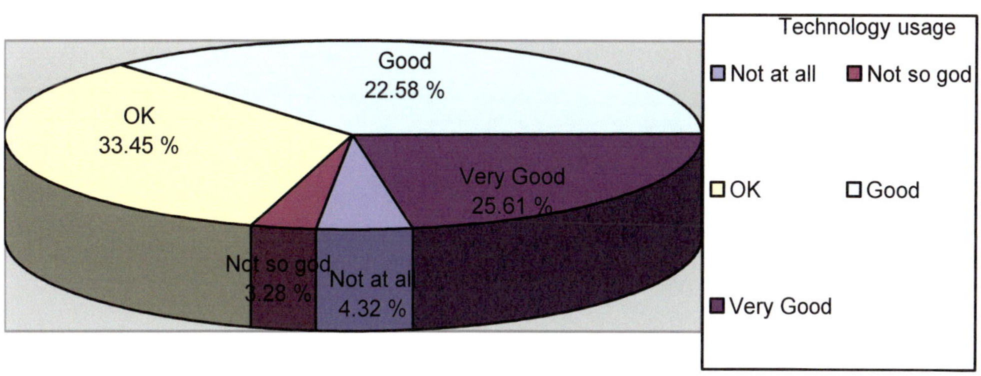

Fig. 30. Moodle LMS - Findings for indicator

7.4.15.3 Discussion of the findings

Most of the respondents, for both Angel and Moodle feel that they have improved their skills using technology and they have classified this as good. Most of the respondents classified their improvement as OK, then fewer respondents classified their improvement as Very Good, while on the other side although few there are some respondents that classified their improvement as Not so good, while fewer as Not at all. This data highlights the importance of technology usage in improving student learner's skills and learning. The learning system usage influenced and improved student learning.

7.4.16 Analyses of indicator: Access to E-learning Material

Describe your access to e-learning material?

7.4.16.1 ANGEL LMS - Findings for indicator: Access to e-learning material

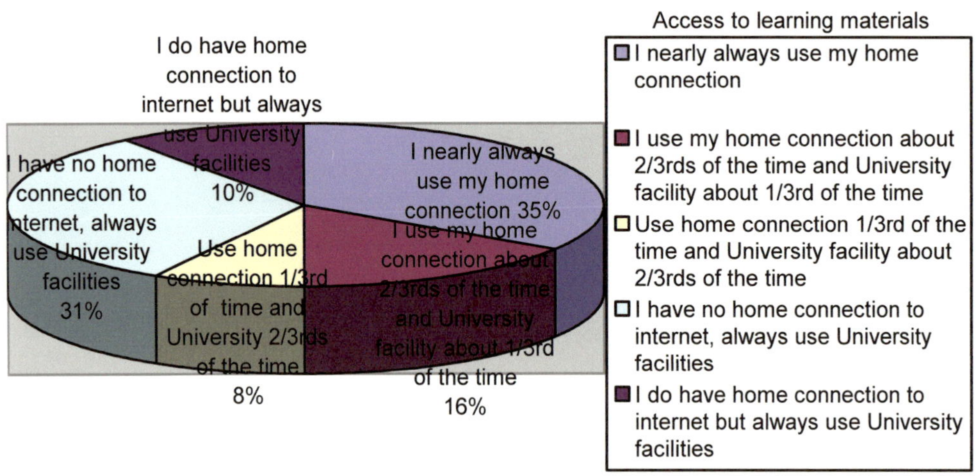

Fig. 31. ANGEL LMS - Findings for indicator

7.4.16.2 MOODLE - Findings for indicator: Access to E-learning Material

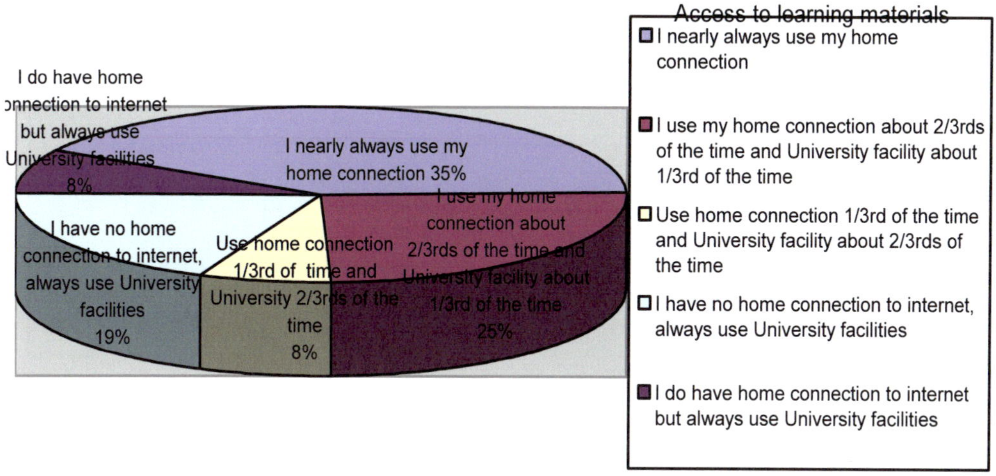

Fig. 32. Moodle LMS - Findings for indicator

7.4.16.3 Discussion of the findings for indicator

Most of the respondents, for both Angel and Moodle prefer using their own home connection to internet, then the largest group have no home connection and use the University facility for connecting online, then use their home connection around 2/3 of the time and 1/3 the University facilities to connect to internet, then few of the respondents use their home connection around 1/3 of the time and 2/3 of the time they use the University facility, and smallest group although do have home connection they always use the University facility to connect to internet.

This data highlights the importance of the factors that drove the learner's decision for choosing e-learning compared to traditional classroom. The most preferred positive option of e-learning for student learners are the facts that they can learn on their own peace, at times suited to their schedule, they can repeat difficult bias and they have more time for reflection.

7.4.17 Analyses of indicator: Online positives

How often do you visit course contents on ANGEL??

7.4.17.1 ANGEL LMS - Findings for indicator: Online Positives

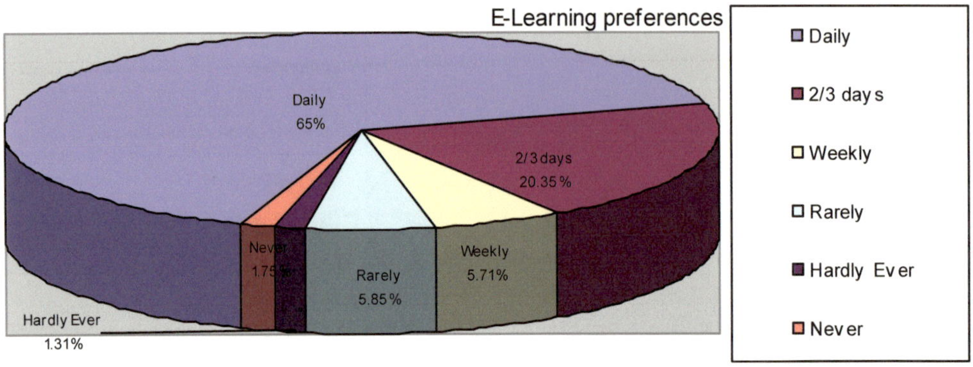

Fig. 33. ANGEL LMS - Findings for indicator

7.4.17.2 MOODLE - Findings for indicator: Online positives - Question 22:

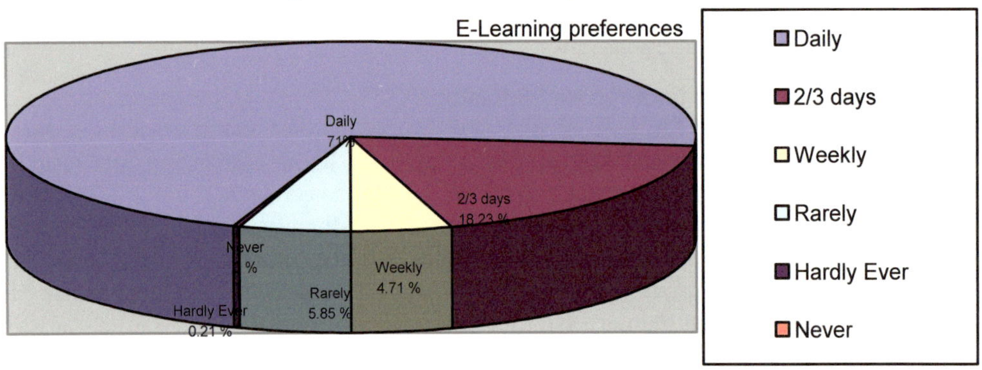

Fig. 34. Moodle LMS - Findings for indicator

7.4.17.3 Discussion of the findings

Most of the respondents, in Angel (65 %) , Moodle (71.09%) access content inn LMS on Daily basis, Angel (20.35 %), Moodle (18.63%) of the respondents access the content each 2 or 3 days, Angel 5.71 % Moodle 4.71% of the respondents access the content on Weekly basis, while on the other hand Angel 5.85 %; Moodle 5.39% of the respondents access the content Rarely, Angel 1.31 % ; Moodle 0.21% access it hardly ever, and Angel 1.31 %; Moodle 0% never access content in LMS.

7.4.18 Analyses of indicator: Learning Outcomes

What is the impact of this e-learning system regarding learning outcomes?

9) Knowledge transfer and understanding; 2) Intellectual (thinking) skills; 3) Practical skills; 4) Transferable skills

7.4.18.1 ANGEL Findings for indicator:

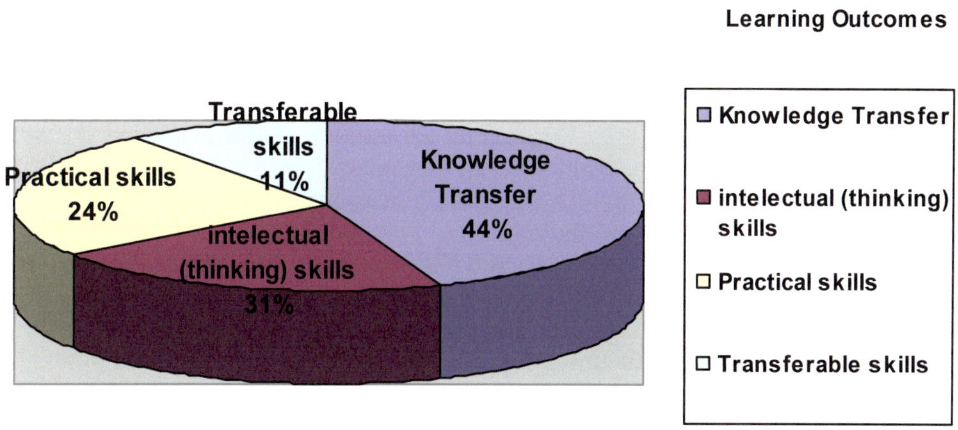

Fig. 35. ANGEL LMS - Findings for indicator

7.4.18.2 Moodle Findings for indicator:

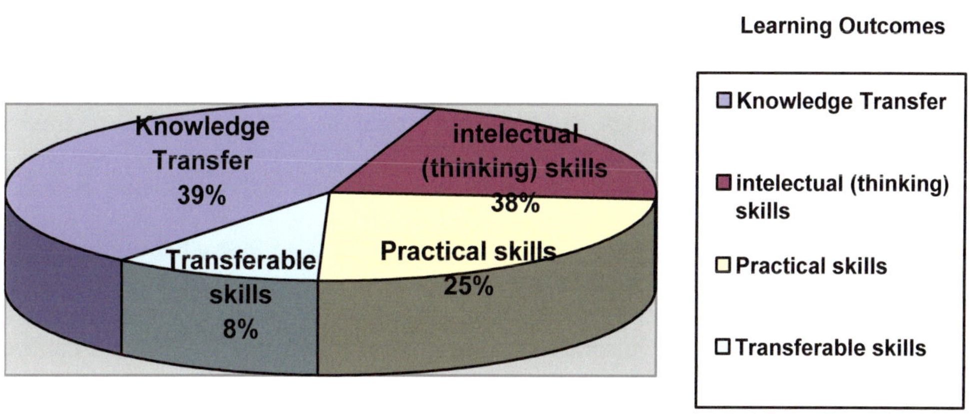

Fig. 36. Moodle LMS - Findings for indicator

7.4.18.3 Discussion of the findings

Most of the respondents, Angel 44 % and Moodle 39 % declared that knowledge transfer was the most important outcome, 31 % in Angel and 38% in Moodle the respondents declared that intellectual thinking skills were the most important outcome, Angel 24 % and Moodle 25% of the respondents think that practical skills were the most important outcome, while only 11 % in Angel and 8% in Moodle the respondents declared most important the transferable skills.

It is a conclusion that both e-learning projects using Angel and Moodle have been rated very similarly regarding the learning outcomes.

7. Conclusion

The research study is following the e-learning trends needs and tries to address the issues and deficiencies from the findings realized in the secondary research. Most importantly the study recognises and tries to address the multidimensional aspects of e-learning. The research study results in several contributions.

The main result of the realised research study was the development of the e-learning indicators methodology that could be used systematically in planning phase of e-learning initiatives and their corresponding e-learning project. Therefore, recommendations are to use the e-learning indicators methodology approach in developing any e-learning initiative and their corresponding e-learning project.

Many current e-learning initiatives follow the "one-size-fits-all" approach just offering some type of LMS to learners. Typically, this approach is related to lack of knowledge of the learner audience or factors influencing that audience and e-learning project overall and therefore fail to provide satisfactory support in the decision making process.

In order to address this issue, an approach dealing with e-learning indicators is proposed, assessed, measured and evaluated. The proposed E-learning Indicators Methodology enables successful planning, comparison and evaluation of different e-learning projects. Above is given comparative analyses of two different institutions using Angel and Moodle and focusing on comparison and evaluation of e-learning indicators of these two e-learning projects. E-learning indicators methodology represents an empirical methodology that gives concrete results expressed through numbers that could be analysed and later used to compare and conclude its e-learning efficiency. With the application of this methodology in e-learning projects it is more likely to achieve better results and higher efficiency as well as higher Return on Investment ROI.

Recommend using the defined e-learning indicators as starting point when developing e-learning initiative and based on the measurements of these e-learning indicators to tailor the specifics of e-learning. Each e-learning initiative is unique and involves specifics that can not be taken under consideration in general in the form of one solution suits all. On the contrary each e-learning initiative should measure the provided indicators and based on them to design and build their e-learning.

From the perspective of all available evidence it points toward growing enrolments and provision albeit from a low starting point. The opinion is that the future quality development in e-learning has to be oriented at the learner's needs and their specific situation that needs to be measured and evaluated using the e-learning indicators.

Regarding the comparative analyses of two distinct e-learning projects: Angel and Moodle the fact is that after analyzing both of the systems, some main problems that these two systems contain, and some suggestions how these problems could be solved or recovered are given below:

As it can be concluded from the data described above, Moodle really has a large number of options that it offers and when these tools come involved into the course they attract the student's attention from his aim. This problem is not faced in ANGEL system, which has a cleaner interface with high usability. As a solution for such a problem, our recommendation is to simplify course pages in the Moodle system, and in this way make it more aesthetic, efficient and attractive. Of course, some necessary tools would have a proper place in a smaller and well readable format.

Another problem of Moodle is that it has a difficult file management. The solution to this problem is allowing managing files and according to the latest news, the professional team of Moodle is currently working on this issue.

ANGEL is not considered to have any problems with the templates and design, but it does not contain a glossary which the Moodle has, and it operates perfectly. I would necessarily put such an item in order to increase its functionality and effectiveness since Moodle is evidence how much it is useful for the learners. Another problem that ANGEL faces is that it does not target a UNIX based system.

All of the above mentioned important issues and problems are the most important and essential ones that student, instructors and other roles mostly care about. That is why their improvements are important as much as their existence. All of the other tools such as surveys, quizzes, language supports and different options are very functional and efficient in both systems and these items are definitely the ones that I would not change in any of them.

Although the e-learning indicators methodology has many positive aspects mentioned above, it also has several drawbacks. Some of the most important identified are:

- Some e-learning projects are running for the entire University while some only for a Faculty or a department. Then the comparison of e-learning projects might not prove to provide accurate insights.
- Comparison of e-learning projects with different types of collectives based on the learning type can not prove satisfactory results. The best results are achieved when comparing similar types of collectives.

Although the methodology tries to capture the multidimensional nature of e-learning some of the indicators could be separated into several others in order to capture more precisely some multiple dimensions of e-learning.

Based on the insights of the research study recommended and proposed is a strategy for implementing E-Learning at South East Europe. The developed strategy takes into account the Universities current mission in achieving a so-called borderless education within the regional Balkans context, but also in a wider European and global context. A number of issues related to such a specific context of the University, such as its multilingual and multicultural environment influenced the developed strategy and its implementation plan.

The main principle of such a strategy is to support the university's mission of borderless education by providing the widest possible access to national and regional excellence in learning and teaching by means of the current and novel technology. That technology includes but is not limited to the Web technologies such as Web-based media and multimedia technologies, broader Internet-based communication and collaboration technologies, as well as more general Knowledge Management technologies. Also, the strategy takes into account the traditional classroom education and classical methodologies and compares the options and possibilities to apply them in combination with the current technologies in a blended manner (Rosenberg, 2004). Following this main strategic principle a number of concrete goals have been defined. Through achievement of these measurable goals the SEE can move towards the fulfilment of its primary mission. Therefore we recommend strategic goals together with a detailed implementation plan for them.

8. References

Bandura, A. (1997), Self -efficacy: The exercise of control. New York. W.H. Freeman.

Bonk, C. J. & Graham, C. R. (2004). Handbook of blended learning: Global Perspectives, local designs. San Francisco, CA: Pfeiffer Publishing.

Coleman, B., Neuhauser, J. & Fisher, M. (2004). Accomplished Methods for Online Collaboration in Graduate Courses. In Proceedings of World Conference on Educational Multimedia, Hypermedia and Telecommunications 2004 (pp. 387-392). Chesapeake, VA: AACE.

Dagger, D, and O'Connor, A,. and Lawless, S,. Walsh, E,. and Wade, V,. (2007) Service-Oriented E-Learning Platforms: From Monolithic Systems to Flexible Services, IEEE Educational Activities Department Piscataway, NJ, USA, May/June 2007 (Vol. 11, No. 3) pp. 28-35

Dumas, J. S., & Redish J. C. (1999) "A practical guide to Usability Testing" revised edition, Pearson Education Limited, pp.55-62

Eklund, J., Kay, M., & Lynch, H. (2003). E-learning: emerging issues and key trends. A discussion paper, Australian National Training Authority.

Felder, R.M. (1993) "Reaching the Second Tier: Learning and Teaching Styles in College Science Education," J. Coll. Sci. Teaching, 23(5), 286--290 (1993).

Fetaji, B. (2006). Issues and solutions in authoring e-learning content in South East European University. In Proceedings of World Conference on Educational Multimedia, Hypermedia and Telecommunications 2006 (pp. 254-259). Chesapeake, VA: AACE.

Fetaji, B. (2007). Assessing, measuring and evaluating e-learning indicators. In C. Montgomerie & J. Seale (Eds.), Proceedings of World Conference on Educational Multimedia, Hypermedia and Telecommunications 2007 (pp. 4640-4649). Chesapeake, VA: AACE.

Fetaji, B., & Fetaji, M. (2007e). "E-learning indicators approach in developing e-learning software solutions" - Accepted and to be published in the proceedings of the IEEE EUROCON 2007 conference, Warsaw, Poland, USA, 09-12 September 2007.

Fetaji, B., & Fetaji, M. (2007g). "E-learning indicators methodology approach in designing successful E-learning" -International E-Learning 2007 conference, Lisbon, Portugal, 06-08 July 2007.

Fetaji, B., & Fetaji,. M. (2007). Assessing, measuring and evaluating e-learning indicators. In P. Kommers & G. Richards (Eds.), Proceedings of World Conference on Educational Multimedia, Hypermedia and Telecommunications 2007. Chesapeake, VA: AACE.

Galotta, C., Zanetti, D., Krejci, D., Oliveira, K. & Rocha, A. (2004). Organizational Learning Based on a Customizable Environment for Knowledge Management Using Intranet. In G. Richards (Ed.), Proceedings of World Conference on E-Learning in Corporate, Government, Healthcare, and Higher Education 2004 (pp. 2626-2633). Chesapeake, VA: AACE.

Harrison, L. & Smith, R. (2003). All I Really Need to Know About E-Content I Learned In Kindergarten: Share and Share Alike. In G. Richards (Ed.), Proceedings of World Conference on E-Learning in Corporate, Government, Healthcare, and Higher Education 2003 (pp. 2004-2006). Chesapeake, VA: AACE.

Helic, D., Hrastnik, J. & Maurer, H. (2005). An Analysis of Application of Business Process Management Technology in E-Learning Systems. In G. Richards (Ed.), Proceedings of World Conference on E-Learning in Corporate, Government, Healthcare, and Higher Education 2005 (pp. 2937-2942). Chesapeake, VA: AACE.

Kumar, P. (2006). Using Universal Design Principles for e-learning. In T. Reeves & S. Yamashita (Eds.), Proceedings of World Conference on E-Learning in Corporate, Government, Healthcare, and Higher Education 2006 (pp. 1274-1277). Chesapeake, VA: AACE.

Liu, L., Maddux, C. & Johnson, L. (2004). Computer Attitude and Achievement: Is Time an Intermediate Variable?. Journal of Technology and Teacher Education. 12 (4), pp. 593-607. Norfolk, VA: AACE.

Mödritscher, F., Gütl, C., Garcia Barrios, V. & Maurer, H. (2004). Why do Standards in the Field of E-Learning not fully support learner-centred Aspects of Adaptivity?. In L. Cantoni & C. McLoughlin (Eds.), Proceedings of World Conference on Educational Multimedia, Hypermedia and Telecommunications 2004 (pp. 2034-2039). Chesapeake, VA: AACE.

Moore, M. G. (1989). Three modes of interaction. A presentation of the NUCEA forum: Issues in instructional interactivity. Presented at the annual meeting of National University Continuing Education Association, Salt Lake City, UT.

Ueno, M. (2004). Animated agent to maintain learner's attention in e-learning. In G. Richards (Ed.), Proceedings of World Conference on E-Learning in Corporate, Government, Healthcare, and Higher Education 2004 (pp. 194-201). Chesapeake, VA: AACE.

Whitehouse, C. (2003). Examining usability issues of e-learning. In P. Kommers & G. Richards (Eds.), Proceedings of World Conference on Educational Multimedia, Hypermedia and Telecommunications 2003 (pp. 2748-2755). Chesapeake, VA: AACE.

Zsifkovits, H. (2003). E-Learning for E-Logistics: Planning and Implementing A Modular Training Program. In G. Richards (Ed.), Proceedings of World Conference on E-Learning in Corporate, Government, Healthcare, and Higher Education 2003 (pp. 845-849). Chesapeake, VA: AACE.

Barriers to Effective use of Information Technology in Science Education at Yanbu Kingdom of Saudi Arabia

Abdulkareem Eid S. Alwani and Safeeullah Soomro
Emails: aalalwani@ieee.org, safee@ieee.org
Yanbu University College
Yanbu-Al Sinaiyah, Yanbu
Kingdom of Saudi Arabia

Abstract

This study examined the barriers to use of information technology (IT) in science education at the Yanbu school district in Saudi Arabia. Sub-domains investigated included: infrastructure and resources, policy and support, science teachers' personal beliefs, and staff development. This chapter is using a survey which shows common barriers encountered by the science teachers were identified. Demographic data enabled description of science teachers based on similarities and differences of gender, location of the school, training, years of teaching experience, and age. Science teachers rated the barriers limiting their use of technology in teaching on a scale ranging from 0 (does not limit) to 3 (greatly limits). We present results which showed that all four domains were highly significant barriers: infrastructure and resources ($M = 2.06$, $p<.001$); staff development ($M = 2.02$, $p<.001$); policy and support ($M = 1.84$, $p<.001$); and science teachers' personal beliefs regarding technology ($M = 1.15$, $p<.001$). The more bariers comes to face the teachers who are related to science and are experienced, the less likely they were to be IT users ($r = -0.16$, $p = .02$). To minimize the impact of these barriers and consequently improve the level of integration of information technology in science education in Saudi Arabia, a well-conceived strategic vision, adequate funding, and good implementation plan are of great importance.

1. Introduction and Related Research

Day after day, the importance of information technology becomes more evident and requires more of our attention. Today's world is one full of information. Through the use of information technology and the Internet, information is now more accessible than ever before. We are swamped with information and increasingly derive knowledge gained from information distributed by the Internet, newspapers, television, computers, magazines, books, radio, etc. Information technology penetrates every corner of our world and our individual lives. What does that mean to us? How can we evaluate the legitimacy of the new "information technology era" and realize its promise of greater knowledge for the many?

The World Wide Web makes our world so small that it increasingly resembles a small village. Internet users tend to know what is going on in their cyber-neighbors' lives; even when that neighbor is often living on the other side of the world! According to Becta (2003) and (Samman, 2003), new technologies might improve our lives in two ways: a) by enabling us to do things better, and b) by enabling us to do better things. Information technologies today significantly affect every society in the world, especially in the field of education.

Successful integration and/or adoption of information technology as well as its rejection depend on several factors. These factors could vary from one place to another depending on the environment where the technology is introduced as well as the purpose and timing of the introduction. Several studies have been conducted on this regard.

The purpose of this study was to examine the barriers that prevent science teachers from Yanbu education district in Saudi Arabia from using information technology in their teaching. This study investigated the degree of IT use and examined the barriers to its use in teaching science.

What are the unique barriers encountered by Saudi educators in the transition to IT-facilitated education? This study outlined an investigation into the barriers that prevent effective use of IT in science education in K-12 public schools in Saudi Arabia, specifically drawing from the perspectives of science teachers. Two research questions were considered:

1. Do science teachers encounter common barriers that prevent them from making effective use of IT in science education in the public schools at the Yanbu education district in Saudi Arabia? And
2. Do science teachers encounter unique barriers (other than the common barriers identified in the first research question) that may prevent them from making effective use of IT in science education in Saudi Arabia?

Weber (1996) surveyed three major themes related to IT barriers: (a) inadequate instruction; (b) inadequate computer systems; and (c) frustration. Examples of barriers that Weber identified include lack of administrative support, financial constraints, policy confusion, logistic limitations, conflicting purchasing decisions, support service deficiencies, and untrained personnel. In addition, he categorized groups of barriers to the use of technology that many researchers have also identified. These are: (a) anxiety; (b) stress; (c) feelings of stupidity, fear of the unfamiliar, and fear of dehumanizing effects; (d) the extreme of computer addiction (microcomputer mania); and (e) the extreme of computer phobia (cyberphobia), potentially involving active resistance, and sabotage.

Beggs (2000) posited that one critical barrier pertains to science teachers' poor preparation and lack of confidence related to IT. While there is some evidence of a history of using technology in science classrooms, not all science teachers are ready to use IT in teaching science. Some instructors, even those well educated and highly competent in the field of science, have been documented as fearing technology, most particularly fearing looking stupid in front of their students by failing in their use of IT. Fear of failure is a very legitimate problem. Ertmer (1999) pointed out that many teachers may ask themselves a hard-to-answer question: "What will I do if the technology fails and I can't complete the lesson as planned?" This may interfere with the adoption of technology in the classroom. Logically, to the extent that teacher training and technical support can answer teachers' questions of what happens when technology does not work, this barrier is reduced.

The U.S. Congressional report as cited in Corbin (2003) reported that the Office of Technology Assessment (OTA) suggested that the lack of experience using technology in the student teaching experience was a major concern. This report goes on to say that to overcome this problem, "K-12 and university educators must work together to integrate technology in the curriculum" (U.S. Congress, 1995, p. 165). Therefore, it is fair to say that the modest level of IT skills in teachers has been a barrier in its implementation in both education in general, and in science education, in particular (Corbin, 2003).

Al-Mohaissin (1993) listed some barriers that prevent effective use of IT in science teaching. The barriers he identified included the fact that poor consistency and compatibility existed between teacher training, available software, and hardware in schools. Most efforts undertaken were to supply hardware. However, the hardware that was delivered to Saudi schools was very limited; consisting of older and limited versions. The hardware installed supported very limited software applications produced by the hardware company. Often, this software did not serve the needs of the science teachers. There is a lack of availability of Arabic computer software for science and what is available is very expensive. Al-Mohaissin did not consider lack of funding a barrier but he indicated that lack of knowledge about IT at the purchasing level resulted in the performance and compatibility barriers experienced. He suggested generic software, like Word and Excel, to overcome the high price of the software programs.

Al-Oteawi (2002) found that there were not enough courses on IT in the colleges, particularly related to computer navigation and Internet skills. No programs existed in the colleges of education that allowed students to learn how to integrate IT in the curricula. Neither there were any in-service training programs in existence that permitted students and educators to develop their knowledge of IT processes.

According to the National Council for Accreditation of Teacher Education (NCATE, 1997), lack of training, knowledge, or familiarity leads to teachers' inability to independently integrate subject matter software with necessary computer hardware. A sizeable amount of literature exists that identifies overlapping barriers, lack of teacher knowledge, and inability to integrate hardware/software reliably. From this literature, a picture can be drawn of the perennial "vicious circle" that illustrates barrier relationships. Teachers' "fear of failure" is reinforced by failure to use IT successfully. The more a teacher internalizes previous failures, the less likely it is that he/she will be able to solve new compatibility issues. The more demands there are on teachers to make IT work in the classroom, the more fear of failure. These issues have implications for supporting science teachers in the IT implementation.

Corbin (2003) identified five barriers and grouped them into three areas: lack of experience in pre-service training, lack of access to computers at school, and lack of on-site technical support. He also stated that the most important barrier most teachers must deal with is lack of access to computers, either in a laboratory setting or in the classroom.

After gathering information through online questionnaires of 170 teachers, Becta (2003) discussed barriers to IT adoption. Arranged from the most to least frequent, these barriers included: lack of confidence, lack of access to quality resources, lack of time, lack of effective training, technical problems, lack of personal access, and age.

Brush (2003), studied what teachers themselves think are the barriers to IT-related instruction. Nine barriers included in his survey were: lack of hardware, lack of software, lack of network access, lack of time to develop courses, lack of support by department or school, lack of salary support during the development period, lack of students' preparation to handle technology, lack of facilities for student laboratories, and lack of central resources.

Al-Moussa (2004) discussed the barriers to integration of IT within Gulf Cooperation Council (GCC) countries. They are: lack of teachers' training programs in the use of the computer, high cost of computer peripherals, and lack of computer technicians in the schools to help teachers and administrators apply IT.

The chapter is an organized as follows. In Section 2 we introduce our methodology which provides procedure to collect our data and shows the findings regarding barriers of IT education in Yanbu. In Section 3 we present the limitation of our analysis method. In Section 4 we present results and discussions. Finally we summarize the chapter with future discussion and recommendations.

2. Methodology

The study was conducted in Yanbu education district in Saudi Arabia. The research designs used were descriptive, comparative, and correlational. Both male and female science teachers at the elementary, middle, and high school levels were asked on their use of IT in the classroom. Comparisons of their survey responses were made. The relationship between demographic information and science teachers' computer experience to their attitudes toward computers was also determined.

The study examined and identified the barriers that hinder the inclusion of IT in science education in Saudi Arabia. The research instrument was developed to replicate this study at future time intervals to monitor trends and the degree of the technology use in Saudi Arabia over a period of time.

Based on the findings from a preliminary focus group of 80 science teachers in Saudi Arabia, common barriers to IT adoption were identified and used to design the survey instrument.

2.1 Variables

There were three categories of variables in the study: (a) dependent variables, (b) demographic variables, and (c) independent variables. The dependent variables of this study were the scores related to degree and frequency of technology use. The instrument used scored measures of amount of technology use, skill levels, and conformity with technology.

The demographic variables came from questions included in the final segment of the survey. These questions include: (a) school location, b) participant's gender, (c) his/her years of teaching experience, (d) pre-service IT training, (e) in-service IT training, and (f) age.

The independent variables focused on four categories of barriers. Each category contained statements designed to test the frequency of the science teachers' responses to determine whether or not it should be considered a barrier. The four groups were: (a) infrastructure and resources, (b) policy and support, (c) science teachers' personal beliefs, and (d) staff development. Participants were asked to add any other barriers they considered important that were not mentioned in the instrument.

2.2 Survey Instrument

The survey consisted of two main parts. The first part investigated barriers to implementing IT in science education in public schools in Yanbu education district in Saudi Arabia. The second part focused on demographic factors.

The first part of the instrument consisted of four sections: (a) infrastructure and resources, (b) policy and support, (c) science teachers' beliefs, and (d) staff development. It also included barriers not previously mentioned in the instrument but added by study participants in response to an open-ended question. Participants evaluated each barrier and rated it according to the values defined in Table 1.

Description	Value
Does Not Limit	0
Slightly Limits	1
Somewhat Limit	2
Greatly Limits	3

Table 1. Limitations of Technology Scale

The second part of the survey contained 12 elements of demographic information. They included: (a) schools' location, (b) gender, (c) years of teaching experience, (d) training, (e) age, (f) grade levels taught, (g) number of classes taught weekly, (h) highest educational degree and year earned, (i) presence of a computer in their home or school, (j) where computers were used (at home or school), (k) where access to the Internet was available (at home or school), and (l) number of computers available in teachers' classrooms and in computer laboratories in schools.

2.3 Participants/Respondents

Study participants included teachers from all K-12 grade levels who were teaching during the School Year 2003-2004. According to the Department of Statistics (2003) in Yanbu Education District, there were a total of 284 science teachers in grades K-12. Survey questionnaires were sent to all schools at the Yanbu education district and distributed by the educational training department to all male and female science teachers who volunteered to participate in the study. Aboutb 176 questionnaires were returned back by 105 male and 71 female science teachers, constituting 60 percent and 40 percent of those solicited, respectively.

2.4 Statistical Methods

The first research question asked was "Do science teachers encounter common barriers that prevent them from effectively using IT in science education in the public schools at Yanbu education district in Saudi Arabia?" The null hypothesis for this question is: Science teachers do not encounter common barriers that prevent them from effectively using IT in science education in the public schools at the Yanbu education district in Saudi Arabia.

This was tested using the sample *t*-test. The domains were tested individually which include: (a) infrastructure and resources, (b) policy and support, (c) science teachers' personal beliefs, and (d) staff development (Table 2). In a Table 2 analysis the statistics and Intercorellation Matrix describing barriers to integration of IT in Science education in Yanbu School as indicated by frequency of IT use.

The average of all participants in every domain was derived. Arranged by perceived importance, the participants reported that most barriers were associated with infrastructure and resources, staff development, policy and support, and the teachers' personal beliefs. SPSS was used to calculate the *t*-statistic and its significance at .05 level.

Variable	Intercorrelation							
	Mean	SD	SEM	IT	IR	PS	PB	SD
Frequency of use of IT	1.13	.78		.88				
Infrastructure and Resources (IR)	2.06	.673	.051	.04*	.93			
Policy and Support (PS)	1.84	.696	.052	-.18*	.48*	.86		
Teachers' Personal Beliefs (PB)	1.15	.682	.052	-.20**	.17*	.39**	.91	
Staff Development (SD)	2.02	.783	.59	-.16*	.67**	.77**	.67**	.92

Table 2. Descriptive Statistics and Intercorellation Matrix

Note: Cronbach's alpha scores of internal consistency are reported in diagonal of correlation matrix

*Significant at .05 level of significance

** Significant at .01 level of significance

The second research question asked was , "Do science teachers encounter unique barriers (other than explicit barriers listed in the second research question) that may prevent them from effectively using IT in science education in Saudi Arabia?" All anticipated major barriers that may prevent science teachers from using IT were explicitly included in the survey. Acknowledging that important barriers may have been overlooked, an open-ended question was included to let the participants express their opinions and thoughts about barriers not mentioned in the survey. Analysis of their answers was conducted by calculating how many times each new barrier mentioned was repeated. After the data were collected, responses were summarized and classified based on location and gender.

3. Limitation

This study was focused only on science teachers from only one educational district covering School Year 2003-2004. Aspects of IT implementation can change over time. Based on the continuous evolutionary development of the computer industry, the degree of technology use this year may be different from that of next year.

This research was limited to a specific region in Saudi Arabia, the Yanbu district. It is hoped that these results could be generalized due to the inclusion of feedback from across Saudi Arabia which was used in the development of the survey instrument. However, one limiting factor of this research is that the results may not be generalized to non-science teachers. The barriers to the application of IT in other fields may be different from those in the field of science.

4. Experimental Results and Discussions

Barriers to IT Integration
Results of a one-sample t-test for all these subdomains of barriers to IT integration are reported in Table 3. All p values for the four subdomains are less than .05 indicating that these common barriers prevent science teachers from effectively using IT science education in the public schools in the Yanbu education district in Saudi Arabia.

	t Value	Significance	Mean
Infrastructure and Resources	40.52	.000*	2.06
Policy and Support	35.11	.000*	1.84
Science Teachers' personal belief	22.36	.000*	1.15
Staff Development	34.13	.000*	2.03

Table 3. Limitations of Technology Scale
*Significant at .05 level of significance

Top ten barriers. To discern trends, specific common barriers were examined in terms of frequency of occurrence. Tables 4 and 5 show the top 10 and top five barriers by frequency of response, respectively.

#	Barrier	Mean	Std. Dev	Sub-Domain
1	No Specific IT Budget	2.48	.88	PS
2	Lack of Finding for Hardware	2.48	.88	PS
3	No Electronic, Science Text Books	2.31	1.01	IR
4	Lack of English Training needed for IT	2.27	.97	SD
5	Not enough Time in School for IT related activities	2.26	1.06	STPB
6	No instructional support for incorporating IT into teaching	2.24	1.13	IR
7	No vision or Strategic plan for IT	2.23	1.01	PS
8	Science Curriculum not compatible with IT	2.18	1.03	IR
9	No access to Internet during School	2.18	1.12	IR
10	Classroom Architecture not suitable for IT	2.17	1.09	IR

Table 4. Top Ten Barriers that limit the Use of IT in Science Education at Yanbu, KSA

Note: Scale runs from "doecn't limit" (0) to "greatly limits". N = 176.
Where
IR = Infrastructure and Resources
PS = Policy and Support
STPB = Science Teachers' Personal Beliefs
SD = Staff Development

Five least frequently cited barriers. There were five statements in the survey that most participants considered to be the least limiting barriers to IT use (Table 6).

The following summarizes the additional barriers as submitted by participants in response to the open-ended question. Most of their responses were focused on the following:

1. No information technology resource centers in education districts and in schools;
2. No specialist trainers to train teachers and students;
3. Busy schedules leave no time;
4. Teaching more than one subject;
5. Shortage of short courses (in-service training); and
6. High cost of short courses.

	Does Not Limit	**Slightly Limit**	**Somewhat Limit**	**Greatly Limit**
	Freq %	**Freq** %	**Freq** %	**Freq** %
No specific budget for information technology in my school (PS)	9 5.1	19 10.8	27 15.3	121 68.8
The lack of school funds to get hardware (PS)	19 10.08	13 7.4	38 21.6	106 60.2
Students don't have access to the internet during the school day (IR)	25 14.2	21 11.9	28 15.9	102 58.0
The architecture of class rooms are not suitable for implementing IT	23 13.1	22 12.5	33 18.8	98 55.7

Table 5. Limitations to Technology integration imposed by Infrastructure and Resources
Note. Where N = 176, IR = Infrastructure and resources, PS = Policy and support, STPB = Science teachers' personal beliefs and SD = Staff Development

It was found that some male teachers from industrial locations and some male teachers from urban locations agreed about the following barriers that prevented them from effective applications of IT. They reported that there was no IT center in the education district or in their schools and there were no specialized and qualified trainers to train teachers and students to use IT in the right way.

Many of the female science teachers from industrial locations experienced the same barriers that male teachers from suburban locations have experienced. These barriers were: busy schedules, teaching more subjects, and doing some work besides teaching. All of these barriers prevent them from applying IT to educational practice. In addition, female teachers from industrial locations have encountered some of the same barriers as male teachers from urban locations, including the shortage of short-course training on how to implement IT into the science curriculum and the high cost they would incur if they choose to pay on their own.

	Does Not Limit	Slightly Limit	Somewhat Limit	Greatly Limit
	Freq %	Freq %	Freq %	Freq %
My School's principal has negative attitudes towards application of information technology. (PS)	9 5.1	19 10.8	27 15.3	121 68.8
The Science supervisor doesn't follow up if I use information technology or not. (PS)	19 10.08	13 7.4	38 21.6	106 60.2
I am frightened of the consequences if I damaged the computer equipments. (PS)	25 14.2	21 11.9	28 15.9	102 58.0
There is no computer specialist at my School. (PS)	23 13.1	22 12.5	33 18.8	98 55.7
The lack of understanding of science supervisors about the important of the information technology. (PS)	23 13.1	22 12.5	33 18.8	98 55.7

Table 5. Bottom Five Barriers to Technology integration imposed by Policy and Support Relating them to gender and location.

5. Conclusion and Future Research

We investigate barriers that prevent teachers from making effective use of information technology in science education in K-12 public schools in the Yanbu education district in Saudi Arabia. Identifying the fundamental barriers encountered by the science teachers in integrating IT into the classroom is the first step towards a solution to the problem. Two related barriers are greatly limiting which are as follows:

1. No specific budget for IT in school; and
2. Lack of school funds to get hardware.

These financial barriers could be minimized by providing support and funds from the Ministry of Education and the Yanbu educational district. This study was not the first to identify these barriers. When Al-Mohaissin (1993) applied his study in Saudi Arabia, one of the barriers he identified was the shortage of computers in the schools. This finding is similar to that of Al-Mohaissin (1993) which revealed that funding is not the first problem that needs to be solved. Hendren (2000) declared that the three important factors affecting science teachers' use of technology in the high school classrooms are: lack of access, insufficient funds, and lack of vision. Carter (1998) found that the two most important barriers are lack of computers in the classroom and lack of time to learn how to incorporate IT into the curriculum. Of the five statements least considered as barriers limiting the use of IT into the classroom, all are related to the subdomain of policy and support. School administration is characterized by some participants as being relatively supportive of the effort to integrate technology into the classroom and not perceived as a primary barrier to technology integration. Barriers rooted in policies and funding require a well-conceived, strategic vision, adequate funding, and implementation plan before much change can be expected.

6. References

Al-Mohaissin, I. A. (1993). Instructions into secondary school science teaching in Saudi Arabia: Teachers' views, some problems and possible solutions. Doctoral dissertation University of Hull.

Al-Moussa, A. (2004). The integration the information technology to Gulf Cooperation Council (GCC) countries [Electronic version]. Al-Riyadh Newspaper, 22 March 2004.

Al-Oteawi, S. M. (2002). The perceptions of administrators and teachers in utilizing information technology in instruction, administrative work, technology planning and staff development in Saudi Arabia, Doctoral issertation. Ohio University.

Beggs, T. A. (2000). Influences and barriers to the adoption of instructional technology. Paper presented at the fifth annual Mid-South Instructional Technology Conference. Retrieved April 11, 2004, from http://www.mtsu.edu/itconf/proceed00/beggs/beggs.htm

British Educational Communications & Technology Department (BECTA). ICT Barriers Survey (2000). Retrieved April 11, 2004 from http://www.becta.org.uk/research.

British Educational Communications & Technology Department (BECTA), (2004). What the research says about barriers to the use of ICT in teaching. Retrieved: April 11, 2004, from http://www.becta.org.uk/ page_documents/ research/wtrs_barriersinteach.pdf.

Brush, T. (2003). Preparing tomorrow's teachers to use technology (PT3). Educational Technology Research & Development, 51(1), 39-128.

Carter, C.W. (1998). An assessment of the status of the diffusion and adoption of computer-based technology in Appalachian college association colleges and universities. Doctoral dissertation, Virginia Polytechnic Institute and State University, Dissertation Abstracts International, 59(10A), 3725.

Corbin, J. F. (2003). The integration of technology into the middle and high school science curriculum, Dissertation Abstracts International. (UMI No. 3081518).

Ertmer, P. A. (1999). Addressing first- and second-order barriers to change: Strategies for technology integration. Educational Technology Research and Development, 47(4), 47-61.

Hendren, K. (2000). The effect of first and second order barriers on the ideal and actual integration of computer technology into the high science classroom, Dissertation Abstracts International.

Hope, W. (1997). Teachers, computer technology, and the change process. Clearing House, 70(4), 191-93. Retrieved April 12, 2004 from http://science.uniserve.edu.au/newsletter/vol11/yeo.html.

Mulqueen, W. E. (2001). Technology in the classroom: Lessons learned through professional development. Education, 122(2), 248-256.

National Council for Accreditation of Teacher Education (NCATE). (1997). Technology and the new professional teacher: Preparing for the 21st century classroom. Retrieved May 1, 2004, from http://www.ncate.orglaccreci/projects/ tech/tech-21.htm.

Samman, B. S. (2003). Towards a Successful Implementation of ICT in the Education System of the KSA. Unpublished master's thesis, University of Leeds, UK.

Weber, R. K. (1996). An identification of barriers to the integration of information technology as perceived by secondary education teacher education students, Doctoral dissertation. Georgia State University. UMI

Yeo, S. (1998). Interactive multimedia in secondary Physics classrooms, Curtin University of Technology, UniServe Science News Volume 11. Retrieved May 11, 2004, from http://science.uniserve.edu.au/newsletter/vol11/yeo.html.

Zakaria, Z. (2001). Factors related to information technology implementation in the Malaysian Ministry of Education Polytechnics. Doctoral dissertation. The Virginia Polytechnic Institute and State University.

3

The Use of Multi-Agents' Systems in e-Learning Platforms

Tomasz Marcin Orzechowski
AGH University of Science and Technology
Poland

1. Introduction

E-learning systems become more and more popular in many areas of education. They enable distance learning as well as allow digital content creators to establish specialized training centres. Such systems are commonly used by numerous governmental organizations as well as commercial content vendors. All these systems share a common purpose: they provide access to on-line learning resources for education. These resources are used by teachers or instructors to create courses in a given subject or topic. As browsing such repositories is inconvenient, inefficient and sometimes impossible, various search engines have been developed to help users retrieve specific data. However, often it is not possible to formulate the search queries alone so that they can pick out the elements, which are of value to a user. The problem of ordering search results by predicted level of interest for the user pertains both to general-purpose Internet search engines and to browsing assistants in specialized repositories. It gets even more severe if elements are very similar as far as their keywords or descriptions are concerned.
The increase in the amount of resources available in e-learning systems will require the need for designing new architecture of such systems. The most important is to provide the ways for sharing resources in accordance with copyrights and to offer possibilities to rearrange course contents consisting of elementary resources.
The main purpose of the presented system was to design and implement the advanced search system, which will allow teachers and pupils to obtain results according to their profiles and interests.
This work was partially supported by the European Commission under the Information Society Technologies (IST) program of the 6th FP for RTD as part of the CALIBRATE project, contract IST-28025.

2. State of Art

2.1 E-learning Systems

The term "e-learning" is commonly defined as this kind of educational approach, where ICT (Information and Communication Technology) is used.

Computers are the basic equipment used in the e-learning process. Different kinds of educational software created and verified by domain specialists and educators allows the implementation of the principles of education, which are the individualization of the trainings and teaching by examples.
Technical capabilities make possible a visualisation of knowledge as well as the alignment of both the pace and structure of the education content to the individual recipient's perception. For example, existing applications, already used in preschool teaching, successfully support the learning of colours, shapes, letters, and perceptivity. Popularity and fast access to the Internet extend learning opportunities both for access to new resources and allow for different kinds of contact such as voice calls, chats, and video transmission among users of the system.
The authors distinguish 2-4 main types of training using e-learning techniques. In this example, Schulmeister (2003) distinguishes between individual - type A and group training - type B, closely related to the form of materials (Fig. 1).

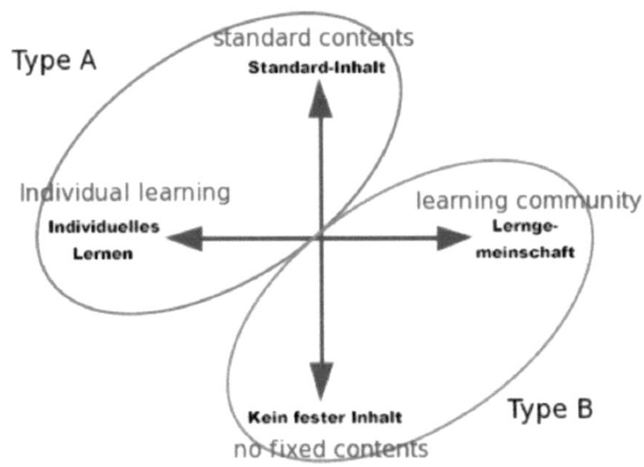

Fig. 1. E-learning types *(orig. "Typisierungvon Lernumgebungen" Schulmeister, 2003, p.16)*

According to Schulmeister (2003), individual trainings - type A - is person-to-standardised content interaction, whilst type B - person-to-person interaction - is the acquisition of knowledge in interaction with members of specific communities of practise (Schlager & Fusco, 2004).
This categorisation is similar to Michael Graham Moore's (1989), considered as an educational theory classic, who suggested three kinds of interactions:

- *learner - content*
- *learner - instructor*
- *learner - learner*

Moore acknowledges as the crucial interaction between student and instructor, who is a domain specialist. This specialist has impact on increasing student's motivation to the course, and acceleration of interest to the presented contents. This specialist is responsible for combining theoretical knowledge with practice to make the knowledge be better assimilated. The amount of taught knowledge is constantly verified during the teaching process.

Hillman, Willis and Gunawerdena (1994) have expanded the list of interaction by adding the learner - interface interaction. They indicate the importance of electronic equipments used in the education process.
Another author also divided e-learning processes into the following three groups:

- *self-study*
- *synchronous education*
- *asynchronous education*

We can also distinguish blended-learning, which is actually the classical learning process extended by some e-learning elements.
The basic unit of electronic content is called Learning Object - LO, which may be either elementary content (Learning Asset) such as: a single image, video, or text file, or may consist of several other LOs respectively associated with each other.
Complex LO could form a single unit such as classrooms, and even the entire course.
A well-described LO by IEEE LOM Standard (IEEE 1484 Learning Objects Metadata, 2005) can be shared not only by members of the given e-learning platform but accessible from various platforms. Currently, there are many standards that describe requirements for various e-learning platforms that can share resources.
The most popular are SCORM (Sharable Content Object Reference Model), specifications provided by IMS GLC, or PENS (Package Exchange Notification Services), or the oldest recommendations defined by AICC (Aviation Industry CBT Committee).

E-learning courses are created, managed, and used facilitating the existing e-learning management systems belonging to following main categories:

- LMS - Learning Management System (Fig. 2);
- CMS - Content Management System (Fig. 3);
- LCMS -Learning Content Management System (Fig. 4).

Sometimes, the following category is also distinguished:

- VCS -Virtual Classroom System.

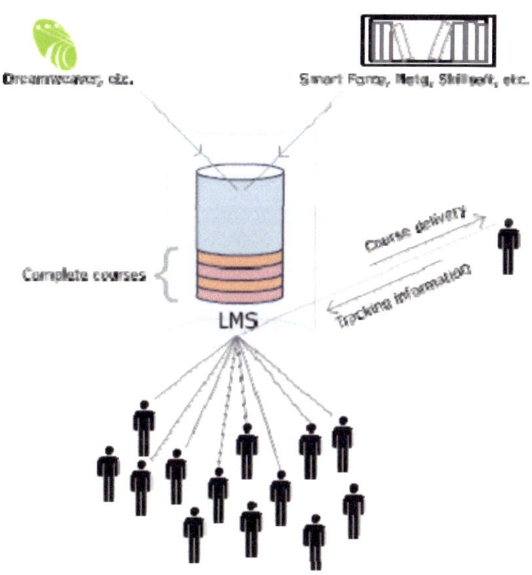

Fig. 2. General Structure of LMS (Nichani, 2001)

LMS is a family of systems, which enables management of all training activities as well as provides presentation of content associated with courses. In particular, LMS systems categorize the users, give them certain permissions to training modules and assign users to specific training groups. In addition, LMS systems offer the ability to monitor the progress of knowledge and skills learned by individual students (Nichani, 2001; Rengarajan, 2001).

CMS is a family of e-learning systems dedicated to creating, storing, managing and presenting content. Significant in this model is to provide opportunities for reusability of Learning Objects, called RLO (Reusable LO) (Nichani, 2001) or content components.
Another feature of CMS is the separation of content from layout (Nichani, 2001).

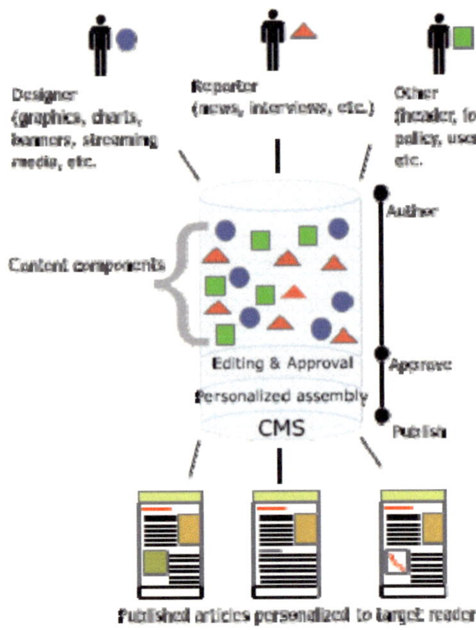

Fig. 3. General Structure of CMS (Nichani, 2001)

It is noteworthy that the LMS can be used only for the teaching process - presenting content and management of students, whilst the CMS assists users to create the content from available elementary components. Development of CMS systems is an example of B2C services (business-to-consumer). Resources collected by these systems may be offered to external institutions.
LCMS is a family of the most technologically advanced e-learning systems. LCMS systems integrate features of LMS and CMS (Nichani, 2001), ensuring both the creation and management of educational content. They provide opportunity for the creation of WBT courses (Web-Based Training) as well as the management and the management of the learning process, taking into account the evaluation of knowledge assimilated by the users (Nichani, 2001; Rengarajan, 2001).

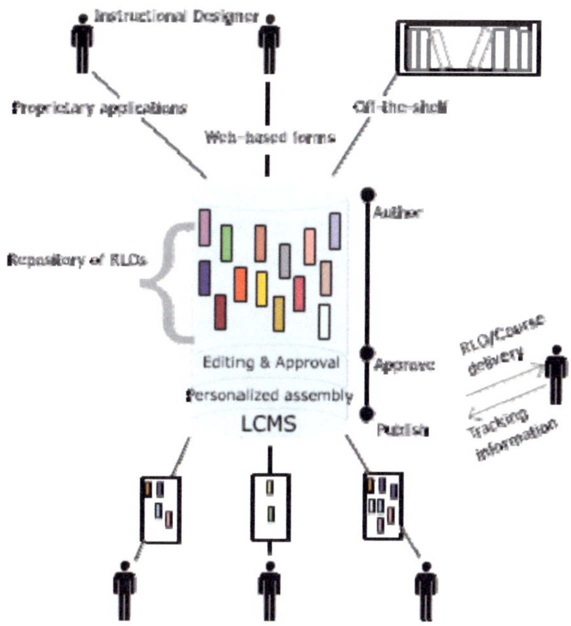

Fig. 4. General Structure of LCMS (Nichani, 2001)

The impact of e-learning trainings on education processes will be expanded. This is caused by fast technology development and the efficiency of this form of training.
Marschall McLuhan Herbert, media specialist, who lived in the period 1911-1980, noted that the media are a key factor in any changes in society. His theory that "the medium is the message" indicates a significant impact on the nature of the medium both on the transmitted content and the quality of the content reception. Media, according to him, may "exclude" (hot media) or "engage" the recipient (cold media).
E-learning systems are able to use the described effect of the transfer of content involving the user's perception almost entirely. Users in constant interaction with content can assimilate the knowledge contained in the received content faster and more efficiently.
The correctness of this prediction was confirmed by the analysis carried out by us at IBM, which pointed out two main advantages of e-learning solution: the effectiveness of training and a real reduction in the cost of training. E-learning trainings allowed this company to reduce training costs by 50-70% and shorten the training time from 11 to 9 weeks, while the productivity of educated workers grew to 100-170%.
It is therefore not surprising that e-learning techniques are becoming popular and are promoted throughout the world.
European Union promotes e-learning techniques under the EU Structural Funds (2007-2013), and within the framework of the "Lifelong Learning Program (LLP).
There are two main problems to be solved when we decide to make a semi-global open e-learning system. The first is: "how to describe and register learning objects (LOs)". The second is: "how to find the LOs that the given user is really interested in".
Independently in both of these two situations we can consider a centralised or decentralised model. The centralised systems are better managed but they are not safe in the case of

scalability. On the other hand, the decentralised systems can solve the problem of scalability but they cannot be managed simply.
A solution is to create a hierarchical structure (semi-centralised) and use the multi-agents' platform to manage this structure and arrange all offered services (Orzechowski & Dziech, 2001a; Orzechowski, 2001b; Orzechowski, 2002).

2.2 Learning Objects in the federation of repositories

The need to provide educational exchange of data has been known for years. The best-known initiatives include:

- ARIADNE Foundation in Europe (www.ariadne-eu.org);
- Multimedia Educational Resources for Learning and Online Teaching (MERLOT) in USA (www.merlot.org);
- LORNET in Canada (www.lornet.org);
- education.au in Australia (www.educationau.edu.au/jahia);
- National Institute of Multimedia Education (NIME) in Japan (www.nime.ac.jp)

These organizations have set up a joint group: "The Global Learning Objects Brokered Exchange" (GLOBE), intended to integrate all standardization work to create and develop open standards for educational data exchange in one integrated brokerage environment.
GLOBE initiative has been met with great interest and now consists of many new members. The most influential institutions are: COSL, EUN, III, KERIS and LACLO.

Two basic standards enabling search in repositories are:

- SQI - Simple Query Interface defines how to access and exchange data among repositories (Simon et al., 2005);
- OAI-PMH - The Open Archives Initiative Protocol for Metadata Harvesting creates independent interoperability framework based on metadata harvesting *(www.openarchives.org/OAI/2.0/openarchivesprotocol.htm)*.

SQI interface is used to transmit queries and results received during the session between the client and repository of metadata. It is fully independent from both query language and format of returned results. Although it is possible to implement SQI to work with any data representation, XML is the most popular. Usually, SOAP, RPC, or RMI are used as exchange protocol between clients and repositories. Session management of SQI is equipped with optional authentication mechanisms. It also supports working in synchronous and asynchronous mode for LOM retrieval, which is important when federation search is used to search the whole federation of repositories at once.
Schema of SQI-oriented communication among clients and repositories is shown in Figure 5. (Simon et al., 2005)

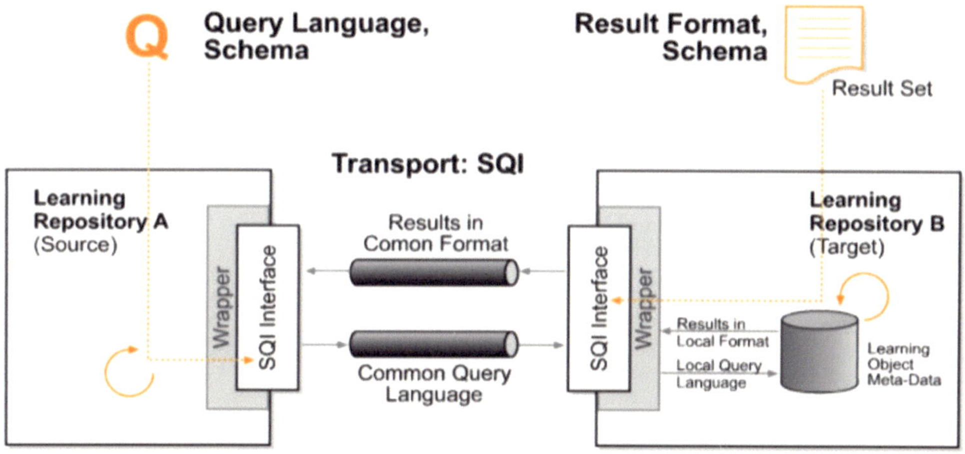

Fig. 5. Communication between components of the system based on the SQI

SQI specification was officially approved during the CEN/ISSS workshop on Learning Technologies in July 2005 by the group of experts working in various EU projects concerning federations of learning resources topics, most specifically: Celebrate, Elena, Ariadne, and Edutella.

One of the languages used to create queries sent via SQI interface is S2QL. S2QL (Simple School Query Language) is a simple query language designed specifically for finding learning resources in different types of repositories. It is abstract language, referring to some abstract pattern, which does not reflect the actual data. Queries in this language cannot be directly processed by the repository. They must be converted to the structure, which is supported by the given database engine of the repository.

S2QL queries are limited only to three possibilities:

- keywords;
- age range; and
- language of learning object.

S2QL schema and namespaces are available in the following locations: http://fire.eun.org/xsd/s2ql-1.0.xsd, and http://fire.eun.org/xsd/s2ql-1.0.xsd.

OAI-PMH is a protocol for the selective gathering of metadata describing learning objects. It allows the automatic exchange of information between systems gathering metadata and their clients. Unlike SQI, OAI-PMH doesn't limit the number of found LOM transferred to the client. Moreover, it is especially dedicated to situations where we actually do not want "to search" by keywords but "to gather" all LOMs by their repository ids, or by the date of deletion, modification or storing in the repository. Communication in OAI-PMH is based on client-server structure and uses HTTP protocol where results are delivered as an XML file. This protocol was used in the ABSS presented in section 3 of this chapter.

The Ariadne Network is a good example of a distributed network of repositories. It was developed by the ARIADNE Foundation that was formed to continue the work and further development of EU projects: ARIADNE and ARIADNE II.

There are also other interesting initiatives such as MACE Project (Metadata for Architectural Contents in Europe 2006-2009). Its aim is to establish the integrated access to repositories containing any data concerning architecture domain, which were the results of other EU research projects such as: DYNAMO, INCOM and WINDS. Actually, MACE project doesn't target to a network of distributed repositories, but to create a single coherent virtual repository of data (Prause et al., 2007; Stefaner et al., 2007). This approach is similar to the one presented in section 3.

The basic element of network structure, Ariadne is a repository that can be searched using SQI. Ariadne Network users can both browse and publish their contents. The structure of the Ariadne network is shown in Figure 6.

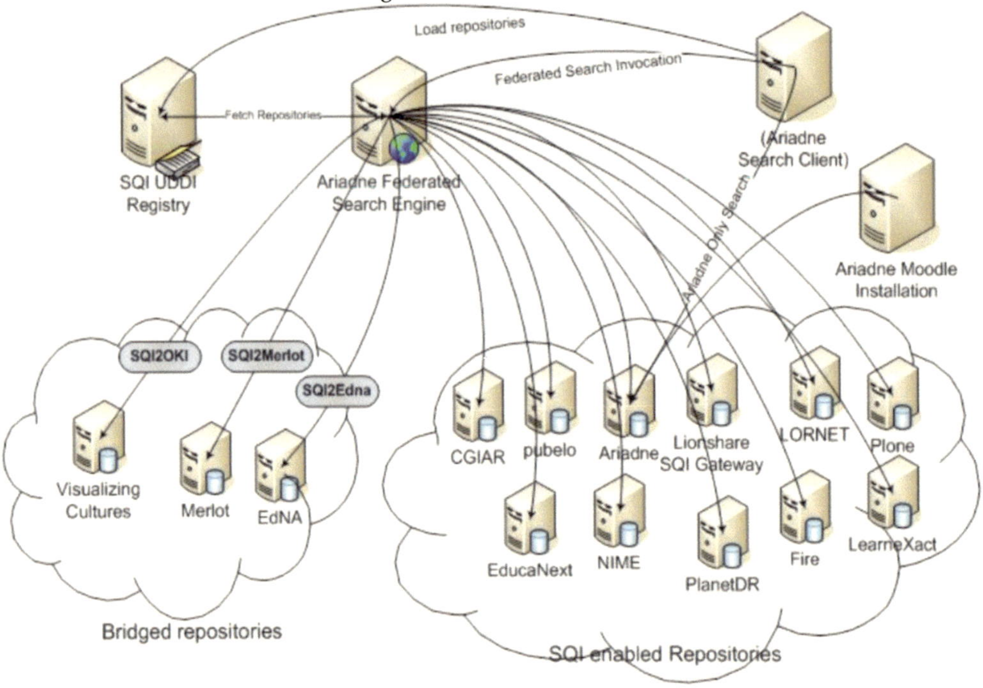

Fig. 6. The structure of the Ariadne Network (http://www.ariadne-eu.org)

Ariadne offers many additional tools, for example Web-Based Learning Environment (WBLE) for the creation and management of educational courses. A person who is responsible for creating a course may use WBLE to create it on the base of LOs collected in the KPS (Knowledge Pool System), which is a distributed database of teaching materials, and then distribute it to students (Van Durm et al., 2001).

KPS consists of resources called Local Knowledge Pool Systems (LKPs) localised in different countries (Najjar et al., 2004). The following APIs were defined to establish the functionality described above: 1. AMI (Ariadne Management Interface) allows teachers access to courses they created, and 2. ALI (Ariadne Learner Interface), which allows access to approved courses (Fig. 7)

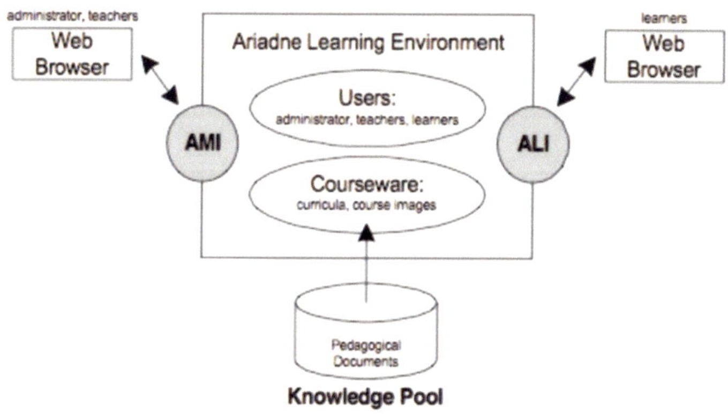

Fig. 7. The Ariadne Web-Based Learning Environment (Van Durm et al., 2001)

An important feature of the Ariadne Network is that it is possible to combine the various repositories in the network by connecting them to the broker. The Ariadne Network is hidden from the end-users' sight under a brokerage layer (Fig. 8).

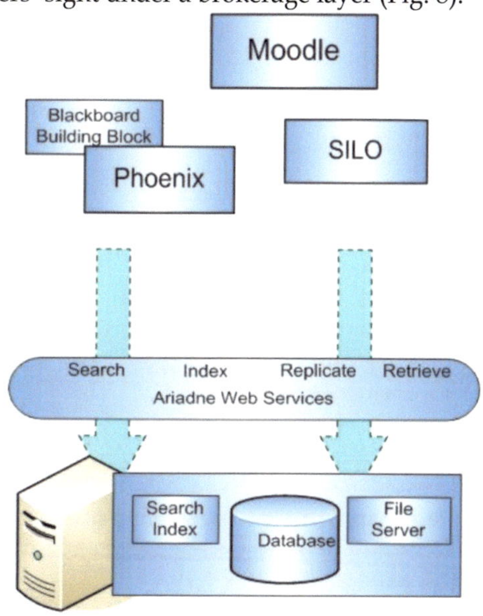

Fig. 8. The schema of communication between clients and the Ariadne Network (http://www.ariadne-eu.org)

Three-layered structure, described above, consists of:
1. Clients - client applications such as tools for queries and indexing, search portals such as PROLEARN, and VLE systems through appropriate plug-ins;
2. Middleware - a layer, which enables Federated Search functionality. It is responsible for sending queries to the repositories, merging received results, sorting them, and then transferring to end-users. Information about repositories connected to this middleware is stored in a UDDI SQI Registry. This register contains information about the active

repositories supporting SQI, and some other additional information such as: - the URL needed to access the Service, - supported query languages, - the type of communication that is supported (synchronous or asynchronous), - contact person responsible for each repository, - a description of the repository, etc.
3. Repositories – Learning Objects Repositories, which are components of the federation and support being searched by SQI.
Federation Search was proposed for the fast search done in real time. It is performed by sending requests at the same time to all repositories connected to the Federation (Simon et al., 2005). All steps of this process are presented in Figure 9.

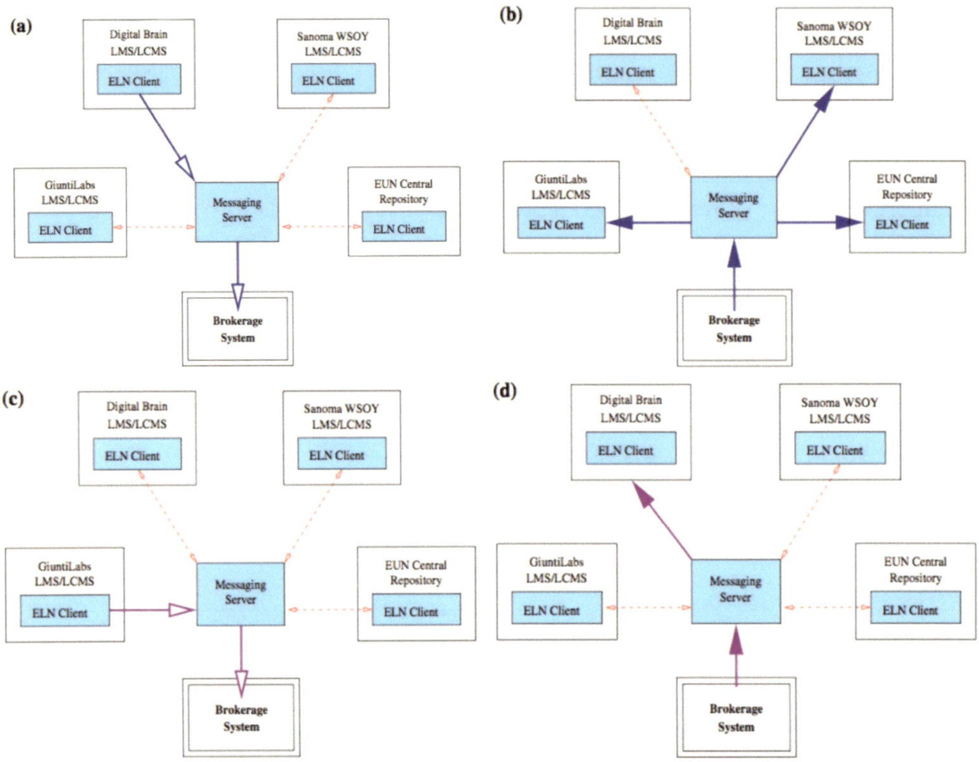

Fig. 9. The schema of Federated Search process (a) sending query by client, (b) distributing query to all repositories, (c) receiving and processing results by broker, (d) sending processed results to client (Van Assche & Massart, 2004).

A well-known disadvantage of this approach is the simple lack of possibility for the introduction of new algorithms into the Federation of Repositories. Implementation of advance search algorithms needs to provide changes done directly at repositories' sites, whilst presented in this chapter, the agents' system approach does not have this kind of limitation.

2.3 Multi-Agents' Platforms

An agent, which is a specific programming entity, is defined as "one who acts" or "one who acts in place of" (Franklin & Graesser, 1997). An agent could be described by the following features: autonomous, reactive, communicative, learning, cooperative, or mobile.

The most important feature of agents is autonomy. According to Franklin & Graesser (1997), "an autonomous agent is a system situated within and a part of an environment that senses that environment and acts on it, over time, in pursuit of its own agenda and so as to effect what it senses in the future". Another definition provided by Jennings (1996) is, "the term is usually applied to describe self-contained programs which can control their own actions based on their perceptions of their operating environment".

Multi-agents' platforms are used for efficient agent managing. The platforms are based on an organizational model of multi-agents' platforms described within a standard that consists of the group of specification documents concerning system architecture, agent communication language, etc. Each platform implements a set of specifications of chosen standard.

Nowadays there are two standards for multi-agents' systems available: MASIF (www.omg.org) and FIPA standard (www.fipa.org). MASIF was dedicated to enable agents travelling among agent systems via CORBA interfaces and does not address inter-agent communication, whilst the FIPA defines specifications for agent communication, agent transport, agent management, abstract architecture and applications.

The core category of the FIPA multi-agents' system is agent communication. FIPA's models do not imply any physical configuration and it is not a scope of FIPA standards to deliver strict guidelines for multi-agents' platform implementation. FIPA standard contains Agent Management Reference Model, being a base for developers who want to design and implement own multi-agents' platform. Architecture of the system contains FIPA's specification of mandatory components for platform managing:

- ACC - Agent Communication Channel;
- AMS - Agent Management System;
- DF - Directory Facilitator.

All of these three components are automatically activated at the agent platform start-up.

There are several FIPA-compliant agent platforms. Very popular, commercial and well described is Tryllian Agent Development Kit. There are also some Open Source Agent Platforms, such as in the examples: April Agent Platform (agents must be written in April programming language), Comtec Agent Platform (it is not developed now), FIPA-OS (not developed since 2003), Grasshopper (official web page is no longer accessible), JADE and JADE-LEAP.

Java Agent DEvelopment Framework *(jade.tilab.com)* is written in Java Open Source and very advanced agent platform, which is fully compliant with FIPA 2000 standard, implemented in pure Java (Bellifemmine et al., 1999). It offers agents mobility, and a highly efficient communication interface based on several different protocols (Chmiel et al., 2005; Shakshuki & Jun, 2004).

The JADE-LEAP extension to JADE allows a wide variety of devices, like mobile phones, to connect to the platform. It also improves communication by adding different protocols including SSL secured ones.

The JADE platform is under continuous development. It was successfully used by many research and commercial organizations including INRIA, Nice-Sophia-Antipolis, ACACIA research team, ATOS Sophia Antipolis agency within the European CoMMA project, CSELT, KPN and Starlab within DICEMAN project, and many more, so the Agent Based Search System presented in the next section was established on the basis of this Platform as well.

3. Agent Based Search System

3.1 Overview

The main purpose of this work was to establish a System, which could improve search quality. Metadata is harvested from remote repositories to gather all needed information in the central repository for further advanced processing (compare with: Chmiel et al., 2005; Chkoliar, 2002, Curry et al., 2003).

The proposed System for use within the e-learning platform contains one multi-agent's layer that is physically divided into two parts: local main core, and remote parts integrated with LOs repositories (Fig. 10).

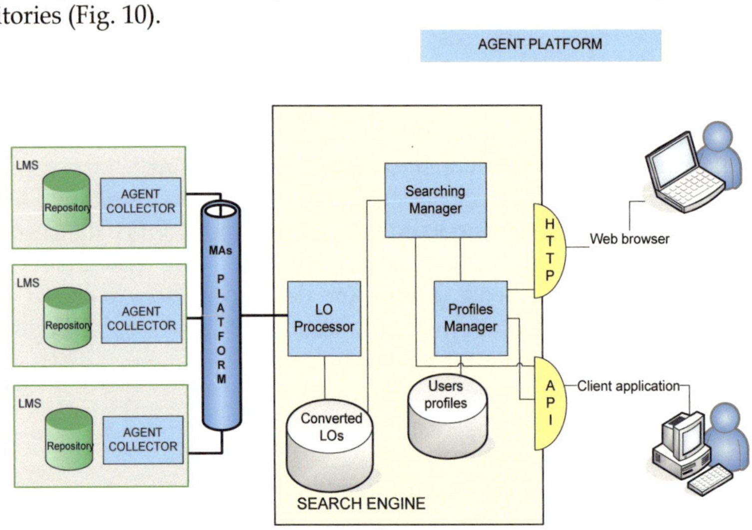

Fig. 10. General System Architecture (Orzechowski, 2007b)

3.2 General Structure

The Agent Based Search System (ABSS) was created on the basis of the Open Source JADE Platform. It consists of two main modules:

- Data Collection Module (Baran et al., 2007), and
- User Management and Resource Search Module (Orzechowski et al., 2007a).

According to functionality the second module could be divided into two functional modules:

- Search Module
- User Profile Module

The structure of the ABSS divided into three modules is presented in Figure 11.

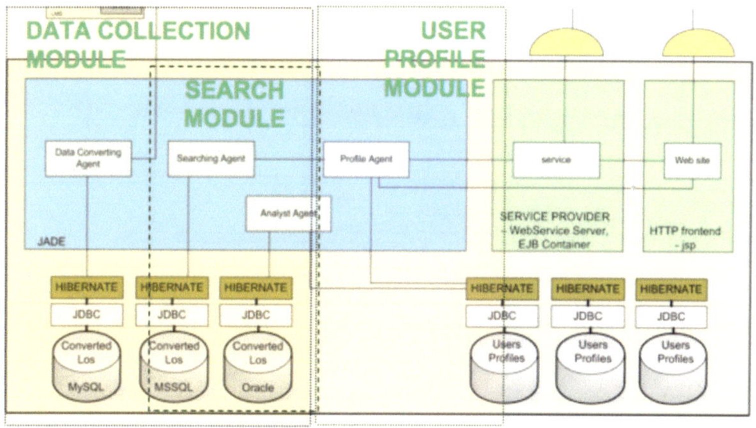

Fig. 11. General System Architecture divided into three modules (Orzechowski, 2007b)

A web interface is also available and it offers accessibility to main features the ABSS. It was built with the intention to calibrate some of the parameters of the Agent Based Search System (ABSS), and to display the most important functionalities of ABSS.

3.2.1 Data Collection Module

The Data Collection Module is responsible for gathering metadata from Repositories (LMS), performing necessary operations on it, and storing it in local databases. The following types of agents were implemented to perform the necessary operations:

- Content Manager Agent (CMA) with Collector Manager Agent (C2MA);
- Collector Agent (CA);
- Converter Agent (CV).

These agents cooperate with agents which are the part of Agent Platform, such as:

- AMS (Agent Management System); It manages agents and containers. CMA uses AMS to trace agent containers and to verify the presence of CA agents in these containers.
- DF (Directory Facilitator). It provides a Yellow Pages service in the Agent Platform so agents can find one another. This service is used by CMA to trace availability of Converter Agents registered in the DF.

The schema of internal interaction among components within DCM is presented in Figure 12.

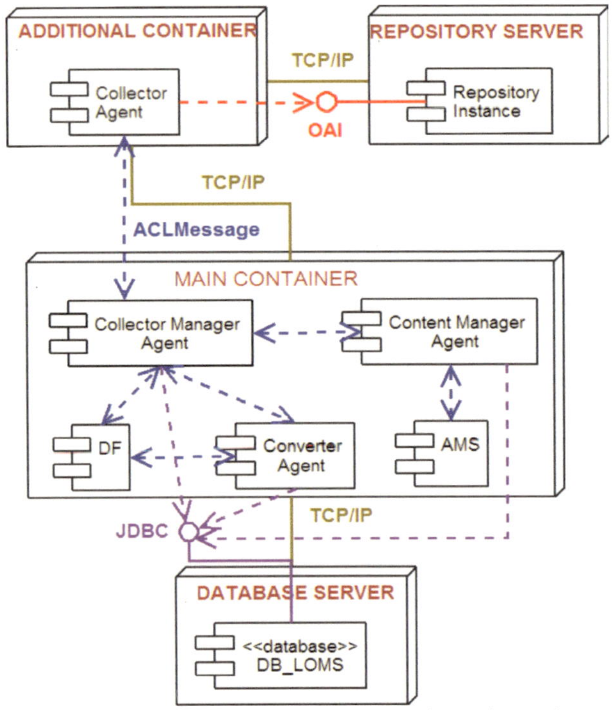

Fig. 12. The schema of the DCM internal structure (Orzechowski et al., 2009)

The Content Manager Agent is the most important agent, which is responsible for communication among all remote parts of the agent platform. There is only one instance of it in the whole system. It maintains an up-to-date list of all connected repositories. After detecting new LMS, the Content Manager creates a new Collector Agent and initializes it. The Collector Agent must be capable of detecting changes in the metadata repository, therefore it needs information about every LO that was previously (last time, when the LMS was connected) present in its database. After the initialization is finished, the Collector Agent moves to the repository and starts observations. When a change of metadata is detected (new LO added, LO deleted or metadata modified), the appropriate information is sent to the Content Manager.

Each Converter Agent, installed in the platform, is associated with a different search algorithm. It must analyse and store received information about LOs, so that it is available in a format that supports fast search. One Converter Agent is usually capable of processing metadata in one language. Each Converter Agent stores results of metadata processing in a separated table or database.

After a new Converter Agent is installed in the system, an initial converting action must be performed. It is very demanding, because every LOM in the adequate language, that has been stored in the local database, must be processed. After that, the Converter Agent publishes its capabilities in the Yellow Pages Service. When the Content Manager receives information about changes in metadata, it informs every appropriate Converter Agent, so that the change is introduced immediately.

Metadata Repositories (e.g. LMS) are accessed via the Open Archive Initiative Protocol for Metadata Harvesting (OAI-PMH).

The OAI-PMH is a lightweight harvesting protocol for sharing metadata between services. The OAI-PMH protocol is based on HTTP. Request arguments are issued as GET or POST parameters. The OAI-PMH supports six request types such as: Identify, ListMetadataFormats, ListSets, ListIdentifiers, ListRecords and GetRecord.
The following scenarios of data harvesting were implemented (Fig. 13):
1. Collector Agent (CA) is sent to a remote repository to perform all actions locally at repository's site. It controls contents all the time and notifies CMA if any changes occur.
2. Collector Agent (CA) is staying and operating locally. In this situation all metadata analysis is performed locally at the ABSS Core host. This approach is designed to the systems, which do not support DCM directly.

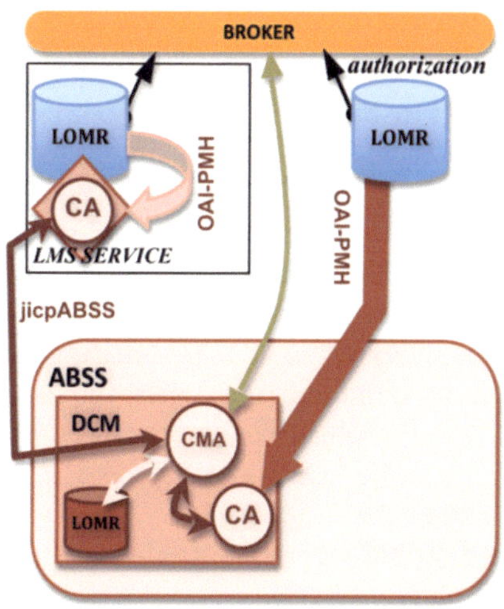

Fig. 13. DCM data harvesting approaches (Orzechowski et al., 2009)

ABSS-LMS is the name of modified JADE-LEAP components and some specialized software intended to be used by administrators of remote repositories to start up DCM components. Services provided by the ABSS-LMS guarantee that communication and registration processes are secure and stable. Security mechanisms include data encryption, achieved by using the SSL/TLS Java protocol and mutual authentication, realized by using digital certificates.
Specialized thread controls guard all platform and communication parameters and correct them automatically if something is out of order. They are responsible e.g. for re-initialization & reconnection of peripheral containers if connection between them and the main container has been lost. They can also kill an agent container, create a new one and register it if connection to the main container cannot be established again.
If the LMS host is part of a private-area network, the proposed and presented solutions (Orzechowski et al., 2009) can omit all of these problems. LMS ABSS-Component creates and runs an agent peripheral container and maintains its registration to the main container. Connections between peripheral and the main containers and communication between CA and CMA agents use specially designed protocol as the extension to existing JADE-LEAP JICP.

The main advantages of the proposed and implemented solutions can be pointed out as:
- Enabling secure communication among agents;
- Introduction of secure data transmission including mobile agents' transmission;
- Introduction of the thread control on each peripheral container;
- Secure registration of new peripheral container connected to DCM;
- Protection of main agent container against fake remote containers;
- Possibilities to connect to remote repository even if it is hidden by NAT;
- Decreasing the number of used ports on peripheral to only two ports.

3.2.2 Search Module

One of the main functionalities of the Multi-Agents' Search System is situated in the Search Module, which is responsible for selecting LOs that are satisfying a given request. The process of selection is performed by algorithms called "search methods" (Baran et al., 2007, Chmiel et al., 2005; Chkoliar, 2002).

The Search components as elements of the Search Module are intended to return the learning object identifiers that match the received query. Communication with other parts of the system is provided by a search agent object, which uses ACL messages to send all necessary information included (Orzechowski, 2007b).

Each search method is implemented by several Search Agents. Usually one Search Agent can perform search of LOMs in one language, as in the case of Converter Agents. The language-based division of local repositories and processing solves several important problems:

- Search algorithms operate on smaller data sets;
- Metadata repository can be distributed;
- Search process can be distributed;
- More popular languages can be supported by larger groups of agents.

The following Search Methods were implemented:

<u>Simple Search Method</u>

After a request is received from a personal agent, all queries are processed to obtain single words set in each category. Query processing eliminates redundant and meaningless words. There is also special character processing. For each language supported in the system a stop words list can be made, which includes words that are omitted in the search process. In English, this list contains e.g.: "for", "on", and "the." Next, a search query is launched for each word from the query in each set (keywords, title, author, description). It's based on comparing keywords and an index describing learning objects (in each - keyword, title, author, and description category). When there is a match - identificator of LOM (lom id) is returned. After a search for all words in a set is finished, results processing is launched in each category. It's based on the local merge mode value, which indicates if results are considered as a union or intersection. Based on results of this merge, there is a rate value assigned to each learning object.

The global merge mode is used as the parameter value to determine how to process results from each category (keyword, description, author, title). Based on this parameter, the next result processing is made.

The next step is to determine if other conditions are sent in the request (age, size, technical role, etc.). If so, actual results are restricted only to those which fulfill all conditions.

<u>Inverted Index Search Method</u>

The Inverted Index method is based on typical strategy of text search. Each word in every category (keyword, title, author, description) is associated to every object it refers to. This search algorithm is based on this relation. After the query is singled out and processed to a set of words (query processing similar as in Simple Search method), the search method finds all learning objects that are associated to those words. Based on the local merge mode ("and" or "or") there are unions or intersections taken and returned. It's done for each category, and after, based on the global merge mode, the next result processing is made.
Sensitive search is a variation of the regular Inverted Index method, which takes into account the multiplicity of repetition of words in a keyword, title or description set. When the learning object is described by one word more than once in one category, and this word is included in the query, the returned results will increase. It also works internally in each category as well as externally, comparing results from all categories (Joung et al., 2005; Su & Widom, 2005).

3.3 UPM – Personalization and offered end-user assistance

UPM is the essential part of the Management and Resource Search Module, which supports: end-users' accounts management including personalized search, and additional functionalities offered for a end-users' recommender system with different implementation of collaborative filtering approach (Orzechowski et al., 2007a; Sarwar et al., 2000) and several internal and external interfaces to the services.
Using a profiling mechanism is essential in e-learning Platforms. Only in this way is it possible to present search results in such a way to suit the end-users' (learners / teachers) expectations. It is necessary to build a local database, which will store information about registered users, including both their interest and the history of their work.
A personal Agent is an agent that will represent a single user. Each registered user can have only one Personal Agent. An unregistered user is also represented by a Personal Agent, but with much reduced functionality.
A Personal Agent is created when a user starts his session in the system. It remains alive, while the user is working. If a longer period of inactivity occurs, the agent stores its state in the database (only if the user is registered), and will die.
The Agent can perform operations on the account, can create, modify or destroy it. Some of these operations are performed automatically as a result of analysis of other user's operations, and some of them can be directly invoked by the user.
The most important function of the Personal Agent is connected with the execution of search requests. The Agent stores a list of recent requests, each associated with a list of results. It must continuously gather the results, valuate and sort them, and return them to the user when asked. In order to perform the search, it must use services offered by the Search Module.
Ranking and Collaborative Filtering component
Most search methods used in Internet repositories match words in the search query and keywords in the known available elements to produce a list of results. As query conformity often isn't enough to order the search results properly, various schemes are used to prioritise the results of the most predicted value for the user. However, people evaluate things on a very subjective basis. Thus, marks on a ranking scale provided by different users may have completely separate meanings. It is impossible to provide a uniform ranking scale that's universal - applicable for all users of a system. The user will always face the question:

"Do the ranks assigned to that element reflect my preferences?"
Collaborative Filtering (CF) is commonly used to organize recommender system on the basis of end-users' behaviour. Introduction of CF into e-learning systems requires adaptation of these general Collaborative Filtering methods in order to improve efficiency (Orzechowski et al., 2007a).
The first step for creation of a CF-based system is selection of data used to predict users' preferences. Analysis of e-Learning object repositories and search systems resulted in establishment of a set of explicit and implicit data collection methods.
The explicit methods include:

- ranking: when the user applies a rank within a given scale to an object,
- labelling: when the user attaches a label to an object.

The implicit methods are:

- selection: when the user clicks a link on the result list; a page with an extended item description is displayed,
- downloading: when the user clicks a link on an item description page; this either displays the Learning Object itself in the browser or downloads the object to the user's computer.

Behaviour vs. profile-based user clustering

Most collaborative filtering systems rely on user behaviour and user actions to determine user preference similarity. The underlying idea is that contents of the objects and characteristics of user profiles are not taken into account (Orzechowski et al., 2007a).
However, characteristics of e-Learning applications require a slightly different approach, for a few reasons. They are connected to the characteristics of e-Learning systems themselves as well as the target audience. Firstly, the most dependable user behaviour data collected by the system - the item rates - are extremely sparse. Secondly, the implicitly collected data has low dependability, as the user may decide at any point that the item is not what they are looking for after all. Because some users of the system are young children (users of type learner), rates may not be reliable, and their action records are prone to be chaotic.
Therefore, it was decided that another approach to user similarity computation was to be designed and implemented. This approach features a new way of grouping users - based on their profiles rather than their behaviour. The following profile elements are taken into account: age, gender, country of education and points of interest.
The procedure is similar to the procedure used in "classic" collaborative filtering. A matrix of size m times n is created. However, columns of the matrix are composed of all possible values for the four profile fields, instead of object ranks/events. In the current implementation, enumerated fields get a '1' if a given value applies, and a '0' if it does not. For other fields, the value is numeric.
To provide balance between the four sections, weights have to be defined for each one of them. This allows the administrator to fine-tune the distribution of users after feature extraction in the n'¬-dimensional space.

Types of user clusters

There is a strict division of users in e-Learning systems into two separate groups: teachers and students (called learners). Therefore, the system should maintain separate clustering schemes for these types of users (Orzechowski et al., 2007a).
Moreover, as presented earlier, the suggested architecture of a ranking system for e-learning consists of two separate approaches towards user similarity assessment: behaviour-based (classic) and profile-based.

Therefore, six different types of user classification are present in the current implementation:
- all users / behaviour-based, - learners / behaviour-based,
- teachers / behaviour-based, - all users / profile-based,
- learners / profile-based, - teachers / profile-based

Calculations are performed independently and separately for each of the cluster types presented above.

Positioning of results using search criteria and profile conformance data

While developing the methods for discovering users' preferences, another problem has been investigated as well. It concerns methods of presenting search results using three different indicators computed by the system (see below) within a single set of results. Output from each of the classification schemes is a set of percentage values, representing the three aspects of conformity of a given LO (search result):

- Search query conformity specifies how the given LO (described in compliance with the IEEE LOM standard) matches a given search method. The system delivers separate sets of results for each of the used search methods.
- User profile conformity specifies how the given LO matches the user's profile, provided upon registration. The system applies values to LOs found previously by the search methods.
- User cluster conformity delivers separate sets of results representing the predicted attractiveness of given LOs within clusters to which the user belongs. Detailed information regarding cluster types and clustering methods have been described in previous sections.

The simplified architecture of the entire result generation system is shown in Figure 14.

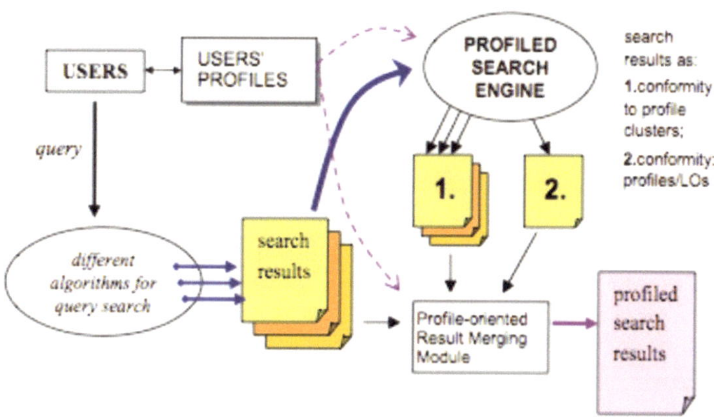

Fig. 14. Simplified schema of merging search results process (Orzechowski et al., 2007a)

A Web GUI was implemented to allow users of the system to choose their preferred way of merging results. Furthermore, an API based on the Web Services technology was implemented to enable utilisation of results generated in our system by external systems (Orzechowski et al., 2007a). As each of the criteria is separate from others, we let users choose which features are used to create the end list of results. These features were divided into two separate parts: search methods relevance (query conformity) and profile relevance (user profile/cluster conformity).

Even if the user decides to utilize all of the offered features, the system prepares two

separate lists of results for each part.
Search method/query conformity
Two different solutions were suggested:

- weighted average - end user can choose the influence of each search method on the end results' list;
- maximum - the maximum value of LO conformity is taken.

Popularity and conformity to profiles and clusters
This part was divided into the following elements:

- conformity to user profiles,
- conformity to clusters determined by user behaviour similarity,
- conformity to clusters determined by multi-dimensional user profiled analysis.
- general popularity (not taking individual users' preferences into account).

For all four elements presented above, the weighted average is used to create a single list of results. Additionally, as ranks for each element can be based on data collected using explicit or implicit methods, the user can choose how these methods influence the computed value for the relevant elements, also using the weighted average
Merging profiles and search methods
The methods presented above generate two lists of results - one sorted by search method conformity, and one sorted by profile conformity. Determination of methods for merging these two lists is a significant problem. While profiling methods are very important in search engines, they should not diminish the importance of conformity returned by the search methods (Orzechowski et al., 2007a).
While research is being performed, the problem has been temporarily solved by using geometric means. Ultimate conclusions in this aspect will require extensive real-life testing and fine-tuning of the production system.

4. Conclusion

The implemented Agent Search System offers new, important features not available in currently used e-learning systems. Simultaneous theoretical research and practical development work open the unique opportunity of testing how new ideas perform in real life and lets us acquire valuable experimental data.
Moreover, analysis of the history of the users' activities, made possible by our system, in connection to analysis of LOM fields, is a significant step towards creation of an intelligent Learning Object search engine, which will present search results in a way as close to the user's expectations as possible.
The Agent Based Search System is stable and easy for management and development thanks to the integration of multi-agent architecture with the stable and scalable EJB JBOSS application Server.
The searcher of Brokerage System, based on the Simple Query Interface (SQI), was optimised.
The proposed Agent Module is the alternative for the existing search module. It has the open character so its work can be easily distributed on all levels, such as (Orzechowski, 2007b):
• FLEXIBILITY
Each new search method can be added to our working system really fast.

• HOT SWITCH-ON
This System provides the easiness of administration of working agents.
• EASY TO DEVELOP & FEEDBACK OPEN
This solution has really spread for adding as many search algorithms and general search functionality as we need.
• ENABLING PROFILED SEARCH AND RECOMMENDATIONS
This System analyses' explicit and implicit knowledge of end-users works with connection to their profiles, improving the positioning for found results and offering different kinds of recommendations.
• OFFLINE SEARCH
Our System allows users to store queries and be informed, i.e. by e-mail, if new LOs, matching user's criteria, will be added to the System.

Some of these tasks could be implemented without an Agent Layer but multiprocessing, distributed data harvesting and inter-components communications makes this agent approach well-founded.

5. References

Baran, R., Zeja, A., Orzechowski, T. M., Dziech, A. & Lutwin, M. (2007). The data collection module of the agent based search system, *Proceedings of WEBIST'2007: "Web Information Systems And Technologies"*, Barcelona, Spain, March 2007

Bellifemmine, F., Poggi, A., & Rimassa, G. (1999). Jade - A FIPA compliant Agent Framework., *Proceedings of 4th International Conference on Practical Applications of Intelligent Agents and Multi-Agent Systems*, 1999

Chkoliar, N. (2002). E-Russia: Programme for the Innovation in Government, *Proceedings of the 10th NISPAcee Annual Conference: DELIVERING PUBLIC SERVICES IN CEE countries: Trends and Developments*, April 25-27 2002, Cracow, Poland

Chmiel, K., Gawinecki, M., Kaczmarek, P., Szymczak, M. & Paprzycki, M. (2005). Efficiency of JADE agent platform, *Proceedings of International Symposium of Parallel and Distributed Computing & International Workshop on Algorithms*, vol.13(2), pp. 159-172, Amsterdam, The Netherlands, April 2005, IOS Press

Curry, E., Chambers, D. & Lyons, G. (2003). A JMS Message Transport Protocol for the JADE Platform, *Proceedings of the IEEE/WIC International Conference on Intelligent Agent Technology, IAT'2003*, Washington, DC, USA, 2003, IEEE Computer Society

Franklin, S. & Graesser, A. (1997). Is it an Agent, Or Just a Program?: A Taxonomy for Autonomous Agents, *Lecture Notes in Computer Science*, 1997, pp. 21-35, Springer, ISBN: 978-3-540-62507-0

Hillman, D. C. A., Willis, D. J. and Gunawerdena, C. N. (1994). Learner-Interface Interaction in Distance Education: An Extension of Contemporary Models and Strategies for Practitioners., *The American Journal of Distance Education*, 8(2) 1994, pp. 30–42.

Jennings, N.R. (1996). Software agents. IEEE Review, pp. 17-20, 1996

Joung, Y.J., Fang, C.T. & Yang, L.W. (2005). Keyword Search in DHT-based Peer-to-Peer Networks, *Proceedings ICSCS 2005*

Moore, M. G. (1989), Three Types of Interaction, *The American Journal of Distance Education*, 3(2) 1989, pp. 1–6.

Najjar, J., Ternier, S. & Duval, E. (2004). User Behavior in Learning Object Repositories: An Empirical Analysis, *Proceedings of The World Conference on Educational Multimedia, Hypermedia and Telecommunications 2004*, pp. 4373-4379, Lugano, Switzerland, AACE, 2004

Nichani, M. (2001). LCMS = LMS + CMS [RLOs], *http://www.elearningpost.com/articles/archives/lcms_lms_cms_rlos*

Orzechowski, T. & Dziech, A. (2001a). Communication between end-users and databases using mobile agent technology, *Proceedings of the IASTED IMSA'2001 Conference: "Internet And Multimedia Systems and Applications"*, pp. 433-436, Hawaii, USA, August 13-16 2001, ACTA Press

Orzechowski, T. (2001b). Concepts of Systems for Information Retrieval, *Proceedings of the IEEE SIBCOM'2001 Conference: "MODERN COMMUNICATION TECHNOLOGIES"*, pp. 39-44, Tomsk, Russia, November 28-29 2001

Orzechowski T. (2002). Meta-data distribution in intelligent databases system, *Proceedings of the IEEE EDM'2002 Conference*, vol.II, pp. 21-24, Erlagol, Russia, July 1-5 2002

Orzechowski, T., Ernst, S. & Dziech, A. (2007a). Profiled Search Methods for E-Learning Systems, *Proceedings of the EC-TEL-LODE Workshop'2007: "2nd European Conference on Technology Enhanced Learning*, Sissi - Crete, Grece, September 2007

Orzechowski T. M. (2007b). The use of multi-agents' systems in e-learning platforms, *Proceedings of the IEEE SIBCON'2007 Conference: "Control and Communication"*, pp. 64-71, Tomsk, Russia, April 2007

Orzechowski, T. M., Zeja, A. & Dziech, A. (2009). Secure Data Harvesting in the Federation of Repositories Managed by Multi Agent Systems, *Proceedings of the IEEE SIBCON'2009*, Tomsk, Russia, March 2009

Prause, C., Ternier, S., de Jong, T., Apelt, S., Scholten, M., Wolpers, M., Eisenhauer, M., Vandeputte, B., Specht, M. & Duval, E. (2007). Unifying Learning Object Repositories in MACE, *Proceedings of The First International Workshop on Learning Object Discovery & Exchange (LODE'07, EC-TEL'07)*, Crete, Greece, September 2007

Rengarajan R. (2001), LCMS and LMS. Taking Advantage of Tight Integration, Click2learn Inc, *http://www.e-learn.cz/soubory/lcms_and_lms.pdf*

Sarwar, B., Karypis, G., Konstan, J. & Riedl, J. (2000). Analysis of Recommendation Algorithms for E-Commerce, *Proceedings of the ACM E-Commerce Conference*, pp. 158-167, 2000

Schlager, M. S., & Fusco, J. (2004). Teacher Professional Development, Technology, and Communities of Practice: Are We Putting the Cart before the Horse?, *Designing for Virtual Communities in the Service of Learning*, Cambridge University Press, 2004

Schulmeister, R. (2003). *Modellversuch Lehrqualifikation für Wissenschaft und Weiterbildung*, (in German), Abschlussbericht, Universität Hamburg, 2003

Shakshuki, E. & Jun, Y. (2004). Multi-Agent Development Toolkits: An Evaluation, *Lecture Notes in Computer Science (Innovations in Applied Artificial Intelligence)*, 3029/2004, pp. 209-218, Springer Berlin / Heidelberg, ISBN: 978-3-540-22007-7

Simon, B., Massart, D., van Assche, F., Ternier, S., Duval, E., Brantner, S., Olmedilla, D., and Miklós, Z. (2005). A Simple Query Interface for Interoperable Learning Repositories, *Proceedings of the 1st Workshop on Interoperability of Web-based Educational Systems*, pp. 11-18, Chiba, Japan, May 2005

Stefaner, M., Vecchia, E. D., Condotta, M., Wolpers, M., Specht, M., Apelt, S. & Duval, E. (2007). Mace - Enriching Architectural Learning Objects for Experience Multiplication, *Lecture Notes in Computer Science*, 4753, pp. 322-336, Springer Berlin, 2007, ISBN: 978-3-540-75194-6

Su, Q. & Widom, J. (2005). Indexing Relational Database Content Offline for Efficient Keyword-Based Search, *Proceedings IDEAS 2005*

Van Assche, F. & Massart, D. (2004). Federation and Brokerage of Learning Objects and Their Metadata, *Proceedings of the IEEE International Conference on Advanced Learning Technologies, ICALT'2004*, pp. 316-320, Washington, USA, 2004

Van Durm, R., Duval, E., Verhoeven, B., Cardinaels, K. & Olivié, H. (2001). Extending The ARIADNE Web-Based Learning Environment,. *Proceedings of World Conference on Educational Multimedia, Hypermedia and Telecommunications*, pp. 1932-1937, AACE, Norfolk

Quality Metrics of an Integrated E-Learning System – students' perspective

Ksenija Klasnić*, Jadranka Lasić-Lazić** and Sanja Seljan**
University of Zagreb - Faculty of Humanities and Social Sciences
**Department of Sociology, **Department of Information Sciences*
I. Lucica 3, 10 000 Zagreb, Croatia
kklasnic@ffzg.hr; jlazic@ffzg.hr; sseljan@ffzg.hr

1. Introduction

As e-learning has become an increasingly important issue in educational systems in the last several years, a considerable number of generic standards, quality guidelines and frameworks have been published relating to better efficiency and quality improvement of the e-learning. While early initiatives were concentrated on the functional understanding and technical skills of ICT use, nowadays they take more into consideration motivation, satisfaction and contextualization which are reflected in the quality of e-learning. In the paper, different views towards the quality of an integrated e-learning have been presented, and the research regarding the quality of the integrated e-learning system (Moodle) introduced by prof. J. Lasić-Lazić and translated into Croatian version (Omega) at the Faculty of Humanities and Social Sciences, University of Zagreb in relation to different European policies.

2. Reference work

Today e-learning systems take important place in formal and less formal educational setting. The first generation of e-learning systems often missed social context and had lack of credibility [1], with exaggerated expectations. Therefore, a number of guidelines, recommendations and surveys aimed to elaborate on quality of e-learning systems. As in Stephenson[2], the quality is easier to describe, than to define, including great number of indicators ranging from purpose, clarity, relevance, technical skills, ease of implementation and consequences up to notions of context, ethics, then cost effectiveness, etc.

---

[1] Quality Assurance and Accreditation For European eLearning: the Case For a European Quality Mark Initiative, EFQUEL Green Paper No. 41 *Brussels, 03/ 2007.* *http://www.qualityfoundation.org/index.php?m1=2&m2=25&view=0*

[2] Stephenson, J. Definitions of indicator of quality on the application of ICT to University Teaching. Tarragona, 2005.

According to the standard ISO/IEC 19796-1[3] designed for learning, education and training one of the first steps in order to harmonize different approaches in e-learning was to develop the new quality standard which should be used in order to define the context in which the system will be used. As stated in the document, this document serves as a reference framework offering orientation to aspects that should be covered and possible solutions supporting adaptation to the specific requirements of the organization. It includes process description (e.g. evaluation of didactic methods) taking into consideration need analysis, framework analysis (of context, resources, organizational context), educational process, production, implementation, realization and evaluation, methods (e.g. identification, alternatives, priorities), objectives (e.g. adequate selection of one or more didactic concepts), target group (taking into consideration their competencies and learning styles), organization, relations, etc.

The European Parliament and the Council have established multiannual program4 for the effective integration of information and communication technologies (ICT) in education and training systems in Europe (eLearning Programme). This program aims to improve the quality of education and adaptation to the needs of the society in the lifelong learning context. The specific objectives include, among others, promotion of digital literacy, social cohesion, and personal development, enhancing intercultural dialogue and European dimension in education and exploitation of the e-learning through innovative teaching methods with the aim to improve the learning quality and to enforce the learner's autonomy.

The aim of the European Survey conducted in 2005 among 600 students5 was to assess the state-of-the-art of the e-learning from the point of view of the main stakeholders: teachers, trainers and learners analyzing four main questions: who are respondents; what is e-learning; how is e-learning rated; what is future of e-learning (last three questions are analyzed through teachers', trainers' and learners' points of views). The survey indicates that e-learning is not seen as isolated, but perceived very positively, as needed and integrated into everyday educational scenario. Attention in this research is given to pedagogical aspect, competence development exceeding technical skills, but stressing critical thinking, learning skill and self-study.

Evaluation of four online courses at the Centre for Research on Learning at Indiana University (Graham, 2000)6 was conducted with the aim to provide feedback regarding active learning, encouraging student-faculty contact and respecting diverse talents and ways

---

[3] Pawlowski, J.M. (2006): ISO/IEC 19796-1: How to Use the New Quality Framework for Learning, Education, and Training. White Paper, Essen, Germany, 2006.

[4] Decision No 2318/2003/EC of the European Parliament and of the Council adopting a multiannual programme (2004 to 2006) for the effective integration of information and communication technologies (ICT) in education and training systems in Europe (*e*Learning Programme). 5. 12. 2003.

5 Aimard, V.; Mc Cullough, C. E-Learning in Europe: How do trainers, teachers and learners rate e-learning? Cedefop, 2006. http://cms.eun.org/shared/data/pdf/report_survey_teachers_and_learners_and_e-learning_final.pdf

6 Graham, C., Cagiltay, B., Craner, J., J. Lim, Duffy, T.M. (2000) Teaching in a Web Based Distance Learning Environment: An Evaluation Summary Based on Four Courses. CILT, Indiana University. http://crlt.indiana.edu/publications/crlt00-13.pdf

of learning. Areas where improvements were mostly needed were students' cooperation, instructor's feedback and interface design. The main problems were inadequate instructors' knowledge on teaching strategies in online environment, great differences regarding asynchronous conferencing, considerable time for instruction managing and limited access to the resources.

"The Five Pillars of Quality Online Education" by Lorenzo and Moore7 include learning effectiveness, student satisfaction, faculty satisfaction, cost effectiveness and access. Quality metrics could be related to the operational level emphasizing ICT practice within traditional teaching program, as in Grahan et al. 8 including student-faculty contact, student cooperation, active learning, prompt feedback, time on task, high expectations, and diverse ways of learning. As in Stephenson (2005), other indicators include online forums for problem discussion. At pedagogical level quality aspects include pedagogical and psychological approaches, epistemology, goal orientation, teacher's role, motivation, program flexibility, learners' control, user activities, cooperative learning, etc. In longer term dimensions, the indicator of return on investment is of the considerable concern at universities which could be measured through reactions at the end of the course, change of learning attitudes, knowledge and skill improvement, change of behaviour, and results of changes in key business. In the learner-centered teaching process, one of the main tasks is learner's responsibility finding the best possible ways to manage their own learning.

3. Integrated e-learning system

The ambition to implement educational reforms in line with educational national policy statements, European standards and guidelines, Bologna declaration and other reference works of the educational paradigm, have resulted by the introduction of the integrated e-learning system and its quality measurement.

Organized into 23 Departments with 111 chairs, offering 10 major and 33 double major undergraduate programs, and a number of postgraduate programs, for more than 6,500 students of whom the majority study at two departments, a constant problem of time and space for lectures and tutorials is present. The Faculty of Humanities and Social Sciences functions almost as a small university and besides organizational and infrastructural constraints, the need for the introduction of an integrated e-learning environment was perceived as a prerequisite for the achievement of future educational reforms.

In 2002, a three year project Organization of Information and Knowledge in the Electronic Learning Environment http://infoz.ffzg.hr/oizeoo) managed by prof. Jadranka Lasić-Lazić has started, funded by the Croatian Ministry of Science with the aim to investigate, test and

7 Lorenzo, G., Moore J.C., (2002) Report to the Nation: Five Pillars of Quality Online Education, The Sloan Consortium, Needham, MA http://www.sloan-c.org/

8 Graham, C., Cagiltay, J. Lim, B., Craner, J., & Duffy, T.M. (2001) Seven Principles of Effective Teaching: A Practical Lens for Evaluating Online Courses. Michigan Virtual University.
http://www.tcc.edu/welcome/collegeadmin/OIE/SOA/review/toolkit/documents/Article_Seven_Principles_of_Effective_Teaching_A_Practical_Lens_for_Evaluating_Online_Course.pdf

evaluate open source (Learnloop, ZOPE, MOODLE…) and commercial solutions (WebCT, Blackboard…) and decide upon the best solution for the needs of the teaching staff of the Department of Information Sciences and in future the Faculty. The fact that Moodle is a free, easy-to-use system (i.e. everyone with basic computer literacy can easily use it) with simple and understandable interface was the main reason for the implementation. Therefore, Moodle interface was translated, customized and implemented for the academic year 2004/2005 under the name OMEGA.

At the moment Omega has been used by more than 3.800 students, more than 200 lecturers, offering more than 400 online courses with around 60GB materials. As Omega e-learning system is used by a considerable number of teachers and students, it is important to determine the degree of Omega's implementation in the educational system of Faculty and also the quality of this implementation.

One of the indicators of efficacy and quality of the implementation and integration of e-learning systems into the educational system is taken to be students' satisfaction with the system and its use. Therefore, a survey was conducted at the Faculty of Humanities and Social Sciences to determine students' attitudes and satisfaction with the use of Omega. Students' attitudes have been defined as the dependent variable.

4. Research

As the number of student and teacher enrollments to the e-learning system is constantly growing and having in mind the need for **complementary teaching tools** unifying traditional teaching methods and ICT, as well as official recommendations, standards, guidelines and frameworks, the research was conducted on quota convenience sample of 148 students at the Faculty of Humanities and Social Sciences, University of Zagreb. As presented in reference works, in a number of surveys a range of different approaches has been implemented taking into account functional understanding, pedagogical approach, practical and social aspects, personal attitudes, context, quantity, quality, etc. Therefore, this research took into consideration four main issues:

1) attitudes regarding the need for better integration of the e-learning into traditional teaching,
2) attitudes regarding better educational quality through the use of e-learning,
3) attitudes regarding quantity and
4) the quality of the e-learning usage.

These four main issues were defined as our main latent dependent variables and were measured by a great number of manifest variables. Independent context was defined with several concepts which are relevant for understanding the complexity of diverse attitudes towards the use of e-learning in educational system.

In this the focus is on description of students' attitudes towards the use of Omega e-learning system in the context of four mentioned dependent variables, also including description of several independent concepts such as students' self-evaluation of own computer competence and satisfaction with this competence, the frequency of computer use in educational and private purposes, evaluation of their teachers' computer competence, frequency of use of ICT by their teachers, satisfaction with Omega's options and general attitudes towards Omega. Mutual relationships between mentioned concepts will be analyzed, and also the relationships between these concepts and some students' socio-demographic characteristics.

5. Methodology and sample

The study was conducted in May 2007. The constructed questionnaire consisted out of 106 variables covering the relevant aspects for analyzing the subject of attitudes towards e-learning and was applied on quota convenience sample of 148 students. There were 74% female and 26% male examinees (which approximately correspond with the Faculty gender structure), all years of study were equally represented in the sample and the greatest numbers of students were from Department of English (34%), Department of Sociology (29%) and Department of Information Sciences (20%).
All analyses were conducted using Statistical Package for Social Sciences, statistical software version 13 (SPSS, Chicago IL).

6. Results

6.1. Independent concepts – description and some mutual relationships

Before presenting the main issues of this paper - four aspects regarding students' attitudes towards the use of Omega e-learning system - firstly, description of some of the variables follow, that by our opinion, constitute an independent context for explanation of diverse attitudes towards the use of e-learning in educational system.

6.1.1. Computer competence and satisfaction with own computer competence – students' self-evaluation

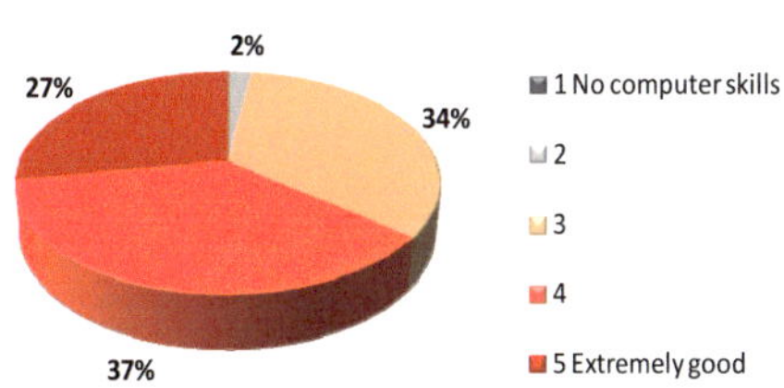

Fig. 1. Self-evaluation of own computer competence (N=146)

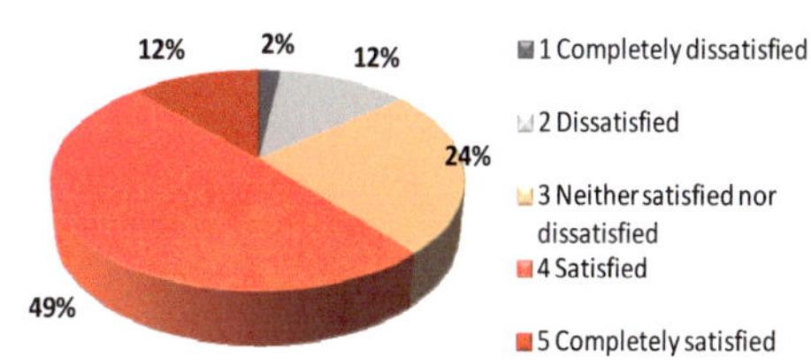

Fig. 2. Satisfaction with own computer competence (N=148z)

Figure 1. shows results of students' self-evaluation of their own computer competence on five-point ordinal scale with ordered response levels from (1) *No computer skill* to (5) *Extremely good computer skills.* Average score was 3.9 (sd=.828), and mod (value that occurs the most frequently) was 4. There was no answer "No computer skills", and only 2% of those with very weak computer skills. Obviously, our students consider themselves to have rather high level of computer competence. Figure 2. shows students' satisfaction with their computer competence on five-point ordinal scale with ordered response levels from (1) *Completely dissatisfied to* (5) *Completely satisfied.* Average score was 3.6 (sd=.926), and mod was 4.
After recoding both variables into three-point ordinal scale the following relation between computer competence and satisfaction with this competence could be noticed (Table 1.):

Satisfaction with own computer competence	Computer competence						Total	
	low		medium		high			
	n	%	n	%	n	%	n	%
low	3	100.0%	14	28.6%	3	3.2%	20	13.7%
medium	0	0.0%	24	49.0%	12	12.8%	36	24.7%
high	0	0.0%	11	22.4%	79	84.0%	90	61.6%
total	3	100.0%	49	100.0 %	94	100.0%	146	100.0%

Table 1. Students' computer competence and satisfaction with this competence

As expected, students with low computer competence are dissatisfied, most students who have medium computer competence have also medium satisfaction, and the majority of students with high computer competence have also a high level of satisfaction (Pearson's chi-square analysis: χ^2 =71.396; df=4; p<.001). Interesting is that some students who evaluate their computer competence as high, are not satisfied with it. This is probably so because they have higher aspirations than other students: they already have good computer skills, but they are not satisfied because they would like to be even better.

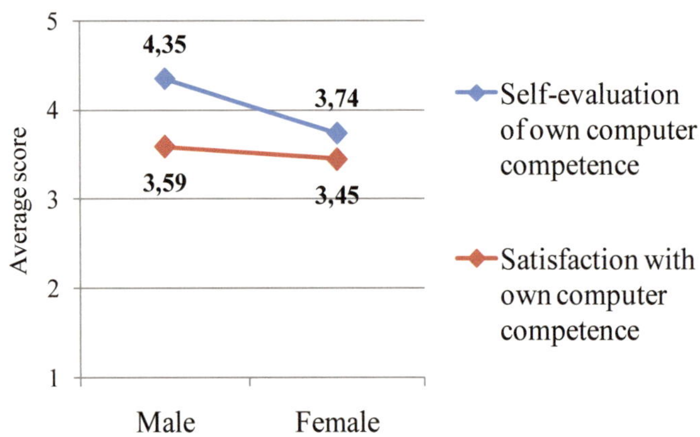

Fig. 3. Average scores of students' computer competence (N=146) and satisfaction with this competence (N=148) by gender Mann-Whitney U test showed a statistically significant difference between male and female students in both variables: male students are evaluating their computer competence higher than female (p<.001) and they are also more satisfied with their own computer competence (p=.001).

6.1.2. Computer use

Figures 3. and 4. show estimates of frequency of computer use in general and in educational purposes on five-point ordinal scale with ordered response levels from (1) Never to (5) Every day. As presented, over 80% of students use computer daily, and over 40% uses computer daily in educational purposes. Average scores for general and educational purposes were 4.78 (sd=.474) and 4.25 (sd=.727) respectively. It should be noticed that all students use computer in educational purposes, and that only one percent does that very rarely (few times a year).

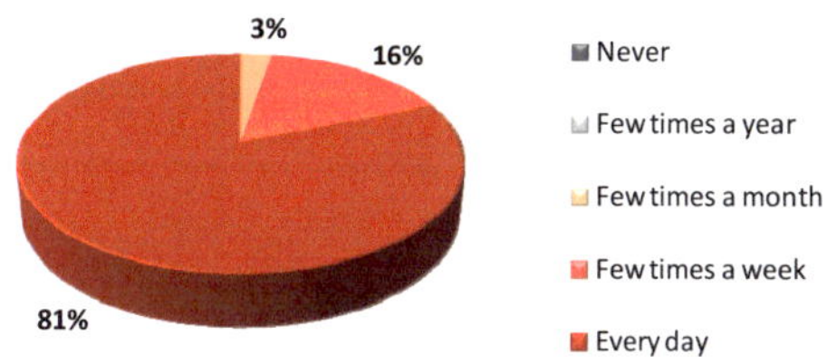

Fig. 4. Frequency of computer use (any purpose) (N=148)

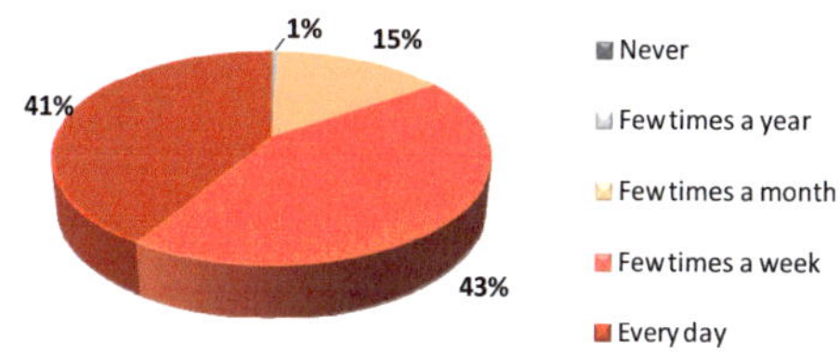

Fig. 5. Frequency of computer use in educational purposes (N=148)

6.1.3. Students' evaluation of their teachers' computer competences

Students also evaluated their teachers' computer competences on the same five-point ordinal scale with ordered response levels from (1) No computer skill to (5) Extremely good computer skills. They have done two evaluations: one for all teachers on their faculty (that is, teachers they have had an opportunity to meet and listen to their courses) and the other evaluation only for those teachers whose courses are enrolled to Omega.

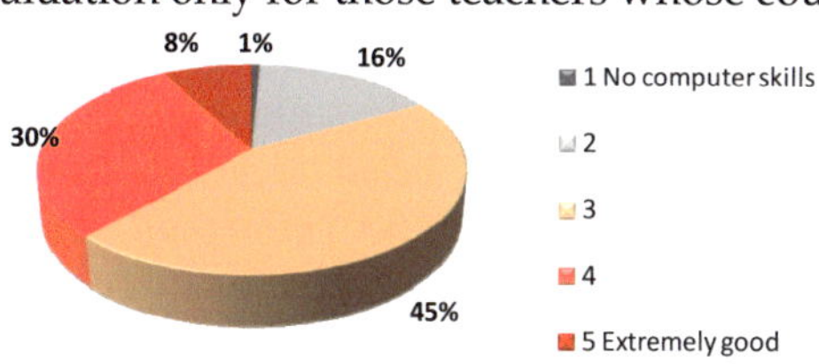

Fig. 6. Evaluation of computer competences - all teachers (N=147)

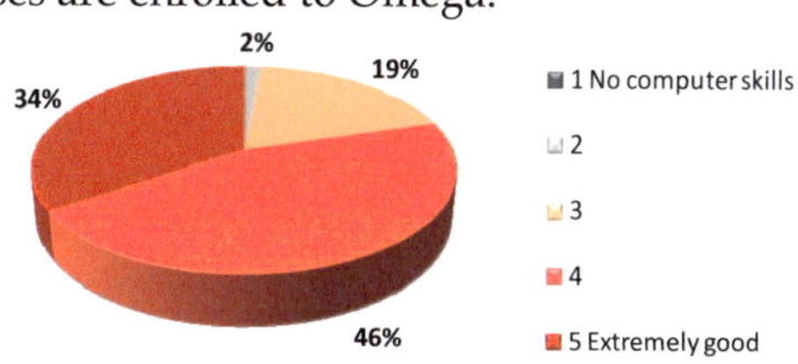

Fig. 7. Evaluation of computer competences - teachers who have courses on Omega (N=132)

When evaluating computer competences of all teachers on the faculty, value that occurs the most frequently is 3 (almost 45% of students gave them grade 3) and when evaluating computer competences of teachers who have courses on Omega, value that occurs the most frequently is 4 (over 45% of students gave them grade 4). Wilcoxon signed-rank test showed that teachers who have courses on Omega are graded statistically higher ($p<.001$).

6.1.4. Frequency of ICT use by teachers

Students estimated the frequency of ICT use by their teachers on an ordinal five-point scale with response levels (1) Never, (2) Rarely, (3) From time to time, (4) Often and (5) Very often. They were given five indicators for evaluation: video projections (PowerPoint presentations, etc.) during lectures, communication with teachers via e-mail, recommendations of exam or seminar materials available on the Internet, the use of Internet for disclosure of information regarding exam results, lecture changes, time of consultations, and uploads of lecture materials on the Internet (see Table 2.).

	(1)	(2)	(3)	(4)	(5)	$\bar{X}$	N
1. Video projections (PowerPoint presentations, etc.) during lectures.	2.7%	12.9%	38.8%	28.6%	17.0%	3.44	147
2. Communication via e-mail.	1.4%	10.8%	36.5%	41.9%	9.5%	3.47	148
3. Recommending exam or seminar materials available on the Internet.	8.9%	28.1%	37.0%	19.9%	6.2%	2.86	146
4. Using Internet for disclosure of information regarding exam results, lecture changes, time of consultations, etc.	0.0%	7.4%	25.0%	40.5%	27.0%	3.87	148
5. Uploading lecture material on the Internet.	2.7%	21.8%	32.7%	25.2%	17.7%	3.33	147

Table 2. Frequency of ICT use by teachers (distributions of percentages, means and numbers of valid answers)

According to our students, the most commonly used information-communication technology by teachers is the use of Internet for disclosure of information regarding exam results, lecture changes, time of consultations, etc. – over 67% of students estimated that their teacher use the Internet for such purposes often or very often. It is followed by communication via e-mail and video projections (PowerPoint presentations, etc) during lectures. The thing that teachers use the least often is literature for seminars or exams available on the Internet.

	Teachers' computer competence	
	rho	p
1. Video projections (PowerPoint presentations, etc.) during lectures.	.269*	.001
2. Communication via e-mail.	.277*	.001
3. Recommending exam or seminar materials available on the Internet.	.360*	<.001
4. Using Internet for disclosure of information regarding exam results, lecture changes, time of consultations, etc.	.299*	<.001
5. Uploading lecture material on the Internet.	.379*	<.001

Table 3. Spearman's correlation: ICT use by teachers and their computer competence
* Correlation is significant at the 0.01 level (2-tailed).

There are positive correlations of teachers' computer competences with all indicators of frequency of ICT use. In other words, students evaluate that those teachers who have higher degree of computer competence more frequently use ICT in their work and communication with their students.

6.1.5. General attitudes towards Omega

For measuring students' general attitudes towards Omega we used five-point Likert scale with ordered response levels (1) Strongly disagree, (2) Disagree, (3) Neither agree nor disagree, (4) Agree and (5) Strongly agree. The scale was constructed out of 14 items[9] presented in Table 4.

Some statements were formulated expressing positive, and some negative attitudes towards Omega.

	(1)	(2)	(3)	(4)	(5)	$\overline{X}$	N
1. Omega is unnecessary addition to the university education.	65.3%	25.2%	6.1%	2.7%	0.7%	1.48	147
2. Omega facilitates distribution of lecture material.	0.7%	1.4%	12.2%	43.5%	42.2%	4.25	147
3. Omega is just an additional burden for students.	38.8%	36.7%	15.0%	8.2%	1.4%	1.97	147
4. It would be better if teachers would personally hand out lecture material instead of putting it on Omega.	27.4%	32.9%	25.3%	11.6%	2.7%	2.29	146
5. Omega should be used only by students from the Department of information sciences.	67.3%	22.4%	6.8%	0.7%	2.7%	1.49	147
6. Omega makes learning easier.	0.7%	3.4%	26.0%	47.3%	22.6%	3.88	146
7. Omega is a helpful addition to the university education.	0.0%	0.7%	11.6%	47.6%	40.1%	4.27	147
8. Omega usage for specific courses raises the quality of lectures.	1.4%	5.4%	31.3%	33.3%	28.6%	3.82	147
9. Omega usage requires too much computer skills.	28.1%	54.8%	11.0%	4.8%	1.4%	1.97	146
10. It would be better if all teachers would use Omega.	0.0%	6.3%	28.5%	34.0%	31.3%	3.90	144
11. Omega usage is a positive step towards higher information literacy amongst students.	0.7%	0.7%	22.1%	42.1%	34.5%	4.09	145
12. Omega usage is too difficult.	36.3%	48.6%	11.6%	2.1%	1.4%	1.84	146
13. Omega is practical because it allows completing some of the obligations without being	2.0%	5.4%	14.9%	44.6%	33.1%	4.01	148

[9] Before the construction of Likert scale, items number 1, 3, 4, 5, 9, 12 and 16 were recoded.

present at the university.							
14. It's more difficult to pass an exam for a course which is on Omega because then professors have higher expectations.	15.5%	37.8%	41.2%	4.7%	0.7%	2.37	148

Table 4. General attitudes towards Omega (distributions of percentages, means and numbers of valid answers)

The majority of students agree with the following statements: "Omega is a helpful addition to the university education." (87.7%[10]), "Omega facilitates distribution of lecture material." (85.7%), "Omega is practical because it allows completing some of the obligations without being present at the university." (77.7%) and "Omega usage is a positive step towards higher information literacy amongst students." (76.6%). It should be noticed that all of these statements express positive attitudes towards Omega.

Statements that have the largest percentages of disagreement are the following: "Omega is unnecessary addition to the university education." (90.8%[11]), "Omega should be used only by students from the Department of information sciences." (89.7%), "Omega usage is too difficult." (84.9%), "Omega usage requires too much computer skills." (82.9%) and "Omega is just an additional burden for students." (82.9%). Notice that all of these statements express negative attitudes towards Omega.

Based on these distributions we may conclude that the majority of students have positive attitudes towards Omega, considering it to be a useful contribution to the university education that facilitates distribution of lecture materials and increases the degree of information literacy. It is also considered to be practical because it allows completing some of the obligations without being present at the university. Moreover, the majority of students do not consider Omega usage to be too demanding, neither in general nor in the context of computer usage knowledge. The majority of students also don't think that Omega should be used only by students from the Department of Information Sciences which is a very important finding because it indicates a fact that the students are aware that technology, and information technology especially, has become an everyday requirement for experts of all professional orientations.

It is interesting to mention that there are some statements that a great number of students can neither agree nor disagree: "It's more difficult to pass an exam for a course which is on Omega because then professors have higher expectations" (41.2%), "It would be better if all teachers would use Omega." (28.5%), "Omega makes learning easier." (26.0%) and "It would be better if teachers would personally hand out lecture material instead of putting it on Omega." (25.3%).

To test the internal consistency reliability of this scale, Cronbach's alpha was computed and found to be .901, indicating very high reliability for this 14 items. The constructed scale was

---

[10] The given percentages are sums of response levels (4) *Agree* and (5) *Strongly agree.*

[11] The given percentages are sums of response levels (1) *Strongly disagree* and (2) *Disagree.*

also tested for normality using the nonparametric one sample Kolmogorov-Smirnov test which showed that the scale is distributed according to normal distribution (p=.347).

General Attitudes Towards Omega in Relation to Computer Use and Competence

To test the hypothesis about the difference in averages on general attitudes towards Omega according to level of students' computer competence and frequency of computer use, we performed one-way analyses of variance and Scheffe post hoc tests for homogeneous variances.

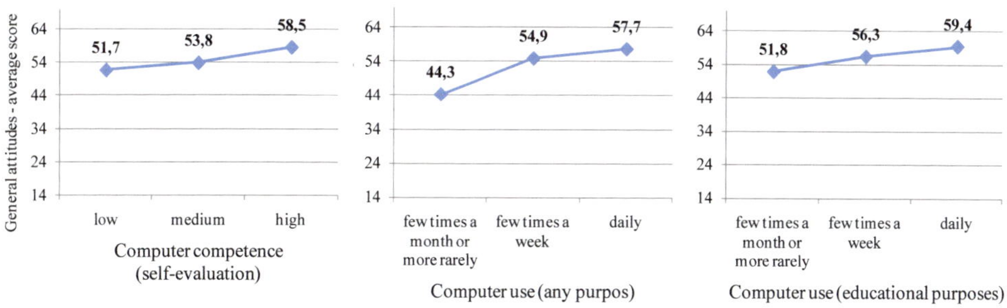

Fig. 8. Average scores on general attitudes towards Omega

The analyses showed statistically significant difference in means between students with medium and the ones with high computer competence (F=6.298, df=2, p=.002): students with high computer competence have more positive general attitudes towards Omega. There is also a statistically significant difference in means between students who use computer in any purpose daily and all other students (F=6.885, df=2, p=.001): students who use computer daily have more positive general attitudes towards Omega. Similarly, there is a statistically significant difference in means between students who use computer in educational purposes daily and the ones who use it only few times a month (F=6.125, df=2, p<.001).

6.1.6. Satisfaction with Omega's options and characteristics

For measuring students' satisfaction with Omega's options and characteristics five-point Likert scale was used with ordered response levels (1) Completely dissatisfied, (2) Dissatisfied, (3) Neither satisfied nor dissatisfied, (4) Satisfied and (5) Completely satisfied. The instrument has been applied only to those students who took at least one course enrolled to Omega. Six different attributes were given for evaluation: visual interface, content organization, possibilities of student-student and student-teacher communication via Omega, amount of lecture material and data access and update.

	(1)	(2)	(3)	(4)	(5)	$\overline{X}$	N
1. Visual interface.	3.8%	13.6%	24.2%	53.8%	4.5%	3.42	132
2. Content organization.	0.8%	12.1%	14.4%	62.9%	9.8%	3.69	132
3. Possibility of intercommunication between	1.5%	12.9%	35.6%	44.7%	5.3%	3.39	132

students.							
4. Possibility of intercommunication between students and teachers.	1.5%	10.6%	34.1%	47.0%	6.8%	3.47	132
5. Amount of lecture material.	2.3%	22.1%	25.2%	40.5%	9.9%	3.34	131
6. Data access and update.	2.3%	18.2%	25.0%	47.7%	6.8%	3.39	132

Table 5. Satisfaction with Omega's options and characteristics (distributions of percentages, means and numbers of valid answers)

All distributions are mildly right asymmetric which means that students tend to be satisfied with Omega's options and characteristics given for evaluation (average scores range from 3.34 for amount of lecture material to 3.69 for content organization).
To test the internal consistency reliability of this scale, Cronbach's alpha was computed and found to be .768, indicating relatively high reliability for this six items. The constructed scale was also tested for normality using the nonparametric one sample Kolmogorov-Smirnov test which showed that the scale is distributed according to normal distribution (p=.167).

Satisfaction With Omega's Options in Relation to Computer Use and Competence

To test the hypothesis about the difference in averages on satisfaction with Omega's options according to level of students' computer competence and frequency of computer use (generally and in educational purposes), we performed one-way analyses of variance. The analyses didn't show any statistically significant differences, so we can conclude that students do not differ in satisfaction with Omega's options on the basis of the variables mentioned above.

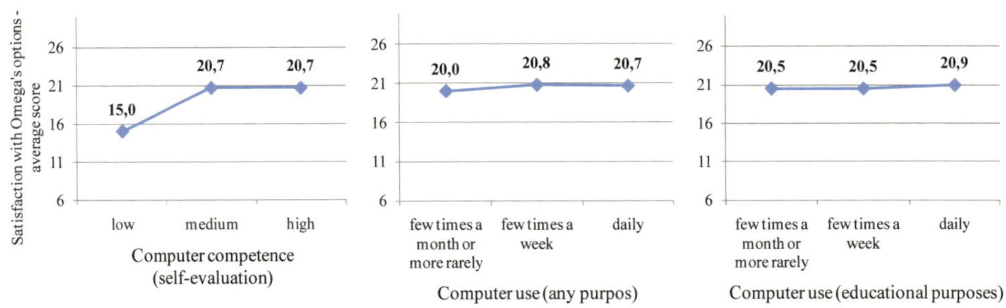

Fig. 9. Average scores on satisfaction with Omega's options and characteristics

6.1.7. Motivation for studying

Motivation for studying was measured with 17 statements covering several groups of possible motives for students to enter and continue their studying on the university such as their own desire for knowledge, their parents' persuasion, their friends who are also students, insurance of a better future etc. Each statement was evaluated on five-point ordinal scale with response levels (1) It doesn't refer to me at all, (2) It doesn't refer to me, (3) I don't know, I'm not sure, (4) It refers to me and (5) It refers to me completely.

	(1)	(2)	(3)	(4)	(5)	$\overline{X}$	N
1. I wouldn't want to quit the university because I wouldn't want to disappoint my parents.	28.4%	16.2%	13.5%	32.4%	9.5%	2.78	148
2. I prefer to study in groups, not by myself.	37.2%	23.0%	17.6%	16.9%	5.4%	2.30	148
3. I like completing my obligations on time so I would have more time for personal amusement.	6.8%	23.0%	20.3%	27.7%	22.3%	3.36	148
4. I like to learn new things and acquire new skills.	0.0%	1.4%	9.5%	46.6%	42.6%	4.30	148
5. I always knew that I want to enroll on the university.	1.4%	2.0%	8.8%	17.7%	70.1%	4.53	147
6. I extremely value my parent's and my family's opinion regarding my progress at the university.	8.8%	16.9%	20.9%	35.1%	18.2%	3.37	148
7. It would really bother me if I had lower grades then my colleagues.	14.2%	23.0%	23.0%	31.1%	8.8%	2.97	148
8. I enrolled on the university because my parents persuaded me to it.	72.3%	16.9%	6.8%	2.7%	1.4%	1.44	148
9. It's very important for me to keep my student's rights.	4.1%	6.8%	21.2%	32.2%	35.6%	3.88	146
10. Passing the exams is my only concern. Grades don't bother me at all.	14.3%	35.4%	21.1%	23.1%	6.1%	2.71	147
11. Most of my friends are students as well.	3.4%	5.4%	14.3%	38.1%	38.8%	4.03	147
12. It's important for me to finish university because it assures me financially more stable future.	3.4%	2.0%	14.2%	41.9%	38.5%	4.10	148
13. I believe that time being a student is the best and the most entertaining time in our lives.	6.8%	4.7%	17.6%	31.8%	39.2%	3.92	148
14. My friends would be very disappointed if I would quit the university.	18.9%	14.9%	29.1%	26.4%	10.8%	2.95	148
15. I'm studying because I think it will provide a better	0.7%	1.4%	9.5%	39.2%	49.3%	4.35	148

future for me.							
16. I think that people who enroll on the university after high school have few more years for „enjoying life".	20.3%	9.5%	23.6%	31.1%	15.5%	3.12	148
17. I tend to pass all my exams in a given period of time because I financially couldn't handle to renrol the academic year.	10.1%	15.5%	24.3%	21.6%	28.4%	3.43	148

Table 6. Satisfaction with Omega's options and characteristics (distributions of percentages, means and numbers of valid answers)

The following statements refer to the majority of students: "I like to learn new things and acquire new skills." (89.2%12), „I'm studying because I think it will provide a better future for me. (88.5%)", "I always knew that I want to enroll on the university." (87.8%), "It's important for me to finish university because it assures me financially more stable future." (80.4%) and "Most of my friends are students as well." (76.9%).
The statements that don't refer to the majority of students are: "I enrolled on the university because my parents persuaded me to it." (89.2%13), „I prefer to study in groups, not by myself." (60.2%), „I wouldn't want to quit the university because I wouldn't want to disappoint my parents." (44.6%) and „Passing the exams is my only concern. Grades don't bother me at all." (49.7%).
We can conclude that the majority of our students enrolled on university because they always wanted to do so, and they didn't do it on anyone's persuasion. One of the main motives for studying and successful study completion is the insurance of better and financially more secure future, but also students' own desire for acquisition of new knowledge. One could say that personal motivation for studying and successful study completion has showed to be a specific combination of extrinsic (better and financially more secure future) and intrinsic (desire for studying and acquisition of new knowledge) motivation factors.
These responses were factor analyzed to determine whether underlying factors might be found that could summarize the results on students' motivation for studying. Items number 1, 6 and 11 were excluded from the analysis because they didn't fulfill Thurstone's principle of simple structure. Extraction method was principal component analysis and rotation method varimax with Keiser normalization. The final varimax solution extracted 6 statistically significant components explaining 65.23% of total variance. The results are presented in Table 7. Only loadings equal or greater than 0.1 are shown.

12 The given percentages are sums of response levels (4) It refers to me and (5) It refers to me completely.
13 The given percentages are sums of response levels (1) It doesn't refer to me at all and (2) It doesn't refer to me.

	Component					
	1	2	3	4	5	6
5. I always knew that I want to enroll on the university.	.858					
8. I enrolled on the university because my parents persuaded me to it.	-.822		.113			-.146
4. I like to learn new things and acquire new skills.	.549		.325	.232	-.119	-.116
12. It's important for me to finish university because it assures me financially more stable future.		.848			-.123	
15. I'm studying because I think it will provide a better future for me.	.129	.772		.191	.218	
3. I like completing my obligations on time so I would have more time for personal amusement.		.553	.314	-.301		
10. Passing the exams is my only concern. Grades don't bother me at all.	-.122		-.839			
7. It would really bother me if I had lower grades then my colleagues.	-.133		.786			
16. I think that people who enroll on the university after high school have few more years for „enjoying life".	-.195			.793		
13. I believe that time being a student is the best and the most entertaining time in our lives.	.321	.173		.733	.151	
14. My friends would be very disappointed if I would quit the university.		-.100		.175	.728	
2. I prefer to study in groups, not by myself.		.179		-.113	.702	.101
17. I tend to pass all my exams in a given period of time because I financially couldn't handle to renrol the academic year.			.182		.216	.772
9. It's very important for me to keep my student's rights.		.182		.149	-.188	.732

Table 7. Rotated Component Matrix(a)

Extraction Method: Principal Component Analysis.
Rotation Method: Varimax with Kaiser Normalization.
(a) Rotation converged in 5 iterations.

First component consists of three items; one of witch has negative loading on the factor. Students prone to this factor always knew that they want to enroll on the university; they didn't enroll on the university on their parents' persuasion and they like to learn new things and acquire new skills. This factor was named PERSONAL DESIRE and it is the only factor based entirely on intrinsic motivation aspects.

Second component also consists of three items. Students prone to this factor want to finish studying because they think it will assure them financially more stable future and better future is the main reason for their studying. They also like to complete their obligations on time so they would have more time for personal amusement. This factor was named FUTURE INSURANCE.

Third component consists of two items; one of witch has negative loading on the factor. Students prone to this factor wish to achieve high grades and they would be really bothered if they had lower grades than their colleagues. This factor was named GRADES.

Fourth component consists of two items. Students prone to this factor think that people who enroll on the university after high school have few more years for „enjoying life" and they believe that time being a student is the best and the most entertaining time in someone's live. This factor was named STUDY TO ENJOY.

Fifth component consists of two items. Students prone to this factor believe that their friends would be very disappointed if they would quit the university and they prefer to study for an exam in group. This factor was named FRIENDS.

The last, sixth factor also consists of two items. Students prone to this factor tend to pass all their exams in a given period of time because they financially couldn't handle to renrol the academic year and it is important for them to keep their student's rights. This factor was named SOCIAL MOTIVES.

We can conclude that there are six independent types of motivation for studying among our students: personal desire, future insurance, grades, study to enjoy, friends and social motives.

The extracted factors were tested for normality using the nonparametric one sample Kolmogorov-Smirnov tests which showed that all factors, except for the first one - personal desire ($p<.001$), are distributed according to normal distribution (p values ranging from .181 for study to enjoy to .947 for friends).

To test whether there is a connection between the type of motivation for studying and general attitudes towards Omega, bivariate correlation analyses were conducted. Statistically significant correlation was found only for the first factor ($rho=.334$; $p<.001$), so we can conclude that positive general attitudes towards Omega are stronger expressed in students with stronger personal desire for studying.

After conducting a sequence of t-tests with each factor as a dependent, and gender as an independent variable and after determining that the test results didn't show any statistically significant difference in means, we can conclude that male and female students do not differ in tendency to neither of extracted motives for studying. Similarly, no differences in means were determined on motives for studying in view of lower and higher study years, except for factor friends which is the preference for students from lower study years ($t=2.685$; $df=142$; $p=.008$).

6.2. Students' attitudes regarding the need for better integration of the Omega e-learning system into traditional teaching

For measuring students' attitudes regarding the need for better integration of the Omega e-learning system into traditional teaching we used five-point Likert scale with ordered response levels (1) Strongly disagree, (2) Disagree, (3) Neither agree nor disagree, (4) Agree and (5) Strongly agree. The scale was constructed out of six items presented in Table 8.

	(1)	(2)	(3)	(4)	(5)	$\bar{X}$	N

1. Omega should be used much more on our faculty than it is used now.	2.0%	4.1%	27.0%	38.5%	28.4%	3.87	148
2. It would be great if all courses were available on Omega.	2.7%	8.8%	30.4%	36.5%	21.6%	3.66	148
3. All teachers should be familiar with Omega's usage and options.	1.4%	1.4%	14.9%	42.6%	39.9%	4.18	148
4. All teachers should be using Omega.	2.0%	6.1%	30.4%	33.8%	27.7%	3.79	148
5. Omega should be used on all departments of our faculty.	1.4%	4.1%	21.8%	38.8%	34.0%	4.00	147
6. Teachers who use Omega are more organized than the ones who don't use Omega.	4.7%	12.2%	35.8%	27.7%	19.6%	3.45	148

Table 8. Students' attitudes regarding the need for better integration of Omega e-learning system into traditional teaching (distributions of percentages, means and numbers of valid answers)

As we can see, students generally agree with all statements supporting the idea of the need for better integration of the Omega e-learning system into traditional teaching (average scores range from 3.45 to 4.18). Generally, over 60% of students agree (4) or strongly agree (5) with given statements. Most students agree that all teachers should be introduced with Omega's usage and options (item 3) and that Omega should be used on all departments of their faculty (item 5).

To test the internal consistency reliability of this scale, Cronbach's alpha was computed and found to be .902, indicating very high reliability for this six items. The constructed scale was also tested for normality using the nonparametric one sample Kolmogorov-Smirnov test which showed that the scale is distributed according to normal distribution (p=.214).

To test the hypothesis about the connection of attitudes regarding the need for better integration of Omega e-learning system into traditional teaching with variables that constitute our independent context, we performed several analyses depending on the type of tested variables.

Independent-samples t-test showed statistically significant difference in attitudes regarding the need for better integration of the Omega e-learning system into traditional teaching in favor of male students (t=2.922; df=145; p=.003): on the scale with variations range from 6 to 30 points, male students have average of 24.8 while average of female students is 22.3 points - although both male and female have rather high average on this scale (that is, both have positive attitudes about this subject), there is somewhat higher positive preference of males.

We determined positive correlation of attitudes regarding the need for better integration of Omega e-learning system into traditional teaching with general attitudes towards Omega (r=.696; p<.001), the number of taken courses that were enrolled to Omega (r=.376; p<.001) and also with the use of ICT by their teachers (r=.315; p<.001). There is also a positive correlation with students' computer competence (rho=.340, p<.001), frequency of students' computer use in educational (rho=.325; p<.001) and private purposes (rho=.250; p<.001) and with students' satisfaction with their own computer competence (rho=.292; p<.001).

Finally, there is a positive correlation of attitudes regarding the need for better integration of Omega e-learning system into traditional teaching with friends as one of the types of motivation for studying (r=.172; p=.040).
In other words, the greater need for better integration of e-learning in traditional teaching is related with male students, with those students who have more positive general attitudes toward Omega and who had more opportunity to get acquainted with all benefits e-learning can produce. It is also associated with greater teachers' usage of ICT in educational purposes probably because teachers who are more competent in ICT use generally, have higher ability to use e-learning system in the way that students can profit the maximum from it. For the same reason, this need for integration is also more expressed in those students who have developed higher level of computer competence and who apply their knowledge and skills daily, whether in personal or educational purposes. Finally, students who believe that their friends would be very disappointed if they would quit the university and who prefer to study for an exam in group also tend to feel greater need for better integration of e-learning into traditional teaching.

6.3. Students' attitudes regarding better educational quality through the use of e-learning

The second issue considering students' attitudes regarding the use of Omega e-learning system referred to students' attitudes regarding better educational quality through the use of e-learning.
For measuring this concept five-point Likert scale was also used with ordered response levels (1) Strongly disagree, (2) Disagree, (3) Neither agree nor disagree, (4) Agree and (5) Strongly agree, and the scale was constructed out of six items14 presented in Table 9.

.	(1)	(2)	(3)	(4)	(5)	$\bar{X}$	N
1. If I miss some classes, it is easer for me to catch up with the class matter if the course is on Omega.	4.1%	8.9%	30.1%	31.5%	25.3%	3.65	146
2. Thanks to distribution of class materials via Omega, there is more time for engaging in discussions and dealing with the subject during lectures.	2.1%	15.1%	31.5%	34.2%	17.1%	3.49	146
3. Use of Omega exonerates lectures because it leaves more time to deal with class content.	2.7%	15.8%	33.6%	32.9%	15.1%	3.42	146
4. It is much more practical to download the class materials from Omega than to write down during lessons.	1.4%	8.2%	15.1%	40.4%	34.9%	3.99	146

14 Before the construction of Likert scale, item number 6 was recoded.

5. Use of Omega compels teachers to be more systematical which helps students greatly.	0.0%	4.1%	28.1%	42.5%	25.3%	3.89	146
6. If all courses were on Omega, students would be overburdened with commitments.	26.0%	24.7%	36.3%	8.2%	4.8%	2.41	146

Table 9. Students' attitudes regarding better educational quality through the use of Omega e-learning system (distributions of percentages, means and numbers of valid answers)

Students generally agree with all statements supporting the idea of better educational quality through the use of e-learning. Most students agree that it is much more practical to download the class materials from Omega than to write down during lessons (item 4) and that the use of Omega compels teachers to be more systematical which helps students greatly (item 5). Very small percentage of students agree that they would be overburdened with commitments if all courses were on Omega (item 6) which indicates that Omega is not seen as a burden, but as a helpful instrument for improvement of educational quality.

This constructed scale was also tested for normality using the nonparametric one sample Kolmogorov-Smirnov test which showed that this scale is also distributed according to normal distribution ($p=.419$).

We determined positive correlation of attitudes regarding better educational quality through the use of Omega e-learning system with general attitudes towards Omega ($r=.651$; $p<.001$), the number of taken courses that were enrolled to Omega ($r=0.337$; $p<0.001$), the usage of ICT by their teachers ($r=.297$; $p<.001$) and with satisfaction with Omega's options ($r=.199$; $p<.001$). There is also a positive correlation with frequency of students' computer use in educational purposes ($rho=.264$; $p=.001$) and with students' satisfaction with their own computer competence ($rho=.195$; $p=.018$).

In other words, positive attitudes about the possibilities of enhancement of educational quality using e-learning system is related (again) with those students who have more positive general attitudes about Omega and who had more opportunity to get acquainted with e-learning because they took more courses that were enrolled to Omega. It is also associated with more frequent teachers' usage of ICT in educational purposes and with greater satisfaction with Omega's options and characteristics. Also, students who use computer in educational purposes more frequently and those who are more satisfied with their own computer competences have more positive attitudes about this subject.

6.4. Students' attitudes regarding the quantity and the quality of Omega e-learning usage

Attitudes regarding the quantity of Omega e-learning usage were assessed on ordinal five-point scale from (1) Completely dissatisfied - Omega is not used enough to (5) Completely satisfied - Omega is used enough, and the attitudes regarding the quality were assessed also on ordinal five-point scale from (1) Completely dissatisfied - the quality of Omega usage is very low to (5) Completely satisfied - the quality of Omega usage is very high.

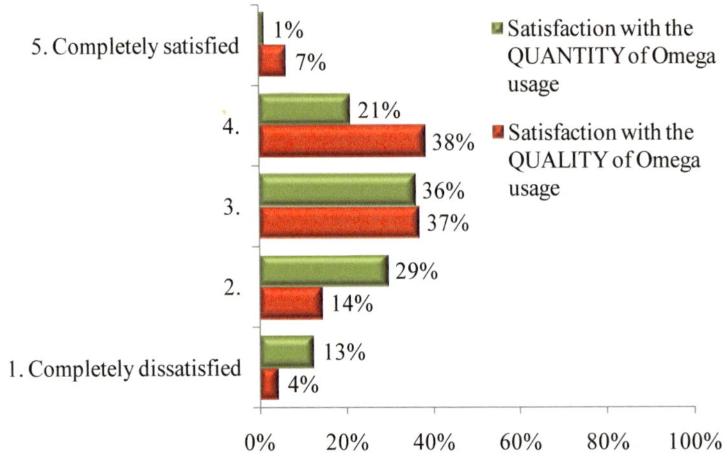

Fig. 10. Satisfaction with quantity and quality of Omega usage

As shown in Figure 10, the most frequent rank for quality of usage is rank 4 (38% of students) and for quantity rank 3 (36% of students).

The average score on assessment of quantity was 2.69, and on assessment of quality 3.28. Wilcoxon signed-rank test showed a statistically significant difference in these two assessments ($p<0.001$) so we can conclude that students are more satisfied with the quality than with the quantity of Omega usage. Over 40% of students think that Omega is not used enough (ranks 1 and 2) which also indicates a students' desire for greater integration of Omega in educational system.

To test the hypothesis about the connection of students' attitudes regarding the quantity and the quality of Omega e-learning usage with variables that constitute our independent context, we performed several analyses depending on the type of tested variables.

6.4.1. The quantity of Omega usage

Nonparametric Mann-Whitney U tests showed statistically significant difference in average ranking of satisfaction with the quantity of Omega usage in favor of male students ($p=.024$) and in favor of students from lower years of study ($p=.002$). Also, there is a positive correlation between satisfaction with the quantity of Omega usage and the number of taken courses that were enrolled to Omega ($rho=.563$; $p<.001$), the usage of ICT by their teachers ($r=.403$; $p<.001$) and satisfaction with Omega's options and characteristics ($r=.244$; $p=.005$). Out of all motivation factors, two are associated with attitudes regarding the quantity of Omega e-learning usage: factor personal desire negatively ($rho=-.178$; $p=.036$) and factor friends positively ($rho=.330$; $p<.001$).

6.4.2. The quality of Omega usage

Nonparametric Mann-Whitney U test showed statistically significant difference in average ranking of satisfaction with the quality of Omega usage in favor of students from lower years of study ($p=.021$). Higher satisfaction with the quality of Omega usage is positively correlated with the number of taken courses that were enrolled to Omega ($rho=.463$; $p<.001$),

the usage of ICT by their teachers ($r=.426$; $p<.001$), satisfaction with Omega's options and characteristics ($r=.410$; $p<.001$) and with better computer competence ($rho=.221$; $p=.010$).
In other words, greater satisfaction with both quantity and quality of Omega usage is connected with students from lower years of study, students who were taken a greater number of courses enrolled to Omega, with students whose teachers more frequently use ICT in educational purposes and with greater satisfaction with Omega's options and characteristics.
Greater satisfaction with the quantity of Omega usage is also connected with male students. In the context of motivation factors, students who tend to factor personal desire, that is those who always knew that they want to enroll on the university, who didn't do it on their parents' persuasion and who like to learn new things and acquire new skills, are less satisfied with the quantity of Omega usage, unlike students who tend to factor friends, that is those who believe that their friends would be very disappointed if they would quit the university and who prefer to study for an exam in groups, who are more satisfied with the quantity of Omega usage.
Greater satisfaction with the quality of Omega usage is also connected with students who have better computer competence.

7. Conclusion

The e-learning system integrated into traditional environment tends to remove, or at least, decrease barriers of the educational process, making it more flexible, enabling acquisition of new skills and competences, but also asking for adaptation, reorganization and investments in order to create better educational scenario. The research on quality measurement of the integrated e-learning system has shown the following:

1. Students generally agree with all statements supporting the idea of the need for better integration of the Omega e-learning system into traditional teaching. Most students agree that all teachers should be introduced with Omega's usage and options and that Omega should be used on all departments of their faculty.
2. The idea of better educational quality through the use of e-learning is generally supported by most of the students. They think that it is much more practical to download the class materials from Omega than to write down during lessons and that the use of Omega compels teachers to be more systematical which helps students greatly. Omega is not seen as a burden, but as a helpful instrument for improvement of educational quality.
3. Students are more satisfied with the quality than with the quantity of Omega usage. Over 40% of students think that Omega is not used enough which also indicates a students' desire for greater integration of Omega in educational system.
4. 45% of students are satisfied with the quality of Omega usage (ranks 4 and 5).

In our attempt to explain these attitudes with some concepts regarding students' experience, knowledge, competence and motivation, we came to conclusion that there are several concepts that are connected to all or some of the four aspects regarding students' attitudes towards the use of Omega e-learning system. These are: the number of taken courses that were enrolled to Omega, frequency of teachers' ICT use in educational purposes, satisfaction with Omega's options and characteristics, frequency of computer use in educational purposes, satisfaction with own computer competence and general attitudes towards

Omega. In addition, male gander and lower study years have also shown to be connected with some aspects of more positive attitudes towards the use of e-learning.
According to the reaction of students the e-learning systems have taken their position in formal and informal setting. Although seen in general with positive attitudes, it lacks social dimension. On the other side, development of new skills next to the sufficient motivation, and possibility of free access offer new role in blended learning.

8. References

Aimard, V.; Mc Cullough, C. E-Learning in Europe: How do trainers, teachers and learners rate e-learning? Cedefop, 2006. http://cms.eun.org/shared/data/pdf/report_survey_teachers_and_learners_and_e-learning_final.pdf

Allen, I. Elaine. Sizing the Opportunity. The Quality and Extent of Online Education in the United States, 2002 and 2003, Sloan-C, 2003. http://www.aln.org/publications/survey/pdf/sizing_opportunity.pdf

Allen, I. Elaine; Seaman, Jeff. Online Nation: Five Years of Growth in Online Learning. Sloan-C, 2007. http://www.sloan-c.org/publications/survey/pdf/online_nation.pdf

Decision No 2318/2003/EC of the European Parliament and of the Council adopting a multiannual programme (2004 to 2006) for the effective integration of information and communication technologies (ICT) in education and training systems in Europe (eLearning Programme). 5. 12. 2003.

Graham, C., Cagiltay, B., Craner, J., J. Lim, Duffy, T.M. Teaching in a Web Based Distance Learning Environment: An Evaluation Summary Based on Four Courses. CILT, Indiana University, 2000. http://crlt.indiana.edu/publications/crlt00-13.pdf

Graham, C., Cagiltay, J. Lim, B., Craner, J., & Duffy, T.M. Seven Principles of Effective Teaching: A Practical Lens for Evaluating Online Courses. Michigan Virtual University, 2001. http://www.tcc.edu/welcome/collegeadmin/OIE/SOA/review/toolkit/documents/Article_Seven_Principles_of_Effective_Teaching_A_Practical_Lens_for_Evaluating_Online_Course.pdf

Klasnić, K.; Seljan, S.; Stančić, H. Quality parameters for the e-learning Omega system // Proceedings of the ITI 2008 30th International Conference on Information Technology Interfaces. Zagreb : Srce - University Computing Centre, 2008.

Lasić-Lazić, J.; Banek Zorica, M.; Pavlina, K. Assessing teaching assessment // Tuning In: Learners of language, language of learners. Istambul : Sabancı University, 2007.

Lasić-Lazić, J.; Špiranec, S.; Banek Zorica, M.; Žunić, S.. Discipline-related information behaviour research: educational policy implications // Proceedings of the 30th Jubilee International Convention : Computers in Education. Rijeka : MIPRO, 2007.

Lorenzo, G., Moore J.C. Report to the Nation: Five Pillars of Quality Online Education, The Sloan Consortium, Needham, MA, 2002. http://www.sloan-c.org/

OIZEOO: Organizacija informacija i znanja u elektroničkom obrazovnom okruženju (2002.-2005.). http://infoz. ffzg.hr/oizeoo/

Omega http://omega.ffzg.hr/

Pawlowski, J.M. (2006): ISO/IEC 19796-1: How to Use the New Quality Framework for Learning, Education, and Training. White Paper, Essen, Germany, 2006.

Quality Assurance and Accreditation For European eLearning: the Case For a European Quality Mark Initiative, EFQUEL Green Paper No. 41 Brussels, 03/ 2007. http://www.qualityfoundation.org/index.php?m1=2&m2=25&view=0

Seljan, Sanja; Banek Zorica, Mihaela; Špiranec, Sonja; Lasić-Lazić, Jadranka. CALL (Computer-Assisted Language Learning) and Distance Learning. Proceedings of 29th International convention MIPRO. Rijeka, 2006. pp. 145-151

Stephenson, J. Definitions of indicator of quality on the application of ICT to University Teaching. Tarragona, 2005.

Stracke, Christian M.; Hildebrandt, Barbara (2007): "Quality Development and Quality Standards in e-Learning: Adoption, Implementation, and Adaptation"; in: Proceedings of World Conference on Educational Multimedia, Hypermedia and Telecommunication 2007 [= EdMedia 2007]; Chesapeake, VA: AACE, 4158-4165. http://www.qed-info.de/docs/quality_standards_qed.pdf

5

Intelligent Interaction Support for e-Learning

Takashi Yukawa and Yoshimi Fukumura
Nagaoka University of Technology
Japan

1. Introduction

Bi-directional communication, which enhances the effectiveness of education through question-and-answer and/or discussion sessions, is important in asynchronous e-Learning systems. Assignments are also important for e-Learning programs to motivate students and track their learning. However, assigned reports in e-Learning programs are submitted online, and it is very easy for students to plagiarize by pasting text from other reports or web sites.

This chapter introduces intelligent interaction support systems including an intelligent bulletin board system (iBBS) and a plagiarism-detecting assignment management system (pAMS). Both systems provide text-based intelligent functions that apply natural language processing and support smooth communication and a fair evaluation of e-Learning classes.

First, for iBBS, a function for the automated detection of important posting notifications (IPNs) is introduced. The IPN function performs information filtering; however, it is not feasible to estimate the statistics of word occurrences, which are required for conventional information filtering techniques, prior to opening a discussion. Nevertheless, since the subjects of discussion in e-Learning classes are always related to the class topic, the ontology is consistent throughout the discussion. A concept-based vector space model, which can virtually capture ontological information from a collection of documents, is therefore effective for the IPN function.

Second, pAMS, an assignment management system with plagiarism detection, is introduced. Students electronically submit their assigned reports using pAMS and the system stores the submitted documents. The system then compares each of submitted reports to other reports and web pages, and detects identical or similar parts of text in the reports. The system then makes the teacher aware of any potential plagiarism. This chapter describes the method for identifying the similar parts of two reports, even if one has been skillfully modified from the other. In addition, the method of retrieving original source materials is introduced. Finally, the evaluation results using a limited set of reports are described.

2. The Bulletin Board System with Intelligent Communication Support: iBBS

2.1 Requirements for iBBS

Inherently, a BBS for an e-Learning course cannot generate active discussions of the subject. If a large number of articles are posted on the BBS every day, reading every article becomes burdensome to both teachers and students, and may cause some students to drop out of the discussion. Therefore, it is desirable to reduce the workload for discussion participants.

To realize this workload reduction, an intelligent communication support function, which is an important IPN function, is embedded in the BBS. We call this system iBBS, and it is achieved with natural language processing techniques.

2.2 The IPN Function in iBBS

The IPN function, illustrated in Figure 1, operates as follows.

1. A participant (student B in the figure) registers his/her words of interest (keywords) into the system.
2. Another participant (student A in the figure) posts an article that includes the content of interest to the student B.
3. The system notifies student B of the posting.

The IPN function must notify the posting of the article by including not only the keywords themselves but also similar words. For example, assume that student B registers an "urgent stop" as a keyword, and student A posts an article including the word "emergency stop." The system must be able to notify student B of this article because the article discusses "urgent stopff even though the poster uses word "emergency stopff to express it.

A message in the BBS has a title line expressing its subject; however, a novice user often uses an irrelevant title, e.g., "question" or "request." Thus, the system has to check the content of the posted message. Consequently, to apply the IPN function, the system must understand the meanings of words.

Although machine-readable dictionaries [3] are commonly used for this purpose, such dictionaries generally consist of words for daily use rather than technical terms used in specialized fields. The authors previously proposed the Concept-based Vector Space Model (CBVSM), which is able to capture the relationships between words used in target texts [14]. CBVSM provides a function that discerns the semantic similarity between words that appear in texts; this capability enables the system to process texts as if the technical terms are understood.

CBVSM and the procedure to construct the concept base are introduced below, and then an implementation of the IPN function of iBBS is described. A performance (accuracy) evaluation of the IPN function is also presented.

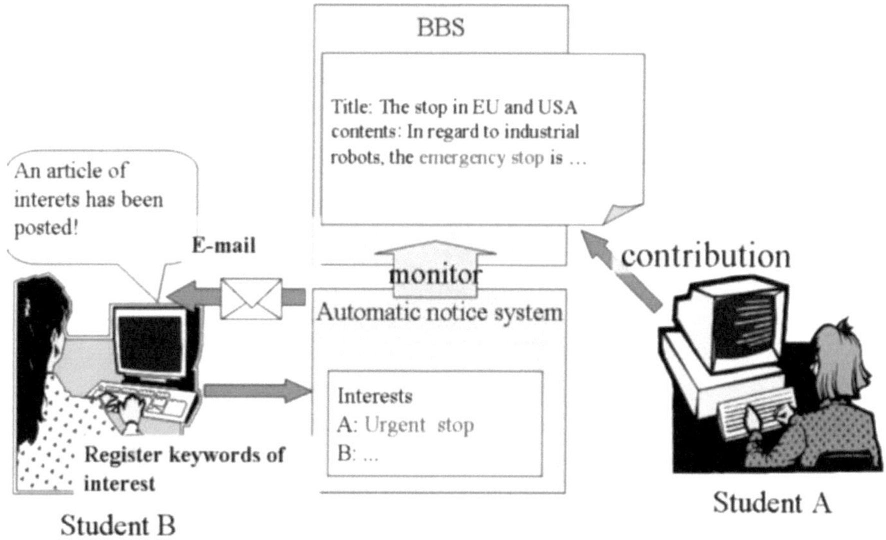

Fig. 1. Notification of Important Postings

2.3 Concept-based Vector Space Model

2.3.1 Concept Base and CBVSM

The purpose of CBVSM is the expressing documents and queries as vectors in a multi-dimensional space and calculating the relevance or similarity as a cosine coefficient between two centroid vectors in order to yield a vector space model.

With a basic similarity discernment scheme exploiting the vector space model, a vector of a document is mapped on a hyper-space, in which each word in a set of documents corresponds to an axis, such that the values along the document axes for the documents correspond to the term frequency-inverse document frequency (TFxIDF) values for the words in the documents [7]. This scheme assumes a vector space in which the words directly correspond to the axes. However, synonyms and/or co-occurrences of words are not considered.

Some improved methods for solving the above problem have been proposed. One is Latent Semantic Indexing (LSI) by Deerwester [2]. This method first counts the occurrences of words throughout the documents and then constructs a word frequency matrix. The rank of the matrix is then reduced using Singular Vector Decomposition (SVD), and the reduced-rank matrix is then used as the document vector space.

Another method is the co-occurrence based thesaurus by Schütze [8, 9]. This method obtains a word vector space based on word co-occurrences in close proximity in documents, whereas LSI creates a document vector space based on word frequencies throughout documents. The words that co-occur in a similar manner throughout documents are expected to be placed close to each other in the hyper-space. The authors refer to a database comprised of pairs of a wordand its associated vectors as the "concept base".

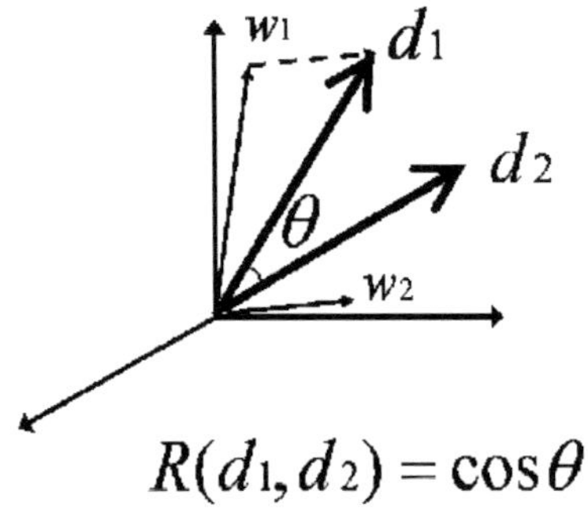

Fig. 2. Concept-based Vector Space Model

The vector for a document is represented as the center of gravity with word vectors constructed from the document. In other words, the document vector is calculated as a normalized summation of the word vectors included in the document, as shown in Figure 2. The similarity between two documents $R(d_1, d_2)$ is calculated as a cosine coefficient between two centroid vectors.

In these methods (LSI and the co-occurrence thesaurus), documents having similar contents provide strong similarities even though the documents do not have the same expressions. This differs from methods based on word occurrences or Boolean full-text searches in that a high similarity degree is obtained only when documents contain similar expressions.

For CBVSM, words and documents that are different in nature from each other are mapped together in the same multi-dimensional space. This means that the methods provide not only similarity between words, but also similarity between words and documents, as well as between documents.

2.3.2 Construction of the Concept Base

The concept base is a knowledge base of words and is comprised of a set of words and their associated vectors. Each word is associated with a high-dimensional vector (a word vector), and the vector is statistically calculated from the target document set. The procedure to construct the concept base is illustrated in Figure 3 and stated in the following steps.

1. List every word that appears in the target documents. Let N be the number of words and w_i be the i-th word in the word list.
2. Create an $N \times N$ zero matrix. Let C be the matrix and C_{ij} be the i-th row and j-th column element in C.
3. Count the co-occurrences of words throughout the documents: if word w_i and word w_j co-occur within a specific distance in a sentence, increment
4. Reduce the rank of C to M using SVD, then obtain the reduced-rank matrix C' (N rows $\times$ M columns).

5. C' forms the concept base. The *i-th* row of C' corresponds to the word vector for word w_j.

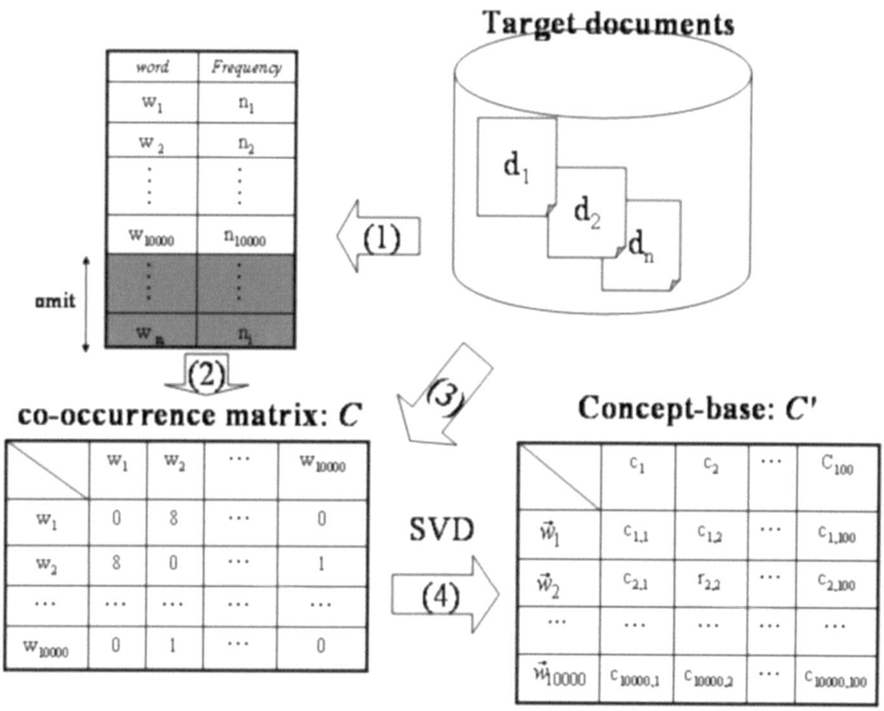

Fig. 3. Procedure to Construct the Concept Base

The maximum value of N is limited by the computing resources. In the case of resource constraints, the word list is truncated based on the occurrence count after step 1. Although M can be 1 to N in theory, we use M = 100 because it has been reported that this value is appropriate for discerning the similarity between words [9].

2.4 Implementation of the IPN Function

The IPN function is achieved by applying CBVSM to an information filtering technique [12]. The system computes the similarity between keywords and every posted article, then sends out alerts for articles that have a similarity degree that exceeds a specified threshold. By using CBVSM for computing, the similarity degree reflects not only occurrences of the keywords themselves, but also occurrences of similar words in an article. Therefore, the method satisfies the requirement for the IPN function, that is, notification of an article which does not explicitly include the keywords but discusses a topic expressed by the keywords.

The procedure for achieving the IPN function is listed in the following steps (see Figure 4).

Preparation 1. Construct the concept base: The concept base has to be generated prior to opening a discussion board. For concept base generation, text documents describing the same areas as the discussion topics are needed. In an e-Learning program, teaching materials include instructional text that can be used for concept base generation.

Preparation 2. Register the keywords of the topic of interest: The user inputs into the system the keywords in which he/she is interested. The system computes the query vector referring to the concept base. A user should have several interests and all students taking a course automatically become users of the discussion board; therefore, the system stores a set of keywords and a query vector for each user.
Step 1. When someone posts an article, the system extracts nouns and verbs from the article, then computes the document vector based on the extracted nouns and verbs referring to the concept base.
Step 2. The following step is iterated while extracting each query vector for each user from query vector storage.
Step.3. The system computes the similarity degree between the query vector and the document vector as the cosine coefficient of these vectors. If the similarity degree exceeds the threshold value, which is defined as a system configuration value, the system notifies the user that an important article is posted.
The concept base generation is a heavily loaded process because it requires the count of word co-occurrences throughout the documents and several matrix calculations. However, this process must be done just one time prior to opening the discussion. For every posting, information filtering based on CBVSM is processed and its cost is identical to that of other methods based on the vector space model.
As stated above, using CBVSM for computing the similarity degree reflects not only occurrences of the keywords themselves, but also occurrences of similar words in an article. For example, assume that student B registers "urgent stop" as a keyword, and student A posts an article including the word "emergency stop." The system described here can notify student B of this article because the similarity degree between words "urgent stop" and "emergency stop" is quite high according to the concept base. In other words, the concept base knows that the words "urgent stop" and "emergency stop" are similar.
The mechanism for adaptation to users is also embedded in the system. To adapt the IPN function to users, a user relevance feedback technique is employed. Because CBVSM is an extension of the vector space model, therelevance feedback technique for the conventional vector space model [1] can be applied directly.

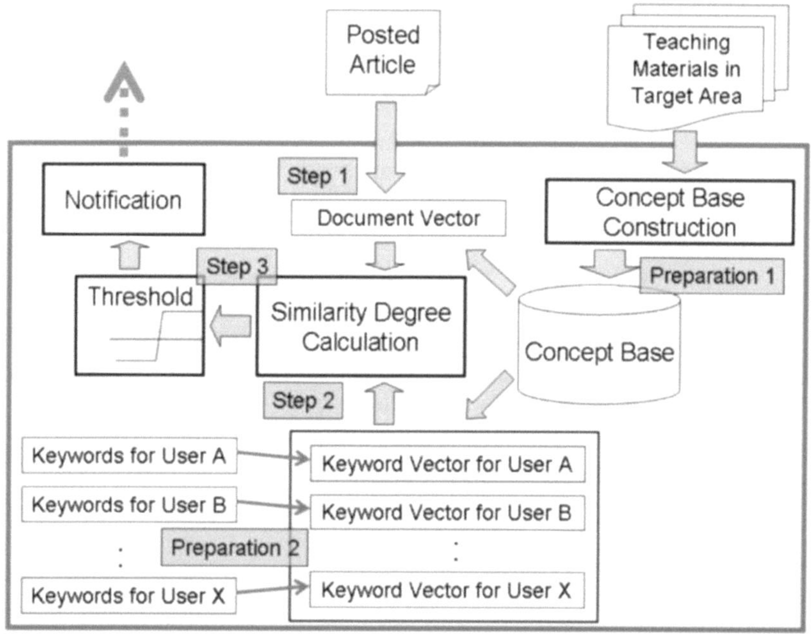

Fig. 4. Implementation of the IPN Function

When a user indicates that an article notified by the system is suitable for his/her interest, the system modifies the query vector to be close to the document vector of the article. Conversely, when a user indicates that an article is incorrectly notified, the system modifies the query vector to be far from the document vector. This modification to the query vector is stored and the system uses the modified query vector hereafter.

2.5 Performance Evaluation

Performance of the information retrieval functions including the IPN function is measured by "precision" and "recall" [1]. These measures are evaluated empirically using actual data sets. Precision corresponds to the measure of reliability and recall corresponds to the measure of completeness. Let N_d be the number of retrieved documents and N_c be the number of correct documents of the retrieved documents. Precision P is defined as

$$P = N_c / N_d.$$

In addition, let N_R be the number of correct documents among all documents in the data set; in other words, the number of complete answer sets. Recall R is defined as

$$R = N_c / N_R.$$

2.5.1 Precision and Recall for the IPN function

In this section, the performance of the IPN function is evaluated using articles posted on the BBS of an actual e-Learning class [11]. If the number of articles is not sufficiently large, the evaluation results for a large number of articles posted on an open BBS on the Internet are also reported. The performance is compared with methods based on conventional models:

TF × IDF vector space model [7] and probabilistic model [5]. The performance improvement with user relevance feedback is also shown.
The articles posted on the BBS of the actual e-Learning course "Information Technology Basics" were used for the performance evaluation. As an example, a teacher requested students to discuss Internet protocols, then 38 articles were posted. The topics of the articles included the collision control technique on the Ethernet, message transfer protocols, and so on. For constructing the concept base, a large size (approximately 8,000 words) of instructional text on information technology was used. The text was used for obtaining statistics for conventional models.
Tables 1 and 2 show the results of the evaluation. "CSMA/CD" was assumed as a word of interest for the results in Table 1, and "NNTP" was assumed in Table 2. Complete answer sets can be constructed by reading all discussions in the BBS and judging whether each article is related, if the number of articles is small. For keyword "CSMA/CD," 10 articles discussed that topic, and 3 articles among them did not include the word "CSMA/CD" explicitly. Table 1 shows that the proposed method found all correct articles as important postings. Therefore, the recall rate and precision rate are 1. In contrast, methods based on the conventional models found only 7 correct articles out of 10 and 1 wrong articleone. For keyword "NNTP," 3 articles discussed that topic, and one article among them did not include the keyword explicitly. The proposed method also found all correct articles for this keyword, whereas the conventional methods found only two articles. The results prove that the proposed method has the capability to find related articles which do not include the keywords explicitly, whereas conventional methods cannot find them.
On the performance evaluation above, the number of articles was quite small. Since the IPN function is useful for the BBS on which a large number of articles is posted, a performance evaluation for a large-scale discussion board is desired. However, the authors had no class with a large-scale discussion of these terms. Instead, an evaluation using articles posted on an active BBS on the Internet was conducted. A total of 5946 articles were downloaded from a BBS discussing the Linux operating system and was assumed to be posted on our BBS. Topics "configuration for wireless LAN" and "detection of a hard disk drive" were assumed to be the users' interest, and the keywords were {"wireless," "lan," "configuration"} and {"hdd" and "detection"}, respectively. In this evaluation, the complete answer set could not be determined, because there were large numbers of articles, and it is not feasible for a human to read and judge every article. What a human can do is to judge whether a notified article is correct. Therefore, the precision rate could be obtained but the recall rate could not.

Method	# Notified	# Correct	Precision	Recall
CBVSM	3	3	1.00	1.00
TF*x* IDF	2	2	1.00	0.67
Probabilistic	2	2	1.00	0.67

Keyword = " NNTP", # correct articles = 3,
# correct articles without word "NNTP" = 1
Table 2. Results for a small number of articles (2)

Method	# Notified	# Correct	Precision	Recall
CBVSM	10	10	1.00	1.00
TFxIDF	8	7	0.87	0.70
Probabilistic	8	7	0.87	0.70

Keyword = "CSMA/CD", # correct articles = 10,
# correct articles without word "CSMA/CD" = 3
Table 1 Results for a small number of articles (1)

Tables 3 and 4 shows the results. The results suggest that the proposed method performs better than conventional methods even for a large-scale discussion board.

2.5.2 Performance Improvement with User Feedback

Performance improvement with user feedback was evaluated using the document set and keywords used above in the large-scale discussion board. Tables 5 and 6 show the results. As shown in the tables, considerable improvement in the precision rate is obtained with user feedback.

Method	# Notified	Precision
CBVSM	88	0.75
TFx IDF	43	0.62
Probabilistic	60	0.19

Keywords = "wireless lan configuration"
Table 3. Results for a large number of articles (1)

Method	# Notified	Precision
CBVSM	37	0.51
TFx IDF	19	0.42
Probabilistic	41	0.43

Keywords = "hdd detection"
Table 4. Results for a large number of articles (2)

# fb cycles	# Notified	Precision
0	88	0.75
1	83	0.80
2	70	0.86
3	63	0.90
4	54	0.93

Keywords = "wireless lan configuration"
Table 5. Performance Improvement with User Feedback (1)

2.5.3 Discussions

The evaluation results suggest that the CBVSM-based method provides superior performance compared with conventional filtering methods for a wide range of sizes of

discussion boards.
The IPN function in iBBS for e-Learning differs from a normal information filtering function in that obtaining statistics on articles is difficult prior to opening the discussion board.

# fb cycles	# Notified	Precision
0	37	0.51
1	34	0.59
2	29	0.64
3	28	0.60
4	25	0.68

Keywords = "hdd detection"
Table 6. Performance Improvement with User Feedback (2)

Instead, the ontology for the discussion articles is implicitly contained in the teaching materials. CBVSM can capture the ontology from the teaching materials virtually, and so the proposed method is expected to provide appropriate judgment even if it for the very first article in the discussion board. In contrast, the methods based on conventional models require statistics on the articles; however, these cannot be obtained in a BBS. Only one instructional text is used for constructing the concept base and obtaining actual statistics of the documents; therefore, the IDF value for every word is constantly 1 in the TF $\times$ IDF model and a priori document probability is also 1 in the probabilistic model. This degrades the performance of conventional methods. As shown in the results in Tables 1 and 2, the proposed method provides perfect precision whereas conventional methods return incorrect articles.
CBVSM is also able to discern the relevance between a topic and an article even though the article does not include the topic keyword, whereas conventional methods basically only detect articles including the keywords. The results show that the CBVSM-based method has a recall rate of 1.0, in contrast to the conventional methods, which cannot detect articles that do not explicitly include the keywords.
In addition, the results prove that user relevance feedback improves the performance, as expected.

3. The Assignment Management System with Plagiarism Detection: pAMS

3.1 Requirements for pAMS

Assignments are important for e-Learning programs to motivate students and track their learning. Since a student of an e-Learning program writes his/her report in electronic form, it is very easy for him/her to copy text from other reports or web sites. Consequently, it is a very heavy burden for a teacher to check for plagiarism in these reports. Therefore, an assignment management system that has a plagiarism detection function is needed. As an added benefit, if students know that the assignment management system automatically detects plagiarism, they will avoid copying text from others. This leads to the prevention of plagiarism.

The plagiarism detection function must have the following capabilities.

- Some students may modify the source text to avoid detection. Therefore, the detection function has to be able to find similar parts in two documents, even if they are skillfully modified and not copied word by word.
- It is not feasible to check the similarity of the target text against every web page on the Internet because of resource limitations. Therefore, the function must be able to narrow down the web pages to suspected ones before checking the similarity.

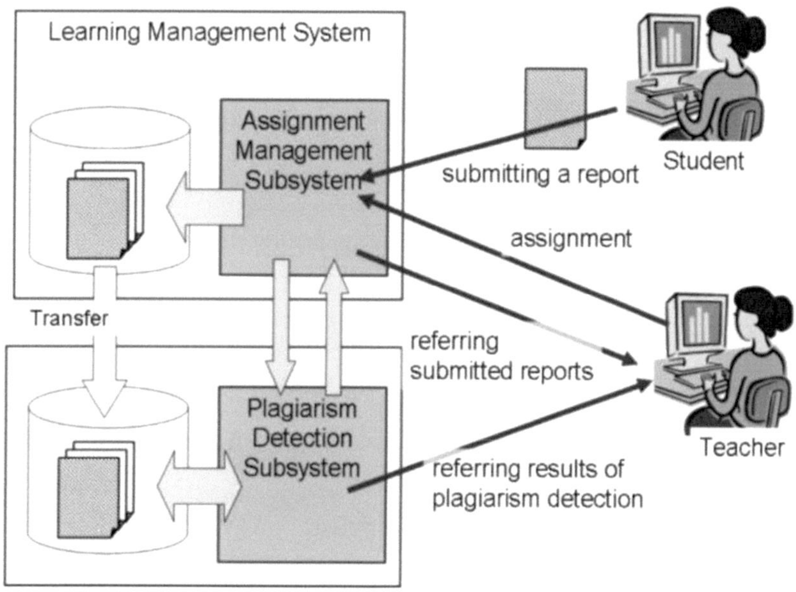

Fig. 5. System Structure of pAMS

3.2 System Structure and Plagiarism Detection Subsystem

The overall structure of pAMS is shown in Figure 5. This system consists of two parts: an assignment management subsystem and a plagiarism detection subsystem [13]. The assignment management subsystem is a module that is compatible with a learning management system (LMS) and provides functions that include assignment configuration, report submission, and submitted report references. The plagiarism detection subsystem detects plagiarism by comparing each pair of reports and web pages.

Figure 6 shows the structure of the plagiarism detection subsystem. When a target report is given, it detects any part similar to other reports and web pages by the following sequence.

1. Extracts the query words from the target document; The words are used for retrieving web pages that are possible source documents if the target report copied text from the web.
2. Issues the query to an Internet search service (e.g., Google), then retrieves and stores N web pages found by the query, where N is a configuration parameter (50 to 100 is appropriate).
3. Compares the target report with each of the other reports and stored web

pages, then finds similar parts; if similar parts are found in the comparison, they are accumulated in the result generation module.

4. When the above step is finished for every document, a list of suspect parts is generated based on the accumulated comparison results.

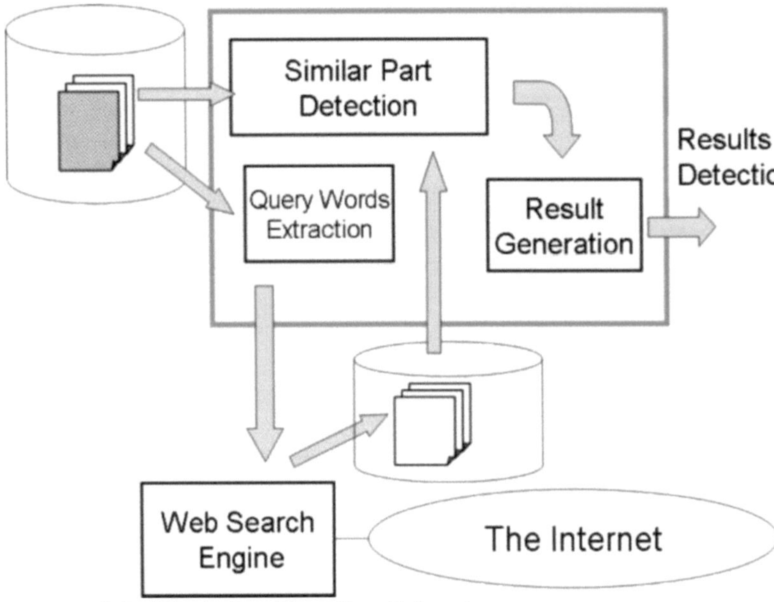

Fig. 6. Structure of the Plagiarism Detection Subsystem

The query words should include words expressing the content of the report and simultaneously the words that are able to narrow the scope of the search. High-frequency words in the document express the main topic and longer words limit the scope. Therefore, the authors employ a combination of high-frequency words and long words as query words. For the detection of similar parts, a combination of the TF× IDF vector space method with the Smith-Waterman algorithm [10, 4, 6] is employed. The TF× IDF vector space model is used for computing the degree of similarity between one sentence and another. Based on sentence-by-sentence similarity degrees, quasi-contiguous parts of similar sentences are found with the Smith-Waterman algorithm. The TF× IDF vector space model technique can recognize the copied sentences revised with the substitution of a word with a synonym, and the Smith-Waterman algorithm can find plagiarized parts revised with word re-sequencing.

3.3 Performance Evaluation

For the performance evaluation of plagiarism detection, students were employed to write intentionally plagiarized reports. Four subjects, including "embedded systems," "copyright," "open source software" and "derivatives," were given, and the students searched web pages describing these subjects, then plagiarized text from these pages. The web pages used for plagiarism were stored in a source document pool and their URLs were recorded for each plagiarized report. A total of 900 plagiarized reports were written. Some of the plagiarized reports were comprised of "dead" copies of parts from one, two, or three web pages. Others were revised with several levels of modification. Non-plagiarized reports were also written. The number of these was 20.

First, to evaluate the accuracy of the plagiarism judgment based on the similar part detection, the web pages used for plagiarism were assumed to be retrieved perfectly. Each of the reports in the test set was input into the system, then the system checked it against web pages in the source document pool and indicated whether it was plagiarized. The precision for plagiarism judgment P_i is defined as

$$P_i = N_C / N,$$

where N is the number of reports in the test set and N_C is the number of reports for which the system with the source document pool gives an correct judgment.

Next, the accuracy of retrieving possible source web pages was evaluated. Each of the plagiarized reports was input into the system, then the system extracted query words for the reports, submitted the query to the Internet search service, and retrieved 100 web pages that matched the query. The precision for suspected web page retrieval P_r is defined as

$$P_r = N_r / N_p,$$

where N_P is the number of plagiarized reports, and N_R is the number of reports for which at least one of the source web pages is included in the retrieved web pages.

Finally, the overall accuracy of the system was evaluated. Precision P_o is expressed as

$$P_o = N_C / N,$$

where N_C is the number of the reports for which the system retrieves web pages and eventually gives a correct judgment.

Table 7 shows the results. Precision P_i demonstrates that if the source web pages can be correctly retrieved, the system can accurately detect plagiarism from the web pages. However, retrieving the source web pages is not sufficiently accurate. This fact decreases the overall precision.

P_i	0.93
P_r	0.54
P_o	0.49

Table 7. Evaluation Results

4. Summary and Future Work

This chapter describes an intelligent interaction support system for e-Learning systems. The support system includes an intelligent bulletin board system(iBBS) and a plagiarism-detecting assignment management system (pAMS) that enable smooth communication and fair evaluation of e-Learning classes.

The functional requirement of the iBBS is clarified, the method using the concept-based vector space model (CBVSM) for the important posting notification (IPN) function is proposed, and evaluation results are reported. The results show that the proposed method provides superior precision and recall rates compared with conventional methods based on the TF×IDF vector model and probabilistic model.

The system structure, pAMS, comprised of an assignment management subsystem and a plagiarism detection subsystem is introduced. The structure of the plagiarism detection subsystem is introduced as a combination of the retrieval of suspected web pages and the detection of similar parts of text. Similarity discernment between sentences based on the TF× IDF vector space model and quasi-contiguous part recognition with the Smith-Waterman algorithm are employed for the similar part detection. A performance evaluation with a limited scale set of intentionally plagiarized reports was conducted. The results show that the overall precision is approximately 50% because of insufficient accuracy in the retrieval of the source web pages.
Improvement of the source web page retrieval capability and performance evaluations with a large-scale set of real plagiarized reports are tasks for future study.

5. References

[1] R. Baeza-Yates and B. Ribeiro-Net. *Modern Information Retrieval.* Addison Wesley, 1999.
[2] S. Deerwester, S. T. Dumais, G. W. Furnas, et al. Indexing by latent semantic analysis. *Journal of American Society for Information Science,* 41(6):391-407, 1990.
[3] S. Ikehara et al. *Goi-Taikei - A Japanese Lexicon, the Semantic Attribute System (in Japnese),* volume 1. Iwanami-shoten, 1998.
[4] R. W. Irving. Plagiarism and collusion detection using the Smith-Waterman algorithm. Technical report, University of Glasgow, Department of Computing Science, 2004.
[5] K. S. Jones, S. Walker, and S. E. Robertson. A probabilistic model of information retrieval: Development and comparative experiments. *Information Processing and Management,* 36(6):779-808,809-840, 2000.
[6] T. Ohta and S. Masuyama. Similar-part detection among term papers. *IEICE Technical Report. Natural Language Understanding and Models of Communication (in Japanese),* NLC2005-112:37-42, 2006.
[7] G. Salton and C. Buckley. Term weighting approaches in automatic text retrieval. In K. S. Jones and P. Willet, editors, *Readings in Information Retrieval,* pages 323-328. Morgan Kaufmann Publishers, 1998.
[8] H. Schütze and J. O. Pedersen. A cooccurrence-based thesaurus and two applications to information retrieval. In *Proc. RIAO '94,* 1994.
[9] H. Schütze and J. O. Pedersen. Information retrieval based on word sense. In *Proc. 4th Annual Symposium on Document Analysis and Information Retrieval,* pages 161-176, 1995.
[10] T.F. Smith and M.S. Waterman. Identification of common molecular subsequences. *Journal of Molecular Biology,* 147:195-197, 1981.
[11] T. Yukawa, H. Amarume, and Y. Fukumura. An important posting notification function in an intelligent bulletin board system for e-learning. In *Proc. Knowledge-Based and Intelligent Information and Engineering Systems: KES2007-WIRN2007,* volume LNAI4694, pages 761-768, 2007.
[12] T. Yukawa, H. Amarume, M. Tochio, T. Kimura, K. T. Nakahira, and Y. Fukumura. An intelligent bulletin board system for an e-learning program for safety engineering. In *Proc. World Conference on Educational Multimedia, Hypermedia and Telecommunications (ED-MEDIA 2006),* volume 2006, pages 2493-2494, 2006.

[13] T. Yukawa and Y. Fukumura. Development of an interaction support system for e-learning. In J. Yoshida and H. Sasabe, editors, *Next Generation Photonics and Media Technologies,* pages 167-170, 2006.
[14] T. Yukawa, K. Kasahara, T. Kato, and T. Kita. An expert recommendation system using concept-based relevance discernment. In *Proc. International Conference on Tools with Artificial Intelligence 2001,* pages 257-264, 2001.

6

Supporting Technologies for Synchronous E-learning

Juan C. Granda, Christian Uría,
Francisco J. Suárez and Daniel F. García
University of Oviedo
Spain

1. Introduction

Recent advances in multimedia technology have enabled new communications possibilities that improve the distance learning experience. Thus, the introduction of multimedia contents in learning materials results in an enhanced learning process. (Steinmetz & Nahrstedt, 1995); (Mishra & Sharma, 2004). In fact, virtual learning environments have an enormous potential (Padmore et al., 2006).

Similarly, enterprise corporations must introduce technical innovations to their production cycle in order to increase their market competitiveness. As a consequence, personal staff must adapt to the changes imposed in the organization to cope with these technical improvements to positively contribute to the corporate success. Thus, it turns essential to design training programs as a part of the corporate policies to keep employees technologically updated. Multiple studies show that interactive training increases knowledge retention and shortens learning curve (Shulman, 1992), and offers great flexibility since training may be provided just-in-time specifically for each user's needs. Interactive learning is even more appropriate to those situations in which an employee manipulates fragile or dangerous equipment. Simulation environments are very suitable to avoid possible misuses and faults that would imply high costs. As an example, in (Mollet & Arnaldi, 2006) the authors propose a virtual reality environment for the training of human staff in a military equipment factory.

Geographical dispersion in multinational corporations constitutes another reason to use e-learning in staff training. Thus, there is no need to maintain a specific training center, so employees do not have to move from their workplace to this center to receive training courses. This implies a cost-saving alternative compared to traditional learning, because displacements are not necessary, so training may be provided just-in-time at the workplace.

Nowadays, e-learning has become a widely used learning strategy in higher education and staff training. In fact, e-learning is one of the most suitable tools for developing training plans in large business corporations in order to establish a continuing education offer to their human resources.

Often, e-learning is divided into asynchronous e-learning and synchronous e-learning attending to the spatio-temporal limitations imposed to the learning process. Thus, asynchronous e-learning allows participants to interact wherever they may be and whenever they may desire. In contrast, attendees to a synchronous e-learning activity must join the virtual session at the same time, so interactions must occur in real time. To accomplish this goal, tools like shared whiteboards, instant messaging, and audio/video conferences are used.

Synchronous e-learning allows multiple remote participants to interact live despite of their geographical location. The instructor and the rest of participants can solve doubts from other participants immediately, providing a sense of co-presence. Therefore, synchronous e-learning promotes learning communities by the interchange of ideas and experiences among learners. In short, synchronous e-learning combines advantages from e-learning such as geographically independence, and benefits from traditional education such as face-to-face interaction.

Audio and video conferencing provide support to synchronous e-learning activities. IETF and ITU-T are organizations that elaborate and promote standard conferencing frameworks and protocols. In this chapter, the main issues of the transport of continuous data over packet networks are explained, especially those related to multicasting and how Real-time Transport Protocol (RTP) copes with the handicaps of this kind of networks (packet loss, latency, jitter, etc.). The next section introduces the characteristics of synchronous e-learning and its advantages over other educational strategies. In section 3, the technological implications of synchronous e-learning are described. In sections 4 to 7, the protocols and recommendations from IETF and ITU-T related to audio and video conferencing are detailed, compared and organized into layers according to their purpose. These protocols are mainly used to establish multimedia sessions between users within a synchronous e-learning session. In section 8, multiple audio and video codecs specifically oriented to synchronous e-learning environments are mentioned. Finally, conclusions are presented in section 9.

2. Synchronous e-Learning

Usually, e-learning systems are classified according to the temporal restrictions imposed on the learning process. Two types of e-learning systems are considered: asynchronous and synchronous systems. The asynchronous e-learning systems do not impose any temporal restriction on the learning process. Thus, there is no need that instructor and learners are connected at the same time, so they can deal with learning materials at their own pace.

In contrast, synchronous e-learning systems imply a temporal synchronization between instructor and learners, but they may be geographically dispersed. The learning experience is guided by the real-time interactions that occur among learners and instructor and among learners themselves. Table 1 compares some relevant characteristics of asynchronous and synchronous e-learning.

Synchronous e-learning presents some features which differentiate it from other learning methodologies:

- Live. Synchronous e-learning activities take place live, that is, they are not previously recorded, but recorded or pre-produced material may be used during the activity.

Asynchronous e-learning	Synchronous e-learning
Intermittent on-demand access	Real-time
Previously recorded or pre-produced	Live
Just in time	Scheduled
Individual or poorly collaborative	Collaborative
Independent learning	Co-presence of learners and instructor
Self-paced	Concurrent learning

Table 1. Differences between asynchronous and synchronous e-learning

- Real-time. Although synchronous e-learning activities may be recorded for a later playback, they are essentially in real time, so they cannot be paused or resumed like self-paced courses.
- Facilitated. Normally, every synchronous session is guided by a facilitator whose mission is to control that interactions between learners are focused on knowledge acquisition. They help to consolidate knowledge.
- Learning-oriented interactions. This differentiates synchronous e-learning from other types of real-time activities like video conferences, or online product demonstrations.

Asynchronous e-learning	Synchronous e-learning
E-mail	Instant messaging
Discussion forums	Online chat
Web-based training	Live webcasting
Podcasting	Audio conferencing
DVD	Video conferencing
Computer aided systems	Web conferencing

Table 2. Examples of asynchronous and synchronous e-learning features

In table 2 the most common features used to provide both asynchronous and synchronous e-learning are listed. The utilization of synchronous e-learning systems has multiple advantages:

- They connect multiple dispersed learners, which results especially appropriate to large multinationals with sites in multiple countries. Corporations may benefit from the ability to train employees at the workplace.
- They allow interactions and collaboration in real time, emulating relations within a traditional classroom. This way, every attendee to the session relates each other more naturally, so the session flows spontaneously. Questions are raised immediately and responses are given directly.
- They provide a sense of immediacy, which is useful to deliver last-minute contents or time-sensitive data. Furthermore, the presence of the instructor is noticeably for

the learners, so anxieties arisen in the learners regarding the non-personal learning experience can be alleviated.

- Learners can share doubts and experiences. This stimulates the sense of connectedness among them. As a result, these tools permit social interactions between learners, which foster learning communities and create a learning synergy. Long-term effects include better teamwork and collaboration skills.
- They promote an egalitarian learning experience among learners. Those extroverts do not dominate class dynamics as in traditional classrooms. Anonymous participation in the e-learning sessions make introvert learners feel more comfortable to participate actively. Due to the avoidance of face-to-face interaction, racial or social differences do not affect the flowing of sessions.

Usually, synchronous e-learning systems provide common features such as audio and video conferencing, instant messaging and presence control, shared whiteboard with electronic ink and telepointers, desktop and application sharing, etc. In (García et al., 2007) a functional evaluation of 20 synchronous e-learning tools is presented. In figure 1, a screenshot of a synchronous e-learning tool (Granda et al., 2008) is shown. This tool provides the most common features of synchronous e-learning systems.

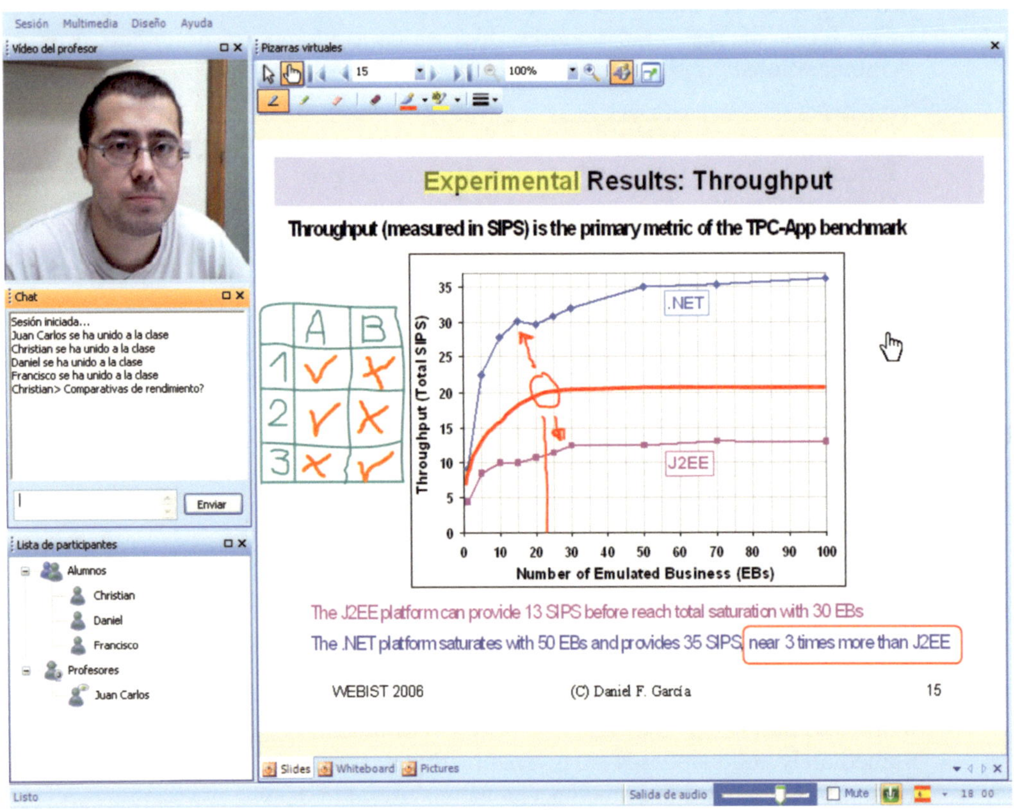

Fig. 1. Screenshot of a synchronous e-learning tool

3. Technological Requirements

In order to provide the functionalities listed in the previous section, synchronous e-learning systems must interchange different types of multimedia data:

- Audio. It conveys the speech from the instructor, which is the most important information in an e-learning session. Thus, it must be prioritized over the rest of data.
- Video. It usually conveys the talking head from the instructor to the learners, so it is less important than audio. Video is used to reinforce the sense of presence of the instructor in the learners to avoid anxieties (Weller, 2007).
- Instant messaging. It allows participants in a synchronous e-learning session to communicate textually. This is very useful for learners to post questions to the rest of the class without abruptly interrupting the class with an oral intervention.
- Presence control. It reinforces the sense of presence of all participants, so the instructor may track the users connected to the session.
- Slide presentation or shared whiteboard. It constitutes the learning materials that support the e-learning session. Formats like PowerPoint and PDF are very common. Most of the tools allow the annotation of the contents by the instructor to provide clarifications.
- Telepointer. It is mainly aimed to point to elements within a slide.

The main goal of a synchronous e-learning tool is to bring instructor's explanations to students and to allow a certain level of feedback from learners to the instructor, so he may provide extra explanations or adapt the pace of the session. Because of this, there must be a two-way traffic among instructor and learners. Furthermore, learners collaborate among them, so traffic turns multipoint, so data generated by a participant must be delivered to the rest of them, increasing significantly the network bandwidth requirements.

However, there is no need to transmit all data within a synchronous e-learning session in a multipoint way. For example, video data is only useful to reinforce the sense of presence of participants, so a multipoint transport may be discarded for video data, and a solution in which only the video from the instructor is delivered to all learners may be adopted. In this situation, video data is transmitted in a one-way fashion from the instructor to all learners. Other types of traffic such as audio data from each participant, instant messages, annotations on the learning contents or telepointers, must be delivered in a multipoint way. Therefore, the speech of a participant must be delivered to the rest of them; the annotations from a participant must be rendered in all session participants' screens, and so on. Nevertheless, this implies higher bandwidth consumption in the underlying network, which is usually the most valuable resource in synchronous e-learning systems. If network multicasting techniques are used, the final bandwidth consumption is reduced significantly.

Audio and video data are the most bandwidth-consuming data in a synchronous e-learning session. In fact, the bandwidth of the rest of data in the session is negligible in contrast to the bandwidth needed to deliver audio and video. Hence, in the rest of the chapter, focus is put on protocols and techniques to deliver real-time audio and video through the Internet.

4. Technological Background

The technologies involved in synchronous e-learning can be grouped in different categories depending on their scope of application. Undoubtedly, the transmission of multimedia streams and the management of user sessions are the most relevant fields and hence the widest range of technological alternatives is focused on them. The great variety of available audio and video coding techniques constitute another significant group, but less important than the aforementioned. In fact, most of the technologies that will be considered here are related to the transmission of multimedia information through the Internet and they belong to the extremely populated group of standards and recommendations on which Internet communications are based. There are two main players in the field of the standardization of Internet communications: ITU-T and IETF.

The ITU-T is a standards development organization (SDO) that is one of the three sectors of the International Telecommunications Union (a specialized agency of the United Nations). ITU-T is responsible for generating worldwide "recommendations" (non-binding standards) for telecommunications. The ITU- T is divided into fourteen Study Groups. Study Group XVI is responsible for generating recommendations for data collaboration and video conferencing.

The Internet Engineering Task Force (IETF) develops and promotes Internet standards, cooperating closely with the W3C and ISO/IEC standard bodies, and dealing in particular with standards of the TCP/IP and Internet protocol suite. It is an open standards organization and its work is usually funded by companies or sponsors.

Both organizations contribute to the technological development of Internet developing recommendations that end up being de facto standards, when not official ones. They usually work together to spread and consolidate their developments but, occasionally, industry pressure can hold up their advances or even confront standards from both organizations.

IETF and ITU-T standards differ in their initial conceptions. While the IETF standards follow a client/server philosophy like most of the Internet protocols, ITU-T recommendations are based on ISDN networks. Both organizations propose their respective protocol stacks for multimedia transmissions, as shown in figure 2. ITU-T has adopted some IETF protocols in its stack: IP, TCP, UDP and RTP. So both organizations agree in the protocols to use at the lower layers. On the other hand, their proposals for managing user sessions are quite different.

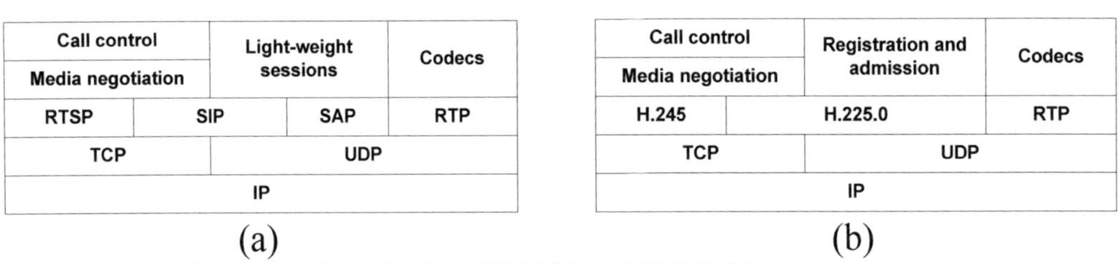

Fig. 2. Multimedia protocol stacks from IETF (a) and ITU-T (b)

5. Network layer

Ideally, multimedia applications should know underlying network characteristics in order to interchange data using the network efficiently. It would be very useful to identify the type of network and its instant congestion to adapt the behavior of the application to the changing state of the network. Applications that cope with the changing conditions of the underlying network are known as net-aware applications.

However, IP networks provide an abstraction layer which hides to applications all information and topology of the underlying network. Thus, applications must measure different metrics in the network to understand its current state. In (Paxson, 1999) traces from multiple connections among several Internet sites are analyzed, so dynamic behavior of the network is estimated according to packet loss, disordered packets, and other metrics. In (Jain & Dovrolis, 2003) a methodology to estimate the network bandwidth available between two hosts connected to the Internet is introduced.

Usually, IP networks are characterized by packet loss, packet replication, packet corruption, network transit time and maximum transfer unit. Nevertheless, there must be taken into account that measurements may vary from one site to another, that is, they depend on geographical location, time of day, network congestion and so on. As a result, multimedia applications must never consider an ideal behavior of the underlying network, and must be prepared to cope with packet loss, different transit times, etc.

5.1 Packet loss

A packet is considered lost when it does not arrive at the receiver. There are few metrics that can be used to measure packet loss in the network. For example, the average packet loss rate may be used to estimate current network congestion, and packet loss correlation may be used to analyze dynamic behavior of the network. Multiple works have demonstrated that the observed average packet loss rate is not constant across the Internet, and it changes smoothly, but the change might be abrupt in rare occasions (Paxson, 1999); (Bolot & Vega-García, 1999); (Yajnik et al., 1999).

It would be ideal for applications that packet loss occurs as isolated events, so they would be uniformly distributed in time. This way, an application can recover from packet loss easily, in contrast to a scenario in which packet loss occurs in bursts. Unfortunately, measurements show that packet loss occurs most of the time as isolated events, but in few occasions it occurs in bursts, so several consecutive packets are lost. Consequently, applications must be designed to tolerate a small fraction of packet loss without affecting their operation significantly.

5.2 Packet replication

Packet replication happens when the same packet arrives multiple times at the receiver. This implies malfunctioned or misconfigured network equipment. However, this must not be a problem for applications; the simplest solution is to discard replicated packets silently. Anyhow, it might become a real problem if the packet replication rate is too high, because it would imply a waste of network resources.

5.3 Packet corruption

Information flowing across networks could be corrupted by the network or by physical phenomena affecting the transmissions. Wireless networks are more prone to packet corruption than wired ones. The receiver identifies corrupted packets by a failure in the

checksum validation at the transport level in the protocol stack. Usually, a corrupted packet is discarded, so applications consider it as a lost packet.
However, depending on the data being carried in a corrupted packet, an application may be interested in receiving the packet regardless it is corrupted. The application might recover the data within the packet partially or totally. This is a very common scenario in audio and video transmission.

5.4 Packet transit time

Transit time refers to the time in which a packet traverses the network from the sender application to the receiver. It is mainly influenced by the length of the path that the packet has to traverse and the length of routers queues. The former refers to the number of routers in the path instead of the physical length of the path. The latter affects the time that a router spends in forwarding the packet to the next router in the path. The longer the queues of the routers are, the more congested the network is. As a result, the transit time is not constant but changes as network status changes.
It is easier for applications to work with a constant transit time. Unfortunately, because of the dynamics of the network, it changes from packet to packet. The variation in the transit time is known as interarrival jitter, and represents one of the challenges that multimedia applications must deal with. To ensure a proper operation, applications usually estimate jitter and have a buffer arranged to bear its effects.
In (Chong & Matthews, 2004) the authors considers a maximum transit time of 150 milliseconds for a successful audio conference among two partners. The same author estimates a maximum interarrival jitter of 75 milliseconds for maintaining an intelligible conversation.

5.5 Maximum Transfer Unit

Packets sent to the network cannot have an arbitrary size. The network technology imposes a maximum packet size. This is commonly known as the maximum transfer unit (MTU). Typical MTUs are 576 bytes for PPP links and 1500 bytes for Ethernet networks.
If a packet is bigger than the MTU of the network, it is fragmented into multiple pieces and they are sent independently to the destiny. Multimedia applications must not delegate to this mechanism delivery of packets bigger than MTU. If an application does so, the loss of any one fragment will make impossible for the receiver to reconstruct the packet. This results in a loss multiplier effect.

5.6 Multicast and unicast delivery

IP Multicast is a bandwidth-conserving technology that reduces traffic by simultaneously delivering the same data to multiple receivers. In addition to synchronous e-learning tools, other applications such as streaming servers or collaborative environments benefit from multicast delivery techniques. In figure 3, both the unicast and multicast delivery techniques are schematized. As shown in the figure, in the unicast delivery it is necessary to replicate data as many times as the number of receptors, while a single copy of data is sent to the network in multicast delivery. In multicast delivery the network is responsible for sending a copy of data to every receptor with as less replication as possible.

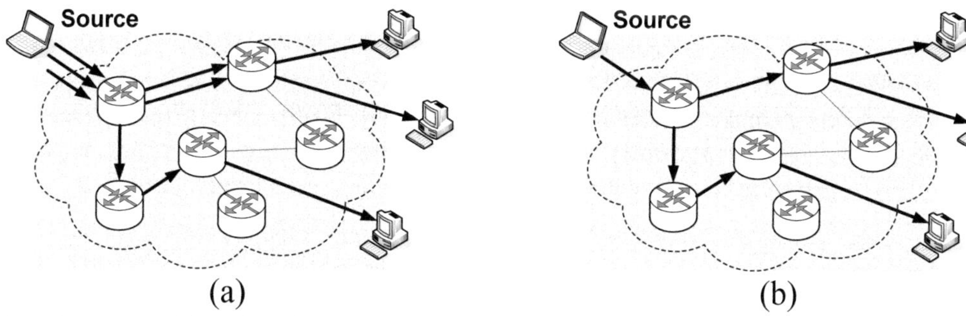

Fig. 3. Unicast (a) and multicast (b) data delivery

IP Multicast is based on the concept of multicast group membership. A multicast group represents multiple hosts that receive the same data stream. This group is not physically or geographically scoped, so receptors may be located wherever in the Internet. A host must register in the multicast group to receive multicast traffic sent to the group. In contrast, any host may send data to the multicast group without registering in the group.

6. Transport layer

Using IP for delivering continuous media has a series of drawbacks as previously explained. In practice, IP is not used directly. Instead, a transport protocol is used over IP to cope with these issues. TCP and UDP are the most commonly used transport protocols in the Internet. TCP is a reliable connection-oriented protocol, while UDP is a connectionless protocol which has the same downsides that IP. Nevertheless, UDP is more suitable to deliver real-time data because it is time-deterministic as opposite to TCP. TCP uses acknowledgments and retransmissions, so the network transit time of a packet may vary significantly.

Today, almost all multimedia tools use UDP for data transport. All advantages of TCP such as flow control, packet loss detection, ordered reception and retransmissions; turn into disadvantages when it is necessary to transmit multimedia streams. In multimedia tools, it is preferable low delays rather than assuring that all data arrive correctly at the receiver. Moreover, IP multicast may be used at the network level with UDP at the transport level, so optimal distribution topologies may be employed.

However, the main problem of UDP is that packets may be lost, reordered o corrupted, exactly as observed for the raw IP service. As a result, mechanisms similar to those in TCP must be implemented in applications to avoid these issues.

6.1 Real-time Transport Protocol

To solve the problems imposed by UDP to the multimedia applications, the IETF has promoted the Real-time Transport Protocol (RTP) (RFC 3550). Although RTP is independent of the transport protocol, it is usually used in conjunction with UDP. It provides services such as packet loss detection and timestamps for timing reconstruction. Multicast delivery may be used if available in the underlying network, so all RTP features are scalable.

The main goal of RTP is to provide end-to-end delivery of time-sensitive data such as audio and video. However, RTP does not guarantee quality of service for real-time services. Therefore, RTP packets may be lost, corrupted or reordered.

RTP was deliberately designed incomplete, so it could be adapted to every application. It offers a set of common functionality instead of specific algorithms; hence it constitutes a framework for developing multimedia applications. The application must implement the specific algorithms to make RTP operate. Thus, in general, RTP is part of the application instead of a separate layer. For this reason, a particular application, in addition to the RTP specification, requires at least the following documents:

- Profile specification. It particularizes different elements that RTP leaves domain-specific and defines extensions to the original RTP specification.
- Payload format specification. It defines the format of the data to be delivered using RTP. For example, the encoding of audio and video and how data must be packetized.

The most common RTP profile is the audio and video profile (RFC 3551). It is intended to support audio and video conferences with multiple participants. In fact, RTP is the de facto standard for voice over IP (VoIP) solutions. RTP is the most appropriate protocol for delivering almost every data in a synchronous e-learning session.
The functionalities of RTP are actually implemented by two protocols, that is, the RTP specification defines two protocols: the transport protocol and the Real-time Transport Control Protocol (RTCP). The RTP transport protocol is responsible for end-to-end data delivery, which includes detection of packet loss, reordered packets and stream timing reconstruction. RTCP monitors quality of service and conveys information about the participants in an on-going session. Moreover, it provides inter-stream synchronization so lip synchronization may be achieved in a video conference. For the operation of RTP two transport addresses are necessary, one for RTP transport packets and the other one for RTCP.
Typically, congestion control is carried out at the RTP level. RTCP packets may be used to estimate network status, because these packets notify the quality of data reception at the receiver side.
Sometimes, especially in low-bandwidth environments when transmitting audio, the RTP packet header has a significant size compared to the audio payload. This implies a high overload that might be unacceptable. In order to reduce the size of the RTP header, and consequently the packet size, RFC 2508 defines a technique to compress RTP/UDP/IP headers, so the final size of the headers is negligible compared to the payload size.
Finally, the IETF has defined a profile for secure RTP transactions (RFC 3711). The secure RTP (SRTP) profile specifies how RTP packets must be encrypted, to guarantee the confidentiality of the communications. Another RTP profile, RFC 4585, provides more feedback from receptors based on RTCP packets, which may be very useful in synchronous e-learning scenarios.

7. Control layer

There are some important tasks that must be carried out in this layer in order to ensure the correct running of a synchronous e-learning activity. The protocols that deal with these issues are signalling protocols because, roughly said, they interchange signals for controlling communications. A signalling protocol must fulfil several tasks:

- Establishment, management and termination of multimedia sessions.
- Handshaking and selection of session features, especially the types and formats of the multimedia information to transmit.
- Management of the session participants, enabling users to log in and log out of a session.
- User localization and address translation; common addresses from different sources like URLs, telephone numbers or e-mail addresses will need to be adapted in order to establish links among them.

The H.323 set of protocols, published by the ITU-T, and the SIP protocol, proposed by the IETF, are the two most widespread signaling protocols. H.323 defines the protocols to provide audiovisual communication sessions on any packet network, but its philosophy is clearly influenced by traditional circuit switching networks. SIP is a lightweight protocol that was designed with the aim of achieving two advantages against H.323: more flexibility and easier implementation. There are countless works that defend, with more or less intensity, one against the other. Some of them are (Schulzrinne & Rosenberg, 1998); (Dalgic & Fang, 1999); (Glasmann et al., 2003). However, although their architectures differ substantially, the latest revisions of both protocols are similar in terms of functionality and the many differences between them have vanished.

H.323 is extremely more complex than SIP. This is because the SIP specification barely imposes any protocol or service to be present in a SIP system. On the contrary, H.323 defines multiple profiles that require the use of several specific protocols and components. From this view, SIP gives much more freedom than H.323 for choosing surrounding technologies. This results in better expansion capabilities. H.323 systems can only handle media formats that have been previously registered by the ITU-T. Thus, trying to use a format unsupported by any H.323 profile can be painful, since ITU-T usually introduces slowly new media formats in its recommendations. Besides, SIP is a text-based protocol, allowing for easy inspection by administrators. On the other hand, inspection of H.323 messages requires specific and more complex tools. It is clear that the high level of specification of H.323 has some drawbacks, but when particular needs match well a specific profile, the deployment and management of an H.323 system can be friendlier than a SIP one, since all elements are perfectly detailed.

The control layer must also serialize the access to shared resources within a synchronous e-learning activity like the audio channel. This task is carried out by floor control protocols.

7.1 Session Initiation Protocol

In contrast to H.323, the multimedia sessions architecture proposed by the IETF is constituted by multiple independent protocols. This architecture includes two Internet specific protocols: SIP and SAP. SIP (RFC 3261) carries out the operations related to session

establishment, modification and termination. The Session Announcement Protocol (SAP) is described in the IETF's RFC 2974; it serves to announce sessions to users or services and was developed for multicast environments. Additionally, IETF and ITU-T worked together to define the H.248 protocol, intended to control the gateways that interconnect networks based on different technologies, e.g. packet switching networks and circuit switching networks. In the nomenclature of the IETF, H.248 is known as the Megaco protocol.
The operation of the SIP protocol is based on request and response messages HTTP-like. It reuses many of the codification rules, error codes and header fields from HTTP. Hence, the call control functions provided by SIP can be deeply and easily integrated in any web infrastructure. In addition, SIP uses the Session Description Protocol (RFC 4566), to exchange the session settings.
The specification of the SIP architecture distinguishes two elements in a SIP network: user agents (UA) and servers. A SIP user agent is a logical network endpoint used to create or receive SIP messages and thereby manage a SIP session. A user agent can perform the role of a User Agent Client (UAC), which sends SIP requests, and a User Agent Server (UAS), which receives the requests and returns SIP responses. These roles of UAC and UAS only last for the duration of a SIP transaction. A SIP transaction consists of a client request message sent to a server and the subsequent interchange of messages until the client receives a definite response from the server. Since SIP servers are only aware of the status of their transactions (i.e. they only know the individual requests and responses that are associated to a transaction), they do not have to keep the status of every call they manage. Therefore SIP systems are stateless and highly scalable.
Although two SIP endpoints can communicate without any intervening SIP infrastructure (servers), this approach is often impractical for a public service as the most advanced functionalities need their presence. The most common duties of servers are user location and address resolution. A server element can perform three different roles that are not mutually exclusive:

- Redirect server. Receives requests from UACs and sends responses directing the client to contact another set of servers.
- Registrar server. Registers the devices at the time they are connected, so it can provide their contact addresses (URIs) when incoming sessions addressed to the devices are received.
- Proxy server. Like HTTP proxies or SMTP mail transfer agents, a SIP proxy server is an intermediary entity that processes transactions on behalf of other user agents. A proxy server primarily plays the role of routing and it is also useful for enforcing policies. A proxy interprets, and, if necessary, rewrites specific parts of a request message before forwarding it.

7.2 H.323 Recommendation

H.323 is an umbrella recommendation of the set of recommendations that the ITU-T elaborated for video conferencing (H.3xx). Of all of them, H.323 is the only suitable for multimedia data transmission through the Internet when there are not any mechanisms to guarantee quality-of-service in the underlying network.
The H.323 system defines several network elements that work together in order to deliver rich multimedia communication capabilities. Those elements are terminals, multipoint

control units (MCUs), gateways, gatekeepers, and border elements. Collectively, terminals, multipoint control units and gateways are often referred to as endpoints.

The terminals are IP network clients and constitute the most basic elements in any H.323 system. Gateways are optional devices that enable communication between H.323 networks and other networks, such as PSTN or ISDN networks. A Gatekeeper is an optional component in a H.323 network that provides a number of services to terminals, gateways, and MCU devices. Those services include endpoint registration, address resolution, admission control, user authentication, and so forth. A multipoint control unit is responsible for managing multipoint conferences and is normally composed of two types of logical entities: one multipoint controller and one or more multipoint processors. A border element is a signalling entity that generally sits at the edge of an administrative domain and communicates with other border element located at other administrative domain.

H.323 is defined as a binary protocol, which allows for efficient message processing in network elements. The syntax of the protocol is defined in ASN.1 and uses the Packed Encoding Rules (PER) form of message encoding for efficient message encoding on the wire. There are four different types of communication flows in H.323 systems:

- Call signaling. Convey all the information related to connections control and supplementary services according to the protocols detailed in the recommendations H.225.0 and H.450.x.
- Call control. Enable control of the transmission of multimedia information and capabilities negotiation, based on the recommendation H.245.
- RAS signaling. The RAS protocol is detailed in the recommendation H.225.0 and is intended to communicate endpoints with gatekeepers.
- Logical Channel Signaling. These flows are media streams indeed; they convey multimedia data using an underlying RTP session for each separate medium.

In the latest revisions of H.323, all flows use unreliable transport protocols, like UDP, except the call control flows, that require a reliable transport protocol, like TCP. Table 3 shows some of the most relevant recommendations included in the H.323 specification.

Recommendation	Purpose
H.245	Call and media control
H.225.0	Establishment and control of the connection
H.332	Management of densely populated conferences
H.235	Security (privacy, authentication, etc.)
H.246	Interworking with services based on circuit switching
H.450.x	Supplementary services (call transfer and diversion, etc.)
H.26x	Video codecs
G.7xx	Audio codecs
T.120	Data sharing (collaborative tools)
X.680	Abstract Syntax Notation One (ASN.1)
X.691	Specification of packet encoding rules (PER)

Table 3. Recommendations included in the H.323 specification

7.3 Floor Control

A high number of attendees usually participate in a synchronous e-learning session. These participants interchange audio, video and other types of multimedia data in real time. Interactions must be coordinated, so data from multiple participants does not interfere. For example, a limited number of users should speak at the same time, so audio streams from multiple participants do not overlap.

In a conference with two peers floor control may be considered trivial. Both peers naturally agree who can speak anytime, so conversation is intelligible. However, as participant number grows, it is necessary to define floor control mechanisms to serialize the access to the audio channel. In general, this applies to every shared resource in synchronous e-learning sessions, such as the shared whiteboard, the video channel, telepointers, etc. It is also interesting to differentiate roles among participants in the session. Usually, the instructor is responsible for granting and revoking privileges to the learners. All these are issues that a floor control protocol must solve.

There are many works about floor control and they are not restricted to synchronous e-learning. In (Dommel & García-Luna-Aceves, 1997) and RFC 4376 the requirements for floor control protocols in large collaborative environments are enumerated. In (Malpani & Rowe, 1997), the authors introduce floor control techniques in very large web seminars.

The Binary Floor Control Protocol (BFCP) was published by the IETF in RFC 4582 to manage joint or exclusive access to shared resources in conferencing environments. It defines different entities: a floor control server, a floor chair and multiple floor participants. The server is responsible for granting and revoking floors to participants. The floor chair decides whether the server must grant or revoke a floor to a participant.

Attendees to a conference may discover floor existence using SIP media negotiation, and consequently BFCP is integrated in the multimedia conferencing framework proposed by the IETF.

8. Media processing

Usually, multimedia data in a synchronous e-learning session imposes important bandwidth requirements, so it is unworkable to send it uncompressed to the network. This is especially noticeable with audio and video. Therefore, it is necessary to encode data in order to reduce the needed network bandwidth. The encoding process is done by audio and video codecs. Those used in synchronous e-learning sessions should exhibit the following characteristics:

- Low latency, so data transmission fulfills real-time requirements.
- High compression ratio in order to consume as less network bandwidth as possible.
- Packet loss resilience to recover from packet loss.

8.1 Audio codecs

Audio conferencing is one of the most important features in synchronous e-learning sessions. It is based on the transmission of the voice of a participant to one or multiple receptors. Thus, it is necessary to capture participant's voice in real time. The capture process implies a digitalization of the analog audio signal and depends on several parameters:

- Sampling rate. It represents the times per second that the analog voice is sampled during digitalization. The number of samples needed is determined by the Nyquist-Shannon sampling theorem. It proofs that the digitalization of an analog signal must be done with a sampling rate twice the maximum bandwidth of the signal. For voice is typical a sampling rate of 8000 Hertz.
- Number of channels. An audio stream may contain one o more independent signals. That is, audio can be mono, stereo or multi-channel. In synchronous e-learning and VoIP, only mono audio is used as it conveys voice from the participants.
- Sample size. It represents the resolution of each sample. The bigger this size is, the higher resolution is obtained in the digitalization process. Typical values are 8 and 16 bits per sample.
- Capture period. Audio capture devices usually have a capture buffer where they keep samples as the digitalization process is taking place. After a period of time, the device returns all samples digitalized to the capturing application. It is important to use a capture period as short as possible to minimize digitalization latency. Typical values for audio conferencing are 20 and 30 milliseconds.

Codec	Sampling rate (Hz)	Bitrate (kbps)	Packet duration (ms)	Packet size (bytes)	Nominal bandwidth (kbps)
G.711	8000	64	20	160	87.2
G.723.1	8000	5.3	30	20	20.8
	8000	6.4	30	24	21.9
G.726	8000	24	20	60	47.2
	8000	32	20	80	55.2
G.728	8000	16	30	60	31.5
G.729	8000	8	20	20	31.2
GSM	8000	12.2	20	-	23.2
	8000	13	20	33	36.4
iLBC	8000	13.3	30	50	28.8
	8000	15.2	20	30	38.4
Speex	8000	2.15 - 24.6	20	Variable	25.35 - 47.8

Table 4. Voice codecs

Depending on the type of audio to encode, different techniques are used. Audio is usually classified into three categories attending to its sampling rate: narrowband, mediumband and wideband. Narrowband audio refers to voice audio, while wideband audio represents music. In synchronous e-learning human voice is used, so only narrowband codecs are employed to encode audio signals.

Particularly, table 4 lists the most commonly used audio codecs in VoIP and synchronous e-learning sessions. This table shows the codec characteristics and the nominal bandwidth, which is the result of considering de bitrate of the audio stream generated by the codec and the RTP, UDP, IP and Ethernet packet headers.

8.2 Video codecs

Video conferencing is another important feature of synchronous e-learning systems. The video from the instructor is delivered to the rest of participants in an e-learning session. Usually a videoconference is point-to-point, but occasionally may be multipoint, so video from multiple participants may be viewed simultaneously. Nevertheless, video is appropriate to reinforce the sense of presence of users; so at least, video from the instructor is delivered to the learners.

Similarly to audio, video is captured in real time and it must be encoded to reduce its bandwidth consumption. Multiple parameters may be configured during video digitalization:

- Image resolution. It represents the dimensions, width and height, of every video frame. The higher the resolution is, the better quality the image has. However, high image resolutions imply high bitrates. A typical image resolution in video conferencing is 320x240 pixels.
- Image format. It specifies the format of every video frame to be captured.
- Frames per second. It represents the temporal resolution of the video. Typical values for video conferencing are 1, 5, 10 or even 15 frames per second.

Audio and video codecs are usually classified into lossless or lossy codecs. The former are used in audio and video edition because they keep the original quality of data. The latter achieve higher compression ratios and they are more suitable to synchronous e-learning sessions. The following are the most widespread codecs for video conferencing:

- MJPEG (Motion JPEG) is a codec in where frames are separately encoded as JPEG images. It is commonly used in IP cameras, but it is not suitable to synchronous e-learning due to its high bandwidth consumption.
- MPEG-4 is a set of standards for audio and video encoding. Similarly to MPEG-1 and MPEG-2, MPEG-4 defines profiles, so different solutions implements different capabilities. Specifically, MPEG-4 part 2 defines the Advanced Simple Profile (ASP) that is very common in video conferencing.
- H.261 is an ITU-T recommendation for the encoding of video signals in ISDN networks. It supports image resolutions of 352x288 and 176x144 with bitrates between 40 Kbps and 2 Mbps.
- H.263 is an evolution from H.261 oriented to low-bandwidth environments. It supports five image resolutions and significantly improves the compression ratio of H.261.
- H.264, also known as MPEG-4 Part 10 AVC, is the result of a joint effort of the MPEG group and ITU-T. It improves ratio compressions of H.263. Thus, it may be used in very-low-bandwidth environments with an acceptable quality. It may also be used for high resolution video. In fact, it is used for encoding video in Blu-ray discs.
- VC-1 is an alternative to H.264 and it is promoted by Microsoft. Its main goal is to provide high bandwidth compression of interlaced video, so it is no necessary to deinterlace it before. In some scenarios it competes with H.264 producing similar results.

9. Conclusions

Audio and video conferencing are two major features of synchronous e-learning systems. The former is used to allow participants to participate orally in the e-learning sessions, while the latter is used to reinforce the sense of presence of users.

IETF and ITU-T are the organizations that promote standards and recommendations for real-time delivery of continuous media over the Internet. IETF has published several RFCs about the Session Initiation Protocol (SIP) in order to define a multimedia conferencing framework in the Internet. ITU-T has developed the H.323 recommendation as an umbrella, so multiple extra recommendations constitute the reference ITU-T framework for multimedia conferencing in the Internet.

However, in spite of these independent conferencing frameworks, both IETF and ITU-T frameworks have in common the Real-time Transport Protocol for the transmission of continuous media in real time through the Internet.

Nowadays, IETF framework based on SIP is more extended that the framework from ITU-T. Almost all software-implemented solutions use SIP and protocols from the IETF, while hardware solutions remain using H.323 recommendation. Nevertheless, both SIP and H.323 are converging to each other, providing the same services, but SIP is still easier to work with than H.323. It is likely that SIP will dominate audio and video conferencing market in the near future.

10. References

Bolot, J.-C. & Vega-García, A. (1996). Control mechanisms for packet audio in the Internet. *Proceedings of 15th Annual Joint Conference of the IEEE Computer Societies. Networking the Next Generation*, pp. 232–239, ISBN 0-8186-7293-5, March 1996, San Francisco, CA, USA.

Chong, H. & Matthews, H. (2004). Comparative analysis of traditional telephone and Voice-over-Internet Protocol (VoIP) systems. *Proceedings of the 2004 IEEE International Symposium on Electronics and the Environment*, pp. 106–111, ISBN 0-7803-8250-1, May 2004, Scottsdale, AZ, USA.

Dalgic, I. & Fang, H. (1999). Comparison of H.323 and SIP for IP telephony signaling. *Proceedings of SPIE Volume 3845*, pp. 106–122, ISBN 0-8194-3438-8, September 1999, Boston, MA, USA.

Dommel, H.-P. & García-Luna-Aceves, J. (1997). Floor control for multimedia conferencing and collaboration. *Multimedia Systems*, Vol. 5, No. 1, pp. 23–38, ISSN 0942-4962, Germany.

García, D. F., Uría, C., Granda, J.C. & Suárez, F.J. (2007). A Functional Evaluation of the Commercial Platforms and Tools for Synchronous Distance e-Learning. *North Atlantic University Union International Journal of Education and Information Technologies*. Vol. 1, No. 2, pp. 95-104, ISSN 1109-9577.

Glasmann, J., Kellerer, W. & Müller, H. (2004). *Service architectures in H.323 and SIP: A comparison*. IEEE Communications Surveys & Tutorials, Vol. 5, No. 2, pp. 32–47, ISSN 1553-877X.

Granda, J.C., García, D. F., Suárez, F.J., Peteira, I. & Uría, C. (2008). A Multimedia Tool for Synchronous Distance e-Training of Employees in Geographically Dispersed

Industries. *Proceedings of 7th IASTED International Conference on Internet & Multimedia Systems & Applications*, ISBN 978-0-88986-727-7, March 2008, Innsbruck, Austria.

Jain, M. & Dovrolis, C. (2003). End-to-end available bandwidth: Measurement methodology, dynamics, and relation with TCP throughput. *IEEE/ACM Transactions on Networking*, Vol. 11, No. 4, pp. 537–549, ISSN 1063-6692.

Malpanim, R. & Rowe, L. A. (1997). Floor control for large-scale MBone seminars. *Proceedings of the 5th ACM International Conference on Multimedia*, pp. 155–163, ISBN 0-89791-991-2, November 1997, Seattle, WA, USA.

Mishra, S. & Sharma, R. C. (2004). *Interactive Multimedia in Education and Training*. Idea Group Publishing, ISBN 1-59140-393-6. USA.

Mollet, N. & Arnaldi, B. (2006). Storytelling in virtual reality for training. *Proceedings of 1st International Conference on Technologies for E-Learning and Digital Entertainment*, pp. 334–347, ISBN 3-540-33423-8, April 2006, Hangzhou, China.

Padmore, M., Hall, L., Hogg, B. & Paley, G. (2006). Reviewing the potential of Virtual Learning Environments in schools. *Proceedings of 1st International Conference on Technologies for E-Learning and Digital Entertainment*, pp. 203–212, ISBN 3-540-33423-8, April 2006, Hangzhou, China.

Paxson, V. (1999). End-to-end Internet packet dynamics. *IEEE/ACM Transactions on Networking*, Vol. 7, No. 3, pp. 277–292, ISSN 1063-6692.

Shulman, R. E. (1992). Multimedia — A high-tech solution to industry's training malaise. *Supermarket business*, Vol. 47, No. 4, pp. 23–24, ISSN 0196-5700.

Schulzrinne, H. & Rosenberg, J. (1998). A comparison of SIP and H.323 for internet telephony. *Proceedings of International Workshop on Network and Operating System Support for Digital Audio and Video*, pp. 83–86, July 1998, Cambridge, UK.

Steinmetz, R. & Nahrstedt, K. (1995). *Multimedia: Computing, Communication and Applications*. Prentice-Hall Inc., ISBN 0-13-324435-0, USA.

Weller M. (2007). The distance from isolation: Why communities are the logical conclusion in e-learning. *Computer & Education*, Vol. 49, No. 2, pp. 148–159, ISSN 0360-1315.

Yajnik, M., Moon, S. B., Kurose, J. F. & Towsley, D. F. (1999). Measurement and Modeling of the Temporal Dependence in Packet Loss. *Proceedings of 8th Annual Joint Conference of the IEEE Computer and Communications Societies*, pp. 345–352, ISBN 0-7803-5417-6, March 1999, New York, NY, USA.

7

Bayesian Agent in e-Learning

Maomi Ueno
University of Electro-Communications
Japan

1. Introduction

The constructivist approach has pervaded the area of educational technology in recent decades. It has been argued in this approach that the responsibility for learning should be increasingly with the learner (Von Glasersfeld, 1995). Therefore, the role of instructor has changed to facilitator from that of teacher (Bauersfeld, 1995). A teacher gives a didactic lecture that covers the subject matter, but a facilitator assists the autonomous learning process. The learner plays a passive role in the former scenario and in the latter the learner plays an active role in the learning process. The emphasis thus shifts from the instructor and content-centred approach toward the learner-centred approach (Gamoran, Secada & Marrett, 2000).

A central feature of this facilitation is individualizing learners and helping them to achieve self-growth through self-evaluation and cooperation with others (Merriam & Brockett, 2007). For example, according to the well known theory by Knowles, facilitation is designing a pattern of learning experiences, conducting these learning experiences with suitable techniques and materials, and evaluating the learning outcomes and rediagnosing learning needs (Knowles, 1983) (Knowles, Holton & Swanson , 1998). e-Learning, which emerged as a method of attaining the learner-centred approach, provides a new autonomous-learning environment that combines 1. multimedia content, 2. collaboration among learners, and 3. computer-supported learning (Ueno 2007). e-Learning should work even if there is no human facilitator and a huge number of learners participate in it. It would essentially be impossible for facilitators to individualize such a huge number of learners and facilitate their learning. The main idea in this paper is that a computational agent in a Learning Management System (LMS) plays the role of facilitator instead of human teachers. The proposed agent uses the learners' history data, which is stored in a database, to individualize learners. A computational agent that learns using machine learning or data-mining technologies from data is called a "learning agent". This paper proposes a learning agent for e-Learning.

First, the agent predicts a learner's final status (1. Failed, 2. Abandoned, 3. Successful, or 4. Excellent) from his/her current learning-history data using a Bayesian network that is constructed from the his/her past learning-history data. The agent compares a learner's learning processes with past excellent learners' learning processes in the database, diagnoses the learner's learning processes, and generates adaptive instructional messages to guide the learner.

In addition, some previous research on learning motivation found that the effects of a mentor's motivational messages were adapted to a learner's status in e-Learning. Visser and Keller (1990) reported that motivational messages could reduce dropout rates and later attempted to improve motivation in e-Learning situations using such messages (Visser, Plomp, and Kuiper, 1999). Gabrielle (2000) applied technology-mediated instructional strategies to Gagne's events of instruction and demonstrated how these strategies affected motivation. Thus, agent messages are also expected to be effective in facilitating learner motivation.

A similar idea to that in this study has been proposed by Ueno (2005). He developed an LMS in which the teacher is substituted for an agent as a virtual facilitator. The intelligent agent provides adaptive messages to learners using learner models represented by the decision-tree model (Quinlan, 1986).

Furthermore, some experiments reported in the Ueno's paper demonstrated the effectiveness of this method, but there are still three main problems:

1. The decision-tree model has a cold-start problem and the agent cannot draw any inferences when we provide new courses.
2. The decision-tree model does not predict the target variable until the data for all the other variables have been obtained, because the decision-tree model cannot deal with any missing data.
3. It is difficult for the decision-tree model to provide the reasoning for prediction.

While on the other hand, the proposed agent based on Bayesian networks has three main advantages:

1. The Bayesian-network model can avoid the cold-start problem by providing a valid prior belief for the network structure, even if there are not sufficiently large amounts of data for learning a Bayesian network.
2. The Bayesian-network model can predict the target variable even if the data for all the other variables have not been obtained.
3. The Bayesian network can provide the reasoning for prediction.

Furthermore, this paper shows that the proposed agent is effective as a virtual facilitator from some experiments and actual data.

2. Related work

Various studies have been done that have applied data-mining techniques to learning-history data in e-Learning.

Becker and Vanzin (2003) tried to detect meaningful patterns of learning activities in e-Learning using the association rule.

Minaei-Bidgoli, Kashy, Kortemeyer, and Punch (2003) proposed a method of predicting a learner's final test score by using a combination of multiple classifiers (CMC) constructed from learning-history data in e-Learning, and they reported that a modified method using a genetic algorithm (GA) could improve the accuracy of prediction.

Talavera and Gaudioso (2004) and Hamalainen, Laine, and Sutinen (2006) proposed a method of predicting final test scores using the naïve Bayes model obtained from learning-history data in e-Learning.

However, these studies only tried to predict the learner's performance in e-Learning from learning-history data, and therefore, they did not discuss how to effectively utilize the predicted data-mining results to improve the learners' results. Furthermore, the data-mining

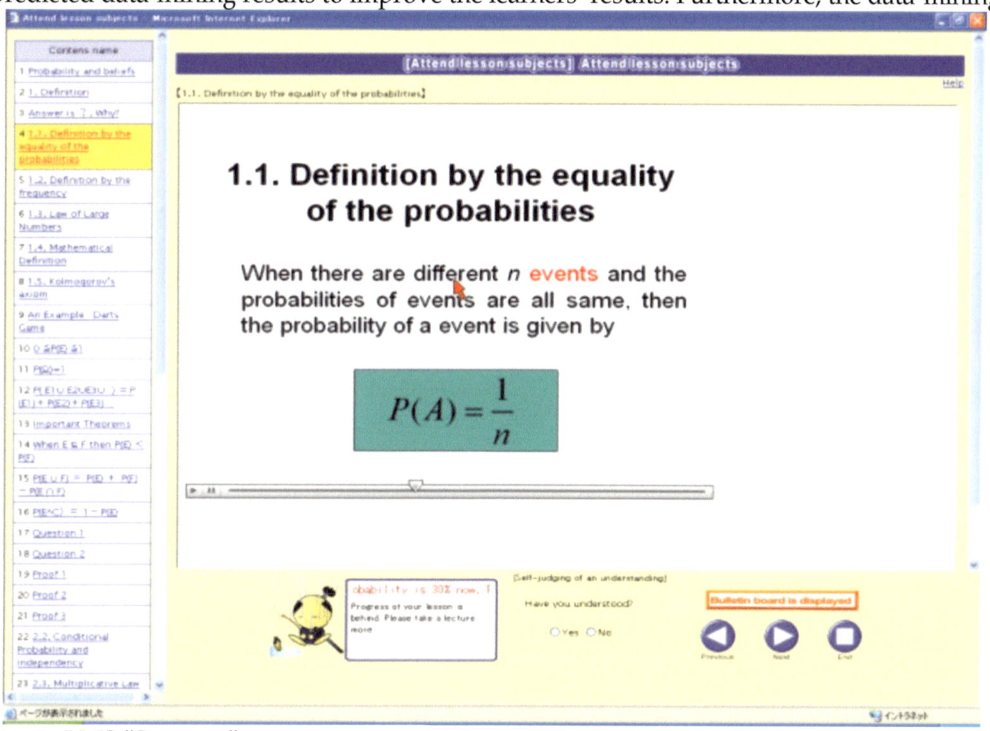

Fig. 1. LMS "Samurai"

engines employed in these studies were not installed into an LMS to automatically analyze the learning-log database.

Here, the author does not simply propose a system of predicting a learner's final status using a data-mining technique, but an agent that acquires domain knowledge related to the content from a learning-history-log database that automatically generates adaptive instructional messages to guide the learners.

3. LMS "Samurai"

The author has developed an LMS called "Samurai"(Ueno, 2004) that is used in many e-Learning courses (128 e-Learning courses are now offered by the University of Electro-Communications through the LMS). The LMS consists of a content presentation system (CPS), a content database (CD), computer supported collaborative learning (CSCL), a learning history database (LHD), and a data mining system (DMS). The CPS integrates various kinds of content and presents the integrated information on a Web page. Figure 1 shows typical e-Learning content presented by Samurai. The content is presented by clicking on the menu button. A sound track of the teacher's narration is also presented based on research by Mayer and Anderon (1991), and the red pointer moves automatically as the narration continues. This lesson co rresponds to a 90-minute lecture at university and includes 42 topics. Although the content i n Figure 1 is text, the system also provides illustrations, animation or computer

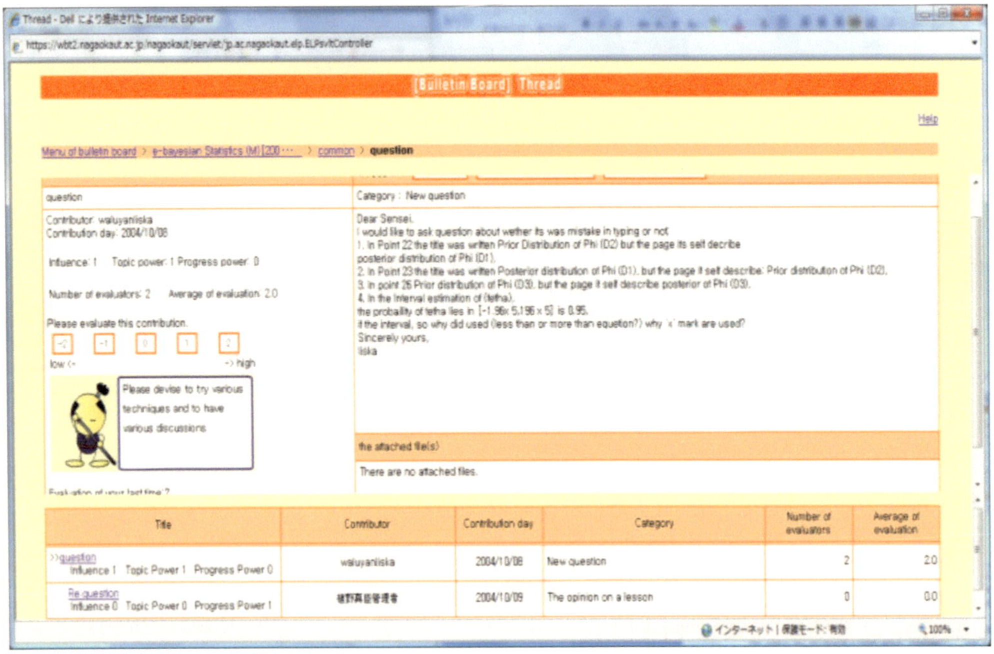

Fig. 2. CSCL in Samurai

lesson corresponds to a 90-minute lecture at the university and includes 42 topics. Although the content in Figure 1 is text, the system also provides illustrations, animation or computer graphics, and video clips. In this lesson, there are 11 items of text content, 11 illustrations, 10 animations, and 10 video clips. The system also presents some test items to assess the learners' degree of comprehension as soon as the lessons have been completed. The CD consists of various kinds of media, such as text, jpeg and mpeg files. The teacher prepares a lecture and saves the content on a CD. Then the CPS automatically integrates the content, and presents this to the learners.

They can also share ideas, questions, and the products of their learning for a given task (e.g., a report or a program source) using the CSCL shown in Figure 2.

The LMS monitors learners' learning processes and stores them as log data in the LHD. The stored data consist of a content ID, a learner ID, the number of topics that the learner has completed, a test-item ID, a record of data input into the DB, an operation-order ID (which indicates what operation was done), a date and time ID (which indicates the date and time that an operation started), and a time ID (which indicates the time it took to complete the operation). These data enable the system to recount the learner's behavior in e-Learning.

4. Bayesian network

A Bayesian network, a Bayesian belief network, or just a belief network is a probabilistic graphical model that allows us to represent and reason about an uncertain domain. A

Bayesian network is represented as a directed acyclic graph of nodes in Figure 3. The nodes in a Bayesian network represent a set of random variables from the domain. A set of directed arcs connects pairs of nodes, representing the direct dependencies between variables. That is, $A \longrightarrow B$ indicates that A causes B. The nodes that the target node depends on are called "parent nodes" of the target node. For $A \longrightarrow B$, A is a parent node of B. Once the topology of the BN is specified, the conditional probabilities corresponding to all arcs should be given. For $A \longrightarrow B$, the value of the conditional probability, $p(B|A)$, should be set. If a node has a known value, it is said to be an *evidence* node. Then, the belief probabilities about all the other nodes in the network are updated using a Bayes theorem from the evidence data.

The Bayesian network is mathematically formulated as follows. Let $U = \{x_1, x_2, \ldots, x_N\}$ be a set of N discrete variables; each can take values in the set $\{1, \ldots, r_i\}$. We write $x_i = k$ when we observe that variable x_i is state k. We use $p(x_i = k | x_j=k', □)$ to denote the probability of a person with background knowledge □ for observation x_i =k given observation $x_j=k'$.

When we observe the state for all variables in set U, we call this set of observations an instance of U. We use $p(Y|Z, □)$ to denote the set of probabilities for all possible observations of Y given all possible observations of Z, where $Y \subset U$, $Z \subset U$, and $Y \cap Z =$ □$.

A Bayesian network represents a joint probability distribution over domain U by encoding assertions of conditional independence as well as a collection of probability distributions.

From the chain rule of probability we know

$$p(x_1, x_2, \cdots, x_N \mid \xi) = \prod_{i=1}^{N} p(x_i \mid x_1, x_2, \cdots, x_{i-1}, \xi) \quad (1)$$

For each variable x_i, let $\Pi_i \subseteq \{x_1, x_2, \ldots, x_{i-1}\}$ be a set of variables called parent nodes that renders x_i and is conditionally independent.

That is,

$$p(x_i \mid x_1, x_2, \cdots, x_{i-1}, \xi) = p(x_i \mid \Pi_i, \xi) \quad (2)$$

A Bayesian network is represented as a pair of a network structure B_S that encodes the assertions of conditional independence in this equation and a set of conditional probability parameters B_P, (B_S, B_P).

Parameter B_S is a directed acyclic graph such that (1) each variable in U corresponds to a node in $B_{S'}$ and (2) the parents of the node corresponding to □ are the nodes corresponding to the variables in Π_i. After this, we will use x_i to refer to both a variable and its corresponding node in a graph. Associated with node x_i in B_S are the probability distributions $p(x_i | \Pi_i, □)$.

B_P is the union of these distributions. When (1) and (2) are combined, we can see that any network for U uniquely determines a joint probability distribution for U. That is,

$$p(x_1, x_2, \cdots, x_N \mid B_S) = \prod_{i=1}^{N} p(x_i \mid \Pi_i, B_S) \quad (3)$$

The problem of learning a Bayesian network can be stated informally as the following: Given training data $X = \{x_1, x_2, \ldots, x_N\}$, find a network, B, that best matches X.

The common approach to this problem is to introduce a scoring metric that evaluates each network with respect to the training data. Then, it is possible to search for the best network according to this function.

Let □$_{ijk}$ be the conditional probability parameters of $x_i=k$ when the j-th instance of the parents of x_i is observed (we write $\Pi_i = j$). Buntine (1991) assumed a Dirichlet prior and employed an unbiased estimator, the expectation of the Estimated A Priori (EAP), as the parameter estimator, $\hat{\theta}_{ijk}$ .That is,

$$\hat{\theta}_{ijk} = \frac{\alpha_{ijk} + n_{ijk}}{\alpha_{ij} + n_{ij}}, (k = 0, \cdots, r_i - 2) \quad , \tag{4}$$

where n_{ijk} is the number of samples of $x_i = k$ when $\Pi_i = j$ and α_{ijk} is the hyper-parameter of the Dirichlet prior corresponding to n_{ijk}, $n_{ij} = \sum_{k=0}^{r_i-1} n_{ijk}$, $\alpha_{ij} = \sum_{k=0}^{r_i-1} \alpha_{ijk}$, and $\hat{\theta}_{ij(r_i-1)} = 1 - \sum_{k=0}^{r_i-2} \theta_{ijk}$.

The predictive distribution is obtained as

$$p(X \mid B_S) = \int_{\Theta} p(X \mid \Theta, B_S) p(\Theta) d\Theta$$
$$= \prod_{i=1}^{N} \prod_{j=1}^{q_i} \frac{\Gamma(\alpha_{ij})}{\Gamma(\alpha_{ij} + n_{ij})} \prod_{k=0}^{r_i-1} \frac{\Gamma(\alpha_{ijk} + n_{ijk})}{\alpha_{ijk}} \quad , \tag{5}$$

where $\Theta = \{\theta_{ijk}\}(i = 1, \cdots, N, j = 1, \cdots, q_i, k = 0, \cdots, r_i - 1)$, and q_i signifies the number of instances of Π_i, $q_i = \prod_{x_l \in \Pi_i} r_l$.

In particular, Heckerman, et al. (1995) presented a sufficient condition for satisfying the likelihood equivalence assumption as the following constraint related to hyper-parameters:

$$\alpha_{ijk} = \alpha p(x_i = k, \Pi_i = j \mid B_S^h), \tag{6}$$

where α is the equivalent sample size (ESS) determined by users and B_S^h is the hypothetical Bayesian-network structure that the user constructs with his/her prior knowledge. These score metrics are designated as Bayesian Dirichlert equivalence (BDe) score mertrics.

That is, even if there is not a sufficiently large amount of data, a Bayesian network can be constructed by using user's prior knowledge. In this paper, we solve the cold-start problem of learning the agent system using these unique advantages of the Bayesian network.

5. Bayesian agent

5.1 Prediction of learner' final status

The main idea here is to apply a data-mining method to the huge amount of stored data and construct a learner model to predict each learner's final status: (1) Failed (Final examination score below 60), (2) Abandoned (The learner has withdrawn before the final examination), (3) Successful (The final-examination score is more than 60 but less than 80); and (4) Excellent (The final examination mark is more than 80.) The well-known data-mining method of the Bayesian network is employed for this propose using nine variables reflecting each learner's status each week:

1. The number of topics that the learner has learned.
2. The number of times the learner accessed the e-Learning system.
3. The average number of times the learner has completed each topic. (This implies the time the learner repeated each topic.)
4. The average learning time for each lecture, which consists of several types of content and runs for 90 minutes)
5. The average degree of understanding for each topic (This is measured by the responses to questions corresponding to each topic)
6. The average learning time for each course, which consists of fifteen lectures
7. The average number of times the learner has changed the answers to questions in e-Learning
8. The number of times that the learner has posted opinions or comments to the discussion board.
9. The average learning time for each topic.

This section explains how Bayesian networks are learned from learning-history data. Fifteen Bayesian-network structures are estimated corresponding to data from learners' learning histories for the fifteen weeks because all courses run for 15 weeks.

Bayesian networks also suffer from the cold-start problem and no inferences can be drawn when we provide new courses. To solve this problem, this paper uses the prior distribution in (6) for learning a Bayesian network. In detail, a Bayesian-network structure is first estimated using data from all learning histories stored in the database; this does not include data corresponding to the target course. Here, this data from learning histories is called "prior data". The main idea is that the estimated structure from the prior data is used for the prior hypothetical structure, B_S^h, in (6). Next, based on this estimated prior hypothetical structure B_S^h, the Bayesian network is learned by maximizing the BDe in (5) from learning-history data corresponding to the target course. This proposed method enables us to solve the cold-start problem when we start a new course. When there are not sufficiently large amounts of data from the learning histories for the target course, the Bayesian agent follows the estimated Bayesian-network structure from all learning-history data, i.e., the prior data. When there are sufficiently large amounts of data for the target course, the Bayesian agent follows the estimated Bayesian-network structure for the target course. The ESS value, α, means the pseudo-sample size reflecting the prior data and this has been determined as 100.0 in this research.

In addition, we employ the Bayesian-network classifer model since the target variable is one variable (Friedman, Geiger, & Goldszmidt. 1997). In detail, we first add arcs between the final status node and all the explanatory variables, and then construct the network structure between the explanatory variables to maximize BDe given the previously drawn arcs. Here, the greedy search algorithm is employed to learn the network structure.

Figure 3 shows the Bayesian network estimated by maximizing BDe in (5) from prior data (data from 4,344 learners in 64 courses). The network in Figure 6 was propagated using the history data from a learner's fourth week of learning. Furthermore, the probabilities of the variables corresponding to the nodes in Figure 3 indicate the prior-belief probabilities for the categories. For example, the node corresponding to the predicted final status of a learner indicates that the probability for "abandoned" is 21.0%, the probability for "failed" is 28.4%, the probability for "successful" is 24.4%, and the probability for "excellent" is 26.2%, when there are no data about the learner.

5.2 Learning Bayesian networks using prior belief

This section explains about how to learn Bayesian networks from learning history data. Fifteen Bayesian network structures are estimated corresponding to learners' learning histories data for the fifteen weeks because all courses run for 15 weeks.

The Bayesian network also has the cold start problem and it can not draw any inferences when we provide a new course. To solve this problem, this paper uses the prior distribution in (6) for learning a Bayesian network. For details, first a Bayesian network structure is estimated using all learning histories data which stored in database and does not include the data corresponding the target course. Here, this learning histories data is called as "prior data". The main idea is that the estimated structure from the prior data is used for the prior hypothetical structure B_S^h in (6). Next, based on the estimated prior hypothetical structure B_S^h, the Bayesian network is learned by maximizing the BDe in (5) from learning histroies data corresponding to the target coourse. This proposed method enables to solve the cold start problem when we start a new course.When there are nor sufficiently large data of learning histories data for the target course, the Bayesian agent follows the estimated Bayesian network structure from all learning histories data, the prior data. When there are

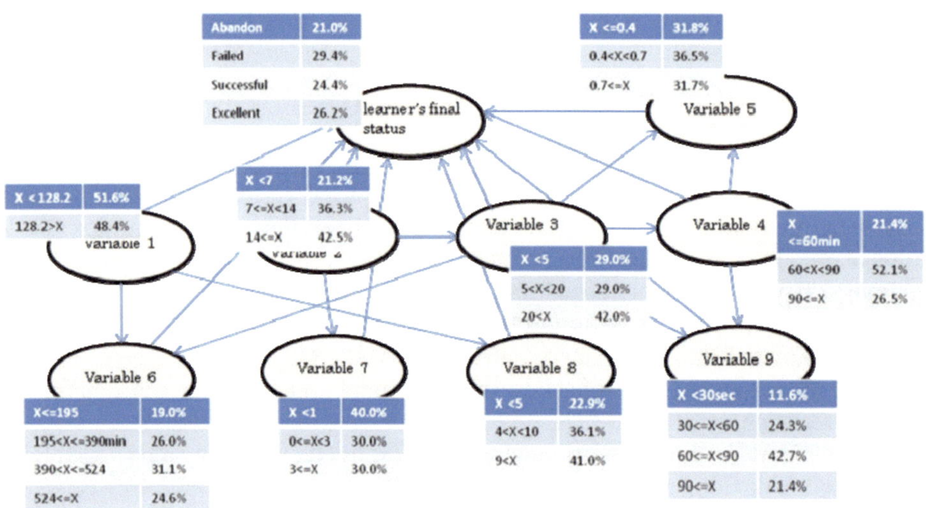

Fig. 3. Example of Bayesian-network structure learned from prior data

Fig. 4. Intelligent agent system (Note that the presented message has not been misspelled. The message is continuously moving within the frame.)

Fig. 5. Various actions by agent

sufficiently large data for the target course, the Bayesian agent follows the estimated Bayesian network structure for the target course. The ESS value α means the pseudo sample size reflecting the prior data and is determined as 100.0 in this research.

In addition, we employ the Bayesian network classifer model since the target variable is one variable(Friedman, Geiger, & Goldszmidt. 1997).

Figure 3 hows the estimated Bayesian network by maximizing BDe in (5) from the prior data (4,344 learners' data to 64 courses). The network in Figure 5 is estimated using 14 weeks of learning history data. Furthermore, the probabilities of the variables corresponding to the nodes in figure 3 indicate the prior belief probabilities for the categories. For example, the node corresponding to the predicted final status of a learner indicates that the probability of "abandon" is 21.0%, the probability of "failed" is 28.4, the probability of "successful" is 24.4, and the probability of "Excellent" is 26.2, when there is no data about the learner.

5.3 Bayesian agent

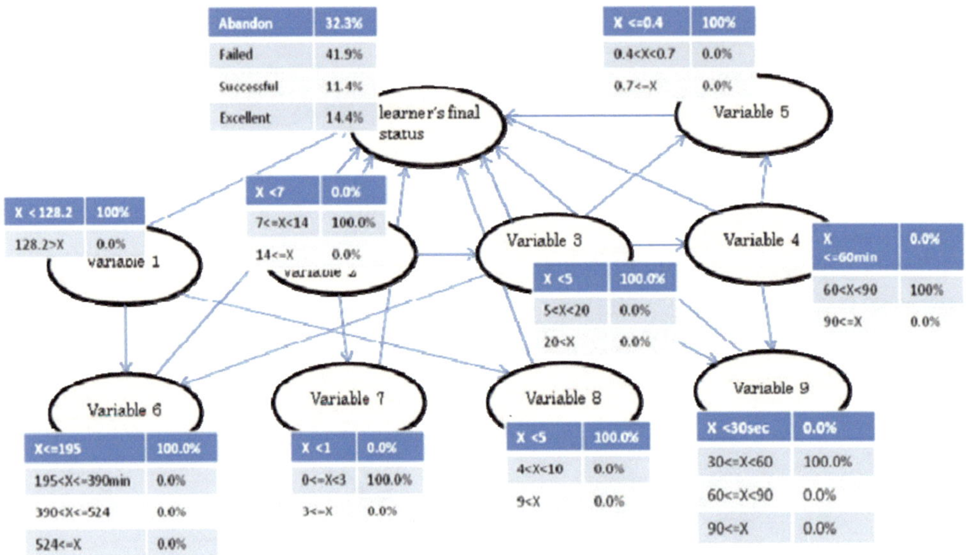

Fig. 6. Final status probabilities propagated by learner's current-history data

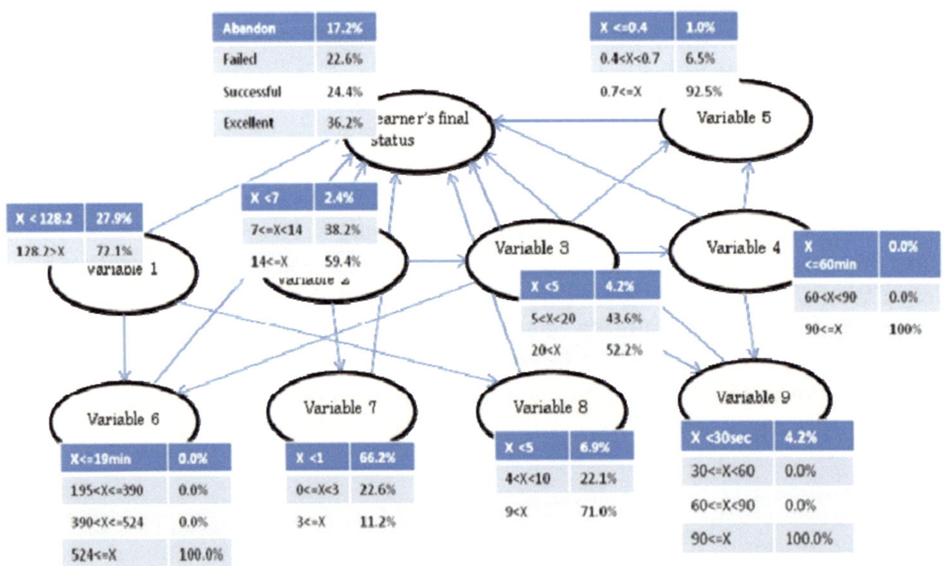

Fig. 7. Retrieved explanatory variables that change predicted final status to "excellent"

This section explains how Bayesian networks are learned from learning-history data. Fifteen Bayesian-network structures are estimated corresponding to data from learners' learning histories for the fifteen weeks because all courses run for 15 weeks.

Bayesian networks also suffer from the cold-start problem and no inferences can be drawn when we provide new courses. To solve this problem, this paper uses the prior distribution in (6) for learning a Bayesian network. In detail, a Bayesian-network structure is first estimated using data from all learning histories stored in the database; this does not include data corresponding to the target course. Here, this data from learning histories is called "prior data". The main idea is that the estimated structure from the prior data is used for the prior hypothetical structure, B_S^h, in (6). Next, based on this estimated prior hypothetical structure B_S^h, the Bayesian network is learned by maximizing the BDe in (5) from learning-history data corresponding to the target course. This proposed method enables us to solve the cold-start problem when we start a new course. When there are not sufficiently large amounts of data from the learning histories for the target course, the Bayesian agent follows the estimated Bayesian-network structure from all learning-history data, i.e., the prior data. When there are sufficiently large amounts of data for the target course, the Bayesian agent follows the estimated Bayesian-network structure for the target course. The ESS value, α, means the pseudo-sample size reflecting the prior data and this has been determined as 100.0 in this research.

In addition, we employ the Bayesian-network classifer model since the target variable is one variable (Friedman, Geiger, & Goldszmidt. 1997). In detail, we first add arcs between the final status node and all the explanatory variables, and then construct the network structure between the explanatory variables to maximize BDe given the previously drawn arcs. Here, the greedy search algorithm is employed to learn the network structure.

Figure 3 shows the Bayesian network estimated by maximizing BDe in (5) from prior data (data from 4,344 learners in 64 courses). The network in Figure 6 was propagated using the history data from a learner's fourth week of learning. Furthermore, the probabilities of the variables corresponding to the nodes in Figure 3 indicate the prior-belief probabilities for the categories. For example, the node corresponding to the predicted final status of a learner indicates that the probability for "abandoned" is 32.3%, the probability for "failed" is 41.9%, the probability for "successful" is 11.2%, and the probability for "excellent" is 14.4%, when there are no data about the learner.

5.3 Bayesian agent

The main purpose of the intelligent agent system is to provide optimum instructional messages to a learner using the previous automatically constructed learner model. The agent appears in the LMS as shown in Figure 4. The agent system also performs various actions based on the learner's current status, as shown in Figure 5. The instructional messages given to a learner are generated as follows:

The agent obtains the learner's current learning-history data and predicts his/her final status using the propagated probabilities in Figure 6. If the predicted most likely final status is "excellent", then the agent provides messages like "Looking great!", "Keep doing your best", and "Your probability of success is xx%". If the predicted status is not "excellent", the agent searches for the explanatory variable that will most increase the probability for the predicted final status by changing the value. Next, the agent finds the explanatory variable that most increases the probability for the predicted final status by changing the value, given the changed value of the explanatory variable. Thus, the agent retrieves the explanatory variables in order for the values to increase the final status probability by changing their values until the predicted most likely final status is "excellent". The retrieved explanatory variables that change the predicted final status to "excellent" corresponding to the learner in

Variables	Instructional messages
1. The number of topics the learner has learned.	1. You are behind in progress in the lesson. Please attend more lectures. 2. Your progress in the lesson is liable to slow. Let's attend more lectures.
2. The number of times the learner has accessed the e-Learning system.	3. You have not participated enough in the lesson. Let's access the system more often.
3. The average number of times the learner has completed each topic.	4. Don't forget previously learned content! Let's review the previous content again.
The average time for learning each lecture, which consists of several types of content and runs for 90 minutes.	5. It seems that you are working through the lectures too quickly. Please spend more time on each lecture.
5. The average degree of understanding of each topic (This is measured by responses to questions that corresponds to each topic.).	6. Was the content of the lesson too difficult? Let's repeat the lecture from the beginning. 7. When there is something you don't understand, let's post questions on the discussion board.
6. The average learning time for each course consisting of fifteen lectures.	8. You have not participated enough in the lesson. Let's access the system and study the content more slowly and carefully.
7. The average number of times the learner has changed answers to e-Learning questions.	9. Your knowledge does not appear to be adequate. Let's repeat the lecture from the beginning.
8. The number of times the learner has posted opinions or comments on the discussion board.	10. Learning is more effective when there is interaction between learners. Let's participate in and contribute to the discussion board.
9. The average learning time for each topic.	11. Did you pay sufficient attention to the lecture? Ordinarily, a lesson should take more time to complete.

Table 1. Instructional messages corresponding to detected variables

NC	BN	DT	SVM	Naïve Bayes
2	89.11(84.27)	75.00(88.70)	80.75(89.25)	75.50(76.25)
3	86.47(66.92)	80.00(84.75)	81.00(88.7)	76.00(77.25)
4	94.00(65.00)	82.00(88.75)	74.00(91.5)	77.00(77.75)
5	96.63(60.57)	80.25(84.75)	78.76(91.5)	76.75(77.75)

Note NC: number of categories; BN: Bayesian network, DT: decision tree model using the ID3 algorithm. The parenthetical values indicate the fitting rates for the training data. network was the most accurate for all NCs.

Table 2. Correct prediction rates (%) obtained in cross-validation experiment

Figure 6 are Variables 4, 6, and 9 as shown in Figure 7. The agent provides messages with the predicted future status, the probability of success estimated by the Bayesian network, and the instructional messages according to Table 1. That is, the agent generates adaptive messages from the gap between the learner's history data and the past-history data of excellent learners.

6. Comparative predictive experiments

Some previous studies have been done on predicting a learner's final test score using several machine-learning methods from learning-history data in e-Learning. Minaei-Bidgoli, Kashy, Kortemeyer, and Punch (2003) compared the accuracy of machine-learning methods (decision-tree model, naive Bayes, and SVM) to predict a learner's final test score from the learning-history data in e-Learning. The decision tree performed the best in the results. However, Talavera and Gaudioso (2004) and Hamalainen et al. (2006) conducted similar experiments and insisted that naive Bayes was the best model.

Finally, Huang et al. (2007) claimed that SVM was the most effective model. Thus, as these previous studies reported different results, this means that the accuracy of prediction depends on the characteristics of the data (i.e., the kinds of variables, data size, domain, and learners' age). Therefore, we also needed to evaluate various models with respect to data obtained from the LMS "Samurai" just as the previous studies had done. We compared the Bayesian-network model with the decision-tree model (ID3), naive-Bayes model, and SVM. Here, we employed the most popular naive-Bayes model, the "multivariate Bernoulli model" (Domingos & Pazzani 1997) and a well known SVM that has a "polynomial kernel" (Vapnik, 2000).

First, the latest data from 800 learners were randomly sampled from the learning-history database for 128 courses in the LMS "Samurai". Furthermore, the learner-history data from 400 out of the 800 learners were randomly sampled as training data, and the remaining 400 learner-history data were used as validation data (test data) for a cross-validation experiment. The cross-validation experiment was carried out to predict learners' final statuses from their learning-history data. The decision-tree (ID3) and naive-Bayes models only use category variables as input data, but the learning-history data use data on continuous variables. Consequently, the data on continuous variables in the learning-history data were categorized as uniformly distributed in each category. Although SVM can use the data on continuous variables for input data, this experiment applied the categorized data to SVM under the same conditions as those for the other models. Here SVM employed the polynomial kernel as a kernel function. To categorize the input data, the range (from the minimum to the maximum value of data) of each variable was divided by the number of categories m into the category ranges. As a result, the continuous data were transformed to category data x_{icj} (if the i-th variable's category c's range includes j-th learner's data then x_{icj} =1, otherwise x_{icj} =0),(i=1,...9, c=1,...,m, j=1,...,N). The number of categories for all variables was increased from two to five in the experiment. In addition, the learninng Bayesian networks in this experiment employed a uniform prior belief for BDe.

The results are listed in Table 2. Each value indicates the correct prediction rates for cross-validation given the number of categories in the corresponding model.

For a large number of categories, DT was very accurate, but not for a small number of categories. For a small number of categories, SVM was very accurate. However, it is clear that SVM overfits the data when there are four or more categories. However, although the decision-tree model is less accurate than SVM when there are fewer categories, it has the best accuracy with four or more categories.

Naïve Bayes has lower correct prediction rates, which can be explained by the variables all having a mutually strong correlation; nevertheless, the model assumed the variables were conditionally independent. The Bayesian network shows the best performances for all NCs. These results indicate the Bayesian network is the most suitable for data stored in LMS "Samurai" because the proposed agent needs to use four categories as variables.

7. Evaluation of prior belief in BDe

One of unique features of the proposal method is to learn a Bayesian agent from learning-history data using BDe that reflects prior belief previously learned from the prior data. Here, it should be noted that the learned prior belief might be quite different from the true structure since the prior data do not necessarily reflect the characteristics of the course. However, no research has been done on how prior belief (where we employ an incorrect hypothetical structure) affects the learning efficiency of Bayesian networks.

Next, let us consider some simulation experiments using the network structure in Figure 3. The procedure in the simulations involves three steps:

1. 100,000 samples are generated from Figure 3.
2. Using MDL, *BDe* with the hypothetical Bayesian-network structures (all possible structures), and Bdeu (BDe with a uniform prior distribution), Bayesian network structures are estimated based on 500, 1,000, and 10,000 samples, respectively, from the datasets for the structures shown in Figure 5. The search method employs the greedy search method.
3. The average number of missing or extra arcs (mean error: ME) was calculated by repeating Procedure 2 ten times.

Table 3 lists the mean errors (ME: the average number of missing or extra arcs in 10 estimates) for BDeu, MDL, and *BDe* for sample sizes of n = 500, 1,000, 10,000, and 100,000. The column "+" indicates the average number of extra arcs in the estimated structures and the column "-" indicates the average number of missing or extra arcs in the estimated structures. The column "ME" indicates the average number of missing or extra arcs in 10 estimates.

The column "*Bde* (best)" indicates the best results by changing the hypothetical structure given the true structure. In contrast, the column "BDe (worst)" indicates the best results by changing the equivalent sample size given a hypothetical prior structure that is most different from the true one. The results for "*Bde* (best)" overwhelmingly have the best accuracies for small sample sizes.

	MDL			Bdeu			Bde (Best)			Bde (Worst)		
N	+	-	ME	+	-	ME	+	-	ME	+	-	ME
500	7.2	8.1	11.3	6.7	2.4	9.1	6.4	2.0	8.4	6,3	3.7	9.9
1,000	5.1	6.7	7.9	4.2	1.3	5.5	4.4	1.7	6.1	4.4	2.2	6.6
10,000	2.0	0.2	2.2	2.0	0.2	2.2	1.8	0.4	2.2	1.8	0.4	2.2
100,000	1.2	0.0	1.2	1.2	0.0	1.2	1.2	0.0	1.2	1.2	0.0	1.2

Table 3. Comparisons of estimates for various score metrics for Bayesian networks

	With agent system	Without agent system
Subject name	Information & Communication Technology	Information & Communication Technology
Students	Undergraduate students (third and fourth years)	Undergraduate students (third and fourth years)
Learning location	Individual student homes	Individual student homes
Credits	2	2
Number of students	74	92
Term	2003, April 10 - July 31	2004, April 10 - July 31
Number of students who withdrew from course	14 (18.9%)	49 (53.2%)
Final test scores	Average: 93.26 Variance: 43.2 (n=60)	Average: 78.74 Variance: 215.24 (n=43)
P-value	1.33E-07	
Total learning time (minutes)	Average: 1045.13 Variance: 71721.8 (n=60)	Average: 801.88 Variance: 65426.9 (n=43)
P-value	1.25E-05	
Average degree of progress per lesson	Average: 0.93 Variance: 0.64 (n=60)	Average: 0.84 Variance: 2.03 (n=43)
P-value for statistical difference test of two averages	0.00031	
Total number of contributions to discussion board	714	928

Table 4. Comparison between classes with and without system

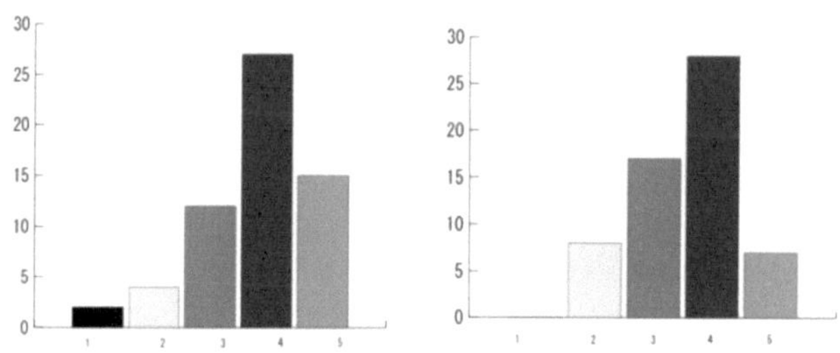

(a) (b)

Fig. 8. Plotted results for Question **A** given to (a) class with system and (b) one without

This means that our valid prior knowledge about the network structure facilitates more efficient learning of Bayesian networks. In addition, even if we set prior knowledge

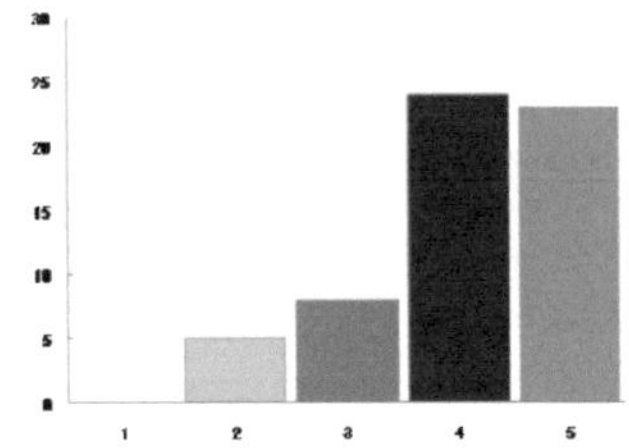

Fig. 9. Results for Question **B**

incorrectly, the results for BDe have better or the same accuracy than one of the traditional MDLs or BDeus. Consequently, the results reveal that the proposed method is effective even if prior belief is quite different from that of the true structure.

8. Evaluation of agent system

The system was evaluated by comparing a class of students that used the agent system with one that did not use it for one semester. The Bayesian network for the agent system was learned using 1,344 histories of learners. The details on the two e-Learning classes are summarized in Table 4. The results reveal that far fewer students withdrew from the class if they had used the LMS with the agent system. In addition, the final test scores, learning-time data, and progress with learning data also indicate that the proposed agent system enhanced learning significantly.

The presentation of the predictive future status of learners and the presentation of adaptive instructional messages help them to maintain the required learning pace. As a result, they can progress until they reach their predicted future status. Furthermore, all learners were asked Question **A:** "How would you rate the system's ability to enhance your e-Learning? 1. Very poor, 2. Poor, 3. Fair, 4. Good, or 5. Very good."

The group with the agent system was asked an additional question, Question **B:** "How would you rate the adequacy of the instructional messages from the agent system? 1. Very poor, 2. Poor, 3. Fair, 4. Good, or 5. Very good." The results for Question **A** are given in Figure 8. The response frequencies for answers 2 and 3, "poor" and "fair" were lower for the class with the system than that without it. This indicates that the system was effective in enhancing learning and the instructional messages had a positive effect on e-Learning. However, it should be noted that the response frequency for "very poor" increased for the class with the system. If we assume that the difference between the results for the two classes are due only to using the agent system, the results mean that learners' opinions about the agent system tended to be polarized compared to the opinions by the class without it.

Figure 9 summarizes the frequency of learners' responses to Question **B**. The results indicate that many learners rated the agent system's messages as "good" or "very good" and this means that the instructional messages from the agent system are acceptable for many learners. However, it should be noted that five learners rated it as "poor".The learners who rated the system as "poor" gave the following reasons :

- "The messages from the agent were too distracting. I couldn't concentrate on my learning due to the agent's incessant actions."

- "The messages from the agent were interfering with my learning because I knew almost all the message content previously even if the agent hadn't sent it."

This means that the messages from the system interfered with some autonomous learners who could learn by themselves. Therefore, we think that the system needs a function whereby learners can hide the agent from the system whenever they need to.

9. References

Becker, K. & Vanzin, M. (2003). Discovering increasing usage patterns in web based learning environments, *Proc. Int. Conf. on Utility, Usability, and Complexity of e-information systems*, pp. 57–72

Domingos, P. & Pazzani, M. (1997). On the optimality of the simple Bayesian classifier under zero-one loss, *Machine Learning*, Vol. 29, 103–137, ISSN:0885-6125

Friedman, N., Geiger, D., & Goldszmidt, M. (1997). Bayesian network classifier, *Machine Learning*, Vol. 29, 131–161, ISSN: 0885-6125

Gabrielle, D. M. (2000). The effects of technology-mediated instructional strategies on motivation, performance, and self directed learning, *Proc. of ED-Media*, pp. 2569–2575, ISBN: 1-880094-40-7

Gamoran, A. Secada, W. G. & Marrett, C. A. (2000). The organizational context of teaching and learning: changing theoretical perspectives, In: *Handbook of Sociology of Education*, Hallinan, M.T. (Ed.), 37–64, Kluwer Academic/Plenum Publishers, ISBN: 0387325174 , New York

Hamalainen, W., Laine, T. H., & Sutinen, E. (2006). Data mining in personalizing distance education courses, In: *Data Mining in e-Learning*, (Eds.) Romero, C. & Ventura, S., 157–171, WIT Press, ISBN: 1-84564-152-3, New York

Huang, C. J., Chu, S. S. & Guan, C. T. (2007). Implementation and performance evaluation of parameter improvement mechanisms for intelligent e-learning systems, *Computers & Education*, Vol. 49, Issue 3, 597–614, ISSN: 0360-1315

Knowles, M. (1983). How the media can make it or bust it in education, *Media and Adult Learning*, Vol. 5, No. 2, 3–4, ISSN: 09152202

Knowles, M., Holton, E. F. & Swanson, R. A. (1998). *The Adult Learner: The Definitive Classic in Adult Education and Human Resource Development* (5th ed.). Gulf Publishing, ISBN: 0884151158, Houston

Mayer. R. E. and Anderson, R. B (1991). Animations need narrations, *Journal of Educational Psychology*, Vol. 83, No. 4. 484–490, ISSN: 00220663

Merriam, S. B. & Brockett, R. G. (2007). *The Profession and Practice of Adult Education: An Introduction*, Jossey-Bass, ISBN: 0470181532, New York

Minaei-Bidgoli, B., Kashy, D.A., Kortemeyer, G., and Punch, W. F. (2003). Predicting student performance: an application of data mining methods with an educational web-based system, *Proc. IEEE conf. on Frontier in Education*, Vol. 1, pp. 13–18

Quinlan., J. R. (1986) Induction of decision trees. *Machine Learning*, Vol. 1, No. 1, 81-106, ISSN: 0885-6125

Talavera, L. & Gaudioso, E. (2004) Mining student data to characterize similar behavior groups in unstructured collaboration spaces, *Proc. of the Workshop on Artificial Intelligence in CSCL, 16th European Conference on Artificial Intelligence, ECAI2004*, pp. 17–23

Ueno, M. (2004) Learning Log Database and Data Mining system for e-Learning, *Proc. International Conference on Advanced Learning Technology,* pp. 194–201 ,ISBN 0-7695-2181-9, IEEE Computer Society

Ueno, M. (2005) Intelligent LMS with an agent that learns from log data, *Proc. of e-Learn2005,* pp. 3169–3176

Ueno, M. (2007). *e-Leanirng in knowledge society* (in Japanese), Baihuukan, ISBN: 4563015733, Tokyo

Vapnik, V. (2000). *The Nature of Statistical Learning Theory,* Springer , ISBN: 0-387-98780-0, New York

Visser, L. & Keller, J. M. (1990). The clinical use of motivational messages: An inquiry into the validity of the ARCS model to motivational design., *Instructional Science*, Vol. 19, 467–50, ISSN: 0020-4277

Visser, L., Plomp, T., & Kuiper, L. (1999) Development research applied to improve motivation in distance education, *Association for Educational Communications and Technology,* Houston, 17–28

von Glasersfeld, E. (1995). A constructivist approach to teaching. In: *Constructivism in Education,* Steffe, L & Gale, J. (Eds.), 3–16, Lawrence Erlbaum Associates, Inc., ISBN: 080581096X, New Jersey.

Data Mining for Instructional Design, Learning and Assessment

Lluís Vicent and Xavier Gumara
Business Engineering School La Salle, Ramon Llull University
Spain

1. Introduction

Statistical analysis is widely used in many different areas: medicine, business, natural and social sciences, and of course, in education.

In this last topic, it is common that teachers make simple statistical analysis on the results of the students at the end of an exam or a course, and this is useful for the evaluation of that course. However a more powerful use of statistics can and must be done if the analyses are used to modify the methodology of learning personalizing contents and methods for groups of students with similar skills. To make a realistic personalization of learning, data mining techniques must be used. They are also useful to manage big amounts of information mainly composed by: contents, skills, tools, grades and students.

In this chapter, we present data mining techniques used in instructional design, in learning and in the assessment of the students. In order to reduce, interpret and classify the information, factor and cluster analysis have been used.

Factor analysis is a technique that extracts few unobserved new variables (factors) from a big number of data. These factors are linear combinations of the observed variables and the expert analyzer must define the information that underlies each factor. Cluster analysis classifies all the information in some sets (clusters) of items with common features.

Let's present here two examples of the use of Data Mining in e-learning:

- **Example 1.** An institution must decide its learning methodology, and it has planned to use a Learning Management System (LMS). Of course, an LMS contains many tools, and teachers and students must learn how to use these tools. But not all these tools add value to learning, and probably many of them are redundant, that is, students can acquire the same competences using different tools. In (Vicent, 2007) teachers were asked to value (from 0 to 3) the performance of each tool (24 were considered) to develop each skill. Using factor and cluster analysis, an LMS of only 5 tools was defined to run an engineering online degree in the European Higher Education Area.
- **Example 2.** If an LMS is used for learning, much information of the students is available: results of questionnaires, number of post in the forums, number of visits to the contents, etc. It is possible to classify the students in function of their behavior with a cluster analysis. This way, lazy, willing, active, brilliant, etc.

students can be detected. Results must be used to modify the behavior of some students if needed.

It is obvious that students have different capacities to learn one topic or skill. And each student is better in some skills than in others. When the teachers create assignments or questionnaires, each of these assignments is assessing one or more skills. Let's assume that at some point of a course, a teacher has collected 500 data of each student: questions answers, grades of assignments, forums posts, etc. Data mining techniques are definitively useful to interpret such amount of information. Factor analysis will simplify these 500 data in a few factors, each factor representing an unobserved variable with a real meaning that must be interpreted by the teacher. This factor will represent a skill or a set of skills. This technique suppose an automatic tool to grade skills, even in the case that the teacher did not define, in the assignment or question, which skills were going to be developed and assessed.

In addition, if a unique teacher manages a big group of students, they can be classified in function of their performance in the skill/s of each factor. Cluster analysis will do this classification. This analysis makes the teacher able to write a good report on the state of learning of their students, giving several grades (one per skill) to their students, and classifying the students in different groups taking into account their performance. If this analysis is done several times during a course, teachers can correct deficiencies in the achievement of some skills. In groups of students, teachers can prepare an adaptive learning plan for each group. This adaptive learning plan should be a must for teachers whose students have to achieve a predefined set of skills. This method can be also applied to a global degree, defining adaptive curricula for different groups of students.

In this chapter, the opportunities that the statistical analysis offer to teachers and managers of learning programs is presented.

2. Why Factor Analysis?

It is easy to understand the value of collecting data from students, but also to realize the need of leveraging this data to create knowledge. Data mining technologies offer a way to recognize and track patterns within data. Normally, there exist similarities between the variables analyzed so it is quite possible that we are dealing with redundant information and therefore it is possible to reduce the complexity of the results. In the world of technology we can find some analogies, for example in certain data compression algorithms applied to images or videos for its broadcast on the Internet.

The multivariate approaches for reducing the dimensions of the information can successfully combine some of the collected variables in a few fictitious variables in order to produce minimum information loss.

Factor Analysis is a common statistical method for extracting general information, as usually, many of data collected are related (correlated) to other data, and do not add significant information. Factor analysis detects these correlations and defines factors, which have meaningful information and are linear combination of the general data. Once the factors are found, the supervision of an analyst is needed to give a meaning to the factors.

Principal Components Analysis (PCA) is by far the most common form of factor analysis and its central concept is summarization; it tries to find the minimum variables: factors or principal components, linear combinations of the original variables that explain, with the minimum information loss, the global meaning of the original variables. The key parameter to estimate the information loss is the variance. A factor with high variance means that it carries a lot of information and vice versa.

So PCA is about sorting the factors taking into account the amount of variance that they explain. If with a few factors the most part of the variables can be explained it will mean that the original variables are correlated and the analysis has succeed, since we have been able to reduce the dimensionality of the problem. On the other side, if the original variables are completely uncorrelated all the factors would have approximately the same variance and we won't be able to reduce the dimension.

For the PCA to work properly, it is necessary to subtract the mean from each of the data dimensions. The mean subtracted is the average across each dimension. So, all the x values have $\overline{x}$ (the mean of the x values of all the data points) subtracted. And the same happens for y, z, and so on. This produces a data set whose mean is zero.

The next step is calculating the covariance matrix. The covariance matrix for an N dimensional dataset would be calculated as shown in (1).

$$C = \begin{pmatrix} \operatorname{cov}(x_1,x_1) & \operatorname{cov}(x_1,x_2) & \cdots & \operatorname{cov}(x_1,x_N) \\ \operatorname{cov}(x_2,x_1) & \operatorname{cov}(x_2,x_2) & & \operatorname{cov}(x_2,x_N) \\ \vdots & & \ddots & \vdots \\ \operatorname{cov}(x_N,x_1) & \operatorname{cov}(x_N,x_2) & \cdots & \operatorname{cov}(x_N,x_N) \end{pmatrix} \quad (1)$$

Since the covariance matrix is square, we can calculate the eigenvectors and eigenvalues for this matrix using a Single Value Decomposition (SVD), diagonalizating the matrix or resolving an eigenvalue equation. The equation for SVD of a matrix X $(m \times n)$ is (2).

$$X = USV^T \quad (2)$$

Where U is an m × n matrix, S is an n × n diagonal matrix, and V^T is also an n × n matrix. The columns of U are called the left singular vectors. The rows of V^T contain the elements of the right singular vectors. The elements of S are only nonzero on the diagonal, and are called the singular values. By convention, the ordering of the singular vectors is determined by high-to-low sorting of singular values, with the highest singular value in the upper left index of the S matrix. This gives the components in order of significance.

Note that for a square and symmetric matrix X (like the covariance matrix), singular value decomposition is equivalent to diagonalization, or solution of the eigenvalue problem.

One way to calculate the SVD is to first calculate V^T and S by diagonalizing X^TX. This process can be seen in (3).

$$\begin{aligned} X &= USV^T \\ X^T &= VSU^T \\ X^T X &= VSU^T USV^T = VS^2V^T \end{aligned} \quad (3)$$

And then, the only incognita left is U, that can be calculated as follows in (4).

$$U = XVS^{-1} \quad (4)$$

It is important to notice that the eigenvectors obtained are unit eigenvectors, that is, their lengths are 1. They are perpendicular to each other and give information about how the datasets are related in order of importance. So, by this process of taking the eigenvectors of the covariance matrix, we have been able to extract vectors that characterize the data. Each component's eigenvalue is called the "amount of variance" the component explains. It turns out that the eigenvector with the highest eigenvalue is the principal component of the data set.

When selecting the number of factors to be extracted it may happen that a minor number of principal components will explain all the variance, which will allow the perfect reconstruction of the original data (even though the number of components found is smaller than the number of original variables). However, in the absence of this event, there is no significance test on the number of principal components to choose.

In (Kaiser, 1960) it is suggested a rule for selecting a number of factors n less than the number needed for perfect reconstruction: set n equal to the number of eigenvalues greater than 1. Several lines of thought lead to Kaiser's rule, but the simplest is that since an eigenvalue is the amount of variance explained by one more factor, it does not make sense to add a factor that explains less variance than is contained in one variable. Since a component analysis is supposed to summarize a set of data, to use a component that explains less than a variance of 1 would be like writing a summary of a book where one section of the summary is longer than the book section it summarizes (Darlington, 1997).

Another criterion to select the number of principal components is to include just enough components that explain some arbitrary amount (typically 80%) of the variance. This can be calculated normalizing the eigenvalues and selecting, in order, the ones that explain the 80% of the variance.

So principal components are linear combinations of the original variables weighted by their contribution to explaining the variance in a particular orthogonal dimension and although the goal of PCA is dimension reduction, there is no guarantee that the dimensions are interpretable. In the next parts of this chapter we present two interpretations of Principal Components Analysis results applied to e-learning.

3. Factor Analysis to Decide which E-learning Tools are Needed in an LMS

3.1 Introduction

In 2005 at La Salle, a group of experts composed by faculty members and technician staff prepared the adaptation of the Engineering programs to the Euopean Higher Education Area (EHEA). As this programes were offered both in the campus and online at La Salle, there was the preocupation of knowing if it was possible to develop all the degrees, taking into account the generic competences the students were supposed to acquire (Tuning, 2001) in a purely on campus way (without the use of an LMS), in a purely online way (with no phisical attendance) or in a blended learning way.

For this reason, on the one hand, all the competences to learn were considered, and on the other hand, an important set of 24 tools for learning (face to face and technological) were stablished. These lists can be seen in Table 1.

Competences	Tools
Conceptual comprehension	Text
Capacity for analysis	Hypertext
Capacity for synthesis	Synthetic video
Planning and time management	Video lesson
Oral communication in the native language	Recording of an on campus class.
Written Communication in the native language	Non teaching purpose videos
Communication in a foreign language	Remote laboratory
Use of information technologies	Simulator
Information management	Virtual library
Ability for mathematical developments	Wiki
Problem solving	Blog
Decision making	Textual forum
Critical and self-critical abilities	Graphical forum
Communication with experts from other areas	Chat
Appreciation of diversity and multiculturalism	Virtual classroom
Teamwork	E-mail and mailing lists
Ethical commitment	News
Ability to work autonomously	Calendar
Adaptation to new situations	Personal folder
Creativity	Working group
Ability for design	Lectures
Leadership	Debate
Initiative and entrepreneur spirit	Interview
Openness to learning all along one's life	Laboratory
Identity, development and professional ethics	
Concern for quality	

Table 1. List of competences and tools considered.

The group of experts wanted to answer 3 questions:

1. Is the face to face class enough to develop the generic competences the Bologna Process indicates?
2. Are the LMS tools enough to develop the generic competences the Bologna Process indicates?
3. Which are the minimum set of tools (online or face to face) good enough to develop all the competences?

To answer these questions experimented face to face and online engineering faculties were polled. The tool was a table in which the resources are placed in the abscissas axis and the competences in the ordinates axis. The faculty were asked to fill the table answering the following question:

"Qualify in an ascending order, from 0 (slightly suitable) to 3 (very suitable), the educational resources in each column, according to their adequacy for the development of the competences indicated in each line:

0: This skill cannot be developed with this resource

1: This skill might be developed with a non conventional use (different from the usual one) of this resource

2: It is possible to develop the skill with a normal use of the resource

3: This resource is very useful for the development of this skill"

The pool was answered by 38 faculty, and the number of data to analyze was of *26 competences x 24 tools x 38 faculty = 23.712 data.*

The first simplification was to caculate the average of the answers of each association competence - tool, obtaining Table 2 (Vicent, 2007).

		Educational Resources																				On Campus resources			
	Skills	Text	Hypertext	Synthetic video	Video lesson	Recording of an on campus	Non teaching purpose vide	Remote laboratory	Simulator	Virtual library	Wiki	Blog	Textual forum	Graphical forum	Chat	Virtual classroom	E-mail and mailing lists	News	Calendar	Personal folder	Working group	Lectures	Debate	Interview	Laboratory
		1	2	3	4	5	6	7	8	9	10	11	12	13	14	15	16	17	18	19	20	21	22	23	24
A	Conceptual comprehension	2,3	2,3	2,6	2,5	2,1	1,5	2,2	2,5	1,3	0,8	1,0	1,4	1,7	1,3	2,2	0,9	0,4	0,2	0,5	0,6	2,6	2,2	1,7	2,5
B	Capacity for analysis	2,4	2,2	2,3	2,2	2,0	1,7	2,2	2,5	1,4	0,9	1,1	1,3	1,5	1,2	2,1	0,9	0,4	0,2	0,5	0,6	2,6	2,3	1,7	2,5
C	Capacity for synthesis	2,2	1,8	2,0	2,0	1,7	1,4	2,0	2,3	1,4	1,1	1,1	1,4	1,6	1,5	2,1	1,0	0,6	0,3	0,7	0,7	2,5	2,5	1,7	2,4
D	Planning and time management	1,5	1,5	0,7	1,2	1,1	0,8	1,0	0,9	0,9	0,8	1,0	1,4	1,3	0,8	1,3	1,7	2,4	3,0	1,7	2,0	1,4	1,4	1,4	1,2
E	Oral communication in the native language	0,9	0,9	0,9	1,7	1,8	1,7	0,5	0,3	0,3	0,4	0,5	0,5	0,4	0,5	2,1	0,4	0,4	0,3	0,3	0,3	2,2	3,0	2,9	1,2
F	Written Communication in the native language	2,3	2,0	0,7	1,2	1,1	0,9	0,5	0,4	1,6	1,2	1,8	2,5	1,4	2,1	1,6	2,0	1,1	0,6	0,7	1,0	1,4	0,8	0,8	0,9
G	Communication in a foreign language	2,3	2,0	1,2	1,7	1,8	1,7	0,8	0,6	2,2	1,1	1,5	2,0	1,2	1,7	1,8	1,8	0,8	0,6	0,8	1,0	1,9	2,0	1,8	1,1
H	Use of information technologies	1,2	2,0	1,9	2,0	1,7	1,6	2,3	2,1	2,5	1,8	2,0	2,4	2,4	2,3	2,5	2,1	1,4	1,4	1,6	1,8	0,9	0,6	0,7	1,4
I	Information management	1,9	2,1	1,2	1,6	1,4	1,2	1,0	1,0	2,4	1,8	1,8	1,7	1,5	1,1	1,5	1,5	1,2	1,2	1,7	2,1	1,2	1,1	0,9	1,0
J	Ability for mathematical developments	2,2	2,1	1,4	1,7	1,6	1,0	1,4	1,9	1,2	0,5	0,6	0,8	1,3	0,7	1,9	0,6	0,2	0,2	0,4	0,5	2,7	1,7	1,4	1,6
K	Problem solving	2,1	2,0	1,7	2,0	2,0	1,0	2,2	2,3	1,4	1,0	0,9	1,7	1,7	1,5	2,2	1,0	0,5	0,2	0,6	1,0	2,7	2,5	1,9	2,5
L	Decision making	1,3	1,4	0,8	1,4	1,2	1,0	2,0	2,2	1,0	0,8	0,9	1,3	1,2	1,1	1,3	1,0	0,5	0,6	0,5	0,8	1,3	2,0	1,6	2,0
M	Critical and self-critical abilities	1,6	1,3	0,8	1,1	1,2	1,0	1,6	1,8	1,0	1,1	1,3	1,9	1,8	1,5	1,7	1,0	0,4	0,2	0,5	0,9	1,4	2,5	2,0	1,9
N	Communication with experts from other areas	1,3	1,2	0,6	0,9	0,9	1,3	1,0	0,8	1,2	1,4	1,6	2,3	2,3	2,2	1,9	2,3	0,6	0,3	0,2	1,3	1,3	2,1	1,5	1,0
O	Appreciation of diversity and multiculturality	1,4	1,3	0,7	1,0	0,9	1,6	0,4	0,4	1,0	1,4	1,7	1,9	1,5	1,7	1,8	1,6	0,5	0,2	0,3	1,2	1,3	2,3	1,5	1,0
P	Teamwork	0,8	0,6	0,4	0,9	0,6	0,9	0,8	0,6	0,6	1,2	1,3	2,0	1,9	2,4	2,2	1,8	0,4	0,2	0,2	1,3	1,5	2,7	2,2	1,6
Q	Ethical commitment	1,2	1,0	0,7	1,0	1,0	1,5	0,8	0,7	0,8	1,1	1,4	1,7	1,6	1,6	1,6	1,4	0,6	0,4	0,6	1,2	1,6	2,3	1,9	1,5
R	Ability to work autonomously	2,4	2,3	2,0	1,9	1,9	2,0	2,6	2,8	2,5	1,1	1,2	1,8	1,8	1,3	2,0	1,2	0,8	0,9	1,3	1,3	1,5	1,4	1,2	2,3
S	Adaptation to new situations	0,9	1,0	1,0	1,0	0,9	1,1	2,0	2,0	1,4	1,2	1,1	1,2	1,2	1,1	1,6	1,2	0,7	0,6	0,6	0,6	1,0	1,7	1,4	2,0
T	Creativity	1,4	1,4	1,3	1,3	0,9	1,1	1,8	2,0	1,1	1,4	1,6	1,6	1,7	1,2	1,6	0,9	0,3	0,2	0,4	0,5	1,2	2,2	1,5	2,3
U	Ability for design	1,7	1,6	1,2	1,4	1,5	1,2	2,0	2,3	1,3	1,0	1,0	1,3	1,5	1,1	1,6	0,9	0,3	0,1	0,4	0,6	2,1	1,7	1,5	2,6
V	Leadership	0,7	0,6	0,4	0,4	0,6	0,4	1,1	0,7	0,4	1,2	1,3	1,9	1,9	2,0	1,7	1,4	0,6	0,3	0,2	1,2	0,8	2,7	1,7	1,6
W	Initiative and entrepreneur spirit	0,8	1,6	0,5	0,5	0,6	0,6	1,4	1,5	1,6	1,4	1,5	1,9	1,9	1,7	1,4	1,4	0,6	0,4	0,4	1,1	1,0	2,7	1,8	1,8
X	Openness to learning all along one's life	1,7	1,5	1,0	1,2	1,2	1,2	1,2	1,4	2,1	1,1	1,2	1,4	1,4	1,1	1,5	1,3	0,7	0,4	0,8	0,8	1,6	1,6	1,4	1,6
Y	Identity, development and professional ethics	1,2	1,0	0,8	0,9	0,9	1,2	0,7	0,7	0,8	1,0	1,3	1,5	1,3	1,3	1,3	1,3	0,6	0,4	0,7	0,8	1,6	2,0	1,8	1,0
Z	Concern for quality	1,4	1,2	0,9	1,0	1,0	0,7	1,2	1,3	1,0	1,0	0,8	1,0	1,0	0,9	1,2	0,9	0,6	0,8	1,0	1,1	1,5	1,5	1,5	1,5

Table 2. Average of the answers of each association.

Looking at this table it is difficult to answer any of the three questions. So, a factor analysis was used to simplify the data. Since the goal is to develop all the competences, these must not be simplified. There is no problem, on the other hand, to use only some of the tools, if all the competences can be learned. So, the factor analysis was applied to the tools.

In these analysis, it was discovered that only 5 factors could explain the 90% of the information of the table. This meant that many of the tools were superfluous and they were not strictly necessary, as they are as usefull as others. In Table 3 the weight of each tool in each factor can be seen.

	Factor				
	1	2	3	4	5
Text	0,539	0,597	-0,035	0,237	-0,335
Hypertext	0,433	0,801	-0,031	0,078	-0,218
Synthetic video	0,738	0,602	0,138	0,001	0,080
Video lesson	0,755	0,552	-0,013	0,267	0,104
Recording of an on campus class.	0,772	0,495	-0,072	0,312	0,097
Non teaching purpose videos	0,394	0,385	0,113	0,533	-0,021
Remote laboratory	0,549	0,499	0,224	-0,568	0,203
Simulator	0,650	0,426	0,192	-0,573	0,085
Virtual library	0,005	0,863	-0,018	-0,029	-0,281
Wiki	-0,654	0,497	0,341	-0,211	-0,093
Blog	-0,712	0,450	0,376	0,122	-0,184
Textual forum	-0,660	0,453	0,511	0,126	-0,014
Graphical forum	-0,369	0,441	0,684	-0,214	0,232
Chat	-0,592	0,219	0,689	0,177	0,121
Virtual classroom	0,347	0,356	0,530	0,399	0,417
E-mail and mailing lists	-0,801	0,397	0,195	0,239	0,063
News	-0,449	0,490	-0,600	0,062	0,350
Calendar	-0,345	0,442	-0,700	-0,049	0,408
Personal folder	-0,181	0,709	-0,601	-0,057	0,173
Working group	-0,674	0,503	-0,244	0,071	0,310
Lectures	0,848	0,008	0,018	0,333	-0,004
Debate	0,246	-0,702	0,411	0,130	0,302
Interview	0,316	-0,764	0,120	0,285	0,347
Laboratory	0,708	0,084	0,317	-0,529	0,177

Table 3. Weight of each tool in each factor.

Therefore, a table where the appropriateness of each factor for the development of any competence was studied. At Table 4 we remark (blue colour) which factor is most suitable for developing each competence.

Many things can be now understood from this table. The first one is that the instrumental competences can be easily developed as the scores of the factors are high. On the other hand, interpersonal and systemic competences are more difficult to develop from the faculty point of view.

An important point in the factor analysis is the sign. Each factor (Table 3.)has positive weights of some tools and negative for others. Then, in Table 4, we can see that maximum scores for each competence can be positive or negative. How must it be read? Let's see an example. *Planning and time management* is well developed by factor 3 in its negative side. It means that the high negative tools of factor 3 (in Table 3.) we see that they are news, calendar and personal folder) are the idoneous tools for developing that competence.

Therefore, in Table 4. we can detect that positive resources of factor 1 are very important in many skills. Positive resources of factor 2 are important in some competences, and negative factors are needed in some systemic skills. Negative resources in factor 3 are indispensable for organization, and positive factors resources are important for interpersonal skills. Positive resources of factor 4 are essential for oral communication.

	Competence	F1	F2	F3	F4	F5
Instrumentals	Conceptual comprehension	1,81	0,66	0,75	0,30	0,39
	Capacity for analysis	1,66	0,56	0,56	0,32	0,10
	Capacity for synthesis	1,17	0,43	0,61	0,14	0,59
	Planning and time management	-0,95	0,47	-3,13	-0,14	2,42
	Oral communication in the native language	1,31	-2,07	-1,20	2,14	0,98
	Written Communication in the native language	-1,17	0,74	-0,19	1,01	-2,24
	Communication in a foreign language	-0,09	0,57	-0,06	2,09	-0,87
	Use of information technologies	-1,00	2,65	0,65	-0,07	1,40
	Information management	-0,91	1,56	-1,33	0,22	-0,78
	Ability for mathematical developments	1,39	-0,36	-0,66	0,08	-1,12
	Problem solving	1,26	0,39	0,72	0,00	1,05
	Decision making	0,40	-0,57	-0,52	-1,26	-0,18
Interpersonals	Critical and self-critical abilities	-0,04	-0,44	0,68	-0,53	0,26
	Communication with experts from other areas	-1,33	-0,01	1,34	0,83	0,13
	Appreciation of diversity and multiculturality	-0,92	-0,42	0,56	1,28	-0,72
	Teamwork	-1,01	-1,11	1,41	0,58	1,54
	Ethical commitment	-0,55	-0,65	0,25	0,68	0,22
Systemic	Ability to work autonomously	0,84	1,80	-0,08	-0,39	0,13
	Adaptation to new situations	-0,03	-0,42	-0,36	-1,54	-0,15
	Creativity	0,10	-0,28	0,71	-1,42	-0,78
	Ability for design	0,85	-0,14	0,22	-1,09	-0,65
	Leadership	-1,22	-1,22	0,79	-0,86	0,80
	Initiative and entrepreneur spirit	-0,97	-0,52	0,70	-1,37	-0,04
	Openness to learning all along one's life	-0,02	0,01	-0,51	-0,21	-1,15
	Identity, development and professional ethics	-0,52	-0,93	-0,48	0,35	-0,63
	Concern for quality	-0,08	-0,69	-1,45	-1,10	-0,70

Table 3. List of suitable factors for developing each competence.

3.2 Cluster Analysis

In spite of the analysis, cluster analysis can be performed to quickly view the relationships between tools. These relationships will show if the tools have a similar behaviour in the development of competences. Applying the cluster analysis as can be seen in (Vicent et al., 2007) we can detect the next 10 clusters:

1. Personal folder, calendar, news
2. Text, hypertext
3. Graphical forum, Chat, Textual forum
4. Working group, e-mail, blog, wiki

5. Not teaching purposes video, recording of an on campus class, video-lesson, synthetic video
6. Interview, debate
7. Laboratory, simulator, remote lab
8. Virtual library
9. Virtual classroom
10. Lecture

If the tools of a cluster have similar behaviour when developing the same competences, we can assume that we can work with only one tool of each cluster if all the clusters are needed. To know if they are needed we must locate the clusters in the factors as can be represented in Table 4.

	F1	F2	F3	F4	F5
+	Cluster 5 / 10	Cluster 2 / 8	Cluster 3 / 9		Cluster 9
-	Cluster 4	Cluster 6	Cluster 1	Cluster 7	

Table 4. Positive and negative location of clusters into factors.

From the factor analysis we can say that negative tools of factor 1, negative tools of factor 4 and factor 5 can be discarded. So, cluster 4 is prescindible: it is e-mail, wiki, blog, textual forum and group folder.

Now, the best tool of each cluster can be selected, and then we can check if with these tools all the competences can be developed. In Table 4 (Vicent et al., 2007), it was shown that with nine tools almost all the competences could be developed" into "In Table 5 (Vicent et al., 2007), it is shown that with nine tools almost all the competences can be developed. Even on that paper, it was explained that the video-lesson and the lecture could be avoided as they are not indispensable for any competence. Looking at that table, answers can be given to the 3 questions:

1. Is the face to face class enough to develop the generic competences the Bologna Process indicates?
   No. The use of the LMS is strictly necessary for some competences as planning or obviously, the use of IT technologies.
2. Are the LMS tools enough to develop the generic competences the Bologna Process indicates?
   No. There are some competences where presence is very interesting as leadership, or ethical commitment.
3. Which are the minimum set of tools (online or face to face) good enough to develop all the competences?
   Only six: Hypertext, Simulator, Graphical forum, Virtual classroom, Calendar, Virtual library and Debate.

Authors of these paper want to point out that these three answers do not necessary represent their thoughts. These answers are given by the collective of faculty that answered the polls.

	Conceptual comprehension	Capacity for analysis	Capacity for synthesis	Planning and time management	Oral communication in the native language	Written Communication in the native language	Communication in a foreign language	Use of information technologies	Information management	Ability for mathematical developments	Problem solving	Decision making	Critical and self-critical abilities	Communication with experts from other areas	Appreciation of diversity and multicultural	Teamwork	Ethical commitment	Ability to work autonomously	Adaptation to new situations	Creativity	Ability for design	Leadership	Initiative and entrepreneur spirit	Openness to learning all along one's life	Identity, development and professional ethics	Concern for quality
Hypertext	2,3	2,2	1,8	1,5	0,9	2,0	2,0	2,0	2,1	2,1	2,0	1,4	1,3	1,2	1,3	0,6	1,0	2,3	1,0	1,4	1,6	0,6	1,6	1,5	1,0	1,2
Video-lesson	2,5	2,2	2,0	1,2	1,7	1,2	1,7	2,0	1,6	1,7	2,0	1,4	1,1	0,9	1,0	0,9	1,0	1,9	1,0	1,3	1,4	0,4	0,5	1,2	0,9	1,0
Simulator	2,5	2,5	2,3	0,9	0,3	0,4	0,6	2,1	1,0	1,9	2,3	2,2	1,8	0,8	0,4	0,6	0,7	2,8	2,0	2,0	2,3	0,7	1,5	1,4	0,7	1,3
Virtual library	1,3	1,4	1,4	0,9	0,3	1,6	2,2	2,5	2,4	1,2	1,4	1,0	1,0	1,2	1,0	0,6	0,8	2,5	1,4	1,1	1,3	0,4	1,6	2,1	0,8	1,0
Graphical forum	1,7	1,5	1,6	1,3	0,4	1,4	1,2	2,4	1,5	1,3	1,7	1,2	1,8	2,3	1,5	1,9	1,6	1,8	1,2	1,7	1,5	1,9	1,9	1,4	1,3	1,0
Virtual classroom	2,2	2,1	2,1	1,3	2,1	1,6	1,8	2,5	1,5	1,9	2,2	1,3	1,7	1,9	1,8	2,2	1,6	2,0	1,6	1,6	1,6	1,7	1,4	1,5	1,3	1,2
Calendar	0,2	0,2	0,3	3,0	0,3	0,6	0,6	1,4	1,2	0,2	0,2	0,6	0,2	0,3	0,2	0,2	0,4	0,9	0,6	0,2	0,1	0,3	0,4	0,4	0,4	0,8
Lecture	2,6	2,6	2,5	1,4	2,2	1,4	1,9	0,9	1,2	2,7	2,7	1,3	1,4	1,3	1,3	1,5	1,6	1,5	1,0	1,2	2,1	0,8	1,0	1,6	1,6	1,5
Debate	2,2	2,3	2,5	1,4	3,0	0,8	2,0	0,6	1,1	1,7	2,5	2,0	2,5	2,1	2,3	2,7	2,3	1,4	1,7	2,2	1,7	2,7	2,7	1,6	2,0	1,5
Maximum online resources	2,5	2,5	2,3	3,0	2,1	2,0	2,2	2,5	2,4	2,1	2,3	2,2	1,8	2,3	1,8	2,2	1,6	2,8	2,0	2,0	2,3	1,9	1,9	2,1	1,3	1,3
Maximum on campus resources	2,6	2,6	2,5	1,4	3,0	1,4	2,0	0,9	1,2	2,7	2,7	2,0	2,5	2,1	2,3	2,7	2,3	1,5	1,7	2,2	2,1	2,7	2,7	1,6	2,0	1,5
Difference	0,1	0,1	0,3	-1,5	0,9	-0,6	-0,1	-1,7	-1,2	0,5	0,4	-0,2	0,7	-0,2	0,5	0,6	0,6	-1,2	-0,3	0,2	-0,3	0,8	0,7	-0,5	0,7	0,2

Table 5. Appropriateness of the optimal tools for the development of all competences.

4. Factor Analysis for Grading Competences

4.1 Introduction

As stated before in this chapter, in the context of the European Higher Education Area (EHEA) teachers are encouraged to evaluate not only the students' knowledge in a subject (contents) but also the skills they may acquire during the learning process (competences).

Contents have always been evaluated through a course by using traditional methods like exams, test questionnaires, continuous evaluation, practical tasks and depending on the subject the list can continue with much more methods.

But since the implantation of the EHEA, teachers must grade competences too. That means they have to evaluate the performance of a student in different skills like capacity of analysis, capacity of synthesis, capacity to assume new concepts from a subject, capacity to make maths developments or even more complex to evaluate skills like the capacity of working on a team.

For example, in a Computer Science subject where the teacher wants to evaluate the basis of Object Oriented programming it is easy to grade concepts like hierarchy, abstraction or interfaces; but it is difficult for them to evaluate how the students are acquiring the previously mentioned and other skills.

Having this in mind, we wanted to focus on question-based tests to try to extract hidden information between the questions to allow the grading of competences; that is because questionnaires produce a lot of information that is not analyzed by the teachers, sometimes because there is such an amount of information that it is impossible to handle it with the naked eye.

For example in a subject where the teacher uses tests every month to evaluate contents, at the end of the year he/she can have up to 500 questions answered by every single student and the only mark that it is being extracted right now from all this information is the mean.

If the assessment of tests is done online with the help of questionnaires tools from the LMS or any other interoperable tool, it is even easier to use the results of an exam to discover new information from the data.

Since teachers are required to have more than one mark per student and subject in EHEA, one of the motivations of the application of data mining in e-learning is to take profit of the automatic recording of the grades in LMS to automatically grade competences. In this context, an interoperable tool named *Stats Engine* has been developed at La Salle and presented in (Gumara et al., 2008).

4.2 Extraction of Competences

As stated before, it is difficult for the teacher to read reports from question-based test from students when they have answered a large number of questions. In order to simplify the understanding of the learning of the students a statistical technique can be applied to the data.

Since the objective is to reduce the amount of data, Principal Components Analysis (PCA) could be applied. PCA describes the variation among many variables in terms of a few underlying but unobservable random variables so it is an appropriate data mining technique that is going to help teachers to better understand test results.

In this study the data used to perform PCA are test results and our base point would be an X matrix (s × q) where the rows represent students and the columns the questions of question-based tests. A cell from that matrix has a specific score from a student to a question of a test. By performing PCA we would get the matrix named V (q × f) storing the eigenvectors from the decomposition where q is the number of questions of the test and f is the number of factors found in the analysis. A cell from this matrix tells us how much of a question is important in a factor.

Besides that we also get S (f × f), a diagonal matrix holding the eigenvalues of the PCA that give information about how important is a factor in explaining the original variables and how much variance explains respect the other factors. This conversion can be seen in Fig. 1.

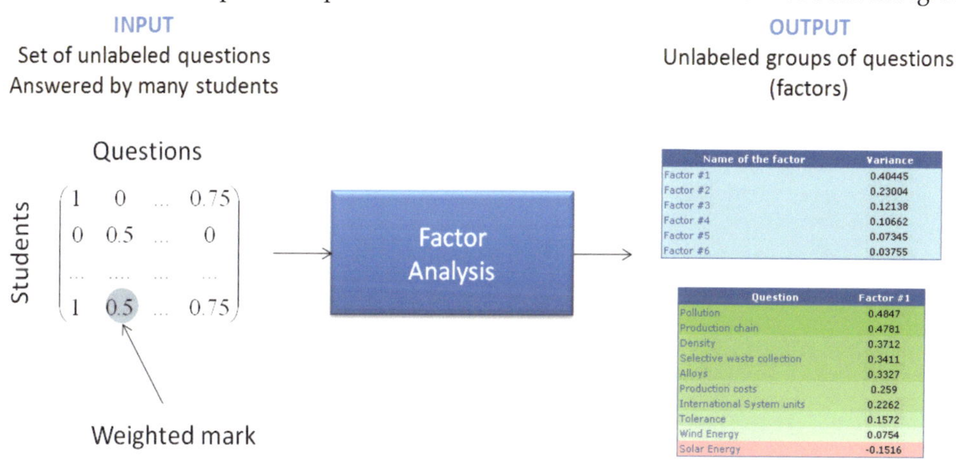

Fig. 1. Use of factor analysis to reduce the dimensionality of tests results.

The aim of our factor analysis is to find those factors which are inferred in the whole imported test dataset if it is reliable enough. For a test data set to be reliable remember that the teacher can reject questions which scores have a negative correlation with the overall scores of the test or that the fact of dropping them from the exam makes Cronbach's alpha to increase.

So, by having a set of unlabeled and reliable questions answered by many students (the more results the better), PCA is able to group questions weightily under a set of unlabeled factors.

We can assume that, if a student has a real skill, he/she will correctly answer the questions related to that skill and vice versa. If the teacher looks carefully to the output from a factor analysis he/she might find some kind of relation between the questions with higher loads, both positive and negative, from the same factor. This relation can be motivated by two facts:

- The questions talk about the same concept, so the students who know about this concept answer correctly the same kind of questions and vice versa, or what is more interesting,
- the questions belong to the same competence or group of competences a student may acquire.

An example of that can be seen in Fig. 2 where an eigenvector for the second factor explaining the most variance is showed. The results belong to an exam of a Data Transmission subject performed at La Salle. The dark green and red questions are the ones that the factor places greater emphasis on; questions 6, 16, 18, 17, 12 and 11 (by this order) are the ones determining the underlying factor #2 as they have the highest positive loads. The dark red marked questions may also be considered by naming the factor if they belong to a clear opposite competence to former questions. Crossed questions belong to the original test but they were rejected from the analysis according to unreliability detection performed by *Stats Engine* and explained at (Gumara et al, 2008).

Question	Factor #2
6. Data communications model	0.5367
16. Analog modems	0.3858
18. Transmission impairments	0.2909
17. Analog modems	0.2267
12. Data communications concepts	0.211
11. Baseband data transmission	0.1034
5. A-Law and PCM (Pulse Code Modulation)	0.0767
10. Error detection and control	0.0586
7. Start bit	0.014
14. ADSL2+	-0.0761
1. ASK Modulation (Data Transmission)	-0.0826
8. Trellis graph	-0.1193
19. HDB (High Density Bipolar)	-0.1353
13. QAM Modulation	-0.1532
15. Modulations	-0.1564
4. Error-correcting codes	-0.2263
9. Data transmission system	-0.467
~~20. TDM (Time-Division Multiplexing)~~	-
~~3. Hamming code (error-correcting code)~~	-
~~2. A-Law and Uniform Quantification~~	-

Fig. 2. Vector of loads of a factor from PCA results.

In this example, the factor can be renamed to"Basic general knowledge in the field" since all the questions were theoretical concepts from Data Transmission as opposite from other factors of the same test that grouped questions that implied the application of basic concepts formulas to be correctly answered. One of these factors was named "Modulation knowledge in practice".

Automatically label questions under skills or competences is a great feature that will surely help teachers when planning their future exams but right now we do not have any information about the performance of a student in each factor.

This performance can be measured with principal components scores. If a student gets a good positive score in "Basic knowledge in the field of study", it will mean that he/she is good in learning concepts by heart.

But scores are not directly generated by PCA, they have to be calculated with the help of the original qualification data and the PCA output.

Let V (q × f) be the matrix of eigenvectors and X (s × q) the original dataset matrix, (Jobson, 1994) uses the relationship Z = XV to find student scores to factors. Z (s × f) contains the principal components scores from each student to each factor. An example of this can be seen in Fig. 3 where principal components scores for a student are shown.

Factor #1	0.794
Factor #4	0.36
Factor #9	0.16
Factor #3	0.153
Factor #2	0.136
Factor #15	0.121
Factor #14	0.116
Factor #16	0.06
Factor #8	0.048
Factor #10	0.021
Factor #6	-0.0050
Factor #5	-0.022
Factor #7	-0.03
Factor #13	-0.052
Factor #11	-0.091
Factor #12	-0.093

Fig. 3. Principal component scores of a student.

Although the application described in this chapter is intended to be used with test results, the fact of extracting skills performance through PCA can be applied to other kind of sources. For example, a teacher would be able to score competences form other kinds of evaluation he/she may assign to the classroom like projects developed, personal interviews, continuous evaluation, etc.

4.3 Cluster Analysis

The objective of cluster analysis in this research is to automatically group students using the previously calculated factors as the data set to execute it. When the students clustering algorithm is fulfilled a set of unlabeled groups of students is given to the teacher as can be seen in Fig. 4.

In order to process the data, each cluster is assigned a vector of means and a vector of standard deviations, each pair of values belonging to a single factor. By looking at the results and having previously tagged factors, the teacher is now able to label groups.

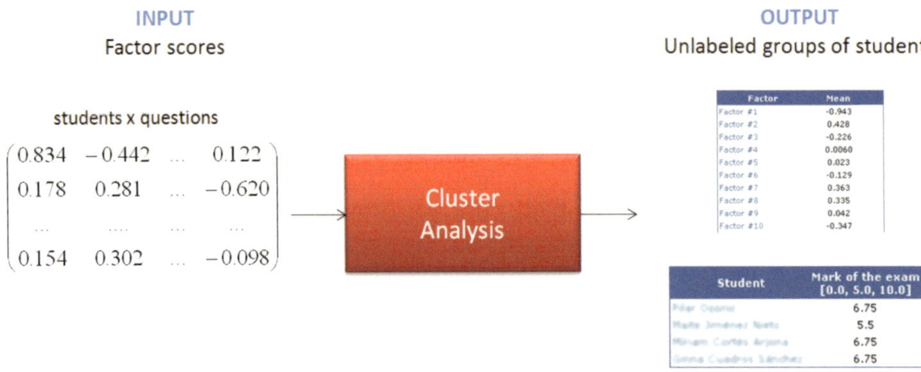

Fig. 4. Use of cluster analysis to group students according to performance on different skills.

5. Conclusions

In this chapter, two examples of data mining applications in e-learning are presented and proved to give knowledge to the teacher.

In the first example, factor analysis has been used in order to set the minimum group of tools for developing an online degree in the European Higher Education Area (EHEA). The research started by polling experienced faculty and then factor analysis was applied to the results to understand their thoughts. Finally, the data from factor analysis was interpreted stating that with a simple LMS of 5 tools and some on campus debates it was possible to cover all the competences. With this analysis it can be understood that a complementariety between face to face classes and online work was needed.

In the second example, a complementary application to questionnaire tools from LMS has been implemented and demonstrated to expand reporting options from open source LMS. The main power of the system is to provide an automatic classification of students according to their performance on different competences. In addition, the system automatically groups the whole group of questions in few factors. Each factor means one or more competences that the student acquires. So this tool becomes a good aid for the competences assessment in the context of an EHEA.

This feature is very useful for the teacher when the scoring periods come. With *Stats Engine* the teacher will not be able to score every single competence required to evaluate (capacity of working on a team may be hard to evaluate with question-based online test results) but will become a great support tool and sure make the scoring of competences and skills easier. The mathematics required have been tested and the algorithms contrasted in order to be suitable for this kind of data.

To summarize, factor analysis is a data mining technique that helped us to reduce a large number of variables in two different problems, both related to learning. By studying the patterns of relationship among many dependent variables, with the goal of discovering something about the nature of the independent variables that affect them, we wereable to give a better interpretation of the data, an interpretation that could not be performed with the naked eye.

6. References

Darlington, R. B. (1997), *Factor Analysis.* Retrieved from http://www.psych.cornell.edu/Darlington/factor.htm

Gumara X., Vicent L., Segarra M. (2008). QTI Result-Reporting Stats Engine for Question-Based Online Tests, *Proceedings of the IEEE ICALT*, pp. 717-721, 978-0-7695-3167-0, Santander, July 2008, CPS, Los Alamitos CA

Jobson J. D. (1994), *Applied Multivariate Data Analysis Volume 2*, Springer.

Kaiser H. F., *The application of electronic computers to factor analysis*, Educational and Psychological Measurement, 1960, 20, pp. 141-151.

Smythe C., Shepherd E., Brewer L. and Lay S. (2002), *IMS Question & Test Interoperability: An Overview*, Final Specification, Version 1.2, IMS.

Vicent, L., G. Bou, X. Avila, J. Riera, J. A. Montero (2007). Which are the best e-learning tools for an Engineering Degree in the European Higher Education area?, *Proceedings of the IEEE ICALT*, pp. 882-886, Niigata, July 2007, CPS, Los Alamitos CA

Tuning (2001). Tuning Education Structures in Europe. http://www.unideusto.org/tuning/

A learning style – driven architecture build on open source LMS's infrastructure for creation of psycho-pedagogically – 'savvy' personalized learning paths

Tania Al. Kerkiri [1], Angela-M. Paleologou [2], Dimitris Konetas [3] and Kostantinos Chatzinikolaou [4]
1. Computer Engineer, University Of Patras, PhD, University of Macedonia, Hellas
2. Assistant Prof. Clinical Psychology & Psychotherapy, University Of Ioannina, Psychological Sector, Hellas
3. Computer Engineer, University Of Patras, PhD Candidate ICT and Distance Education Laboratory, University of Ioannina, Hellas
4. PhD, Tutor at the Regional Training Institute of Hellas

1. Introduction

A host of research has been devoted to the way individuals acquire and perceive educational material in relation to their personality profile (Wallace et al, 2007). However, when e-learning is the case, the same issue becomes more complex than the traditional face-to-face learning process (Graf et al., 2008). Classic teaching approaches do not typically necessitate stern alignment to the learners' skills, aptitudes, preferences, perceptiveness, capacity and/or special abilities -how much more, to any fine inherent differences among knowledge recipients, mostly because they rely on the arbitrariness allowed or tolerated in any live contact. In contrast, it is now widely acknowledged that e-learners do differ in this variety of qualities (Jonassen et al., 2000) in so distinct and challenging ways that e-environments should at some point adjust to them -and this appears more pressing than ever, if effectiveness of e-education is the operative goal, since e-communication entails incalculably heightened demands from both e-tutors and e-learners being notably exposed through the medium. Contemporary e-educational methods are oriented towards satisfying this prerequisite to meet special characteristics of admittedly savvy e-learners and this tendency is reflected in the current web-based e-learning systems (Hauger et al., 2007).
The e-Learning Management Systems (e-LMSs) are most popular in the knowledge provision efforts made, and are constantly evolving, based on contemporary ICT research results, such as multimedia and broadband Internet, as well as offering flexibility in terms of the users' time-management and e-environment familiarization in order to facilitate e-learning processes within recognizable educational settings. They have thus found wide applications in an increasing number of educational institutions. Still, enough issues have to

be additionally addressed and solved before firm assessments of the efficiency of such approaches are satisfyingly conclusive. Such issues are here seen to pertain mainly to two major axes: **a)** the refinement of the very e-system itself by deepening meaningful methodologies of treating e-information and **b)** the expansion of its points of reference by seriously taking into consideration principles, tenets and actual applications of neighboring disciplines, with psycho-pedagogy being dominant in this account. A closer look to recent developments follows to highlight these issues. Emphasis is put in merging the former with the latter axis, with attention paid to the personalization of the content that the e-learner seeks for, and, correspondingly, the personification of the quest of the very same e-learner.

To avoid commonsensical traditional learning methods of the 'one-size-fits-all' approach and to consequently adapt to the users' personalized needs, the e-LMSs structures employ adaptive hypermedia systems (AHS) methods (Brusilovsky, 1996). Current e-Learning platforms have begun to benefit from these innovations. The availability of a variety of learning objects (digital resources that can be shared and accessed through the Internet and reused in multiple teaching and learning contexts) also boosts their wider acceptance. In addition, educational standards such as LOM, SCORM, IMS, and PAPI, have been implemented and lead up to their further development.

Progressively, however, a most interesting shortcoming arose, that an open source LMSs lacked features of personalization and subsequent dedication of learning paths for the individual learner. This limitation highlighted a closely related additional need: any features of personalization that would eventually emerge from research oriented towards satisfying such newly arising requirements should be structured by paying close attention to, and taking action for incorporating features which would directly and functionally reflect psycho-pedagogical theory in hard practice - indeed, using an automated procedure. Early efforts that approached provision of personalised learning paths were either based on the performance of the learner (Carchiolo et al., 2007), or on indications of her/his preferences (Graf et al., 2008). Many existing open source LMSs (e.g., Moodle) still confine their personalization approaches to adapting their interface to the preferences of the learner - a feature, which, however positive might be, does not, however, escape the peril of overgeneralization, thus leaving a considerable gap in the field of multidimensional provisions that become progressively essential for the contemporary e-user's needs. In addition, the mode of tracking e-learners' preferences has in many such instances risked breaching of personal data and confidentiality.

In this light, the current work firstly examines psycho-pedagogical principles connected to Technological Enhancement Learning in some detail, in order to tackle issues of interest in helpful tools and features of a capacity to be exploited for further improvements. It then proceeds in proposing an architecture that can be applied upon the current structure of any LMS and may contribute to a more integrative, even holistic approach of personalization. To this end, key-learning psycho-pedagogical theories with an emphasis on dialectic cognitive-constructivism are earlier discussed pointing at an effective knowledge provision favouring personalization; the theoretical background of adaptation is examined as the basis for their implementation; research done towards this purpose is selectively reviewed; and learning styles are inspected as a palpable method to concretize outcomes from the amalgamation of influential tenets which were selected as superior on personalization-relevant precepts.

2. Background

2.1. Psycho-pedagogical theories in Technological Enhancement Learning (TEL)

Technology Enhanced Learning systems (TEL) is a term referring to the actual activity of learning with the support of technology as inferred to be constantly evolving to incorporate increasingly sophisticated functions for the best interest of e-users. Important enhancements in this respect may well be signified by solidification of psycho-pedagogical precepts into e-provisions for advancing e-learning efficacy. This area will be hereafter looked at.

Each learning process may be perceived as a cognitive encapsulation of transformed information that is offered by different sources into new forms of (brain/thinking-) patterns /schemata. The nature of these transformations distinguishes the type of the pertinent learning strategy applied each time for elaboration. Each strategy in its own right constitutes a descriptor of this process. Largely, learning theories have evolved from behaviorism, holding that the 'student' is an 'empty container', but have eventually been scrutinized within the realm of cognitive approaches, averring that the process is dependent on brain functioning due to thinking activity in response to the information that is imported. A radical development of these conceptualizations has been relatively lately offered by the constructivist view according to which the 'student' creates his/her own milieu of significance (Ally, 2004). By concretization of the cognitivist metaphor: 'mind as computer' in both i) positivist methodological and ii) symbolic theoretical precepts, constructivism has gradually evolved to delineate with cognitive schemata, analyses and met-analyses, thus becoming a major learning paradigm, eventually termed cognitive constructionist approach (Wallace et al., 2007). This tenet places constructivism at the core of the most dynamic conception of contemporary management of learning, notably as it has lately encompassed a social milieu notion, wherein meaning is created by virtue of the learner's frame of reference as multiply related to people, places and objects plus to self- and time- dimensions.

Simpson (2002) credibly argued that constructivism is a psychological and philosophical perspective, and an epistemology rather than merely a learning theory. Indeed, without refuting certain behaviourist tenets, it is predominantly referred to as a learning theory in line with cognitivism (see, e.g., Schunk, 2003), in that it fosters active involvement of the student in the learning process that is offered within a democratic, dialectic environment aiming at essentially 'extracting' knowledge from within the individual, as structured or 'semi-structured' mental schemata allow for building new concepts upon 'preexisting' patterns. Notably, the latter are highly subjective, hence have to be regarded as (treatable as) individualized. It is foreseeable that increasingly educators and institutions will tend to adopt this line of thinking when handling educational issues especially in the realm of e-education, and to eventually challenge the traditional passively-lectured-trainee view, with a growing appreciation of different ways of prompting students to 'knowing the world'.

Constructivism acknowledges the active role of the learner in interpreting reality (Larochelle et al. 1998), challenging the objectivist view which suggests that 'facts speak for themselves' and it thus offers an alternative philosophy, according to which constructions and views of the world are not stable, but are in continuous change being largely built upon past experiences and potentially directed by the learner's degree of initiative to precisely energize alternative interpretations at each given moment of the knowledge experience. Unfolding in time constructivism has well passed its initial 'versions' of moderate/ exogenous approach, which dictated a close inspection of the learner by a tutor still bound to exert increased control over both the knowledge recipient and the teaching content. The theory's two major consecutive phases/versions, though, have underlined the importance of gradual suspension of directiveness, at first favouring the radical/endogenous facilitation of knowledge acquisition, wherein democratic processes ease accessibility to knowledge. At its latest articulation, the approach inclined favouring the furthest conception of dialectic constructivist recourse, where a tutor acts as a mediating 'scaffold' remotely guiding the student near conquering, beyond knowledge, the alternating paths to it (Dalgarno, 2002).

Even though current theories embed elements originating from behaviorism and cognitivism, however, emerging online strategies tend to place emphasis on participation in online collaborations and in fact move to set as a goal the implementation of constructivism (Jonassen, 1999). With the support of rapid technological developments these modern trends in education lead to new methods of knowledge delivery. Ally (2004) claimed that all three approaches of learning can be used successfully at the process of designing online learning environments, by using "behaviourist strategies to teach 'what' (facts), cognitive strategies to teach 'how' (processes and principles) and constructivist strategies to teach 'why' (higher level thinking that promotes personal meaning and situated and contextual learning)".

Consequently, TEL should ably support and adapt to various psycho-pedagogic methods, as well as to the different functional requirements provided by these approaches (Lee, 2008).

Even though Dalsgaard (2005) partly concurred with Ally (2004) in the prospect of combining theoretical tenets, however, he also suggested that it is not possible to construct a generic-catholic-universal framework for TEL, because it should be founded on a specific learning theoretical approach, which, nevertheless, cannot give answers to all questions of educational design. Dalsgaard accordingly proposed the development of three consecutive frameworks based on three adjunct theoretical tenets on learning:

a) The cognitivist approach: having grown into a doctrine based on the various time-, empirical observation-, and hard data of field research evidence- proof, that there are mental structures underlying not only thought, but also emotion, as well as the very perception and interpretation of both, inner/internal and outer/external source information (Lazarus, 1999). Gardner (1993), whose multiple intelligence theory is based on cognitivism, asserts that mind consists of numerous fairly specific and independent computational mechanisms, and it is in this context that research on learning styles has also been promoted. Based on cognitive learning theory, the structure of content of the cognitive matter should be organized hierarchically. Relevant research (Deshler, 1986) has surely led to the conclusion that students learn mainly from the progressive and relation-linked construction of knowledge. This approach may well find applications in a Learning Management System (LMS) with a psycho-pedagogically driven learning path creation module.

b) The radical, as interlocked with the dialectic, constructivist approach: holding that learning is a subjective and internal process of construction of (subjective) meanings and is considered as a result of the organization and the adaptation of new information in already existing knowledge. Students are able to structure their mental forms from facts (experiences) filtering them through their previous experiences. The individual determines how to proceed based on his or her unique needs, perceptions, and experiences, distinguishes known from unknown, identifies resources available to support learning efforts, and formalizes and tests personal beliefs (Hannafin et al., 1999).

This constructivist view is cogitated in the work of Ernst von Glaserfeld (1984), the psychologist who depicted it as "... a radical theory of knowledge" –knowledge, as seen not to reflect an objective, ontological reality, "but exclusively an ordering and organization of a world constituted by our experience" (p.24). Learning here is not taken as a phenomenon of the "stimulus-answer" type. The challenge faced by the teacher is how to build hypothetical model(s) for the diverse cognitive worlds of students, which might be extremely different to those initially 'predicted' (von Glaserfeld, 1996) -a challenge, that may well be met by LMSs. Lastly, the third framework advised to function in synergy by Dalsgaard was:

c) The activity theory approach: interpreting the *actions* of the individual as components of wider *activities* that are meaningful in social and practical situations of the physical world. Actions actually produce novel mental forms and structures that can be viewed as tools of interactive usefulness. Such powerful tools, in turn, may shape the basis of knowledge and learning, especially e-learning (Nardi, 1996). In this perspective, designers of a learning resource system implementing constructivism have to analyze human activity systems based on psycho/socio-cultural, psycho/socio-historical criteria focusing on the interaction of human activity and consciousness within its relevant environmental context. Educators have started to conceive the interesting possibilities of using technology (Fjeld et al, 2002), but the change in the psycho-pedagogical focus and the variety of psycho-pedagogic requirements import new prerequisites in the way in which the technology should be applied as well as in the way by which such an ideal psycho-pedagogical design should be realized by technology. Even today, technology still supports behaviourist approaches emphasizing instruction and practice rather than learning to learn -how much more, learning self-regulation towards learning. Learning technology should become more flexible, combining progress in both psycho-pedagogical methods and technological tools.

Consequently, a logical question arises: how can e-Learning systems be developed and used so as to apply such concepts, which, however complex they may be they nonetheless constitute an appealing challenge if the best interest of e-learners is to be the ultimate goal? According to the Hannafin et al. (1997) creed, as shown in Figure 1 (borrowed from their work), a pedagogical e-learning system can be founded on a) a learning theory, b) learning principles, and c) the use of technology (and other materials) for different activities in the learning environment. These dimensions represent three clashes of abstraction -the magnitude and depth of which are ideally expected to be reflected on the work of a designer of a learning object system while targeting e-learning success.

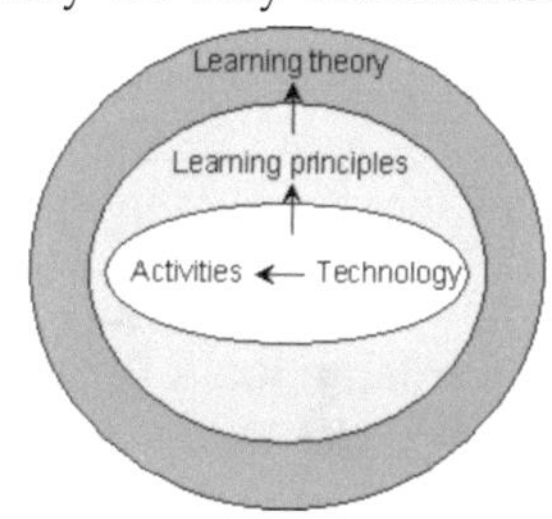

Fig. 1.Hannafin et al (1997) Founds of a pedagogical e-learning system

To the best of the current work's knowledge, a learning object system based in theoretical approaches steeped in cognitive constructivism has not yet been fully developed. The application, though, of processing theory and cognitive-constructivist principles in a parallel mode may surely offer a new perspective on the development and retrieval of learning object systems and it has been accordingly suggested that e-students should be encouraged to become actively involved in such a dynamic system in a manner that they can be creatively engaged in the very design of the repository of these learning objects: this can be achieved by stimulating representations of their knowledge -indeed, on a wide collaborative basis (Bannan-Ritland et al., 2000). In the same spirit, the process rather than the outcome is the optimal focus, with an aim to generalizing individualized gain-scend rather than any over-generalized trite-trend. Thus, an advanced learning objects system would provide the desired process-based frameworks and guidance to harmonize the various resources and approaches - ergo assist the e-learner to make the best use of an authentic constructivist learning environment for a meaningful accessibility to knowledge.

2.2. Learning Management Systems (LMSs)

This most prolific stream of cognitive-constructivist thinking (Vygotsky, 1978; Brown et al., 1989; Jonassen et al., 2000) treats learning as an active collaborative process led by the learner her/himself and steered by problem-solving activities. Nowadays, a very popular means to provide knowledge is through information technology-based systems developed to support electronic delivering of knowledge. These systems are widely known as Learning Management Systems (LMSs), and, as Lee (2008) explained, they are a wide range of systems that organize and provide access to online learning services for students, teachers, and administrators, and which, as a wide-range set of services, usually include access control, learning content provision, communication tools, and organization of user groups. It is therefore precisely these systems that ought to align with, and keep up the cognitive-constructivist approach for the best interest of e-users.

The LMS are chiefly capable of offering services for administration and management of the learning processes/courses/Learning Resources (LRs), by being based on, rather than straightforwardly providing downright psycho-pedagogical explicit activities (Ismail, 2002). In this sense, psycho-pedagogical context is envisaged as circumscribed within the content of the Learning Resource (LR). Subsequently, the essential constituents of the application logic containing the psycho-pedagogic material are to be coded into the digital learning content. The actual systems designed to support teaching and learning over the Internet are known as Virtual Learning Environments (VLEs). Nevertheless, the common use of the term LMS is to describe the actual role of the VLMs. Henceforth, the term: "e-Learning Management System(s)", abbreviated as: 'e-LMS(s)' is adopted to describe the functionalities of the VLMs.

2.3. Adaptation & Personalization in e-LMSs

Adults, the main recipients of e-LMSs provisions especially when solely e-learning requirement is the case, have specific needs regarding their e-training, as they face specific restrictions, mainly connected to time, personal obligations and vocational duties, along with possible limitations in terms of the degree of their familiarization with knowledge accessibility and fast-track acquisition tactics as well as possible ambiguities and even insecurities on refining their vision and prospects for developing their professional career - especially as the latter is increasingly connected to pertinent educational needs, which, in turn, are mainly incited within a rapidly evolving era towards life-long-learning demands and reforms. Moreover, adult e-learners are fairly seen as of a more-or-less solidified personality (Rogers, 1999), with more-or-less rigid cognitive schemas and with a more-or-less reluctance if not resistance to re-evaluate attitudes and re-script interpretations. These as challenges are to be met by the e-LMSs. To fulfill these needs e-LMSs have to be adaptable to the e-learners' current state/profile. Adaptive Hypermedia Systems (AHSs) do provide the theoretical principles of adaptation sought for (Brusilovsky, 1996) being the systems that can alter the interface or their content in accord with the attributes of their user. Web-based e-Learning systems are AHS with applicability especially in educational settings.

Adaptation techniques can be largely distinguished into two categories: i) those that provide navigation support and ii) those that provide presentation support. Several implementations of these techniques are on the whole based on facets of the direct navigation of the user, potentially differential interfaces for each user, etc. An adaptive system that supports such aspects must be designed so as to take into consideration:

A. the user's goal or user's task as related to the context of the hypermedia system,
B. the user's background, i.e., his/her previous experience beyond the subject of the hypermedia system, which is relevant enough to be considered –including lemmas such as the user's profession, experience of work in related areas, etc, and, finally,
C. the e-user's preferences as understood here to include learning styles and indications on profiling any additional number of their properties.

Features of the first category match the situational dimensions of the e-use ad hoc.

Features of the second category concern the content presented in each user. It is here deemed that an adaptive e-LMS emphasizing content personalization should contain:

1. a learner history profile, on details about his/her broadly relevant background, history of thematic preferences, degree of past (un)successful exploitation of the medium, demographic characteristics such as age, gender, family status, training objectives, as well as alternative objectives envisaged and/or hoped for in the course of the e-search
2. a learning resources (LRs) detailed description, with records of existing contents and capabilities plus updates on additional auxiliary and/or supplementary tools, and
3. a correlation function associating e-learner's characteristics with characteristics of the LRs during the learning process - that is, a function that accounts for various facets of the effect that several LRs characteristics have (and had) upon the e-learner. Finally,

Features of the third category refine and deepen the conditions of e-use by pondering into the e-learner's qualitative characteristics, her/his capabilities in knowledge acquisition that is described by his/her learning style, traits and trends regarding e-content uses, etc.

2.4. Learning resources and their role in personalization in e-LMSs

As indicated, a LR is adequately described as any digital entity which can be used, reused and/or referenced during a technology-mediated learning process - hence useable for learning, educational, and/or training purposes. The LRs are in the core of a e-LMSs with the latter being the apt vehicle for the LRs to be provided in a most discernible and at the same time flexible formulation for education and practice.

Their probably most generative method is their capability to construct small, independent units that can be (re)used and (re)arranged in taught e-courses. The creation of different courses is an apposite combination of these e-course units. Moreover, in current e-LMSs several methods are available to create the same educational result, as they provide i) a variety of LRs formats (docs, html, ppt presentations, video/audio files, different kinds of questionnaires etc) and ii) a vast collection of tools, as for assessment (particularly of types automatically scored and stored, as multiple choice), discussion forums, chat, file sharing, video conferences, shared whiteboards, message, e-portfolios, content uploading, students' work return, peer assessment, student groups admin, their grades' collection and clustering, questionnaires, tracking tools, etc. Most recently developed features in these systems include wikis, blogs, RSS and 3D virtual learning spaces. This variety allows the e-tutor to comfortably select from a wide range of facets in order to address each e-learner's learning needs - on the basis of significant findings (Graf et al., 2008) establishing that the learning process is highly and effectually facilitated when the learner learns the way s/he prefers.

2.5. Learning standards

Notwithstanding their indisputable assets, the reusability and interoperability of learning objects has been presented as a major problem in adaptive learning, inasmuch solutions of their technical linking are not directly presupposed. Standards have been thus adopted by the e-learning community to facilitate and foster interoperability and reuse of learning artifacts among different e-learning platforms. The pertinent use of predefined sets of metadata promotes the exchange of LRs among different e-learning systems and content providers, while offering higher potentials for finding existing learning content as well. Such standards for the learning resources are Learning Object Metadata (LOM) and Sharable Content Object Reference Model SCORM[1]. Standards have likewise been developed for the description of learners as well, such as LIP, PAPI, Dolog LP, FOAF[2].
LOM and PAPI are important to briefly review in the present account, as viewed to not only be popular, but also concentrate the most interesting characteristics for multi-purpose LMS applications in accord with psycho-pedagogical cognitive-constructivist principles.

2.5.1. Learning Object Metadata (LOM) standard

Indeed, most broadly used for the description of the LR is the Learning Object Metadata (LOM) standard. Its specifications can be found on the Learning Technology Standards Committee (LTSC) of IEEE (2002), the certified body that originally promoted LOM, in order to provide structured descriptions of every digital entity, namely, the LR, precisely towards learning, education, and/or training usability. To describe the content of LRs, LOM is stratified into a pre-defined vocabulary classified in nine main categories:

1. general, which groups the general information that describes the resource as a whole,
2. life-cycle, referring to the history- and current state- related resource features, and those that have affected this resource during its evolution,
3. meta-metadata, on information about the meta-data per se,
4. technical, about the technical requirements and characteristics of the resource,
5. educational, which groups the educational and pedagogic features of the resource,
6. rights, defining the rights and conditions of use for the resource,
7. classification, which describes the taxonomy of the resource, and finally,
8. annotation, offering and storing history of comments on the LR's educational use.

These categories treat a given object in an inclusive way, thus allowing easy usage of them in an e-Learning system.

2.5.2. Personal And Private Information (PAPI) Standard

The Personal and Private Information (PAPI) standard presents the learner's educational and professional progress. The PAPI descriptors refer to the learner's:

1. educational level, learning experiences, and background,

---

[1] specifications of SCORM can be found in Advanced Distributed Learning (ADL, 2004).

[2] a brief comparative presentation of these standards can be found in Ounnas et al. (2006).

2. performance in different educational topics, certificates, qualifications, licenses, diplomas, skills granted by authorized institutes,
3. rights to access information (herein suitable to enrich by ethical standards insertion)
4. preferences, as for, e.g., written/spoken language, favored document format etc, or LRs.

2.6. Learning Styles

Keefe (1991) asserted that learning style is both a student characteristic and an instructional strategy. As a student characteristic, learning style indicates how a student learns and likes to learn. As an instructional strategy, it informs about cognition, context, and content of learning aspects. Roy & Chi (2003) examined whether the way a learner approaches the educational process, the way s/he searches for information, and even the LRs' format and content, contribute to improving his/her learning performance. Mitchell (1994) identified more than 100 proposed models which claim to depict the e-learners learning styles.
From the available learning style models, the Felder and Silverman model prevailed for the current account, chiefly due to its clear-cut multidimensionality. This model distinguishes two styles of learning, physical and sensing, and contradistinguishes their subtypes by discerning special properties: For each style, 5 different learning types of learning are further defined: sensing-intuitive, visual-verbal, deductive-inductive, active-reflective, and sequential-global. It also provides clear relationships between the different characteristics of the LRs and the learning characteristics of the learners, as shown on Table 1.

Learning style	LR properties	Learning style	LR properties
Sensing	Experiments, data, facts, LRs of high interactivity	Intuitive	Pictures, diagrams, flow charts, primitives, concepts, theories, LRs of high semantic density
Visual	Books, printings, diagrams, flow charts, videos, avi, presentations, timelines, demonstrations, films	Verbal	Case studies, experiments
Deductive	Books, diagrams, presentations	Inductive	Text, books, pictures, videos, avi
Active	Experiments, tutorials, presentations	Reflective	Papers, books, self-assessments
Sequential	Books, flow charts, algorithms	Global	Maps, pictures, novels

Table 1. Felder-Silverman learning types and their preferred LR characteristics

Outcomes of the learning style models have been used in several experiments (Graf et al., 2008; Kerkiri et al. -in press) as a method to provide personalization.
3. Determinants of an architecture built upon open-source LMSs
Incentives: Stepwise following the evidence examined above, the currently proposed model of content personalization, by employing TEL enhancements linked with psycho-pedagogical tenets, is triggered by a number of key-factors, including: **a)** the desired availability of a variety of well annotated LRs for the same educational purpose, with each one: **i)** having different characteristics that shall feed the LMS, and **ii)** being able to be contained in either an internal or an external repository; and **b)** the preferable and advisable

large number of capabilities that would yield automated matching of the characteristics of LRs on the one hand, and e-learners' on the other.
Additionally posited here is that the desired automated matching is to be guided by proper description of the LRs properties. Such directly generated knowledge indicates the LRs' educational capabilities and it also eases their automatic discovery from software agents.
Initially, to tackle any availability of such capabilities in the open source LMSs, the most popular of them were exhaustively evaluated. Open source LMSs were focused upon mainly because: i) a great number of the educational institutes satisfyingly support their curricula by them and ii) a great number of resources are already available for them.
Trailing: Still, on the pretty colloquial, yet ratified whim: 'better is the enemy of the good', it was postulated that at least three e-attributes on provisions to e-learners could be closely inspected: First, the existence (or not) of a shielding umbrella-formation keeping essential structures of the already existing fundamental framework both intact and operable without jeopardizing the system's accord. Second, the existence (or not) of any kind of supporting platform furnished with tools, concepts and features well-coordinated to offer qualitative services via a quantitatively rich range of educationally valuable materials (e.g., e-teaching modules); such a platform would not merely function as a pallet of 'assorted' supplies, but as a stage of action in terms of the required interoperability of these materials. A third, and equally critical determinant to trail - and, if not found, to create anew in favour of e-learners' satisfaction and progress - would be a robust mathematical formula, namely, an algorithm, which would be designed in a psycho-pedagogic spirit and be performed so that it would unambiguously rule, stem and sort information, material, and sequences for the best interest of all e-users engaged in an electronically conducted educational interaction.
Since these prerequisites point at, and almost directly presuppose personalization processes, a transitory trailing of favourable features would involve exploration of the capabilities of the existing open source LMSs for fostering such complex entities, equipment and operations. Results of this search are briefly presented in the following paragraph.

3.1. Open source LMSs personalization capabilities

To experiment on the open source e-LMSs capabilities towards personalization the most popular of them were installed: ATutor, Ilias, Claroline, Dokeos, Docebo, Moodle (Kerkiri & Paleologou, 2009). To explore their pertinent capabilities several apt criteria emerging from the definition of personalization systems as stipulated above (see section 2.3) were set: Thus, it was examined whether: i) these systems have a user model, ii) the LR is described as an autonomous entity, iii) these LMSs use properties to describe LRs and learners, iv) they create and/or handle repositories and lastly, vi) they employ a personalization algorithm.
Hence, the same course was created within each one of them. Some interesting findings emerged from this comparative research:
1) by and large, all LMSs contain a sufficient number of different kinds of resources and activities, as, e.g., forums/chats, questionnaires, quizzes, html/doc/pdf documents, surveys etc. This capability may potentially support different kinds of LRs which can better fit with different learning style types. This large, yet fairly scattered, variety, though, may well be seen as confusing for, e.g., an inexperienced e-tutor, who might be puzzled as to what and how to chose from, and technically, even as a 'l'art-pour-l'art' almost inconsequential feature, not necessarily functional for e-users;

2) in examining their storage-structure, each of these LMSs surfaced to lack consistency in supporting each LR and learning activity; besides, storage is not performed uniformly for all material. Albeit standards, such as SCORM, are often adopted as mediators for the transfer, yet, the observed storage disparities tend to complicate sharing between the several LMSs;
3) these e-LMSs do not support a storage-structure to maintain the properties of the LRs. Although Ilias was a brilliant exception, able to record LRs properties, and to follow the LOM standard, still, it did not seem to further utilize them. So, the e-tutor is deprived from seeing these properties during a course creation, and thereafter s/he is somewhat impeded to clearly decide on selecting over various features of, e.g., their quality, their place in a learning chain, etc, and, generally, feels uncertain of their value in an educational section.
4) only some of them, as, for instance, Docebo, Claroline, and Dokeos, as well as Ilias, do support repositories containing LRs, thus allowing their reusability. Also, the same e-LMSs support a tree structure (learning path) to build the course, while their capability to incorporate LRs from external repositories does not reach a full hierarchical taxonomy - so they tend to treat the LRs as rather unstructured, dispersed repository for the course; also,
5) no one of them managed to provide an automated method of creating the course - how much more to render genuine and serviceable personalization methods.

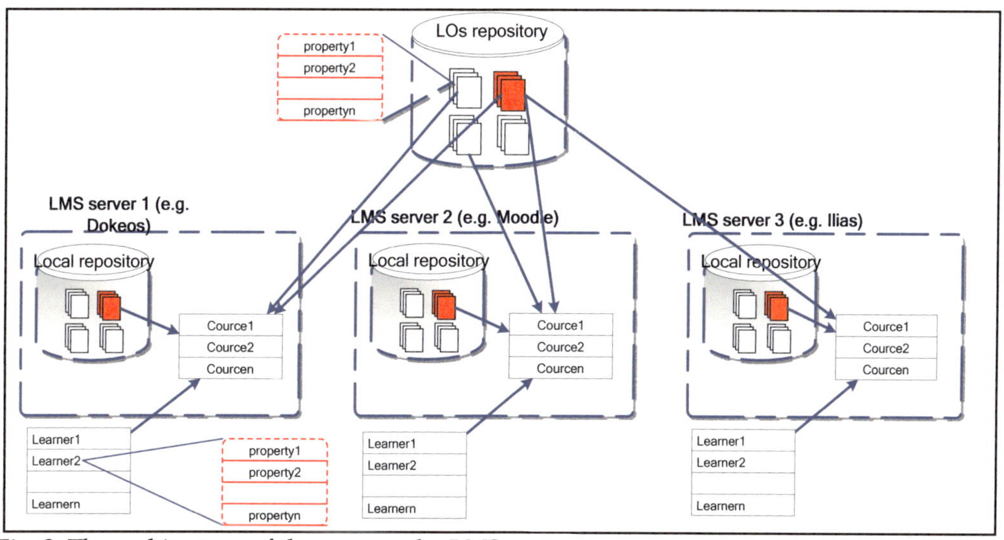

Fig. 2. The architecture of the proposed e-LMS

The herein proposed use of the LRs in e-LMSs is seen in Figure 2, displaying the relationship between the LRs and the e-LMS. As seen, this design ensures that properties of the LRs are obvious at a glance, facilitating their manual or automatic selection for even highly dedicated courses based on the e-learner's profile and their educational outcomes.

4. The structural components of the proposed architecture

To build a reliable personalization algorithm in open source-LMSs and in chorus keep these LMSs intact within their current structure, a concrete course of action is here submitted, chiefly pertaining to the creation of: **I.** a super-structure, **II.** an integrative platform, planned to encompass certain key- functions and modules, and **III.** a bridging algorithm aiming at cognitive constructivist-founded personalization. This process is stepwise described below:

I. Creation of a super-structure, which would uphold the LRs properties and subsequently describe the factors that determine their capabilities. It is here suggested that upholding the properties may be attained by using metadata selected from an educational standard. This information is tied to the LR and is swept along the LR during its export from the LMS, henceforward being available in other LMSs through its import to them. This makes the LR both reusable and self-defined, thus reducing the LRs' creation cost. In a similarly developed additional structure, apposite information for the learner would be maintained as well.

Technologies that can identify an entity as a knowledge-structure along with its properties, their values, cardinalities, and constraints are those of the Semantic Web (Berners-Lee et al., 2001). In its framework, to define an entity a unique id (Unified Resource Identifier -URI) is ascribed and its properties described through metadata. For each instance of these entities a unique URI is also defined, and several properties are attached to it, via the format:

`<resource Id><propertyName><property value>`

e.g.

`<LR-#201><hasDifficulty><Very Difficult>`

which means that the LR having URI=LR#109 has the property: 'hasDifficulty', and the value of this property is 'Very Difficult'.

This method allows the extension of the LR's description, without affecting the whole model, with properties which have not been initially predicted.

II. Design of an integrative platform based on these two structures and automating the course creation. The modules accommodated in the platform of this architecture are seen in Figure 3, where input/output, functionality of each module, as well as their intermediate informational flow, are graphically shown as staged in a dynamically interoperable manner.

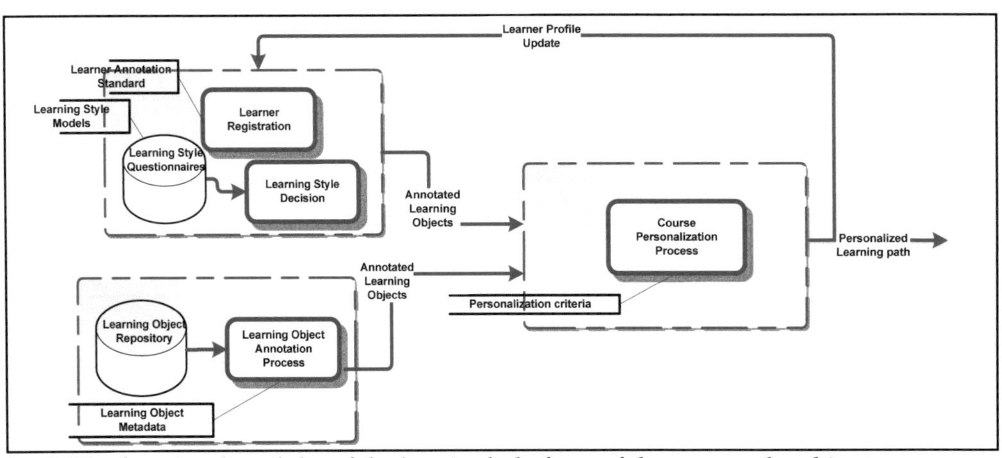

Fig. 3. The functional modules of the 'staging' platform of the proposed architecture

One by one, these modules are reviewed below:

a) learner profiling module: this module creates and maintains in a repository various learner-related demographic information (e.g., age, gender, learner's current goal and interest in the educational material), navigational history, etc. (Muntean & Muntean, 2008). These entries are maintained in a continuous and uninterruptible process via:

i) personal direct registration: securing information about the user's demographic details and (dis)likings, as time availability, appealing material format, means of delivery, etc.

ii) indirect updating derived from his/her navigation in the e-LMS. This type of information may relate to his/her progress, preferences, constraints, inclinations, etc.

Current LMSs, even the open source ones, keep tack of a number of a learners' actions, e.g. the time s/he spent over a course, the order in which s/he was engaged with several LRs and activities, the scores s/he made on quizzes, etc, thus tracing evidence on what might affect his/her professional carrier and on how his/her profile might be shaped. However, such records: are typically stored without being further utilized in a maximally productive way; remain independent entries far from being interoperable with other LMSs features; are invariably static, based on fixed characteristics of the e-user, not easily, flexibly, or at all correlated (e.g., tag a change of her/his navigation habits); and are not incorporated within the existing infrastructure in order to improve quality of her/his access to knowledge.

In contrast, one of the most important functionalities of the module submitted here is the learners' learning style specification, usually achieved by issuing the germane questionnaire. On the basis of its partial and total scores, the learner's profile is then manually updated.

Certain efforts have been made (Tuparov & Dureva, 2008) to enhance LMSs with the proper infrastructure and the functionality of learning style-decision oriented web-sites. Graf and colleagues (2008) reached extraction of the learning style based on the LRs that a learner has preferred. Generally, though, invariably using indirect updating of the learner's profile risks some considerable ambiguity. In this respect, perhaps the only reliable property for claiming valid results is the e-learner's performance per se - again, only when his/her examinations marks, and course/semester grades can be electronically delivered.

As learning approaches and strategies are still over implementation; tackling effect(s) of several factors such as learning style is under investigation; and concurrent e-LMSs are still under development; it appears that the safest method to trace the e-learners' learning style is an immediate update through a well-designed questionnaire.

If $C = \{c_1, c_2, ..., c_n\}$ defines the proffered structure describing the learners of an LMS, each learner c_i has k properties, posed by the ordered vector $c_i = \{p_1, p_2, ... p_k\}, \forall\ i = 1, ..., n$. Every one property of the learner assumes a value from a well-defined domain. Explicitly, if:

```
hasPreferredLanguage, hasPreferredFormat, hasCertification, hasUserRole,
hasIntendeduserRole, hasLearningStyle, has Age, hasGender, hasLearningTime,
hasPerformance, hasClassification
```

are all part of the description properties of a learner. Their corresponding domains are:

```
PreferredLanguage={el, en, fr, …}
PreferredFormat={pdf,doc,wav,avi,...,txt}
Certification={Vocational Training, Higher Education, MSc, PhD, Continuous Formation}
UserRole={Beginner, Pro-Intermediate, Intermediate, Post-intermediate, Advanced}
IntendedEnduserRole={Lecturer, Learner, Trainer, Trainee}
LearningStyle={Sensing/Intuitive, Visual/Verbal, Deductive/Inductive,
Active/Reflective, Sequential/Global}
AgeRange={5-8, 9-12,13-15,16-18, 19-23,24-29,30-40,41-50,51-60,60-70, …}
Gender={m,f}
LearningTime={0:30-1,1-2, …}
Performance={ {lessonId, Grade} }, Grade E [0,10]
```

and then his/her profile is:

```
Ci ={hasPreferredLanguage, hasPreferredFormat, hasCertification, hasUserRole,
hasPerformance, hasIntendedEnduserRole, hasLearningStyle, hasAgeRange, hasGender,
hasLearningTime, hasPerformance}
```

Consequently, the vector of the specific learner c_i having id='URI2-User' is:

```
Ci ={User-2,http://www.uom.gr/eLearning/user2.htm,{el,en}, {doc,avi}, MSc, Advanced, 7, Learner, Active/Reflective, 24-29, m, 5-8, {Multimedia,7,6}, {H.2.5.2, Photoshop-Masks} },
```

and his/her description using the ontological language Web Ontology Language (OWL) is:

```
<oxml:instance id="a:L#09"><oxml:instanceOf concept="a:Learner"/>
 <oxml:hasAttribute relation="a:name"><oxml:value>User 2</oxml:value>
 </oxml:hasAttribute>
 <oxml:hasAttribute relation="a:learnerURI">
   <oxml:value>http://www.uom.gr/eLearning/user2.htm</oxml:value>
 </oxml:hasAttribute>
 <oxml:hasRelation relation="a:hasPreferredLanguage" instance="a:el"/>
 <oxml:hasRelation relation="a:hasPreferredLanguage" instance="a:en"/>
 <oxml:hasRelation relation="a:hasPreferredFormat" instance="a:doc"/>
 <oxml:hasRelation relation="a:hasPreferredFormat" instance="a:avi"/>
 <oxml:hasRelation relation="a:hasCertification" instance="a:MSc"/>
 <oxml:hasRelation relation="a:hasUserRole" instance="a:Intermediate"/>
 <oxml:hasRelation relation="a:hasPerformance" instance="a:7.0"/>
 <oxml:hasRelation relation="a:hasIntendedUserRole" instance="a:Learner"/>
<oxml:hasRelation relation="a:hasLearningStyle" instance="a:Active/Reflective"/>
<oxml:hasRelation relation="a:hasAgeRange=" instance="a:13-15"/>
<oxml:hasRelation relation="a:hasGender=" instance="a:f"/>
<oxml:hasRelation relation="a:hasLearningTime=" instance="a:5-8"/>
</oxml:instance>
```

b) learning resource treatment module: the functionality of this module is to create and maintain a repository of well-annotated resources which can be used alternatively to teach the same topic. Towards this aim it has to record a set of LRs and clearly and specifically define their properties, so that each one shall be a self-described entity. These properties can describe their suitability for a specific type of learner, their suitability for a particular course, their potential classification in a learning path, their learning outcomes and educational aims/objectives. Using the various existing standards, e.g., Learning Object Metadata (LOM), or Sharable Content Object Reference Model (SCORM) is a very popular modus operandi to facilitate the LRs description.

A notable advantage of this module is the classification of the LRs in a hierarchical structure. Even the simplest taxonomy which only supports the: is-A relationship provides semantics as to the connection of the classified entities. In this case, a hierarchy is used to describe the learning path of a course, with each node of this hierarchy describing the course sections. This hierarchy also defines pre-requisition chaining (precedence-succession relationships) between the LRs. This categorization and the arrangement in a hierarchical node are further facilitated by usage of existing taxonomies, e.g., ACM especially for the Informatics. Thus:
Let the LRs of a repository be shown by the structure $L = \{l_1, l_2, ..., l_m\}$, where each l_j has l properties $l_j = \{p_1, p_2, ..., p_l\}, \forall\ j = 1, ..., m$. The properties and their domains D consist of the corresponding data elements chosen from educational standards, e.g., LOM. Indicatively, if using the LOM standard, the LR is described as:

```
lip={title, author, hasClassification, hasFormat, hasLanguage, hasResourceContext, hasLearningResourceType, hasInteractivityLevel, isForEndUserRole, hasSemanticDensity, hasCoverage, hasDifficulty, isForLearningStyle}
```

where the domains of these properties are correspondingly:

```
Description,
Classification={H.5.1.1 Web Design Tools, H.5.1.2 Image Processing Tools, ...},
ResourceContext={Vocational Training, Higher Education, MSc, PhD, Continuous
Formation},
LearningResourceType={Exercise, Figure, Book, Lecture, Tutorial, Paper, Diagram,
VideoAudio, Presentation, Lecture, Simulation, Questionnaire, Graph, Index, Slide,
Table, Narrative Text, Experiment, Problem Statement, Self-Assessment},
InteractivityType={Active, Expositive, Mixed},
InteractivityLevel={Very Low, Low, Medium, High, Very High},
SemanticDensity={Very Low, Low, Medium, High, Very High},
Coverage={Very Low, Low, Medium, High, Very High},
Difficulty={Very Easy, Easy, Medium, Difficult, Very Difficult},
isForLearningStyle={Sensing/Intuitive, Visual/Verbal, Deductive/Inductive,
Active/Reflective, Sequential/Global}
hasPerformance={ {lessonId, Grade} }
TypicalLearningTime
```

etc, where Format, Language, UserRole, IntendedEndUserRole, LearningStyle are defined as earlier and the 'lessonId' is derived from the curriculum of each educational institute. Consequently, the description metadata of an LR is:

```
<oxml:instance id="b:LR#201"><oxml:instanceOf concept="b:LearningResource"/>
 <oxml:hasAttribute relation="b:title"><oxml:value>Photoshop CS3</oxml:value>
 </oxml:hasAttribute>
 <oxml:hasAttribute relation="b:description"><oxml:value>Try this illustrated
reference guide ... available information during the exercises</oxml:value>
 </oxml:hasAttribute>
 <oxml:hasRelation relation="b:hasClassification" instance="b:H.5.1.2 Photoshop"/>
 <oxml:hasRelation relation="a:hasFormat" instance="b:html"/>
 <oxml:hasRelation relation="a:hasLanguage" instance="b:en"/>
 <oxml:hasRelation relation="b:hasLearningResourceContext" instance="b: MSc "/>
 <oxml:hasRelation relation="b:hasLearningResourceType" instance="b:SelfAssessment"/>
 <oxml:hasRelation relation="b:hasLearningResourceType" instance="b:Tutorial"/>
 <oxml:hasRelation relation="b:hasLearningResourceType" instance="b:Exercise"/>
 <oxml:hasRelation relation="a:hasInteractivityLevel" instance="a:High"/>
 <oxml:hasRelation relation="a:isForUserRole" instance="a:Pro-Intermediate"/>
 <oxml:hasRelation relation="b:isForIntendedEndUserRole" instance="b:Trainer"/>
 <oxml:hasRelation relation="b:isForIntendedEndUserRole" instance="b:Trainee"/>
 <oxml:hasRelation relation="a:hasCoverage" instance="a:Very High"/>
 <oxml:hasRelation relation="a:hasDifficulty" instance="a:Medium"/>
 <oxml:hasRelation relation="ab:isForLearningStyle" instance="a:Sensing/Intuitive"/>
 <oxml:hasAttribute relation="b:hasPerformance"><oxml:rId>DatabasesII</oxml:rId>
....................
 <oxml:grade>9.81</oxml:grade>
 </oxml:hasAttribute>
</oxml:instance>
```

So, an LR is an entity having a set of properties, which are directly and immediately shown, and can be straightforwardly combined to the properties of the learners, using a set of rules that are derived from the outcomes of the educational system.

c) personalization module: the adjacent personalization module is engaged with applying the proper parameters that connect the learners' characteristics to the ones of the LRs.

The functionality of this module is shown in Figure 4.

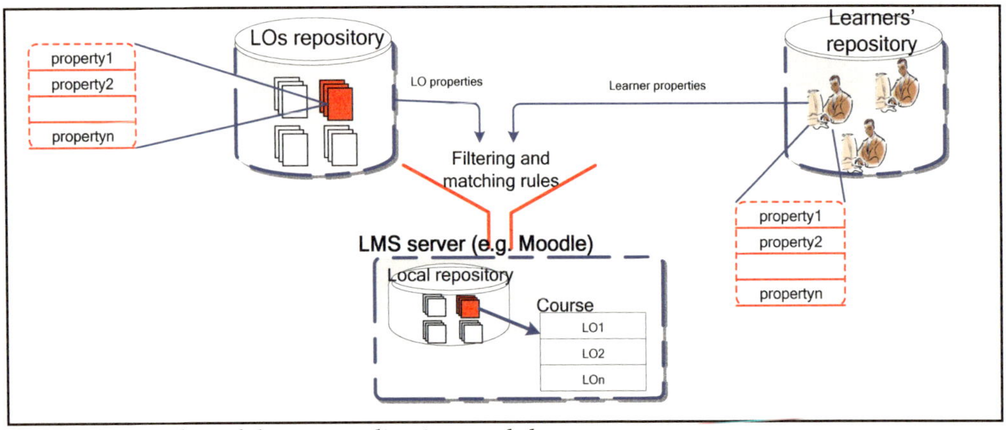

Fig. 4. Functionality of the personalization module

As seen in Figure 4, for a specific learner the personalization module uses the properties of each LR and the intermediate alignment structure that contains the matching rules, while selecting the most suitable learning resource from each node.

To create personalized learning paths the most apt LR is discerned from each node of the hierarchy for the specific learner depending on a number of chosen parameters. To this aim, an intermediate structure is created, used to combine characteristics of the two entities. This structure is of the form:

```
<alignenment>
  <LearnerPropertyId> </LearnerPropertyId>
  <weightL> </weightL>
                              //weight by which it participates in the matching
  <weightl,pr-id> </weightl,pr-id>
  <LRPropertyId></LRPropertyId>
  <weightLR> </weightLR>
                              //weight by which it participates in the matching
<weightlr,pr-id> </weightlr,pr-id>
                              //weight of this instance of the LR property
</alignenment>
```

Indicative entries of this structure are shown in Table 2:

Properties deriving from heuristic rules based on learning style						
Learner properties			Learning resource property			
hasUserRole	0.55	Beginner	hasDifficulty	0.33	Very Easy	0.9
hasUserRole	0.55	Beginner	hasDifficulty	0.33	Easy	0.7
hasUserRole	0.55	Beginner	hasDifficulty	0.33	Medium	0.5
hasUserRole	0.55	Beginner	hasDifficulty	0.33	Difficult	0.3
hasUserRole	0.55	Beginner	hasDifficulty	0.33	Very Difficult	0.1
hasUserRole	0.55	Intermediate	hasDifficulty	0.33	Very Easy	0.3
hasUserRole	0.55	Intermediate	hasDifficulty	0.33	Easy	0.5
hasUserRole	0.55	Intermediate	hasDifficulty	0.33	Medium	0.9
hasUserRole	0.55	Intermediate	hasDifficulty	0.33	Difficult	0.5
hasUserRole	0.55	Intermediate	hasDifficulty	0.33	Very Difficult	0.1

Table 2. Indicative entries connecting learner and LRs properties

This structure is used to create rules that match learners and LRs. Each rule indicates that a learner of given properties identified by the: <LearnerPropertyId> participates in the match with a specific weight <weight$_{L}$> and these are connected with specific properties of the LR having, e.g., id: <LRPropertyId> which also participates with a specific weight <weight$_{LR}$>. The connection between these properties becomes more accurate by also linking the intermediate values of these properties, which bare their own specific weights: <weight$_{lr,pr\text{-}id}$> and <weight$_{l,pr\text{-}id}$>. This structure combines propertyIds of LRs and learners respectively for each specific value of these properties. As seen in the scenario of Table 1, the properties: 'hasUserRole' of the learner and 'hasDifficulty' of the LR are combined, where the property: 'hasUserRole' participates with a weight of 0.55 (weight$_{L}$), while 'hasDifficulty' with a weight of 0.33 (weight$_{LR}$). Moreover, following the same scenario, the intermediate values of each one are aligned to the intermediate values of the other. The weights defined for each intermediate value of these properties, e.g., weigh$_{LR,1}$=0.9 being the weight of the value 'Very easy', for the beginner learner show the % that a 'Beginner' would prefer an 'Easy' LR against a 'Very Difficult' one. In the specific scenario, a Learner having "UserRole"="Beginner" prefers LRs having "Difficulty"="Very Easy", in a percentage 90%, while the preference of the same Learner for "Very Difficult" LRs is 10%.
Adoption of this LRs/learners description and their alignment, as seen in the previous examples, results in that: the learner L#09, prefers LRs of "SemanticDensity"="High", "Difficulty"="High" and "Format"="avi". While examining the LRs of a specific node to find the most suitable ones for this learner, with the LR having, e.g., URI="LR#201", then the following alignment document is going to be created based on the matching of Table 1:

```
<alignenment>
<LearnerPropertyId> L#09 </LearnerPropertyId>
  <connection-to-LR>
  <LRId> LR#201 </LRId>
  <weight>
     <LearnerPropertyId > UserRole, Pro-Intermediate </LearnerPropertyI>
     <weight_L> 0.55 </weight_L>
     <LRPropertyId > Difficulty, High < /LRPropertyId>
     <weight_LR> 0.33 </weight_LR>
     <weight_LR,pr-id> 0.1 </weight_LR,pr-id>
  </weight>
....
  <weight>
     <LearnerPropertyId > UserRole, Pro-Intermediate </LearnerPropertyI>
     <weight_L> 0.55 </weight_L>
     <LRPropertyId> Interactivity,high </LRPropertyId>
     <weight_LR> 0.55 </weight_LR>
     <weight_LR,pr-id> 0.5 </weight_L,pr-id>
  </weight>
...
  <connection-to-LR>
...
</alignenment>
```

By having so far explained the entire integrative platform described above as aimed at resembling a stage of action rather, than merely an assortment pallet, the prospects of its structuring may now be more clearly understood: Along with its modules, this platform carries a number of notions encapsulated in each step of its processes that are here believed to ensure both its expansiveness and its compliance with cognitive constructivist principles. The third component of the proposed architecture is presented below.

III. The bridging algorithm refers to a method that would be robust enough to unambiguously rule, stem and sort information, material, and sequences while being generated in a creative psycho-pedagogic spirit by respect to cognitive constructivist tenets, that would in turn allow the attempted personalization be implemented in the best interest of all e-users involved in the educative e-interactivity.

It is stipulated that this algorithm is not to serve as merely a static formula for connecting different entities of the proffered platform or for linking its contents with existing structures of the Semantic Web; it rather is designed to function as a circuit amid them, thus ensuring interoperability, hence efficacy. It markedly uses the enhanced super-structure offered here, and is shaped in a mature psycho-pedagogic milieu inscribing eclectic methods of the platform that emerged, in a conscious orientation to wisely use the vast pool of the learning objects so as to choose which of the latter shall offer the e-user the optimal learning path.

The personalization algorithm of the presently proffered framework bares different content for the individual learner, so it highly depends on the existence of different LRs for the same educational topic. On this account, in each node of the hierarchy several educational objects are attached and can be used alternatively to teach the same didactic subject to learners of different profiles. The algorithm that selects the most suitable LRs for a dedicated learner follows:

Step 1: For a specific learner, his/her properties are compared to the properties of all the learning resources of each node through the alignment-structure,

Step 2: For each LR of the specific node the weights of all matching properties are multiplied,

Step 3: For each LR a total weight is calculated (formula 1) by summarizing all the intermediate results,

$$weight_{li} = \frac{\sum_{k=1}^{t}\left(w_{lr,i} * w_{LR,k} * w_{L,k}\right)}{\sum_{k=1}^{t}\left(w_{LR,k} * w_{L,k}\right)} \tag{1}$$

where w_{LR} and w_L are the $weight_{LR}$, and $weight_L$, as defined in the alignment structure, the weight $wl_{r,i}$ is the total weight of the instances of the LR, and k is the number of the records of the alignment-structure for which the properties of the LR l_i are matched to this learner. As seen, the weight $w_{l,m}$, ,i.e., the weight of the learner, does not participate in this formula.

Step 4: From each node the LR having the greater weight is selected,

Step 5: The process is repeated for the LRs of the ontology.

This method selects the best ranked LR from each node according to the selection-criteria; consequently, the whole learning path turns out to be the most suitable one.

The concluding choice to be made in this module is a custom-made learning path based on characteristics of the specific learner.

The use of weights is brainwave approach as the fluctuation of their values is very easy. In this way examination of the influence of these parameters can be done, and the promotion of the desired parameters is feasible. For example, if it were supposed that one has to examine whether or not the property "semanticDensity" influences the "Performance" of a specific type of learner, e.g. the one who has "MSc", then, the same course can be delivered twice: firstly using a high weight to this parameter, and later a lower one. For the specific course, inspection of the outcomes of his/her "Performance" as run in parallel results in that the influence of the characteristic "semanticDensity" is checked.

5. Implementation

To attest these proposals a web-based application was implemented and used in parallel with the most popular open source LMS, the Moodle. The software was used to implement the personalization algorithm and Moodle was used to deliver the ensuing course. This application implements the proposed super-structures that store the properties of the LRs and handles these metadata. The maintenance of the LRs properties is seen In Figure 5.

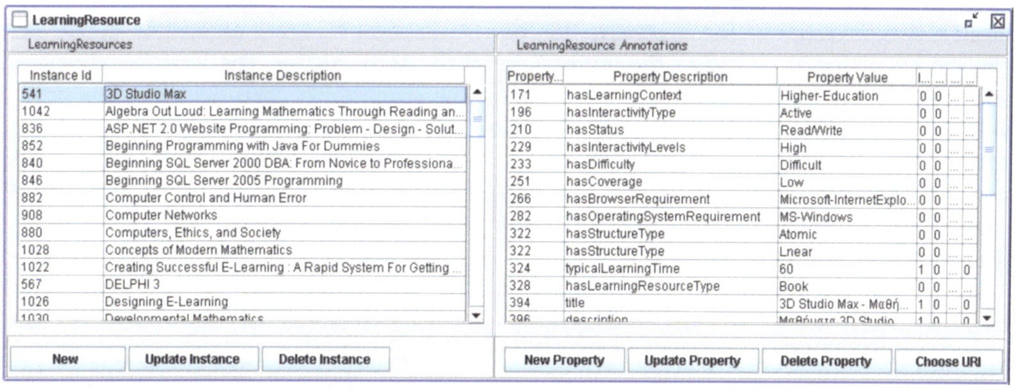

Fig. 5. The LRs Repository and the treatment of their properties

As seen, the properties of the LRs are described using the LOM educational standard. The available resources of the repository used here are shown on the left side and the number of the available properties of a single LR of the repository is shown on the right.

To create the e-course hierarchy, the web was exhaustively searched to discover suitable LRs that met the experiment specifications for alternative learning resources varying in formats, interactivity degree, semantic density degree, context type, etc. While planning the courses, a great effort was put to include a variety of LRs categorized into 20 scrutinized educational activities, intended to cover the overall experimental prerequisites. The ensuing material was thoroughly inspected, evaluated and accordingly attached to the ontology. The adopted personalization method was based on the Felder and Silverman (1998) learning style model. The factors under examination in the pertinent experiment were the effect of the "UserRole" to "Difficulty", "InteractivityLevel", "SemantciDensity" and the effect of "LearningStyle" to "InteractivityLevel", "Format", "LearningResourceType" and "SemanticDensity".

The weights that were used to connect these factors are shown in Table 3.

Combination of properties of LRs - Learners based			
Learner property		LR property	
hasUserRole	0.55	hasDifficulty	0.33
		hasInteractivityLevel	0.33
		hasSemanticDensity	0.33
hasLearningStyle	0.45	hasInteractivityLevel	0.25
		hasFormat	0.25
		hasLearningResourceType	0.25
		hasSemanticDensity	0.25

Table 3. Combination of properties of Learners and LRs

From a specific node of the hierarchy this personalization bridging algorithm 'chose' one specific LR which is picked as the optimal object for each learner. The final learning path was provided to each individual. After the course completion, two decisive dimensions were examined: **i)** the satisfaction of the learners from their participation in the experiment and **ii)** the difference of their performance in this course lesson as compared to the performance of other students, who had not participated in the experiment. Albeit these indicators could hastily be viewed as insufficient for a denotative feedback, however, due to the novel and purely tentative character of the experiment per se, they were reckoned as reasonably fitting the aims of the whole effort. This was thought because the current effort in its entirety, was, as initially indicated, primarily centered in the theoretical and mathematical verification of merging two important axes: on the one hand, **a)** the potential refinement of the e-system supporting educational actions and activities by pondering into its technical methodologies and attempting mathematical manipulations that would perhaps endow further sophistication to its treating e-material, and, on the other hand **b)** the potential expatiation of even the very theoretical framework of cognitive constructivism along with the prospects of its applications into its largely unfamiliar e-environment, via precisely an algorithmic expression. This vision would have been adequately proven even if a single case-study was involved in the experimentation process, of a pair of a single e-tutor interacting with a single e-learner together dealing with the existing system's capacity and the currently proposed intervention's ability to: store information, retrieve material and process e-education in a smooth and functional manner.

Again, in this light, the success indicators selected for the present purposes could prove sufficient, provided that the relevant measurements would be markedly high in the gauge. Indeed, the related hypotheses were confirmed, with outcomes of these experiments being considered as very promising: i) the percentage of the participants who reported great satisfaction with taking part in the project reached a quite impressive 78%, and ii) their mean performance in the course increased against the mean performance of the control group at a considerable 18%.

Further Improvement Tactics: Consecutive steps for improving results in both i) quantitative and ii) qualitative terms are readily conceivable: i)For example, more indicators on outcomes would include general course performance ratings, intermediary grades, marks on midway assignments, participants' assessments of partial provisions, time management pointers, and gauges on speed of retrieval of information. It was also deemed that in order to arrive at even more reliable results, the experiment would have to be continued and enriched towards qualitative improvements: ii) For example, variables which should also be included at such a future phase include: variety of several courses assessed in parallel, larger and varied (e.g., in demographics) samples of e-learners, a greater quantity of educational material qualitatively assessed as for, e.g., the conditions of delivery of its components, the appropriateness of the format of its components as ascribed to different users, the degree of users' satisfaction in the cooperation with specific e-tutors, different weights in the properties that are examined, etc. More specifically, given that the proffered architecture has satisfactorily inter alia shown its expansiveness due to its integrative platform of operations as conjunct with its bridging algorithm; and given that it does provide the capability to easily: i) change values of the existing parameters included in the system and ii) add more in order to cover a wider spectrum of characteristics to each tally, improvement tactics as the aforementioned should and could (Kerkiri et al, -in press) be promptly followed.

6. Conclusions

The present work attempted to abridge tentative, yet influential findings and concepts of two distinctly disparate doctrines traditionally ascribed to ICTs and psycho-pedagogy respectively. By focusing on relevant illustrative evidence it aspired to primarily provide some indication as to the feasibility of linking these two seemingly unrelated fields of study in a way that would benefit the end-users of this alliance. The open source LMSs as a fertile environment on the one hand and the cognitive constructivist approach on the other were purposefully selected as it was deemed that almost by definition they could be exploited in synergy with respect to the contemporary needs of savvy e-users. Although certain exemplary theoretical studies have been asserting the legitimacy of such alliance in the past (e.g., Dalgarno 2002), however, no one known to the current one has proceeded beyond theoretical to empirical experimentation, which was the general objective of the present effort. On a consecutive layer, this work chose to deal with the popular, yet delicate issue of contemporary e-educational methods addressed to undeniably savvy and demanding e-learners, whose special, idiographic characteristics craving for e-material personalization did not appear to be practically taken into account by most of the thoroughly investigated existing e-systems that support electronically conducted teaching processes. In this way, it not only hoped to trail this shortcoming, but also to offer a viable solution for it. The focal point of interest in this study being indeed the issue of personalization, it was accordingly led to advance beyond examining the capacity, yet inertia of the most popular open source LMSs to cover individual e-learners' needs for effective knowledge accessibility, and thus to present a coherent architecture of novel factually interoperable components that were ad hoc attested to efficiently serve such personalization purposes by applications compatible to the existing e-LMSs. These components were **I.** the creation of a superstructure that would secure fundamental functions of the LMSs environment on which the proffered architecture would unfold, **II.** the design of an integrative platform that would stage methods, tools and features derived from both the theoretical and empirical realms in question, and finally **III.** a bridging algorithm, that would function as a circuit amongst these features in order to uphold, not only interoperability, but also expansiveness of the spectrum of tools and services provided –again, not only to the e-learners themselves, but also to their e-tutors.

In the research involved in this work an architectural structure and a personalization algorithm for e-Learning systems were presented focusing on a gradually apparent need of e-users for what was here depicted as a double concern: namely, the personalization of the content that the e-learner seeks for, and, likewise, the personification of the quest of the very same e-learner. The underlying concept dictates that once the characteristics of a learner are fed into a psycho-pedagogically founded and indeed cognitive constructivism-inspired e-system, it is not only the system itself that would take care of the user by supplying her/him with information suitable to his/her type by use of the proposed architecture; it would automatically empower the user to choose and change the type of the e-educational material that s/he seeks for, by simply altering/modifying/enriching the previously stored information about him/her. A significant finding in this research aspect of the study is that the proposed architecture also appeared to promise cost-effectiveness, inasmuch as it was shown that it can be also applied even in already developed LMSs.

The design of this system is coordinated through the utilization of learning style outcomes (Kritikou et al., 2008), educational standards (cf LOM, SCORM, PAPI, LIP), Semantic Web technologies (Berners-Lee et al., 2001; Kerkiri et al., 2009). The capabilities of this design rely on the creation of self-defined LRs. This leads to i) appreciating and exploiting their educational properties at a glance and ensuring their suitability for a specific learner by abiding to a multidimensional matrix of parameters, ii) promoting its characteristics so that they can be discovered by proper software (e.g. s/w agents), through an aptly computerized process, and iii) steering their automate classification in the right position of a learning path.

The personalization algorithm of the proposed system is based on divergent properties of equally divergent weights for the matching. This offers the maximum flexibility to a researcher to produce a dedicated course for the individual, as s/he can easily change these parameters depending on the outcomes s/he wants to examine. In this work's future plans the layered development of a number of functionalities are scheduled. Accordingly, next steps to be taken aim primarily to the creation of a repository of alternative LRs for a number of courses. A collation of courses shall follow which are to be created from the personalization algorithm with, and without evaluations. To this end, the relevant evaluation strategy shall be more refined and based on evaluating both educational approaches, observing students that follow the learning-styles approach courses and those that do not. With all the outcomes of the first experiment having being very promising, an even deeper examination is foreseeable, so that in the long term using different LRs, and a number of learner profiles of a wide variety of learning styles may well be available to extensively serve a multitude of users in progressively more meaningful ways.

7. Future Orientations

In an effort to respond effectively to e-learners' increasing demands and at the same time follow the Dalsgaard's three-fold proposition by also upholding Hannafin and colleagues' suggestions while continuously verifying the capacity of this architecture for meaningful expansiveness, it is further postulated that the hardiness model could be employed in the future, as the next step for an even more inclusive, unifying framework, that combines these qualities by actually coordinating distinct principles into an applicable instrumentation.

Hardiness theory holds that three distinguishable, yet interoperable and, ideally well balanced, personality components are interwoven in the cognitive schemata construction modes of each individual in the form of a highly idiographic/personalized frame of (subjective) reference. The latter may be reconstructed, inasmuch flexibility is encouraged or

not by use of, both, inner and outer, inherent and interpersonal/communicable resources. These components are defined as [self-]Control, Commitment -Responsibility and Challenge- Enthousiasm, repsectively (Maddi, 1980). Found in both, balance and, fairly, but not excessively, high levels in the individual profile, these "3C's" ensure i) good general, both mental and physical health, ii) fulfilling goal-setting, iii) adept goal-pursuing, iv) effectual stress-management, v) emphatic interpersonal/communicational skills and vi) general successfulness in an overall vii) productive, creative and pleasing quality of life. In contrast, when detected at both, imbalance and low levels in the individual profile, their fusion entails Alienation, i.e., aloofness and widespread hazy dissatisfaction with the self, others and any future prospects (Paleologou, 1996). Regardless of the degree of sturdiness indicated and irrespectively of the breadth of balance between these '3C's', the hardy-vs-alienated profile is portrayed as the compass of a person's navigation in life. Because repeated scrutinization of its components and consequent adaptations to the concurrent measurements of individual and group profiles have been optimized through three decades of study and applications, this theory's revisions and enrichments have led to detailed systemization of i) principles and ii) practical steps aiming to reconstruct a) dysfunctional schemas underlying the attitudes of alienated profiles and b) functional, yet potentially upgradeable, hardy profiles towards bettering their already satisfying lifestyle (Paleologou, 2001). The constellation of the emerging cognitive re-scripting approaches is now at a stage that may be addressing and treating information and interpretation processing that secures body, mental, social and spiritual harmoniousness of a person's inter-, and intra- cohesion in competency (e.g., idem, 2009). This structural system appears to be appealing to serve as a common denominator for an effective stabilization of both theoretical psycho-pedagogical plus learning principles and e-tools as well as functions of LMSs in favour of e-users.
Hence, almost by definition, the hardiness components seem appropriate for a concrete future inclusion in the currently proposed architecture at a level beyond mere profiling of the e-learners' individual persona, but by proceeding to aid them also in corrective actions towards precisely improving their learning style, capacities and future projections

8. References

ACM Computing Classification System: Top 2 Levels, (1998), Valid through 2009, [Internet], Available At <http://www.acm.org/class/1998/overview.html>, Last Accessed [1/4/2009]

Advanced Distributed Learning, (2004), SCORM, Available at: <http://www.adlnet.gov/scorm/>, [Last Visit 14/02/099].

Ally, M. (2004). Foundations of educational theory for online learning. In: *Theory and practice of online learning*, Anderson, T., Elloumi, F. (Eds.), Athabasca, AB: Athabasca University

ATutor, http://www.atutor.ca, [Last Visit 01/01/09]

Bannan-Ritland, B., Dabbagh, N. & Murphy, K. (2000). Learning Object Systems as Constructivist Learning Environments: Related Assumptions, Theories and Applications. In: *The Instructional Use of Learning Objects, Association for Instructional Technology and Association for Educational Communications and Technology (AIT/AECT)*, D. Wiley (Ed.), <http://www.reusability.org/read/>

Berners-Lee, T., Hendler, J., Lassila, O.: The Semantic Web. Scientific American, Vol. 20, pp. 34-43

Brown, J.S., Collins, A. & Duguid, P. (1989). Situated Cognition and the Culture of Learning. *Educational Researcher*, Vol. 18, No. 1, pp. 32-42

Brusilovsky, P., (1996), User Modeling and User Adapted Interaction. *Special issue on adaptive hypertext and hypermedia, Methods and techniques of adaptive hypermedia*, Vol. 6 No. 2-3, pp. 87-129

Carchiolo, VS., Longheu, A., Malgeri, M. & Mangioni G. (2007). An Architecture to Support Adaptive E-Learning. *International Journal of Computer Science and Network Security*, Vol. 7, No. 1, 166-178.

Claroline, http://www.claroline.net/, [Last Visit 01/04/09]

Dalgarno, B. (2002), Constructivist computer assisted learning: Theory and techniques: http://www.ascilite.org.au/conferences/adelaide96/papers /21.html

Dalsgaard, C. (2005). Pedagogical quality in e-learning - Designing e-learning from a learning theoretical approach. *E-learning and education (eleed) Journal*, Vol. 1

Deshler, D. (1986). Learning strategies: An instructional alternative for low achieving adolescents. *Exceptional Children*, Vol. 52, pp. 583-590.

Docebo, http://www.docebolms.org/doceboCms/, [Last Visit 01/04/09]

Dokeos, http://www.dokeos.com, [Last Visit 01/04/2009]

Felder, R., Silverman, L. (1988). Learning and teaching styles in engineering education. *Engineering Education*, Vol. 78, No. 7, pp. 674–681

Fjeld, M., Lauche, K., Bichsel, M., Voorhorst, F., Krueger, H. & Rauterberg, M. (2002). Physical and Virtual Tools: Activity Theory Applied to the Design of Groupware. In: *Activity Theory and the Practice of Design*, A Special Issue of Computer Supported Cooperative Work (CSCW), B. A. Nardi & D. F. Redmiles (Ed.), Vol. 11, No. 1-2, pp. 153-180, Netherlands

Gardner, H. (1993). *Multiple Intelligences - The Theory in Practice*, BasicBooks, ISBN-10: 046501822X, New York

Graf, S., Kinshuk, Liu, T.-C. (2008). Providing Adaptive Courses in Learning Management Systems with Respect to Learning Styles, *World Conference on E-Learning in Corporate, Government, Healthcare, and Higher Education Proceedings*, pp. 482-486, ISBN: 978-0-7695-3167-0, July 2008, Santander, Cantabria

Hannafin, M., Land, S. & Oliver, K. (1999). Open Learning Environments: Foundations, Methods, and Models, In: *Instructional-Design Theories and Models: A New Paradigm of Instructional Theory*, Reigeluth, C. M. (Ed.), Vol. 2, pp. 215-239

Hauger, D., Köck, M. (2007). State of the Art of Adaptivity in E-Learning Platforms. *Proceedings of the 15th Workshop on Adaptivity and User Modeling in Interactive Systems*, pp. 355-360, Halle/Saale, Germany, Sep 2007

IEEE Learning Technology Standards Committee, Retrieved online 01/03/2009 at: http://ltsc.ieee.org/wg12/files/LOM_1484_ 12_1_v1_Final_Draft

IEEE P1484.2.1/D8, 2001-11-25, Draft Standard for Learning Technology Sponsored by the Learning Technology Standards Committee of the IEEE Computer Society. Retrieved online 01/09/2008 at: http://ltsc.ieee.org/wg12/files/LOM_ 1484_12_1_v1_ Final_Draft

ILIAS, http://www.ilias.de, [Last Visit 01/04/09]

Ismail, J. (2002). The design of an e-learning system, beyond the hype. *Internet and Higher Education*, Vol. 4, pp. 329 - 336

Jonassen, D.H. & Grabowski, B.L. (2000). *Handbook of Individual Difference, Learning, and Instruction*. Hillsdale, NJ: Lawrence Erlbaum Associates

Jonassen, D.H. (1999). Constructing learning environments on the web: Engaging students in meaningful learning. *EdTech 99: Educational Technology Conference and Exhibition 1999: Thinking Schools, Learning Nation*

Kerkiri T. & Paleologou A.-M. (2009). Do open source LMSs support personalization? A comparative evaluation. *Proceedings of the 2nd WSKS 2009*, LNCS/CCIS Springer Verlag

Kerkiri, T., Konetas D., Paleologou, A.-M. & Mavridis, I. (in press), Semantic Web Technologies Anchored in Learning Styles as Catalysts towards Personalizing the Learning Process, *International Journal of Learning and Intellectual Capital*, ISSN (Online)

Kerkiri, T., Mavridis, I. & Manitsaris, A. (2009). How e-Learning systems may benefit from ontologies and recommendation methods to efficiently personalize knowledge, *International Journal of Knowledge and Learning* ISSN (Online): 1741-1017 - ISSN (Print): 1741-1009

Kritikou, Y., Demestichas, P., Adamopoulou, E., Demestichas, K., Theologou, M. & Paradia M. (2007), User Profile Modeling in the context of web-based learning management systems. Science Direct, *Journal of Network and Computer Applications*, Vol. 12, No. 6, pp. 603-627

Larochelle, M. & Bednarz, N. (1998). Constructivism and Education: beyond epistemological correctness. In: *Constructivism and Education*, Larochelle, M. Bednarz, N. and Garrison, J. (Ed.), ISBN 0521621356, 9780521621359, Cambridge, Cambridge University Press

Lazarus, R.S. (1999). *Stress and emotion: A new synthesis.* NY: Springer Publishing Co, Inc.

Lee, S. (2008), The Gates Are Shut: Technical and Cultural Barriers to Open Education, In: *Opening Up Education: The Collective Advancement of Education through Open Technology, Open Content, and Open Knowledge*, Iiyoshi, T., Kumar, V., John Seely Brown (Ed.), Publisher: The MIT Press, ISBN-10: 0262033712, London, England

Maddi, S.R. (1980). Myth and Personality. *The Journal of Mind and Behavior*, Vol. 1, No. 2, 145-154

Mitchell, D.P. (1994). Learning style: critical analysis of concept and its assessment. In: *Design for learning: educational technology aspects*, R. Hoey (Ed.), UK: Kogan Page

Moodle, http://www.moodle.org, [Last Visit 01/04/2009]

Muntean, C., H. & Muntean, G., M. (2008). End-User Quality of Experience-Aware Personalized E-Learning, In: *Architecture Solutions for E-Learning Systems*, S. Clarke (Ed.), pp. 281-301, Dublin, Ireland

Nardi, B.A. (1996). Context and Consciousness: Activity Theory and Human-computer Interaction. MIT Press, Cambridge, MA

Nash, S., S. (2005). Learning objects, learning object repositories, and learning theory: Preliminary best practices for online courses. *Interdisciplinary Journal of Knowledge and Learning Objects*, Vol. 1, pp. 217-228, Available at http://ijklo.org/Volume1/v1p217-228Nash.pdf

Ounnas, A., Liccardi, I., Davis, H. C., Millard, D. E. & White, S. A. (2006). Towards a Semantic Modeling of Learners for Social Networks, *Proceedings International*

Workshop on Applications of Semantic Web Technologies for E-Learning (SW-EL), (AH'06), Dublin, Ireland

Paleologou, A. - M. & Dellaporta, A. (2009). Hardiness vs Alienation Personality Construct Essentially Explains Burnout Proclivity and Erroneous Computer Entry Problems, World Academy of Science Engineering Technology Proceedings, Vol. 40, pp. 1-17.

Paleologou, A. - M. (1996). *Hardiness Manual on Stress Management. R.* Athens: ELKEPA

Paleologou, A. - M. (2001). *Orientations in Clinical Psychology,* Athens: Ellinika Grammata

Rogers, A. (1999), *Teaching Adults,* Open University Press, ISBN 960-375-015-8

Roy, M. & Chi, M. (2003). Gender Differences in Patterns of Searching the Web. *Journal of Educational Computing Research,* Vol. 29, No. 3, pp. 335-348

Schunk, D. H. (2004). *Learning Theories: An Educational Perspective,* ISBN:0-13-038496-8, Upper Saddle River, New Jersey

Simpson, T. L. (2002). Dare I oppose constructivist theory?. *The Educational Forum,* Vol. 66, No. 4, pp. 347- 354, ISSN-0013-1725

Tuparov, G. & Dureva, D. (2008). Learning Styles Testing in Moodle. *Procedures of CompSysTech '08,* Bulgaria

Von-Glasersfeld, E. (1984). An introduction to radical constructivism. In: *The Invented Reality,* P. Watzlawick (Ed.), pp. 17-40, New York: W.W. Norton & Company

Vygotsky, L. S. (1978). *Mind in Society: The Development of Higher Psychological Process,* M. Cole, V. John-Steiner, S. Scribner, & E. Souberman (Ed.), Cambridge, Harvard University Press.

W3C Recommendation Web Ontology Language -OWL. (2004). Retrieved online 14/09/2008 at: http://www.w3.org/TR/owl-features/

Wallace, B., Ross, A., Davies, J.B. & Anderson, T. (2007). *The Mind, the Body and the World: Psychology after Cognitivism.* Imprint London: Imprint Academic

10

E-learning in information accessibility of disabled assistanttechnology

Chunlian Li and Yu Sun
Changchun University
China

1. E-learning in information accessibility of disabled assistant technology

1.1 The disabled higher education and network teaching

1.1.1 Development of higher education for the disabled

Around the 18th century, the European started to take cognizance of disability and disabled people scientifically. In 1864, American congress passed a resolution on merging the Washington schools for the blind and for the deaf into Gallaudet University, and it became the first university in the world for the disabled.

The famous IDEA (the Individuals with Disabilities Education Act) is mainly about the stage of compulsory education for the disabled students. But the protected by the Act also includes the people who accepted higher education. The Act strengthened the disabilities' awareness on right to protect the personal needs and use the facilities in higher education, enhanced the people's awareness of the possibility and legitimacy on the disabled sharing the higher education. Data shows that the U.S. has more than 1500 universities that accept disabled students, almost one the thirds of the American university. In 1995, almost all the disabled people at the proper age enrolled into the universities or colleges. And there were 42.8 million disabled students in American colleges in 1999. For example, in the famous University of Michigan, there are 200 disabled students among each 3500 ones.The colleges provide all kinds of services for disabled students to adapt their special needs of material conditions, such as the use of braille books, reading software, etc. Each school has its accessible environment for the various needs of the special students.

In Japan, the higher education for disabilities follows the principles of democratic education with neither special preferential policies nor the restrictions. While in previous Soviet Union, it runs in two ways, study together with the common students or in the special education institute. After the collapse of the Soviet Union, Russia retained partial special schools. In the United Kingdom and some other countries, almost all the people with disabilities study in ordinary colleges or universities in ordinary class. Most of the people with disabilities of Yugoslavia have obtained higher education levels, many of them became masters or doctors. Any chance is equal to people with disabilities in the aspect of education. In China, the higher education for people with disabilities can be traced back to the early 20th century. The government approved the establishment of the formal department for the blind and dumb schools, and the excellent graduates will be sent to the special educational college of

National Central University without examination. After new China was founded, Communist Party of China and the government attached great importance to the cause of the handicapped and the higher education for the disabled. Higher education for the disabled planed by government began after the mid-1980s in China. Since the recent 20 years, there has more than 30000 disabled students studying in Chinese universities and the Changchun University keeps the Chinese level on special higher education.

1.1.2 Network resources of higher education for disabled

In most countries, people with disabilities shared equally college education with common students. So the services provided by library must meet the different needs arisen due to all kinds of physiological defects. The first digital library for the blind of Paraguay is created in 2007 offering free service for the blind in Spanish. At the web site, a reading-software called JAWS is available to help the blinds "view" pages or "read" electronic books.

Another digital library for the blind where the visually impaired can listen to electronic books, music or on-line lectures for free has been opened in the National Library of China. About 200 electronic books, 500 audio programs and 500 video programs are available in the library, covering ancient Chinese culture, medicine, modern literature and daily life. Some of the materials were provided according to the requests from the blind. The library plans to add at least 200 electronic books, 30 lecture videos and 500 audio programs every year.

Australia, Canada, Croatia, Denmark, Japan, Korea, Netherlands, South Africa, Sweden, UK and the USA have joined to issue a report on the governance and funding of library and information services for visually impaired people. The report is aimed to support a long-term dialogue among stakeholders about how to meet opportunities and challenges for widening access to reading materials for visually impaired people best.

The professional membership organization AHEAD (Association on Higher Education And Disability, http://www.ahead.org) is organized for individuals involved in the development of policy and in the provision of quality services to meet the needs of people with disabilities involved in all areas of higher education. Nowadays, it has more than 2,500 members throughout the United States, Canada, England, Australia, Ireland, Northern Ireland, New Zealand, South Africa, Sweden, Japan and Greece. In addition to the international membership, AHEAD has formal partnerships with 30 regional affiliates and numerous other professional organizations working to advance equity in higher education for people with disabilities. Since 1977 AHEAD has delivered quality training to higher education personnel through conferences, workshops, publications and consultation. AHEAD members represent a diverse network for professionals who actively address disability issues on their campuses and in the field of higher education.

There are many websites of "Educational Resources", "Job Training/Placement", "University Resources" for people with disabilities in higher education. Such as "College Funding for Students with Disabilities" at http://www.washington.edu/doit, "Financial Aid for Students with Disabilities" at http://www.finaid.org/otheraid/disabled.phtml, "Scholarships Available for College Students with Disabilities" at http://www.spinalcord.org/ , "On-line Disability Information System (ODIS)" at http://dll.umaine.edu/cd/html/online.html, etc. The National Science Foundation, the State of Washington, and the U.S. Department of education have provided the primary funding for DO-IT (Disabilities, Opportunities, Internetworking, and Technology) to serve to increase the successful participation for people with disabilities in challenging academic

programs and careers. ODIS is created by the center for Community Inclusion and Disability Studies of the University of Maine to offer courses in many disciplines throughout the year. Courses are delivered through various technologies and formats including interactive television, compressed video, internet, intranet, video streaming technologies and combinations of these systems. Depending on the technology utilized, students participate in the class "live" or asynchronously through materials archived online.
Besides, some universities have open courses that are offered by Tufts Open Course, UMass Boston Open Course, MIT Open Course, Utah State University Open course Yale Open Course, Notre Dame Open Course, UcIrvine, Johns Hopkins Open Course, etc.
Also, some other university resources are available at George Washington University , Iowa State University, Johns Hopkins University, Northwestern University, Oklahoma State University, Ohio State University, Oklahoma State University, Tarleton State University, University of Delaware, University Of Georgia, University of Illinois at Urbana-Champaign, University of Iowa Division of Developmental Disabilities, University of Kansas Medical Center, University of Minnesota, University of New Hampshire, University of Virgina, University of Washington, Victorian University, Wright State University.

1.2 The e-learning system

1.2.1 The ideas and goals of e-learning

E-learning is a new education concept which has been applied in various fields beyond formal education, such as adult education, corporate or enterprise training, business training institutions. The original interpretation of e-learning refers to the study action assisted by electronic means and that the learning process is usually created by interaction with digitally delivered content, network-based services. These lessons can be made more interesting using multimedia i.e. combination of text, graphics, sound and animation. Lessons can be delivered to the learner via various means e.g. CD-ROM, video conference, Internet. Nowadays, the much talked about e-learning is referred to its narrow sense that the learning by Internet.
The main goals of e-learning are to make learning more convenient, more effective, to reduce more educational cost, and what's more to do great benefit to the resource sharing throughout the world. It deliveries the digital content, provides a learner-oriented environment for the providers and learners. It promotes the construction of life-long learning opinions and learning society. To both the provider and the learner, web-based learning options offer terrific flexibility and cost savings. The learning process can be carried at anytime, anywhere by anyone via any media and anyway. Benefit from the powerful combination of audio, animation and software simulations that produce highly engaging multimedia training. Courses today use realistic simulations, hands-on exercises, and role-playing scenarios to help learners "learn while doing".
As a Internet-based learning, e-learning has the following three characteristics:

i. Network: Knowledge can be updated in time, and meanwhile ensuring knowledge consistency.
ii. Personalization: The terminals can be computers or mobile telephones. Learners can arrange personal progress according to his (her) time, can decide the appropriate

content he (her) need.

iii. Trackability: All learning activities can be recorded as the basis for the assessment of the learning result and the analysis of training needs.

1.2.2 Some typical e-learning systems

The original concept of e-learning is presented about 30 years ago, and the narrow concept is appeared about over 10 years ago, but its real use began only few years ago. In the most recent period, especially since 1998, network-based "e-Learning" concept began frequently in the mass media as well as in the industry, and gradually become a "popular language". The application spreas rapidly around the world. Learning management systems (LMSs) and course management systems (CMLs) are the two similar modes of e-learning.

1.2.2.1 LMSs

LMSs refer to software that primarily acts as an electronic registrar by electronically performing various enrollment and related tasks. LMSs were originally designed for workplace learning environments, and specifically perform some or all of the following tasks:

- Registration
- Track participation (classroom attendance, sign-ons and sign-offs of online courses)
- Track of completions (including final scores or grades)
- Testing
- Follow-up discussions with participants
- Aggregated reports, such as the number of people registered for particular courses
- Transfer of information to other systems, such as human resource information systems
- Process charges for courses, such as tuition payments and transfer payments among departments
- Course catalog
- Skills management.

From a participant perspective, an LMS provides a central point from which learners access activities. It provides a list of courses available, and lets learners enroll in courses. If learners must complete prerequisite courses, the system can check that. After learners enroll in a course, the system can automatically generate an enrollment confirmation and, later, a reminder about the class. After class, the system can be used to test knowledge, record a course completion, and send the information to the learner's permanent employment record, as well as send follow-up correspondence to the learner. For an e-learning course, the system can launch the course, track student progress, record completions, and send information to learner's permanent employment record

For administrators, LMSs can be used to manage both classroom courses and e-learning. For e-learning, the system starts the course after the learner registers in the course. For classroom courses, the LMS can provide a variety of resources, including schedules for individual classrooms (that is, facilities tracking capbilities) and class lists for instructors. LMSs can also be used to record and assess training satisfaction (Level 1). In addition, LMSs can generate a number of reports, from the number of students enrolling in particular courses to aggregated records of student performance in particular courses.

Many LMSs are available on the market. Here, we will take the SkillSoft PLC, Saba, and SumTotal Systems as examples.

Case 1: SkillSoft PLC[http://www.skillsoft.com]

SkillSoft was incorporated in Ireland on Aug. 8, 1989. After completing a merger with SmartForce in 2002 became known as SkillSoft PLC. It is a leading provider of e-learning and performance support solutions for global enterprises, government, education and businesses with small to medium-sized. SkillSoft enables business organizations to maximize business performance through a combination of comprehensive e-learning content, online information resources, flexible learning technologies and support services. Their products offer the most comprehensive content alongside the most experienced and qualified consulting team in the e-learning industry. Content offerings include business, IT, desktop, compliance and consumer/SMB courseware collections, as well as complementary content assets such as Leadership Development Channel video products, KnowledgeCenter™ portals, virtual instructor-led training services and online mentoring services. The main models include the following.

- Digitized business books and reports, learning management system and virtual classroom
- Online business and IT training
- SkillPort: learning management system
- Books 24x7: online business and technical books resource
- SkillSoft Dialogue: web collaboration tool

Case 2: Saba[http://www.saba.com]

Founded in 1997, Saba is the premier global provider of strategic human capital management (HCM) software and services. Saba 's people management solutions are used by more than 1,300 organizations and over 17 million end users worldwide. Saba 's solutions increase organizational performance by aligning workforce goals with organizational strategy; developing, managing and rewarding their people; and improving collaboration. Here, we introduce Saba learning suite.

Saba learning suite is the most comprehensive solution available for addressing the strategic goals of learning organizations. It delivers effective formal and informal learning that is tied to clear business outcomes and strategic human capital management initiatives. Combined with Saba Centra, Saba Learning Suite is the first product from a single company that offers the full continuum of learning methods - formal, informal, self-paced, live, and a blend to provide seamless and truly effective learning that builds organizational competencies. The suite gives learners the ability to target competencies and capabilities, measure improvements, and assess the impact of those improvements on performance, revenues, and cost savings.

The Saba Learning Suite includes capabilities for: enterprise learning management, Certification management, For-profit customer education, Learning content management systems, Content authoring tool, Saba Centra: Virtual classrooms, Informal learning and collaboration, Career and competency management.

Case 3: SumTotal Systems[http://www.sumtotalsystems.com]

SumTotal Systems, Inc. is a global No.1 provider of learning, performance, and talent management solutions[http://www.hiray.net/No.1-a.htm], its partners spread over Asia Pacific, Europe, Middle East, Africa, Latin America, North America. Their Learning Management System (TotalLMS) is an industry's leading and the backbone of SumTatal's learning management offerings. TotalLMS combines best-of-breed functionality with simple configuration to help companies easily administer a variety of learning activities for both internal and external audiences. By providing the latest information, training and certifications, companies can help their customers to use their products more effectively, become productive more quickly and decrease their need for support. SumTotal's customer education solutions provide global, scalable capabilities to maximize the effectiveness, coverage and consistency of training to a company's customers. The recently released ResultsOnDemand Learning provides a best-of-breed learning management platform in an easy-to-use, rapidly deployed solution. This Software-as-a-Service (SaaS) solution provides organizations a low risk opportunity to leverage the robust functionality in ResultsOnDemand Learning. More than 1,500 organizations, large and small, depend on SumTotal learning solutions to improve learning management efficacy, meet training compliance requirements, and report on training's impact.

1.2.2.2 CMSs

CMSs are online systems that were originally designed to support classroom learning in academic settings, such as universities and high schools. CMSs provide instructors with the ability to perform the following tasks:

- Place course materials online: Most CMSs provide pre-programmed buttons for the course syllabus, course schedule, and course materials linked to specific lessons, such as copies of readings and PowerPoint slides from lectures.
- Track student progress through assessment features, which enable instructors to give quizzes and tests online, and an online grade book, where instructors can post student grades
- Discussion board, where instructors and students can discuss readings and continue class discussions between formal class sessions
- Other communication tools, which let instructors send announcements to classes and communicate individually with students
- Lock box for students, where students can store class materials in a safe place—either a presentation to give later in class or backing up class assignments in a safe place
- Course statistics, which provide information on the use of the course site, including who and when used the course site

Because CMSs enable instructors to easily create a course website by following a template and uploading existing documents in PowerPoint, Word, Excel, Acrobat and other popular formats without converting them to a web format (like HTML), they require few specialized skills. As a result, CMSs are easy to learn and were quickly adopted by instructors, even those who might claim to be luddites. Indeed, some universities report that well over 70 percent of their instructors have created course websites using CMSs.

CMSs also have been proven popular in managing asynchronous academic distance courses, too, because of their ability to manage discussions. In addition, given that CMSs were already installed and in wide use only adds to their popularity. When using a CMS to manage a distance course, instructors post a core lesson—a master script, of sorts, that guides students through readings, discussions, and learning activities—instead of merely posting readings and PowerPoint slides for each lesson,. Instructors then use the discussion board to manage the course discussions, which are usually more extensive than those used in classroom courses.

Examples of CMSs include the commercial products Blackboard and WebCT (emerged with Blackboard), and the open source system, Moodle, but not limited to these. The following are the simply introduce to them.

Case 4: Blackboard Learning System [http://www.blackboard.com]

The Blackboard Learning System of Blackboard Inc. is an industry－leading software application used to power virtual learning environments, supplement classroom education and as a platform for distance learning programs. Featuring a robust core set of capabilities that enable instructors to efficiently manage courses, author content, create assignments, and foster collaboration, among other key functions, the Blackboard Learning System help institutions accomplish mission-critical objectives related to instruction, communication and assessment. These key capabilities include:

- Course Management
- Content Authoring
- Adaptive Release
- Syllabus Builder
- Learning Units
- Online Textbook Content (Course Cartridges)
- Teaching and Learning Tools
- Personal Information Management
- Discussion Board
- Virtual Classroom / Collaboration Tool
- Group Projects
- Assessments and Surveys
- Assignments
- Gradebook
- Reporting and Performance Dashboard
- Enterprise Scalability
- Multi-Language Support
- Standards
- Blackboard Building Blocks (Open APIs)
- System Integration

Case 5: Moodle [http://moodle.org]

Moodle is an Open Source Course Management System (CMS), also known as a Learning Management System (LMS) or a Virtual Learning Environment (VLE). It has become very popular among educators around the world as a tool for creating online dynamic web sites for their students. To work, it needs to be installed on a web server somewhere, either on one of your own computers or one at a web hosting company. The current version is 1.9, which was released in March of 2008. It has been translated into 61 different languages. Major improvements in accessibility and display flexibility were developed in 1.5. As of March 2008, the Moodle user community with over 400,000 registered users on their site alone. As there are no license fees or limits to growth, an institution can add as many Moodle servers as needed. The largest single site has reported over 19,000 courses and over 41,000 students, and the Open University of the UK is building a Moodle installation for their 200,000 users. Its capabilities will be divided into two aspects, i.e. the system management functions and the network teaching functions.

Ⅰ The system management functions

- •Site integration
- •The easy-to-use design
- •Dynamic modular design
- •The role management
- •User Registration Management
- •Styles in a variety of themes
- •Multi-language supported
- •Well opened
- •Perfect management tools
- •Other new technical features

Ⅱ Network teaching functions

- •Multiple types of courses supported
- •Flexible curriculum management
- •Tracking analysis of study record
- •Classing and grouping functions
- •Courses resource management
- •Two-way evaluation
- •Test & item bank
- •Multi-styles online teaching module
- •Industry-standard supporting
- •Other new features

1.2.3 Discussion on the application of e-learning in the HEFD

As we covered at the beginning of section 1.2.1, the much talked about e-learning is referred to the learning by Internet, and which has contributed a lot to the higher education. In this part we will review the application among universities around the world.

1.2.3.1 E-learning in higher education

Since the middle of the 1990s, the number of colleges and universities which provide courses and degree programs via e-learning has been growing dramatically. Internet-based e-learning has become one of the most concerned paths for people to acquire their expected knowledge. More and more universities have been invested a huge amount of resources to implement their Internet-based e-learning platform or environment. Many universities established its e-learning system based on the commercial platforms. Following are the details.

Cornell University offers over 2,000 SkillSoft courses in information technology and business-related topics such as administrative support, communication, customer service, human resources, leadership, management, personal development and team building. The University of Houston became SkillSoft's first enterprise-wide education partner in the United States in 2004, offering the SkillChoice Complete business skills, IT and desktop solution to the entire campus community. University of North Carolina Wilmington had used SkillSoft IT courseware since 1998. In 2005, the university became enterprise-wide users and began offering SkillSoft's SkillChoice Complete solution of business skills, IT and

desktop courseware, etc. to all faculty, staff and students. Besides, The Western Governors University and Minnesota School of Business are all the costumers of SkillSosft. What's more, SkillSoft has extended its service to Chinese market. East Carolina University puts a new face on academic outreach with Saba Centra Live, Hosei University Builds a New Education Model With Saba Centra Live, University of Tennessee Nearing a Decade of Distance Education Using Saba Centra Live. The University of Manchester, a Blackboard client since 2003 recently made a strategic decision to adopt the Blackboard Managed HostingSM solution for its Blackboard Learn - Vista™ delivery. The University of Manchester aims to be one of the top 25 universities in the world and is committed to achieving this by 2015. Moodle is an open source system and its known sites have reached to 55,499 till January in 2009.
Besides the commercial platform-based ones, there are also various kinds of e-learning systems around the world. The first pioneer intelligent and adaptive Web-based educational systems were developed in University of Pittsburgh 1995-1996 by Brusilovsky[1] named Adaptive and Intelligent Web-based Educational Systems (AIWBES). Since then many interesting systems have been developed and reported. In 2004, Brusilovsky presented a distributed architecture for adaptive e-learning: Knowledge Tree[2]. Subsequently, He worked out the ontology-based framework for user model interoperability in distributed learning environments in 2005 [3].
In 2001, the Department of Education, Training and Youth Affairs (DETYA) commissioned one of the largest educational research projects ever undertaken in Australia, to focus on innovation in schools [4]. The Innovation and Best Practice Project (IBPP) consisted of research into 107 schools throughout Australia in relation to teaching and learning toward a 'knowledge society'. Through the innovation of e-learning environments, teachers found they were more able to cater to the differences of different students than previously attempted in the conventional classroom.
Jianming Yong [5] proposed a new method to design an efficient Internet-based e-learning platform by combining an Internet-based e-learning environment with the Internet-based workflow mechanism in University of Southern Queensland, Australia. The whole system can be divided into four parts, Teaching Workflow System (T), Learning Workflow System (L), Admin Workflow System (A), Infrastructure Workflow System (I). Mirko Cesarini [6] has described a platform designed on the power of process management abstractions provided by WFMS. When teachers set a course, they can benefit of the flexibility, expressiveness and control capabilities. At the same time a student, having its learning process driven by a workflow designed by a teacher, earns the possibility to customize her/his learning path while maintaining it within the bounds of practicability and usefulness. Teachers' effort in creating courses for the new platform is eased by some visual tools and by improving reusability. Every created course can be a topic of another course. A new visual designed course is translated into workflow code through intermediate representation levels. These levels allow a teacher to customize the course for different situations by explicitly cutting some branches in the resulting learning paths. The use of an orchestration engine allows enrich a course not only with static learning material but also with the services provided by third programs or institutions.
Fox an Trinidad (2006)[7] developed a structural framework to assist educationalists implementing e-learning or as they refer to "technology-enhanced learning". This framework is based on the work of Herrington (2001) [8] and describes three components of

importance when developing new resources and providing professional development for staff. These components are resources, pedagogies and delivery strategies. The resources are the learning content and forms of information that are provided to the learner. These resources are best provided as a variety of forms, which need not be all online. Pedagogies are the activities used to engage the learner. This underpins the manner in which the environment is structured and should include opportunities for people with disabilities learner to construct their own meaning through collaboration and a learner-centred environment. The delivery strategies element refers to the reliability and accessibility to the e-learning environment. The ability to design inclusively for learners who may be geographically located from the teacher is critical to this component (Oliver & Herrington, 2001) [9].

Since 1999, the Chinese Ministry of Education has authorized 67 ordinary universities and the central committee Radio and Television University does the modern distance learning pilot work, allows them to develop the certificate and non-certificate education. Related resources are available at the site http://www.ceta.edu.cn/Plone/resource.

1.2.3.2 E-learning in the HEFD

The advantages of the online learning have been widely described in the literature. However, the prospect promised with the digital era has not become the reality for most people with disabilities, especially in educational context. Some studies of the statistical accesses of e-learning web pages of the major organizations have revealed a high percentage of inaccessible pages. A large number of organizations have realized the importance of the services for people with disabilities.

A survey on e-learning for disabled people is been make by Electronic Training Village (ETV) (http://www.trainingvillage.gr). In the survey over 320 respondents across Europe gave their views about accessibility to e-learning for people with disabilities. Over one fifth of disabled e-learners require voice or speech recognition software to communicate with computers. Half the respondents thought e-learning would offer users with disabilities more opportunities to learn. 54.8% expected it to open up new and innovative opportunities. From the survey it appears that most people still believe modern e-learning involves merely reading off a screen. In fact e-learning technology has now evolved into a set of interactive multimedia applications.

The Web Accessibility Initiative of W3C has presented the Web Content Accessibility Guidelines and its current version is 2.0 (WCAG2.0). WCAG 2.0 covers a wide range of recommendations for making Web content more accessible. Publicly Available Specification (PAS) 78 has been developed by the Disability Rights Commission (DRC) in collaboration with BSI. This PAS outlines good practice in commissioning websites that are accessible to and usable by disabled people.

Besides, various actions have been taken to help disabled persons attain the e-learning education they deserve. In European Union, the "European Network for Visually Impaired Training, Education and Research" has worked a lot including the completed and actual projects, the following are the detailed.

□MEBUS/Let's Vitalize (1998-2000)

Developing a training course for IT trainer to educate ViP.

□MARQUISA/UMBRELLA (1998-2000)

Developing a training course long term unemployed ViP.

□EVASA (2000-2002)

Developing a training course long term unemployed ViP with low qualification

□PROBAT I-III (2000-2003)

Developing a helpdesk software for Microsoft Office optimized for blind computer-user.

□PROBIQ (2000-2003)

Developing a BORLAND 5.0 C++training course for ViP

□SOBES (2003-2005)

Developing interactive & case-sensitive diagnosis software to analyze the optimal computer setup for computer users with visual handicaps

□E-Learn-ViP (2005-2006)

Evaluation of available E-Learning products for ViP.

□PROVIPTRAIN (2004-2006)

Developing a modular training course for trainer in institutes for ViP.

□PROZESS (2006-2007)

Self diagnosis software for eye test considering computer setup and driving licence

□PRIAMOS (2006-2007)

Pilot project for empowering people with low vision to achieve a driving licence by using Bioptics and technical driving assistance systems

□SEE-ViP (2005-2007)

An E-Learning project aimed to develop an accessible LMS and CBT. Creating blended learning courses for the subjects English and Information Management.

□ValorViP (2007.1-2007.2)

Evaluation of EC funded project for the target group of visually impaired people.

□DICOMP-S.NET (2007.1-2008.6)

Developing a free screenreader.

□Discovering Hands (R) (2006.8-2008.7)

Education of blind women as doctors assistant in palpation diagnostics.

□AHVIIT-ACCESS (2006.10 – 2008.9)

Developing innovative audio-tactile learning materials

□eYES (2006-2008)

Creation of an e-learning interface for the blind and the visually impaired

□KnowProViP(2007.10-2009.9)

Developing a Knowledge Management and training system for trainers who educate:

- visually impaired
- and elderly people
- immigrants

□E-COVIP (2006.10-2008.9)

Developing a network and certified blended learning course for E-Learning Coaches for visually impaired people Developing a network and certified blended learning course for E-Learning Coaches for visually impaired people

Apart from the above, Margaret E.S [10] describes a case study undertaken by the University of Dundee at its library in 2006-2007 in which an e-learning module was developed to support library staff training in disability awareness. Jane Seale published a book named "E-learning and Disability in Higher Education" [11]. Examining the social, educational and

political background behind making e-learning accessible in higher and further education, this book considers the role of, and provides advice for, the key stake-holders involved in e-learning provision: lecturers, learning technologists, student support services, staff developers and senior managers. M.Arrigo[12] introduces an online learning environment designed for blind students based on the client-server model. F. Colace, et. al.[13] presented a standardized design approach to e-learning contents for people with disabilities based on the use of accessibility and usability guidelines.
In America, 54 million Americans with disabilities use information technology (IT) at colleges and universities, which accounts for 20 percent of the population. So there starts a movement on many college campuses to become more proactive in using e-Learning as a strategic tool for students with disabilities.

1.2.4 References

[1] Peter Brusilovsky , Christoph Peylo. Adaptive and Intelligent Web-based Educational Systems, International Journal of Artificial Intelligence in Education 13 (2003) 156–169
[2] Brusilovsky, P. (2004) KnowledgeTree: A distributed architecture for adaptive e-learning. In: Proceedings of The Thirteenth International World Wide Web Conference, WWW 2004 (Alternate track papers and posters), New York, NY, 17-22 May, 2004, ACM Press, pp. 104-113
[3] Brusilovsky, P., Sosnovsky, S. & Yudelson, M. (2005). Ontology-based Framework for User Model Interoperability in Distributed Learning Environments. In G. Richards (Ed.), Proceedings of World Conference on E-Learning in Corporate, Government, Healthcare, and Higher Education 2005 (pp. 2851-2855)
[4] Department of Education, Training and Youth Affairs. (DETYA) (2001). School innovation: Pathway to the knowledge society. Canberra: Commonwealth of Australia.
[5] Jianming Yong, Internet-based E-learning work flow process, 9th International Conference on Computer Supported Cooperative Work in Design (CSCWD 2005) Computer Supported Cooperative Work in Design II, 0302-9743, 2006: p.516-524
[6] Mirko Cesarini; Mattia Monga; Roberto Tedesco, Carrying on the e-Learning process with a Workflow Management Engine, Association for Computing Machinery(ACM) Annual Symposium on Applied Computing(SAC 2004) vol.2; 20040314-17; Nicosia(CY) Applied Computing 2004 vol.2, 2004
[7] Fox, R., & Trinidad, S. (2006). Technology's role in leveraging curriculum reform. Paper presented at the Conference on ICT in Teaching and Learning, ICT2006, July 7-10, Hong Kong.
[8] Herrington, A., Herrington, J., Oliver, R., Stoney, S. & Willis, J. (2001). Quality guidelines for online courses: The development of an instrument to audit online units. In G. Kennedy, M. Keppell, C. McNaught & T. Petrovic (Eds.), Meeting at the crossroads: Proceedings of ASCILITE 2001 (pp.263-270). Melbourne: The University of Melbourne.
[9] Oliver, R. & Herrington, J. (2001). Online learning design for dummies: professional development strategies for beginning online designers. In P. Barker & S. Rebelsky (Eds.), Proceedings of EDMEDIA 2002, World Conference on Educational

Multimedia, Hypermedia and Telecommunications. Norfolk, VA: AACE, (pp 1500-1505).
[10] Margaret E.S. Forrest, E-learning to support the development of disability awareness skills: a case study, WORLD LIBRARY AND INFORMATION CONGRESS: 74TH IFLA GENERAL CONFERENCE AND COUNCIL 10-14 August 2008, Québec, Canada
[11] E-learning and Disability in Higher Education (Paperback), by Jane Seale (Author) , UK, Routledge Tavlor & Francis Group, 2006, USA & Canada, New York, NY
[12] M.Arrigo. E-Learning Accessibility for blind students. Recent Research Developments in Learning Technologies, 2005, 1-5
[13] F. Colace, M. De Santo, P. Rocca Comite Mascambruno, E-Learning Contents for People with Disabilities: a Standardized Design Approach, ICTA'07, April 12-14, Hammamet, Tunisia,109-114

1.3 Technology of information accessibility

1.3.1 Solutions to information accessibility

Accessibility is initially used in the environment construction referred to that the surrounding environment is accessible to all kinds of people with disabilities to live, study and work. Then it is introduced into the field of information science and technology which generates the concept of information accessibility. Information accessibility refers to that any one (whether disabled or not, whether young or not) at any circumstance can equally, conveniently, accessibly access and make use of information. Information accessibility including two main areas, one is the accessible design of the hardware and software related to the electronic and information technology and its assisted products and techniques, and the other is the network accessibility which included the accessibility of web site content, web application, etc.. In this chapter we will pay much attention to the accessibility with the help of computer technology especially the network technology.

Most people today can hardly imagin life without the internet. It provides access to news, email, shopping, and entertainment, at any hour of the day or night. But these are all based on the facts that you can use a mouse and see the screen and hear the audio—in other words, if you don't have a disability of any kind. So the solution to information accessibility is to do everything to make all people with various kinds of disabilities can easily access the web. And it can be concluded into the category of web accessibility.

Web accessibility [1] refers to the practice of making websites usable by people of all abilities and disabilities. When sites are correctly designed, developed and edited, all users can have equal access to information and functionality. For example, when a site is coded with semantically meaningful HTML, with textual equivalents provided for images and with links named meaningfully, this helps blind users using text-to-speech software and/or text-to-Braille hardware. When text and images are large and/or enlargeable, it is easier for users with poor sight to read and understand the content. When links are underlined (or otherwise differentiated) as well as colored, this ensures that color blind users will be able to notice them. When clickable links and areas are large, this helps users who cannot control a mouse with precision. When pages are coded so that users can navigate by means of the keyboard alone, or a single switch access device alone, this helps users who cannot use a mouse or even a standard keyboard. When videos are closed captioned or a sign language version is available, deaf and hearing impaired users can understand the video. When flashing effect is avoided or made optional, users who prone to seizure what has been caused by these effects are not put at risk. And when content is written in plain language and illustrated with instructional diagrams and animations, users with dyslexia and learning difficulties are better able to understand the content. When sites are correctly built and maintained, all of these users can be accommodated while not impacting on the usability of the site for non-disabled users.

The needs that Web accessibility aims to address include:

i. **Visually impaired:** Visual impairments including blindness, various common types of low vision and poor eyesight, various types of color blindness;

ii. **Motor/Mobility:** e.g. difficulty or inability to use the hands, including tremors, muscle slowness, loss of fine muscle control, etc., due to conditions such as Parkinson's Disease, muscular dystrophy, cerebral palsy, stroke;

iii. **Hearing impaired:** Deafness or hearing impairments, including individuals who are have difficulties in hearing;

iv. **Seizures:** Photo epileptic seizures caused by visual strobe or flashing effects.

v. **Cognitive/Intellectual impaired:** Developmental disabilities, learning disabilities (dyslexia, dyscalculia, etc.), and cognitive disabilities of various origins, affecting memory, attention, developmental "maturity," problem-solving and logic skills, etc.

Individuals living with a disability use assistive technologies such as the following to enable and assist web browsing:

i. Screen reader software, which can read out, using synthesized speech, either selected elements of what is being displayed on the monitor (helpful for users with reading or learning difficulties), or which can read out everything that appears on the computer (used by blind and vision impaired users).

ii. Braille terminals, consisting of a Refreshable Braille display which renders text as Braille characters (usually by means of raising pegs through holes in a flat surface) and either a QWERTY or Braille keyboard.

iii. Screen magnification software which enlarges what is displayed on the computer monitor, making it easier to read for vision impaired users.

iv. Speech recognition software that can accept spoken commands to the computer, or turn dictation into grammatically correct text - useful for those who have difficulty using a mouse or a keyboard.

v. Keyboard overlays, which can make typing easier and more accurate for those who have motor control difficulties.

1.3.2 International developing process of information accessibility

Every region in the world has experienced over 100 percent growth in Internet usage in the last five years according to the table of World Internet Usage and Population Statistics provided by Internetworldstats.com. With the Internet becoming a more important part of society throughout the world, many countries are recognizing and acting upon the need to ensure access to the web for people with disabilities.

It seems as if each nation is taking a slightly different approach to the problem of Internet access for people with disabilities. Some have established laws that provide human or civil rights. Others, like the United States, have addressed the access issue through the technology procurement process. One fairly common approach throughout the world is for nations to support and adopt the Web accessibility guidelines (WCAG 2.0) created by the Web Accessibility Initiative (WAI).

In 1998 the US Congress amended the Rehabilitation Act to require Federal agencies to make their electronic and information technology accessible to people with disabilities. Section 508[2] was enacted to eliminate barriers in information technology, to make available new opportunities for people with disabilities, and to encourage development of technologies that will help achieve these goals. The law is applied to all Federal agencies when they develop, procure, maintain, or use electronic and information technology. Under Section 508, agencies must give disabled employees and members of the public access to information that is comparable to the access available to others.

Summary of Section 508 technical standards：

i. **Software Applications and Operating Systems:** include usability for people that are visually impaired, such as alternative keyboard navigation.

ii. **Web-based Intranet and Internet Information and Applications:** assure accessibility to web page graphics by the visually impaired using assistive technology such as screen readers and refreshable Braille displays. This is accomplished by using text labels and descriptors for graphics.

iii. **Telecommunications Products:** address accessibility for people who are deaf or hard of hearing. This includes technology compatibility with hearing aids, assistive listening devices, and TTYs.

iv. **Videos or Multimedia Products:** include requirements for captioning of multimedia products such as training or informational multimedia productions. Captioning or video descriptors must be able to be turned on or off.

v. **Self Contained, Closed Products:** product with embedded software, such as information kiosks, copiers, and fax machines, cannot be used with assistive technology. This standard requires that access features be built into these systems.

vi. **Desktop and Portable Computers:** discuss accessibility related to mechanically operated controls such as keyboards and touch screens.

The Disability Discrimination Act 1995 (c.13) (DDA 1995) [3] is an Act of the Parliament of the United Kingdom which makes it unlawful to discriminate against people in respect of their disabilities in relation to employment, the provision of goods and services, education and transport. It is a civil rights law. Other countries use constitutional, social rights or criminal law to make similar provisions. The Equality and Human Rights Commission provides support for people with disabilities Act. Equivalent legislation exists in Northern Ireland, which is enforced by the Northern Ireland Equality Commission. In 2001, the United Kingdom passed the special education regulations of disabilities, requiring all educational institutions and education-related services necessary to anticipate on people with disabilities in the educational services required. For example, while organizations do not have the visually impaired access to services, but they have required the agency to provide services immediately when necessary.

Some internal companies involved into the area of information accessibility at a very long time ago. For example, IBM began hiring the employees with disabilities in 1914.

IBM has eight research centers all over the world, the IBM global accessibility center "IBM Ability and Accessibility Center" is linked under the rank of IBM's research centers. The essential mission is to collect the best and the most advanced technology from the 8 centers to serve the R&D of accessibility. Up to date, IBM has established information accessibility centers in America, Japan, German, France and Australia.

Microsoft introduced two ways to support the technology of information accessibility. One is to adding accessibility performance to the popular products. Such as pre-setting some APIs to extend the products' existing practicabilities, some accessible products are developed for the people with disabilities. In addition, Microsoft has associated with more than 100 companies for the accessibility on the products R&D and manufacturing, so that its windows and other products can provide better services for all people. In Chinese, Microsoft has been a partner of China Braille Press on promoting application of information technology for the blind. On Microsoft's website, there are accessibility information technologies pages providing mass free resources for the developers.

1.3.3 Design criterion for network recourses accessibility

The World Wide Web Consortium (W3C) [4] is an international consortium where member organizations, a full-time staff, and the public work together to develop Web standards and guidelines designed to ensure long-term growth for the Web. Over 400 organizations are members of the consortium. W3C is jointly run by the MIT Computer Science and Artificial Intelligence Laboratory (MIT CSAIL) in the USA, the European Research Consortium for Informatics and Mathematics (ERCIM) headquartered in France and Keio University in Japan, and has seventeen outreach offices worldwide.

W3C's Web Accessibility Initiative (WAI) [5] works with organizations around world to make the web more accessible for people with disabilities and older users. WAI pursues web accessibility by ensuring that web technologies support accessibility; developing guidelines for Web content, browsers and media players, and authoring tools; developing resources to support improved evaluation tools; developing resources for education outreach; and coordinating with research and development efforts that can affect future accessibility of the Web. WAI is supported in part by the U.S. Department of Education's National Institute on Disability and Rehabilitation Research (NIDRR), European Commission's Information Society Technologies Programmed, HP, IBM, Microsoft Corporation, SAP, and Wells Fargo.

On 11th December 2008 W3C announces a new standard that will help Web designers and developers to create sites that better meet the needs of users with disabilities and older users. Drawing on extensive experience and community feedback, the Web Content Accessibility Guidelines (WCAG) 2.0[6] improve upon W3C's groundbreaking initial standard for accessible web content.

This new standard from the WAI will advance accessibility across the full range of Web content (such as text, images, audio, and video) and Web applications. WCAG 2.0 can be more precisely tested, yet it allows Web developers more flexibility and potential for innovation. Together with supporting technical and educational materials, WCAG 2.0 is easier to understand and use.

Web Content Accessibility Guidelines (WCAG) 2.0 defines how to make Web content more accessible to people with disabilities. Accessibility involves a wide range of disabilities, including visual, auditory, physical, speech, cognitive, language, learning, and neurological disabilities. Although these guidelines cover a wide range of issues, they are not able to address the needs of people with all types, degrees, and combinations of disability. These guidelines also make Web content more usable by older individuals with changing abilities due to aging and often improve usability for users in general.

WCAG 2.0 is developed through the W3C process in cooperation with individuals and organizations around the world, with a goal of providing a shared standard for Web content accessibility that meets the needs of individuals, organizations, and governments internationally. WCAG 2.0 builds on WCAG 1.0 [WCAG10] and is designed to apply broadly to different Web technologies now and in the future, and to be testable with a combination of automated testing and human evaluation.

The individuals and organizations that use WCAG vary widely and include Web designers and developers, policy makers, purchasing agents, teachers, and students. In order to meet the varying needs of this audience, several layers of guidance are provided including overall *principles*, general *guidelines*, testable *success criteria* and a rich collection of *sufficient techniques, advisory techniques*, and *documented common failures* with examples, resource links and code.

The WCAG is of the most effect all over the world. And many other standards made by many countries have made references to it. The Disabilities' Right Committee and the British Institute of Standard have set down a criterion about the web accessibility and the government has introduced it into the technology standard for governmental stock. In Jun 2004, Japan Industry Standard Association released JISX 8341. In its third section, accessible demands on web service are regulated according to the WCAG.

1.3.4 Some cases of information accessibility

- **Kyoto City Web**

The challenge: Leverage the Internet to increase tourism in Kyoto City, a large, culture-rich metropolis in Japan. Help make sure that the Kyoto City Web site is more accessible to all people regardless of ability or disability. Include both foreign language support and text-to-speech functionality for Japanese, English, Korean and Chinese.

The solution: IBM Easy Web Browsing technology is being offered, at no charge to end users, on the Kyoto City Web site, to allow users who have low vision to enlarge text or read text aloud.

The benefit: follows the direction and "Grand Vision" of Kyoto for the 21st Century. Helped establish an accessible Web site that is attracting the global community. Increased traffic on the Web site.

1) Kyoto City government uses Easy Web Browsing as part of its 'Grand Vision' for 21st Century：

Seeking to create a direction for civic life and city development, the Kyoto City government devised a "Grand Vision" for the 21st Century. In 1978, the city made a declaration to the world that Kyoto would be "a city open to the free exchange of world cultures." As part of the plan to achieve this ideal, Kyoto formulated "The Master Concept of Kyoto City" in 1983 with the aim of meeting many of its goals by the year 2000. This Master Concept asserts that the city will keep developing, but at the same time preserve its tradition. From Kyoto City Web site: (see Figure 1)

Fig. 1. Kyoto City Web site home

"To attract the world's cultures, Kyoto City created a Web site that allowed all people, regardless of their abilities or native language, to be able to access information. The Web site is available in four languages, and uses IBM Easy Web Browsing technology to enlarge text and read it aloud. The technology is very easy to use and is offered free to the user. Senior citizens, who often have vision difficulties such as low vision or cataracts, can now access all the information on the Kyoto City Web site through enlarged text or as a "screen reader." The screen size can be customized from 50% to 600%. It also enables the user to change the color of the Web site background to help those with color blindness and other color-related vision impairments. For children and non-Kyoto natives, the IBM Easy Web Browsing "reading aloud" function helps increase comprehension. Offering this enhanced communications functionality as part of its Web site increases the user's comfort level with technology – even for novice users."

2) Vision for the future of Kyoto City

In the coming years, government agencies, local municipalities and private companies will plan how to prepare their Web content in various languages – such as English, Hangul and Chinese – in order to enhance global information transmission. They can use the Kyoto City Web site as the model. By adopting the multilingual text-to-speech technology from IBM, Easy Web Browsing can be used to help those agencies address the needs of their constituents.

1.3.5 References：

1、http://en.wikipedia.org/wiki
2、http://usability.gov/web_508/tut-b.html
3、http://www.york.ac.uk/admin/hr/resources/policy/disability_dda_1995.htm
4、http://www.w3.org/
5、http://www.webaim.org/
6、http://www.w3.org/TR/WCAG20/
7、http://www-03.ibm.com/able/index.html

1.4 Higher education grid for disabled

1.4.1 Grid and education

Grid is the forefront technology in the field of IT and Internet. It is considered the most significant breakthrough at computer architecture, operating system, user interface since 1995 to 2010. It integrates the whole Internet into one huge super computer and will keep it to share the resources of compute, storage, data, information, knowledge, expert, etc. There is no fixed definition for grid but the following features:

- Distribution and Resource Sharing
- High degree of abstraction
- Self-similarity
- Dynamic nature and diversity
- Autonomy and the multiple of management

The classified method of grid can be various. According to the type of managed resources, grid can be categorized into compute grid, data grid, information grid, service grid, knowledge grid, semantic grid, etc. Applying the grid to education to provide all kinds of educational resource becomes the education grid. Here, the educational resources include the course ware and very type of media materiel as well as the computing ability, storage space, databases, sensors and demote devices.

China Education and Research Grid (ChinaGrid[1]) is an important project of the fifteenth national "211 project" and is responsible by Chinese Ministry of Education. Up to now[2], it has integrated a large number of grid resources of 20 famous universities from 13 provinces and cities, the computing power of polymerization is more than 16 trillion times per second, the storage capacity is more than 170 TB, it has become one of the world's largest super grid. Five application grid have been developed successfully on the bioinformatics, image processing, computational fluid dynamics, mass information processing and online university courses.

There are more than 120 types of bioinformatics software tools, 30 kinds of services related to database, about 100,000 medical images, 10,000 pieces of diagnostic data. Chinagrid supports the typical grid application such as the optimized design of digitized virtual man and aircraft, integrates digital museum resources of 18 universities, provides more than 300 college courses and approximately 3,500 hours course videos. It can provide many grid services such as the video-on-demand education system through the 22 servers distributed in 17 cities.

The Kerala Education Grid Project is a path-breaking initiative of the Kerala government to provide quality education to all the students pursuing higher studies in the state. The project vision is to provide quality education to all, independent of geography. The project aims to facilitate multiple independent course-specific collaborative information and knowledge networks across distributed servers over the Internet as well as affordable and pedagogically effective online assisting learning environment for the colleges in any subject.
American Education Grid Portal[3] is provided as a platform for the educational community to support generation and sharing of education resources across the different institutions, universities and colleges of higher education. The portal is also intended to facilitate collaboration, sharing of knowledge, best practices and co-operation to improve the quality of education offered in the colleges and in the open learning mode. In many ways, Education Grid is complementary to the National Program on Technology Enhanced Learning that is being executed by the IITs and IISc to develop content in large number of courses for engineering colleges. It provides development and deployment of systems and processes that use NPTEL and other open content for conducting quality education in the colleges.

1.4.2 Grid resources for special education

1.4.2.1 The status of higher special education

The higher special education in China began in the medium 80s in 20th century. From 1985, limb-impaired students have been recruited by Shandong Binzhou medicine college. In 1987, the special education school of Changchun University was established and became the first higher special education academy in China. Till now, there are more than 10 high schools recruits the various disabilities.
There are four manners exist present, such as establishing special education academy or setting the corresponding department and major in common colleges, let the people with disabilities study together with the healthy students, setting up some junior colleges to recruit people with disabilities and is managed by the cooperation of independent vocational school and adult education college, and all other regular and irregular network education forms [4].
The prevalent computer & network technology has penetrated into the high special education colleges to assist the teaching and researching and many relevant works have been reported. In the teaching application of network technology in higher special educational colleges, study on how to exert the function of multimedia and how to make full use of the advantages that network resources made to teaching is worth to investigate. Studies show that information technologies have laid out obvious advantages at the compensating the dumps for their physiology limitation and increasing the interests in study.
British Staffordshire University began the development of virtual learning system COSE in 1996 and now the third version is come into birth. In 2001, an e-learning junior college was held in Shenzhen Radio & Television University that is serviced to the people with disabilities and is aroused strong reverberation. It shows that modern distance education model is the efficient method to make the disabilities get the equality education and obtain employment. Subsequently the education academy for disabled people of central Radio &

TV University is established. But the e-learning study on the high special education in high school is of no reports.
According to the result of the second countrywide disabilities sampling investigation, the total number of disabled people in China is 8296 and it takes the portion of 6.34% to the national total. Throughout the country there are only more than 10 colleges that recruit disabled students. Under the whole background of constructing socialism harmonious society, it is of most important to resolve the equality education for the disabled. Engaging in the study of special education e-learning system in common colleges can benefit to the development of our national special education and also can make more people with disabilities obtain higher education.

1.4.2.2 Implementation of e-learning system for higher special education based on grid

Distance education is one of the most important aspects of informationization education. It can enable the special needs group breakthrough the limitation of traditional teaching mode and obtain high-quality education. It's well known that the distance education system is of a distributed circumstance in which the men and men, men and computer can share the information independent of the time and space limits. As the third generation network technology, grid can provide better platform for resources sharing. Grid is a new technology based on the internet and mean while integrates the whole internet into a vast super computer to realize the comprehensive sharing of computer resources, data resources, information resources, knowledge resources and expert resources. Resource sharing is the most importance feature of grid and it can efficiently manage and schedule the processor time, memory, network and storage. International grid technology develops quickly and the distance education research reports based on grid are familiar, such as the Birmingham Grid for Learning, the education grid of Washington University, etc. Although they are not specialized for the special education, they provide some convenience offers to the people with disabilities and all kinds of users to meet their needs in it. By contraries, the research on high education service based on grid in Mandarin China is appeared lately. But several institutes and colleges have taken their work into different degree. The work of Beijing Jiaotong University, Zhejiang University of technology, Guangzhou University, etc. are reported. China-grid plan also includes the relevant content about distance education. By reading through all the available literature, a conclusion can be drawn that there is no instance of study on e-learning system for higher special education based on grid in colleges.

1.4.3 A case study on special higher education grid

In this section we will introduce the layout of e-learning teaching resources for higher special education worked by our group. It expands the application fields of grid and meanwhile wishes that the more convenience network study circumstances is offered to more and more people with disabilities.

1.4.3.1 Grid structure

The main purpose of the proposed grid is to establish a distributed and massive education resource library, offer a set of resource sharing and storage management mechanisms by which users can conveniently and quickly access network information anytime and

anywhere. Because of that the service objects is the special needs group, a special dealing is necessary to the preparation of educational resources and the offered services also has its special feature. The structure of the proposed system is shown in fig. 2.
Education resource servers distributed in different regions will continue to input the corresponding information into the e-learning grid included network courseware, video on demand (VOD), assistant study information and assistant supports. User can capture all kinds of information service by distance logging in and upload or storage some resources to share with other users. The physical position and topological structure of the whole network are transparent to all users. So users do not need to know that where the coursewares were stored. The relevant work is done by grid middleware. In this system, high reliable service can be obtained as far as there is one grid node in work.
The assist support module at the server end will offer the client downloading and video format transferring function. All the resources provided by the grid will suite to all persons including the visual impairments. So the downloaded client will offer text-to-speech function. Network courseware and VOD files can be played online or in local machine. The function of video format transferring is equipped in any grid node. Storing format

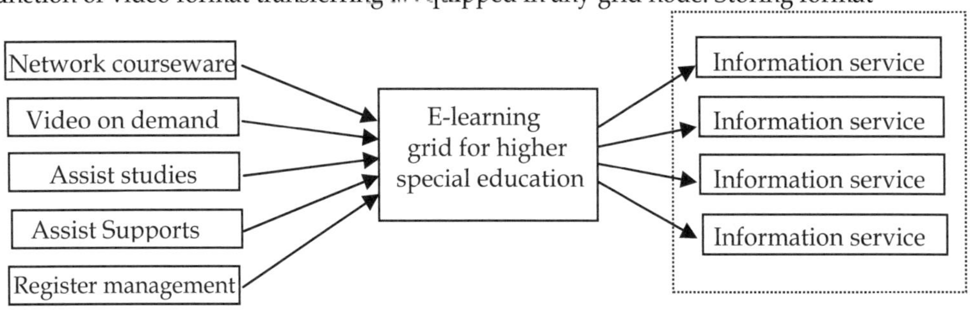

Fig. 2. Structure of e-learning grid for higher special education

transferring makes that the downloaded video can be played in computer, mp3 and even portable cellular phone. Register management is accomplished by main grid node and it includes the log in for node user and member user. Two kinds of users can share the grid service. Besides, the node user can storage its private resources or offer some service and the member users can give its own resource storage in the grid and share it with all the other users.

1.4.3.2 Grid components and its access model

Three components exist in the grid, they are grid client, grid manager and grid node. There is an integrative web server at grid client but it can only send the requirement to the grid manager. In the grid node, Java technology is adopted to deal with the requirements came from client or grid manager. Grid manager is responsible to the whole grid management. It not only deals with the web requirement but also the grid database.
Grid client can directly access the grid node to obtain various services. This scheme is useful to keep the load balance. See fig. 3 for the access model.

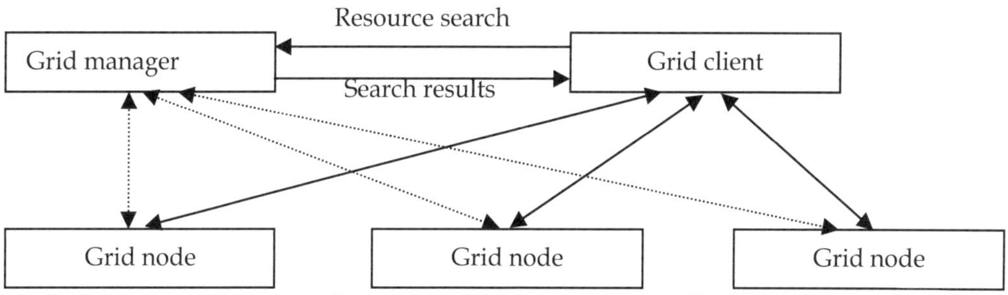

Fig. 3. Access model of e-learning grid for higher special education

From the above fig. we can see that the first role of the grid is resource storage. Both the grid node and client can submit its own teaching resource to the grid and the grid manager decides which node will be used. During the operation, the requirement is first transferred from grid node or client to grid manager, then the manager searches the management database to confirm which node can offer the service according to the requirement and then sends the result (including the node ID) to the required node or client. When the required end got the responds information it can directly get connection with the grid node signed by node ID. The second role of this grid is to offer information service. When the service requirement is sent to the grid manager from client, the grid manager also searches the inner information to find the grid nodes which can meet the needs and then send all the available nodes' IDs to client. The client can select one node, but the default setting is to connect with the first node of the nodes list. Grid manager in this access model is the kernel of the whole grid system. So we take a special server as the grid manager and its service management function is baked up in the main node. The grid manager responds to the client's requirements regularly and once the exception occurred, the main grid node takes the place of grid manager immediately. As for the important or the unique resources of the grid, it always is stored a copy on server or other nodes. The grid system can be regularly run as long as one node is in work.

The data storages at the grid manager include:

(1)Node user information table: userID, userName, password, realName, address, nodeParameter.

(2)Member user information table: userID, user-Name, password, realName, address, memberLevel.

(3)Resource information table: ResourceID, cap-tion, metadata, nodeIDs.

Among the resource information table, "Resource-ID" is used to sign every teaching resource. It is confirmed when the resource is registered or uploaded. "caption" signs the resource name and "metadata" refers to the feature parameters of the resource such as the size, storage format, knowledge-point, content introduction, etc. "nodeIDs" shows the nodes' IDs that storage the resource.

1.4.3.3 Design of grid resource library

The particularity of the service object determines the particularity of resource library in the proposed e-learning grid. Every teaching resource in the grid can be lies in both the video and audio media. Such as the network courseware is played as video by default and its service objects are deaf-and-dumb students. Before playing these kinds of resources user can make selection whether needs the speech support. On the contrary, video on demand resources will be played by default for visual impairments. So before playing user can make selection that whether needs the text-caption support. The resource storage names is the integrated identifier which is composed of resource ID, course identifier, resource type, knowledge point. Each part is separated by "-". Resource ID is the unique and uniform code of all resources and is consists of year (4bits), month (2bits), day (2bits) and an order number (3bit). Course identifier implies the course name and it is expressed by the first spelling letter of Chinese word. Resource type refers to the network courseware or VOD media, etc. In this system is coded by two bits number such as 01. Knowledge point is also expressed by the first spelling letter of Chinese content. For example, if the resource code is 20060122001-jsjwhjc-01-gaishu,it means that the resource is a network courseware for computer basic knowledge (in Chinese is : ji suan ji wen hua ji chu), the knowledge point is summarize (in Chinese is: gai shu) and it is the first resource submitted on January the 22nd in 2006. The system resource list will be shown to the user when the client access grid server. The total meaning of the resource code can benefit to both the user and the management people.

1.4.4 References：

[1] http://www.chinagrid.edu.cn
[2] http://news.xinhuanet.com/newmedia/2006-07/25/content_4875147.htm
[3] http://www.edugrid.ac.in
[4] YU Huiyun, WEI Xiaoman. A Review of Researches on Higher Special Education in China. Chinese journal of special education. 2006, 4:66-70(in Chinese)

11

Application of Data-Mining Technology on E-Learning Material Recommendation

Feng-Jung Liu and Bai-Jiun Shih
Tajen University
Ping Tung, Taiwan

1. Introduction

"Information overload" problem is even more emphasized with the growing amount of text data in electronic form and the availability of the information on the constantly growing World Wide Web (Mladenic et. al., 2003). When a user enters a keyword, such as "pencil" into a search engine, the result returned is often a long list of web pages, many of which are irrelevant, moved, or abandoned (Smith et. al., 2003). It is virtually impossible for any single user to filter out quality information under such overloading situation (Shih et. al., 2007).
Designing appropriate tools for teaching and learning is a feasible approach to reduce the barriers teachers might encounter when adopting technology in their teaching (Marx et. al., 1998; Putnam & Borko, 2000). With potentially hundreds of attributes to review for a course, it is hard for the instructor to have a comprehensive view of the information embedded in the transcript (Dringus & Ellis, 2005). Computer-based systems have great potential for delivering learning material (Masiello, Ramberg, & Lonka, 2005), which frees teachers from handling mechanical matters so they can practice far more humanized pedagogical thinking. However, information comes from different sources embedded with diverse formats in the form of metadata, making it troublesome for the computerized programming to create professional materials. (Shih et. al., 2007).The major problems are:
(1)Difficulty of learning resource sharing.
Even if all E-earning systems follow the common standard, users still have to visit individual platforms to gain appropriate course materials contents. It is comparatively inconvenient.
(2) High redundancy of learning material.
Due to difficulty of resource-sharing, it is hard for teachers to figure out the redundancy of course materials and therefore results in the waste of resources, physically and virtually. Even worse, the consistency of course content is endangered which might eventually slow down the innovation momentum of course materials.
(3) Deficiency of the course brief.
It is hard to abstract course summary or brief automatically in efficient way. So, most courseware systems only list the course names or the unit titles. Information is insufficient for learners to judge quality of course content before they enroll certain courses.

To solve the problems mentioned above, we propose an automatic inquiring system for learning materials which utilize the data-sharing and fast searching properties of LDAP. Our system not only emphasizes friendly search interfaces, but also excavates the association rule from log data of learning activities. Meanwhile, collaborative filtration is employed to improve the reliability of the searching results.
However, the result lacked meaningful associations or visual accessibility in current approach. We then intend to employ some AI techniques to improve the results. A topic map seems to be a good solution. Fisher, Wandersee and Moody (2000) said that a topic map presents a group of assets in a network structure; the knowledge network is completed by interlinked conceptual nodes, and spread out in a framework. It not only involves sets of concepts but also the organization of concepts in terms of their inter-relationships.
In this Chapter, we will give a brief review of what has been done on addressing the information overload problem on e-Learning, and explain how related techniques were applied. After then, a detailed description of the system implementation will be provided, followed by pedagogical application suggestions to possible alternatives for the integration of the technology into the learning field. Both the technical and educational evaluations of the system were discussed. At last, our conclusion brings some ideas and suggestions to the alternative possible integration of technology into learning in all fields.

2. Literature Review

A key factor of hypermedia-based learning is customizable cognitive style as it suffices users' information processing habits, representing individual user's typical modes of perceiving, thinking, remembering and problem solving. Cognitive psychologists recognize that knowledge has a basic structure which presents the inter-relationships between concepts. Anderson (1980) distinguished knowledge into declarative and procedural types to identify their characteristics as abstract or practical functions (Anderson, 1980). In understanding knowledge, Ausubel (1968) provided two strategies including progressive differentiation and integrative reconciliation for making meaningful learning focusing on the systematic methods to learning (Ausubel, 1968). The implication of these theories is two-fold; one, knowledge has an internal structure to sustain itself; two, systematic retrieval and understanding of knowledge is an effective method for learning (Shih et. al., 2007).
In order to effectively use technology to assist the education process, helping learners to collect, process, digest, and analyze the information, we introduce data mining, association and collaborative filtering technologies, describing how the technology facilitates the processing of data, and how the dynamic map can achieve the pedagogical goal.
Generally speaking, there are two approaches to organize and present knowledge: top-down and bottom-up. Top-down approaches consist of supervised-learning. They require human-experts to define knowledge ontology (Noy & McGuinness, 2001) and taxonomy (Bruno & Richmond, 2003). Accordingly, the machine classifies the knowledge by those predefined rules, based on co-occurrence and ANN (Artificial Neural Network). Inversely, bottom-up approaches are fully-automatic and represent unsupervised-learning, including SOM (Kohonen, 2001) and knowledge maps. However, most applications took hybrid approaches, that is, a human expert (SME: subject material expert) to predefine ontology and taxonomy and then clustering and organizing the knowledge by using ANN or SOM. This is sometimes called reinforcement learning. (Bruno & Richmond, 2003)

2.1 Data Searching, Storage and Retrieval

The Lightweight Directory Access Protocol, LDAP, is an application protocol for querying and modifying directory services running over TCP/IP. LDAP was originally intended to be a "lightweight" alternative protocol for accessing X.500 directory services through the simpler (and now widespread) TCP/IP protocol stack. The advantages are:

(1) fast searching: LDAP utilizes the properties of data hierarchy, caching technology and the innovative index technology to offer fast inquiry service;

(2) Extendable Data schemas: The data schema mainly describes and defines the attribute of entries in the directory tree. LDAP allows users to define data schemas by themselves and let schema specification more flexible;

(3) Multiple access permissions and data encoding: Except that be able to establish the access permissions according to users' specifications individually, LDAP also supports some security mechanisms, such as SSL (Secure Socket Layers), TLS (Transport Layer Security) and SASL (Simple Authentication & Security Layer);

(4) Suitable for the inquiry of a large amount of data: The directory database is designed under the assumption that the frequency of reading is greater than frequency of writing. It can improve the usability and dependability of data by duplicating data extensively.

XML and Java technology are recognized as ideal building blocks for developing Web services and applications that access Web services. JAXB (Java Architecture for XML Binding) is an XML binding model that defines the way of automatic mapping XML documents into objects in a programming language. Two major processes, marshalling and unmarshalling, take care of the mapping between Java objects and XML documents, which makes JAXB surpass traditional SAX and DOM approaches. Its advantages are:

(1)Simplicity: It is Java procedure too to derive the classification (Schema-Derived Classes & Interfaces) through the outline that Binding Compiler compiles out, so does not need to deal with XML file by oneself, and does not deposit and withdraw the content tree without according to the order;

(2)Extensibility: The programmer can revise the schemas and derive the classification independently, and let the procedure accord with systematic requirements even more. Additionally, when XML Schema is changed to some extents, it just needs to recompile Schema, and increase some more procedures newly, instead of needing to revise the original procedures,

(3)Efficiency: Because all of data of the content tree are produced of JAXB according with the definition of XML Schema, there not exist any invalid methods or objects. Even it could use the Unmarshaller class to verify whether XML file is effective.

2.2 Data Association

The Apriori algorithm(Agrawal, 1993) is one of the most representative algorithms of association rule. Its key steps are: (1) produce the candidate set from the database, and then find out the largest item-set according with the minimum support degree; (2) find out the items from the large item-set derived in previous step, in accord with the minimum confidence degree.

However this approach is time-consuming because the database are usually scanned too many times. Therefore, many algorithms, like the DIC algorithm (Brin et. al., 1997), DHP algorithm(Park. et. al., 1995) , are proposed successively to improve the performance. We suggest using association rule mining techniques to build an e-learning material recommendation system that intelligently recommend on-line learning activities or shortcuts in the course web site to learners based on the actions of previous learners to improve course content.

2.3 Collaborative Filtering

Collaborative filtering is one of recommendation mechanism for personage, also called "people to people correlation". Currently, it is applied to all kinds of e-commerce extensively to infer user's interest in other products or the service through the analysis of user's materials or the behavior. Currently, the filtration technologies are classified into the following three methods:

(1)Rule-based filtration:
By the questionnaire or other ways to obtain the data, such as user's preference, or interest, etc. which will be made use of the reference as recommending.
(2)Content-based filtration:
The system recommends other relevant contents according to the user's selected content. And, the recommended content mostly were used and hived off or consulted by other user's experience before.
(3)Activity-based filtration:
By collecting user's activity information, infer the relation of some contents. Such mechanism is usually applied on these websites without member system.Prior works in collaborative filtering have dealt with improving the accuracy of the predictions. In the proposed system, we adopted the collaborative filtering instead of the complicated content processing, and provided recommendation on possible keywords of contents with the accuracy.

3. Implementation

We utilized the techniques of the LDAP directory server and JAXB to reduce the load of development of search engine and the complexity of parsing the contents (Li et al., 2005). The data-mining techniques will be applied to support the e-learning materials recommendation. Relevant techniques including LDAP, JAXB, association rule and collaborative filtering are illustrated below.

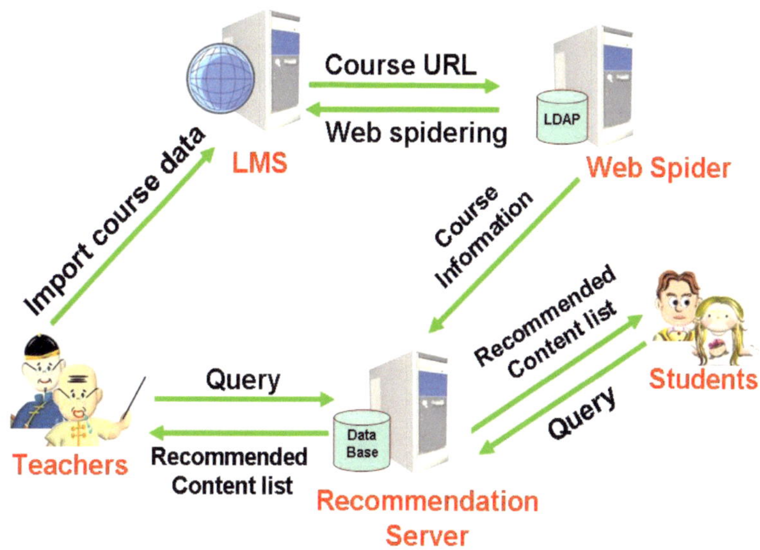

Fig. 1. System architecture.

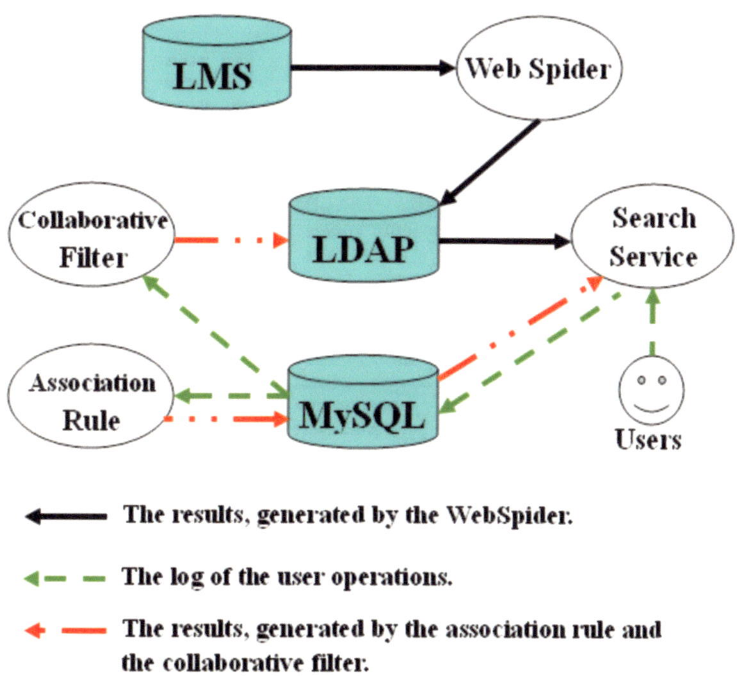

Fig. 2. The data flow of the recommendation system.

In the recommendation system, it consists of three participants: learning management system, web spider and recommendation server as shown in Figure. 1. Learning management system, LMS, not only manages and provides the content services, but also registers the content URL address to web spider for collecting content index data. Through the URL address of content, the web spider will visit and parse all of the content recursively and store resulting contents into LDAP server. This scheme is applicable for all of e-learning content accessible by HTTP protocol. At last, a web-based querying system is presented to the users for friendly learning.

As shown in the Figure. 1, while teachers or content providers uploaded their learning materials to the LMS systems, the background process stored in the LMS will pass the pathname or URL address of the uploaded materials to the web spider-like process for collecting index data. The web spider parses and traces all linked documents of the course contents. As an example of course content made by StreamAuthor package (CyberLink. http://www.cyberlink.com/multi/products/main_7_ENU.html), the content mostly consisted of a lot of HTML document translated from MS Powerpoint formatted files. In implementation, we defined and realized the PptHtmlParser class derived from HtmlParser interface to parse the materials created by the StreamAuthor package. The web spider will recursively visit these links embedded in the parsed documents. In Figure. 2, it describes the data flow in the recommendation system including three data sources.

In implementation, we developed the backend program for collecting user behavior-related data in the JAVA programming language. In addition to the sake of the properties of cross-platform and easy usages, JAVA can directly utilize the abundant packages with powerful functions, such as HttpClient in Apache Jakarta project (http://jakarta.apache.org/commons/httpclient/), HtmlParser (http://htmlparser.sourceforge.net/) created by Derrick Oswald, etc.., is good for reducing the cost of system implementation. Additionally, we adopted the JAXB mechanism to transform the result, generated by HtmlParser process, to the XML documents, fit to the predefined schema as shown in Figure. 3. Because of the unmarshalling mechanism, it is easy to access data elements in XML documents with the minimum burden of programming.

```
<xs:element name="LearningResource" type="LRTy...
<xs:complexType name="LRType">
  <xs:sequence>
  <xs:element name="url" type="xs:anyURI"/>
  <xs:element name="title" type="xs:string"/>
  <xs:element name="topic" type="xs:string" minO...
  <xs:element name="content" type="xs:string" min..
  <xs:element name="oriContent" type="xs:string"/>
  </xs:sequence>
</xs:complexType>
```

Fig. 3. The schema of JAXB.

The proposed recommendation system is achieved with the four jobs: collecting indexing data, inquiring services, association rule and collaborative filtering as shown in Figure. 2. We will have detailed descriptions as follows.

3.1 Index Data Collection

Collecting data index is similar to other web spider searching engines. The parser will automatically search the complete course content and distinguish the topic from the content body by HTML tags. Moreover, it transform the data into the XML documents compliant to the XML schema by utilizing the Marshaller mechanism of JAXB (Ed Ort et al., 2003) as showed in Figure. 4. Besides, it is easy to validate and access XML documents by JAXB unmarshalling functions by JNDI (java naming and directory Interface). The processed data are stored into the LDAP database at last.

```
public static void Html2Xml(HtmlParser hp,String ...

//Create LRType  Object, from the derived class from JAXB
    LRType lrt = new LRType();
    lrt.setUrl(hp.getURL().toString());
    ......
    JAXBContext jc = JAXBContext.newInstance...
    JAXBElement<LRType> lrElement =
    (new ObjectFactory()).createLearningResource(lrt);

//Create the Marshaller Oobject and store the LRType in a file
    Marshaller mar = jc.createMarshaller();
    mar.setProperty(Marshaller.JAXB_FORMATT...
    mar.marshal(lrElement,new FileOutputStream...
                                        ....
}
```

Fig. 4. Parts of the program for JAXB Marshaller mechanism.

3.2 Inquiring services

Usually, learners in the e-learning system concern about learning resources related to the topics. Through the data sharing mechanism of the LDAP, the metadata of the learning materials distributed in several platforms are stored into the same directory database. With such a deployment, teachers can easily inquire the related learning resource and enrich them. The learners can now search through the common interfac for materials orginally distributed among different LMS sites.

Collecting the users' operating behavior, including searching strings, entry links, etc., is another task. We treated each searching string (keywords) issued as a transaction. Then, these transaction logs are used to mine the association rule with user behaviors. Additionally, the usage logs created by students following the resource links will be stored for collaborative filtering.

3.3 Association rule mining

Both the Apriori Algorithm(Agrawal et. al., 1994) and the Tree-based algorithm are employed to develop the association rule for the learning material recommendation system. An itemset can also be seen as a conjunction of a sequence of searching keywords by a learner in the same session. If an itemset satisfied minimum support, then it is a frequent itemset. It means that most of learners used those keywords in the frequent itemset to look up their interested contents. The minimum support threshold and minimum confidence threshold are influent on the reliability of filtered results. If set to the less, the reliability of conducted results will be reduced; otherwise, it will cause the number of the resulted data become too small and fail to infer to the accuracy prediction.

We used the SQL language to filter and sort the large one-items according to minimum support. And then, to make the combination of these filtered items and to calculate the number of transaction records in database which have the same elements as ones of the composed subset. The pseudo code for association rule mining is shown in Figure. 5.

In the association rule, an item-set is called a frequent itemset if it satisfies the minimum support threshold. And more, the reasonable items will be derived if these items satisfy the minimum confidence threshold. As to the settings of the minimum support threshold and the minimum confidence threshold, it is worth mentioning that the settings of the minimum support threshold and the minimum confidence threshold have much influence on the reliability of the filtered results. If these thresholds are set to a smaller value, the reliability of conducted results will be reduced; otherwise, it will cause the amount of the resulted data become too small and cannot infer to the accuracy prediction.

```
d=new array
t="select distinct session as s"
foreach(t as row){
  w="select word where session=row.s"
  foreach(w as item){
    arr=combination(item)
    foreach(arr as i){
      if(i contains d)
        i.count++
      else
        d.add(i)
    }
  }
}
```

Fig. 5. Pseudo code for association rule mining.

3.4 Collaborative filtering

The general collaborative filtration recommends the related information to the users. We used such a mechanism to discovering out and providing the corresponding keywords to these courses. Text mining techniques could also be used to find out the keywords in a context. However, related algorithms are sometimes too complicated to implement. Thus, we inferred the possible keywords of the course contents by analyzing the transaction logs of learners' searching strings. The steps of the proposed mechanism are shown as following.

```
u=new array
t=select distinct url
foreach(t as row){
  u.add(row.url)
  u[row].k=new array
  w=select word where url=row.url
  foreach(w as key){
    if(key contains u[row].k)
      u[row].k.count++
    else
      u[row].k.add(key)
  }
}
```

Fig. 6. Pseudo code for collaborative filtering.

Step 1: Calculate the frequency number of keywords used to inquire the preferred subjects by learners.
Step 2: By utilizing the result of the step above, filter the items by minimum threshold, and to store into LDAP server.

In the system implementation, the association rule is mainly adopted to find out the relations between these keywords learners used for searching the content. And, the collaborative filtration is applied to automatically filter the correct keywords of each course. The psuedo code for collaboratve filtering is shown in Figure. 6. Such mechanisms will greatly benefit learners on searching out their interested materials quickly and correctly. We believe that as the amount of material grows, the better the performance of the content the navigation recommendation system will provide to the learners will become.

4. Results

In our system, main page shows a simplified table of contents with multiple levels of embedded categories. Learners can search contents by using multiple keywords concurrently like in regular search engine. Meanwhile, queries based on content creator, topic, content body are also allowed. Users start from the first-level keyword search, the related material will be tabulated just like the regular search engine. Below each topic, the collaborative filtered keywords will be presented. Users can follow the link to reach associated topics (course material). In this way, users can recursively trace down the topic tree with virtually infinite search levels.

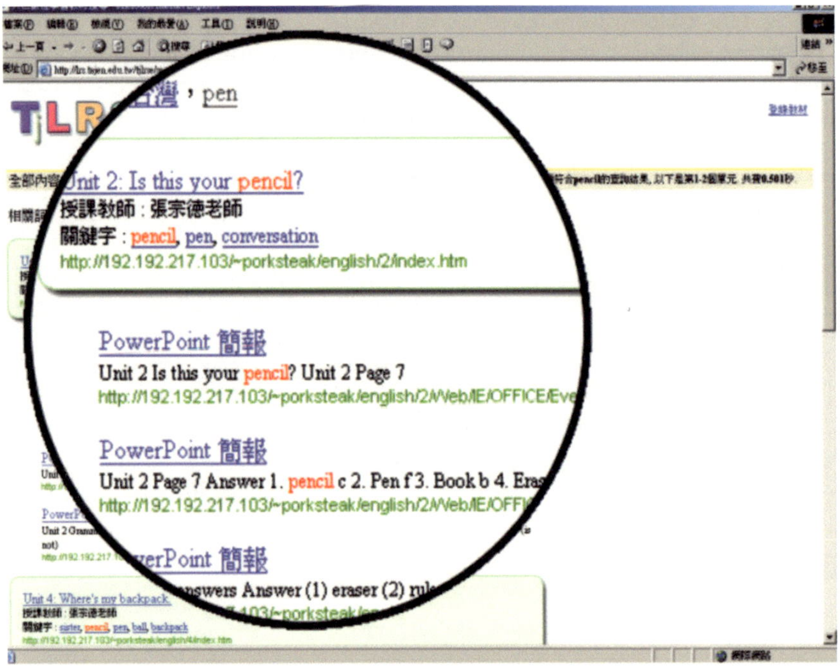

Fig. 7. The result conducted by searching with the "pencil" word.

Fig. 8. The associated words with the "pencil" word.

All results are presented in XML form and comply with the SCORM (SCORM 2004. http://www.adlnet.gov/) requirement. In Figure. 7, we demonstrate a search result for the keyword "pencil". Users first type in the keyword and the system reposes with "Unit 2: Is this your PENCIL?", which is a unit with the title containing target keyword. Below that, two keywords, "pencil" and "Conversation", defined by the teacher of Unit 2 or filtered by collaborative filtration, are cited also. Users can click on the hyperlinks and read the course content or explore the recommended topics.

Meanwhile, the system had found related topics generated from the user log. We can easily see these related topics in our system, previous users are interested with "pencil" and the teacher's name (of course, learners can trace down the link if he/she want to). As shown in Figure. 8, it shows the associated words with the "penceil" word on the top of screen.

While teachers upload their learning materials to the LMS systems, it will pass the pathname of uploaded material to the web spider for collecting index data. Then, we adopt the JAXB mechanism to transform the result generated by HtmlParser process into XML documents fitting to the defined schema. Bye Unmarshalling mechanism, it is easy to access data elements in documents.

There are currently more than 28 URLs of courses registered in the recommendation system. It contains more than 574 course units in total. According to the usage logs, users get into their content search by 2~3 keywords (averaged 2.39). And, each query request spends about 0.65 seconds.

To access the association efficiency, we observe the usage log in one hour period and found that 317 out of 517 queries followed system recommendation links, that is, approximately 60% or two-third of the users followed the system recommendation. This fact also implies a high "hit-rate" of association which we intent to exploit in a future survey.

5. Conclusion and Future Works

The proposed LMS supports systematic learning as well as constructive learning, which can effectively guide users through systematic browsing and inquiry. With this function, it works more as a dynamic researching tool than static learning material. On the other hand, the LMS sustains constructive learning. Although the functionality of a topic map is formulaic and systematic, it is also feasible for task-based learning. From the constructive point of view, learners need resources from multiple sources for the purpose of independent research. The mechanism can suffice the exploration of various learning styles, tendencies of interests, and professional abilities. More importantly, this guidance is not provided by teachers working in the classrooms, but by an autonomous system which is supported by a professional team with a wide array of resources. It turns learning into an information-guided dynamic. Therefore, this material helps users to "discover" new knowledge by presenting explicit and implicit knowledge so that they are able to see ideas and concepts that are most unexpected. This process matches the basic principles of constructivist learning.

In present E-learning scenes it is difficult to integrate all e-learning platforms from various vendors. However, as digital contents explosively grow, a resource-sharing mechanism should not be built solely for material-inquiring service across diverse e-learning LMS platforms. Thus, we proposed an integrated learning activity-based mechanism to assist users with automatic material recommendation. Thus, we established a prototype and proposed an integrated learning activity-based recommendation system. Currently, we proceed to collect a large number of user learning logs and to evaluate the effectiveness of the material recommendation system. We believe such a deployment will be helpful in achieving the better learning performance and a higher learner's satisfaction.

The techniques of the LDAP and the JAXB greatly reduced the load of development of search engine and the complexity of the content parsing. The material recommendation system improves the learning performances based on the learning activities of previous learners. From the educational perspective, teachers can effectively use this system to collect, process, digest, and analyze information. Learners can gain an overview of the subject matters while surfing the course contents.

From the usability perspective, we see that the LMS can carry out autonomous processing and presentation. It provides teachers and learners with an autonomous abstract environment. Even facing substantial documents, computers can replace human labor to efficiently process the tedious algorithm, but maintain high-level humanistic and professional analysis. Teachers can apply it on the teaching websites, and let the system compile thematic materials for them, saving time of copying and pasting, coding, and rewriting. It is customizable and interactive. The interface interacts with users, opening up layers of information upon every selection and inquiry. Hence, the route taken by every user is different, and the system returns with different results upon every choice. The system has proper support for customized learning. Best of all, it is easily manipulated. Most search engines, websites, and databases are designed to carry documents with different formats, content areas, and inquiry methods. Users who are unfamiliar with each system can get lost in it, and every inquiry can take up much energy and time. By the way, it is easy to use, and simple for users to grasp the key terms generated from the knowledge content. Users do not need to spend much time and energy to get a hold of the main theme of the massive resources. Even learners without prerequisite knowledge or sufficient subject understanding to reach into the depth of content, can still get on the system quickly, starting from the search item.

Educational evaluations are scheduled in the forthcoming year after accumulating threshold amount of user-experience. We plan to investigate the usability and instructional value of the LMS, which includes the presentation of material categories and the trouble-free search for materials; the convenience of data retrieval; the meaningfulness and usefulness of resources; the value of the system's assistance in new knowledge discovery; the usefulness of instructional needs; the appraisal of the overall conceptual presentation of large amount of information; and the level of acceptance and comprehensive understanding of the learning materials, and so forth. At the same time, a focus group performs interview to gather more feedbacks in depth.

6. References

Agrawal, R., and Srikant, R. (1994) Fast Algorithms for Mining Association Rules. Proc. of the 20th VLDB Conference, Santiago.

Agrawal, R., Imielinski, T., and Swami, A. (1993) Database mining: A performance perspective. IEEE Transactions on Knowledge and Data Engineering, 5(6):914-925. Special Issue on Learning and Discovery in Knowledge-Based Databases.

Anderson, J. R. (1980). Cognitive Psychology and Its Implications. San Francisco: W. H. Freeman and Company.

Apache Software Foundation. Jakarta Project-HttpClient. Available at http://jakarta.apache.org/commons/httpclient/.

Ausubel, D. P. (1968) Educational Psychology: A Cognitive View. New York: Holt, Rinehart & Winston.

Berry, M. A., & Linoff, G. S. (2000). Mastering Data Mining. NY: John Wiley & Sons.

Brin, S., Motwai, R., Ullman, J.D., and Tsur, S. (1997) Dynamic Itemset Counting and Implication Rules for Market Basket Data. ACM SIGMOD Conference on Management of Data, pp. 265-276.

Bruno, D., & Richmond, H. (2003). The truth about taxonomies. Information Management Journal, 37(2): 44-51.

Chen, H., Houston, A.L., Sewell, R.R., & Schatz, B.R. (1998). Internet browsing and searching: User evaluation of category map and concept space techniques. Journal of the American Society for Information Science, 49(7): 582-603.

Chen, K. J., & Liu, S. H. (1992). Word identification for Mandarin Chinese sentences. Proceedings of the 15th International Conference on Computational Linguistics. Nantes, France.

Chien, L. F. (1997). PAT-Tree-Based Keyword Extraction for Chinese Information Retrieval. Proceedings of the 20 International ACM SIGIR Conference on Research and Development in Information Retrieval. Philadelphia, PA, USA, July 27-31, 50-58.

CyberLink StreamAuthor. Available at http://www.cyberlink.com/multi/products/main_7_ENU.html.

Derrickoswald and Somik. HTML Parser. Available at http://htmlparser.sourceforge.net/

Dittenbach, M., Merkl, D., & Rauber, A. (2000). The Growing Hierarchical Self-Organizing Map. Proceedings of the Int'l Joint Conference on Neural Networks (IJCNN'2000), vol. VI: 15-19. Como, Italy: IEEE Computer Society Press.

Dringus, L. P., & Ellis, T. (2005). Using data mining as a strategy for assessing asynchronous discussion forums. Computer & Education, 45, 141-160.

Ed Ort, and Bhakti Mehta (2003) Java Architecture for XML Binding (JAXB). Available at http://java.sun.com/developer/technicalArticles/WebServices/jaxb.

Fisher, K.M., Wandersee, J. H., & Moody, D. (2000). Mapping Biology Knowledge. Boston: Kluwer Academic.

Fox, E., Hix, D. L., Nowell, T., Brueni, D. J., & Rao, D. (1993). Users, User Interfaces, and Objects: Envision, A Digital Library. Journal of the American Society for Information Science, 44(8), 480-491.

Govindasamy, T. (2001). Successful implementation of e-learning; pedagogical considerations. The Internet and Higher Education, 4(3-4), 287-299.

Han J., J. Pei, and Y. Yin (2000) Mining frequent patterns without candidate generation. Proc. of the ACM SIGMOD Conference on Management of data.

J.S Park, C.Ming-Syan, and S.Yu.Philip (1995) An Effective Hash Based Algorithm for Mining Association Rules. Proc. of ACM SGMOD, pp. 175-185.

Kiang, M. Y., & Kumar, A. (2001). An evaluation of self-organizing map networks a robust alternative to factor analysis in data mining applications. Information Systems Research, 12(2), 177-194.

Klemke, R. (2000). Context framework - an open approach to enhance organizational memory systems with context modeling techniques. Proceedings of the Third International Conference on Practical Aspects of Knowledge Management (PAKM2000), Basel, Switzerland, 30-31 October.
Kohonen, T. (2001). Self-organizing Maps. (3rd ed.). New York: Springer-Verlag.
Li, Sheng-Tun and Lin, Chu-Hung (2005) On the distributed management of SCORM-compliant course contents. Advanced Information Networking and Applications, AINA 2005. 19th International Conference on Volume 1, Issue, 28-30 March, pp. 221 - 226 vol.1.
Lin, X., Soergel, D., & Marchionini, G. (1991). A self-organizing semantic map for information retrieval. Proceeding of 14th the ACM SIGIR Conference Research and Development in Information Retrieval. Chicago, Illinois, USA, October 13-16, 262-269.
Liu, D.-R., & Hsu, C. (2004). Project-based knowledge maps: combining project mining and XML-enabled topic maps. Internet Research,14(3), 254-266.
Liu, F.J. & Shih, B.J., E-learning activity-based material recommendation system, Interactive Technology and Smart Education, VOl. 4, Issue: 4, P.200-P.207, 2007, 11.
Malhotra, Y. (1998). Deciphering the knowledge management hype. Journal for Quality & Participation, 21(4), 58-60.
Marx, R. W., Blumenfeld, P. C., Krajcik, J. S., & Soloway, E. (1998). New technologies for teacher professional development. Teaching and Teacher Education, 14, 33-52.
Masiello, I., Ramberg, R., & Lonka, K. (2005) Attitudes to the application of a Web-based learning system in a microbiology course. Computer & Education, 45, pp. 171-185.
Mladenic, D., & Grobelnik, M. (2003) Feature selection on hierarchy of web documents. Decision Support Systems, 35, pp. 45-87.
Nonaka, I., & Takeuchi, H. (1995) The Knowledge-Creating Company - How Japanese Companies Create the Dynamics of Innovation. NY: Oxford University Press.
Noy, N. F., & McGuinness, D. L. (2001). Ontology development 101: A guide to creating your first ontology. Stanford Knowledge Systems Laboratory Technical Report KSL-01-05 and Stanford Medical Informatics Technical Report SMI-2001-0880, March.
Putnam, R. T., & Borko, H. (2000). What do new views of knowledge and thinking have to say about research on teacher learning? Educational Researcher, 29, 4-15.
Rasmussen. E. (1992). Clustering Algorithms. In W. B. Frakes and R. Baeza-Yates (eds.) Information Retrieval Data Structures and Algorithms. NJ: Prentice Hall.
Rath, H. H., & Pepper, S. (1999). Topic maps: introduction and allegro. Proceedings of the Markup Technologies 99, Philadelphia.
Rauber, A., & Merkl, D. (1999). Automatic Labeling of Self-Organizing Maps: Making a Treasure-Map Reveal its Secrets. Proceedings of the 3. Pacific-Asia Conference on Knowledge Discovery and Data Mining (PAKDD'99). Beijing, China, April 26-28.
Roussinov, D., & Zhao, J. L., (2003). Automatic discovery of similarity relationships through Web mining. Decision Support Systems, 35, 149-166.
Salton, G. (1989). Automatic text processing. MA: Addison-Wesley.
SCORM 2004 3rd Edition. Available at http://www.adlnet.gov/.

Shih, B. -J., Shih, J. -L., & Chen, R. -L. (2007) Organizing learning materials through hierarchical topic maps: An illustration through Chinese herb medication. Journal of Computer Assisted Learning, Dec 07 issue, Volume 23, Issue 6, pp. 477-490.
Smith, K. A., & Ng, A. (2003). Web page clustering using a self-organizing map of user navigation patters. Decision Support Systems, 35, 245-256.
Veerasamy, A., & Belkin N. J. (1996). Evaluation of a Tool for Visualization of Information Retrieval Results. Proceedings of the 19th International ACM SIGIR Conference on Research and Development in Information Retrieval, (SIGIR), 85-92.
Wong, K. F., & Li, W. J. (1998). Intelligent Chinese Information Retrieval - Why Is It So Difficult? Proceedings of the First Asia Digital Library Workshop. 47-56.
Yang, C. C., Chen, H., & Hong, K. (April, 2003). Visualization of Large Category Map for Internet Browsing. Decision Support Systems, Special Issue on Web Retrieval and Mining, 35(1), 89-102.
Yoon, B.-U.,Yoon, C. -B., & Park, Y. -T. (2002). On the development and application of a self-organizing feature map-based patent map. R&D management, 32(4), 291-300.
Zamir, O., & Etzioni, O. (May, 1999) Grouper: A Dynamic Clustering Interface to Web Search Results. Computer Networks, 31(11-16), 1361-1374.

12

Loosely-Tied Distributed Architecture for Highly Scalable E-Learning System

Gierłowski and Nowicki
Gdansk University of Technology
Poland

1. Introduction

Vast majority of modern e-learning products are based on client-server architecture and utilization of web-based technologies (WBT). Such approach permits easy creation of e-learning systems that do not require a complex, operating system dependant client software. All possible mechanisms are moved to a system's server, while client side software is severely reduced and implemented by use of operating system independent WBTs (thin-client architecture). That way any user with a decent version of any popular operating system is able to access learning resources and services, providing operator of the system with a widest possible user group. Overall costs of system deployment are also significantly reduced by eliminating a need for a client software installation.

Unfortunately there are also drawbacks of such solution. Because of the majority of mechanisms are located on the server, its usage levels trend to build up quickly leading to limited system scalability. Moreover, WBTs utilized to create thin-client part of e-learning system, depend on constant, reliable network connectivity to system's server. Any disruption of such connectivity can lead to lack of service, client instability or even worse - presentation of malformed results, which is unacceptable in didactic tasks. To make things worse, thin-client element of the system cannot include advanced error handling and recovery mechanisms.

While web-based thin-client architecture works well in case of uncomplicated e-learning content distribution, its limitations will negatively impact functionality of more sophisticated systems (such as systems utilizing didactic simulation or providing advanced knowledge assessment capabilities) and are not prepared to handle limited/unstable network connectivity scenarios.

In the following chapter we describe a novel, distributed e-learning system architecture. It still utilizes web-based technologies, but its design differs radically from currently popular e-learning solutions which rely almost exclusively on thin-client architecture. In our design we employed loosely-tied distributed system architecture, full-client approach, strict modularity, and our original communications package called Communication Abstraction Layer (ComAL) - specifically designed to support communication functions of e-learning systems in diverse network conditions (including fully offline environment).

Instead of reducing client software sophistication and moving all possible mechanisms to a server part of a system, we propose to divide its functionality into self-sufficient blocks (called modules) and define methods of communications between them. Such approach gives us a number of unique advantages: system can be deployed gradually and not all of its elements need to be deployed (partial deployment); modules (which provide server or client functions) can be connected and disconnected from the system at will without disrupting its operation; the system is also resistant to network environment changes and can function as a managed entity even when there is no network connectivity whatsoever (offline scenario).
Furthermore, system scales very well and can support setups starting from a single client (without a server part), to big corporations consisting of many independent organizational units, hundreds of system's servers (each running a chosen set of modules) and thousands various clients. Integration with third party products is also easy, and third party applications can be used as system's clients or even integrated in its internal data paths.
We present our solution using our original knowledge assessment system, created according to this new architecture, as an example. The system was deployed and tested in production environment on Faculty of Electronics, Telecommunications and Informatics, Technical University of Gdansk with great success, reducing staff workload and increasing efficiency of didactic process. Included tests results also show system's versatility as the system was deployed in environments of classroom, remote and blended learning.
In the following section of the chapter we describe our motivation for creating a dedicated system for handling knowledge assessment related tasks. A basic system design considerations are included in the next section, followed by presentation of our original Communication Abstraction Layer (ComAL), designed specifically to handle communication tasks in eLearning systems. As the system is created in modular fashion a description of its architecture and existing modules is provided next. Modules are divided into server and client modules, with a special section devoted to a simulation-based ones. Next, we present description of a few possible configuration scenarios and present results of a practical deployment conducted on Gdańsk University of Technology. The chapter closes with conclusions gathered both from theoretical analysis of the new architecture and practical deployment of our distributed, ComAL-supported knowledge assessment system.

2. System motivation

The task of knowledge assessment is one of the fundamental elements of didactic process. It was also one of the first didactic tasks to be conducted by various electronic learning devices employed to support didactic process. Currently there are many e-learning solutions supporting knowledge assessment both as their main functionality or as an additional module ("Sakai...", 2008) , ("Moodle...", 2008). Almost any advanced e-learning tool offers this functionality. In light of those facts we could conclude that this area of e-learning is a well explored one and suitably supported by practical e-learning products.
Our experience with e-learning systems both as their users and designers, leads us to conclusion that the above statement is far from correct. Vast majority of currently available electronic knowledge assessment tools are extremely similar and offer strictly limited functionality. Such products offer almost exclusively knowledge assessment based on various choice tests and their automatic grading mechanisms most often are not very comprehensive and fit to support different grading scenarios.

In complex e-learning systems knowledge assessment functionality is treated as mandatory element, but also receives no special consideration, which often results in a simple implementation of choice test. Specialized knowledge testing solutions (employed for example by Microsoft during their computer proficiency exams) include more advanced mechanisms, like adaptive question selection, but they are few and still do not go beyond the basic scenario of choice test (Bersin & Accociates, 2004), (Jesukiewicz, P. et al., 2006).

Apart from these weaknesses, one of the most serious problems with currently available products and especially the most popular ones based on web-based thin-client architecture, is their strict dependence on network connectivity. Majority of such products require constantly active network connection during e-learning session and few are fit to function under other circumstances, such as periodic or no network connectivity, and still remain a part of managed e-learning system. The quality of network service is also a factor in case of many of such products (Gierłowski K. & Gierszewski T., 2004).

Apart from characteristics directly connected with didactic process, there is also a deployment phase of the system to consider. Designers of e-learning do not pay sufficient attention to this subject, and such approach often results in lack of user interest in good e-learning products or deployments unsuccessful despite otherwise correct choice of the system's functionality.

From our experience, the most common reasons for e-learning system deployment problems fall into one of these categories:

1. lack of required or expected functionality of the e-learning solution; user interface design,
2. incompatibility or lack of integration with other systems being used in organization,
3. inability to provide a smooth transition from previously used product.

In case of large organizations we can also add:

4. performance/availability problems,
5. extensive unification of didactic process due to deployment of a single, organization-wide system.

The first point is self-explaining and well known - choosing the correct functionality of the system is a basic step in deployment process and any lacking functions will lower users' opinion. In the event where any advantageous function is missing from the product it can be provided by external applications if the system has been designed with ease of integration in mind (see point 3).

User interface is the element of e-learning system which has direct contact with its user and, as such, directly influences the user's opinion about the product - in case of knowledge assessment systems that includes both teachers and students. Efficient and friendly user interface has a paramount impact on system deployment. Moreover, if we are deploying a new system in place of previous solutions, serious differences in menu layout will most likely be received unfavorably by users.

An e-learning knowledge assessment system most often functions in parallel with other computerized applications - grade archives, resource planners, payment/finance systems, content repositories, library indexes etc. In many cases our system can benefit from information from these sources or we need to make results of knowledge-assessment available to such outside systems. A special care should be taken to provide means of integration between such systems, as lack of this functionality will drastically reduce usefulness of e-learning system and create resentment of users each time an additional work to transfer the data will be required. A system able to integrate with its environment can also be easily extended with new functionality, when a need arises (see point 1), which makes this characteristic even more important.

Very rarely an e-learning knowledge assessment system will be deployed as a first such solution in a given organization - more often it would be deployed in place of some previous solutions. From our experience, providing a smooth transition from previously used products is the most important requirement necessary for a successful deployment. To fulfill this goal administrators need to consider its technical and organizational aspect.

Technical aspects of a successful deployment include such critical elements as uninterrupted service and good system performance. The service provided by e-learning system should be available to all interested users continuously, even during the period when an old solution is deactivated and new service commences its operation. Moreover, care should be taken to maintain a good system performance despite a heightened load of the system, which is expected shortly post-deployment.

Organizational aspects of smooth transition are even more important and difficult - users are accustomed to their familiar ways of conducting e-learning tasks. If the deployment of our new system is to be successful, the users must have necessary information about its operation (for example: courses, manuals etc.).

It is also very probable, that teachers organized their work in a way, which allowed them to efficiently utilize the previous system - if the new proposition will require drastic changes in work organization the chances of successful deployment will be low. There is also a possibility, that users augmented the basic system's functionality with third party applications, which they loosely integrated with the system (for example they use MS Excel to analyze results exported from the system).

Moreover, users would probably have a considerable amount of data collected in the previous system (for example: test content, grades history etc.), which must be possible to transfer to a new one.

If we are plan to replace many independent solutions used through an organization with a single system, we face the most difficult scenario for successful deployment: there will be different data sets and formats to migrate to a new system and hard to evaluate functionality and performance requirements. Users from different organizational units and with different needs will be required to unify they work organization to match functionality provided by a new system and depend on centrally managed and maintained solution, where any modification of system's operation is much more complicated, time consuming and thus unlikely. Moreover, while consolidating data from different organization units can be difficult, the opposite operation (separation a from shared data store) can prove even more work consuming.

The above analysis shows that, apart from the obvious requirement of providing necessary functionality, interoperability of an advanced e-learning system is its key characteristic. Also, all methods which would enable a gradual deployment, differentiation of system operation between organizational units in large organizations and provide high performance/reliability are highly recommended.

Having analyzed above limitations of currently available knowledge assessment products and difficulties of deploying a new solution in already functioning environment, we designed and created our own dedicated knowledge assessment system. It was designed to provide highly modifiable platform for various knowledge testing tools, able to provide its functions in any network connectivity conditions (including no connectivity scenario). The system can scale from very simple setup (adequate for servicing a single exercise) to a large, distributed solution fit to support an enterprise. Strictly modular architecture allows users to employ only a selected set of its mechanisms and extremely easily integrate it with third-party solutions. The selection of employed modules depends completely on user needs - there is no mandatory control module or management platform which must be present.

We created a number of client modules with full support for low/no-connectivity scenarios, for example:

1. the classic, but highly configurable and versatile, multiple choice knowledge testing solution,
2. a simple simulation-based module, addressing security of Ethernet switches,
3. an unique simulation-based knowledge and skill assessment module, dedicated to exercises concerning Asynchronous Transfer Mode (ATM) and Frame Relay networks,
4. a number of modules allowing a real-time grading of students performance during exercises.

Our system also addresses security aspects of remote, computer based knowledge testing, in both test distribution and results gathering preserving user anonymity to unauthorized parties.

As an key element of the system, we have created an innovative Communication Abstraction Layer (ComAL) - a set of mechanisms designed to provide e-learning system designers with API containing a comprehensive set of communication functions which can make an e-learning system independent of underlying network connectivity conditions. ComAL completely isolates e-learning solution programmer from the details of network communication and can be employed to easily create networked e-learning solutions, allowing creation of an integrated, managed e-learning system even in environment without network connectivity.

3. Overall system design

During design and creation of our system we aimed to provide a solution fit to accommodate needs to assess students knowledge in the widest possible set of scenarios. To fulfill this task we considered its following aspects:

1. compatibility with a widest possible set of hardware and operating systems,
2. ability to function in variety of network connectivity environments (including lack of such connectivity) while still retaining capability to function as globally managed solution,
3. security and reliability of the system, including safety of the system itself, test content, students' solutions and personal data,
4. information storage and manipulation capabilities, to allow creation of central database of results and grades, complete with easy access methods,
5. knowledge assessment functionality including: multiple choice tests with highly customizable automatic grading and real time grading by a teacher,
6. comprehensive management interfaces for administrators and teachers,

7. ease of deployment, customization, modification and integration with third-party solutions.

To fulfill these requirements, we have chosen a client-server architecture for our system, which is a pretty standard solution today, but in contrast to the most common practice we decided to abandon thin-client technology in favor of full-client approach.

From our experience, web-based thin-client architecture despite its undisputed compatibility and ease of deployment, is not especially well suited for knowledge assessment systems, as it requires a constant network connectivity for operation and lacks a sufficient degree of control over user environment, which impairs system reliability and allows unauthorized actions on part of the users. Operating system and web browser security mechanisms are also an important issue here, as their incorrect configuration can lead to abnormal client software behavior (Nowicki K. & Gierłowski K., 2004).

Full-client approach allows client to conduct much wider range of operations compared to thin-client. This allows inclusion of more advanced internal mechanisms providing improved functionality, much better reliability and security of client operation. With proper design full-client utilizing web-based technologies can also operate independently of server which gives our system versatility, necessary to handle limited network connectivity scenario. It also facilitates creation of a strictly modular system architecture and providing of high level of scalability (as many tasks can be conducted client-side and data transfers minimized).

The most serious limitations of full-client approach, deployment and system compatibility, are also possible to over-come by employing easily deployable, platform in-dependent clients (for example Java-based). Such solution allows for all advantages of full-client and web-based technologies, while still retaining high level of hardware and system compatibility and easy (even web-based) deployment.

The second of our fundamental design decisions was maintaining a strict modularity of our product. All basic elements are constructed as modules capable of operating independently, that's why we call the architecture of our system – a loosely-tied distributed architecture.

Moreover, we are employing only standardized, self-descripting data format for inter-module data transfer - Extensible Markup Language (XML).

Modular system structure complicates design and implementation, as it requires the use of additional inter-module communication mechanisms, but these difficulties are easily compensated by our ComAL API, described in later section.

On the other hand modular structure brings enormous advantages, as it is possible to substitute customized solutions in place of some standard modules or include additional elements into standard system data paths to provide additional data analysis/translation functionality (Figure 1). Advantages of these possibilities are clear, as they allow easy modification and customization of the system, including creation of dedicated interfaces for third-party systems and applications. Furthermore, there are already many solutions accepting XML input and providing XML output (for example MS Office, OpenOffice etc.).

There is also a possibility which had proven even more useful then these mentioned above during test deployments of our system – it is possible to deploy only selected elements and/or integrate it directly with third-party solutions supporting XML language.

An ability to deploy only a chosen set of modules allows for deployment precisely tailored to individual needs. If system user is interested only in simple multiple choice solution for a small number of students there is no need for a system server – it is enough to deploy only a testing/grading module and read resulting offline data files directly with MS or Open Office. In an opposite situation, where the user is interested only in system's data storage and access functions, he can easily deploy the system's server part, substituting its clients with his own, as long as they support XML output or can provide appropriate translating interface.

Fig. 1. Integration with external applications.

This partial-deployment ability also makes transition to new system much easier, as it can be conducted in phases, by gradually exchanging existing infrastructure with modules of the system.

The most common usage scenarios include:

1. No server-side / third-party scenario - client modules are operating independently or export results to a third-party application/system.
2. Single server scenario - client modules are managed by client communication module and access central database, all data storage and control functions are available.
3. Multi-server distributed architecture - able to support large number of clients (performance) and allows different organizational units to operate independent (but integrated) servers.

As you can see, a loosely-tied distributed architecture, where all modules are able of independent operation and communications are handled with a well-known, versatile data format, satisfies many of critical development requirements, difficult to fulfill with, currently the most popular, centralized thin-client approach. Gradual (or even partial) deployment is possible, as well as easy integration with third party applications and modification of system's functionality.

A detailed description of system architecture, found in the later section, will also show that the system's operation in separate organizational units can be differentiated in a significant degree, and that high performance/reliability level is relatively easy to maintain.

4. Communication Abstraction Layer

One of key elements of modular system are inter-module communication mechanisms. The task of providing local communication (between modules on the same machine) is relatively simple, because we can precisely predict environment characteristics.

Remote connectivity (communication between modules on different machines) is another matter. It is dependent on various characteristics of available network infrastructure. Providing reliable communication and satisfying quality of service requirements of an e-learning system in wide range of network scenarios and conditions is a difficult and work intensive task (Gierłowski K. & Gierszewski T., 2004). Its complication and cost most often lead

to abandoning such attempts and creation of products which require constant and stable network connectivity lacking mechanisms for handling other scenarios (for example: the popular thin-client architecture) or employ no advanced communication functions at all.
While such approach may be sufficient for didactic content distribution systems, knowledge assessment requires a higher degree of communication between client (which interacts with user) and server part of the system (usually responsible for control, management, task assignment and results gathering).
To help developers in building a robust, networked e-learning systems we have created a set of mechanisms called Communication Abstraction Layer (ComAL) specifically designed to provide network communication functions required by e-learning environment (Figure 2). This set of mechanisms can employ a variety of communication methods, automatically choosing the one most appropriate for current working conditions, and is responsible for all communication tasks - both local and remote. It isolates e-learning system developer from particulars of implementing a network communication mechanisms by providing him with high level API.
From our experience in developing networked e-learning systems, we divided most often encountered network conditions into four scenarios:

1. Local Area Network - efficient and reliable, permanent network connectivity.
2. Internet - an environment where we have a permanent network connectivity at our disposal, but there are no Quality of Service (QoS) or reliability guarantees.
3. Periodic connectivity - most commonly encountered in case of dialup connections.
4. Offline - there is no network connectivity, but there is still a possibility of communication by offline methods (floppy, CD/DVD, USB-storage...).

ComAL provides dedicated means for maintaining a stable communication in all of these environments, and is able to detect the correct scenario automatically and keeps monitoring the situation to detect if the scenario changes.

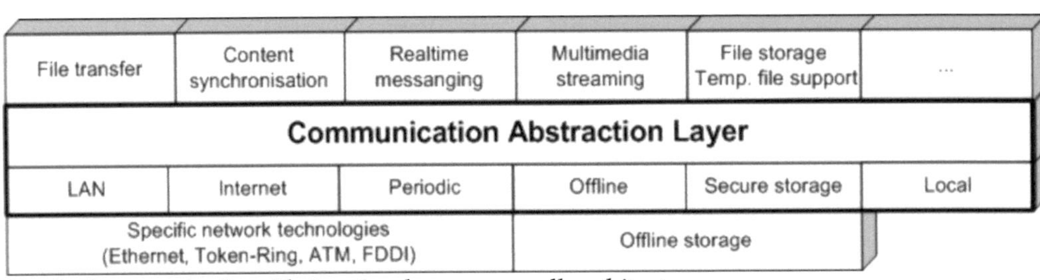

Fig. 2. Communication Abstraction layer - overall architecture.

Communication functions provided by ComAL to e-learning system creator can accommodate a wide variety of application types, ranging from sending a simple messages, through high volume file transfers and content synchronization, to reliable, real-time interactive message exchanges and multimedia transmissions. Of course, not all of these functions can be made available in all of the above scenarios. To deal with such limitations, ComAL provides feedback mechanisms informing higher application layers about functionality available under current network conditions, state of currently conducted communication activities, overall status of network connectivity and its changes.
For transport of data ComAL currently employs (Figure 3): direct TCP and UDP connectivity, SOAP over HTTPS, encrypted SOAP over SMTP and advanced, automatic,

secure file export/import functions. Some of these methods (SMTP and file-based) allow communication between system modules behind NAT. Moreover, we are currently developing a media proxy module functionality, allowing destinations behind NAT to communicate with TCP/UDP and indirect (but still secure) SOAP over HTTPS.

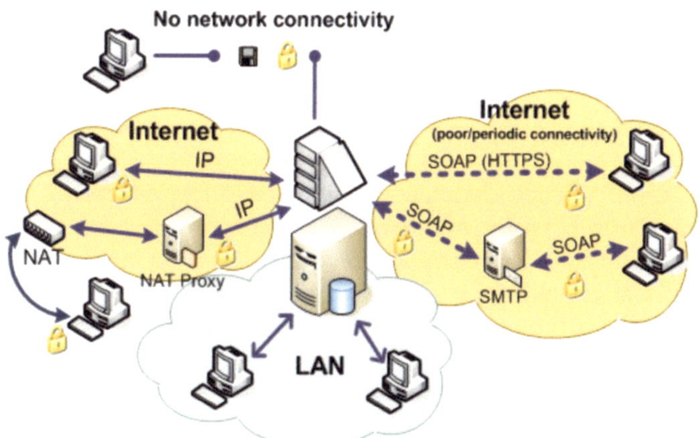

Fig. 3. Communication scenarios supported by e-learning systems with use of ComAL.

All communications can be protected with use of strong security mechanisms, ensuring their confidentiality, integrity and mutual authentication of communicating parties. The communication can also be digitally signed to ensure non-repudiation of submitted data (for example test solutions). The ComAL utilizes both symmetric and public-key cryptography and supports automatic key/certificate generation for clients.

Due to similarities between mechanisms required in case of the Offline communication scenario and committing data to a high security storage, ComAL can also be easily employed for that purpose. To provide user with such functionality, we have defined a fifth (special) communication scenario - Secure Storage. It provides a considerable range of cryptographic functions and tamper protection mechanisms:

- In-memory file storage - files are stored exclusively in memory, optionally in encrypted and signed form. It minimizes the chances of recovering protected data from disk.
- Automatic secure delete - mechanisms to securely delete files from disk - both on demand (in case of regular files) and automatically in case of temporary files. The delete procedures are somewhat relaxed in comparison with ones advised for high security solutions, in order to prevent an excessive hardware degradation while still retaining a decent level of security.
- Symmetric/asymmetric encryption and data signing - well known and widely used cryptographic mechanisms, based on OpenSSL libraries.
- File attributes verification - all file attributes (read only, archived, system, creation data, modification date etc.) can be employed in encryption/signing process, to prevent user from modifying them.
- File location verification - low level information from filesystem directory and allocation table can be employed in encryption/signing process, to prevent users from modifying/backing up/coping/overwriting protected files. For example: file

needs to be placed in the same exact disk sectors as it was initially written to, if it is to be correctly decrypted.

- Access counters - information about all operations (reads/writes) can be included with the file in secure manner.
- Date/time monitoring - dedicated mechanisms detect and report any suspicious changes of system time/date.

These advanced secure storage functions were added to ComAL for use in e-learning products deployed in remote learning / remote knowledge assessment scenario. An example of their use can be an upgraded version of our choice-test module, described in a later section.

We believe that creation of such abstraction layer, able to free e-learning system developers from difficult, specialized, costly and work consuming design and implementation of network communication functions can encourage creation of advanced solutions, taking full advantage of potential provided by a networked environment. It has been utilized in a number of our e-learning products (Nowicki K. & Gierłowski K., 2004), ("QTI…", 2008), (Gierłowski K. et al., 2003), greatly reducing design complexity and implementation work required. It was also successfully employed to extend functionality of strictly local e-learning solution, to allow network based management.

ComAL has been designed to isolate high level e-learning system designer and programmer from specifics of network connectivity. Our experiments with various new e-learning technologies and functionalities confirmed our belief that such isolation is an advantage in most cases, but they also suggest that the layer should not block programmer/designer from accessing low level functions and statistics of network interfaces if he wishes to. Such functions should be kept as network technology independent as possible, but should be available. An excellent example of e-learning product which requires such access is the mobile version of our real-time grading module (described in later section) - it requires access to low level parameters such as radio signal strength or hardware address. To support this requirement, we decided to extend ComAL with ability of a very simple SNMP (Simple Network Management Protocol) agent, which provides such information to higher layers in standardized form.

ComAL is a basis of all inter-module communication in our knowledge assessment system, enabling our system to function as manageable entity in most diverse communication scenarios.

5. System architecture

As our knowledge assessment system follows a client-server design, its modules can be divided into two basic groups: client and server modules. Communication between system elements is conducted with use of ComAL to support various network environments.

Client modules interact directly with student or teacher during didactic process and are responsible for providing majority of system's functionality in accordance with configuration information obtained from servers and under their control. Results of knowledge assessment conducted by client modules are returned to servers for processing and storage.

There can be many client modules providing different types of knowledge assessment or supporting functions - their design and functionality is described in the following sections.

All of these modules are able to function as independent applications and support full ComAL capabilities, including strictly offline scenario - in such case configuration and test packages are provided to them as cryptographically protected files (automatically generated by server), and results are returned to server in the same way. Also they are able to monitor presence of network connectivity and initiate automatic upload of results gathered in offline mode.
Server part of the system is a distributed database containing both didactic content and system's complete configuration information. A single server consists of a database (most often an SQL server) and at least one of two modules: system maintenance module and/or client communication module.
A system maintenance module is responsible for creating and maintaining distributed information base. It also provides a web-based administrative interface allowing administrator to create and control the system.
An administrator is responsible for creating a distributed system architecture by defining communication links between system servers, and deciding which of ComAL transport mechanisms are permitted for each link. If a server cannot maintain current transport mechanism it will switch do less demanding one if such is permitted, otherwise it will mark link as down. A simple link-state path selection protocol is then used to ensure communication between all nodes, utilizing as link metrics information from ComAL network monitoring mechanisms.
Over such communication structure works a data indexing mechanism, allowing full access to distributed information base from any system node. This distributed database includes complete information about system-wide configuration (system structure, global users and access rights, link states, distributed database state) which is replicated to all servers and didactic content (test content, grading rules, student lists, test results and grades etc.) which is kept locally on specific server and is not replicated (however, creating mirror servers is possible), but can be searched and accessed from any server if there is connectivity present, and access rights are sufficient (Figure 4).

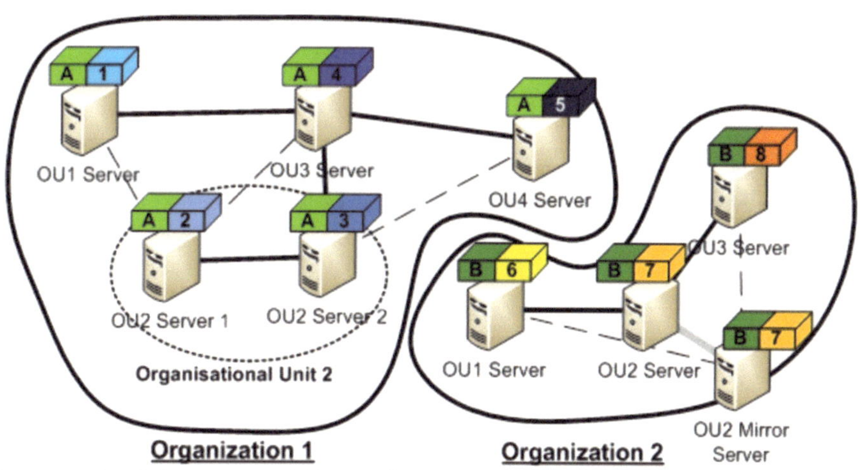

Fig. 4. Server side of the system: A,B – configuration content (replicated) in organization; 1,2,… - didactic content (indexed or mirrored).

Such architecture allows largely independent operation of a particular server (supporting for example a single course or organization department), while still allowing administration of the system as a whole and easy access to information stored on different servers. It will give various teachers or departments the freedom of independent operation and still provide means of global data access. As a result servers can be connected and disconnected from the distributed system at will with no negative effect for them or the system (other than loss of access to disconnected resources).
If a given server will communicate with client modules, it must include a client communication module. It is responsible for communication with other modules using ComAL, supplying client modules with configuration and didactic content, gathering and processing incoming results and providing teacher's interface to the system.
Teacher's interface allows its user to create test packages and assign it to specific combination of students, network workstations or time frames - it is possible to provide student witch a choice of available tests. Such test package contains all information to conduct a test, namely: test content adequate for specific client module, grading rules and additional information concerning test execution (time limit, randomization of content, means of results upload etc.).
Teacher's interface allows a full read access to gathered results and ability to modify or add data concerning teacher's own tests, as well as generation of basic reports and statistics. There is also an option of importing external data in XML format into the system and exporting system data in the same format.
Described structure of the distributed database addresses important requirements necessary for easy and efficient system deployment in large organizations. It can be deployed gradually and its operation can be significantly modified in different servers while overall system's integrity remains intact. Performance problems can be easily solved by deploying more servers. Reliability level also remains very high, as server failures simply cause system to reconfigure its data paths and the only resources that are unavailable are these maintained exclusively (not mirrored elsewhere) on the malfunctioning server.
Furthermore, despite all these advanced functions and possible configurations, deployment in simple scenarios remains uncomplicated.

6. Client modules

Client modules are critical for the system as they are its point of contact with the student, responsible for many essential tasks, such as presentation of test content, en-forcing configured test conditions (time, test randomization, etc.), performing it and sending all necessary information back to the system for processing and storage, etc. The grading of tests can be conducted client-side, by client modules, or server-side, by client communication module. Server side grading is more secure but less scalable and versatile solution.

6.1. Test-based knowledge assessment module

This first and most often employed client module of our system allows knowledge assessment by means of diverse choice tests. While the method itself is very popular in case of e-learning products, we designed this module to provide functionality unique among similar products.

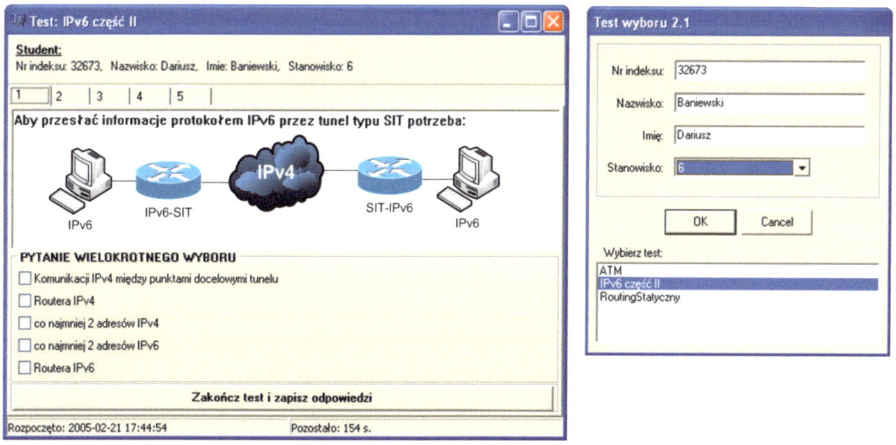

Fig. 5. Choice-test knowledge assessment module - user interface.

Module's user interface (Figure 5) allows presentation of wide range of multimedia content including formatted text, bitmap and vector graphics, sound and movies which provides teacher with great versatility when preparing test content. Test questions can be randomly selected from a larger set, and order of both questions and answers can be randomized.

Automatic grading mechanisms support both single and multiple choice questions in single test, and use simple scripting language which allows to utilize any of popular methods of assigning points for test answers. The total test result can be normalized to a provided value and/or mapped to a grade. The module returns to server or external application a complete information about student's solution (which can be later used by, for example, server side grading mechanisms), such as: personal data, test id, timeframe of test, client-side grading results of all questions and total grade, all answers, operating system computer name and user name, IP address etc.

Module configuration allows teacher to enforce various additional test characteristics, such as necessity of solving questions in order, lack of ability correct already answered questions, time limit for a whole test or every single question etc.

Apart from already described functionality, one of our primary priorities was to take full advantage of ComAL communication capabilities allowing the software to function as part of managed system even without network connectivity. Such scenario is most often ignored by de-signers of modern e-learning solutions as it prohibits the use of web-based thin-client architecture. At the same time it is a very popular scenario in case of network-related courses, as obtaining network connectivity is often the final goal of laboratory exercises on the subject.

The module is fully capable of independent offline operation according to encrypted and protected configuration files and course packages. In such case results are stored in similar, protected files and can be decrypted by the module at teachers request for manual transfer to the server or other application such as MS Excel. The module can also detect available network connectivity and update its status by obtaining new configuration settings/course packages from the server and uploading cached test results automatically.

After through testing of this module and over one year of its extensive usage in real didactic environment, we decided to upgrade its functionality to better support a remote learning environment. Even in its initial version, the module can support remote knowledge assessment activities, but it does not incorporate any dedicated mechanisms for the task, except these required to support various connectivity conditions.

Knowledge assessment in remote learning scenario is a very difficult task, because teacher has no direct control over student's working environment or even reliable information about it - for example, there is no guarantee, that the test was completed by a given student, that no prohibited resources were utilized (calculators, books, etc.), that it was attempted only once, that the questions were unknown prior to test, etc.

There were many solutions proposed to solve these issues (including real-time video monitoring and similar, difficult and costly solutions) but any of them can be bypassed with at most moderate difficulty, and their deployment and maintenance can be called "troublesome" at best. In this situation we decided to test a number of new approaches to the problem of enforcing test conditions in remote learning scenario, but none of them has been designed to provide guarantees - only to protect against most common exploits, but without inconveniencing student or teacher.

In our opinion there are 3 basic security elements of remote knowledge assessment:

1. Reliable and secure communication - aforementioned information should be transmitted to and from client in a secure (confidential an unmodified) and reliable way.
2. Stored data security and confidentiality - sensitive data, such as test content, answers and results need to be protected against unauthorized access, modification and deletion.
3. User identity verification - there should be some way to verity identity of a person taking the test.

The first two requirements can be easily solved with the new ComAL version, supporting Secure Storage functions. Secure communication mechanisms were included in ComAL from the beginning as a common requirement for e-learning systems. New Secure Storage procedures can prevent users from obtaining unauthorized access to local module data (encryption, signing, in memory file storage, secure delete), including a significant level of protection against multiple test attempts performed by backing up and restoring module data (file attribute/location verification, access counters).

To provide some means of user identification confirmation, we decided to employ keystroke dynamics analysis (Sungzoon C. et al., 2000) - method of identification based on measuring timing relations between keystrokes. This method is employed during user logon and in course of the test, if there are any questions that require typing. During our test deployment (about 100 tests), the method showed over 90% efficiency in detecting attempts to impersonate users. The required identification data (necessary to train underlying neural network) has been collected during preceding classroom exercises.

As a result we have at our disposal one of the most advanced (apart from adaptive choice tests) knowledge testing products utilizing choice test method, which can function as a standalone application or as a part of managed system regardless of network connectivity available, due to integrated ComAL functionality and provides dedicated support mechanisms for remote knowledge assessment.

6.2. Real-time grading module

Real-time grading module has been designed to support classical theoretical and laboratory exercises. It is an inter-face for a teacher, allowing him to grade students during such activities, by marking their progress through assigned tasks.

The main element of the module's user interface (Figure 6) is a table containing all students participating in the current class in the rows and task numbers in columns. A teacher can assign percent grades (including above 100% for exceptional performance) for specific tasks, and the system will calculate resulting total grade automatically and in real-time.

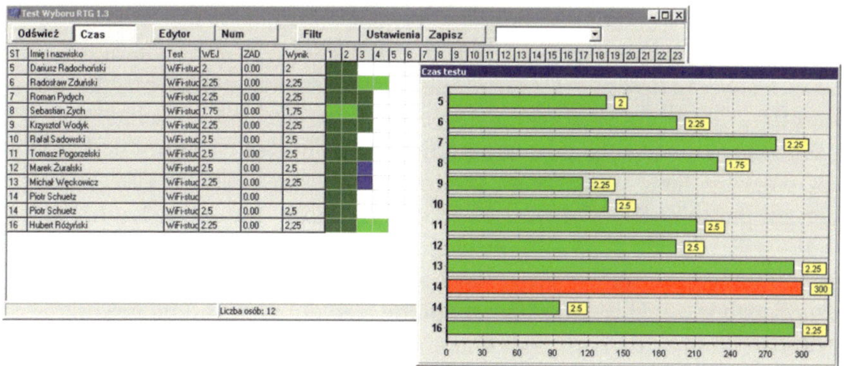

Fig. 6. Real-time grading module - user interface.

The list of students can be obtained from the system server or any other application with use of any ComAL-supported mechanisms including offline files. For example, if students are required to take an entry test before the class, their list, complete with additional information such as their place number and entry test grade will be displayed. Of course other means of creating such list can also be used (such as dedicated system module for checking in or a teacher prepared list) and provided to module by the server automatically or by simple file import.

Apart from user list, module can also take into account different point weights for different tasks, and such information is obtained by the module in the same way as the list of students.

This module can be an enormous help for a teacher, as he has complete information about his students at his disposal including name, place, and if entry test was taken, its result. That way he knows the entry level of theoretical knowledge of his students and can assign his attention accordingly. Also student's progress during current class is easy to track and graded automatically. Results can be uploaded to system server via any of ComAL transport methods.

6.3. Real-time grading module (mobile version)

Practical deployment of the system at Gdansk University of Technology proved great usefulness of Real-time grading module. It has been successfully utilized in a number of scenarios, including lectures, both theoretical and laboratory exercises and seminaries. An ability to easily grade activity of students, without interrupting the flow of lecture/exercise (to ask for student's identity, for example) is a great asset. However the deployment also uncovered several limitations of the product – the most important being its dependency on a

computer hardware able to run full blown Java applications and equipped with standard console: high resolution monitor, full keyboard and optionally mouse.
Because of these limitations and aware of high popularity of Symbian based mobile phones, we decided to start development of a mobile version of real-time grading module. It supports all console types available in mobile phones: standard phone keyboard, full keyboard and touch screen.
The module utilizes a simplified version (only two communication models: online and offline) of ComAL for Symbian 6.0 v3 (still under early stages of development) which can provide connectivity with use of WiFi, GPRS/EDGE…, and Bluetooth. It is also able to transmit ComAL offline communication files through IrDA.
In online mode the module exchanges information with system in real-time, while offline mode allows teacher to download/upload information packages on demand.
Apart from the support for new console types, we also decided to include a new mode of entering the grades, which has proven an efficient one in case of large number of students. Instead of marking their progress on the graphical list (X axis/Y axis: tasks/students), teacher can simply enter ID in "row number/chair number" format, task number and grade. The module will provide him with student identity and information about his current grading along the way, if such information is available to the module.
With help of such module the most troublesome element of real-time grading is obtaining and entering an identification of place that a given student occupies. To help with the task, we are currently developing and testing two different solutions, both utilizing low level integration with wireless technologies.
The first mechanism, designed for computer laboratories, utilizes Bluetooth interface. It works by measuring the strength of Bluetooth signal from interfaces present in student's computers. Hardware address of a Bluetooth interface with the strongest signal is then checked with a list of such addresses to obtain a computer number (place number). In practice it means that all a teacher has to do is to approach a student instead of entering place ID manually - the module will display student's information and allow teacher to enter the grade.
The second one, designed for larger environments (for example lecture halls) is only available to the module in online mode. In contrast with the Bluetooth-based solution described above, it depends on WiFi access points (APs) and their ability to measure WiFi client's signal. Our test proved, that with 3-4 APs (we used Cisco Aironet 1100 APs) deployed in a simple (as far as radio propagation is concerned) environment (lecture hall) it is possible to pinpoint location of wireless client with about 5 meter accuracy. It is insufficient to identify a particular place in the hall, but the module uses this information to narrow down the list of possible place ID, which it provides to teacher to choose from.
Both of above solutions are in testing phase, but they are already functioning fairly stable. The main problem concerns a proper configuration of the required infrastructure: Bluetooth interfaces should be of the same type or at least transmit with similar power, they need to be configured as "shown" (as opposed to "hidden" where they will not transmit their identity information), the table of Bluetooth hardware addresses and their corresponding place IDs need to be constructed as well as the table allowing translation of WiFi signal strengths to locations, etc. To offset this problem, we are currently working on tools designed to automate many of the above tasks.

6.4. Script-based automatic grading framework

We have observed, that solutions of many tasks in laboratory environment can verified with use of automatic programs or scripts. In case of our area of expertise - computer networks - we often employ such tools to verify the correctness of student's solutions. Simple scripts can check connectivity, measure network performance statistics (such as throughput, error rate, delay etc.), monitor availability of services (such as, for example HTTP, FTP, DNS, SMTP, POP, IMAP servers) or even remotely login into computers to check correctness of the configuration files. Such automation is an enormous help for a teacher, allowing him to both easy grade students and help them troubleshoot their solutions.

Seeing the usefulness of such tools, we decided to integrate them with our knowledge-assessment system. The main difficulty of this task originates from a multitude of available scripting engines, additional required libraries etc.

To offset this difficulty, we decided to implement the module as a framework designed to run scripts and programs supported by an underlying operating system and then capture and parse their returned results.

The module obtains configuration from a system server (through ComAL) or from a local XML file. Teacher can configure what programs and scripts are to be executed, how often and how to interpret their results, for example: "Every minute run iperf.exe with a number of parameters to measure network throughput through a student configured system. If the throughput is over certain threshold, mark task 5 as completed in 100%. If it is below this threshold, but here is connectivity mark task 5 as completed in 50%.".

Many programs and scripts can be used to verify a single task creating complex and detailed checks - in such case checking scripts are chained with OR / AND conditions.

Teacher can also organize tasks in a hierarchical way, by defining a prerequisites for a given task - for example: "Completion of task 6 is not checked until task 5 is marked as completed". It prevents unnecessary checks and possible "false positives" by allowing the teacher to clearly specify the moment the task begins and/or correct starting configuration for a given task.

Test deployment of the framework in computer networks laboratory proved that it allows a completely automatic grading of many complex exercises, provided that teacher analyzes students' workflow and prepares a well designed and tested module configuration. However, as a results of a test deployment we decided to mark automatically assigned task grades in system's database as such, for optional verification and confirmation by a teacher.

7. Simulation-based client modules

A simulation product can be of great service in didactic process (Chwif, L. & Barretto, M.R.P., 2003) (Reichlmayr T., 2005) - it has its use in both remote learning (Kindley R., 2002) (Chiaming Y. & Wu-Jeng L., 2003) and classical learning activities (Lainema T. & Nurmi S., 2006) (Henning K. et al., 2005). Of course there are many types of simulation products, each suitable for different tasks: there are simulators devoted to detailed modeling of physical processes (often employed in scientific research), simulators created to train users in operation of various machines (for example: flight simulators), and a great many other products.

In our work at Gdansk University of Technology we find simulation an effective tool in both research and didactic tasks. Its usefulness in computer network science research is obvious and there is a wide variety of products available. Unfortunately, in case of didactic simulation the situation is not as good as in case of research devoted products. The choice of products currently available on the market is extremely limited, if we disregard a number of simple products employing scenario-based model (Kindley R., 2002), while still called "simulation". These products, while often applicable in web-based remote learning, provide only fraction of possibilities that a simulation approach provide.

Such situation coupled with vast usefulness of simulation-based products in technical higher education, leads us to believe that care should be taken to promote development of well designed and implemented didactic simulation solutions. Our research shows, that proposed modular architecture can also be employed internally in more complicated system's modules (to which didactic simulation modules certainly belong) with considerable gain in ease of deployment, usage and future update or modification. In such scenario, mechanisms of a system's module is divided into several separate building blocks. The need to provide inter-block communication will, of course, complicate development, but ComAL mechanisms can be utilized here also, facilitating the task. In contrast with our overall system architecture, in which modules are only loosely tied (can operate independently and do not need other modules to provide their functionality), in case of a single system module composed of smaller building blocks, they need to be strongly integrated, as all of them are required for a module to function.

The need for a strong integration between module's building blocks does not mean that they are bound to be located on the same physical machine. As ComAL is used to handle internal communication, all of its communication modes can theoretically be utilized and building blocks can be distributed across the network while still operating as a single system's module. In practice it is unfeasible to employ ComAL modes such as offline or periodic – they do not provide the required degree of integration between building blocks. The remaining modes of ComAL communication (local, LAN and Internet) have proven to function quite well in such usage scenario.

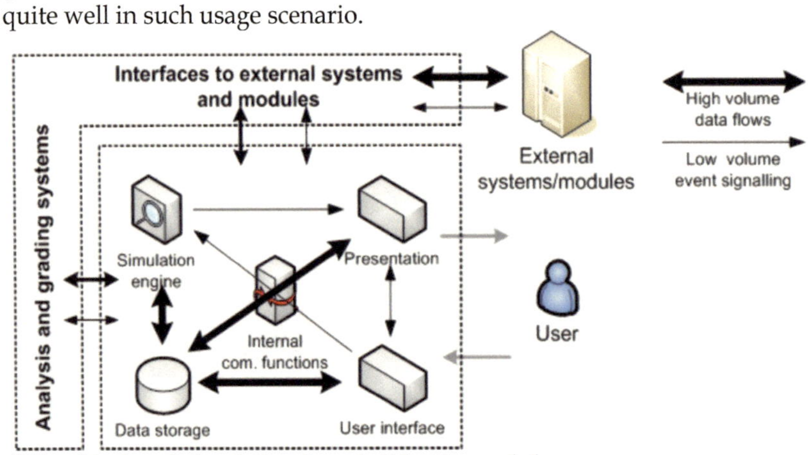

Fig. 7. Building blocks of simulation-based didactic module.

Didactic simulation product structure

Based on our experience and research, we recommend a division of didactic simulation module into four main building blocks:

1. simulation engine,

2. user interface,
3. data presentation mechanisms,
4. information storage.

They all need to cooperate to form a single system's module (or a standalone didactic product), but in design of any of them we can take various approaches. This, coupled with fact that different approaches can also be taken in connecting these modules together with the use of ComAL, present us with variety of choices and possibilities.

Simulation engine

The simulation engine is a central element of didactic simulation, controlling all activity occurring in simulated environment. It should communicate with:

- data storage to be aware of a current state of all simulated mechanisms, to change it and to store history of their operation,
- (directly or indirectly) user interface to accept user input,
- (directly or indirectly) data presentation mechanisms to provide user with visualization of current system state.

Communication with user interface and data presentation mechanisms is often implemented indirectly, by use of a global data storage, with which all modules interact. This architecture allows modularity and helps to make the product easier to implement, maintain and upgrade, but induces its own challenges, especially in real-time simulation products.

Complexity of simulation engine determine how close to reality our simulated environment can possibly be. More complex simulation engine allows us to provide user with higher level of realism and make our product more universal, as complex and detailed simulation engine can be used in many scenarios and tasks without need to modify and upgrade it.

Unfortunately raising complexity of simulation engine will also negatively impact our product because it multiplies its costs.

We should also remember that the simulation engine itself does not determine the quality of our product. Is should be coupled with equally sophisticated user interface and data presentation mechanisms to make a complete learning solution. So with simulation engine complexity growth, we should expect similar growth of complexity in these areas. Also multiplied communication activity between these components is to be expected, further raising product costs and infrastructure requirements.

The main difference between didactic and other simulator types is that, more often than not, we can make significant simplifications in the simulation model, without any loss of functionality of the final product. Such approach is highly advisable, because it allows us to reduce product hardware requirements and implementation effort.

The reason for this situation is the fact, that in case of didactic simulation, user never interacts directly with simulation engine - he always does it with assistance of advanced user interface and presentation mechanisms, which completely isolate him from internal workings of the model. However, we need to carefully balance possible simplifications and short-term work conservation against universality and future utility of the model.

User interface and data presentation mechanisms

Among the most crucial parts of didactic simulation products are user interface and data presentation mechanisms. They are elements of the product which interact directly with its user, and as such, their importance can easily rival that of simulation engine itself.

User interface is a set of mechanisms which allow user to interact with simulation model. It directly determines what actions user can perform, and also an exact way in which user must behave to perform a given action.

Data presentation mechanisms take information returned by simulation engine and create a simulated environment for user to interact with. They provide him with information about every important aspect of simulated reality and give feedback of his actions.

User interface and data presentation mechanisms interact directly with user, which makes them the most important elements from didactic point of view. If we analyze their function, we can see that they exactly fulfill the role of a teacher: they have a set of knowledge at their disposal (contents of data storage and output from simulation engine) and need to transfer this knowledge to user in the most efficient way. What makes simulation based didactic product even more effective (and interface and presentation modules even harder to make) is the ability to transfer not only knowledge, but also "practical" skill and experience.

Their proper design and functionality directly determines the path and outcome of learning process. It is evident how much care and theory of learning skill and experience should be employed here.

In case didactic simulation product, it is user interface and data presentation mechanisms that directly determine the outcome of didactic process. It is the main difference between other classes of simulation products and didactic simulation. These mechanisms are the most important elements of didactic simulation products and therefore a special care should be taken with their design and implementation. We face not only significant technical challenges here, but we should also take into account the theory of learning in their creation, to maximize the didactic efficiency of our product.

As the amount of information that a modern simulation engine can provide can be significant we are rarely interested in such data in its full scope and raw form. That makes the efficient data analysis mechanisms are an essential element. Their task is to provide presentation mechanisms with exact information necessary to generate a desired user experience.

Such task requires an efficient data connection with simulation engine, and possibly static information store. Next, a significant computational power is needed for data analysis and format conversion. Then, prepared information needs to be send to data presentation mechanisms.

Data presentation mechanisms are responsible for creating the view of simulated environment that is available to user. The main requirements here are sophisticated, multimedia-display capabilities, which can sometimes need to be supplemented with support for external user interface devices. There are many possible solutions, that can be employed here, but web-based technologies (WBT) seem well suited for the task, which makes it easy to implement this functionality as client-side element of thin-client system.

User interface provides user with ability to control the simulated environment and determine the set of actions available to him. It needs to be well designed, both in terms of implementation and logical design and layout. Web-based technologies can provide such functionality, but in this field, native operating system solutions perform significantly better (Nowicki K. & Gierłowski K., 2004).

It is also advised, that the client portion of the system should be aware of its working environment, to remedy problems with improper configuration of user's workstation. Problems in these areas are highly probable and can lead to variety of ill effects, starting from malformed display, to complete client part failure. This is the most challenging requirement, if we plan to use WBT mechanisms - for the security, universality and reliability reasons WBT mechanisms are executed in virtual environment, isolated from the operating system.

These characteristics make it advisable to consider further division of user interface and presentation mechanisms to optimize performance and reliability of the system. Such need largely depends on chosen system architecture.

For example, in case of thin client architecture, it may be advisable to locate the analysis element on the server, to minimize client computation load and amount of data that will be transmitted between client and server.

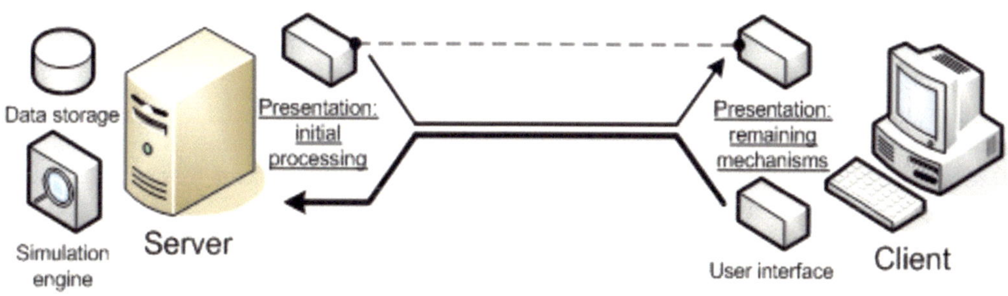

Fig. 8. Client-server architecture with divided presentation mechanisms

There is also an interesting solution, in which we exploit the fact, that presentation and user interface elements can be further divided into two components: mechanisms that simply collect physical user activity information (key presses, mouse activity…) or physically display multimedia content (display or sound driver…) and mechanisms that analyze user actions and prepare multimedia content to be displayed.

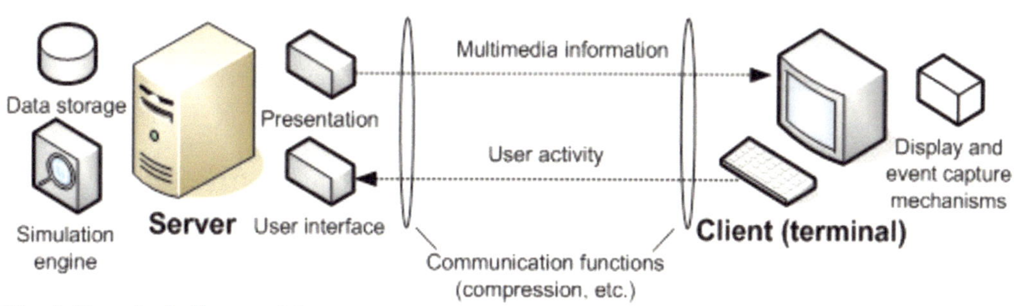

Fig. 9. Terminal client architecture

It enables us to create a thin-client solution which locates only physical display and user activity detection on the client - in other words: a remote terminal. In such case all system

activity is conducted on the server, and client only obtains graphics to be displayed, and sends user actions like keyboard or mouse activity.
It would seem that amount of data transmitted between client and server will be quite high, but it is also possible to precisely predict this amount and there are many, very efficient, optimization solutions available. In such scenario, we gain easy design and deployment, excellent management, reliability and independence from client environment, at a cost of significant server load resulting in poor scalability.
This solution allows the mount of control of user environment at level of native operating system, fat-client solutions and the best possible from user environment.

Information storage
All modules of the system need to store search for and access various types of information. It can take many forms and be required for various purposes: from data directly connected with didactic material provided to user, to a range of configuration or internal processing information. Due to complexity and vast variety of possible data storage solutions, we will not discuss this topic here in detail, however ComAL layer provides a number of secure storage functions.

7.1. Simulator of attacks on Ethernet switching devices

Another example of a product created according to described guidelines is "Simulator of attacks on Ethernet switching devices". It is a much simpler solution that our previous example, as this product only provides simulation of a single, isolated Ethernet switching device.

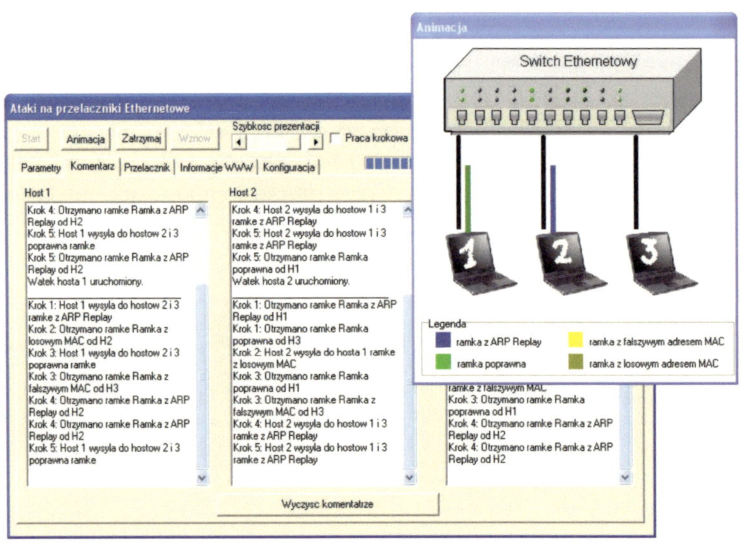

Fig. 10. User interface and presentation mechanisms

With use of provided graphical user interface, user can choose the type and parameters of external input, that will be send to switching device and set the timing of these actions. He can also activate or deactivate various security mechanisms that can protect the switch from certain attacks.

When the attack scenario and desired defense mechanisms are ready, user can decide to perform a simulation of attack. State of key device subsystems and parameters along with all events occurring in the system are presented to user as a number of detailed lists and readouts. Application also provides graphical visualization of key events on device schematic, and simulation can be performed in step-by-step or continuous fashion.
The application was created in modular form, with all its building blocks functioning independently as separate threads and communicating through ComAL.

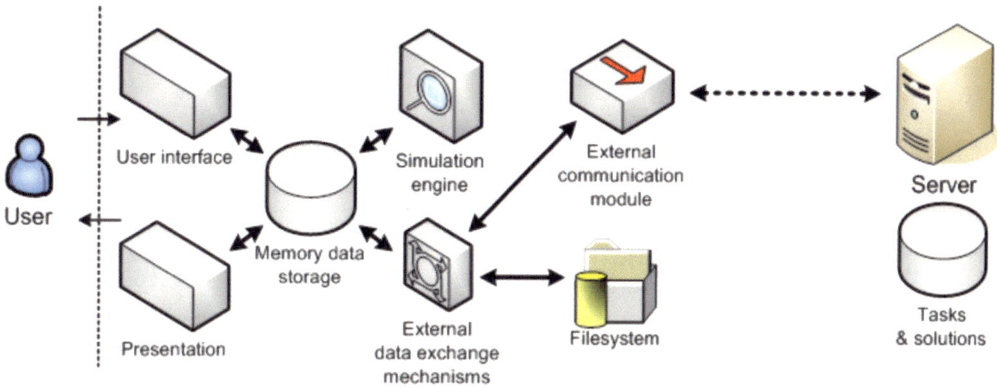

Fig. 11. Simulator of attacks on Ethernet switching devices - building blocks and overall structure.

To communicate with outside world the module utilizes a dedicated data exchange subsystem: it handles data conversion and communicates with external communications module (conducting communication with the server) and local filesystem (allowing saving and restoring data locally).
Described product serves successfully as pre-laboratory training help for students, allowing them to get a better grasp of the subject, before interesting but requiring set of laboratory exercises concerning local area network security.
The example of "Simulator of attacks on Ethernet switching devices" proves that our proposition of module structure composed from independent building blocks and accompanying guidelines can be useful even in case of simple products. This tool, designed and created with such rules in mind, can be easily upgraded or extended.

7.2. Didactic model of connecting LAN systems by WAN networks

"Didactic model of connecting LAN systems by WAN networks" (Figure 11) has been developed as a part of our re-search concerning simulation-based didactic and e-learning tools. It is a didactic simulator (Kindley R., 2002) , designed and implemented according to results of our original research of such educational tools (Nowicki K. & Gierłowski K., 2004), (Gierłowski K. & Nowicki K., 2002).

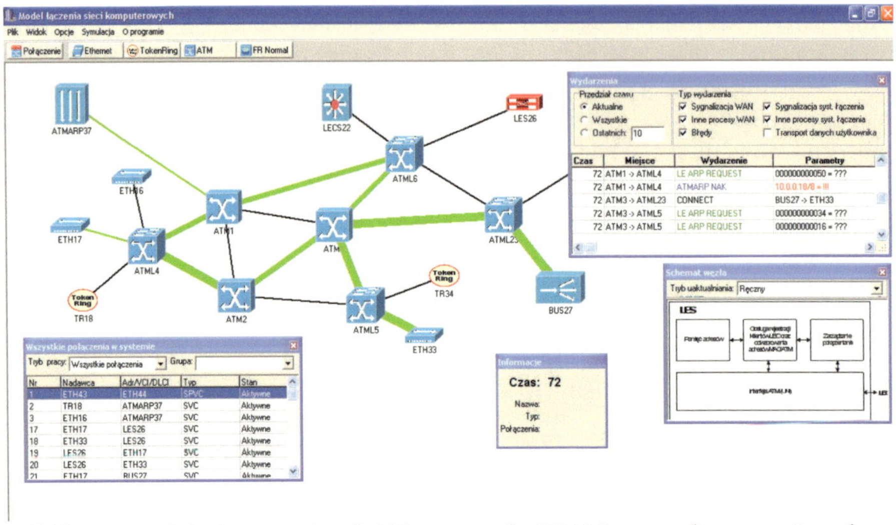

Fig. 11. Didactic model of connecting LAN systems by WAN networks - user interface.

Our simulator covers various technologies that allow computer data traffic through Asynchronous Transfer Mode (ATM) and Frame Relay wide area networks, for example: Classical IP over ATM (CLIP), LAN Emulation (LANE) or Multiprotocol over Frame Relay (MPoFR).

Due to its original design (Gierłowski K. & Nowicki K., 2002) it can be employed in a variety of didactic roles:

1. knowledge distribution - a comprehensive, context sensitive help system is included, containing theoretical information concerning various elements of simulated environment. Coupled with simulator's ability to illustrate the knowledge with interactive, modifiable examples it creates a highly efficient knowledge distribution solution.
2. skill development - didactic simulation product is one of the best tools for building practical skills on the base of theoretical knowledge, bridging theory and practice.
3. self study and experimentation - didactic simulation product (with its ability to save and restore simulated system state) can be used by students for self study, as they are able to experiment in real-like environment without fear of damaging or critically misconfiguring the equipment.
4. design, troubleshooting and optimization exercises - ability to interact with much more complicated systems than possible under laboratory conditions allows for these highest level exercises, able to build not only basic skills but also give user experience in efficiently dealing with these complex tasks.

Among these roles a knowledge and skill assessment can also be found - our simulation product includes mechanisms for automatically measuring various aspects of simulated system performance (available bandwidth, data loss, transmission delay etc.), which allows automatic grading mechanisms to assess competence of simulated system's designer and administrator.

The module is able to receive task files by ComAL from the server. A tasks file consists of a starting simulation setup, a set of goals which user must reach (for example: create

connectivity between selected devices, optimize system efficiency by a certain threshold etc.) and grading rules. User's solutions along with their grades are uploaded to the server.
The module was originally created as a standalone application supporting SCORM-compliant data files ("SCORM ...", 2007), but by employing a dedicated interface interacting with product's information store and ComAL communication functionality it has been upgraded to a networked product, able to fully integrate with our knowledge assessment system (Figure 12).

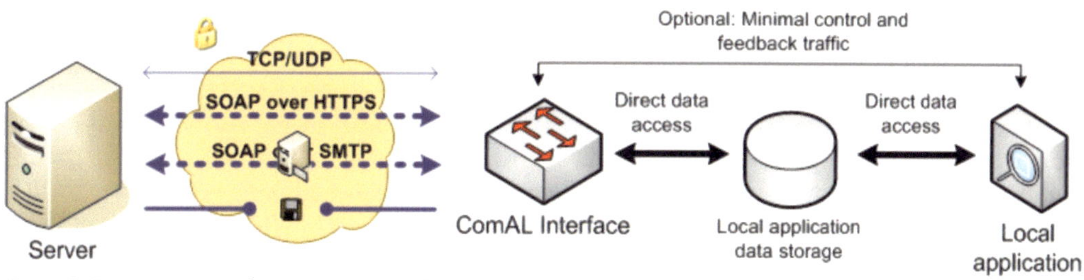

Fig. 12. Integration of proprietary e-learning solution with the system by employing ComAL-database interface.

Modifications of product code were not necessary to archive that result, and that fact can be considered as another evidence of ComAL vast usefulness and versatility. A number of minor user interface modifications were also made to improve functionality of the product.
A didactic simulator can be a powerful e-learning tool as its capabilities cover wide range of scenarios. Its inclusion of as a module in our system offers us a unique ability to test not only theoretical knowledge, but also student's ability to employ it in a given situation (user's skill), and even his efficiency in dealing with various real-life situations (experience). These test can be conducted in both simple and very complex systems, which would otherwise never be available for didactic tasks.

8. Additional server modules

Apart from already described server modules responsible for creation of a distributed system (system maintenance module) and communication with other modules (client communication module), we have developed two additional ones which provide supporting functionality for our knowledge assessment system: web publication module and analysis module.
They both require a database to function and as such are categorized as server modules. However, to access the system's resources they interact with client communication module through ComAL - such approach is required to reliably access the distributed database.
As independent modules they can also interact with other data sources, apart from our distributed database system, as long as correct (XML-based) data format is supported.
Both of these modules, while functional, are currently undergoing research and development works and were not yet released to a production environment.

8.1. Web publication module

This module is responsible for communication with system's living users (not software clients) and allows teacher to easily publish test related information to his students. The module provides its own teacher's interface (which can be integrated into client communication module's interface) and can operate on the entire distributed data store.

fulfill this task the web publication module requires a web server with PHP language support as its working environment. The module can be divided (Figure 13) into management part (which provides teacher's interface and manages publications) and publishing part (which provides services to users) - they interact with use of a shared database space.

The most important function of this module is a knowledge assessment results publication. The teacher can easily create and publish on the web automatically generated lists of results from system's database. Two methods of list creation are supported: manual selection of results to include or using a rule which automatically publishes matching results.

The lists can contain results of a single or a number of exercises in which case each of them is represented as additional table column. Moreover, a final grade can be calculated from a set of exercises.

Another possible form of results publication is a student oriented one. After providing correct login information student can access all his grades stored in the system.

Results published in any form can also be automatically supplemented with additional information present in the system, for example: teacher's contact information, correct solutions of test questions, cross references to study materials etc.

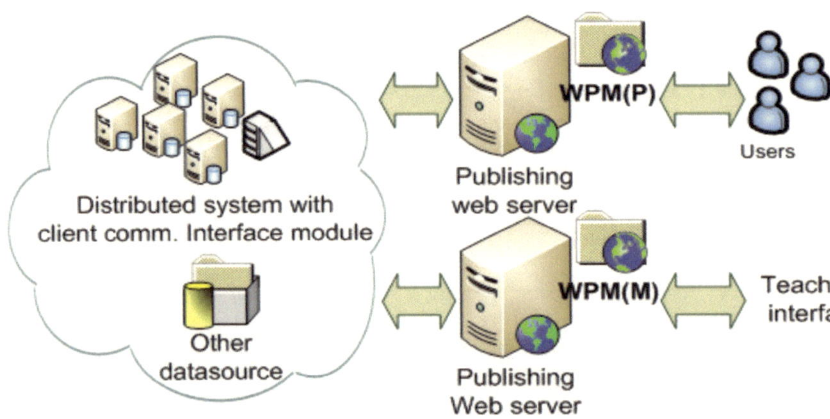

Fig. 13. Web publishing module (WPM) divided into management (M) and publishing (P) parts.

Each publication can be configured by the teacher either as local or universal. Local publications are available only from the web publication module from where there were configured. Universal publications are available from any web publication module in the system (if its configuration allows such usage).

Functionality described above allows students to easily track their progress through multiple exercises on many separate subjects, consult their teachers and revise their knowledge. Moreover, the fact that any and all web publication modules can be used to access all the information stored in the system, provide students with easy and reliable

access to a complete and current (all changes in the database are instantly visible) grading information in uniform layout.
in turn gain very easy, work conserving and error resistant method of result, solution and contact information publishing.
The second function of the module is to provide strictly web-based choice test functionality. The module allows teachers to use test packages prepared for knowledge assessment module described in chapter 6.1 (full-client) in thin-client environment. The test can be are carried out with any modern web browser with JavaScript enabled. Of course all described limitations of thin-client approach apply and only a subset of the full-client module's functionality is available. Still, it is a good tool to conduct simple tests without preparations or in emergency situations.
The last function of web publication module is the web-based deployment of full-client software to client computers. It is currently under development and will provide web-based guide and wizard (Java) to check client computer configuration, advise user in necessary system configuration changes and automatically install desired (and allowed by administrator for a particular user) full-client modules.

8.2. Analysis module

This module is devoted to a detailed analysis of test packages and gathered knowledge assessment results stored in the system database (Figure 14). Additionally it allows monitoring of system operation and usage.
Its functionality consists of: statistical analysis of test results and student grades, assessment of test quality based on test results (under development), semi-automatic generation of didactic content, helpful in acquiring knowledge appropriate to a given test, creating reports concerning system operation and usage.
The first option allows teacher to calculate various statistical properties of knowledge assessment results, such as maximum/minimum/mean grade, percentage of students passing the test, grade distribution etc.
Choice test results can also be used to assess quality of the questions (defined as correct level of their difficulty and high discrimination). We are currently testing our own analysis engine for the task, based on experiences described in (Costagliola G. et al., 2007) and other works referenced there.

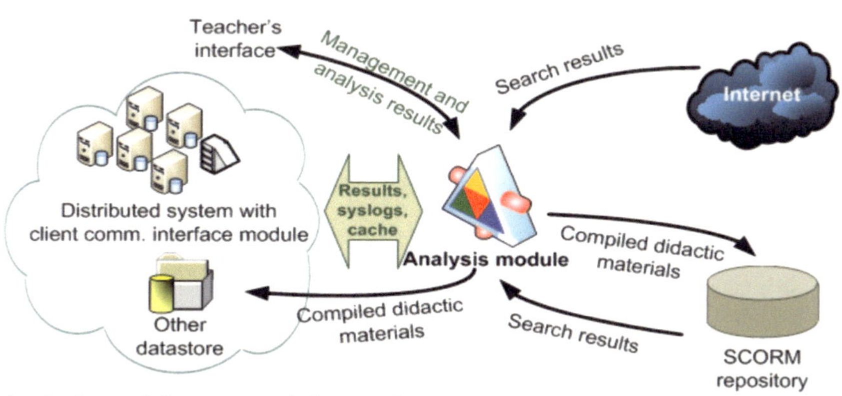

Fig. 14. Analysis module - external data exchange.

The third of module options can be used to semi-automatically prepare electronic learning material appropriate for a given choice test. It can then be used for pre-assessment study or during test results revision. To fulfill this useful and usually time-consuming task we use three basic methods.

In case of the most direct approach, learning content can be included directly in XML test definition. It can be linked to a test as a whole, or to separate questions and even answers. As such method is obviously not the most efficient one (in terms of data management), learning content objects can also be referenced by URI links, instead of including them directly. In such case the system compile an appropriate learning package fully automatically. Un-fortunately it is also a work intensive solution for a teacher.

The second and third methods are based on automatic search of appropriate material on the Internet using highly configurable Google search engine ("Google...", 2007) or in a repository of SCORM compliant material ("SCORM...", 2007).

The second method requires test author to provide keywords in XML test definition. They can be supplied as separate XML elements or just as marked parts of questions and answers. Such information is then used in the search.

The third method does not require any additional input except test definition. The search phrases submitted to search engines are automatically constructed from test definitions by removing popular words, and obtaining keywords by means of: word frequency analysis, checking word positions in sentences, comparing results of searches for candidate key-words with remainder of test definition.

As these automatic methods can produce unpredictable results (which is especially true in case of Internet search) a teacher's revision of results is necessary. The module provides teacher with a preview of search results which should be manually verified and can be subsequently used to construct a SCORM compliant package. The teacher constructs such package by connecting desired materials with SCORM sequencing and navigation relations ("SCORM...", 2007) using module's web interface. Resulting SCORM package can be utilized in a wide variety of SCORM compliant e-learning systems.

Apart from these education-related tasks, the module is also able to gather event logs and usage statistics from the system nodes, to create overall reports concerning its operation, efficiency, usage and to inform administrator about important events occurring in the system.

9. Deployment results

To test its efficiency in production environment we deployed the system in selected classes (mainly computer science and computer networks) of Faculty of Electronics, Telecommunications and Informatics, Technical University of Gdansk during the last three years. A total of over 3500 students participated in the tests generating about 32000 separate test results.

The system allowed to drastically reduce workload of the teachers by automatically creating attendance list, conducting and grading tests and generating lists of results. It lowered time consumed by knowledge assessment related tasks from over 10 min. to 1 min. on average, for a single laboratory group. It also allowed to minimize number of errors occurring in this process (for example: name mistypes, lost results,) by about 70%, which makes the resulting

error rate almost null (1-2 mistakes for about 4000 test results). It was also well received by our students, which is visible in the opinion poll results presented below.
A combination of test-based knowledge assessment and real-time grading modules, has been particularly effective during laboratory exercises, as it allowed to instantly grade exercises composed of theoretical test and practical laboratory work. Its ability to function in offline environment and upload results when connectivity becomes available made it suited even for computer networks laboratories.
To guide us in further development of our system, we conducted an opinion pool amongst the students and teachers using it. Overall results are presented in tables 1-3.
Of a 200 students participating in the poll, 83% think that deployment of the system was a desirable change (from classical pen and paper tests and assorted computerized knowledge assessment solutions), 15% is indifferent, and 2% preferred previous methods employed for the purpose.

	Better	**Indifferent**	**Worse**	**Total**
Students	166 (83%)	30 (15%)	4 (2%)	200
Teachers (early post-deployment)	6 (50%)	3 (25%)	3 (25%)	12
Teachers (6 month post-deployment)	10 (84%, +34%)	2 (16%, -9%)	0 (0%, -25%)	12

Table 1. Results of a survey concerning deployment of the proposed system - Gdansk University of Technology.

The most common positive remarks concerning the system include (in order of frequency): very fast publication of results, a single, well known location and universal format of results, an uniform knowledge testing interface for many subjects and teachers.
As a downside of the system students pointed to its strictness in enforcing test limits (such as time limit or need to answer the question in order) and tendency to overdo such limitations by the teachers.
Of 12 teachers using the system for about a year, 10 rate it as a better solution that the ones they employed before and 2 are indifferent. It is a significant improvement over the first teacher's opinion poll, conducted one month after the system was deployed - the opinions then included: 6 for better, 3 indifferent, and 3 for less useful than previous solutions. We attribute that results and their subsequent change to an additional work required to learn operation of the system and prepare didactic materials (tests definitions etc.).

Strict time limit enforcement	10%
Too many enforced limitation during test	8%
Choice test as a method of knowledge assessment	8%
Change from previously known solution/UI	6%
Other remarks	2%

Table 2. Most popular positive student's remarks concerning deployment of proposed knowledge assessment system.

Fast publication of results	41%
Single, well known location of results	23%
Choice test as a method of knowledge assessment	22%
Lack of technical problems during knowledge testing	16%
Low level of grading/publishing mistakes	10%
Uniform knowledge testing interface	10%
Multimedia tests support	6%
Instantaneous publication of any modifications	5%
Other remarks	7%

Table 3. Most popular positive student's remarks concerning deployment of proposed knowledge assessment system.

That conclusion is supported by remarks provided by the teachers. They include, in order of importance to pool respondents and frequency: almost fully automatic and very easy result gathering and publication, ability to perform test in non-networked environments, easy and automatic test deployment and execution.
As a drawback teachers mentioned the need to learn how to use a completely new tool of advanced functionality.
Also, no irreversible data loss (in storage and in transmission) occurred in 3 years of system operation. There are also no indications of successful security breach in any element of the system.

10. Conclusions

In this article we described a dedicated knowledge assessment system, designed to supplement existing e-learning solutions, as they implement such functionality in inadequate manner. The design of our system includes a number of original solutions and often exceeds similar products in terms of functionality. Our system relies heavily on web-based technologies (Java, XML, HTML, standardized media files, streaming media, SOAP, SMTP, MIME, etc.), but their usage differs from currently popular trends.
The uniqueness of our e-learning solution lies in use of independent modules, full-client approach, loosely-tied distributed architecture and inclusion of ComAL functionality.
As a result we have a system which can be deployed fully or partially and easily integrated with third party solutions. Possible deployment scenarios range from a single workstation with knowledge testing module exporting results to MS Excel, to a collection of interconnected servers (each controlling a large number of knowledge-testing client modules) allowing global information searches. The system has proven to be extremely scalable. Complication of system configuration also scales, which means that simple setups are as easy to prepare and maintain as installing and running a standalone application, while only more advanced require additional system configuration and administration.
Distributed server part configuration is also easy due to automatic information routing mechanisms. System servers function independently and can be connected and disconnected from the system almost at will with no impairment of their basic functionality, apart from global search ability. That independence allows various departments of an organization to autonomously organize their own elements of the system and retain access to full system information base.

Client modules are implemented in full-client version, as our research proves it to be superior to thin-client approach in case of knowledge assessment systems, in contrast with systems mainly devoted to didactic content distribution.
Our, currently implemented, client modules allow:

- classical knowledge assessment by use of choice tests,
- unique functionality of skill assessment by employment of didactic simulation-based tool,
- easy grading students during classroom exercises,
- ability to utilize external scripts and applications to automatically grade students during practical laboratory excercises,
- easy import/export XML data between the system and external sources,
- advanced and instantaneous results publication.

Moreover, we are currently developing additional server modules which will handle supporting tasks, such as statistical analysis, question quality assessment and semi-automatic didactic material compilation.
As a separate thread of our research, we are developing methods of utilizing information provided by low-level network mechanisms, to provide additional functionality without sacrificing layer separation provided by ComAL. In this research we are concentrating mainly on wireless technologies as they seem to provide many unique advantages.
All system modules employ our original ComAL communication package designed especially for e-learning systems. Allows e-learning product designers to use communication functions independent of available network connectivity, and allows dynamic environment detection and automatic selection of data transmission mechanisms including strictly offline methods (automatically controlled file import/export). Such functionality allows creation of centrally managed systems even in environment where there is no network connectivity available.
All of these traits make our system one of the most versatile, expandable and easy to deploy knowledge assessment solutions available and positive feedback from its users seems to confirm our confusions.
Usefulness of the system has been verified by its successful deployment in production environment, where over 30000 test were processed, and by means of student and teacher opinion pool. The results confirmed its value in various learning environments and provided us with further development directions.

11. References

Bersin & Associates. (2004). Study: Learning Management Systems 2004, Bersin & Associates, http://www.bersin.com/

Chiaming Y. & Wu-Jeng L. (2003). Web-based learning and instruction support system for pneumatics, Computers & Education, Vol. 41, No. 2, pp. 107-120, ISSN 0360-1315

Chwif, L. & Barretto, M.R.P. (2003). Simulation Models as an Aid for the Teaching and Learning Process in Operations Management, Proceedings of the 2003 Winter Simulation Conference, ISBN 0-7803-8131-9, New Orleans, December 2003, IEEE Explore

Costagliola G. et al. (2007). A Web-Based E-Testing System Supporting Test Quality Improvement, Proceedings of the 6th International Conference on Web-based Learning, pp.190-197,
Gierłowski K. & Nowicki K. (2002). Simulation of Network Systems in Education, Proceedings of the XXIVth Autumn International Colloquium Advanced Simulation of Systems, pp. 213-218, ISBN 80-85988-77-1, Krnov, September 2002, MARQ, Ostrava.
Gierłowski K. & Gierszewski T. (2004). Analysis of Network Infrastructure and QoS Requirements for Modern Remote Learning Systems, Proceedings of the 15th International Conference on Systems Science, ISBN 83-7085-805-8, Wroclaw, September 2004, Oficyna Wydawnicza Politechniki Wrocławskiej, Wroclaw
Gierłowski K. et al. (2003). Didaktische simulationsmodelle für E-learning in der IK-ausbildung, Proceedings of 7th Workshop Multimedia für Bildung und Wirtschaft, pp. 77-82, ISSN 1436-4492, Ilmenau, Septamber 2003, Tech. Univ. Ilmenau, Ilmenau.
Google Documentation, (2007), http://www.google.com/
Henning K. et al. (2005). Blended Learning in Computer Science for Students of Mechanical Engineering, Proceedings of Computers and Advanced Technology in Education, ISBN 0-88986-522-1, Oranjestad, August 2005, ACTA Press, Oranjestad
Jesukiewicz, P. et al. (2006). ADL Initiative Status and ADL Co-Lab Network, Academic ADL CoLab archives, http://www.academiccolab.org/
Kindley R. (2002). The Power of Simulation-based e-Learning, The e-Learning Developers' Journal, https://www.elearningguild.com/showfile.cfm?id=95.
Lainema T. & Nurmi S. (2006). Applying an authentic, dynamic learning environment in real world business, Computers & Education, Vol. 47, No. 1, 94-115, ISSN 0360-1315
Moodle Course Management System Documentation, 2008, http://moodle.org/
Nowicki K. & Gierłowski K. (2004). Implementation of Didactic Simulation Models in Open Source and SCORM Compliant LMS Systems, Proceedings of XXVIth International Autumn Colloquium, Advanced Simulation of Systems, pp. 161-166, ISBN 80-86840-03-4, Sv Hostyn, September 2004, MARQ, Ostrava
QTI Public Draft Specification Version 2, (2008), http://www.imsproject.org/question/
Reichlmayr T. (2005). Enhancing the student project team experience with blended learning techniques. Proceedings 35th Annual Conference Frontiers in Education, ISBN 0-7803-9077-6, Indianapolis, October 2005, IEEE Explore
Sakai: Collaboration and Learning Environment for Education Documentation, (2008), http://sakaiproject.org/
SCORM 2004 3rd Edition Documentation, (2007), Advanced Distributed Learning Initiative, http://www.adlnet.gov/
Sungzoon C. et al. (2000). Web based Keystroke Dynamics Identity Verification using Neural Network, Journal of Organizational Computing and Electronic Commerce, Vol. 10, No. 4, pp. 295-307, ISSN 1091-9392.

Evolution of Collaborative Learning Environments based on Desktop Computer to Mobile Computing: A Model-Based Approach

Ana I. Molina, William J. Giraldo, Francisco Jurado,
Miguel A. Redondo and Manuel Ortega
University of Castilla-La Mancha
Spain

1. Introduction

In the last years a great amount of collaborative applications have been developed. These applications can be framed in the paradigms of *Computer Supported Cooperative Work* (CSCW) or *Computer Supported Collaborative Learning* (CSCL) according to their specific purpose (group work or learning in-group). On the other hand some of them have been developed according to the paradigm of mobile computing. Advances in wireless technology and its integration on mobile devices offer support to user-to-user interaction on the move, becoming any place a potential collaborative learning scenario.

Most of mobile collaborative systems are carried out in the same manner as other applications are developed, without taking into account the special characteristics of these paradigms. Therefore, the requirements that characterize these paradigms may not be considered in the most appropriate way; in special, in relation to user interface (UI) development and the perception of the context of the application. From our point of view we need appropriate frameworks and tools (methodologies, processes, specification techniques, CASE tools, etc.) to help in the analysis and design processes of these complex applications. However the current approaches do not offer an integrating and efficient solution that tackles jointly mobility, learning and group work issues. With the aim of obtaining an appropriate support for the development of multi-platform groupware applications we propose to use a model-based approach for the development of interactive groupware applications. In particular we propose to use a proposal called CIAM (Molina et al., 2009). This is a methodological framework supported by a set of notations for modeling and designing interactive and collaborative tools. This approach can be used for supporting the evolution of existing systems based on desktop metaphor towards mobile support (Eisenstein et al, 2001). In this chapter we show the application of this method to a case study. We will take as a starting point a collaborative e-learning environment called Domosim-TPC (Redondo & Bravo, 2006) and show the application of our method.

This chapter is structured as follows. Section 2 presents the related works in the field of modeling of interactive and collaborative issues, as well as proposals for automation and model-based generation of user interfaces. In the following section, our model-based evolution process is presented. This process is based on the use of conceptual specifications using the CIAN notation. This notation has been proposed in the context of a methodological approach called CIAM. In this section the CIAM methodological approach is shown, enumerating its several stages, and the aspects that are specified in each. Finally we will show the evolution process of a CSCL system, called Domosim-TPC, towards PDA support and we will draw some conclusions.

2. Related Works

There are several solutions to the problem of *building device-independent user interfaces*. An interface model for separating the user interface from the application logic and the presentation device is necessary. There are several markup languages that help in this purpose, as for example UIML (Abrams, 1999). This kind of languages allows the production of device-independent presentations for a range of devices. But these solutions do not provide high-level guidance guaranteeing quality across multiple versions of applications. Other alternative is the use of a model-based design of UI (Paternò, 1999), which focuses on the tasks supported. The idea is that task analysis provides some structure for the description of tasks or activities, thus making it easier to describe how activities fit together, and to explore what the implications of this may be for the design of user interfaces. A number of approaches to task modeling have been developed (GOMS (Foley et al., 1991), HTA (Annett & Duncan, 1967), CTT (Paternò, 2004), etc.). The logical decomposition of tasks is reflected in the selection, consistency and grouping of elements in the UI obtained. The new context of use implies reconfigurations of the UI that are beyond the traditional UI changes (Eisenstein et al., 2001), such as the redistribution of widgets across windows or tabs in a tabpanel, the reduction of a full widget to its scrollable version, without using a sophisticated widget, to replace a interactor with a smaller alternative, etc. The technique of automatically selecting an appropriate interactor while considering screen resolution constraints has already been investigated and shown to be feasible (Eisenstein & Puerta, 2000).
The process of generating a user interface in a model-based system can be seen as that of finding a concrete specification given an abstract one (well-known as the "*mapping problem*") (Limbourg & Vanderdonckt, 2004). When we deal with the evolution of an application (in particular, the user interface) towards devices with limited interaction capacities (mobiles phones, PDAs,...) or new interaction modes (tactile screen, use of pen for pointing), the *mapping problem* is more complex, and especially, so is a possible generalization. The transformation process must take into account device restrictions, but without constraining the application usability in the adaptation process to the new context. Selecting the best interaction element (or widget), as well as the arrangement of them in the screen area, is becoming the main problem to be solved. The user interface development is a very subjective process, which depends a lot on the designer's experience, creativity and aesthetic opinions. Complete generalization of this process is complex and, in fact, there is not much success in this sense. Normally, developed applications are very closed in specific domains. Several systems have attempted to automatically generate user interfaces in a model-based environment (UIDE (Foley et al., 1991), Mecano (Puerta, 1996), Trident (Vanderdonckt &

Bodart, 1993). The idea of these systems was to try to automate as much as possible the interface generation process from a task model. However, these systems usually delegate to the designer the responsibility of selecting the interface final appearance. The system assists about possible alternatives applicable to a certain case.

Besides, there are several proposals that have tackled the *problematic of the conceptual modeling of work in-group applications*. These proposals come from different fields: (1) the Human-Computer Interaction community (the CTT notation (Paternò, 2004) and the GTA framework (van Welie & van der Veer, 2003) are some examples); (2) the CSCW systems and, in particular, *workflow* systems, as for example the APM notation (Carlsen, 1998); and (3) the Software Engineering (as for example the COMO-UML (Garrido, 2003). The study of these proposals has allowed us to detect the following limitations: (a) the need for *theoretical and computational models* that allow specifying the activities in group supported by a computer in a suitable way; (b) the lack of notations that allow MODELING the existing *differences between cooperative and collaborative tasks* accurately, according to Dillenbourg's remarks[1] (Dillenbourg et al, 1995); and (c) the scarce variety of *notations* that support in a joint way interactive and work in-group aspects. These limitations cause the semantics of the specifications of collaborative applications to be incomplete and confirm the lack of a methodological framework supported by a coherent set of notations for modeling and designing collaborative tools of interactive nature.

3. From desktop support to mobile support: A Model-Based Evolution Process

With the aim of obtaining an appropriate *support for the development of multi-platform CSCL applications* we propose to use a *model-based approach* for the development of interactive groupware applications, called CIAM. This is a methodological framework supported by a set of notations for modeling and designing interactive and collaborative tools. This approach can be used for supporting the evolution of existing collaborative learning systems based on desktop metaphor towards mobile support. Also we are interested in the identification of guidelines that facilitate the creation of a complete semi-automatic environment that generates CSCL and mobile tools, independent of the study domain and of the platform.

3.1 CIAM: A methodological approach for modeling interactive groupware applications

In this section the CIAM (*Collaborative Interactive Application Methodology*) proposal is briefly presented. CIAM is a methodological approach for the development of CSCW applications that takes into account the modeling of group work and interaction issues. Unlike other existing proposals in the fields of conceptual modeling of CSCW systems and modeling of issues related with the Human-Computer Interaction, CIAM considers the joint modeling of both issues, as well as the differentiation between the concepts cooperation and collaboration. A more detailed description can be looked up in (Molina et al, 2009).

---

[1] These differences affect the division of tasks, the roles participation in the tasks and the product obtained as a result of a joint activity.

The most important elements of CIAM are the following ones: (1) A *methodological approach* that defines the set of phases that compose the proposal, as well as the set of specification techniques to use in each of them (figure 1); and (2) A *notation*, called CIAN (*Collaborative Interactive Application Notation*) that allows expressing the peculiarities of the interactive groupware systems by means of a conceptual modeling (figure 2).

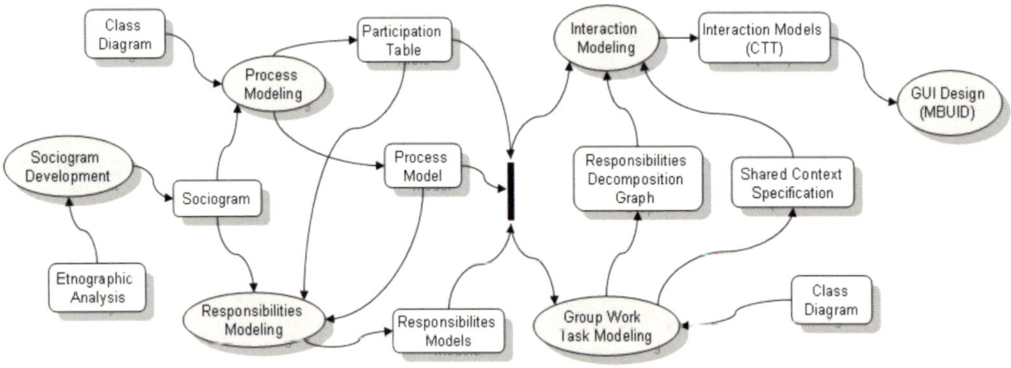

Fig. 1. The CIAM proposal and the products obtained in each of its stages.

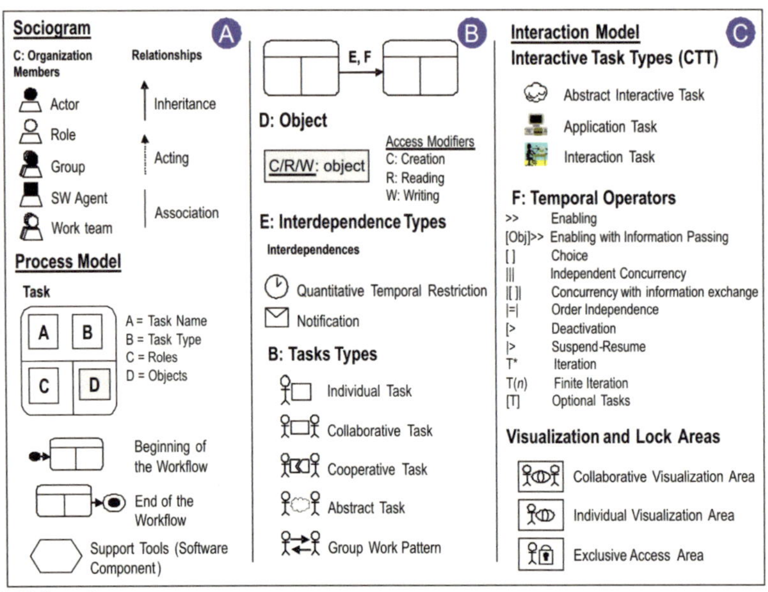

Fig. 2. CIAN Notation

The stages in CIAM and their objectives are enumerated next:

- In the ***Sociogram Development*** stage the organizational structure is modeled, as well as the relationships that exist between its members. The members that form the organization are in one of the following categories: *roles, actors, software agents*; or groupings of the previous ones, giving rise to *groups* or *work-teams*. Elements in this diagram can be interconnected by means of three kinds of basic relationships: *inheritance, performance* and *association*.

- In the following two stages (***Responsibilities Modeling*** and ***Process Modeling*** stages) the abstract tasks (or processes) that define the work in-group developed in the organization, as well as the temporal and data dependencies that exist among them are described. It is created the so-called *participation table,* which provides an initial idea about the division of the work at the highest level of abstraction. Once the participation table has been constructed, the *Responsibilities Model* can be defined. It specifies in more detail and under an individual perspective the responsibilities associated to each one of the roles in the organization, adding to its shared responsibilities those that are exclusive to it. The information specified in these two stages is supplementary, being necessary for both models to be coherent. Once the main tasks that characterize the group work and the responsibilities for each role have been defined, it is created the *process model.* This model uses a diagram (a graph) that allows relating all the information defined (the roles, the objects generated and accessed, and the main tools used for supporting the work in-group) by means of the two previous techniques. It shows the order of accomplishment of the tasks.
- In the ***Group Work Task Modeling*** stage the group tasks identified in the previous stages are described in more detail. Two different kinds of tasks are distinguished and modeled in a distinctive way: the *collaborative tasks* and the *cooperative tasks.* The *cooperative task modeling uses* the called *Responsibilities Decomposition Graph.* The notation used for cooperative task modeling is similar to the one used in the stage of creation of the *process model.* This way, we maintain coherence in the notations. The nodes of the graph represent individual tasks in which a single role is involved. The *collaborative tasks* specification is based on the *shared context* definition (Ellis et all, 1991), that is, the set of objects that are visible to the users and the actions that can be performed.
- Finally, in the ***Interaction Modeling*** stage the interactive aspects of the application are modeled. For each task of individual nature detected in the previous stages of the process, an *interaction model* is created. The notation used for the interactive models is the *interactive tasks decomposition tree* from CTT. As for the collaborative tasks, CIAM allows obtaining the interactive model directly from the *shared context* definition. The *interaction model* obtained facilitates the obtaining of the final UI.

4. A case study: The learning of Domotics

4.1. The starting system: Domosim-TPC

In Spain the new regulation for *Technical Training* ("Formación Profesional" in Spanish) takes professional profiles into account and training in Domotics is considered a must. Some learning stages in electricity and electronics courses are centered on the study of the design and maintenance of singular installations and automation of buildings dedicated to housing. In this area the design of domotics installations have a fundamental role. In this kind of training, the realization of practical experiments is especially important. However, the material necessary to carry out these assignments is usually expensive and in many cases it is not adequately provided. This problem gets worse with the difficulty to bring the student closer to real situations, to replicate accidents and to simulate those chaotic situations which may happen in the real world. In order to soften this problem by means of the use of technology, we have developed a distributed environment with support for distance learning of domotics design: DomoSim-TPC (Redondo & Bravo, 2006). Using the DomoSim-

TPC system (figure 3), the activities of practical learning of domotical design are structured in three clearly differentiated stages. In each of them diverse cognitive exercises are carried out and approached and representations of expert knowledge are used.

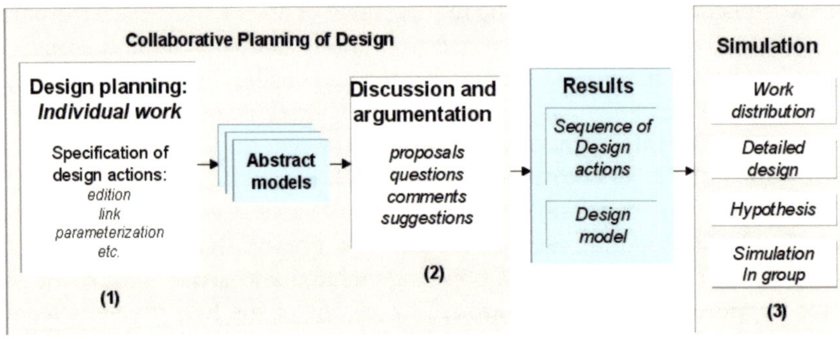

Fig. 3. Stages and tasks of domotical design learning carried out in an experience with DomoSim-TPC.

The *collaborative planning of domotical design* is divided in several phases, supported in three different workspaces in Domosim-TPC:

- *Individual Planning stage* (figure 4). In this stage the students, in an individual way, reflect and plan the steps to build a model satisfying the requirements proposed in the problem formulation. The strategy traced by the user is dynamically contrasted with an optimal plan of design for this problem.

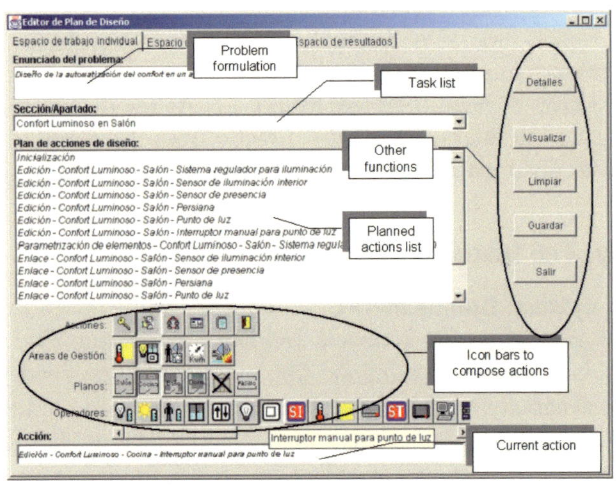

Fig. 4. Plan Editor in Domosim-TPC

- *Discussion Stage* (figure 5). The discussion process is a social task in which participants in an activity reflect about the model built, exchange ideas, propose a resolution mechanism, acquire new knowledge and purify their contributions. From this process a proposal (model) is obtained, reflecting the viewpoint of each participant.

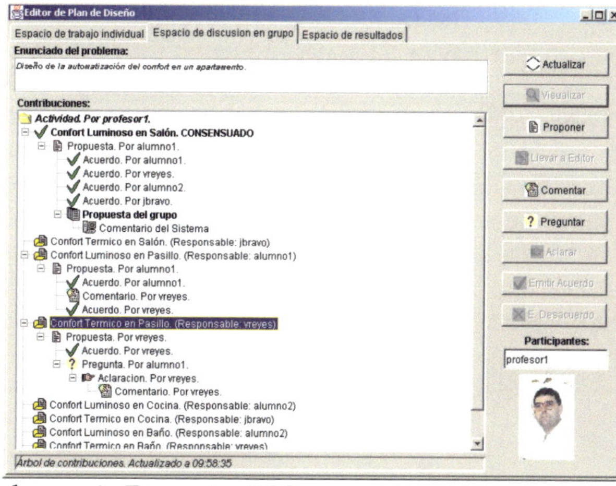

Fig. 5. Discussion workspace in Domosim-TPC

- *Result stage*. Finally, the space of results facilitates the visualization and perception of the parts of the activity that the group has already developed and agreed. The participants can observe the results and solutions obtained during the process, independently of the discussion and of the development process necessary for their achievement (this is the main goal of a *groupware* tool). Alike the discussion space, the results space has a tree-shaped hierarchical structure, used to organize the information relative to the results obtained in the activity. The application allows visualizing the results in a textual and a graphical way.

We are interested in the effective use of mobile computing devices for collaborative learning. There are tasks in the system Domosim-TPC which are susceptible of improvement through mobile computing. In particular, the *Collaborative Planning of Design* is a asynchronous and reflexive task which could be improved using mobile devices.

4.2. Applying CIAN for adapting collaborative tasks in Domosim-TPC to mobile computing

We intend to obtain the mobile version, and in particular, the PDA version of the individual plan edition space in Domosim-TPC (figure 4). The evolution process proposed is based on the use of *conceptual models* of the starting system. Next, we describe the analysis and modeling of the main tasks in asynchronous workspace of Domosim-TPC using the CIAN notation. The models, created in the context of CIAM, allow adapting the user interface of Domosin-TPC to mobile computing support. Also, these conceptual models are used for automating and generating this evolution process.

First we are going to explain the creation of the *sociogram* and the *process models* associated with the system Domosim-TPC. In figure In figures 6 and 7 we can see the appearance of both. In the ***Sociogram*** *Development* stage, the organization structure is modeled, as well as the relationship between its members. In the example we have the following roles: *Teacher*, *Student*, *Observer* and *System* (that adds expert knowledge to the learning process). We identify some specialized students called *Planner* and *Designer* that take part in the two main tasks in the environment. The inheritance relationships can be enriched with the definition of *conditions*. For example, we show that a *Student* can be specialized in the *Designer* role in the context of the *"Design"* Task. The *Planner* role has several subroles (*Plan Designer, Critic* or *Specialist*). A *Planner* can play any of them depending on the *"Task Allocation"* chosen for the activity. Once the *inheritance* (generalization / specialization) *relationships* among roles established, the *actor-role acting relationship* is added for the main roles in the diagram. This kind of relationship can be labelled when we want to express the cardinality (minimum and maximum) in the cases in which the specification establishes restrictions on the matter. The diagram can also show the relationships among roles that can, at a certain moment, work together. These relationships are expressed by means of *association relationships*. In figure 5 we can see that the *Student* role and the *Teacher* role are associated, creating work group. This indicates that there are tasks in which both with their respective responsibilities take part.

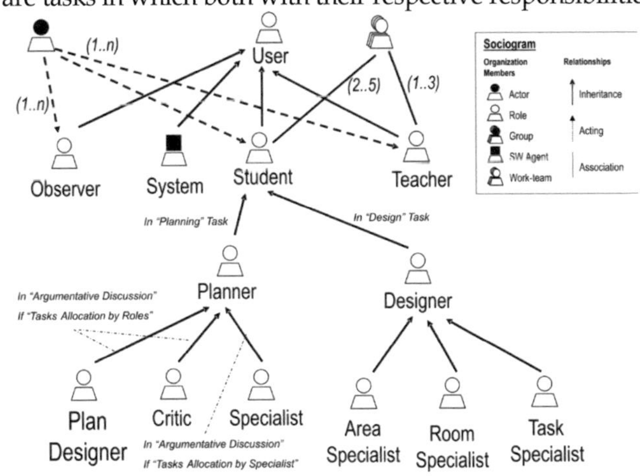

Fig. 6. *Sociogram* of Domosim-TPC

In the following two stages (***Responsibilities Modeling*** and ***Process Modeling*** stages) the workflow that defines the work in-group developed in the organization is described. Figure 7 shows the *process model* associated to the system taken as example. In this example we use a symbol to express *Abstract Task* (7.d), that is, group work tasks that can be decomposed into others in a lower level of abstraction and of different kinds (7.g and 7.h). Collaborative and Cooperative tasks must specify the roles involved in its execution (7.a), whereas in the individual tasks only a role must appear. For all the tasks the objects manipulated and their access modifiers are indicated (7.b). For each task we can specify the so-called *Domain Independent Support Tool* (7.c). These are the supporting tools that implement well-known patterns or interaction protocols. Between the tasks *Configure Experiences* and *Planning* we can see temporal and data dependencies (7.c), indicating that the data *Activities* are transferred and the relation between these tasks is sequential (>>). Between task *Planning* and *Design and Simulation*, there is a period dependence (7.f) and a condition that must be checked (7.e).

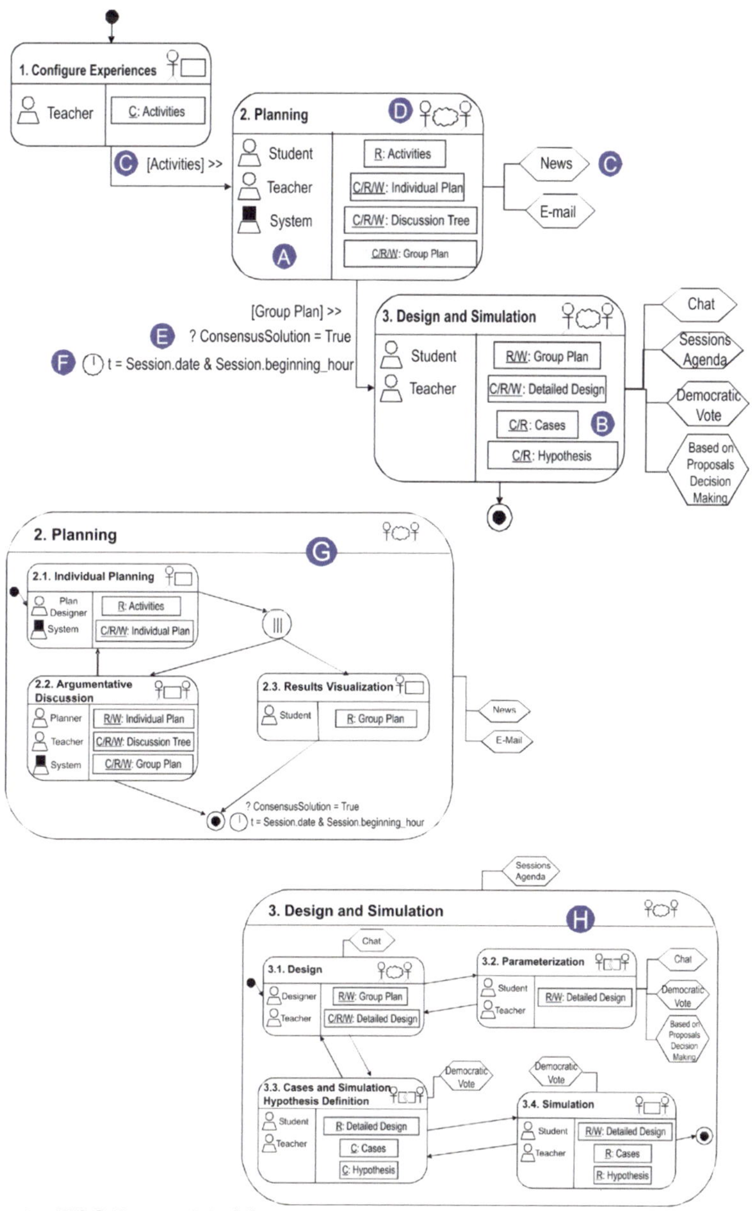

Fig. 7. Domosim-TPC *Process Model*

Figure 8 shows the ***Interaction Model*** (task model in CTT notation) for individual task "*Individual Planning*" (task 2.1 in figure 7). To obtain the version for PDA of the individual workspace, temporal relationships among the tasks and the domain-manipulated objects must be taken into account. This information allows creating the interface in which both the widgets (user interface objects) that show domain application objects (internal objects) and the widgets that allow executing certain actions applicable to these internal objects must appear together. In the design plan editor (individual workspace) two internal objects are handled: the *DESIGN_ACTION* and the *INDIVIDUAL_PLAN* (a collection of design actions). Figure 8 shows the names (in uppercase) of both objects. They are part of the name of the tasks that manipulate them.

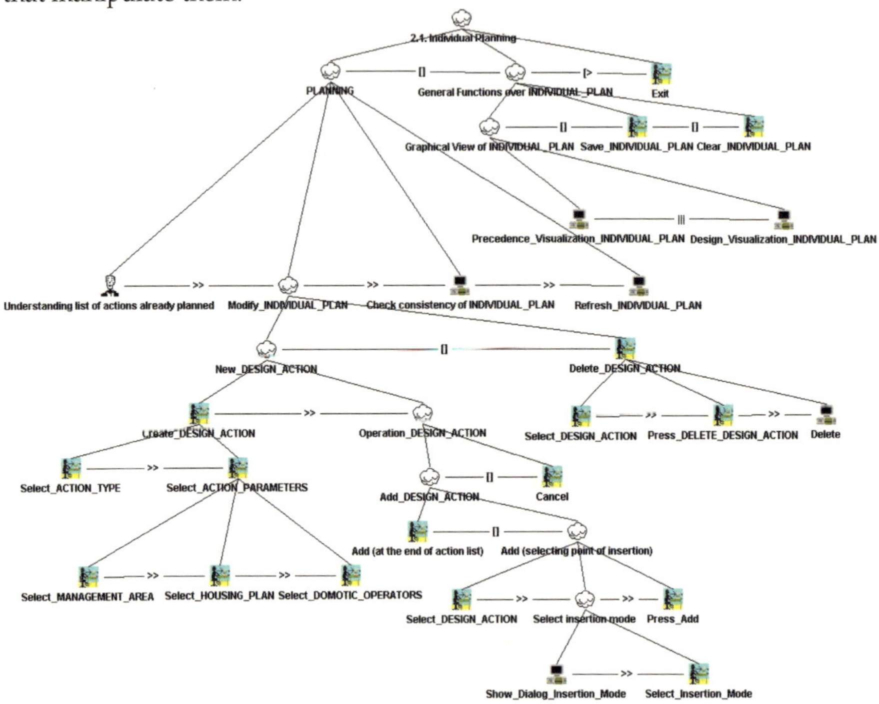

Fig. 8. Modeling of abstract task "2.1 Individual Planning".

Diagram in figure 8 shows the general functions that can be performed on the individual plan. It can be shown graphically. There are two modes of *visualization*: a list of nodes (a node represents an action) connected by arcs (representing precedence relationships); and the design of the scene that is created for executing the planned actions list. We can also *save* the individual plan. The option *Clear* eliminates all the information contained in the actions list. These actions are applicable to the *INDIVIDUAL_PLAN* object. These must appear in the user interface next to the object related (the list box that shows the sequence of steps in the plan). The resulting PDA interface of this subset of tasks is shown in figure 9 (a). In addition, the individual plan editor handles *DESIGN_ACTION* objects. In the diagram shown in figure 8 the actions *Add_DESIGN_ACTION* and *Delete_DESIGN_ACTION* are included. The first one has certain complexity. When a task (that means an operation over a internal object) is of the interaction type, the mapping to a perceptible object (a widget in the interface) is more direct. This kind of operations can be represented by means of buttons, options in a menu or a contextual menu. It has been applied to the mapping of the *Delete_DESIGN_ACTION* operation, or the aforementioned generic functions, which the user can perform on the *INDIVIDUAL_PLAN* object.

However, when a task has a certain complexity, i.e., when a task is represented by an abstract task, with several abstraction levels and several interaction tasks (this occurs in the *New_DESIGN_ACTION* task), more complex visual components are necessary (a panel, in a

PC version of the interface; or in a PDA, where there are display resolution constraints, a dialog box is a better choice). This occurs in the task that allows creating new design actions, as we can see in figure 9 (b). This dialog box appears whenever a new design action is created.

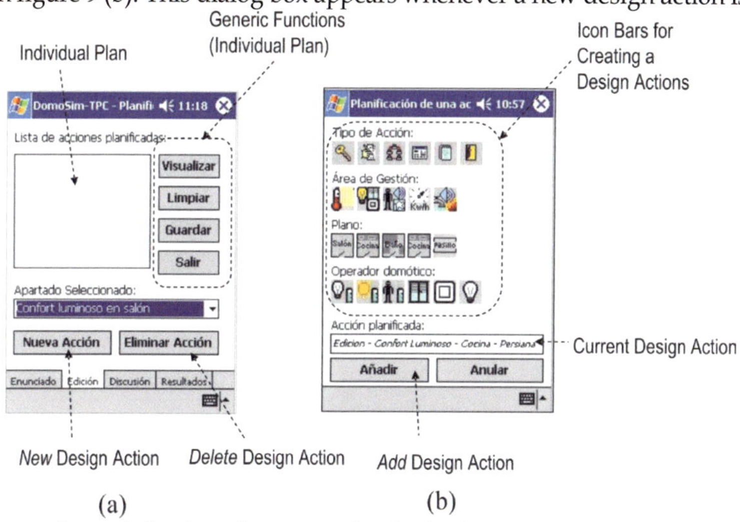

Fig. 9. PDA version of the interface to individual plan edition. (a) Interface that allows showing and performing actions on the *INDIVIDUAL_PLAN*. (b) Dialog box that allows the creation of a new *INDIVIDUAL_ACTION*.

4.3. The obtained system: Domosim-MOB

The system Domosim-Mob has been obtained as result of applying the aforementioned method for generating the PDA User Interface version of the Domosim-TPC system. It is important to point out that the functionality supported in PDA devices is a supplement of the original system. Domosim-Mob is an extension developed to add mobility to the learning process ("*learning anywhere and at anytime*"). Whilst mobility in learning processes favours the involvement of students in the task in question, the use of these devices does, however, mean paying the price of visualization limitations. In figure 10 we can see the appearance of the user interfaces for supporting the *result stage*.

The tasks supported in Domosim-Mob are similar to Domosim-TPC tasks, but the access to them has been improved, as a consequence of there being greater flexibility. However using mobile devices, beside the features characteristic of the discussion process, creates additional problems due to the fact that it offers the possibility of participating in the discussion without the need for the device to be connected to the server: that is the synchronization with the rest of the members in the group. One-to-one synchronization, in other words, synchronization of a mobile device with the system, is quite well resolved. However, in our case a synchronization of order *n to m* is necessary. Our approach to solving the problem is by applying a variation of the Schiper-Eggli-Sandoz algorithm for the exchange and ordering of messages in distributed systems respecting a causal order based on a model of logic clocks. The diagram in figure 11 shows the global structure of the Domosim-Mob application. The new context of use entails the appearance of several work modes in the application:

- *Connected work session* (Figure 11-1). The mobile application accesses the information server, although not at the same time as other participants of the group. The information associated with the group process and the history of the group is recorded and filed at a central location. Information exchange is based on XML files.
- *Disconnected work session (off-line)* (Figure 11-2), in which the user works with local information available in the mobile device. Students can work in isolation. They reflect on and construct the solution of the problem, which is stored in the PDA.
- *Synchronization session* (Figure 11-3). This one appears as a result of the previous work mode. Students send updated information to the server (individual contributions in the discussion process and their answer to the proposed problem) with the aim of providing and storing consistent information about the collaborative experience. The server distributes this information to the rest of the members of the teams. In order to guarantee confidentiality when accessing the server, an authentication process is necessary.

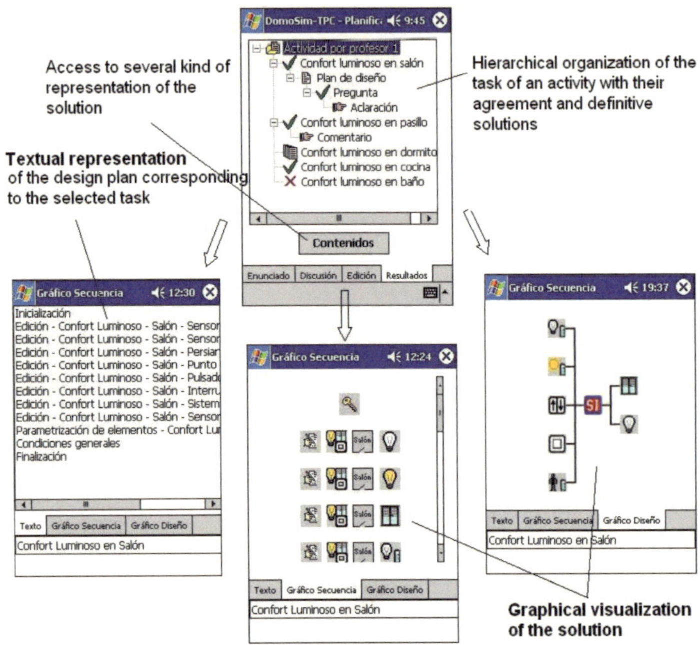

Fig. 10. PDA version of the interface to result visualization

5. Conclusions and Future Works

The main goal of the work presented is to incorporate the mobile computing paradigm in the teaching and learning of domains with a high experimental degree in order to take into account mobile computing possibilities. There are a lot of applications based on desktop metaphor that can be adapted to mobile computing support. We propose to use a model-based approach for the development and evolution of the graphical user interface of CSCL applications. Using a model-based approach allows the production of device-independent specifications of starting systems in this evolution process. In particular we propose to apply

the specification techniques proposed in the context of CIAM. CIAM is a methodological approach that guides the designer following different phases from modeling to reaching interaction models of groupware systems. CIAM is based on the CIAN notation that allows users to accurately describe the features of a collaboration process (roles, responsibilities, tasks, shared context, etc). We have shown the application of CIAM in the design and evolution process of the user interface that supports the task of *collaborative planning of design* in the context of a CSCL system, called Domosim-TPC. We have obtained a mobile version of this system, called Domosim-Mob.
The results in the application of this method show the necessity to include those aspects closely related with *context modeling* and the *synchronization* of contents; that is why we make an outline of the way to take into account these characteristics as a future work.

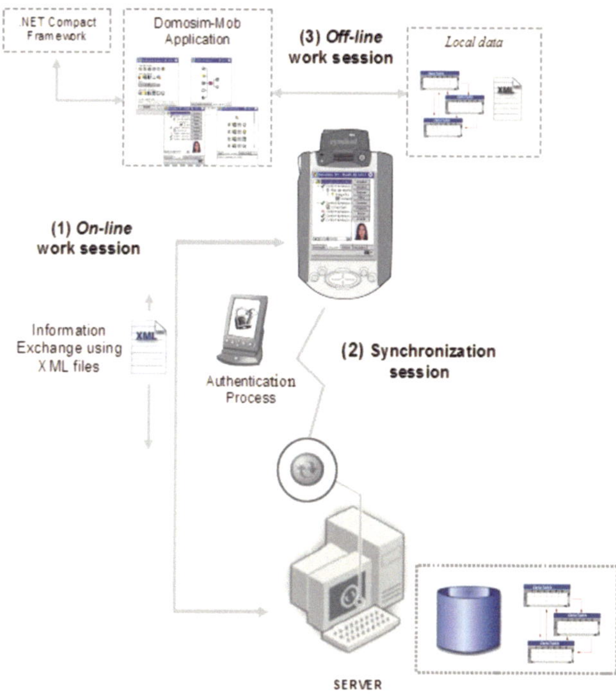

Fig. 11. General structure of Domosim-Mob

6. Acknowledgments

Work supported by the Castilla-La Mancha University and the Junta de Comunidades de Castilla-La Mancha in the projects mGUIDE (PBC08-0006-512) and M-CUIDE (TC20080552).

7. References

Abrams, M.; Phanourious, C.; Batongbacal, A.L.; Williams, S. & Shuster, J. (1999) UIML: An appliance-independent XML user interface language. In A. Mendelson, editor, *Proceedings of 8th International World-Wide Web Conference WWW'8* (Toronto, May 11-14, 1999), Amsterdam, Elsevier Science Publishers.

Annett, J. & Duncan, K.D. (1967). Task Analysis and Training Design, *Occupational Psychology*, 41, pp. 211-221.

Carlsen, S.: (1998) Action Port Model: A Mixed Paradigm Conceptual Workflow Modeling Language. *3rd IFCIS International Conference on Cooperative Information Systems.*

Dillenbourg, P.; et al., (1995) The Evolution of Research on Collaborative Learning, ed. P. Reimann, Spada, H. Vol. Learning in humans and machines. *Towards an interdisciplinary learning science.* pp. 189- 211.

Eisenstein, J. & Puerta, A. (2000). Adaptation in Automated User-Interface Design. *Proc. of IUI'2000* (New Orleans, 9-12 January 2000), ACM Press, New York, pp. 74-81.

Eisenstein, J.; Vanderdonckt, J. & A. Puerta. (2001) Applying model-based techniques to the development of user interfaces for mobile computers. in *ACM Conference on Intelligent User Interfaces IUI'2001.* Alburqueque.

Ellis, C. A.; Gibbs, S. J. & Rein, G. L.. (1991). Groupware: Some Issues and Experiences, *Communications of ACM* 34(1) 38-58.

Foley, J.; et al., (1991). UIDE-An Intelligent User Interface Design Environment, *in Intelligent User Interfaces*, J. Sullivan and S. Tyler, Editors. Addison-Wesley. pp. 339-384.

Garrido, J. L. (2003). AMENITIES: Una metodología para el desarrollo de sistemas cooperativos basada en modelos de comportamiento y tareas, *PhD-Thesis*, Departamento de Lenguajes y Sistemas Informáticos, Granada, Universidad de Granada. *Spain.*

Limbourg, Q. & Vanderdonckt, J.(2004). Addressing the Mapping Problem in User Interface Design with UsiXML. *Proceedings of the 3rd annual conference on Task models and diagrams (TAMODIA 2004).* Czech Republic.

Molina, A.I.; Redondo M.A. & Ortega, M. (2009). A methodological approach for user interface development of collaborative applications: A case study, *Science of Computer Programming* 74 (9), pp. 754-776

Paternò, F. (1999). *Model-Based Design and Evaluation on Interactive Applications.* Springer Vergal, ISBN 1-85233-155-0.

Paternò, F., (2004) ConcurTaskTrees: An Engineered Notation for Task Models., in The *Handbook Of Task Analysis For HCI*, D. Diaper and N.A. Stanton, Editors. LEA, Mahwah, NJ., p. 483-501.

Puerta, A.R. (1996). The MECANO Project: Comprehensive and Integrated Support for Model-Based Interface Development". in *CADUI96: Computer-Aided Design of User In-terfaces.* Numur, Belgium.

Redondo, M.A. & Bravo, C. (2006) DomoSim-TPC: Collaborative Problem Solving to Support the Learning of Domotical Design. *Computer Applications in Engineering Education.* Ed. John Wiley & Sons, vol. 4, N°1, 9-19.

Vanderdonckt, J.M. & Bodart, F. (1993) Encapsulating Knowledge for Intelligent Automatic Interaction Objects Selection. In *InterCHI'93*: ACM Press.

van Welie, M. & van der Veer, G. C. (2003). Groupware Task Analysis. *Handbook of Cognitive Task Design.* E. Hollnagel. LEA., NJ, pp. 447-476.

14

From the discovery of students access patterns in e-learning including web 2.0 resources to the prediction and enhancement of students outcome

Raquel Hijón-Neira and Ángel Velázquez-Iturbide
Universidad Rey Juan Carlos
Spain

1. Introduction

This chapter explains a new tracking system for the web 2.0 eras developed based on the knowledge gained about similar systems development (Hijon et al., 2007) and on the approaches for further assessment of interactions data developed, such as visualizations and statistical analysis (Hijon & Velázquez, 2008). Thus, it explains how teachers can benefit from the information it would provide to keep an eye on students while working beyond their reach. The system is been used during the current academic year in our university and some of it is also shown. There is also the description of an assement process teachers can follow through the system to be able to obtain the information needed. Therefore, how the system can be used to gain the knowledge about students' interactions, and ways to predict and enhance their students outcome.
Firstly, there is a review of the state of the art in analysis of interactions, and specially in Learning Management Systems.
Secondly, a there is the description of the problem analysis. Where, there is an explanation of the reasons the host LMS to develop the integrated tracking system for the web 2.0 has been Moodle. And, there is a description of the objectives this tracking system may pursuit, namely: give teachers a more accurate perspective of how their students are working, therefore improve the teacher learning process; also, to improve Moodle analysis of interaction features with open queries, and improve the visualizations of this interactions data providing a 'birds eye view'; of course, offering of interactive visualizations of this interactions data that would be catchy and engaging to encourage teachers analysis. Once decided the host LMS was Moodle, there is an evaluation of new already developed modules for it that may fulfill the desired functionality the new module may include. And finally, there is a clear description of the new system functionality development and the knowledge teachers can easily obtain from it.
Thirdly, there is an explanation of how the system can provide the required knowledge to teachers by simply interacting with the system. Some examples of knowledge gaining and interpretation of data to predict and enhance students´ outcome are explained.

Finally, conclusions about using this new module developed for Moodle and the importance of prediction of students' outcome to enhance teaching and learning.

2. Previous Research in Analysis of Interactions

Determining learning behaviour in electronic media is a complex problem. A difficulty is that students mostly use these environments away from the classroom and out of sight of their educators. Without the informal monitoring that occurs in face-to-face teaching it is difficult for educators to know how their students are using and responding to these environments. Educators have had to seek new ways of obtaining information about the learning patterns of their students. This requires the development of effective methods of determining and evaluating learner behaviour in electronic environments.

For example, an analysis of student use of a courseware website by (Peled & Rashty, 1999) found out that the most popular online activities were passive and involved getting information rather than contributing. Their conclusion is that the students were very goal oriented in their use of the web site. Further information can be gained from knowing when students access resources (Sheard, et al., 2005). This can help educators understand student's preferred learning patterns. A study carried out by (McIsaac., et al., 1999). explored interactions of doctoral students with an online environment and they concluded that student interactions were goal focussed. For instance, in a study of student use of a first year geology website by (Hellwege, et al., 1996)., log file analysis showed that students accessed the most recent lecture notes first, picking up a couple of key slides, before returning to a previous lecture. As a result, it was shown that students were accessing resources according to immediate need. In this way, another study (Hijón & Velázquez 2006) of this characteristics showed that the average connections to the CMS was over thirty minutes. Particular navigation patterns may also indicate the lack of, or prominence of, navigational mechanism available.

Analysis of learner interactions may also be used to compare learning behaviours of different groups of students. Some studies have found a relationship between learning outcomes and web site usage. Like (Comunale, et al., 2002) found evidence to suggest that higher course grades are related to more frequent website use or another one that found no correlation (Hernández-García, et al., 2008). Another studies (Dimai & Ebner, 2003), (Dowming, et al. 2005) where participation and implication grades are measure through indicators such as emails sent, forum participation, total connection time to the LMS. An example of more subjective measures such as interactions' quality was obtained in (Barbour & Collins 2005). In some empiric studies made it is highly remarkable the importance on time and dedication to the course habits (Nian-Shing & Kan-Min, 2002), the connection time (Kickul & Kickul 2002) and the total number of accesses to the system (Ramos & Yudko 2008) (Moreira, et al. 2005).

A study by (Lu, et al 2000) which analysed log file interactions with different resources on a courseware website found a relationship between frequency of assess to learning resources and final exam scores. They content that this provides evidence that the use of relevant Web content improves learning. A more recent study (Gao & Lehman 2003) investigated learning outcomes of students using Web-based learning environments providing different levels of interactivity. Log file analysis showed that the students in the proactive and reactive interactions groups spent more time on task. Interview data revealed that the students in the interactive groups spent more time reviewing and reflecting and learning content and this resulted in greater learning outcomes. On the other hand, in (Nickles 2005)there is a study of six measures of student behaviour in a CMS which did not consistently correlate with their grades.

Although there have been various gender based studies of the use of the Web, there are a scarcity of studies which report on differences in courseware usage based on gender. A study by (Peled & Rashty 1999) found differences in the type of resources accessed by males and female students. The males used interactive resources significantly more than the females; whereas, females used passive resources more than males. Another study by (Hijón et al., 2008b) found important differences on the students' accesses patterns on the morning and evening courses, also among students with different exam performance and on courses that run over the year or just only a semester to select some of them.

Analysis of learner interactions may also be used to compare learning behaviours of different groups of students. Some studies have found a relationship between learning outcomes and web site usage.

2.1 In Learning Management Systems

Teachers need more and more an aid from the e-learning system that provides information about how students interact with it. Thus, some applications that try to resolve the problem of keeping an eye on the student while working out of sight of the educator have already been developed in different areas of e-Learning, such us. (Ramani & Rocha 2000) describe tools for letting instructors easily view student participation in a Web-based class using charts and graphs to display student participation. (Reffay & Chanier 2002) identify clusters and cliques within the online class. These tools focus not on the individual student, but rather on class activity as a whole. Althougth both sets of tools are interesting and potentially useful in aiding the understanding of Web Based discussion forums, they aren't build on an analysis of the discussion evaluator's workflow, which is a critical requirement for improving online teaching effectiveness.

In (Mazza & Dimitrova 2005) had developed an Application CourseVis that visualized interactions of students with an e-learning site, and then they moved towards moodle and offered what they have called GISMO which is an application that can be installed into Moodle and shows basically different types of graphical information (bar charts, and matrix visualizations…) basically 2D graphical information about the overall classroom accesses or the detailed information from a specific student. All it is offered are graphs of the accesses, the 2D visualization may have a third dimension that is color (from light two dark shows the quantity of accesses), or shape (bigger circles show a larger amount of contributions from the student). Even though their visualizations are more advance than Ramani and Rocha's, they still lack of interactions and improvement. Thus, in (Hijón & Velázquez, 2008a) important improvements have been obtain by using interactive visualizations to monitor students interactions.

In University of Edinburgh they have made tracking and visualization of student use of online learning materials (Hardy, et al. 2007). Their tracking tools are non-invasive, whilst providing information not available in standard web server logs, the tools also allow the tracking of non-standard page elements such as inlines and allowed a great measure of control over what information is recorded. Their tracking process could thus be divided into two main phases largely independent of each other: data collection and data analysis. The data captured was for three main types of event: page accesses, the viewing or hiding of inline and the firing-up of popups, each event storing relevant information on the tracking server. Each event had a common data set. User and session identifiers were captured from a WebCT cookie. Information such as the client machine was captured using JavaScript commands and client IP and domain information via the HTTP header. An internal page identifier for the page accessed was also recorded as well as the URL used to access the given page. In addition to this information, page access data was also recorded; the referrer URL which could be used to determine the path a student used navigate through the course; a start and end time for a page access – this time was measured at the client. This provided temporal information as to when the course was being viewed. Inline events were also recorded: an internal inline identifier unique to a given page; the event time at which the inline was revealed or hidden together the even type, which could be one of: reveal, hide, reveal all and hide all. This would provide feedback as to how inlines were used by students.

It is clear the importance of analysis users' interactions in order to improve and facilitate the information offered through a web site. Furthermore, since the analysis of web usage for understanding learners behaviour is an important task in the enhancement of the teaching-learning process, it has already been done by authors trying to find out hints that lead them to the discovery of behavioural access patterns, but as said, it is very difficult and time consuming for teachers to thoroughly track and assess all the activities performed by all students.

Thus, despite there are some research on data generated on e-learning systems, there is still lack of standard methods that provide, first, with the required information about interactions, second, with the overall method to make that the information obtained could be automatically related with additional data on the learning process and storaged in an unique database system, and third, that provides methods of treating the information and visualizing it that results in greater and quicker teachers' comprehension of what is happening.

3. Problem Analysis

It has been developed an application into the Moodle LMS, called Merlin-Mo, since it is worldwide widespread and offers very good service for e-Learning (Aberdour, 2007) where Moodle scored 79% for its use in Higher Education among the more than 50 open source platforms. A summary of the features that also has leading us to make that decision are: It is fully open source software (a GNU license regulates download, usage, modification and redistribution of the code). It is platform an independent environment, flexible, easy to use, available in multiple languages and open to customization. Its architecture and user interface are focused on "activities" rather than on "Content", so large number of activity modules is available, allowing for a wide range of pedagogical settings. It features a nice user-friendly interface both for students, teachers and administrators. From a technical point of view, it is design with a very strong modular structure, a fundamental module for those willing to integrate additional functions or upgrade existing functions. The community of Moodle developers and users is very lively and is actually offering a very good support through a dedicated web site and a number of specialized web forums. Also, a lot of high quality technical documentation is available. The source code has been judge of very good quality by programmers. The Figure 1 shows an example of how this new module fits into the Moodle system.

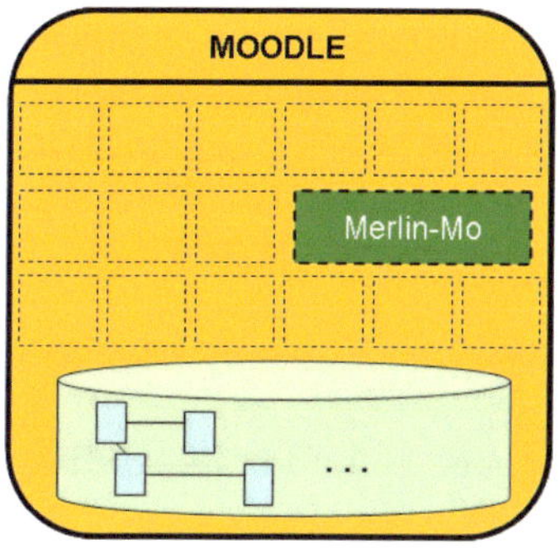

Fig. 1. Merlin-Mo into Moodle

The new module should offer a fully automatic installation in any running Moodle system. Therefore after its installation the module should offer very complete statistics and visualization of students' interactions. Thus, the integration and compatibility should allow using the Moodle database and all the Moodle preset services, such as, administration and security services. Finally, it should be developed under a GNU license, allowing its use by all the developers community and, of course, Moodle users.

3.1 Objectives

The general objective is to offer teachers a more accurate perspective of how their students are working that would result in a better teaching-learning process. Therefore, a partial objective is to improve Moodle analysis of interaction features with open queries that would lead to a precise information gathering. Furthermore, to improve the visualizations of this interactions data providing a 'birds eye view' that would result in a much more easy to follow way for the teacher to do the analysis. Moreover, offer interactive visualizations that would be catchy and engaging, and would lead to 'want to know more' offering nicely built and easy to use interfaces. Finally, and not less important, since Moodle lacks also of statistical analysis it would provide statistical visualizations that would easily give an overall impression of the question placed to the system. Therefore, the list of objectives of Merlin-Mo:

- Detailed data of what students are doing within the course in a selected time period.
- Representation of students work through the year. Obtaining of time graphs with interactions.
- Detailed information about accesses to different resources. As they may be very different in structure and in the way students interact with them, possibility of selection of visualizations; otherwise, the system should offer the most appropriate.
- Analysis of different types of actions a student can do when reaching different resources.
- Easily identification by the teacher of what parts or resources are more and less used, and how are they used.
- Identification of lurkers or proactive students.

- Identification and way of analysis of cooperative students, how they do this participation and cooperation in the different web 2.0 resources Moodle has (eg. Forum, chat, wiki).
- Offering of different interfaces according to the previously selected data, therefore *ad-hoc* interface customization to the user.

The general objective that this module should accomplish into the Moodle system should be the offering of all this new functionality but also the obtaining of a total integration of this module into Moodle, to do it, it would be necessary to obtain the following partial objectives:

- Use of Moodle security system to allow only teachers of the specific course to see the analysis.
- Synchronization of the language and other user settings of this new module with the general configuration settings Moodle offer for users and courses.

3.2 Evaluation of existing applications

Once decided that the Host LMS was Moodle, the applications that should be analyzed were the module for analysis that comes in the standard version, and try to find out new modules, if have been developed, for this LMS. So this was what it was done, firstly deeply analyze the standard Moodle module for tracking students' interactions, finally, check in the already developed modules as add-ons if there were some that covered these functionality.

On the one hand, the module for analysis is very poor; it just offered a data table structure where teachers can ask for hits to his/her courses in a very poor interface. Furthermore, the data is visualized just as a tabular format with all lack on improved visualizations that would include simple or complex graphs, statistics or interactive visualizations that would help teachers on the analysis.

On the other hand, when checking if some modules that covered all or any of this functionality were already developed for moodle, there were found out the followings blocks (as Moodle calls them):

Most Active Users: It is a block that lists the most active users of the LMS along with a ranking. Each user is given a rank according to the number of hits made by him. The rank is simply the Z score of the number of hits made by the user. It just offers a rank with the top ten higher workers within a course. Much more is still needed for a teacher to set up policies that encourage students to learn and participate in different resources.

Inactive users: this block shows the teacher users who haven't logged in to their course for a set amount of days. Teacher can also choose to display this information to students or not. It gives the teacher a good vision of who are the inactive users within a course. It is a good feedback from the LMS but not enough.

Online users' Google map: this block displays who are the users currently online. It is very useful when teaching e-Learning, not so necessary on hybrid learning. It uses the geographical information from users' profiles to display the locations of online users on a Google map. The geocoding of locations are cached in the Moodle database and updated when cron runs. As its precedent, it may be very useful in e-learning, where students can be geographical far apart, but no so necessary in blended learning.

Raw records count: It is a simple course report that generates one list with the number of records in the log for each student in the course. The data table can be exported to ODS, Excel and CSV. The module improves a little bit the information that standard Moodle offers, since it adds totals to the tabular information it already offers. Thus, it is better than do not have any type of summary about the tracking information teachers need, but is indelible not enough.

Register: Register activity organizes logs of courses in sessions; each session has login and logout. If register is in a normal course, it will calculate only logs from that course, if it is in a metacourse, it' will calculate all logs of courses in that category. Login is the first log for the course (or of categories) if there are not any other logs before the timeout period, "register activity" creates a logout. The module improves the information standard Moodle had up until now by offering sessions analysis, not only accesses or hits. After all, it is a step further on this analysis since it offers a new concept, but the information is displayed in the same tabular format, and represents nothing much.

3.3 Module for Students' Interactions Assessment

A new module for the Moodle LMS has been developed that covers all required functionality explained before in the objectives section.

The new tracking and visualization system of students' interactions for Moodle LMS has been divided into two main applications. Both of them, represent different types of information, offer interfaces designed ad-hoc to the selection of the information required, and present the data visualizations in a much different way. The Figure 2 shows the main interface of the new module called Merlin-Mo.

Fig. 2. Main Interface of Merlin-Mo

Once the tracking system is reached just be clicking in the Moodle menu option, the user has two main options: on the left hand side, the Ad-Hoc Interaction Assessment System (AIAS), and on the right hand side, the Preset Interaction Assessment System (PIAS). In the first one, teachers can find a wide open interface to place queries to the system about how their students are working, also, in some cases, the way to represent the information can be selected. In the second one, there is a complex analysis easy to do, since queries and interactions can be selected through a guided interface that would offer the visualization that best suits the data. Following to this, there is a detailed explanation of each system.

Ad-Hoc Interaction Assessment System

The partial functionality derived from the objectives, within the tracking system, this application fulfils are the following: Detailed data of what students are doing within the course in a selected time period; Visual representation of the students' amount of work through the year; Obtaining of time graphs with interactions; Detailed information about accesses to different resources. As they may be very different in structure and in the way students interact with them, possibility of selection of visualizations; otherwise, the system should offer the most appropriate. Analysis of different types of actions a student can do when reaching different resources. Easily identification by the teacher of what parts or resources are more and less used, and how are they used.

The information can be represented in two different ways, in 2D tables and in 2D graphs depending on the query data to be shown and on the user preferences.

The main interface of the system is shown in Figure 3, where user can identify three sections:

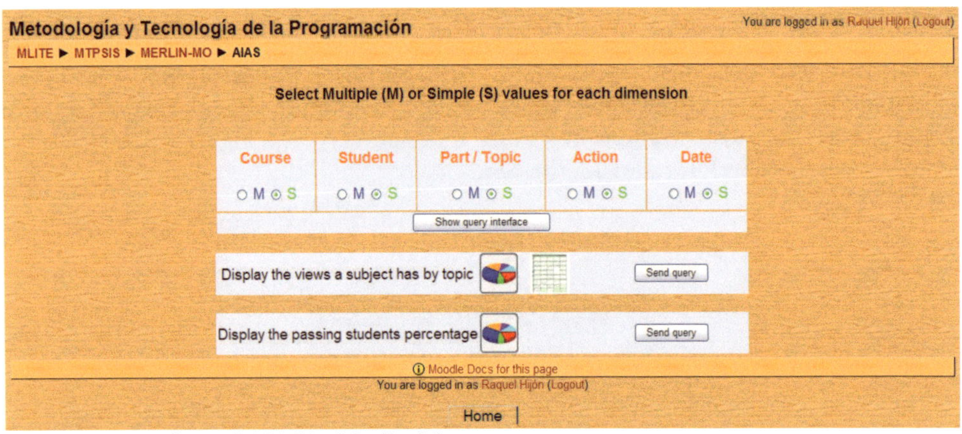

Fig. 3. Main Interface of AIAS in Merlin-Mo

The first section asks the user to fulfil some values in five different boxes that would dynamically generate the following interface. Therefore, this interface uses the values that have been selected or left by default. In this sense, the "M" stands for multiple values that would be able to be chosen afterwards, this is to say, more than one course, student, part/topic, action or date; and "S" stands for "simple" values, this means, just one value would be selected in the next interface. The five boxes stand for the five different dimensions users can ask for, those are:

Course: Stands for the courses the teacher would like to ask for, of course, it only includes courses the user role is teacher, this means that he/she is authorized on that course.

Student: represent the students enrol in the course/s previously selected.

Part/Topic: allows the selection of a resource included in the course, it could be either a type of document (word, adobe, excel...) or a forum, chat, wiki... related to the whole course or specific chapter in it.

Action: includes all actions students can do within the LMS, this is: view, add, update, etc.

Date: permits the selection of a time period in the analysis. As explained before, if "M" is clicked on this interface, a date range can be selected in the following interface, otherwise, only dates as constant can be selected, as "last week", "last month", "today" and so on.
As a result of the user selection in every box, the interface would allow those values to be picked afterwards, and what is more important, it would offer the user to pick between one type of representation or another, depending in the number of variables selected, the system would dynamically offer only tables, or both, tables and graphics.
The second and third sections are preset queries that, for its importance, have been already formed and are offered to the user without more interaction than just by clicking. The first of them shows the list of resources accessed and activities done within a course detailing the number of accesses. As it can be observed by the icons on the section, the information would be displayed in a sector graph representation and in a tabular linked chart. The second of this section, offers the overall results of students passing the course; thus, it offers the teacher the big picture of results, more detail can be obtained in the following results section. In this last case the information would be displayed in a sector representation.
When user fulfils the first section, it offers a second interface based on the options the user has previously marked, this is to say, the multiple or simple values for each part or dimension he/she has clicked on would be dynamically rearrange the data to be shown in the second interface. Therefore, bellow each element it would appear "M" or "S" respectively indicating values that could be chosen (see Figure 4) as well as the visualization type to choose from depending also, on the values selected in each dimension; in this example, user can pick from tabular, graphical or the combination of both representation.

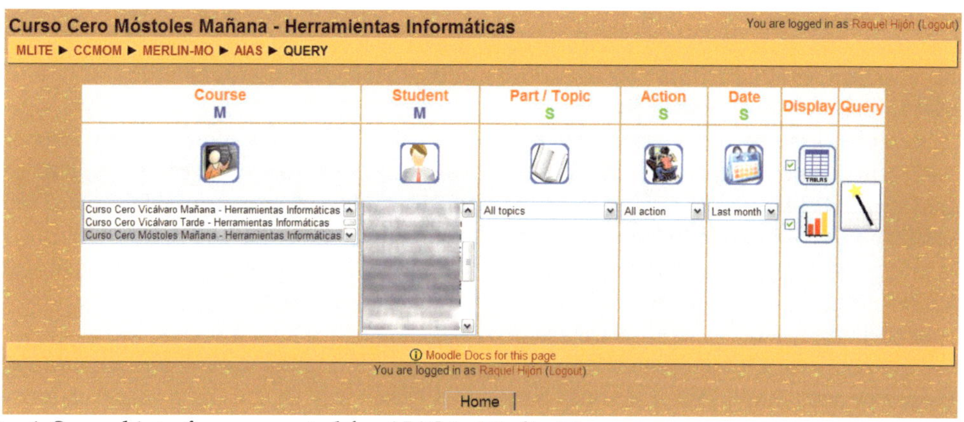

Fig. 4. Second interface generated for AIAS in Merlin-Mo

In the second interface generated only selected students were picked from the marked course (the interface has been generated to allow multiple values for "Course" and "Students" options); no restrictions were marked on the part/topic and action, which means "all topics" and "all action" options and "last month" where marked in the Date option (only simple values were allowed on this options); both types of the possible representations have been marked, graphs and tables. Therefore, results of the query after the user has filled the options appear when users click on the wand icon, Figure 5 shows them.

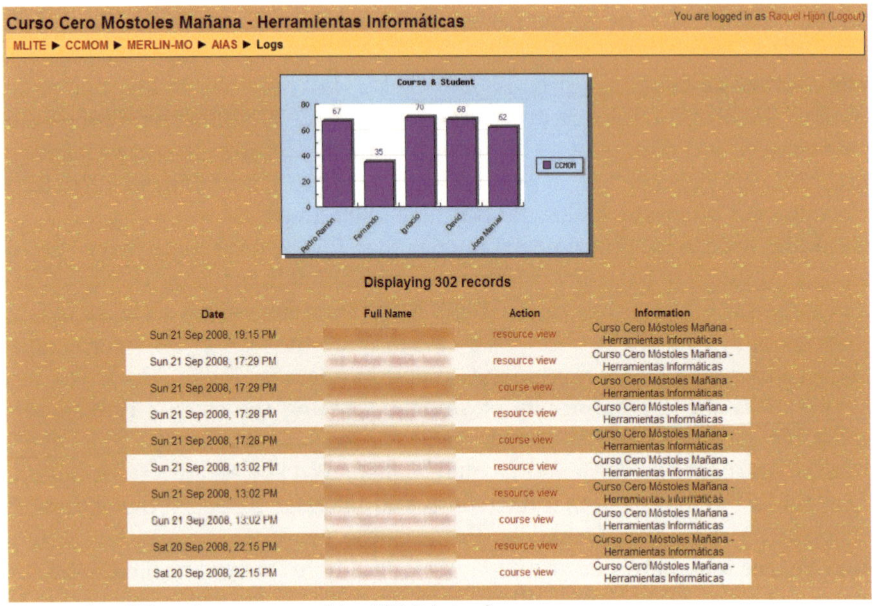

Fig. 5. Example of Results generated in AIAS interface

Further information about each register listed can be obtained just by clicking, either on the student name or in the action, which would automatically expand the data details about students and the specific action, respectively. Therefore, when clicking on the student name, the system would lead to more information about the student, and the clicking on the specific action and implicit part would show specific details that register about.

Preset Interaction Assessment System

This module of the tracking system offers a system with a different interface, also easy and intuitive, and would offer the user a richer visualization of students' interactions. This part includes interactive visualizations allowing them to represent more variables in the same visualization, which leads to two general objectives: one is the obtaining of a wider analysis and interpretation of data; and the other one is the higher teacher engaging with the analysis since results should reorganize or change by interacting with them.

The partial objectives this module tries to fulfil are:

Offer the possibility of analysis of students' interaction data grouped and also individually. It would be very important if it could be tracked either way in the same visualizations or graphs. Evolution of students (as before, individually, grouped or both ways) acceding to selected course resources through a time period selected, offering visualizations that differ from the traditional table representation. Study of the overall class results at a birds eye view first, what would offer a very good overview to the teacher; and secondly, possibility to "dig into data" to know more about what students have performed one way or the other. Since teachers usually teach more than one course, it would be important being able to compare course performance in different views and courses, which would possibly result in the obtaining of different access patterns. Students' analysis of interactions along arrange of courses. And also the offering of data for comparing, studying and analyzing students' performance through different academic years. Grace comparison through visualizations that would promptly give results to teachers within a course.

The module is divided in little applications that display a second interface depending in the functionality and the users' desire for analysis. These interfaces have been created to easily divide different functionality offering a modularity that would result in usefulness, easiness of use and user satisfaction. The main interface of this application is shown in Figure 6 where the information to be shown is grouped as follows:
Visits: it offers the information about students' accesses to the resources of a selected course.
Social Network Discussions: visually represents in a social network how students write posts in forums within the course. It should offer the social network of the conversation among them identifying threads of discussions clearly identifying who is who so teachers can make decisions of amount and quality of work done by them.
Participation: represents how students cooperate and participate in tasks that implies "learning by doing" more than simply "passively listen and reading"; this is to say, participative activities such as writing on a chat, wiki, forum, as resources of the Web 2.0 that clearly implies participation.
Most common route: who being a teacher would like to know what is mostly done by students when entering the site? It would be important towards where to set an important announcement in the LMS or getting to know, how quick a message is gotten to most of the students. It is a way, of kind of knowing what path and what delay have teachers' messages into the LMS.
Performance: quantitative feedbacks for teachers are the course results, which are measured by the grades students make in the course, after all. Offering a clear way of representing them as tree view visualization with the identification of the students would be a good "big picture" of results as well as detailed information when needed.
Course Comparison: visualizes different access pattern of different students groups. It could compare two different shifts of the same course, e.g. morning and evening one; or the same students acceding totally different courses in the same academic year or different. As seen, the possibilities are endless, but the wider the system, the wider the sample and therefore, the analysis and results.

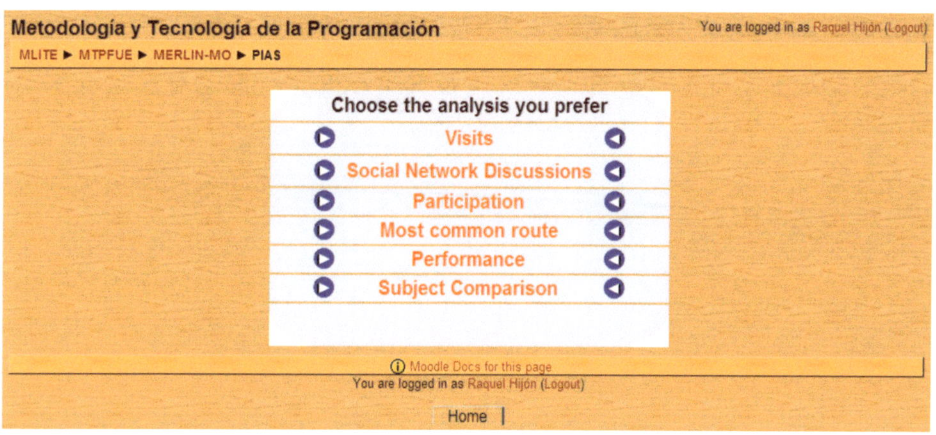

Fig. 6. Main Interface of PIAS in Merlin-Mo

When clicking on the second option, "Social Network Discussion", the system offers the possibility of analysis of how are the students participation in a particular forum associated to a course selected. Figure 7 shows its interface. Firstly, on the left hand side a course must be selected, and also a forum from the ones created within the course (usually there are more than one). Secondly, on the left hand side, information about the different representations has to be picked either a Social Network display, containing how each student has answered to others or has started a thread; or a Radial Graph that always sets in the centre the student that has been clicked on.

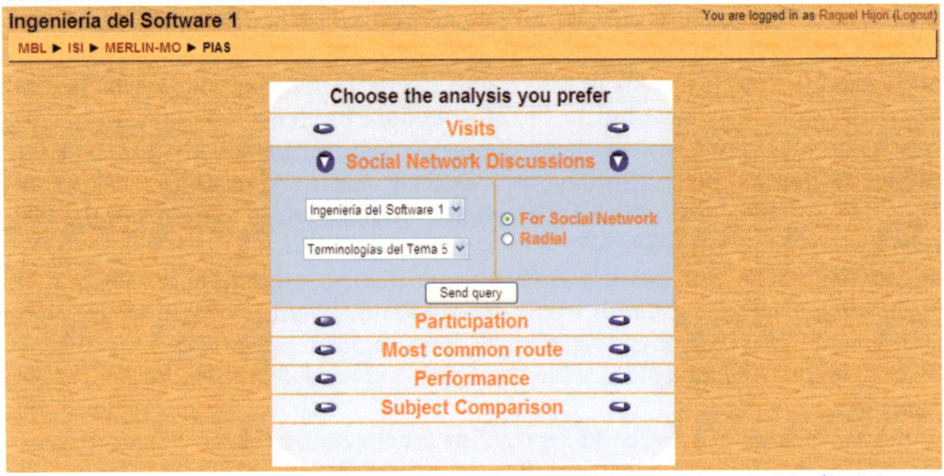

Fig. 7. Second interface generated for PIAS Social Network Discussions in Merlin-Mo

In this second interface of the PIAS system, named 'Social Network Discussion', the user has to select a course and a forum within the course, in this example the selected course was 'Software Engineering I' and among the forums to pick, the one on 'Design Patterns' have been clicked; Then, two visualizations can be selected, by clicking on the first one, 'Social Network' or 'Radial' that show differently the links among students participating in the discussion. The Figure 8 shows the first representation where the students are the nodes. Then, the user can move the image throughout the screen; pick on a node (student) that would highlight in red, as well as the nodes connected to it that would highlight in orange. This is particularly useful when the network is very crowded and it is difficult to detect relationships.

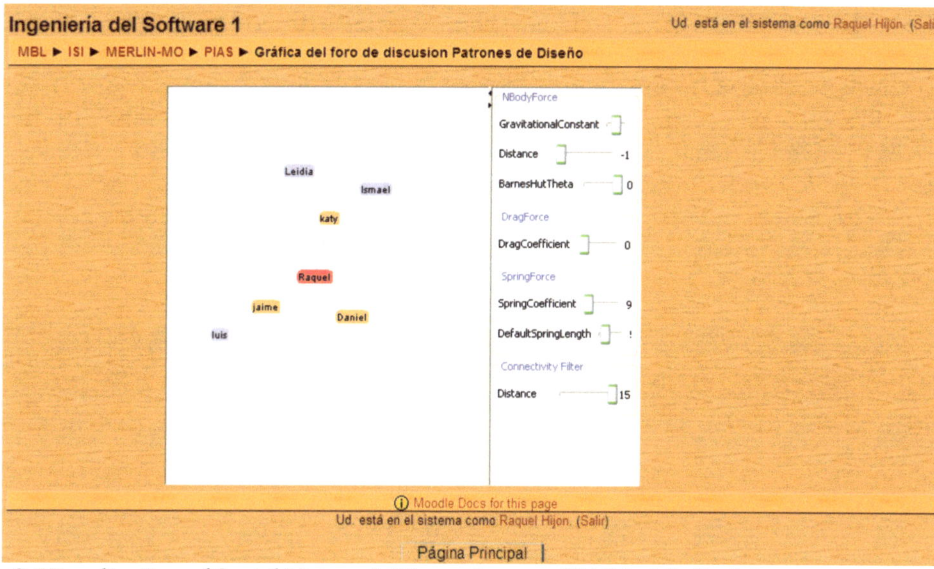

Fig. 8. Visualization of Social Network Discussions on PIAS in Merlin-Mo

In the third interface of the PIAS system, "Participation", the selected course was 'Software Engineering I' and the selected chat within the course is the 'Chat de Dudas' one (see Figure 9).

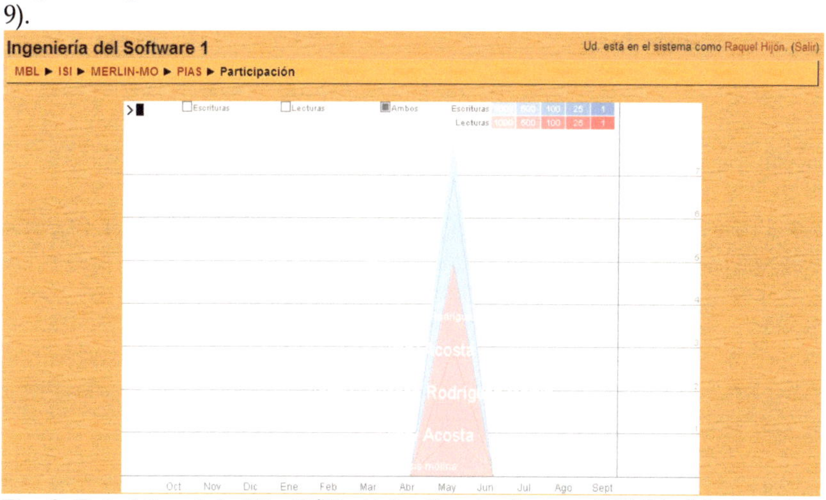

Fig. 9. Data Mountain Vis. Of Participation in chats on PIAS in Merlin-Mo

In this case results are shown in a Data Mountain visualization, where the x-axis offer the time frame those chat messages have taken part (in the example, two months, April to June) and the y-axis the amount of messages. As everyone knows, chat messages can be either read or written; the top centred interactive boxes allow the user to see both (as in the example) or only written messages or read ones. Also, on the top left side, a specific student can be selected, and the interactive graph would show the chart of only that student. The third interactivity option within this visualization is than by clicking on any coordinates of the 'Data Mountain' data clicked highlights offering detailed information about that specific dot (or student).

In the fourth interface of the PIAS system, named 'Most Common Route', user has to select a course and a student or group of them registered on that course. Figure 10 shows the results of the most common route follow by the sample students into the Software Engineering Course. As it is shown on the graph, each node acceded is labelled by the resource type (chat, survey, forum, etc) and the name within the type and course. When the chart is too crowed and want to look for something that identifies a node, the window on the left bottom part can help us to do so by highlighting the matches.

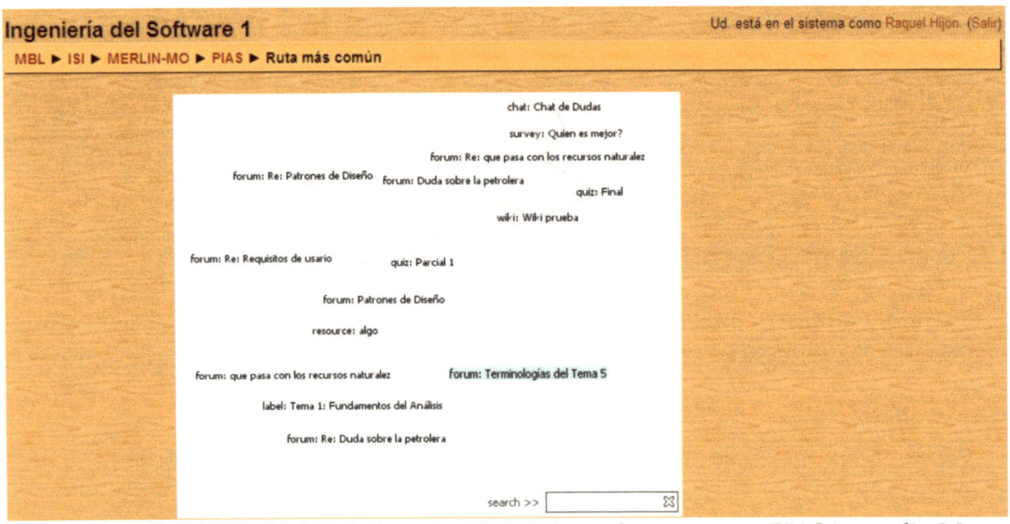

Fig. 10. Visualization of the Most Common Route through a course on PIAS in merlin-Mo

In the fifth interface of the PIAS system, named 'Performance', user has to select a course and an exam result to analyze on that course. Then, he/she would have to pick among the possibilities of representation. First option is represented on Figure 11 for 'By grade' visualization that offers a Congress Visualization with the overall of the exams the course had on the x-axis and the grades on the y-axis. These results can be modified by selecting a specific student on the left bottom window, or a specific exam on the right bottom window.

Fig. 11. Congress Vis. of the Performance in all exams within a course on PIAS in Merlin-Mo

Second option is represented on Figure 12 for the 'Social network' one that offers a the representation of the final exam results on the selected course.

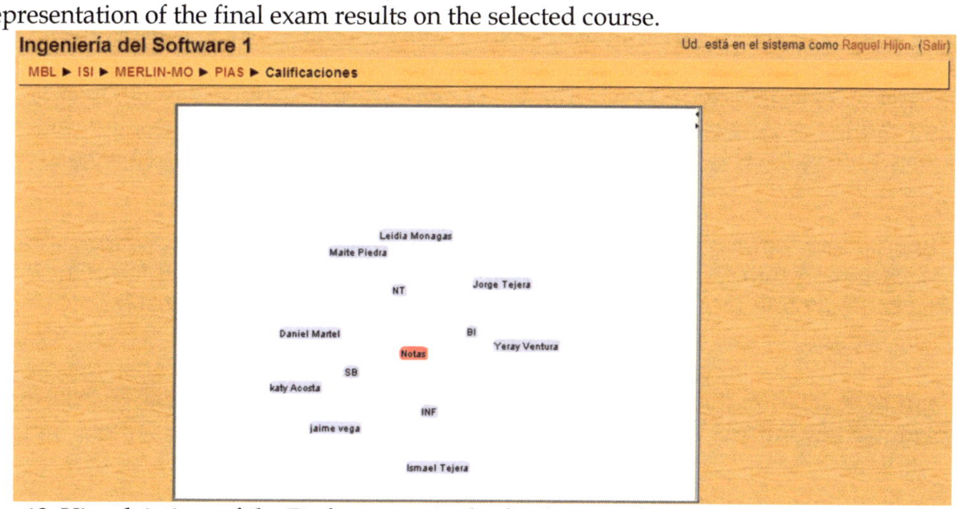

Fig. 12. Visualziation. of the Performance in the final exam of a course on PIAS in Merlin-Mo

As it can be seen each group of student obtaining the same grade are grouped together by the linking to the node containing their grade. Then, users can pick on a node and it will be highlighted as well as the linked ones, which results in a really easy understanding of the results when the network is too crowded or some grades or students want to be looked at; other options like zooming permit the enlarging of the images as well.

4. Prediction and Enhancement of Students Outcome

From the correct interpretation of the information the system provides to the teachers, those can predict and therefore enhanced their students' outcome. Examples of the questions teachers can make to the Merlin-Mo system are:

4.1 Do students have different access patterns if they are in the morning or in the evening courses? Is there a difference that is common to all the morning/evening courses?

Teachers can ask the system the option "subject Comparison" in the PIAS interface and select two courses, one taught in the morning and the other one in the evening. The system would offer the comparison between the access patterns of students in the morning classes, usually full time students, to the ones in the evening classes, usually older and with other concerns in their lives than just attending university.
Teachers can also ask the system for "performance" also in the PIAS interface on the same courses. And probably different accesses patterns are found between the course shifts, such as those in the morning/evening sessions work harder, possibly because they have more spare time, or fail also more, probably because they do not make the most of their time. Or that the ones in the morning/evening sessions get better grades, probably because they are more brilliant students, or with better skills, hence most of them also have jobs outside university.
All in all, possible conclusions of this partial analysis is that students in the morning/evening classes get better grades, probably because they are more brilliant students, or with better skills, hence most of them also have jobs outside university. Therefore, teachers and educators should set out policies to prevent the morning/evening class from absenteeism in the final exam when detected, and both booster motivation and enhance attitudes towards the course; by handing out more assignments and practical exercises during term time, and periodic refreshers to keep them up to date with class.

4.2 Do students that have a similar exam performance have a similar access patterns to the courses? Can it make a difference among them? Is there a difference if the course last only one semester? And if it is the first or the second semester?

Teachers can ask the system for "performance" and "participation" in the PIAS interface in different courses, for instance, when considering first/second semester courses or courses that run over the year, it can probably be observed that the amount of access of the groups tends to rise towards the end of the course, and therefore the exam. Teachers can find out how different grades groups increase their participation differently when they obtain different grades (*pass*, *good* and *very good* grades). Probably the ones that get *good* grades are the ones that, as time passes, most increase the amount of work done in the course. Those students who are *absent* probably do not show such a dramatic improvement.
Probably results such as, students that pass are more constant in keeping up with their work as the year goes by, than those that do not pass. Or, students that pass work harder over the year, increasing the amount of work done towards the final exam than the rest. Finally, if there is a higher percentage of *absenteeism* in the morning/evening probably explains that they are less/more motivated or have more time to expend studying.
To prevent failures and abandoners, teachers and educators should encourage students to start working sooner on the course and to maintain the amount of work done constantly, since it may lead them to get a better exam performance.

4.3 Do students tend to work more in peak periods? When are them? Are they similar among different courses and/or shifts? Does the exam performance make a difference among them?

Teachers can ask the system for the detailed amount of access by student within a course using the AIAS interface in Merlin-Mo and setting a concrete range of time. To make a comparison among the exam performance, the "performance" in the PIAS interface can contribute.

There may be found a tendency in several courses to work more towards the exam dates or at the end of the academic course, which would result in a better performance in second semester courses or courses that run over the year.

By looking at the access data from the first stages of the course, different groups of students can be identified; therefore teachers can put in place measures to prevent *absent* students from not taking the final exam and potential failing students not doing as much work as is required to pass.

Teachers pace or course plans could probably be changed in order to ask students to do some extra work, such as: assignments, midterm exams, etc, during the first stages of the course, since it has been corroborated that during the first months of the course, or the first part of the year (whatever is first), less work is usually done.

5. Conclusion

Firstly, a new software module for analysis of students' interactions has been developed. It largely enhances the standard Moodle reports. The module, called Merlin-Mo, covers all the initial functionality required to meet users' needs. It offers very good and easy to use interfaces that enclose potent search engines into the data model to look and organize dynamically data about interactions. Data is treated with useful statistical and interactive visualizations that generate good and easy to understand representations of data to help teachers in the process of analyzing students learning patterns. The module has been developed following Moodle standards to obtain a perfect automatic integration into a running Moodle LMS. Merlin-Mo module has been developed to support two languages, English and Spanish; those and other server settings are automatically adopted from the host Moodle user settings. Lastly, it has also been adjusted to be seen in the main market browsers.

Furthermore, teachers can predict and enhance students' outcome by analyzing how students acceded the different parts of the courses, where significant differences can be observed. By adopting policies that prevent from wrong students behaviors on early stages much better results can be obtained. To help in the analysis of learning behaviors using the system many, the results can be analyzed grouped in three general types of access' patterns, namely: differences among morning and evening sessions, amount of accesses by exam performance, evolution of the access patterns through out the year.

6. Acknowledgements

This research was supported by the Spanish MEC project TIN2008-04103/TSI.

7. References

Aberdour, M. (2007). "Open Source Learning Management System". EPIC Whitepaper. http://www.epic.co.uk/content/news/oct_07/whitepaper.pdf (Accessed April, 17, 2009)

Barbour, M. K. & Collins, M. (2005). Online Writing as an Indicator of Student Performance. *Journal of Instructional Technology and Distance Learning*, Vol. 2. No.8. August 2005.

Comunale, C. L., T. R. Sexton, et al. (2001-2002). "The effectiveness of course Web sites in higher education: An exploratory study" *Journal of Educational Technology Systems* v.30 n.2 p.171-190.

Dimai, B., Ebner, M. (2003) Community without a vision won't work. *1st Global Conference, Interactive Convergence: Research in Multimedia*, 2003.

Dowing, Y., Chun-Hsiung, L., Pei-Chen S. (2005) The analysis of learning records and learning effect in blended e-Learning. *Journal of Information Science and Engineering* 21, 973-984 (2005).

Gao, T. and J. D. Lehman (2003). The effects of different levels of interaction on the achievement and motivational perceptions of college students in a web-based learning environment. *Journal of Interactive Learning Research* v.14 n.4 p.367-386.

Hardy, J., Bates, S., Hill, J., Antonioletti, M. (2007). Tracking and Visualization of Student Use of Online Learning Materials in a Large Undergraduate Course. *International Conference in Web Based Learning ICWL 2007.* Edinburgh, UK, pp.280-287.

Hellwege, J., A. Gleadow, et al. (1996). Paperless lectures on the Web: An evaluation of the educational outcomes of teaching Geology using the Web. *Proceedings of 13th Annual Conference of the Australian Society for Computers in Learning in Tertiary education (ASCILITE '96)*, Adelaide, Australia, University of South Australia.

Hernández-García, Á., Iglesias-Pradas, S., Chaparro-Peláez, J., Pascual Miguel, F. (2008). Influencia en el rendimiento académico de la interacción en línea de los alumnos: estudio y análisis comparativo entre diferentes modalidades de enseñanza. *SIIE'08 (X Simpósio Internacional de Informática Educativa 2008)*

Hijón, R., Velázquez, A. (2006). Web, Log Analysis and surveys for tracking University Students. *Proceedings of IADIS International Conference on Applied Computing*. ISBN: 972-8924-09-7, pp 561-564.

Hijón, R., Velázquez, A. and Herrera-Cabanillas, V. (2007). Blended Learning Tools for Assessing Students Interactions. *Proceedings of CEDI 2007 – II Congreso Español de informática, VIII Simposio Nacional de Tecnologías de la Información y las Comunicaciones en la Educación – SINTICE*, pp. 11-14. Zaragoza, Spain, September 2007.

Hijón, R., Velazquez, A. (2008). How to Improve Assessement of Learning and performance through interactive visualization. *Proceedings od the 8th IEEE International Conference on Advance Learning Technologies ICALT*. Santander, Spain, July 2008.

Hijón, R., Velazquez, A. (2008a). How to Improve Assessement of Learning and performance through interactive visualization. *Proceedings of the 8th IEEE International Conference on Advance Learning Technologies ICALT*. Santander, Spain, July 2008.

Hijón, R., Velazquez, A. , Barn, B., Oussena, S. (2008b). A Comparative Study on the Analysis of Students Interactions on e-Learning. *Proceedings of the 8th IEEE International Conference on Advance Learning Technologies ICALT*. Santander, Spain, July 2008.

Kickul, J., Kickul, G. (2002). New pathways in e-learning: the role of student proactivity and technology utilization. *Midwest Academy of Management Proceedings 2002.*

Lu, A. X. Y., J. Zhu, J. H., et al. (2000). The use and effects of Web-based instruction: Evidence from a single-source study. *Journal of Interactive Learning Research v.*11 n.2 p.197-218.

Mazza, R. and Dimitrova, V. (2005). Generation of Graphical Representations of Student Tracking Data in Course Management Systems, *iv*, pp. 253-258, *Ninth International Conference on Information Visualisation (IV'05)*, 2005.

McIsaac, M. S., J. M. Blolcher, et al. (1999). Student and teacher perceptions of interaction in online computer-mediated communication. *Educational Media International* v.36 n.2 p.121-131.

Moreira, P., TEIXEIRA, V., VALENTE, H., et. al. (2005) Elearning in human nutrition: a pilot study. *EUNIS 2005 Proceedings.*

Nian-Shing C., Kan-Min L (2002). Factors affecting e-learning for achievement. *Proceedings of IEEE International Conference on Advanced Learning Technologies (ICALT 2002).*

Peled, A. and D. Rashty (1999). Logging for success: Advancing the use of WWW logs to improve computer mediated distance learning. *Journal of Educational Computing Research* v.21 n.4 p.413-431

Nickles, G. M. (2005). Correlations of student grades and behavior while using a course management system under different contexts. *Proceedings of the America Society for Engineering Education Annual Conference & Exposition* .Portland, OR.

Ramani, L., Rocha, H. (2000), Interaction Map: Information Visualization Techniques in Web-based Distance Education Environments, *tech. report IC-00-17, Universidade Estatual de Campinas*, Brazil, Oct 2000.

Ramos, C.; Yudko, E. (2008) "Hits" (not "Discussion Posts") predict student success in online courses: A double crossvalidation study. *Computers & Education 50* (2008) 1174-1182.

Reffay, C., Chanier, T. (2002) Social Network Analysis Used for Modelling Collaboraion in Distance Learning Groups. *Proc. Intelligent Tutoring System Conf.*, Springer-Verlag, 2002, pp. 31-40.

Sheard, J, Albrecht, D.W., Butbul, E. (2005): ViSION: Visualization Student Interactions Online, in A. Treloar & A. Ellis (Eds.), *Proceedings of the Eleventh Australasian World Wide Web Conference*, Gold Coast, QLD, Australia, 2-6 July 2005, Southern Cross University, Lismore, NSW, Australia, ISBN: 0975164430, pp 48 - 58.

15

Dependable e-learning systems

Ali Al-Dahoud[1], Marek Woda[2] and Tomasz Walkowiak[2]
[1]*Al-Zaytoonah University, Jordan, aldahoud@alzaytoonah.edu.jo*
[2]*Institute of Computer Engineering, Control and Robotics*
Wroclaw University of Technology, Poland, Tomasz.Walkowiak@pwr.wroc.pl,
Marek.woda@pwr.wroc.pl

1. Introduction

Education in nowadays fast changing world is a very important aspect. The need of gaining more professional knowledge, shortening the time available for stationary methods of learning (esp. when somebody works) resulted in the development of distant learning methods [UNDP, 2002]. In a more widely usage of internet and development of internet based techniques for distributing multimedia materials a modern distant learning [M. Woda, 2006] is commonly known as e-learning.

E-learning is being more willingly and widely employed [W. Baranski W., Walkowiak T., 2003],[Ch. Dean, 2002]. Therefore, in an effort to diversify this form of sharing knowledge, it is common to use various available tools given by the available technology. We can safely say that Internet is at present the most interesting and dynamically expanding medium for providing educational contents in a truly distributed fashion for different actors.

E-learning becomes also very important for traditional universities. On one hand development of e-learning gives universities opportunity to reach potential wider audience. On the other there is a large need from students for supporting traditional way of teaching by a internet based one (so called blending learning).

During the last decade necessity of education, that facilitate gaining new abilities in IT and High Tech related professions, was exposed. The job market situation constantly changes; this state enforces constant skill improvement and also people retraining whose jobs are being replaced by automated processes. A lot of universities create new educational services based on different e-learning solutions. This situation resulted in growing interest of jobless community and youth toward alternative forms of learning. This form of teaching, when well organized, gives new undisputed opportunities for many social strata.

Despite of the fact that e-learning already proved its great usefulness, it suffers from many childlike deficiencies. We can count, among other things, to these drawbacks lack of the coherent vision for learning process accomplishment, practical guidelines how to organize consistent learning content. Due to these disadvantages e-learning is being perceived ambiguously and incorrectly implemented in e-systems, which leads to limitation its reliability. Usually, in reality, theory and practice are not on the par, same situation is clearly visible in e-learning theory and its implementations. In e-learning, whole pressure was put on the theory of learning, and there is no restrictions or even practical guidelines

present in field of its technology and implementations, which in many cases has negative influence on newly developed e-systems. Currently, most of the college teachers, government and many schools notice the need of standardization and rationalization this type of teaching. More and more is being told about so called e-education systems. Therefore, in this paper we would like to focus on technical aspects of e-learning i.e. e-learning systems.
From the point of view of computer engineering nowadays e-learning systems are examples of a web base application and us other information systems it's dependability aspects are very important. Dependability evaluation of e-learning in general, ought to be based rely on following pillars: (high) availability, usability, scalability, interoperability, stability and security [J. Hall, 2004].

2. Important

This work is devoted to dependability aspect of e-learning systems. Authors present technical aspects of the software part of e-learning systems (e-learning platforms, distant lectures, multimedia presentations and virtual laboratories). Next, a high availability approach to hardware part is discussed. It is followed by a short analysis of several dependability aspects (availability, usability, scalability, interoperability, stability and security) with a conclusion that business continuity is a crucial factor. Therefore, the analysis of the e-learning system monitoring techniques is given. It is followed by a proposition of a new technique of monitoring: the virtual user representative. At the end original and inexpensive method of lectures is presented.

3. E-learning systems

The core of each e-learning system is an e-learning platform. This is a tool that is a virtual equivalent of a university (understood as institution, facility) that has to meet four essential functions as: student's management, dissemination of knowledge, testing progress of its absorption and communication between e-learning process actors (students and teachers).
On one hand there exist a large number of e-learning platforms to mention only: Learning Environment Online (LEO), IBM Lotus Learning Management System, Blackboard Learning System, TopCalss e-Learning Suite, WebCT Campus Edition, R5, Oracle i-Learning, Manhattan Virtual Classroom, Moodle. On the other one can noticed a large integration of e-learning platform market. In case of commercial products and the university like education Blackboard Inc. after fusion with WebCT is a leading producer of e-learning platforms with really no competitors. In case of company training the leading products are by IBM and Oracle. Whearas the open-source leader is Moodle.
All modern e-learning platforms are a three tier Internet application. The uses HTML with CSS and JacaScript for a user interface. In the middle tier a large number of script languages are used, for example: Perl (WebCT), ASP (R5), PHP (Moodle) or JSP (Lotus LearningSpace). In the data tier a large number of different database systems are used. In case of Open Source products the most popular are MySQL or PostgreSQL (Moodle), among commercial ones Oracle (Oracle i-Learning), MS SQL (Blackboard, TopClass) or IBM DB2 (Lotus LearningSpace).

E-learning platforms can be deployed enterprise-wide to supplement the traditional classroom or for pure distance programs. Use of them allows the university to efficiently leverage campus resources to both extend their offerings and enhance the teaching and learning experience. One of the many benefits of using e-learning platforms includes the ability to offer an "always on" environment, providing more time for the student to interact with professors and classmates as well as with the course material in an efficient, engaging and effective manner. Moreover, their functionality allows to perform self test and quizzes allowing to check the level of the student knowledge.

Other elements of e-learning systems like multimedia presentations, recorded lectures and virtual laboratories are launched from inside the e-learning platforms. In case of multimedia presentations Adobe products like Authorware and Flash are the most popular. Delivering lectures through internet is based on media-streaming technologies (Microsoft Windows Media, RealNetworks, Quicktime, Flash Media Streaming) or Adobe FLV video format. Virtual laboratories [T. Walkowiak, 2005] could be developed in two different way by a designing a simulator in general purpose language or by a usage of a general purpose simulation software. The first solution is usually based on Java technology. The second uses general purpose software that allows to simulate complex systems like LabView, Matlab, Mathematica , MathCAD or Maple.

To summaries e-learning systems uses a large number of different software technologies. Moreover, an e-learning system provides the platform for the enterprise's online learning environment by enabling the management, delivery and tracking of blended learning (i.e., online and traditional classroom) for employees, and customers. Therefore, a robust e-learning system should integrate with other systems, so administrative and supervisory tasks can be streamlined and automated and the overall cost and impact of education can be tracked and quantified [J. Hall, 2004].

4. Model of high-availability e-learning system

To meet these nowadays requirements, an e-learning solution must be based on a scalable hardware and software architecture that can be easily optimized to deliver high performance while improving the utilization of IT resources and reducing power, cooling and floor space requirements.

The numerous core e-learning services require multiple computing platforms to meet various needs of multiple commercial and open source systems, while the internal operations typically need OS environment including an email server and a file server, resulting in a wide range of computer hardware and software. Therefore, these diverse computing needs cause a complex computing environment, where a wide range of hardware, operating systems (OS), and applications co-exist [Y. Han, 2004]. Such environment requires choosing the right hardware to support and maintain business continuity of the system.

Most of the e-learning system implementation is being based on one of the following models:

Cost Performance Model - which was designed for cost-conscious learning institutions looking for the best performing system at an affordable pricing structure. It is not a minimum requirement, but rather a recommendation that will support cost concerns institutions while efficiently supporting their usage and load.

High-Performance - aimed at institutions, primarily concerned with performance over cost. Most configurations consist of highly-available recommendations. The purpose for multiple servers at the various tiers within the technology stack is to support distributed, parallel processing.
High-Availability Model - aimed at institutions primarily concerned with uptime and availability. Highly-available models can be cost conscientious and/or high-performing.
In this chapter will focus on last model. Right choice for a suitable hardware for e-learning system for an organization could be really a challenging task. Now, we may present some advice that might be worth to consider. There are a number of vital questions to ask, but given below are ones that must be asked:
Users influx and increase of courses within the institution;
Archive strategy, meaning the removal of data from the system that no longer applies/valid;
Lease or purchase terms on equipment (hardware is typically turned over every x academicals years);
Concurrency of user community (number of online concurrent user);
System performance expectations;
Expected availability / redundancy expectations.

Generally speaking, high availability system should be resilient to common failures (system as a whole should be resilient not its components), easily maintainable should provide alerting / monitoring mechanisms that allow to warn when system enters in danger state to prevent its collapse. It has to support recovery automation after an outage and have built-in procedures that prevent unrecoverable data lost.
E-learning system that could be called dependable should meet number requirements as [Optimizing eLearning, 2007]:
High service levels—Systems must operate 24X7 with little downtime, planned or unplanned and must be able handle spikes in user demand without degrading response time;
Low TCO—Systems must be cost-effective to own and manage when considering;
everything from hardware and software license costs to the system's impact on datacenter power and cooling costs;
Scalability—With a growing population of students and an ever-growing demand;
for online delivery, the eLearning infrastructure must be easy to scale in support of higher levels of throughput, more users and more online courses;
Easy to manage—With limited IT staff to assign to the project, it must be easy to deploy and manage the solution so that service levels can be met without an extensive IT staff.

High reliability unfortunately is tightly connected with initial cost, which is usually very steep. By with passing of time, the cost incurred, will bring massive savings, due to low maintenance and exploitation costs and for unparalleled reliability (hardware redundancy, which reduce the downtime by allowing for component replacement without entire system turn off).

5. Dependability aspects of e-learning systems

E-learning system must be robust enough to serve the diverse needs of thousands of learners, administrators, content builders and instructors simultaneously (availability).
The infrastructure should be flexible enough to support future system growth, both in terms of the materials size number of students (scalability).
In order to support a number of highly personalized services, such as self-paced and role-specific learning, the access, delivery and presentation of material must be prepared in easy to use and highly intuitive way (usability).
To cope with a common problem how to join a content from different sources and multiple vendors hardware/software solutions, e-learning system ought be based on widely known, accepted and what is most important open, industry standards, like Web based one (XML, SOAP, JAVA, EJB) and support the major learning standards (AICC, SCORM, IMS and IEEE) (interoperability).
Since e-learning system main tasks are to reliably and effectively manage a huge datasets and provide hassle free access for numerous users from a different time zones it should be able to run outages free twenty four hours per week (stability).
One of the key aspects of e-learning, and very often neglected or forgotten is confidentiality / security. Each e-learning system must provide essential security mechanism that prevent from identity theft, frauds, system misuse or personality spoofing (Security).

6. Monitoring for dependability analysis

One of major concerns in e-learning is to have the working system, and prevent outages or slowdowns since it has a great impact on learners. Since business continuity of e-learning system is crucial factor, all the underlying services may not be disturbed in any manner. Therefore many precautions should be undertaken. And versatile safety measures should be involved to keep the system in a working state. Any unexpected system behaviors are reflected in stress for users, and in the end impact their learning experience. Therefore, there continuous monitoring of the e-learning system is a very important aspects.
With improvement of administration in mind, many software companies offer commercial tools for network monitoring. One of the most advanced monitoring tools is IBM Tivioli Monitoring. This is very complex platform that provides professional tools for gathering data and presents it to administrator in very convenient graphical diagrams. This feature helps to have a quick view of what is happening on the network. This software is also supplied with special feature that may inform administrator about any threats like i.e. bottlenecks. Additionally Tivioli makes possible to use gathered data in data mining researches because all data are stored in data bases. Tivioli architecture is divided in three layer with top level manager, through middle layer to low level agent layer. It provides support for Windows and UNIX like platforms and has very professional help desk support from IBM.
Other solutions are not as advanced as IBM Tivioli software, however there is some interesting software like OpManager (http://manageengine.adventnet.com/products/opmanager) that provides interface for monitoring network traffic, CPU usage, memory and disk usage. It can also generate daily (weekly) statistics. Producer assures that it can cooperate with SNMPTRAP mechanism that makes possible to supervise system, by receiving information from SNMP server. According to data from product web site, there is

free version of this software. However, it does not contain any interesting features like mentioned SNMPTRAP handling, report generation or CPU usage monitoring.

AdRem NetCrunch (http://www.adrem.com.pl/netcrunch) is another monitoring platform. This system is dedicated for network data analyzing basing on SNMP protocol. It makes possible to gather system statistics characteristic for monitored workstation (i.e. memory usage). It available many interesting features like physical and logical topology recognition. This is achieved through ICMP scanning and SNMPGET queries. It is also supplied with alert mechanism, a dedicated event manager that handles with events like network interface state monitoring or filtering syslog - logs exchange standard in IP networks. Moreover it has very well developed network monitoring interface, among other things capacity monitoring. Still this product has its disadvantages. System statistics are gathered by enquiring other devices, except SNMPTRAPS that are triggered from SNMP servers.

From free software there are usually local applications like top - a command line tool that presents system statistics of the local workstation for Linux/Unix or Task Manager for Windows. There is also network version of the top application called RPCTOP, however like original top it can only read CPU and memory usage.

The main player on open-source market of network management software (which has network monitoring capability) is OpenNMS (http://www.opennms.org/).OpenNMS is a truly distributed, scalable platform for all aspects of the FCAPS network management model (FCAPS is a network management functional model defined by ITU-T and ISO in specification M.3400 - http://www.itu.int). Currently, OpenNMS focuses on three main areas:

Service Polling - determining service availability and reporting on same.

Data Collection - collecting, storing and reporting on network information as well as generating thresholds.

Event and Notification Management - receiving events, both internal and external, and using those events to feed a robust notification system, including escalation.

All mentioned commercial and free products can, and are applied for monitoring e-learning system. However, all of them have one important drawback – they monitor the system from the inside. In case of many information systems and especially in case of e-learning systems the most important are users. It could happen that the system is operating well from the inside but could be not accessed from Internet, for example in case of some error in external DNS system. Therefore there is large need to monitor the e-learning system from the outside. Authors proposed the use a User Virtual Representatives (UVR) [M. Woda, T. Walkowiak, 2007]. It functions as a substitutes of a user, acts like human users, perform regular human actions in pursue to detect service unavailability. When service, which agent is ascribed to, is no longer responding, and UVR agent give can't itself recognize the culprit, it could give commands to lover tier monitoring agents in order to recognize the situation, which of component services.

7. The low-cost and universal approach to reliable lectures delivery

One of the most important ways of teaching is a lecture. In the case of distant learning, usually, TV transmission or video tape is used. Nowadays, DVD discs or internet transmissions using streaming servers are rather more common.
Currently, the most popular form of lecture is slide presentation, where whiteboards or multimedia animations are very rarely present. So, to make from such lecture from multimedia e-learning material, only the lecturer has to be recorded. Presented slides can be taken directly from power-point presentation or pdf (or other) files. In this chapter, the authors present an approach to produce internet lectures in a simple and inexpensive way.

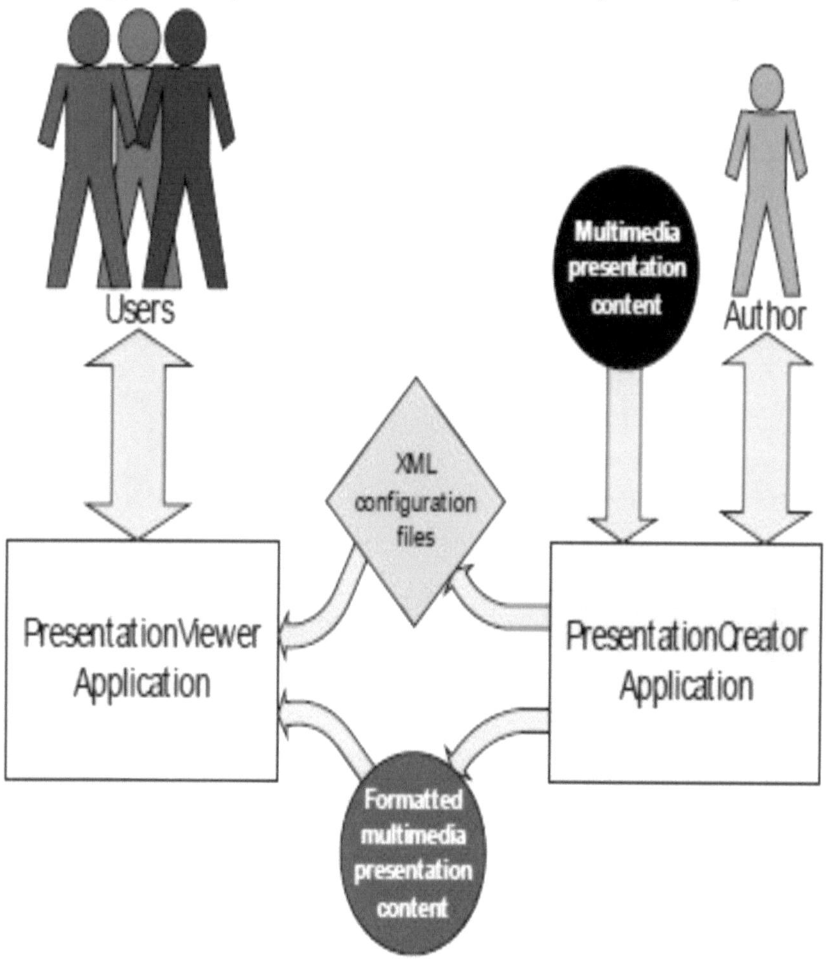

Fig. 1. Solution architecture

Two applications have been developed: PresentationViewer and PresentationCreator. The first of them allows users to explore and watch multimedia lectures. The second application helps lecture authors to save their lecture recordings and slides as the PresentationViewer application content and makes possible to easily configure the look and feel of the PresentationViewer.

In some aspects, it is similar to the approach taken in ([Dean, Ch. 2002],[English, J., 2006]), but it does have more functionalities and does not need any, especially commercial, streaming server. It uses new technology: Adobe Flash 8 environment. The authors assumed that the internet lecture should be available for everyone who has internet connection, without any additional software. Due to Adobe Flash environment, the PresentationViewer application was created. It meets requirements and is easy to use. Even adding new content to the PresentationViewer application or configuring it to users' preferences is very simple and fast due to XML based configuration files and thanks to the authors who created this user-friendly PresentationCreator application. Thanks to Adobe FLV video format, the authors avoided using streaming servers and any commercial applications that would have been possible needed to convert standard AVI video files to streaming formats. FLV video files can be placed even on the simplest HTTP server and play in Flash application on user side while downloading. The PresentationViewer application uses this feature. Furthermore, no commercial application is needed to convert video files to FLV format.

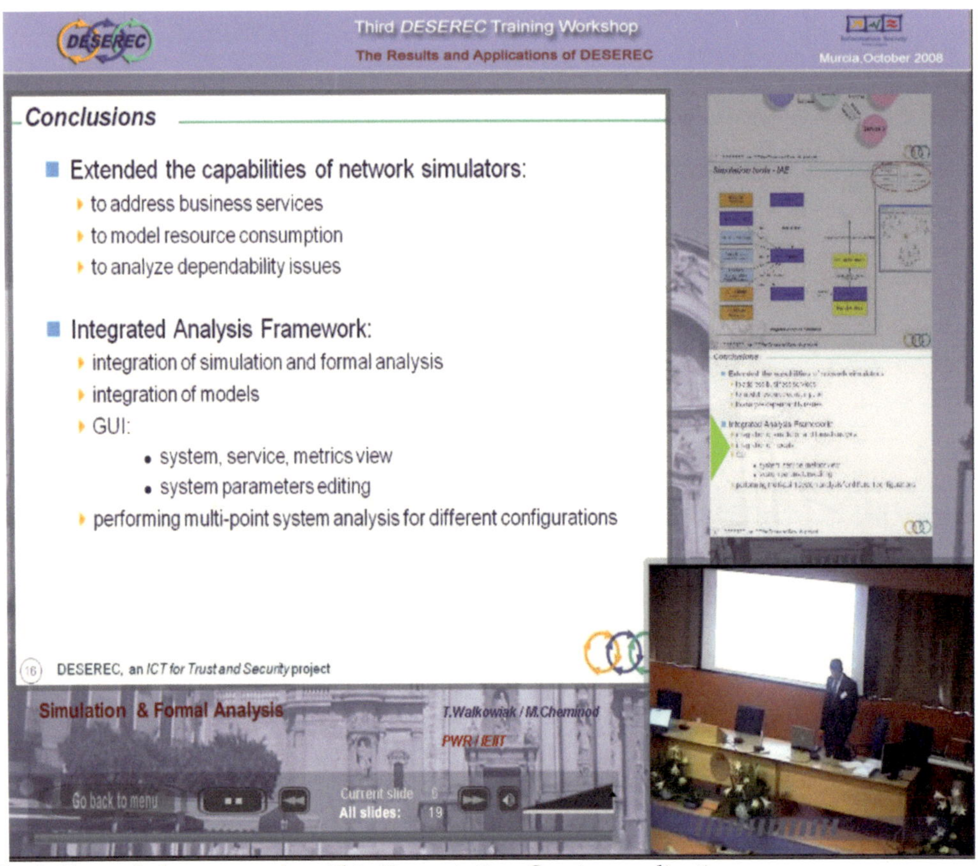

Fig. 2. Example lecture made within Presentation Creator application

8. Conclusion

The paper presented dependability aspects (availability, usability, scalability, interoperability, stability and security) of software and hardware components of e-learning systems. The authors proposed the business continuity of e-learning system as a crucial dependability factor. Therefore, the hardware high availability approach was presented and methods of monitoring the underlying services is given.
Authors presented an inexpensive platform for reliable online lectures creation, which assures lectures delivery in timely and desired by a student way, that makes learning more convenient and the same time more efficient.

9. References

"Blackboard Hardware Sizing Guide" - http://library.blackboard.com/docs/r6/6_1 /admin/ bbls_rel61_hardware_sizing_guide.pdf, Blackboard Inc, 2004.

Ch. Dean, Technology based training & On-line learning. An overview of authoring systems and learning systems available in the UK, December 2002.

Dean, Ch.) 'Technology based training & on-line learning. An overview of authoring systems and learning systems available in the UK', December 2002.

English, J., (2006) Macromedia Flash Professional 8 Training from the Source, Macromedia Press, Peachpit, Press, Berkeley, CA, USA.

M. Woda," Conception of Composing Learning Content into Learning Tree to Ensure Reliability of Learning Material", Proceedings of International Conference on Dependability of Computer Systems. DepCoS - RELCOMEX 2006, Szklarska Poręba, 25-27 May 2006, IEEE Computer Society, pp. 374-381, 2006.

M. Woda, T. Walkowiak, "Multi agent event monitoring system", The 3rd International Conference on Information Technology. ICIT 2007. Al-Zaytoonah University of Jordan, Amman, Jordan, May 9-11, 2007.

J. Hall, "Assessing learning management systems", Oracle University. http://www.clomedia.com/content/templates/clo_article.asp?articleid=91&zoneid=29, 2003.

"Optimizing eLearning", http://www.sun.com/third-party/global/blackboard/collateral/SunBlackboardWP10_1_07.pdf, Sun Microsystems, 2007.

"Poland and Global Information Society: Logging on. Human Development Report", UNDP, Warsaw, 2002.

T. Walkowiak "Applications of virtual laboratories in teaching at technical universities", Journal of Digital Information Management, vol. 3, nr 3, pp. 202-204, 2005.

W. Baranski W., Walkowiak T., Multimedia approach to distance learning, First International Conference on Soft Computing Applied in Computer and Economic Environments. ICSC 2003, January 30- 31, 2003 Kunovice, Czech Republic, pp. 150-158, 2003.

Y. Han, "An Integrated High Availability Computing Platform" The Electronic Library. http://dlist.sir.arizona.edu/1052/, 2004.

Ontology-driven Annotation and Access of Educational Video Data in E-learning

Aijuan Dong[1], Honglin Li[2] and Baoying Wang[3]
[1] *Hood College, Frederick, MD 21704, USA*
[2]*AOL Video Search, 333 Bush Street, San Francisco, CA 94104, USA*
[3] *Waynesburg University, Waynesburg, PA 15370,USA*

1. Introduction

In the past decade, we have witnessed unprecedented advances in multimedia technology. As a result, an unprecedented amount of multimedia data is being generated. Among the myriad types of multimedia data, presentation videos from lectures, conferences and seminars, and corporate trainings are of particular interest to this chapter.

The need for specific solutions in this field comes from the popularity of e-learning systems. Recent years, there have been extensive efforts at both universities and colleges on developing e-learning systems to support distant learning. Based on Sloan Consortium survey (Allen & Seaman, 2008), over 3.9 million students were taking at least one online course during the fall 2007, which accounts for over 20% of all U.S. higher education students. Online enrolments continue to grow at rates far in excess of the total higher education student population, with the most recent data demonstrating no signs of slowing down. For example, the online enrolment growth rate for 2007 is 12.9%, while the growth rate for the overall higher education student population is only 1.2% for the same period (Allen & Seaman, 2008). In addition, there are e-learning systems for military, medical, and cooperate trainings (Smith, Ruocco, & Jansen, 1999; Fan, Luo, & Elmagarmid, 2004). For example, Microsoft supported 367 on-line training lectures with more than 9000 online viewers in the year of 1999 alone (He, Grudin, & Gupta, 2000). These e-learning systems enhance learning experiences and augment teachers' work in and out of traditional classrooms (Abowd, Brotherton, & Bhalodai, 1998; Flachsbart, Franklin, & Hammond, 2000). Working professionals as well embrace e-learning programs due to their convenience and flexibility (Kariya, 2003). However, due to unstructured and linear features of videos, the essential instructional content of most e-learning systems, the presentation videos, has not been fully exploited. People often feel difficulties in locating a specific piece of information in a presentation video. Sometimes they have to play back and forth several times to locate the right spot. To ensure effective exploitation of these video assets, efficient and flexible access mechanisms must be provided.

Video annotation data play a critical role in video systems. The richer the annotation data are, the more flexible the video access becomes, and thus the more effective the video data can be utilized. We view video annotation as a two-step process: video segmentation, and video annotation data extraction and organization. The former divides a continuous video stream into a set of meaningful and manageable segments, and the latter extracts various annotations from these segments and organizes them in a way that facilitates efficient video access. In the following sections, we will examine the existing systems or approaches with regards to these two aspects.

A variety of techniques have been proposed on segment presentation videos. Earlier work from the Cornell Lecture Browser (Mukhopadhyay & Smith, 1999) uses feature differences between binary slide images to segment a slide video stream. Later, Yamamoto et al. (2003) propose topic segmentation of lecture videos by computing the similarity between topic vectors obtained from a textbook and a sequence of lecture vectors obtained from a lecture speech. In 2003, a content density function is proposed based on the observation that topic boundaries coincide with the ebb and flow of the "density" of content shown in videos (Phung, Venkatesh, & Dorai, 2002). Using various visual filters, Haubold and Kender (2003) utilize key frames in instructional video segmentation. Extracted key frames are first assigned a media type. Key frames are then clustered based on visual contents. Recently, Lin et al. (2005) investigate a linguistics-based approach for lecture video segmentation. Multiple linguistic-based segmentation features from lecture speech are extracted and explored. Similar approach has been explored in this paper, where segmentation positions are estimated with comparisons of successive indexes using dynamic programming (Kanedera, Sumida, Ikehata, & Funada, 2006). Related work in this field also include these (Onishi, Izumi, & Fukunaga, 2000; Rui, Gupta, Grudin, & He, 2002; Liu & Kender, 2002; Ngo, Wang, & Pong, 2003). Despite many successes, most approaches described above focus on linearly segmenting video streams into smaller units using information from single modality. In this paper, we investigate how to combine visual and textual information in the hierarchical segmentation of presentation videos.

After a video is segmented, video annotation data can be extracted from the video and its segments. In our study, we find that one of the problems in current video systems is that there exists a gap between users' information needs and video content representation. On one hand, users from different domains or with different backgrounds perceive video content from different perspectives and are only interested in particular type of information. On the other hand, most existing video systems have only one representation of video content. Thus, it is very difficult for these systems to provide multiple and customized views to users from different domains. As a result, the degree of video retrieval relevancy is low. Another overlooked problem in most video systems is the organization of video annotation data. Syntactic relations and semantic constraints are not sufficiently enforced in current annotation data organization. Thus, it is difficult to extract relevant information from the ever-growing multimedia data collection.

Research has been conducted to address these problems. Relevance feedback has been used widely in image retrieval to adjust user queries and provide better approximation to the users' information needs (Rui, Huang, Mehrotra, & Ortega, 1998; Cox, Miller, Omohundro, & Yianilos, 1996; Cox, Miller, Minka, & Yianilos, 1998; Papathomas, et al., 1998; Minka & Picard, 1997). However, this technique is proposed under the assumption that high-level semantic concepts can be captured by low-level multimedia features, which is not always the case (Cox, et al., 1996), such as high-level abstract concepts in scientific domains. Therefore, relevance feedback cannot be used to approximate users' information needs under these situations.

With the development of semantic web, several ontologies have been developed to annotate and represent multimedia content in recent years (Khan & McLeod, 2000; HyvAonen, Styrman, & Saarela, 2003; Schreiber, Dubbeldam, Wielemaker, & Wielinga, 2004; Bao, Cao, Tavanapong, & Honavar, 2004; Hauptmann, 2004; Tsinaraki, 2004; Hollink, Worring, & Schreiber, 2005). Despite many initial successes, one problem with most existing approaches is that one ontology targets one specific domain or data collection. A new ontology is generated by combining domain specific knowledge with a multimedia ontology. The ontology is then used to annotate multimedia data in an effort to integrate domain knowledge into multimedia access and increase the degree of retrieval relevancy. As a result, such an ontology only works for users from one specific domain and it cannot meet the information needs of a variety of users. In this paper, we propose multi-ontology based multimedia annotation. Although this multi-ontology annotation model applies to multimedia in general, we focus on our discussion on presentation video data.

Based on the discussion above, we propose a framework for ontology-driven presentation video annotation and access in this study. The rest of chapter is organized as follows. Section 2 introduces the framework for ontology-driven video annotation and access. Section 3 discusses multi-mode video segmentation. We detail the hierarchical segmentation of presentation videos through visual and text analysis. Section 4 proposes multi-ontology based video annotation. After video is segmented and metadata is extracted, Section 5 describes ontology-driven video access. Section 6 implements an experimental video access platform to demonstrate the idea. Section 7 concludes the research and highlights the opportunities for future work.

2. The Ontology-driven Framework

In this section, we present the ontology-driven framework. The framework provides the readers with a high-level view of the research and lays the foundation for subsequent discussions.

The ontology-driven framework is proposed based on annotation-driven video systems. In a typical annotation-driven video system, video data is the combination of video production data (i.e., video raw data) and video annotation data (i.e., video metadata). Users interact with annotation data and then locate raw video data through the time stamps that are associated with the annotation data. As can be seen, it is the availability of the video annotation data that determines the functionalities and flexibilities of a video system.

The ontology-driven framework integrates ontologies into video annotation and access. In this framework (Figure 2.1), video data consists of both video production data and video annotation data, the same as that of annotation-driven video access. However, video annotation (i.e., the process of assigning various indices or annotations to a video) interacts with both video production data and ontology; video access operates on video production data, video annotation data, and ontology. Depending on applications, multiple ontologies can be incorporated. The goal is to integrate ontology into video systems in an effort to improve users' video access experience. We argue that ontology-driven video annotation and access can improve users' video access experience. The integration of ontology has the following advantages. First, ontology describes concepts and their relationships in a formal way. By semantically refining video queries based on these relationships, relevant concepts can be extracted. Since such relevant information is extracted directly from ontology where domain knowledge is embedded, there is a potential to increase the degree of video retrieval relevancy. Second, in the ontology-driven framework, multiple ontologies can be integrated. Different ontology describes the same video content from different perspective. This enables multiple content representations of the same video content. Thus, different users' information needs are addressed. Third, the controlled vocabulary of ontology is exploited to annotate and access video data, which alleviates the problem of inconsistency in annotation data and thus enables information sharing and exchange among different parties. In other words, ontology facilitates information retrieval over collections of heterogeneous and distributed information sources. Finally, ontology represents knowledge in a machine-processable format, which means that we can use computer programs/user agents to process information and infer knowledge. This is especially important when a large amount of videos are disseminated over the web.

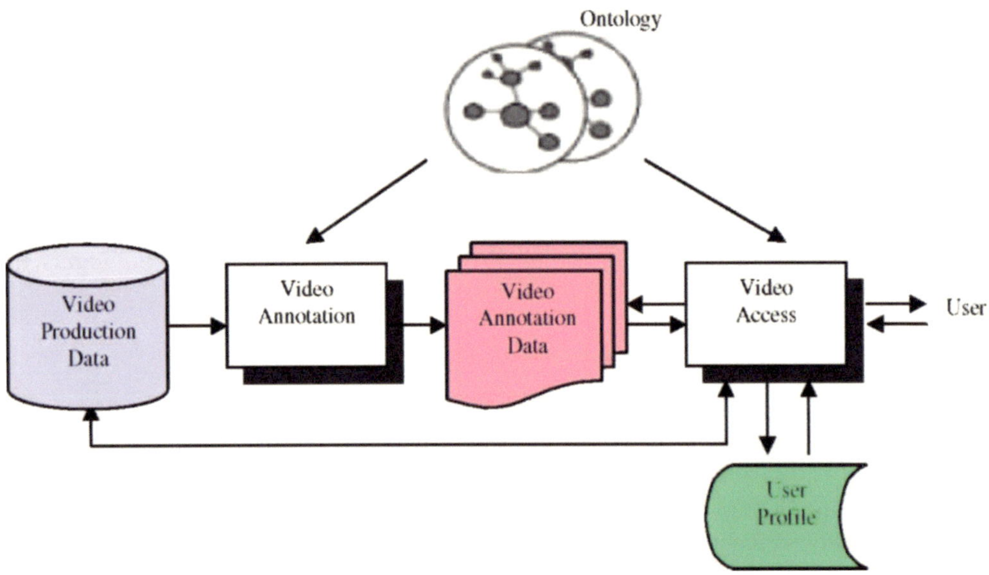

Fig. 2.1. The framework of ontology-driven video annotation and access.

3. Hierarchical Segmentation of Presentation Videos through Visual and Text Analysis

Video segmentation addresses the issue of granularity and answers the question of what to index. Thus, video segmentation is the first and one critical step towards automatic annotation of digital video sequences. In our study, we observe that a presentation usually consists of many subtopics, and each topic covers several slides. For convenience, we simply use the word topic instead of subtopic. This inherent structure enables hierarchical segmentation, indexing, and access of presentation videos. Moreover, most presentations have the following two data sources: PowerPoint slide video stream (i.e., the video stream captures slide activity during presentation) and PowerPoint slide file, also called a PPT file. Both of them contain rich information about the video content. Thus, it is logical to use both of them in the segmentation of presentation videos.

3.1 Overview of the Approach

According to the discussion above, this section proposes a hierarchical segmentation procedure for presentation videos through visual and text analysis (Figure 3.1). Specifically, a two-level video segmentation is investigated: topic-level and slide-level. Slide-level segmentation operates on slide video streams captured by a stationary camera, while topic-level segmentation makes use of extracted slide text.

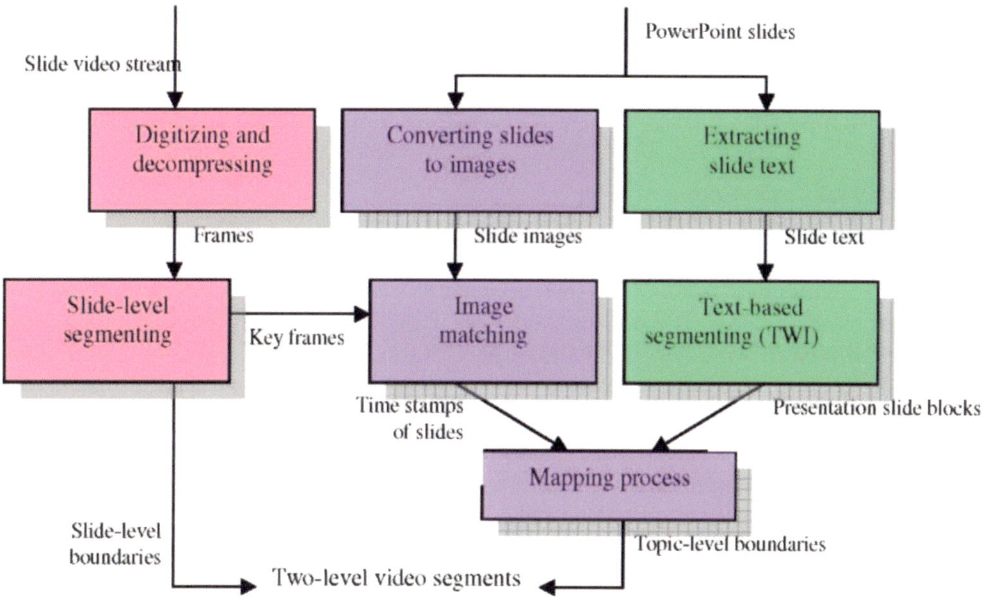

Fig. 3.1. The segmentation of presentation videos.

Figure 3.1.shows that the first step in topic-level segmentation is text-based segmenting through Topic Words Introduction (TWI) that will be discussed later. TWI generates a sequence of slide blocks, each of which discusses one topic. To associate each slide block with its corresponding topic-level video segment, the temporal relationship between a slide video stream and slides must be established. This is accomplished by matching slide images converted from PowerPoint slides with key frames extracted from slide-level video segments. Based on timing information of each slide, slide blocks can be mapped with topic-level video segments, thus achieve hierarchical video segmentation. In the following subsections, we discuss in detail slide-level segmentation and topic-level segmentation.

3.2 Slide-level Video Segmentation

Slide-level segmentation divides a continuous slide video stream into a set of video segments, each of which matches one slide. More formally, given a presentation video stream V and a set of n slides,, compute a set of video segments $vs_{slide-level} = \{ vs_{0,slide-level}, vs_{1,slide-level}, \ldots vs_{i,slide-level} \}$ such that the projected slide image of each video segment $vs_{i,slide-level} (0 \le i \le m)$ does not change.

Notice that this definition only requires that each video segment vs_i displays the same slide, but it does not impose that two adjacent segments display different slides. Thus, extra segments (false positives) are acceptable. If the matching process detects the same slide is shown in two consecutive video segments, then these segments will be combined. By allowing extra segments, it is less likely that slide transitions go undetected.
To segment presentation videos at slide-level, the feature of local color histogram is employed. We compare the local color histograms of adjacent successive frames. When the difference exceeds the pre-defined threshold, a slide-level boundary is declared. This approach is simple, but works well for presentation videos. This is because most slide transitions are abrupt cuts, and presentation videos do not have special video effects, such as fading, dissolve, and wipe.

3.3 Topic-level Video Segmentation

In our study, we observe that most presentations tend to follow a basic structure in spite of differences in contents and formats. A typical presentation, especially a conference presentation, starts with a title slide, then an outline/overview slide, which is followed by a number of content slides. The outline/overview slide of a presentation summarizes major topics that will be covered in content slides. In addition, the first-time introduction of a new topic in the content slides generally uses terms that are the same as or very similar to what occur in the outline/overview slides. Actually, most presenters intentionally construct such a structure in an effort to guide their presentation and engage the audience. Based on this observation of the presentation structure, we propose a text-based segmentation algorithm—Topic Words Introduction (TWI).
TWI segments a presentation into topically coherent slide blocks. More formally, given a presentation p and a set of n content slides,, compute a set of slide blocks $SB = \{sb0, sb1, ..., sbk\}$, such that the topic of each $sbi(0 \le i \le k)$ does not change. TWI algorithm works on slide text that is automatically extracted. Specifically, for each PPT slide file, extract slide content from its outline/overview slide and slide titles from its content slides. With the extracted text, TWI algorithm consists of three main phases: morphological analysis, lexical score determination, and boundary identification.
Phase one: morphological analysis. The purpose of this phase is to determine the terms to be used in the following phases. Two major processes in this phase are tokenization and stemming.
Tokenization refers to the process of dividing the input text into individual lexical units.
With a regular expression recognizer and a stop-word[1] list, punctuation and uninformative words are removed. And the remaining slide text is converted to streams of tokens, including words, numbers, and symbols. Stemming is the process of reducing tokens to their roots, also called stems. The Porter's stemming algorithm (Porter, 1980) is used here for this purpose. It removes the common morphological and inflected endings from English words. Thus, the result of it is a set of word stems. These stems are considered the registered terms of a presentation.

---

[1]A stop-word is a word that lacks significance to the determination of the subject of a document.

An example output of morphological analysis for extracted slide text is illustrated in Figures 3.2 and 3.3. Line numbers are manually added for clarity. In Figure 3.2, each line correlates to one bullet/list in the overview/outline slide, while in Figure 3.3, each line associates with the slide title of a content slide.

1. background
2. barrier
3. experi gridblast keck center
4. lesson learn
5. acknowledg

Fig. 3.2. Slide content from the outline/overview slide of a presentation.

......
4. barrier
5. keck center
6. origin nongridawar configure keck center
7. scal large compare genom
8. schemat view web portal
9. current gridawar configure
10. compon gridblast
......

Fig. 3.3. Slide titles from the content slides of the same presentation.

Phase two: lexical score determination. The purpose of this phase is to measure the similarity between a topic and a slide.

Since most presenters summarize their major topics in the outline/overview slides, analyzing extracted text from the outline/overview slide can identify the topics of a presentation. In our study, for each presentation, we take each natural line of text from its outline/overview slide as one topic (Figure 3.2). For example, "lesson learn" is one identified topic. If there is more than one level in the outline/overview slides, then the content of the first level is used. A dictionary of word-stem frequencies is constructed for each line of text and is represented by a vector of frequency counts. These vectors are called topic vectors in our discussion.

Content slides are summarized by their titles. Therefore, in the TWI algorithm, slide titles are used to represent the content slides of a presentation. For example, "scal large compare genom" in Figure 3.3 is such a slide title. Similarly, a dictionary of word-stem frequencies is constructed for each slide title. This is again represented as a vector of frequency counts. These vectors are called content vectors in our discussion.

To segment presentations at the topic level, we calculate the lexical scores between topic vectors and content vectors. Lexical score measures the lexical similarity between two vectors and is represented by cosine similarity measure (Formula 3.1)(Hearst, 1994).

$$score(i,j) = \frac{\sum_t w_{t,ti}\, w_{t,cj}}{\sqrt{\sum_t w_{t,ti}^2 \sum_t w_{t,cj}^2}}, \tag{3.1}$$

where t_i is a topic vector, C_j is a content vector, t ranges over all the registered terms of t_i and c_j, w_{t,t_i} is the weight assigned to term t in topic vector t_i, and w_{t,c_j} is the term weight assigned to term t in content vector C_j. Here, the weights on the terms are simply their frequency counts. For a presentation with k topics and n content slides, each topic has n lexical scores, and the total lexical score calculation is $k * n$.

Phase three: boundary identification. The method for boundary identification is based on lexical cohesion theory, which states that text segments with similar vocabulary are likely to be in one coherent topic. Thus, the more words two vectors share, the more strongly they are semantically related.

A lexical score between a topic vector and a content vector measures how strong these two are related, and is used here to determine topic boundary. The larger the score, the more likely the boundary occurs at that content slide. Steps for boundary identification are stated in Figure 3.4.

For each topic i, if there exists lexical score(s) greater than zero (line 2), then its boundary is set where the first maximum lexical score occurs (line 3), i.e., the position where the topic is first introduced. Otherwise, if the lexical score equals to zero, the algorithm locates its previous and subsequent boundaries, and calculates the lexical scores of adjacent content vectors within these boundaries. After that, set a boundary where the lexical score is greater than threshold T1 (line 4-7). Instead of comparing with zero (line 2), a threshold may be used. Due to limited terms in both topic vectors and content vectors in the case of presentations, we found zero is a reasonable threshold here.

1. For each topic $i(0 \le i \le k)$
2. If there is lexical score(s) greater than zero
3. Set the boundary i where the first maximum lexical score is
4. Else
5. Locate the boundary $i-1$ and boundary $i+1$
6. Calculate lexical scores of adjacent content vectors within these two boundaries
7. Set a boundary where the lexical score is greater than the threshold $T1$
8. End if
9. End for

Fig. 3.4. Boundary identification.

To map segmentation results of TWI back to video segmentation, image matching between key frames extracted from slide-level video segments and slide images converted from PowerPoint slides is preformed (Figure 3.5). Most key frames extracted from slide-level video segments have borders and/or overlaid presenter images. Unlike slide-level segmentation that works on frames that are captured using the same stationary camera, image matching with local color histogram difference cannot give satisfying results. Thus, image matching reported here is accomplished through image edge detection and analysis.

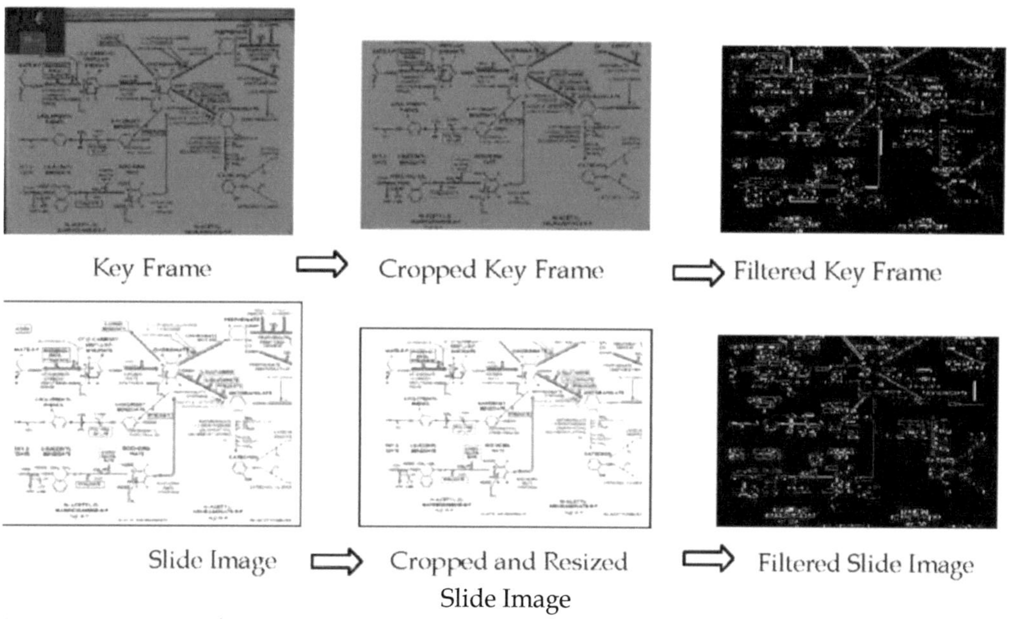

Fig. 3.5. Image matching.

The first step in image matching is to align extracted key frames with converted slide images. We first crop key frames and slide images. Since all frames are captured with the same stationary camera, the clipping factors only need to be determined once per presentation. Then we resize the cropped slide image to the same size as the cropped key frames, or vice versa. Bilinear interpolation is applied in this process.
The next step is to extract edge information of both key frames and slide images. There are many ways to perform edge detection. In this paper, we apply Sobel filter on both images. The Sobel method is a gradient method and it finds edges using the Sobel approximation to the first derivative. It returns edges at those points where the gradient is maximum.
Based on work in (Mukhopadhyay, et al., 1999), the difference between a filtered key frame and a filter slide image is then computed as follows:
Given Sobel-filtered key frame $f1$ and Sobel-filtered slide image $s1$, let b1 be the number of black pixels in $f1$, $d1$ be the number of black pixels in $f1$ whose corresponding pixel in $s1$ is not black, b2 be the number of black pixels in $s1$, and $d2$ be the number of black pixels in si whose corresponding pixel in $f1$ is not black, then the difference Δ is defined as

$$\Delta = \frac{d1 + d2}{b1 + b2} \tag{3.2}$$

The pair with the smallest Δ is considered as a matching pair. When multiple key frames extracted from adjacent video segments match the same slide image, their corresponding segments are combined.

Image matching adds timing information to each slide. Based on this timing information, slide blocks from TWI are associated with topic-level video segments. Moreover, the relationship between slide-level and topic-level video segments can also be inferred.
Formally, given a presentation p , its slide video stream V, and a set of n slides, let
$S_{slide-level} = \left\{ vs_{0,slide-level}, vs_{1,lide-level}, ..., vs_{m,slide-level} \right\}$ be a set of video segments generated from slide-level segmentation, $SB = \left\{ sb_0, sb_1, ..., sb_k \right\}$ be a set of slide blocks produced from Topic Words Introduction, then,

$$vs_{topic-level} = \left\{ vs_{0,topic-level}, vs_{1,topic-level}, ..., vs_{ktopic-level} \right\}$$

where

$$vs_{i,topic-level} = \left\{ \begin{array}{l} vs_{j,slide-level} \mid 0 \le j \le m, \text{ and the projected slides} \\ \text{of } vs_{j,slide-level} \in sb_i \end{array} \right\} (0 \le i \le k)$$

Therefore, hierarchical segmentation of presentation videos is achieved.

4. Multi-ontology Based Video Annotation

After a video is segmented, video annotation data can be extracted from the video and its segments. In this section, we propose a multi-ontology based multimedia annotation model in which a domain-independent multimedia ontology is integrated with multiple a domain dependent ontology in an effort to better address different users' information needs. We first describe the process of ontology development and then introduce the strategy to integrate the domain-independent multimedia ontology with multiple domain ontologies. A term extraction procedure is proposed as a mechanism to extract domain-specific annotations.

4.1 Developing Ontology

To realize multi-ontology based multimedia, the first step is to develop ontology. Two types of ontologies are involved: a domain-independent multimedia ontology and domain ontologies.

Multimedia ontologies describe multimedia entities, structure, and content that are shared by all domains. Several multimedia metadata standards have been proposed in the literature (Martinez, 2004; n.d.; The Dublin Core Metadata Initiative, n.d.; Isaac & Troncy, 2004). MPEG-7 (Martinez, 2004), developed by the Moving Picture Expert Group (MPEG), is one of the most widely accepted standards for multimedia content description. MPEG-7 provides a rich set of description tools to describe multimedia assets from various aspects, such as content generation, content description, content management, navigation and access, user interaction, and so on. Several multimedia ontologies have been developed based on the MPEG-7 standards (Hunter, 2001; Tsinaraki et al., 2004; Garcia et al., 2005). Hunter's ontology is the first MPEG-7 ontology and it covers the upper part of the Multimedia Description Scheme (MDS) part of the MPEG-7 standard. Starting from the ontology developed by Hunter, Tsinaraki's ontology covers the full MDS part of the MPEG-7 standard. Compared to the previous ones, Garcia et al. developed the most complete MPEG-

7 ontology. The proposed Multimedia Ontology (MO) here is based on MPEG-7 standards but focuses on the aspect of content description.
Three steps are followed to develop MO. First, we identify classes of the ontology. In general, classes describe concepts in the domain and are the focus of most ontologies. There are three types of classes in the proposed multimedia ontology (Figure 4.1): multimedia entities, non-multimedia entities, and descriptor entities. Multimedia entities are further classified into image, video, audio, audiovisual, and multimedia. Non-multimedia entities include agent, place, time, and instrument. Descriptor entities include visual descriptors, audio descriptors, structure descriptors, and semantic descriptors. In Figure 4.1, "Multimedia" refers to composite information that combines other multimedia elements such as image, audio and video. "MultimediaSegment" describes a segment of such media. Figure 4.1 gives the big picture of the MO, and some of the classes are not shown due to the limited space. Classes can have subclasses, for example, video segment is a subclass of Video. The subclass/superclass relationship may go several levels deep depending on the domain. In Figure 4.1, all arrows are labeled with "subClassOf," which depicts this relationship.

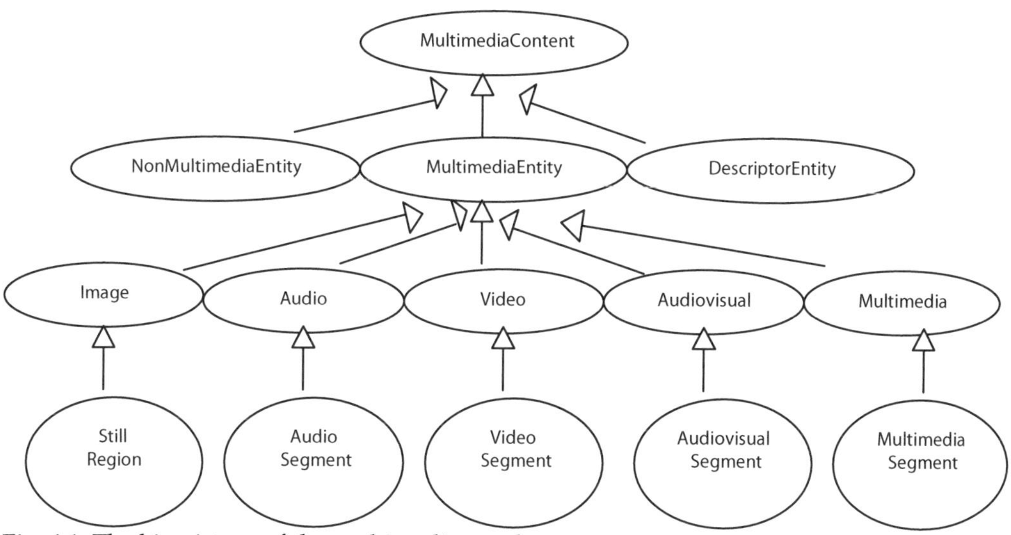

Fig. 4.1. The big picture of the multimedia ontology.

We then arrange all classes in a hierarchy. This concept hierarchy describes various relationships among classes, for example, multimedia entities are disjoint with non-multimedia entities and descriptor entities, and video segment is a subclass of video.
The last step is to define properties for each class. These properties further define the permitted relationships among multimedia entities, descriptor entities, and non-multimedia entities. Figure 4.2 shows an example of one video segment property. In Figure 4.2, "hasDominantColor" is a video segment property. This property correlates "VideoSegment" class, a multimedia entity, with "DominantColor" class, a descriptor entity. "DominantColor" is a subclass of "Color" and "Color" is a subclass of "VisualDescriptor." By following this subclass chain, "VideoSegment" class is further related to "Color" class and "VisualDescriptor" class, both of which are descriptor entities. Properties can also be viewed as links among individuals from domain and individuals from range. Properties can have

sub properties and each property can have multiple constraints. More details about general ontology development can be found in this paper (Noy & McGuinness, 2001).

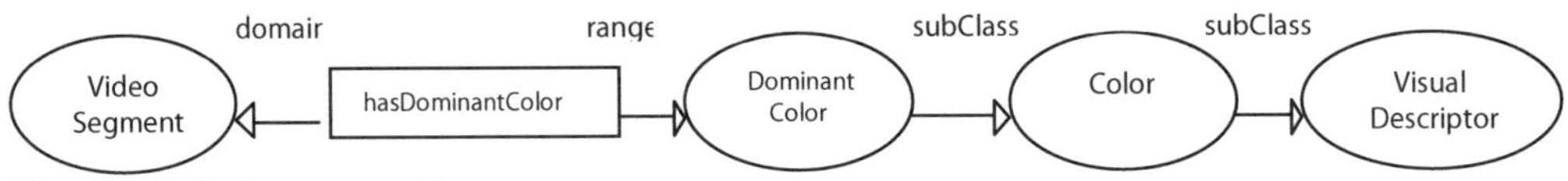

Fig. 4.2. Defining properties.

Domain ontologies can be either adopted or developed from the scratch. Each domain ontology defines domain concepts, concept properties, and concept relationships that are specific to that domain. These concepts and concept properties, called ontological terms in our discussion, form the controlled vocabulary of that domain ontology.

4.2 Integrating the Multimedia Ontology (MO) with domain ontologies

To integrate MO with domain ontology, we use controlled vocabulary of that domain ontology to annotate multimedia content. Specifically, the ontological terms from a domain ontology are added as properties to instances of multimedia entities at different levels, which allows us to annotate multimedia content with domain-specific concepts at different levels.

Figure 4.3 illustrates the basic idea at ontology structure level. Again, only a small portion is displayed here. In Figure 4.3, "VideoSegment" is a multimedia entity. Three of its properties defined in MO are listed, i.e., "hasStartTime," "hasAbstract," and "hasDominantColor." Data Mining Ontology (DMO) and Gene Ontology (GO) are two domain ontologies that are integrated with MO. "hasDMOAnnotation" and "hasGOAnnotation," from DMO and GO respectively, are added to "VideoSegment" class as two properties. "hasDMOAnnotation" annotates instances of "VideoSegment" with ontological terms from DMO, while "hasGOAnnotation" annotates instances of "VideoSegment" with ontological terms from GO.

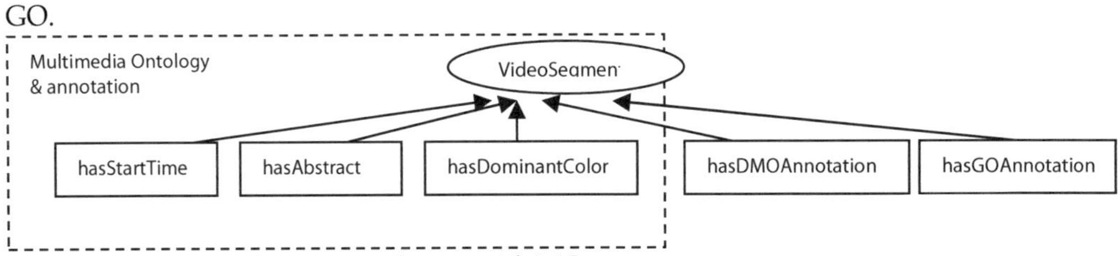

Fig. 4.3. Integrating domain ontologies with MO.

MO can integrate with multiple domain ontologies. The relationship between them is one-to-many. In the case of a new ontology joining the system, properties are added to multimedia entities at the right level. This process does not affect other parts of the system.

Since one instance of MO can be annotated with multiple ontological terms of a given domain and one ontological term of a given domain can annotate multiple instances of MO, the relationship between instances of MO and ontological terms of a given domain is many-to-many. The cardinality of the relationship modeled in Figure 4.3 is one-to-one, i.e., one instance of "VideoSegment" is annotated with one and only one ontological term from GO, that is "hasGOAnnotation" is a single-value property. It is a simplified version. The many-to-many relationship described above can be modeled using intermediate relations.

To realize this integration strategy, i.e., adding ontological terms of a domain ontology to instances of MO, we must address the issue of how to automatically annotate multimedia entities with ontological terms of a specific domain ontology. To annotate multimedia with semantic concepts, most approaches in the literature are model-based. Various statistical models are built and used as semantic concept detectors. This approach works well when it is easy to build statistical models and the number of possible concepts is small. In this paper, we present a term extraction procedure (Figure 4.4) that can be used to automatically extract ontological terms from multimedia textual resources for situations where it is very difficult to build statistical models, such as conference presentations, and/or the number of terms is so big that it is infeasible to build concept detectors for all possible concepts.

During the development of the term extraction procedure, we realize that professionals do not talk or write with ontologies in mind. Therefore, it is very rare to find exact ontological terms in their writings or talks. The main idea of the term extraction procedure is to find the longest sub-word sequences in input text that partially matches ontological terms. To this end, we utilize regular expression pattern matching in the procedure. Especially, Java regular expression standards[2] are followed. The expression \w matches a word character: [a-zA-Z_0-9], \s a white space character, * zero or more times, and + one or more times. Parentheses are used to group expressions. Before term extraction, uninformative words and punctuations are removed from input text. The detailed procedure is explained as follows.

```
1. Initialization
2.    Let W := {w_1 , w_2 ,..., w_n } ;; W is a word sequence of length n , and w_i ,
                1 ≤ i ≤ n , is a single word.
3.    Let T := {ontological terms}
4.    Let C := φ ;; for extracted ontological terms.
5.    Let start := 1 ;; start with the first word.
6. while (start ≤ n )
7.    Let step := 0 ;; variable for term expansion.
8.    while (start + step ≤ n and T.size > 1)
9.          pattern :=
(\w*[\s-]) + w_start ([\s-] \ w*) + w_start+1 ...w_start+step ([\s-] \ w*) +
10.         Let T':= matchPattern(pattern, T )
11.         if ( T'.size >= 1)
12.               T := T'
13.               step := step + 1
14.   end of while
15.   if (step >= 1)
16.         add terms in T but not already in C to C
17.   start := start + step
18. end of while
```

Fig. 4.4. The term extraction algorithm.

[2] http://java.sun.com/j2se/1.4.2/docs/api/java/util/regex/Pattern.html.

Given an input word sequence $W := \{w_1, w_2, ..., w_n\}$, the objective is to extract all ontological terms from W and store them in collection C. The procedure starts with initialization (line 1-5). For each word in input text, first design the matching pattern (line 9). Then match the pattern against all ontological terms (line 10). If one or more ontological terms are found to match the pattern, then expand the word or word sequence with the word that follows (line 11-13). Continue doing this expansion until the text input is exhausted or no more ontological terms can be found (line 8). Store extracted ontological terms in collection C. The pattern definition in line 9 finds ontological terms that contain every word of the word sequence in specified order. But subsequences are not necessarily continuous sub-strings of ontological terms. For example, "ribosomal large subunit assembly and maintenance" is a matched ontological term for the text input "ribosomal assembly." We apply the above term extraction algorithm with ontological terms from different domain ontologies and, thus, get different domain-specific annotations for the same multimedia content.

With this multi-ontology based multimedia annotation, different sets of annotation data are used in information retrieval. If a user is a biologist, then GO-based annotation is used; if a user is a computer scientist, then DMO-based annotation is used. As a result, multimedia information retrieval can be tailored towards different users' information needs.

5. Ontology-driven Video Access

After videos are segmented and annotation data are extracted, this section introduces ontology-driven video access. The key idea is to integrate ontologies into video browsing, searching, and filtering. The goal is to increase video retrieval relevancy and enhance users' video access experiences.

Ontology-driven video access works on video annotation data and refines or generalizes user queries with relevant domain concepts extracted from domain ontologies. To extend ontology-driven video access to external heterogeneous data sources, web services are explored.

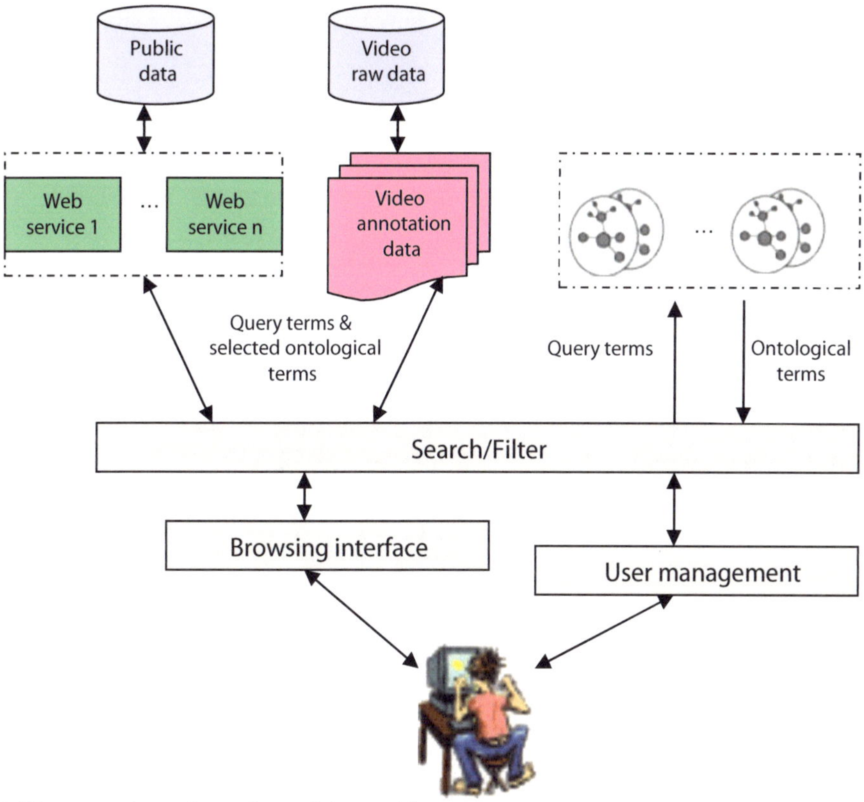

Fig. 5.1. The overview of ontology-driven video access.

Given query terms, the system first sends these query terms to a selected domain ontology, and retrieves relevant ontological terms/concepts based on the relationships embedded in that domain ontology. After that, both query terms and extracted ontological terms/concepts are fed into the selected set of video annotation data and web services, which then return relevant materials from both internal video collections and external data sources that are publicly available. Based on the proposed architecture, one single search pulls out all the relevant material both internal and external, which simplifies and reduces work on the users' side.

The purpose of user management in Figure 5.1 is to manage user profiles. By knowing learning habits or access preferences of users, there is a better chance that a video system can present relevant information of more interest to users.

6. Experiment

To experience ontology-driven video annotation and access proposed, we use VCGB as our test bed and build a Ontology-driven Video Access Platform for Virtual Conferences (OVAP).This system is proposed in the broad context of virtual learning/ researching environments, such as virtual conferences, virtual seminars, and virtual classrooms. Virtual learning/researching environments overcome geographical and economical limitations, and enable students and researchers alike to learn new technologies, participate in high quality meetings, and share research ideas easily.

6.1 Multi-ontology video annotation

We use the Multimedia Ontology (MO) developed in Section 4.2, Gene Ontology (GO) and an experimental Data Mining Ontology (DMO) to demonstrate multi-ontology based multimedia annotation.

GO provides controlled vocabularies for describing gene products in terms of their biological process, molecular function, and location in a cellular component. The standardized GO terms facilitate the annotation of gene products and allow for uniform queries to be performed across different scientific databases. The DMO is developed from the scratch, following the same process as described in Section 4.2. Figure 6.1 illustrates this ontology structure with a high-level view. All the arrows in Figure 6.1 are labeled with "subClassOf," which depicts subclass/superclass relationships. Details on classification and ARM (Association Rule Mining) are not shown.

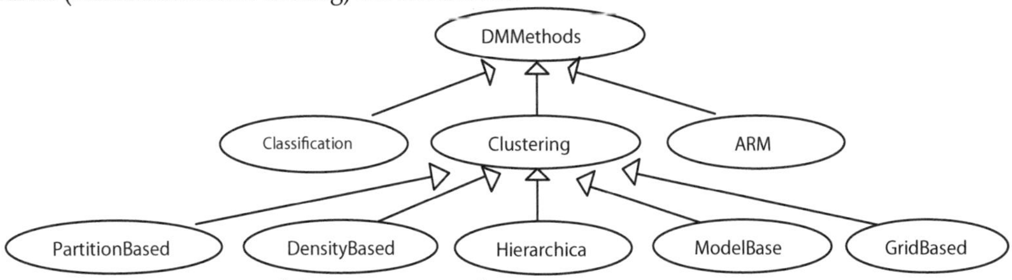

Fig. 6.1. The big picture of data mining ontology.

Both MO and DMO are developed using the Protégé 3.1.1 ontology editor. Due to limited query facilities and non-web query interface of Protege, we convert MO and DMO into database schemas from their ontology XML outputs. As for GO, we use its MySQL format downloaded from http://www.geneontology.org/. To realize the integration of MO with GO and DMO, two intermediate tables are created to model the many-to-many relationships existing between instances of MO and ontological terms from GO and DMO respectively as described in Section 4.2.

After setting up ontologies and their storage structures, the next logical step is to extract MO-based, GO-based, and DMO-based annotations.

To perform ontology-driven video annotation, the first step is video segmentation. The segmentation of presentation videos uses the exact same procedure as described in Section 3. Slide-level segmentation operates on slide video streams, while topic-level segmentation makes use of extracted slide text. At the end, slide-level segmentation creates a sequence of slide-level video segments. Within each such segment, the projected slide image does not change. Topic-level segmentation generates a sequence of topic-level video segments, each of which covers one or more slides. Within each such segment, the topic does not change. Since the presenter video stream and the slide video stream have the same presentation timeline, the presenter video stream is segmented as well based on this temporal relationship.

To extract annotation data from a presentation video and its segments, we apply multi-ontology based multimedia annotation as discussed in Section 4. Three levels of annotation data are extracted: presentation-level, topic-level, and slide-level. For MO-based annotation, at the presentation-level, words or terms in presentation titles are used; at the topic-level, words or terms in topic vectors are used; at the slide-level, words or terms in content vectors are used. For GO-based and DMO-based annotation, the term extraction algorithm introduced in Section 4.2 is applied on presentation titles, outline/overview slides, and content slides. Besides these data, other annotation, such as presenter information, presentation durations, video segment start time and end time, key frames, and so on, are all stored in the annotation database.

Before term extraction, uninformative words and punctuations are removed from the extracted slide text. To find uninformative words in input text for GO-based annotation, we perform a word frequency study on GO terms. Gene Ontology of version January 2005 has 19,455 terms and more than 70,000 words. Some words, such as activity (6657), regulation (1939), biosynthesis (1084), occur much more often than others and are uninformative words to the domain. Based on the word frequency analysis result of GO, we pick those terms with very high frequency and combine them with a common stop-word list, and use the combined list to remove uninformative words from input text. As for DMO-based annotation, we use the common stop-word list only.

6.2 Ontology-driven Video Access

Typical video access involves browsing and searching. To facilitate browsing, OVAP provides links for abstract, full paper, PowerPoint slide, video summary with key frames, and whole presentation for each virtual presentation (if available) in a hierarchical manner according to the ease of access. Regarding the search operation, one search pulls out relevant documents regardless of the format and sources. Search results are presented in multiple levels. In addition, relevant documents from PubMed (Sayers & Wheeler, n.d.) and Google (Google Inc., n.d.) are dynamically extracted with the corresponding web services. Figure 6.2 describes the general search process.

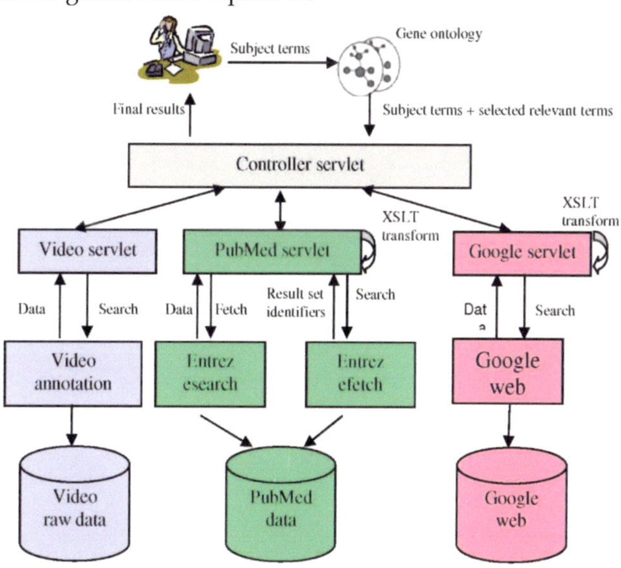

Fig. 6.2. The ontology-driven search.

The following interactive steps describe this process:

- A user enters query terms; the application sends them to Gene Ontology.
- The application extracts relevant GO terms from Gene Ontology and displays them to the user an ontology-based browsing space.
- The user selects GO terms of interest, and the application feeds both query terms and relevant GO terms to the controller servlet. Servlet here refers to the software agent developed in Java.
- The controller servlet sends all these terms to VCGB servlet, PubMed servlet, and Google servlet to extract relevant materials from the VCGB video collection, PubMed literature collection, and Google web sources, respectively.

In the VCGB branch, GO-based annotation data are used. As indicated in Section 6.1, GO-based annotation data have three levels: presentation-level, topic-level, and slide-level. The servlet first searches presentation-level annotation data. If there is a match, it searches topic-level and slide-level annotations of that presentation. Slide-level video segments with matching topic-level annotations are searched before those with no matching topic-level annotations. Then, the servlet searches the rest slide-level video segments with no matching presentation titles. Finally, the VCGB servlet organizes video data using SMIL (W3C, n.d.), RealText, and RealPix (RealNetworks, Inc., n.d.), links it to an HTML page and returns that HTML page to the controller servlet.

In PubMed servlet, the servlet first calls the *esearch* utility of PubMed web service by sending out an HTTP GET request with a URL containing all required parameters, *esearch* returns XML data that contain result set identifiers. PubMed servlet then extracts QueryKey and WebEnv from the XML data and sends out another HTTP GET request with a URL containing all required parameters. This request calls *efetch* utility, and *efetch* returns data to PubMed servlet. PubMed servlet transforms the results to HTML using XSL and returns them to the controller servlet.

In Google servlet, the servlet executes *doSearch* with a Google license key and other query parameters. Google Web APIs sends back query results with structured data format. Google servlet then converts structured data to XML and transforms XML data to HTML using XSL. Finally, it returns HTML results to the controller servlet.

The controller servlet compiles the results from the three servlets and sends back the final result as an HTML page to the user/ program. Figure 6.3 is an example of HTML pages sent back to users.

Fig. 6.3. Search result presentation.

7. Conclusion and Future Work

The explosive growth of video data demands efficient and flexible access mechanisms. In this paper, we propose an ontology-driven framework for video annotation and video access. The goal is to integrate ontology into video systems in an effort to improve users' video access experience.

The ontology-driven video annotation is a two-step process: video segmentation, and video annotation data extraction and organization. In video segmentation, we propose and utilize multi-mode segmentation procedures for presentation videos. In this procedure, the semantic-rich textual modality is integrated with the visual modality.

To extract annotation data from videos and video segments, and organize them in a way that facilitates video access, we employ a multi-ontology based multimedia annotation model. In this model, a domain-independent multimedia ontology is integrated with multiple domain ontologies. The goal is to provide multiple, domain-specific views of the same multimedia content and thus meet different users' information needs.

With extracted annotation data, we propose and implement ontology-driven video access. In ontology-driven video access, a user can select which ontology to interact with. The selection of ontology determines the set of annotation data and the group of relevant terms/concepts. As can be seen, ontology tailors the video access to users' domain-specific information access needs. To extend ontology-driven video to external heterogeneous data sources, web services are explored in this dissertation. Our experience shows that web service is an effective way to extract relevant documents from assorted, publicly available data sources.

In this paper, we focus our discussion on presentation videos. But the general concept of ontology-driven video annotation and access is applicable to many other areas as well, for example, digital libraries, the Web and corporate video collections. To improve the work and also extend the concept of ontology-driven to other fields, we identify the following areas for future work:

- To apply multi-ontology based multimedia annotation model on different types of multimedia assets, the issue of extracting domain-specific annotation need to be further addressed.
- Information-rich text modality is important in semantic segmentation of videos. We would like to integrate intelligent text analysis techniques that integrate natural language processing, machine learning, and artificial intelligence. We envision that such techniques will provide a viable solution to text-based segmentation.
- Ontology-driven video annotation and access incorporates ontology into video systems. To apply this concept on a large scale, other issues, such as redundant information across ontologies and external ontology inference engine integration, need to be further addressed.
- Formally evaluating a video access system is an important issue. Most approaches in the literature are survey-based. We would like to investigate other ways to assess our system in the future.

Video plays an important role in today's education. With the increasing growth of video data, we envision that there will be more extensive research conducted to effectively segment, annotate, and access these data, thus making them fully benefit the advance of society.

8. References

Abowd, G. D., Brotherton, J. A., and Bhalodai, J. (1998). Classroom 2000: A system forcapturing and accessing multimedia classroom experiences. *CHI' 98 Demonstration Paper,* pp. 20-21.

Allen, I. E. and Seaman, J. (2008). Staying the Course: Online Education in the United Statee. Available online at http://www.sloan-c.org/publications/survey/staying_course. Last access time June 23, 2009.

Bao, J., Cao, Y., Tavanapong, W., and Honavar, V. (2004). Integration of Domain-Specific and Domain-Independent Ontologies for Colonoscopy Video Database Annotation. *Proc. of 2004 International Conference on Information and Knowledge Engineering (IKE 04),* pp. 82-90.

Bianchi, M.(1998). AutoAuditorium: A fully automatic, multicamera system to televise auditorium presentations. *Joint DARPA/NIST Smart Spaces Tech. Workshop,* 1998.

Brotherton, J. A. and Abowd, G.D. (2004). eClass: Assessing automated capture and access in the classroom. *ACM Trans. on CHI,* pp. 121 - 155.

Cox, I. J., Miller, M. L., Minka, T. P., & Yianilos, P.N. (1998). An optimized interaction strategy for Bayesian relevance feedback. *Proc. of IEEE conf. on Computer Vision and Pattern Recognition,* pp. 553-558.

Cox, I. J., Miller, M.L., Omohundro, S.M., and Yianilos, P.N. (1996). Target testing and the pichunter Bayesian multimedia retrieval system. *Advanced Digital Libraries Forum,* pp. 66-75.

Fan, J., Luo, H., and Elmagarmid, A.K. (2004). Concept-oriented indexing of video databases: Toward semantic sensitive retrieval and browsing. *IEEE Trans. On Image Processing,* July 2004, pp. 974-992.

Flachsbart, J., Franklin, D., and Hammond, K. (2000). Improving human computer interaction in a classroom environment using comptuer vision. *Proc. of the 5th international conference on Intelligent user interfaces,* pp. 86-93.

Garcia, R. and Celma, O. (2005). Semantic Integration and Retrieval of Multimedia Metadata. *Proc. of the 5th International Workshop on Knowledge Markup and Semantic Annotation,* November 2005.

Google Inc.(n.d.). Google SOAP Search APIs. Available: http://www.google.com/apis/api_faq.html.

Haubold, A. & Kender, J. R. (2003). Analysis and interface for instructional video. *Proceedings of International Conference on Multimedia and Expo,* pp. 705-708.

Hauptmann, A. G. (2004). Towards a large scale concept ontology for broadcast video. *Proc. of the 3rd Int. Conf on Image and Video Retrieval (CIVR'04),* pp. 674-675.

He, L., Grudin, J., and Gupta, A. (2000). Designing presentations for on-demand viewing, *Proc. of CSCW'00,* pp.127-134.

Hearst, M. A. (1994). TextTiling: Segmenting text into multi-paragraph subtopic passages. *Computational Linguistics,* Vol. 23, No. 1, pp. 33-64.

Hollink, L., Worring, M., and Schreiber, G. (2005). Building a Visual Ontology for Video Retrieval. *Proc. of the ACM Multimedia,* pp. 479- 482.

Hunter, J.(2001). Adding Multimedia to the Semantic Web - Building an MPEG-7 Ontology. The 1st International Semantic Web Working Symposium (SWWS'01), pp. 261-281.

HyvÄonen, E., Styrman, A., & Saarela, S. (2003). Ontology-based image retrieval. *Poster Proceedings, the 12th International World Wide Web Conference.*

Isaac, A., and Troncy, R.,(2004). Designing and Using an Audio-Visual Description Core Ontology. *Proc. of the 14th International Conference on Knowledge Engineering and Knowledge Management,* October 2004.

Kanedera , N., Sumida, A., Ikehata, T., and Funada, T. (2006). Subtopic segmentation in lecture speech for the creation of lecture video contents. *Syst Comp Jpn,* 37(10), pp.13-21.

Kariya, S. (2003). Online education expands and evolves. *IEEE Spectrum.* 40(5): 49-51.

Khan, L. & McLeod, D. (2000). Audio structuring and personalized retrieval using ontologies. *Proc. IEEE Advances in Digital Libraries (ADL2000),* p. 116.

Liu, T. and Kender, J. R. (2002). Rule-based semantic summarization of instructional videos. *International Conference on Image Processing,* pp. 601-604.

Lin, M., Chau, M., Cao, J., & Nunamaker, J. F. (2005). Automated video segmentation for lecture videos. *The International Journal of Technology and Human Interaction (IJTHI),* Vol. 1, No. 2, pp. 27-45.

Rowe, L.A., Harley, D., Pletcher, P., and Lawrence, S. (2001). BIBS: A Lecture Webcasting System. *Center for Studies in Higher Education.* Paper CSHE4-01. http://repositories.cdlib.org/cshe/CSHE4-01.

Martinez, J. M. (2004). MPEG-7 Overview. Available: http://www.chiariglione.org/mpeg/standards/mpeg-7/mpeg-7.htm .

Minka, T. P. & Picard, R. W. (1997). Interactive learning with a 'society of models'," *Pattern Recognition.* Vol. 30, No. 4, pp. 565-581.

Mukhopadhyay, S. & Smith, B. (1999). Passive capture and structuring of lectures. *Proceedings of the 7th ACM International Conference on Multimedia,* pp. 477-487.

Müller, R. and Ottmann, T. (2000). The 'authoring on the fly' system for automated recording and replay of (Tele)presentations," *ACM/Springer Multimedia Systems Journal*, Vol. 8, No. 3, pp. 158-176, 2000.

Ngo, C., Wang, F., and Pong, T. (2003). Structuring lecture videos for distance learning applications. *ISMSE*, pp. 215-222.

Noy, N., McGuinness, D. (2001). Ontology development 101: A guide to creating your first ontology. *Technical Report SMI-2001-0880*, Stanford University School of Medicine.

Onishi, M., Izumi, M., and Fukunaga, K. (2000). Blackboard segmentation using video image of lecture and its applications. *International Conference on Pattern Recognition*, pp. 615–618.

Papathomas, T. V., Conway, T. E., Cox, I. J., Ghosn, J., Miller, M. L. , Minka, T. P., et al. (1998). Psychophysical studies of the performance of an image database retrieval system. *IS&T/SPIE Symposium on Electronic Imaging: Science and Technology, Conference on Human Vision and Electronic Imaging III*, pp. 591-602.

Phung, D., Venkatesh, S., & Dorai, C. (2002). High level segmentation of instructional videos based on content density. *Proceedings of Multimedia '02*, pp. 295-298.

Picard, R. W. & Minka, T. P. (1995). Vision texture for annotation. *ACM Multimedia Systems*, 3 (1), pp.1-11.

Porter, M. (1980). An algorithm for suffix stripping. *Program*, Vol. 14, No. 3, pp.130-137. RealNetworks, Inc.(n.d.). Real networks production guide. Available: http://service.real.com/help/library/encoders.html#productionguide.

Rui, Y., Gupta, A., Grudin, J., and He, L. (2004). Automating lecture capture and broadcast: technology and videography. *Multimedia Systems*, pp. 3–15.

Rui, Y., Huang, T. S., Mehrotra, S., & Ortega, M. (1998). Relevance feedback: A power tool in interactive content-based image retrieval. *IEEE Transaction on Circuits and Systems and Video Technology*, Vol. 8, No. 5, pp. 644-655.

Sayers, E. and Wheeler, D. (n.d.). Building customized data pipelines using Entrez programming utilities (eUtils). Available: http://www.ncbi.nlm.nih.gov/books/bv.fcgi?rid=coursework.chapter.eutils.

Schreiber, A. T., Dubbeldam, B., Wielemaker, J., & Wielinga, B.(2004). Ontology-based photo annotation. *IEEE Intelligent Systems*, Vol. 16, No. 3, pp. 66-74.

Smith, T., Ruocco, A., and Jansen, B. (1999). Digital video in education. *Proc. of the Thirtieth SIGCSE Technical Symposium on Computer Science Education*, pp. 122-126.

The Dublin Core Metadata Initiative. (n.d.). Dublin Core metadata initiatives. Available: http://dublincore.org/.

Tsinaraki, C., Polydoros, P., and Christodoulakis, S. (2004). Interoperability support for Ontology-based Video Retrieval Applications. *Proc. of 3rd International Conference on Image and Video Retrieval*, pp. 582-591.

Yamanoto, N., Ogata, J., & Ariki, Y. (2003). Topic segmentation and retrieval systems for lecture videos based on spontaneous speech recognition. *Proc. of EUROSPEECH 2003*, pp. 961-964.

W3C(n.d.). Synchronized Multimedia Integration Language (SMIL 2.0). Available: http://www.w3.org/TR/SMIL2/.

17

When a robot turns into a totem: The RoboBeggar case

Gaetano La Russa, Erkki Sutinen
University of Joensuu
Finland
Johannes C. Cronje
Cape Peninsula University of Technology
South Africa

1. Introduction

After her kingdom had been devastated by a prolonged famine in 1649, Queen Christina of Sweden commanded that wooden "beggar" statues be set up in the entrance of churches to collect money for the poor (Saariholma (a), 2001). Figure 1 shows two surviving examples of these wooden begging statues. These statues, known as "begging man/men" (*vaivaisukko* or *vaivaisukot* in Finnish), have slits through which donors are able to push coins. They continued to be used under the Russian domination of Finland and were, until a few decades ago, quite a common sight in the west of Finland where people still used them to deposit charitable donations. One hundred and eight examples of these wooden beggar statues are currently extant (Santaholma (b), 2001). Of these, only one, in the Lutheran Church at Soini (Etelämäki, 2000), has female features (Fides, 2002).

Fig. 1. Two wooden begging statues (*vaivaisukot* in Finnish)

A decision was taken with 3rd sector at the University of Joensuu in 2002 to research the potential of the RoboBeggar as a fundraising tool and to combine that research with the university's R&D program in the field of human-robot interactions. The initial design of the RoboBeggar prototype was limited in some ways by its intended similarity to historic Finnish *vaivaisukot*. It was in fact the original intention of the designers to construct a robot that the public would immediately recognize as being similar to the ancient wooden statues that were once a common sight in the porch entrances of Lutheran churches (Fides, 2002; Kouvolansanomat, 2001; Wanha, 2007). One of the aims of the research project was also to determine the extent to which the classical Finnish *vaivaisukko* that was used in earlier centuries to raise funds for charity might be replicated and modernized as a digitally controlled humanoid robot.

We devised a series of research questions to highlight the educational and technological advantages of the planned robot over the traditional *vaivaisukko*. Table 1 compares certain salient features of the traditional *vaivaisukko*, the RoboBeggar and two other electronic fundraising systems. The table elucidates how two fundamentally different technological fundraising systems illuminate specific issues and motivations in RoboBeggar research. Column 4 indicates the features of the online fundraising system (Online UNICEF) that is used by the United Nations Children's Fund (UNICEF) to raise funds to finance activities such as the construction of schools in Africa or to buy mosquito nets for people who live in malarial areas (UNICEF, 2007). Column 5 shows how the Securegive "Hercules" (2007), an automated teller machine (ATM) compares with the other systems when they are used in donation kiosks. The ATM Hercules has been used at various times by the Swedish Lutheran Church and The Swedish Church Mission (Svenska Kyrkans Mission) to receive and process funds for charitable causes (Palo, 2006; Terhemaa, 2006).

Feature/Function	Vaivaisukko	RoboBeggar	Online UNICEF	ATM Hercules
Interaction	No	Yes	Yes	No
Ease of donation	Yes	Yes	No	Yes
Ability to act as a reminder to donate	Yes	Yes	No	No
User learning support	No	Yes	Yes	No
Emotional appeal	Yes	Yes	No	No
Donor satisfaction	No	Yes	Yes	No
Donor encouragement	No	Yes	No	No
Ability to stimulate a repeat donation	No	Yes	No	No
Digital illiterate	Yes	Yes	No	Yes

Table 1. Comparison of four fundraising systems

Table 1 also highlights features that researchers need to include in a robot so that non-expert users might be encouraged to make donations. One of the axioms of this kind of research is that it is necessary to support interactions with online help (Mondi et al., 2007; Swan, 2004) so that users will be *encouraged* to donate while simultaneously being *rewarded* with some degree of personal feedback and gratification.

The physical dimensions and the appeal of the robot were dictated by the fact that the hardware had to be both *anthropomorphic* and *relatively small in stature* in comparison with the average human being. The height of the RoboBeggar was therefore fixed at 150 cm. The robot also needed to be able to collate information by means of visual, aerial and hypermedia devices that could create and process fundraising target data, statistics, graphics, sociological data, and other specific interactions. The robot also needed to be capable of giving e-learning feedback to users about fundraising targets and goals, the reasons for the fundraising, the targets fixed by the local community, and the reasons why it is ethical to donate money to help needy people. The design of the software was conceptually complex because it was necessary for the money-collecting functionality to operate in combination with the e-learning functions so that users could complete the donation process with ease. A full-graphic and intuitive donation interface was designed for this purpose. The use of "plastic money" (i.e. bankcards) added features to the hardware (namely a bankcard reader for donations), and these posed some interesting problems about the desired resemblance to the *vaivaisukko*. We also decided to give the anthropomorphic robot a female rather than male form even though only one female *vaivaisukko* survives in Finland. We justified this decision by pointing to the fact that it is mainly women who bear the material and occupational brunt of poverty in developing countries throughout the world (De Haan & Lipton, 1998; Hulme et al., 2001; Harcourt, 2001). And since the usability tests of the robot were mostly scheduled to be undertaken at fundraising events on behalf of developing countries, it seemed a natural choice to make the robot female in appearance.

In early Spring of 2004 the female (i.e. *gynoid*) robot called RoboBeggar (the term gynoid is derived from *gynē*, the Greek for woman, and the –oid suffix which indicates similarity in English) was tested in experimental circumstances in the Kupittaa Mall, an urban shopping mall in Turku (the main town on the southwest coast of Finland), which is frequented by a large number of users. The robot was set up to the one side of the walkway of the main hall of the mall so that it would be visible to and accessible by the thousands of people who shop daily in the Kupittaa Mall. The OP Bank Group (the largest financial services group in Finland, known by their acronym OKO) graciously cooperated by funding the basic transportation costs of the robot and by allowing the robot to be situated next to their bank in the Kupittaa Mall. The Cancer Association of South-West Finland (*Lounais-Suomen Syöpäyhdistys* or LSSY in Finnish) was designated as the beneficiary of the robot's fundraising activities.

In the paragraphs that follow we describe the basic architecture of the robot, the adjustments made to the software on the basis of experience, the logistics and agreements concluded for the conduct of the research, a description of how the robot was run. We also evaluate the effectiveness of the robot as a fundraising tool, undertake an analysis and evaluation of all relevant collected data and, finally, draw conclusions about what kind of procedures might work best in future interactions between human beings and fundraising robots.

2. The RoboBeggar architecture used in the Kupittaa event

The architecture of the robot in the Kupittaa event was essentially the same as it was in June (Faggiano & La Russa, 2004) and September 2003 (La Russa, 2009), with the main variations being the touch screen interface and the audio components. Figure 2 shows a schema of the robot architecture and its activity flow. The robot, which consisted of a combination of software (for internal and external operation management) and hardware, had the following components:

(1) *The software.* The software manages and controls both the programmed behaviour and the communications that take place among the robot's components and between users and the transaction system. The e-learning module (*e-module*), which creates a connection between fundraising requirements and the necessity to heighten donor awareness, sympathy and response, presents a condensed version of essential information about the cancer organization that is the beneficiary, the disease itself, its incidence in Finland and the extent to which children are at risk of contracting cancer.

(2) *The touch screen.* The touch screen is the interface between the users and the robot and presents the e-learning information in modular form. The touch screen gives users the option of selecting their preferred operation. The options are to donate funds, to be presented with more information or to close the transaction.

(3) *The bankcard reader* (or card reader). The card reader is an electronic device that is capable of reading the magnetic tape of bankcards. If a user decides to make a donation, software transmits the information provided by the user to the bank. The bank then responds by setting up secure conditions for the transmission of data so that the user's donation can be received by the fund. The user is then given an opportunity to select the precise amount of the donation in a simplified window (see Figure 3 for details). The window allows the user to make a donation only in accordance with predetermined donation amounts (i.e. 1, 2, 5, 10, 20, 50 and 100 €). The RoboBeggar and the bank system are connected by means of GSM connection.

(4) *The sound card and the speakers.* These are necessary so that the robot can talk and so give audible feedback to donors. The robot's ability to speak makes its resemblance to a humanoid more convincing.

(5) *The printer.* The printer offers the donor a printed receipt which functions both as a receipt and as a reminder of the donor's charity. Although the printer is actually a constituent part of the bankcard reader, external separate equipment could just as well be used to produce better quality printouts.

(6) *The micro controller and the servomotors.* The servomotors, which move the arms and head of the robot, give continuous feedback to the software about the latest position and situation of the robot. The servomotors are controlled by a programmable microchip (a micro controller) that receives orders from the software through a serial port. The software commands are "interpreted" in the micro controller and transformed into motor action. The RoboBeggar is capable of gestures that are correlated to the sound card and to a speakers' activity.

(7) *The robot shell.* The shell, constructed from twelve bolted aluminium plates, provides the robot with a body to which the limbs and head are attached. The computer and its components, the micro controller and the loudspeakers, are all allocated space inside one of the two chambers into which the shell is subdivided. The shell can

easily be disassembled in its two constituent parts: the lower and upper sections (which hold the limbs, the head and the touch screen structure). All the servomotors are located inside the tubes that comprise the limbs and the neck with a total of 6 degrees of freedom (DOF). In engineering and mechanics (as well as in robotics), a *degree of freedom* defines the capacity of a rigid body to rotate on one of its axes or move along it (Zhang et al., 2007). Since rigid bodies have three axes, the maximum number of DOFs in a three-dimensional rigid body is 6. It is obvious from this that the DOF of systems such as robots can increase to a higher number (the human arm alone, for example, is considered to have seven DOFs).

Because the software is the core and heart of the robot, it needs to synchronize the robot's motors with its speech so that the robot's speech might appear to be as natural as possible. It also needs to take care of the e-module flow and to ensure that any bankcard's communication data will be transferred securely and efficiently.

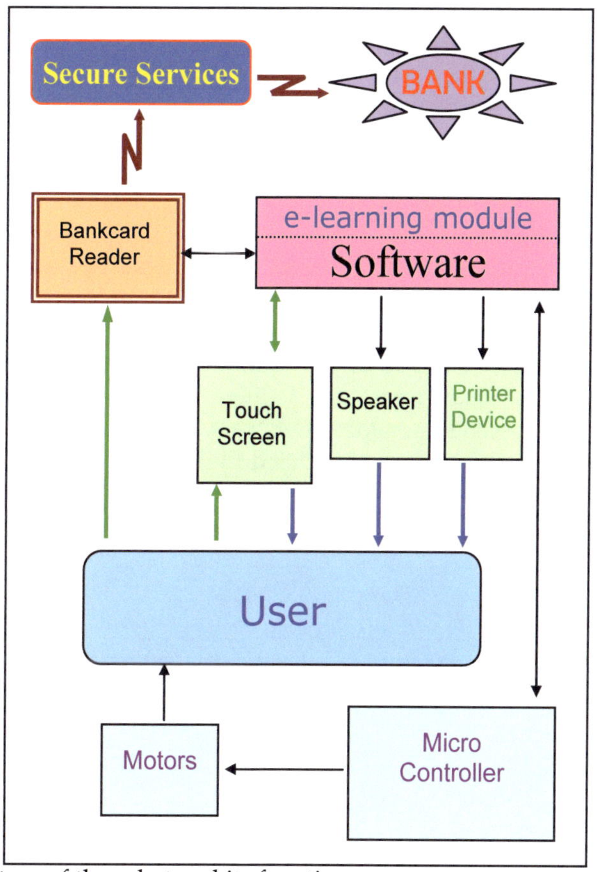

Fig. 2. The architecture of the robot and its functions

3. The RoboBeggar in the Kupittaa Mall experimental event

The choice of giving the robot a gynoid appearance was not motivated by sexist considerations but by the relative success of women in media and communication (Stratton,

2001). Because it has been proved that robots make a positive educational impact in learning environments (Pfeifer, 1997; Miglino et al., 1999), the gynoidal appearance of the RoboBeggar should be considered to be a compromise between an indigenous Finnish tradition (Santaholma, 2001; Fides, 2002; Etelämäki, 2000), technology (Naidu et al., 2002; Papert & Harel, 1991; Vo et al., 1995; La Russa et al., 2004) and sociological studies that privilege and showcase the role of women (De Haan & Lipton, 1998; Hulme et al., 2001; Harcourt, 2001).

3.1 The robot interface

Because the user interface had to be as simple as possible (Marwedel, 2003; Cooper & Reimann, 2003) while offering a highly intuitive interface for the e-learning module (Norman, 2002), the LSSY was asked to express their preferences about the style of graphic interfaces and the information that they would present to prospective donors. Because LSSY is experienced in fund-raising activities and possesses accurate information about their average user interaction time (estimated to be approximately 60 seconds for the human-robot interactions) (Card et al., 1986), the e-learning module was reduced to four basic informative windows (see Figure 4, 5, 6 and 7) with additional direct access to the iconic window that mediates the donation activity (see Figure 8). Three other windows were dedicated to the human-robot introduction (the welcome window - see Figure 3 for the template) and the donation process (see Figure 9 for an image of the bankcard reader information window). The remaining (final) window of the donation process thanks the donor with a text that is randomly extracted from a list of twenty possible choices.
The use of the euro icons was dictated by the fact that it is necessary for users to be well-informed about the size and value of the monetary value of the donation that they intend to make (Huang et al., 2002) - in spite of the limited time at their disposal for making a decision. The euro icons make it easy for a donor to choose the size of the donation according a progressive ascending value order from left to right and top to bottom. The icons were also visually weighted and distributed in the iconic window in accordance with their representative values (see Figure 8).

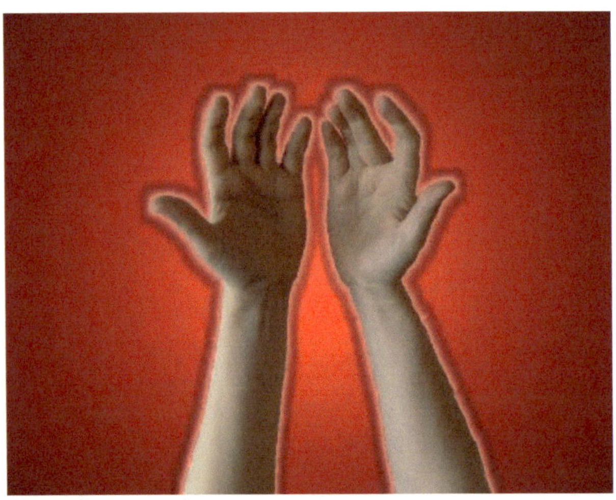

Fig. 3. The welcome window template

Fig. 4. The main LSSY window which introduces the *campaign to eliminate cancer*

The frame of Figure 4 reads "*Voluntary Work to Fight Cancer*" (*Syöväntorjuntatalkoot* in Finnish). The buttons are programmed with the following links:

(1) "Syöpä?" (*cancer*) leads to the e-module "Syöpä lyhyesti" (*in brief about cancer*). See Figure 5.

(2) "Lasten syövät" (*kids' cancers*) leads to the e-module "Lasten syövät" that is shown in Figure 6.

(3) "LSSY ry" leads to the descriptive e-module of "Lounais-Suomen Syöpäyhdistys" organisation (*The Cancer Association of South-West Finland*) that is shown in Figure 7.

(4) "Takaisin" (*back*) is for going back to parent e-module.

(5) "Käyttöohjeet" (*instructions*) leads to the system usage information e-module. In the other e-modules this button is substituted by "Lahjoittaa" (*make a donation*) which straightly leads to the iconic window of Figure 8.

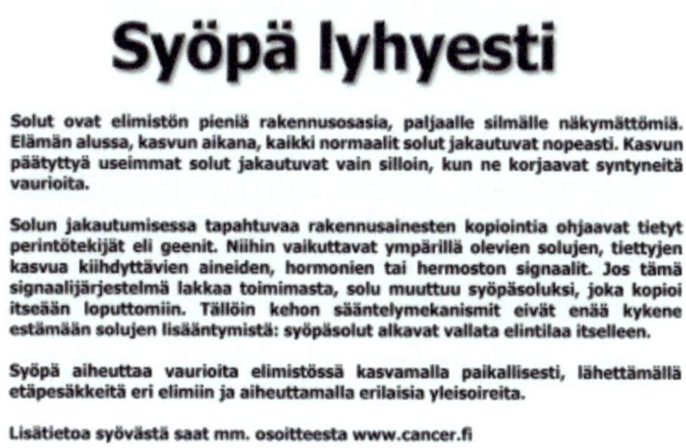

Fig. 5. A brief overview *about cancer*

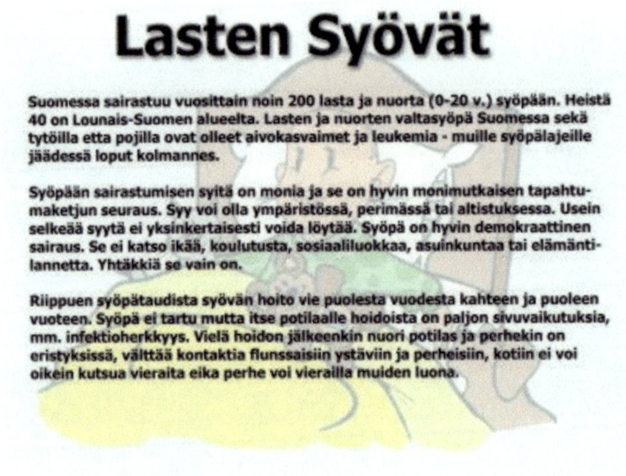

Fig. 6. An explanation of how *Children get cancer*

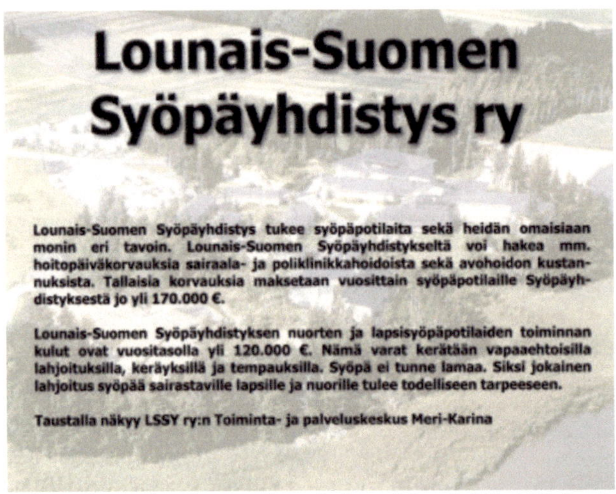

Fig. 7. The window describing the *Cancer Association of South-West Finland*

The *iconic window* of Figure 8 informs the user of the opportunity to donate a given amount of money by touching the correspondent monetary icon. It also tells that after having chosen a donation value a new window (see Figure 9) will guide through the bankcard operation to complete the donation process which would be confirmed by the robot. The confirmation is given via receipt printing and a final informative e-module containing the donation data (the current user's donated amount as the overall donated amount), some extra activity hints and the verbal thanking of the robot.

Fig. 8. The *iconic window* controlling the donation process

Fig. 9. The bankcard reader information window with written instructions

3.2 How the RoboBeggar was used in practice

The LSSY was entrusted with the care and public management of the robot for a period of two weeks in late February 2004, and as much information as was considered necessary was given to the representatives of the bank and the cancer organization about the software and hardware of the robot. In addition to this, the robot's software was simplified compared to previous usage events because it was too expensive for the robot's designers to manage the robot directly themselves (the distance between the research institute and the mall was about 600 km) and because there were no available local robotic technicians to undertake the task. The designers therefore automated the uploading of the robot software to coincide with the initialization of the computer system so as to obviate as much as possible the need for any kind of direct administrative management of the robot.

The economic need to create a partly self-managing robot that was not under the direct control of the academic staff nevertheless created some unexpected consequences that gave its designers additional socio-cultural data that they were obliged to take into consideration when considering how they might modify the robot to cope the range of likely human-robot interactions in the future.

3.3 Data and feedback information

The robot, suitably attired in woman's clothing, was eventually carefully positioned next to the OKO Bank on the one side of the main hall of the Kupittaa Mall. From that position it was possible for the bank's employees to observe and monitor what was happening to the robot from their own work stations. The robot was switched on in the mornings and off in the evenings by means of an electric cable that was connected to the main power supply of the bank. Members of the LSSY organization volunteered to stand near the RoboBeggar so that they could help and encourage passers-by to approach the robot and begin a human-robot interaction.

On the eve of the usage period the research team assembled and tested the robot in situ in Kupittaa Mall and briefed those members of the bank's staff who would be involved in the care of the robot with whatever they needed to know about the running of the robot (such as its activation and deactivation, and its stability). OKO Bank also took responsibility for maintaining the integrity and safety of the robot. The management of the RoboBeggar was then handed over to a representative of LSSY, and everything looked fair for full use and data collection starting the following day. The robot was positioned with its back to the bank and its front toward the mall pathway. This was the prelude to two weeks of testing and fundraising that would follow.

What follows below is a description of the event feedbacks that were obtained from three different sources: (1) the OKO Bank's employees, (2) a local newspaper article, and (3) the Multiple Choice Question forms that were intended to be offered to donors.

3.4 Feedback from the employees of the OKO Bank

Three employees of the bank reported the following information during the course of interviews:

(1) For unknown reasons and at unpredictable moments the robot would stop functioning. This made it necessary for the LSSY attendees to restart the robot's program by unplugging and then plugging in the power cable again.

(2) In the first few days tens of people interacted with the robot and made donations through the medium of the robot.

(3) Even while the robot was functioning, hundreds of people approached the robot and the LSSY attendants because the RoboBeggar's had attracted their attention with its rather distinctive voice calling from the speakers (the axis of the pathway in the mall was only about ten meters away from the place where the robot stood).

(4) Fewer than twenty people experienced difficulty in sliding their bankcards through the bankcard reader slot at a speed that would allow the magnetic tape to read the data on the bankcard. Sometimes this operation had to be repeated to be successful and sometimes people turned to make a cash donation directly to the LSSY attendees who were armed with donation tins.

(5) There was a distinct increase over the period of the experiment in the number of people who were attracted by the RoboBeggar and who approached it either out of curiosity or to make a donation.
(6) After about a week the LSSY volunteers decided to keep the RoboBeggar switched off and resorted to collecting money by using only the LSSY donation cans. They did this because they said that the robot had already become known to the users of the mall and because many of them were approaching the robot before it had even called them. The LSSY volunteers also eventually concluded that it was easier and simpler for them to collect money directly in donor boxes than to wait for users to complete the interaction processes. In the meantime an additional vest that displayed LSSY fundraising information (see Figure 10) was placed over the robot's chest.
(7) During the sixteen days of the fundraising experiment, many hundreds of people came over to examine the RoboBeggar and to ask about its function, and these people collectively donated thousands of euros to the LSSY organization.

3.5 Feedback from the local newspaper

During the experiment the local Turkulainen newspaper published an article (Pitkänen, 2004) that described the fundraising robot and offered opinions about its functions and usability. The picture in Figure 10 accompanied this article and it is reproduced here with the permission of the newspaper. The article highlighted the following points:
(1) People perceived the gynoid as a charming lady with green eyes that focused on passersby. (Author's note: For this experimental event, the robot had been repainted for a third time. This inspired the research team to consider the possible future use of intelligent tissues, which are substances capable of reproducing humanoid skin-like behaviours.
(2) The calling voice of the robot proved to be so effective in attracting people that its volume had to be reduced. Many passersby became alarmed because they thought that a real person was in some kind of trouble and approached the robot area offering their help.
(3) The robot had very good manners and would thank people courteously for their donations.
(4) The use of "plastic money" was a necessary component in the fundraising campaign because many people who did not carry cash wished nevertheless to make donations.
(5) The robot offered people a choice of beneficiaries for their donations (i.e. they could specify whether their donation should be diverted to child or adult care).
(6) The robot was not capable of carrying out a conversation (dialogue). It was evident that donors had an emotional need to tell the robot about their own experience of cancer.
(7) The robot was occasionally switched off.
(8) LSSY attendants supplemented the fundraising activities of the robot.

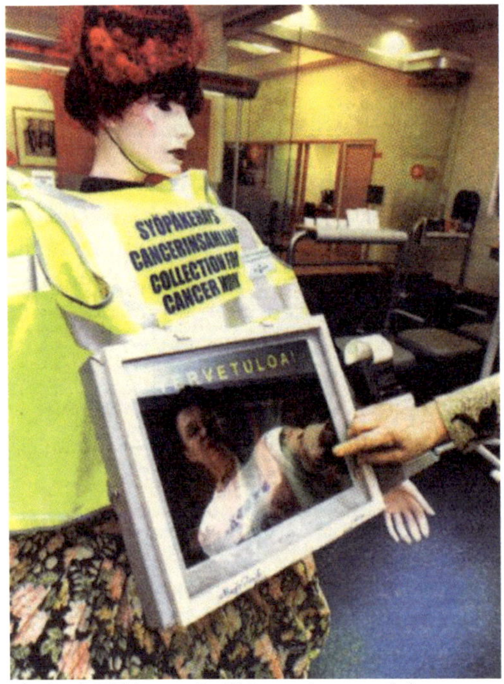

Fig. 10. The RoboBeggar in its LSSY vest (still in active mode)
Photograph reproduced by kind permission of the photographer, Pasi Leino.

3.6 Feedback from users

A Multiple Choice Question (MCQ) form was designed to be offered to people who approached the robot and who had initiated an interaction process. The form was intended to provide the researchers with additional data for analysis and evaluation. The information collected by the form related to:

(1) Gender
(2) Age group
(3) The functionality of the robot (seven questions)
(4) The effectiveness and influence of the robot (four questions)
(5) User evaluations and assessments (five questions)
(6) The donation system application (four questions)
(7) A blank space for any additional messages to the researchers and/or the designer of the robot (users were instructed by a message in bold letters at the bottom of the front of the form to write any additional personal contributions on the reverse side of the form).

According the type of question being asked, users could respond in one of two possible ways (Uebersax, 2006):

(1) They could express their opinion in terms of the following scale:
1 = completely of different opinion
2 = partially of different opinion
3 = it cannot be determined
4 = partially of the same opinion

5 = fully of the same opinion

(2) They could choose one of the following three options:

No

It cannot be determined

Yes

Only five multiple-choice feedback forms were returned to the research team by the LSSY volunteers at the conclusion of the fundraising test campaign. The reasons for this poor feedback are explained in the following section.

4. Analysis and assessment of the data material

It was a defect in the research design that the LSSY volunteers focused mainly (if not solely) on fundraising to the exclusion of a prior agreement also to collect research data. The research element would have involved them in encouraging users to fill in the feedback forms which were designed to provide vital information about the way in which the RoboBeggar was being used. If a similar misuse of the robot is to be avoided, communication between the research institute and the LSSY needs to be much more clear and unambiguous. If communication had in fact been clearer before the test event, the necessary users' feedback information would have been collected (Pitkänen, 2004).

The feedback that was collected provided a variety of data relating to different aspects of how the robot was used and how users approached it. The feedback obtained comprised 75 answers to questions about the quality of the robot's functions and its efficiency, and 15 expressions of personal opinion. The analysis in the graphics in Figures 11, 12 and 13 are presented as percentages of the related data population. Most noteworthy among the results is the following feedback obtained from an analysis of user responses (set out in comparison with results obtained from a previous test event in June 2003 (La Russa et al., 2004) :

(1) When users were asked to express an overall opinion about the functionality of the robot (the user interface, the donation process, the provided information, etc.), 74 % of their replies pointed out that it had been totally successful, and 23 % that it had been successful (see graphic in Figure 11). In a previous test event carried out by La Russa (La Russa et al., 2004), the corresponding values had been 78 % for totally successful and 15 % for successful.

(2) When asked their opinion about whether the robot was successful in its interactive tasks, 80 % of responses were yes and 20 % were no (see Figure 12). In the previous test event, 94 % of the answers were yes and 6 % were unsure.

(3) In response to a question about whether the robot had been successful in creating a "fun" situation, 40 % of the answers indicated that it had been totally successful while 60 % indicated that it was successful (see Figure 13). In the previous research event by La Russa, the corresponding values had been 78 % for totally successful, 14 % for successful, 4 % for unsure, and 4 % for totally unsuccessful.

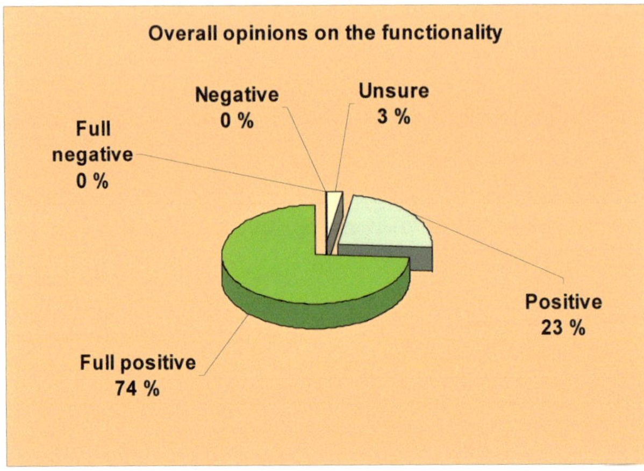

Fig. 11. Users' assessments of the robot's functionality

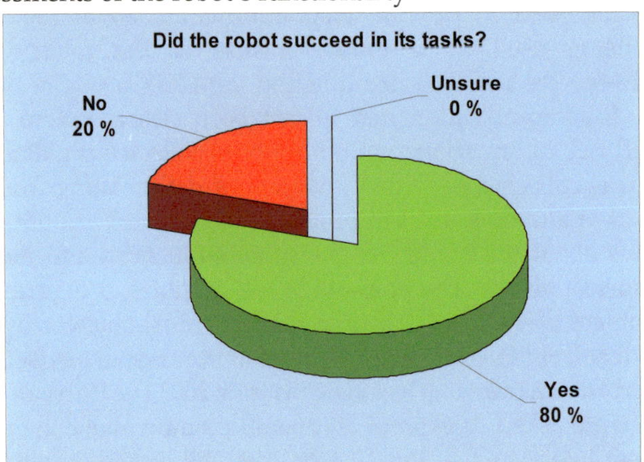

Fig. 12. Users' assessments of the robot's success in carrying out its tasks

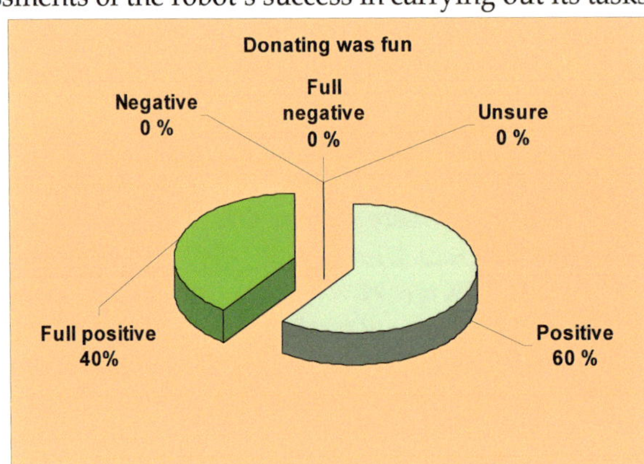

Fig. 13. The extent to which users enjoyed using the robot to make a donation

The researchers introduced a new set of questions for the Kupittaa Mall test event to evaluate users' perceptions and their appreciation (or otherwise) of the robot's donation system features. Figure 9 displays the results (45 % of the answers were a global positive response and 35 % a global negative response).

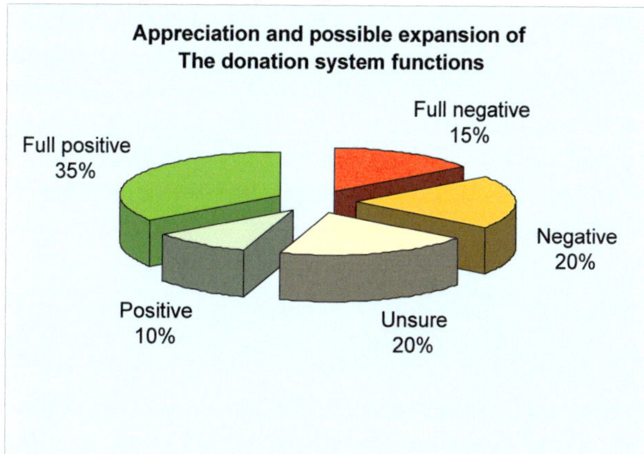

Fig. 14. Users' appreciation of the robot's donation system application and potential for expansion

The feedback obtained from participant OKO Bank employees and the Turkulainen newspaper tended to be in agreement: users initially perceived the robot as a living being and then, when it had become inactive, as a catalyst for emotional reactions and conceptual creativity.

5. RoboBeggar as a digitalized totem

It was noticeable was that the robot had so stimulated a number of passersby that they wanted it to act as a confidant with whom they could verbally share their experiences. The emotional reaction of people towards the robot was in fact so strong that many experienced it as *almost* human (Pitkänen, 2004). The calling voice of the robot was so successful in attracting the attention of passersby that many felt compelled to come to its aid (they assumed that the robot was in fact a person in trouble and they came to question the LSSY volunteers about its function).

During the first week of the fundraising campaign the robot made a strong social impact on passersby who knew about the its presence, purpose and role as a technological agent for raising funds for combating cancer. The RoboBeggar had thus in fact become a successful catalyst for collecting funds for the fight against cancer. Even after the LSSY had switched the robot off, the RoboBeggar continued to create a strong *momentum* as a catalyzer or emotional totem that served the interests of the cancer-fighting organization (Gareth, 1997). The LSSY participants *adopted* the robot by dressing it as one of their volunteers and by using its undoubted attractiveness to encourage people to make donations (Figure 10 shows the striking yellow LSSY vest with which the robot was clothed). The existence in people of unconscious ideations that can be concretized in, for example, symbols or totems has already been widely studied in psychological, sociological and educational research (Starr-Glass, 2004; Fiske & Fiske, 2005). The Merriam-Webster's Dictionary defines **totem** as *an object (as an animal or plant) serving as the emblem of a family or clan*. This definition implies that the RoboBeggar achieved the status of a totem.

Despite occasional failures in the technological functioning of the RoboBeggar, valuable information was nevertheless collected from the three means of feedback about donor behaviour and attitudes towards the robot. That data confirms that the robot's humanoid appearance and verbal skills were successful in affecting the emotional and cognitive behaviour of the people who came into contact with it. After it had been there for a while, the robot even began to assume a living role in the imagination of people who frequented the mall. People accepted the role of the robot as a catalyst in the campaign against cancer and as a means that people could use to make donations to combat the disease. In other words a purely technological robot was accepted by people and transformed into a highly emotive social totem.

6. Conclusions

Despite some unwanted and unforeseen conditions and events, the robot RoboBeggar received mainly positive reactions from users with regard to its functionality, its interactive tasks and its ability to create fun and amusement during the interactive learning process. The robot was successful in its essential fundraising and supportive purposes.

An analysis of the assembled data (from interviews, the newspaper article and from user and participant feedback) highlights the reasons why and the mechanisms by means of which the robot was transformed into a social totem that elicited some highly emotional reactions. It is apparent that the humanoid appearance of the robot and its verbal skills and appeal were among the main elements that elicited emotional responses from people and influenced their subsequent behaviour. This research tends to confirm that is through the agency of human imagination and perception that a robotic tool (in our case, the RoboBeggar) can be transformed into a totem of social value and effectiveness. It also became clear to the researchers that it is not only design and implementation that are important for the successful operation of a fundraising robot but that the robot's self-presentation and social aura are also crucially important factors for an overall understanding of why such a robot may be successful. The test case conducted in the Kupittaa Mall clearly shows how presentation and social aura compensated for the partial failure of the RoboBeggar's implementation. It is also clear that interpersonal and cultural elements influenced the way in which people perceived, accepted and responded to the robot as a potential personal interlocutor.

It is now clear that future developers of this model might do well to look at the possibility of technological improvement in the interface and e-learning modules. It is also clear that additional studies are required to investigate the emotional and psychological responses of users to advanced technological equipment that elicits emotional responses in human beings. It is also fundamentally important to be able to define exactly how influential both the hardware and software are in human-robot interactions so that effective guidance can be given to the designers of anthropomorphic robots of this kind. It is also important to be able to define the effect that particular physical environments and locations have on the efficiency of a humanoid robot's function so that it will be possible to place a robot in optimal situations for interacting with human beings.

7. Acknowledgments

Our special thanks are due to Osku Kannusmäki who assisted with the development of the RoboBeggar and its subsequent modifications.

8. References

Card, S.K., Moran, T.P. & Newell, A. (1986). The psychology of human-computer interaction, Published by Lawrence Erlbaum Associates, 1986. ISBN 0-89859-859-1, Hillsdale, NJ, US

Cooper, A. & Reimann, R. (2003). About Face 2.0: The essentials of interaction design, John Wiley & Sons Publishers., ISBN: 0-7645-2641-3, Indianapolis, IN, US.

De Haan, A. & Lipton, M. (1998). Poverty in Emerging Asia: Progress, Setbacks, and Log-jams. Journal of Asian Development Review, vol. 16, no. 2, 1998 pp. 135-176, ISSN 0116-1105

Etelämäki, T. (2000). Tiekirkot avaavat ovensa hiljentymiseen.(in English: Road-Churches open their doors to silence). Kirkon Tiedotuskeskus, Suomen Ev.Lut. Kirkko, 2.6.2000. Retrieved February 18, 2008 from: http://www.evl.fi/kkh/kt/uutiset/kes2000/tiek-00.htm

Faggiano E. & La Russa G. (2004). Robo-eLC: Enhancing Learning Hypermedia with Robotics, Proceedings of ICALT, IEEE Advanced Learning Technologies, pp. 465-469, ISBN 0-7695-2181-9, Joensuu, Finland, 30 August - 1 September, 2004, IEEE Computer Society, Washington, DC, US

Fides (2002). Katolinen hiippakuntalehti, 65 vintage, 3/2002, p. 6, ISSN 0356-5262

Fiske, A. P. & Fiske, Susan T. (2005). Social relations in our species and our cultures. Forthcoming in S. Kitayama and D. Cohen, Eds., *Handbook of Cultural Psychology.* New York: Guilford. 2005.

Gareth M. (1997). *Images of Organization,* SAGE Publications Inc., ISBN 0761906347, Thousand Oaks, CA, US

Harcourt, W. (2001). The capabilities approach for poor women: empowerment strategies towards gender equality, health and well-being, *Proceedings of Justice and Poverty: examining Sen's Capability Approach Conference*, Cambridge, United Kingdom, 2001.

Huang, S-M, Shieh, K. K. & Chi, C-F (2002). Factors affecting the design of computer icons, *International Journal of Industrial Ergonomics,* Volume 29, Issue 4, April 2002, pp. 211-218, ISSN 0169-8141

Hulme, D., Moore, K. & Shepherd, A. (2001). *Chronic poverty: meanings and analytical frameworks.* CPRC Working Paper 2. Institute of Development Policy and Management IDPM, ISBN 978-1-904049-01-2, Manchester, United Kingdom

Kouvolansanomat (2001). Archive, Old Culture, 2001/05/15. Retrieved May 17, 2007 from: http://www.kouvolansanomat.fi/arkisto/vanhat/2001/05/15/kulttuuri/juttu1/sivu.html

La Russa, G., Myller, N. & Sutinen, E. (2004). Robo-eLC: a learning appliance for e-commerce, *Proceedings. of IADIS International Conference on Applied Computing,* pp. 371-378, Lisbon, Portugal, 23-26 March 2004

La Russa, G. (2009). Manuscript available by author.

Marwedel, P. (2003). *Embedded System Design.* Springer; 1st edition, October, 2003, ISBN 1402076908, Kluwer Academic Publishers, Netherlands.

Miglino, O., Lund, H. & Cardaci, M. (1999). Robotics as an Educational Tool, *Journal of Interactive Learning Research*. Vol. 10, Issue 1, pp. 25-47, ISSN 1093-023X .

Mondi, M., Woods, P. & Rafi, A. (2007). Students' 'Uses and Gratification Expectancy' Conceptual Framework in relation to E-learning Resources, *Journal of Asia Pacific Education Review*, Vol. 8, No.3, pp. 435-449, ISSN 1598-1037.

Naidu S., Cunnington, D. & Jasen, C. (2002). The Experience of Practitioners with Technology-Enhanced Teaching and Learning, *Journal of IEEE Education Technology & Society*, Vol. 5, No.1, January 2002, pp. 23-34, ISSN 1436-4522.

Norman, D.A. (2002). *The Design of Everyday Things*, Basic Books, ISBN 0465067107, New York, NY, US.

Palo, M. (2006). Modern technology to help collecting: In Uppsala (Sweden), It's possible to donate with bankcards, *The Christian Democrats Newspaper*, 21 December 2006, Finland.

Papert, S. & Harel, I. (1991). *Constructionism*, Ablex Publishing Corporation, ISBN 0893917869, Norwood, NJ, US.

Pfeifer, R. (1997). Teaching powerful ideas with autonomous mobile robots, *Journal of Computer Science Education*, Vol. 7, No. 2, 1996, p. 161-186, ISSN 1744-5175.

Pitkänen, L. (2004). Robotti kerää tukea (*in English* "Robot collects support"), *Turkulainen*, 21 February 2004, p. 8.

Saariholma, K.. (a) (2001). Vaivaisukot - Tummatukka ja kirkonäijät, *Kirkonpalwelija*, 3/2001, p. 6.

Santaholma, K. (b) (2001). Vaivaisukot, *Multikustannus Oy*, 2001.

Starr-Glass, D. (2004). Exploring Organizational Culture: Teaching Notes on Metaphor, Totem, and Archetypal, *Journal of Management Education*, Vol. 28, No. 3, pp. 356-371, ISSN 1052-5629.

Securegive "Hercules" (2007). Website accessed July 13, 2007: http://securegive.com/gallery.html

Stratton, J. (2001). *The Desirable Body: Cultural Fetishism and the Erotics of Consumption*, University of Illinois Press, US, ISBN 9780252069512.

Swan, K. (2004). Relationships Between Interactions and Learning in Online Environments, *Sloan-C Editor for Effective Practices in Learning Effectiveness*. Retrieved March 17, 2008 from: http://www.sloan-c.org/publications/books/pdf/interactions.pdf.

Terhemaa, T. (2006). Pankkikortilla taivaaseen (*in English*: From bankcard to heaven), *Sakset ristissä*, The Evangelical Finnish Lutheran Church, 10.12.2006. Retrieved March 1, 2008 from: http://195.236.185.74/ktuutiset.nsf/9eba8c4dc67d4937c2256ca9004dc04d/e3dfce8af806d359c225723a003503dd?OpenDocument.

Uebersax, J.S. (2006). *Likert scales: dispelling the confusion*. Statistical Methods for Rater Agreement website. 2006. Retrieved April 12, 2009 from http://ourworld.compuserve.com/homepages/jsuebersax/likert2.htm

UNICEF, (2007). Website accessed July 13, 2007: http://www.unicef.ch/

Vo, M.T., Houghton, R., Yang, J., Bub, U., Meier, U., Waibel, A. & Duchnowski, P. (1995). Multimodal Learning Interfaces, *Proceedings ARPA 1995 Spoken Language Technology Workshop*, Austin, TX, US, January 22-25, 1995, Morgan Kaufmann publishers, San Francisco, CA, US.

Wanha Karhunmäki Centre (2007). Retrieved May 20, 2007 from: http://www .wanhakarhunmaki.net/rophengelk_eng.html

Zhang, Y., Finger, S. & Behrens, S. (2007). *Introduction to Mechanisms*. Retrieved July 13, 2007 from: http://www.cs.cmu.edu/~rapidproto/mechanisms/chpt4.html

Virtual patients as a practical realisation of the e-learning idea in medicine

Andrzej A. Kononowicz[1] and Inga Hege[2]
[1] *Department of Bioinformatics and Telemedicine, Medical Faculty, Jagiellonian University, Kraków, Poland*
[2] *Medical Education Unit, Ludwig-Maximilians University, Munich, Germany*

1. Introduction

Medicine has long been regarded as a discipline impossible to teach online. The complexity of the human organism and the intricacies of the patient-doctor interaction seemed beyond the reach of 'soulless' computers. However, a brief glimpse at recent advances in medical education reveals a different picture. The technically savvy Generation Y has entered medical school and their expectations of learning methods are different from previous generations'. Electronic devices like laptops, palmtops and smartphones are no longer expensive gimmicks, but have become indispensable elements of everyday life. This evolution coincides with significant changes in the healthcare sector. The ageing population demands increasing attention from medical personnel, resulting in a reduction in the time that can be devoted to teaching activities. In addition, the trend towards decreasing lengths of patients' stays in hospitals reduces the possibilities for medical students to observe the treatment process. It is in this context that harnessing computers to support the learning process by simulation of clinical scenarios may be very helpful, especially in the case of rare conditions.

Virtual patients (VPs) are "interactive computer simulations of real-life clinical scenarios for the purpose of medical training, education, or assessment" (Ellaway et al., 2006b). They offer a wide variety of (anonymous) patient-related data including medical history, physical and technical examinations, as well as laboratory tests. In most cases, the goal of the student is to find the right diagnosis and propose a correct medical treatment based on the data presented. Virtual patients provide a training opportunity in a risk-free environment before students are allowed to take part in bedside teaching. They may also be used to document the fact that all students have been exposed to all diseases defined by curricular objectives. The first virtual patient systems emerged in the early 70's (Harless et al., 1971) and since then have evolved significantly, taking advantage of new possibilities offered by the Internet and multimedia technologies. Research has shown that such systems enable students to learn clinical problem-solving more efficiently (Lyon et al., 1992). Increasingly, more and more medical schools are utilising virtual patients and indeed embedding them into their curricula.

As is often the case with new terms their meaning may vary in the community, which sometimes leads to misunderstandings. For that reason it is imperative to differentiate between the definition of a virtual patient as presented in this chapter and related concepts. Most virtual patients are entirely computer-based and should not be confused with standardised patients - i.e. human actors playing the role of patients (Barrows, 1993), nor with high-fidelity computer simulators connected to realistic robot mannequins (Bradley, 2006). However, some learning scenarios use a combination of these techniques. Also beyond the scope of this chapter are computer simulations of biological processes for research purposes, and electronic versions of patient health records created for medical documentation (Ellaway, 2004). Virtual patients consist of a set of patient-related medical data that can be organised in various forms, thereby allowing its division into different classes of systems. In linear systems the information is displayed in a fixed, predefined order. A user's decisions do not have an influence on how a case unfolds. Such cases can be created, for instance in the virtual patient system CASUS® (Figure 1) (Fischer, 2000).

Branched systems offer the students various paths to the solution of a case. The user is confronted with a clinical situation and may select one from a set of options. The user's decisions affect the treatment of the patient, which may in turn result in different outcomes. The underlying model of this virtual patient class is a directed graph with nodes presenting the current status of the patient, while the edges visualise the possible transitions between states. A model of a branched virtual patient is presented in Figure 2. A good example of a system from the class of branched models is Open Labyrinth (WWW_12).

Template-based systems (e.g. CAMPUS (Garde et al., 2007) or Web-SP (Zary et al., 2006)) offer students a very wide choice of possible options. The user may select from hundreds of interview questions, laboratory exams, physical examination and treatment methods. Most options contain standard values, but some have been changed manually by the case's author to reflect the characteristics of the condition in question. Many pre-built templates use standardised terminology, which assures high quality and completeness of the data. The core of virtual patients may also be implemented as a complex mathematical model enabling the simulation of physiological regulations such as renal function, respiration or body-fluid balance. The system GOLEM devised at Charles University in Prague is a set of nearly 40 non-linear differential and algebraic functions that describe almost 200 input and output variables (Kofránek et al., 2003). Using GOLEM allows many different clinical scenarios to be simulated (e.g. circulation insufficiency, renal disorders, diarrhoea). This enables students to learn by experimenting with the basics of physiology. Knowledge-based virtual patient systems (e.g. Docs'n Drug or D3 WebTrain) are created dynamically from declarative data by means of a knowledge interpreter (Holzer et al., 2005). A recent trend in the authoring of virtual patients is to embed them as 3D-characters in virtual worlds, like for example, Second Life (Conradi et al., 2009). In such an environment the user may work on the cases collaboratively with fellow students through the Internet. Margaret Bearman (Bearman & Cesnik, 2001)(Bearman et al., 2001) attempts to summarise the variety of virtual patient models by dividing them into two major groups: problem-solving and narrative models. In the former a student has to deal with a large set of raw information and has to decide by himself what is relevant. In the latter, a patient's personal storyline is presented. The first model allows more freedom in information collection, whereas the second encourages reflective learning through experience gained in observing the correct medical treatment patterns.

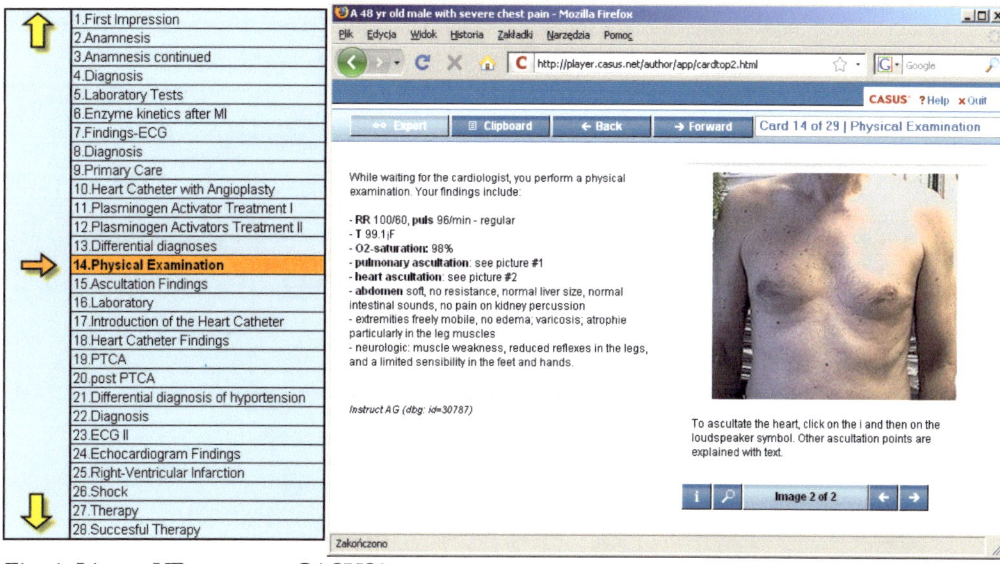

Fig. 1. Linear VP system – CASUS®

The introduction of virtual patients offers several advantages in comparison to the traditional methods of teaching clinical skills. The learning materials, following the e-learning paradigm, are accessible anytime and from almost anywhere. Once available they potentially require fewer personnel and resources to conduct the courses, depending on the level of integration with face-to-face teaching. They may help in solving some of the ethical problems arising with bedside teaching. Mistakes made by students have no significant consequences, which enables less stressful learning. Situations that involve strong emotions (like breaking bad news or dealing with violent, aggressive patients) may be practised in a safe-environment. Fewer students in operation theatres or clinics also reduce the danger of hospital infections. Virtual patients are more standardised in teaching than human actors and may convey a significantly higher amount of didactic information (Triola et al., 2006). The knowledge presented by these systems can also be rapidly updated when it is necessary to do so. Additionally, multimedia presentations, combining images, animations, video and audio clips are more stimulating than plain books, thus contributing to more efficient learning (Prensky, 2001). It has been demonstrated that virtual patient systems can be used to foster not only the learning of clinical and bioethical decision making, but also basic doctor-patient communication and history taking (Kenny et al., 2007)(Stevens et al., 2006).
Nevertheless, it is imperative to acknowledge that artificial models are not equivalent to encountering real patients and cannot entirely replace traditional bedside teaching. Modern state-of-the-art simulations are still a long way from the realism of symptoms exhibited by real world patients. Learning at home using virtual patients requires a lot of self-discipline and motivation, which is not always given. Deterioration in enthusiasm for learning can also be caused by a lack of personal face-to-face feedback from the tutor and easy interaction with fellow students. Computers connected to the Internet tempt users with the wealth of

distractions available online (as is also the case in other branches of e-learning). The current design of curricula in many medical schools makes it difficult to align the virtual patients properly with other didactic activities. A lack of computer skills and difficulties in accessing broadband Internet connections are sometimes still a hindrance.

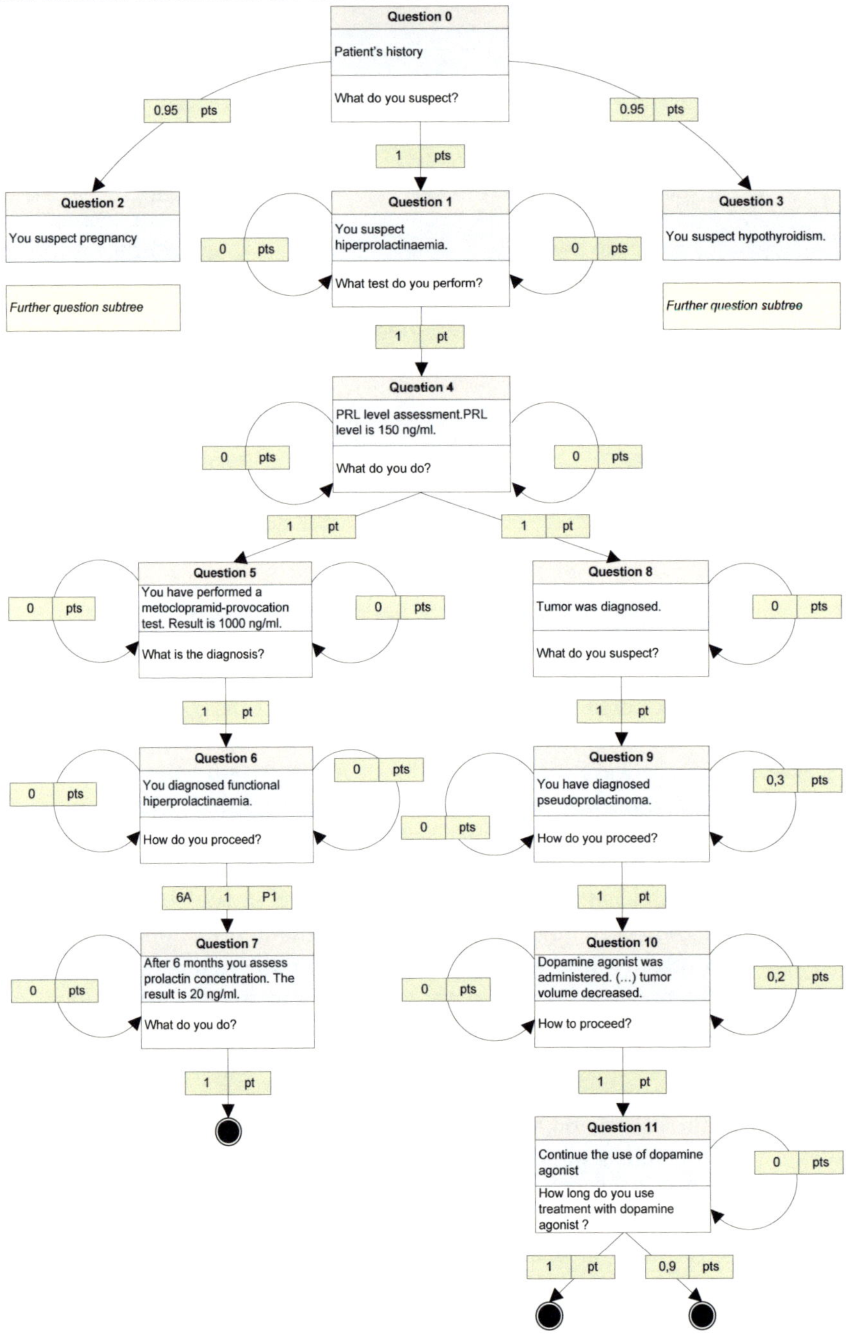

Fig. 2. Fragment of a branched model of a VP (simplified) (Kononowicz et al., 2005)

It is hard to decide which type of virtual patient is the best. The answer depends on many factors - e.g. learning objectives, concrete implementation of the model, applied learning scenarios. Our experience includes active development of virtual patient systems and participation in creation of their educational content in both linear (CASUS® (Fischer, 2000), (Hege et al., 2009)) and branched models (BIT Exam (Kononowicz et al., 2005)). Thanks to the participation in the European project eViP (→ section 7) we have also learnt in practice the usage of template-based systems such as CAMPUS or Web-SP. Each model has its strength and weaknesses. Based on our experience, we may conclude that linear models tend to be easier to implement and explain to content matter experts than branched. More than 1000 cases have been created within the CASUS® system and deployed at various universities around the world, whereas the usage of branched systems is, so far, less propagated. On the other hand linear models do not give students the freedom of choices they have in clinical practice. It seems more difficult to show realistically the consequences of actions in linear models than in branched. Template-based systems provide the learners with an abundance of choices but due to limited guidance they may not be an optimal choice for novice students, but more suitable for continuing medical education (CME). However, all of the above mentioned issues need to be formally tested by studies higher up the Kirkpatrick's levels of training evaluation (Kirkpatrick, 1998). This requires large scale and long term multi-centred studies that hopefully will be conducted in the coming years.

2. Virtual Patient Systems

Most virtual patient systems include a player, authoring tool, administration component, storage system, indexing facilities and assessment tools, all of which will be described in more detail in the following section.

2.1 VP Players

Virtual patient players are applications for displaying the content of patient cases. The player decides how the medical data should be presented to the student and how the user may interact with the system. Virtual patient systems exist which offer alternative players presenting the same underlying content in various ways (e.g. the CAMPUS system offers a resource intensive Classic Player and a fast, light-weight Card Player (WWW_02)). According to a survey by Huang et al. (Huang et al., 2007) most of the virtual patient players require an Internet connection. Offline VP courses distributed via CD-ROM and DVD-ROM have gradually been replaced by web applications running in generic web browsers. This trend can be easily explained by the advantages offered by fast updates to the content which are possible in centralised server-based installations. The disadvantages of web solutions, such as latencies in the transmission of multimedia rich content are compensated for by the increase in bandwidth of Internet connections and optimised media codecs.

Navigation in VP players most commonly involves selection of options with the mouse pointer. Depending on the data model, the case unfolds linearly or branches according to student choices. However, there are also players which are navigated by natural language recognition (Bergin & Fors, 2003). The learner types in questions to the virtual patient, orders medical examinations or therapy activities, and the systems tries to respond accordingly. The most technically advanced systems go even further by offering speech recognition (Kenny et al., 2007) or even analysis of a student's movements and gestures by video cameras (Stevens et al., 2006).

M-learning is a recent trend in distance learning which aims to miniaturise devices used for displaying educational content. This approach is also found in the design of virtual patient players, of which the first pilot projects are currently being implemented. In Figure 3 two prototypes are presented. The first one displays virtual patients in a generic web browser on a palmtop, but modified by XSLT transformation to fit the size of a small portable device. The second example shows a VP player implemented as a J2ME Midlet.

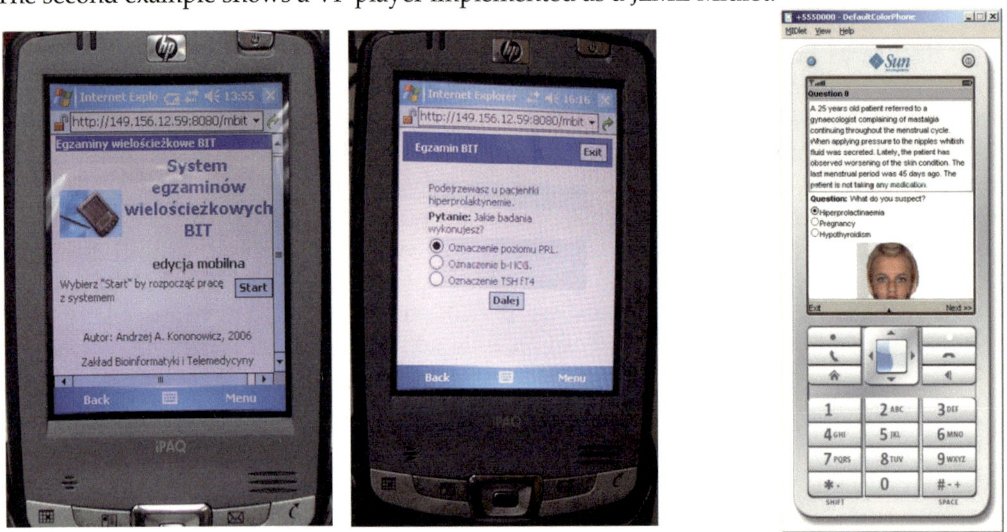

Fig. 3. Virtual patient players on mobile devices for palmtop and mobile phones (Kononowicz, Pękała, unpublished) - pilot project

The majority of publicly available virtual patient players only support content that conforms to the VP system's proprietary data model (Holzer et al., 2005). The attempts to build a generic VP player have not been very successful so far. However, new hope for a common solution that will facilitate interoperability between VP systems has been raised by the introduction of the MedBiquitous' MVP standard (→ section 5) (Smothers & Azan, 2008). A profile of this standard has been implemented by four systems used in the eViP project (→ section 7).

2.2 VP Authoring Tools

Virtual patient authoring tools are software components required for the creation of new content, or modifications to existing cases. The authoring tool usually reflects the characteristics of individual VP models. The goal often striven for is to design the authoring environment in a way that would enable a medical subject matter expert to construct and modify the core features of the virtual patient single-handedly without advanced IT skills. A good example of an easy to use authoring environment is provided by the CASUS® system (Figure 4).

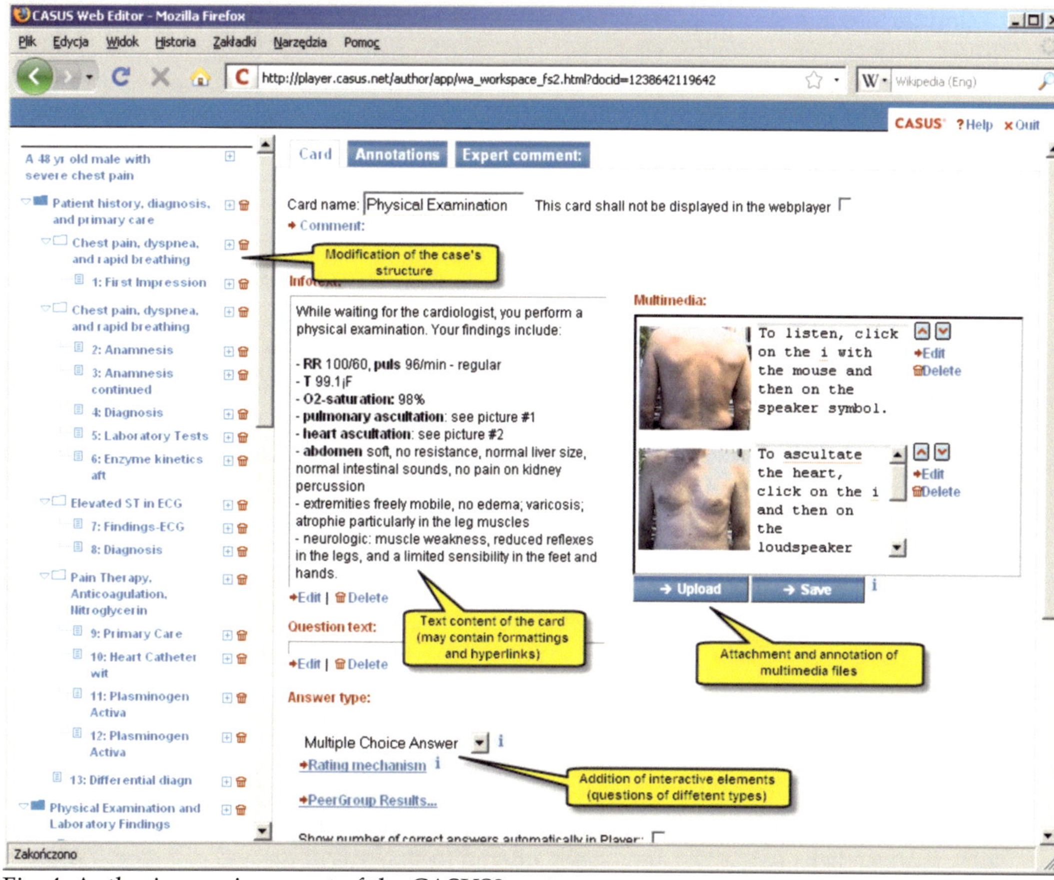

Fig. 4. Authoring environment of the CASUS® system

Operated by a standard web browser, it enables the authoring of cases from different locations without additional software installations. The simple linear structure is easily understood and supports fast development of cases. In the experience of one of the authors, post-graduate students who were assigned their own cases to create only required a quick 1-2 hour tutorial to sufficiently explain the basics of the tool, thus allowing the autonomous development of VPs.

External tools that were initially designed for other purposes are reused by some VP systems for the authoring of cases. A good example is the branched system Open Labyrinth utilised at St George's University of London. The graph-like structure of a case is designed in the Visual Understanding Environment (VUE) - an open source tool implemented at Tufts University (Kumar & Saigal, 2005). VUE facilitates the creation of conceptual maps of structured digital information. A map of a VP case developed in VUE is then imported into the Open Labyrinth environment for further processing (eViP's TRG, 2009).

2.3 Course Managers

Virtual patients are usually clustered into learning courses. Students are enrolled individually or in groups by tutors. More sophisticated solutions are based on federated identity-based authentication and authorisation infrastructure (AAI), which enables single sign-on (SSO) access to all e-learning services (e.g. SwitchAAI (Hämmerle, 2006)). Access to virtual patients should be protected for patient privacy reasons (→ section 6). Grouping patients into courses facilitates the fulfilment of didactic goals. An instructor may guide students along the recommended learning path by controlling the timing of virtual patient availability. Individual tutors and administrators may also be assigned to courses, thus helping to assure the scalability of the system.

2.4 Student Assessment Tools

One potential use of virtual patients is in student assessment (→ section 5). A role of virtual patient systems is to provide the teacher with an insight into students' activity in the learning module. Parameters such as login time and count, session length, percentage of visited content, answers given and their correctness are often monitored. One advantage of exporting the results into a universal format (e.g. CSV, Excel) is that it enables complex analysis of the results in external statistical packages, which in turn facilitates research into the effectiveness of virtual patients in teaching.

2.5 Reviews/Evaluation

High quality virtual patient content is a prerequisite to achieving good learning results. Virtual patient systems often incorporate internal or external evaluation tools; both for subject matter experts who review the content, as well as for end-users learning from the resources. Evaluation questionnaires, as developed by the eViP consortium (de Leng et al., 2009), (Huwendiek et al., 2009) are usually offered to students at the end of a case. They can be very tightly integrated with the VP system (e.g. in CASUS system) or be handled by external survey tools integrated with the evaluation.

2.6 VP Repositories and Referatories

Virtual patients can be disseminated by repositories and referatories. Repositories are electronic catalogues containing virtual patient packages that can be reused. Referatories, on the other hand, are collections of metadata describing the cases. They may contain information about the condition, learning objectives, licence agreements and prerequisite knowledge needed to solve the case, but do not actually contain the educational resource. For instance the eViP consortium creates their own referatory of cases which collects metadata regarding virtual patients published and repurposed within the project. Both institutions of the chapter authors contribute actively in the project by reporting their work in the referatory.

The presented overview of different types of tools available in virtual patients systems gives an insight into the diversity of functions required for virtual patient usage. There is a constant need for adding improvements in the already presented tools. However, while developing new or upgrading existing tools, backward compatibility to existing systems, which already have been well integrated into the curriculum, cannot be forgotten.

3. Virtual patient authoring

In this section we will highlight the didactical and medical steps which are important for the creation of virtual patients and a virtual patient curriculum.

3.1 Preparatory steps

In their article "A practical guide to developing effective web-based learning", Cook et al define four important steps which must be carried out before commencing with VP creation (Cook & Dupras, 2004). Although focused on web-based medical education courses, most of the steps apply to all kinds of VPs.
As a first step they recommend a needs assessment to identify problems and learners' and educators' needs. It is also recommended to think about the educational scenario in which the VP will be integrated. For example it could be used in a problem-oriented learning (POL) seminar, as a self-directed learning unit or for assessment (see next section for further information). This also determines the approximate length or learning time of the VP.
Steps 2 and 3 focus on determining the technical resources and needs of both educators and students. It is important to choose an appropriate learning system, which best meets the requirements defined in step 1. Most often the system already implemented at the local institution is used, but as seen in section 1 and 2 of this chapter there are numerous systems with different educational approaches already available. Related to this aspect is the choice of the VP model as described in the introduction.
In step 4 the commitment of all potentially involved staff and learners should be secured and potential barriers identified. Greenalgh suggests a team-based multidisciplinary approach as a successful model and emphasises the importance of incentives and rewards for all actively involved staff (Greenalgh, 2001).

3.2 Metadata definition

For the authoring of a virtual patient it is recommended to define educational metadata which includes learning objectives. The topic of a VP could be either a relevant disease which should be taught using a VP before a real patient is encountered, or a more exotic disease which is unlikely to be seen in a real patient.
As recommended by Fall et al (Fall et al., 2005), a crucial preparatory step before starting the creation of a VP is the definition of the clearly written learning objectives it should deliver. Cook et al. not only recommend concentrating on medical knowledge, but also on the skills and attitudes which the VP is designed to engender (part of step 1) (Cook et al., 2004).

A very good definition of a learning objective is given by Mager:
"An objective is a description of performance you want learners to be able to exhibit before you consider them competent. An objective describes an intended result of instruction, rather than the process of instruction itself." (Mager, 1962) and the Mager model (Mager, 1975). This model recommends that learning objectives should fulfil the following three requirements:

- should have a measurable verb (e.g. "explain", "demonstrate", "define", instead of "know")
- should give a specification about what the learners are taught

- criteria for success and competence shall be defined.

There are also numerous learning objectives catalogues which can be used as guidelines, for example the Swiss Catalogue of Learning Objectives (Bloch & Burgin, 2002) or the Objectives for the Qualifying Examination published by the Medical Council of Canada (WWW_11).
The target group is an important piece of metadata to define, because this has a major impact on the level of difficulty of the VP. Possible target groups are, for example, undergraduate medical students (pre-clinical, first year, final year, etc), interns and residents (continuing medical education - CME), nurses or physiotherapists.

3.3 Creation approach

When collecting material for the creation of VPs, there are three approaches used independently from the learning system:

- Taking a real patient's history and use his/her findings as base for the VP (e.g. implemented in the CASEPORT project (Holzer et al., 2005))
- Invent a patient history and collect/create all relevant findings (e.g. implemented in the CLIPP project (WWW_04))
- Repurpose an existing VP and adapt and enrich it to the curricular needs (e.g. implemented in the eViP project (WWW_06))

Of course for all approaches the copyright and patients consent aspects have to be considered (→ section 6).
For the first and the third approach the patient history might need to be adapted or reduced to match the learning objectives which are to be achieved by the VP. Using the second approach the continuity of the VP has to be considered (e.g. when collecting findings - especially images - the age, gender of the patient has to match!). Using the third approach can save time and money, if there is a VP which already meets most of the aspects defined previously.

3.4 Writing a VP

It is recommended by Fall et al. that a multi-institutional approach is used for creating VPs or VP curriculum, especially when they are to be distributed to other institutions other than your own. This enhances the applicability of these VPs at other institutions (Fall et al., 2005).
Although most of the VP systems offer an authoring system to enter VPs easily, there are also other possibilities to consider. For example the CLIPP project uses a word processor template for the authors to enter their VP which was transferred into a VP system after the final expert review. This offers authors the option to working offline, and no system-specific training is necessary. Using a wiki could be useful for a shared VP creation with more than one author.

Concerning the "real" text creation for the VP there are some aspects to consider.

- Use first or second person narrative wherever possible to directly engage the learner (Clark & Mayer, 2003).

- Multimedia can significantly increase the effectiveness of the VP (Marinopoulos et al., 2007) provided it is essential to the learning process and not just decorative (Masters & Ellaway, 2008).
- Include interactions in the form of quizzes, self-assessment or interaction with other participants is crucial (WWW_04).
- Consider the needs of students with disabilities. A good starting point for more information is the website of Equal Access to Software and Information (http://people.rit.edu/easi).
- Include evidence-based key-teaching points and references (Fall et al., 2005).
- For the linear model the structure of the VP is typically standard history, examination, investigation, diagnosis, treatment (HxExIxDxTx) (Ellaway et al., 2008).

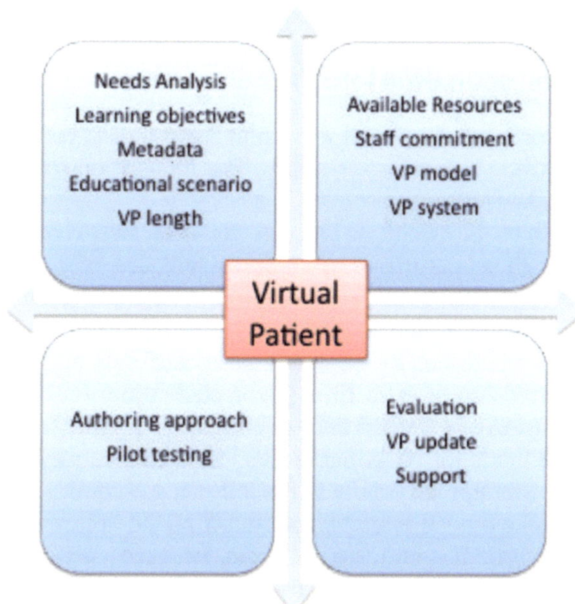

Fig. 5. Steps involved in the creation of a VP

3.5 Amount of time and money

A survey conducted by Huang et al. including 142 medical schools found that one third of virtual patients cost more than $50,000 and 80% cost more than $10,000. The median production time was 17 months (Huang et al., 2007). As an example, the CLIPP project had an overall production time of 310 hours per VP (60 hours/VP for writing) with costs of about $18,000/VP.

After having completed the VP creation, it is advised to have a content and didactic review.

Steps 8 to 10 suggested by Cook include the following:

- A formative and summative evaluation of the developed e-learning material should be planned (step 8). An evaluation during the integration period will give important feedback on the acceptance of the VP within the target group.
- Concerning implementation a pilot test among the target group of the developed material should be conducted (step 9). For example, a focus group can be used.
- Especially required time, how well the learning objectives have been covered, navigation and overall satisfaction should be evaluated.
- Step 10 recommends maintenance planning. This includes (depending on the chosen system course) moderation and monitoring, technical support, testing of external hyperlinks and, most importantly, the regular update of the content (Friedman, 1996).

Following similar guidelines more than 1000 virtual patient cases have been already developed or repurposed at the Ludwig-Maximilians-University in Munich or Jagiellonian University Medical College (e.g. in projects like NETWORM or eViP,→ section 7).

4. VP implementation scenarios into the curriculum

An important issue which, as mentioned in section 3, should be considered before creating the VPs, is their integration into the curriculum. The integration strategy is a fundamental aspect of acceptance by learners.

As mentioned by Cook et. al. (Cook & Dupras, 2004) as step 7 of developing e-learning courses, it is not enough to assume that students will use offered e-learning resources without enhancing their participation. This is in line with many other studies (Hege et al., 2007), (Baumlin et al., 2000), (Cahill et al., 2002).

The three major aspects mentioned by Cook are the accessibility and user-friendliness of the system/website, the provision of extra time ("protected" time) for the learners to complete the course and the inclusion of a reward and/or consequences mechanism.

There are numerous methods for introducing VPs into a curriculum, each with its own pros and cons which will be highlighted briefly in the following section.

The easiest way is to make the VP available as a self-directed voluntary module without any specific strategy of reward. It could, for example, be used to compliment a face-to-face teaching unit. But, as mentioned above, without encouragement the participation of learners the use of the VP will be very low (Hege et al., 2007). Therefore, for example, Fischer et al recommend the proper integration of computer-based cases into a face-to-face learning curriculum in combination with the assessment framework (Fischer et al., 2005a).

Another option is the integration of VPs as an obligatory self-directed learning module. This is often applied in undergraduate curricula. Successful work with a VP can, for example, be mandatory for passing a course, but this extrinsic motivation of students does not necessarily lead to a thorough working through of the VP (Hege et al., 2007).

To foster a more intrinsic motivation of learners the offering of incentives is an option. Student acceptance can often be as high as for obligatory VPs when they are motivated by the relevance of the content to an exam (e.g. for an OSCE), or by the use of VPs as a preparatory tool for courses like seminars, tutorials or bedside-teaching. At the medical school of the LMU in Munich we have had very good experience implementing VPs in the curriculum in internal medicine as self-directed preparation for the weekly seminar (blended-learning approach) and introducing exam relevance of the VPs' content.

A different integration approach is Learning by Teaching (LBT) or a student authored approach, which means that one or more learners create a VP (or parts of it) as an educational activity (Ellaway et al, 2008), (Kononowicz et al., 2008). For instance postgraduate medical students at the Jagiellonian University Medical College create virtual patients as one of their assignments in the computer science seminar. Creating the clinical scenarios autonomously involves a deep understanding of the condition of the patient and didactic expertise. It is recommended that the VP creation is supported by an expert tutor. After expert review these VPs can be integrated into the curriculum as learning cases.

Apart from integrating VPs as single encounters, they can be included in a curriculum many times with a development over the time. This might be especially applicable for complex VPs (Ellaway et al, 2008).

Communication between learners is encouraged for several reasons. For example, Lou et al. found evidence that collaborative learning is a more effective way of learning (Lou et al., 2001). As mentioned by Valcke et al. research results suggest that adding a communication component like a discussion board to an information component like a VP results in better student performance (Valcke & De Wever, 2006).

Integrating VPs successfully into a curriculum often takes years. For example at the LMU VPs have been used for undergraduate medical education since 1993, but students' acceptance at the beginning was very low. Only after years could VPs be established as an integral component of the curriculum. Currently 15 VP courses (consisting of 5-15 VPs) in 13 different content domains are included in the curriculum in different educational settings.

4.1 Assessment using Virtual Patients

In recent years the introduction of virtual patients for assessment purposes has increased. Courteille et al. (Courteille et al., 2008) conducted a pilot study on using an interactive simulation of patients (ISP (Bergin & Fors, 2003)) for an OSCE-based exam. They showed that the VP could reliably differentiate between the performances of the students. An important prerequisite for successful integration is the training of students in mastering the exam tool. They also found a surprising influence on the students' performance by the human assistants.

At the University of Ulm an online assessment tool (OAT) on the basis of the virtual polyclinic "Docs´n drugs" was developed including three clinical scenarios implemented for an assessment study. They found a moderate correlation with written exams (r=0.36) and a higher correlation between the three scenarios (r=0.50-0.56) (Waldmann et al., 2008).

Even for the United States Medical Licensing Examination (USMLE) Step 3 examination a computer-based case simulation (CCS) has been introduced. Dillon et al. report on the research findings in this case. They conclude that CSS can be used for large-scale high-stakes testing and represents a unique contribution to the overall assessment of physicians, but the administration of such complex assessment formats is a challenge (Dillon et al., 2002).

Another implementation scenario is the key-feature approach (Bordage et al., 1995). A key-feature is defined as "a critical step in the resolution of a problem". Two corollaries were added by Page and Bordage: It focuses on a step in which examinees are most likely to make errors in the resolution of the problem, and it is a difficult aspect in of the identification and management of the problem in practice (Page & Bordage, 1995).

A study by Fischer et al. introduced a 15-item key feature exam for assessing clinical decision-making skills in undergraduate students (Fischer et al., 2005b). They found that their modified key-feature exam (designed according to the guidelines provided by the Medical Council of Canada) was a reliable, valid and feasible method for assessing clinical decision making skills. The acceptance of students was intermediate and according to Fischer et al. could be improved by enhancing the curricular integration of such electronic case-studies.

5. Standards in virtual patients

Technical standards in e-learning establish norms which may help in achieving high quality content and foster the interoperability of educational resources. Since the development of virtual patients is expensive, standardisation efforts are in general very welcomed by the community. In order not to reinvent the wheel, standardisation bodies often reuse existing well-established specifications and extend them with new features characteristic for the given field of application. A keystone of many e-learning projects is the ADL SCORM(Sharable Content Object Reference Model) specification (WWW_01) which aggregates methods for describing the way learning resources may be packaged, structured and run in virtual learning environments.

A conceptual model for defining metadata of educational resources has been proposed in the IEEE 1484.12.1 Standard for Learning Object Metadata (LOM) (WWW_07). Having its representation in XML or RDF languages, the model presents a hierarchy of description items. Semantics of the leaf elements are defined by a branch of parental elements in the LOM description tree. The specification constrains the possible values of the items by defining permitted data types and controlled vocabularies. Allowing a high degree of flexibility in the usage of its elements, the standard supports the creation of its application profiles that represent the needs of individual communities.

The disadvantage of distributing virtual patients as generic SCORM sharable content objects with LOM metadata is the loss of descriptions characteristic for this kind of resource. A compromise between the adherence to well established standards and the addition of new features characteristic for medical education and VPs has been proposed by MedBiquitous. The MedBiquitous Consortium is a non-profit organisation aiming at establishing interoperability standards in healthcare education (Smothers et al., 2008b),(WWW_09). This organisation publishes profiled versions of well known e-learning specifications, such as IEEE LOM and SCORM, while also proposing new specifications e.g. for Activity Reporting and Medical Education Metrics. A particularly interesting proposal is the MedBiquitous' Virtual Patient (MVP) specification (Smothers & Azan, 2008a) which defines a format for exchanging case-based educational resources in medicine. Clinical and demographic data of a patient are saved in a Virtual Patient Data (VPD) document separately from the media resources (MR). A large set of predefined attributes characterising the virtual patient is defined, containing sections such as Medication, Interview Item, Physical Exam or Diagnosis. Media Resources are referenced in an IMS manifest file. The Data Availability Model aggregates both virtual patient data and media resources and makes them available for presentation in an order defined by the Activity Model (AM). The package's metadata can be expressed in Healthcare LOM - a profiled version of the IEEE Learning Object Metadata format. The MVP data is expected to be displayed in a run-time environment designed according to the MedBiquitous Virtual Patient Player specification (WWW_10). Figure 6 presents the relations between all elements of the MVP specification.

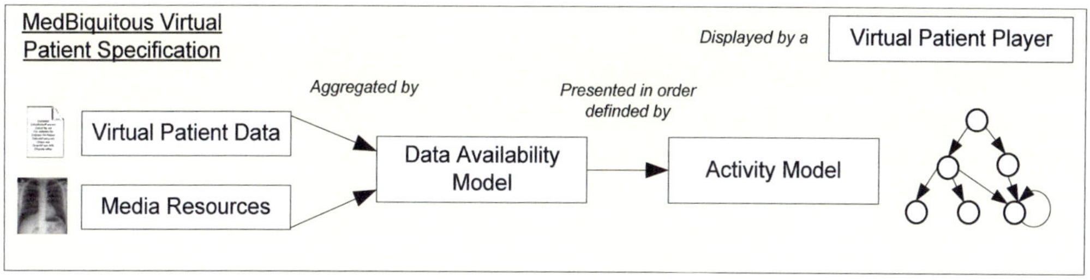

Fig. 6. Elements of the Mediquitous' Virtual Patient Specification

The MVP model has its binding in XML syntax. Together with files containing the Data Availability Model, Activity Model, Media Resources and metadata files, the content is inserted into a SCORM (IMS CP compliant) package which may be transferred between virtual patients systems. The Mediquitous' Virtual Patient Specification allows the exchange of VPs with different models including linear, branched or template-based types at different conformance levels (Kononowicz et al., 2009b). This has been successfully tested by the eViP project in which a profile of the MVP has been implemented in four VP systems (Zary et al., 2009). Unfortunately, due to high-level semantic differences, the import functionality still needs human intervention for some actions (e.g. while converting from branched to linear models).

There are also aspects of virtual patients which are not yet directly supported by the MVP specification. This applies, for instance, to question and assessment items which are frequently used by some VP systems (e.g. by CASUS). For such elements the use of external e-learning specifications is recommended (eViP's TRG, 2009). For instance, questions of various types may be easily implemented with the IMS Question and Test Interoperability (QTI) specification (WWW_08). This standard has been in development since 1999 and offers a data model for representing questions, tests and its results in a format that is independent of the authoring tool and assessment system. This enables storage of questions and their interchange regardless of the currently available e-learning infrastructure. Assessment items supported by the specification may be simple types (e.g. MCQ, MAQ, Sorting, Text Entry, Hot Spot, etc.) or be combined into more complex, customised types (i.e. composite items). The abstract QTI data model has its binding in XML syntax. The QTI specification is supported by many learning and assessment delivery systems (e.g. Moodle, Dokeos or Sakai). There are also implementations of this standard in VP systems (Pfähler & Holzer, 2009).

A further important problem that could be potentially solved by using standards is the integration of virtual patient systems with the existing e-learning infrastructure of universities (Holzer et al., 2005),(Kononowicz et al., 2009a). The SCORM Run-Time specification can be used to implement communication between a virtual learning environment (e.g. Blackboard or Moodle) and a virtual patient system. A Single Sign On (SSO) mechanism for various virtual patient tools can be implemented using Security Assertion Markup Language (SAML) implemented by the Shibboleth middleware (WWW_14). The Swiss Virtual Campus (SVC) is an example of an initiative aimed at the sharing of e-learning resources between Swiss universities (including medical faculties) via a federated identity-based authentication and authorisation infrastructure based on Shibboleth (SwitchAAI) (Hämmerle, 2006).

6. Intellectual property rights (IPR) and patient data safety in virtual patients (Miller et al., 2009)(WWW_15)

Intellectual property rights (IP) (WWW_16) are legal property rights over intellectual creations, such as books, movies, music, paintings, photographs, and software. Common types of intellectual property are, for example, copyrights, trademarks, patents and industrial design rights.

The IPR applicable in the context of virtual patients is copyright, which protects the expression of ideas or information. For a work to be protected by copyright, it has to be original and be expressed in a fixed material form, for example printed or electronically.

In Europe one does not have to register the copyright in the work before it is protected, but copyright is applied automatically. It gives the copyright holder the exclusive right to control the reproduction or adaptation of his work for a certain period of time.

The growing use and sharing of virtual patients in under- and postgraduate medical education increasingly brings into question the issue of how to protect digital content with the intention of it being shared among institutions, even worldwide. In the medical field apart from IPR issues there is the additional complexity of ensuring the patients' anonymity, since in most VPs clinical recordings such as images, x-rays or videos are included. If the patient-related data does not allow identification of the patient the media may be used without obtaining permission. However, due to advances in identification technology, and also because of the danger of missing a characteristic feature of the patient, it is always advised to get written consent from the patient.

To obtain permission from patients to use their personal medical information for a defined purpose a consent form is used. A considerable volume of litigation in many countries has focused on the issue of consent and as a consequence the doctrine of informed consent is assumed (Schachter & Fins, 2008).

Important initiatives to address these problems are described in the following section.

6.1 Creative commons (WWW_05)

Creative Commons (CC) is a non-Profit-Organisation, which develops and provides ready-made licensing contracts for the publication and distribution of digital media. CC is neither publisher nor contract partner of the copyright owners. For the simplest license the licensee only has to give the name of the grantor of the license. Modifications can be made depending whether commercial use is allowed or forbidden and whether edited versions can be distributed under the same conditions. This leads to six different licensing models with a combination of the following options:

- commercial/non-commercial use
- editing allowed/forbidden
- (no) redistribution under the same conditions

Which license form applies is clearly identifiable from the works' metadata, so normally there is no need for direct communication between creator and user. Despite its distinct advantages and overwhelming popularity, the CC is not ideal for sharing patient specific data in the form of digital content because it does not address the patient consent or withdrawal of consent and the scope of permission (Miller et al., 2009). More information can be found on the CC website http://www.creativecommons.org.

6.2 The CHERRI project

The 'CHERRI' (Common Healthcare Educational Recordings Reusability Infrastructure - Practice, Interoperability and Ethics) project has carried out surveys in the UK of existing practice, researched the medico-legal context and developed a consent and licensing model that is anticipated to meet the needs of all those concerned (Ellaway et al., 2006).
The following problems were identified: "lack of common process and standards at institutions, lack of connection between terms of consent and subsequent use, unnecessary duplication in local contexts as a safety measure, and a pervading culture of risk and uncertainty that is leading to both individual and institutional anxiety and loss of utility". CHERRI has developed a conceptual Consent and Licensing Model that is based on the CC model and which addresses both the uncertainty and the disconnectedness of current practice.
Several recommendations have been published in the CHERRI report, including that all creators and users of clinical recordings for academic non-clinical settings should be better educated and supported in a normalised way for quality assurance reasons.

6.3 Report on the Management of Intellectual Property in Virtual Patients by the eViP project (Miller et al., 2009)

Any project aimed at sharing work across several jurisdictions faces the challenge of having a mutually accepted exchange system. In addition to considering existing works, this system must also clarify how to share works that are jointly created or repurposed.
The European project about Electronic Virtual patients (eViP) that is described in more detail in section 7 aims to enhance the sharing of VPs among European healthcare institutions. Since traditional ownership of content and jurisdiction differs in the participating countries a major challenge for the project has been to come to a common IPR and patient privacy agreement. The report on the management of IP in virtual patients addresses these different legal situations. Miller et al. found that although there are undoubtedly disparities between countries, measures can be adopted to prepare and protect digital information which is intended to be shared. The project has adopted a framework for a licensing model and outlines a five-step process for preparing and protecting digital content in the medical and healthcare area:

- Step 1: Review IP and copyright status in partner countries. Since Copyright is handled differently under each country's national laws and is regulated throughout Europe via a complex web of international conventions, treaties, agreements, and European Community (EC) Directives, a review of IP and copyright status was conducted for each partner country.

- Step 2: Compare copyright issues between partners to identify both, similarities and differences. Apart from many similarities in eViP partner countries, the main differences that have been found relate to duration and ownership of copyright. This shows that sharing copyright protected works among partner institutions is feasible.

- Step 3: Create a common consent form for recording patient information based on similarities between partnering countries which is compliant with national regulations and institutional policies. Such a form is a simple document establishing who may gain access to the information, the purpose of the study, an explanation of the uses, disclosures and what kind of teaching is involved. Within the eViP project a generic consent form has been created (Miller et al., 2009). The consent form has been translated into all partners' languages and reviewed by the legal departments of each partner's institutions.

- Step 4: Implement common consent. The eViP project came up with a model describing how this issue should be tackled. The clearance model which was devised is not just for signing off existing VP content, it is also meant as a best practice guideline to clear new content for medicine and healthcare. A problem arises if a patient's consent is not available for existing VP content, for example, because it was given orally, or does not cover its use within the intended project. To obtain new consent from that patient can be be time-consuming or even impossible in some cases. The model, developed that the responsible clinician at the institution in question, should now evaluate the risk and decide whether to sign off the information. For this decision it is important to bear in mind the type, scope, quality and age of consent and the context in which is was obtained, and the value of the information and whether documentation exists. The advantage of this approach makes it less complex to decide how to handle valuable and difficult information, where otherwise the issues might not be addressed or the information discarded.

- Step 5: Adopt a simple and robust licensing model. Due to the limitations of CC concerning patients' consent and the scope of permission, the eViP project decided to develop an eViP common licensing model based on the current CC framework in cooperation with CCLearn [WWW_03].

Of course the results from the limited number of countries involved with eViP are not representative of jurisdictional differences or copyright laws throughout Europe. However, this process proved to be a very successful start in initiating and informing discussions with other countries, not just in the EU but also across the world. The process of introducing VPs at universities requires the support of the schools' leaders who need to clearly define the institutions' policies in creation and usage of these resources. Regulations regarding the ownership of the created cases, legal constraints in usage of patient-related data (consent form), possibilities for VP exchange, incentives for VP authors, the VP review process and a clear motivation for students to use VPs need to be thoroughly discussed. From our experience we have learned that such a process cannot be accomplished instantly but requires step-wise changes that can be introduced only in the course of a few years.

7. Virtual patient initiatives

As it has been pointed out in the third section of this chapter, the development process of virtual patients is expensive and time consuming. It involves collaboration of many technical and subject matter specialists, alignment of the content with the curriculum, as well as a thorough review by experts and evaluation by students. A possible solution to that shortcoming is to share the development costs among a group of institutions which would then share the new resources. Rather than reinventing the wheel by duplicating existing resources, part of the work could be acquired from common databases. Some learning and virtual patient initiatives are presented below to give an overview of the projects contributing to the popularity of virtual patients. By analysing their experience, conclusions for future e-learning projects (also for types of resources other than virtual patients) may be drawn.

7.1 Digital libraries and catalogues

In the course of the past years millions of web pages have been published on-line. The value of resources varies considerably. In order to find something valuable just by a plain Google search the educator needs to waste lot of time on separating the "digital" wheat from the chaff. Even when appropriate content has been found, a lack of clarity in copyright clearance may often prevent the resource from being used. Fortunately, initiatives like the digital library MERLOT (McMartin, 2004) attempt to solve this problem by establishing large collections of free, peer-reviewed educational assets. The MERLOT (Multimedia Educational Resource for Learning and Online Teaching) initiative was launched in 1997 at the California State University Center for Distributed Learning and supports the sharing of learning materials from a large number of disciplines beyond health sciences (like business sciences, history, mathematics, physics, etc). However, there are also projects that focus explicitly on medical content. A good example is the HEAL (Health Education Assets Library) project initiated around 1998 by a consortium of American medical colleges (Candler et al., 2003). The database enables educators to search and retrieve digital multimedia objects and reuse them in, for instance, the authoring of virtual patients. The majority of the catalogued assets is peer-reviewed and indexed by relevant controlled vocabularies (like MeSH). After submitting a query a list of resources is displayed consisting of a thumbnail picture of the asset and a set of metadata. External collections of multimedia items can be attached on request to the central HEAL server. The MedEdPORTAL initiative also belongs to a group of peer-reviewed educational healthcare resource repositories (Reynolds & Candler, 2008). In the scope of this portal are larger assets than are usually available via HEAL. Single multimedia items are regarded in MedEdPortal as educationally incomplete and need to be extended by more detailed didactical instructions. The content does not necessarily need to be digitalised since paper-based learning materials are indexed as well. An interesting fact is that MedEdPortal host a large collection of references to over 80 virtual patients (AAMC Virtual Patient Collection), from well-known medical centres like Harvard Medical School, the University of Pittsburgh and New York University School of Medicine. The resources in the MedEdPORTAL are available on request under Creative Commons licences. The portal promotes the authoring of resource-intensive materials by facilitating scholar acknowledgement of the work. This includes the establishing of a strict peer review process (25% submissions rejected, 41% accepted with revisions) and a uniform citation mechanism.

7.2 eViP

Electronic Virtual Patients (eViP) is a project co-founded by the European Commission aimed at establishing a large collection of virtual patients (over 300 cases) from institutions across Europe (Balasubramaniam & Poulton, 2008) (WWW_06). The project started in 2007 and is planned to run for three years, but one of the project goals is to propose a sustainability model that will ensure the continuation of the database after the year 2010. Consisting of nine partner institutions from five countries: United Kingdom, Germany, Sweden, the Netherlands, Poland and Romania, the initiative guarantees that the content will be diverse in terms of the language and healthcare culture. Since the institutions are using four different virtual patient systems (CAMPUS, CASUS, Open Labyrinth and Web-SP) the resources need to be transferable between different data models. The shared resources are repurposed by the participating universities to enable the use of their content in the local conditions of the partner institutions (Stachoń et al., 2008). This involves translation of the content, and changes to reflect the characteristics of the national healthcare system and the medical curriculum. As part of this process the content is often additionally enriched by new medical data, media resources or formative assessment items. The problem of making the content transferable between different data models was solved by implementing the eViP application profile of the MedBiquitous Virtual Patient (MVP) specification (Zary et al., 2009). The quality of the import/export process is assessed by a four level conformance testing metrics (Kononowicz et al, 2009b) and may (to a certain level of semantic complexity) be tested automatically by software tools. The process of transferring content between institutions also touches upon patients' privacy and copyright issues, and these are examined by the project in the context of different legal systems (Miller et al., 2009). Finally, the project will evaluate the success of the introduction of the created and shared content into the curricula, but these results are not yet available at the moment of writing.

7.3 CLIPP

Clerkship directors from thirty northern American medical schools participated in the three year long programme Computer-assisted Learning in Paediatrics Project (CLIPP) (Fall et al., 2005). A set of 31 virtual patients covering all learning objectives published by the Council on Medical Student Education in Pediatrics (COMSEP) was developed, implemented on the CASUS platform and extensively tested. Currently about 100 medical schools in the U.S. and Canada have subscribed to use the paediatric curriculum of CLIPP with about 20,000 users per year. The price of a set of CLIPP cases pre user was approximately equal to a price of a text book which made the project economically reasonable. A further reusage of these resources will reduce this cost even more.

7.4 PREVIEW

The increasing popularity of online, multi-server virtual environments (MUVEs) has encouraged educators to use them as platforms to engage students in e-learning. The most well known MUVE in use today is definitely Second Life (WWW_13). There are already many locations available in this environment specially destined for medical education (e.g. Healthinfo Island or VNEC) (Boulos et al., 2007). The enormous simulated world created by Second Life users also potentially provides a great opportunity to implement virtual patients. The goal of the PREVIEW project is to deliver problem-based learning scenarios in the world of Second Life (Conradi et al., 2009). A set of four PBL scenarios developed by St George's University of London for paramedic students uses virtual patients. Students - represented in the virtual environment by their avatars - work collectively on problem-based sessions involving the administration of first aid in a street accident, as well as in life-endangering situations simulated in the underground and a night club. Provided with a paramedic equipment box, participants of such session may carry out various observations and examinations on virtual patients. An interesting feature of the PREVIEW's virtual patients is the fact that they are implemented following the MedBiquitous MVP standard. This in turn allows part of their content to be imported automatically from other virtual patient systems. Since learning in virtual worlds is gradually becoming more and more natural for the new generation of 'digital natives' (Prensky 2001), the way of presenting VPs demonstrated by the PREVIEW project may become increasingly important in the future.

7.5 Other projects

The selection of initiatives presented above shows the diversity of projects fostering virtual patient development. There are plenty of further programmes involving the usage of computerised case-based simulations in medicine that could not be described here in more detail. Worthy of attention are the European NETWORM project – a set of virtual patients in occupational medicine (Radon et al., 2006), REViP - an Anglo-German project focussing on the embedding of repurposed and enriched Virtual Patients (VPs) within a Paediatrics curriculum (Balasubramaniam et al., 2009), CASEPORT - a national platform for virtual patients in Germany (Holzer et al., 2005) and the virtual patient collection managed by the International Virtual Medical School (IVIMEDS) (Harden & Hart, 2002), (Davies et al., 2006).

8. Summary

The goal of this chapter was to present the concept of virtual patients – i.e. computer-based simulations of clinical scenarios for educational purposes. Basic models and the technical aspects of both virtual patient creation and administration have been introduced, as well as standards for uniformly describing and sharing virtual patients. We have also touched briefly upon the underlying pedagogic concepts, including an overview of fundamental scenarios of virtual patient introduction into medical curricula. Since virtual patients deal with very sensitive data, the topic of patient consent and intellectual property rights in medical e-learning has also been discussed. This chapter has outlined many of the e-learning initiatives that have already emerged in supporting the creation and exchange of virtual patients. The outcomes of those initiatives give a valuable source of ideas on how to introduce virtual patients into educational settings successfully. Many aspects of virtual patients are relevant to case-based learning in general, including content domains outside of medicine and life sciences. We hope that some practical conclusions for non-medical e-learning applications can be drawn from this chapter. Despite their history, virtual patients are in many universities still poorly represented in curricula. We hope that our chapter will foster the usage of this learning method at medical schools.

9. Acknowledgements

The authors wish to thank Michael Timberlake and Prof. Dr. Harold C. Lyon for revising the paper linguistically. The authors are also grateful to Chara Balasubramaniam from St. Georges University in London, Dr. med. Martin Fischer and Daniel Tolks from the Private

University in Witten-Herdecke, Germany, Prof. Dr. Irena Roterman-Konieczna and Dr. Aleksandra Stachoń from the Jagiellonian University, Poland for their encouraging support and a thorough review of the chapter. Many thanks also to the eViP team for many fruitful and inspiring discussions.

10. References

Balasubramaniam, C. & Poulton, T. (2008). eViP: Electronic virtual patients. *The Newsletter of the Higher Education Academy Subject Centre for Medicine, Dentistry and Veterinary Medicine,* 01.16, pp. 6-7.

Balasubramaniam, C.; Poulton, T. & Huwendiek S. (2009). Repurposing Existing Virtual Patients; an Anglo-German Case Study. *Bio-Algorithms and Med-Systems*, 5, 9, 2009 ,pp.91-98.

Barrows, H. S. (1993). An overview of the uses of standardized patients for teaching and evaluating clinical skills. AAMC. *Acad Med*, 68, 6, pp. 443-51

Baumlin, K. M.; Bessette, M. J.; Lewis, C. & Richardson, L. D. (2000). EMCyberSchool: an evaluation of computer-assisted instruction on the Internet. *Acad Emerg Med.*, 7, 8, pp. 959-962.

Bearman, M. & Cesnik, B. (2001). Comparing student attitudes to different models of the same virtual patient. *Stud Health Technol Inform*, 84, 2, pp. 1004-1008.

Bearman, M.; Cesnik, B. & Liddell, M. (2001). Random comparison of 'virtual patient' models in the context of teaching clinical communication skills. *Med Educ*, 35, 9, pp. 824-832.

Bergin, R. & Fors, U. (2003). Interactie simulaed patient - an advanced tool for student-activate learning in medicine and healthcare. *Computers&Education,* 40, pp. 361-376

Bloch, R; Burgin, H (2002). The Swiss Catalogue of Learning Objectives. *Med Teach,* 24, pp. 144-150.

Bordage, G.; Brailovsky, C.; Carretier, H. & Page, G. (1995). Content validation of key features on a national examination of clinical decision-making skills. *Acad Med*, 70, pp. 276–281.

Boulos, M. N. K.; Hetherington, L. & Wheeler, S. (2007). Second Life: an overview of the potential of 3-D virtual worlds in medical and health education. *Health Info Libr J*, 24, pp. 233-245.

Bradley, P. (2006) The history of simulation in medical education and possible future directions, *Med Educ*, 40, pp. 254-262.

Cahill, D.; Cook, J., Sithers A., Edwards, J. & Kenkins, J. (2002). Evaluation of an online postgraduate education programme. *Med Teach.* 24, 4, pp. 425-428

Candler, C. S.; Uijtdehaage, S. H. J. & Dennis, S. E. (2003). Introducing HEAL: the Health Education Assets Library. *Acad Med*, 78, pp. 249-253.

Clark, R & Mayer, R. (2003). *e-learning and the science of instruction*. Pfeiffer, San Francisco

Cook, D.A. & Dupras, D. M. (2004). A Practical Guide To Developing Effective Web-based Learning. *J Gen Intern Med*, 19, pp. 698-707.

Conradi, E.; Kavia, S.; Woodham L.; Poulton T. & Savin-Baden M., (2009). PREVIEW: Problem-based learning in virtual worlds. *The Newsletter of the Higher Education Academy Subject Centre for Medicine, Dentistry and Veterinary Medicine,* 01.18, pp. 20-22.

Courteille, O.; Bergin, R., Stockeld D., Ponzer S. & Fors U. (2008). The use of a virtual patient case in an OSCE-based exam - A pilot study. *Med Teach,* 30, pp. e66-e76.

Davies, S.; Smith, S. R.; Harden, R.; Boucheny, T. & Allan, S. (2006). The IVIMEDS approach to virtual patients. *The Newsletter of the Higher Education Academy Subject Centre for Medicine, Dentistry and Veterinary Medicine,* 01.12, pp. 30-31.

de Leng, B.; Donkers, J.; Brasch, C.; Huwendiek, S. & Kononowicz A. A. (2009). Evaluation instruments to support educators in making deliberate choices when they use virtual patients to teach clinical reasoning, *International Conference of Virtual Patients,* ICVP'09 Kraków.

Dillon, G. F.; Clyman, S. G; Clauser, B. E. & Margolis, M. J. (2002). The Introduction of Computer-based Case Simulations into the United States Medical Licensing Examination. *Acad Med,* 77, 10, pp. 94-96.

Ellaway, R. (2004). Modeling virtual patients and virtual cases. *E-Learning Discourse,* MedBiquitous.

Ellaway, R.; Cameron, H.; Ross, M.; Laurie, G.; Maxwell, M. & Pratt, R. (2006). Clinical Recordings for academic non-clinical setting. http://www.cherri.mvm.ed.ac.uk [accessed 01.04.2009].

Ellaway, R.; Candler, C.; Greene, P. & Smothers, V. (2006). An Architectural Model for MedBiquitous Virtual Patients. *Technical report,* MedBiquitous, Baltimore

Ellaway, R.; Poulton, T; Fors, U.; McGee, J. & Albright, S. (2008). Building a Virtual Patient Commons. *Med Teach,* 30, pp. 170-174.

eViP's Technical Reference Group (2009). Best Practice Guidelines for the eViP application profile and associated conformance metrics, http://www.virtualpatients.eu [accessed 01.04.2009].

Fall, L. H.; Berman, N. B.; Smith, S.; White C. B.; Woodhead J. C. & Olson A. L. (2005). Mulit-institutional development of a computer-assisted Learning Program for the Pediatrics Clerkship: The CLIPP project. *Acad Med,* 80, 9, pp. 847-855

Fischer, M. R. (2000). An authoring and learning tool supporting diagnostic reasoning; Use of Computers in Medical Education (Part II), *Zeitschrift für Hochschuldidaktik,* chapter CASUS, pp. 87-98.

Fischer, M. R.; Aulinger, B. & Kopp, V (2005a). Implementierung von Computerlernfällen in das Curriculum der Inneren Medizin. *GMS Z Med Ausbild* 22, 1, Doc12

Fischer, M. R.; Kopp, V.; Holzer, M.; Ruderich, F. & Jünger, J. (2005b). A modified electronic key-feature examination for undergraduate medical students: validation threats and opportunities. *Med Teach,* 27, 5, pp. 450-455.

Friedman R. B. (1996). Top ten reasons the World Wide Web may fail to change medical education. *Acad Med,* 71, pp. 979-981.

Garde, S.; Heid, J.; Haag, M.; Bauch, M.; Weires, T. & Leven, F. J. (2007). Can design principles of traditional learning theories be fulfilled by computer-based training systems in medicine: the example of CAMPUS. *Int J Med Inform* 76, 2-3, pp. 124-129.

Greenalgh, T. (2001). Computer aided learning in undergraduate medical education. *BMJ,* 322, pp. 40-44.

Harden, R. M. & Hart, I. R. (2002). An international virtual medical school (IVIMEDS): the future for medical education? *Med Teach,* 24, pp. 261-267.

Harless, W. G.; Drennon, G. G; Marxer, J. J.; Root, J. A. & Miller, G. E. (1971). CASE: a Computer-Aided Simulation of the Clinical Encounter. *J Med Educ,* 46, 5, pp. 443-448

Hämmerle, L. (2006). SWITCHaai: Shibboleth-based Federated Identity Management in Switzerland. *Proceedings of CESNET 2006 Conference,* Prague

Hege, I.; Kopp, V.; Adler M.; Radon, K.; Mäsch, G.; Lyon, H.& Fischer MR (2007). Experiences with different integration strategies of case-based e-learning. *Med Teach,* 29, 8, pp. 791-797

Hege, I.; Kononowicz, A. A.; Pfähler, M.; Adler M. & Fischer, M. R. (2009). Implementation of the MedBiquitous Standard into the learning system CASUS. *Bio-Algorithms and Med-Systems,* 5, 9 ,pp. 51-55

Holzer, M.; Hörnlein, A.; Atzmueller, M.; Singer, R.; Schlott, S.; Leven, F.; Puppe, F. & Fischer, M. (2005). Interoperability of case-based training systems in medicine: The CASEPORT approach. *Proceedings of eLearning in der Medizin und Zahnmedizin,* pp. 3-12, Quintessenz Verlag, Berlin

Huang, G.; Reynolds, R. & Candler C. (2007). Virtual Patient Simulation at U.S. and Canadian Medical Schools. *Acad Med,* 82, 5, pp. 446-451

Huwendiek, S.; Haider, H.; Tönshoff, B. & de Leng, B. (2009). Evaluation of curricular integration of virtual patients: Development of a student questionnaire and a reviewer checklist within the electronic virtual patient (eVIP) project. *Bio-Algorithms and Med-Systems,* 5, 9, pp. 35-44

Kenny, P.; Parsons, T.; Gratch, J.; Leuski, A. & Pizzo, A. (2007). Virtual Patients for Clinical Therapist Skills Training. *Lecture Notes in Computer Science* 4722, pp. 197-210

Kirkpatrick, D. L. (1998). Evaluating training programs: the four levels, Berrett-Koehler Publishers, ISBN 1576750426, 9781576750421, San Francisco

Kofránek, J.; Andrlík, M. & Kripner, T. (2003). Virtual patient behind the screen using computer simulator GOLEM. *Proceedings from the 5th IFAC Symposium on Modelling and control in biomedical systems,* pp. 473-477, Melbourne

Kononowicz, A. A.; Żabińska-Popiela, M.; Roterman-Konieczna I. & Krzysiek J. A Case-Based Examination System with Multiple Answer Paths. *Proceedings of AMEE 2005,* Amsterdam

Kononowicz, A. A.; Stachoń, A. J.; Romanowska-Pawliczek, A.; Obtułowicz, P.; Pyrczak, W. & Roterman-Konieczna, I. (2008). Learning-By–E–Teaching: Experience from Involving Students in Preparation of E-Learning Materials. *Bio-Algorithms and Med-Systems (in press)*

Kononowicz, A. A.; Hege, I., Adler, M., de Leng, B., Donkers, J. & Roterman I. (2009a). Requirements on Virtual Learning Environments generated by the use of Virtual Patients. *Proceedings of the KU KDM'09 Conference,* pp. 52-54, Zakopane

Kononowicz, A. A.; Heid J.; Donkers J.; Hege I.; Woodham L. & Zary N. (2009b). Development and Validation of Strategies to Test for Interoperability of Virtual Patients, *Accepted for MIE 2009 Conference,* August 30 - September 2, 2009, Sarajevo

Kumar, A. & Saigal, R. (2005). Visual understanding environment. *Proceedings of the 5th ACM/IEEE-CS Joint Conference on Digital Libraries JCDL '05.,* pp. 413, June 7–11, 2005, Denver, Colorado, USA

Lou, Y.; Abrami, P. C. & D'Apollonia, S. (2001). Small group and individual learning with technology: a meta-analysis. *Rev Ed Res* 71, pp. 449-521

Lyon, HC.; Healy, JC.; Bell, JR.; O'Donnell, JF.; Shultz, EK.; Moore-West, M.; Wigton, RS.; Hirai, F. & Beck, JR. (1992). PlanAlyzer, an interactive computer-assisted program to teach clinical problem solving in diagnosing anemia and coronary artery disease. *Acad Med* 67(12), pp. 821-828

Mager, R. (1975). *Preparing Instructional Objectives*. Belmont, CA: Fearon-Pitman Publishers.

Mager, R. (1962). *Preparing Instructional Objectives*. Palo Alto, CA: Fearon Publishers.

Marinopoulos, S.; Dorman, T.; Ratanawongsa, N., Wilson, L., Ashar, B., Magaziner, J.; Miller, R.; Thomas, P.; Prokopowicz, G.; Qayyum, R. & Bass, E. (2007). *Effectiveness of continuing medical education*. Rockville, MD: Johns Hopkins Evidence-based Practice center, Evidence report/Technology Assessment No. 149. Agency for Healthcare Research and Quality.

Masters, K. & Ellaway R., (2008). e-learning in medical education Guide 32 Part 2: Technology, management and design. *Med Teach*, 30, pp. 474-489

McMartin, F. (2004). MERLOT: A Model for User Involvement in Digital Library Design and Implementation. *Journal of Digital Information*, 5, 3, http://jodi.tamu.edu/Articles/v05/i03/McMartin/

Miller, A.; Balasubramaniam, C. & Fischer, M. R. (2009). Report on the Management of Intellectual Property in Virtual Patients by the eViP project. http://www.virtualpatients.eu [accessed 01.04.2009]

Page, G & Bordage, G. (1995). The medical council of Canada's key features project: a more valid written examination of clinical decision-making skills. *Acad Med*, 70, pp. 104–110

Pfähler M. & Holzer M. (2009). Erweiterung des QTI-Standards zur Unterstützung von LongMenu-Fragen sowie Abbildung spezifischer Metadaten in QTI 2.1. *GMS Med Inform Biom Epidemiol*. 2009;5(1):Doc06.

Prensky M. (2001). Digital Natives, Digital Immigrants. *On the Horizon*, NCB University Press, 9, 5.

Radon, K.; Kolb, S.; Reichert, J.; Baumeister, T.; Fuchs, R.; Hege, I.; Praml, G.; Fischer, M. & Nowak, D. (2006). Case-based e-learning in occupational medicine-The NetWoRM Project in Germany. *Ann Agric Environ Med*, 13, pp. 93-98

Reynolds, R. J. & Candler, C. S. (2008). MedEdPORTAL: Educational scholarship for teaching. *Journal of Continuing Education in the Health Professions*, 28, 2, pp. 91-94

Schachter, M. & Fins, J. J. (2008). Informed Consent Revisited: A Doctrine in the Service of Cancer Care. *The Oncologist*, 13, 10, pp. 1109-1113

Smothers, V. & Azan, B. (2008a). MedBiquitous Virtual Patient Specifications and Description Document; Technical report, MedBiquitous Consortium, Baltimore.

Smothers, V.; Greene, P.; Ellaway, R. & Detmer, D. E. (2008b). Sharing innovation: the case for technology standards in health professions education. *Med Teach*, 30,2, pp. 150-154.

Stachon, A. J.; Kononowicz A. A.; Roterman-Konieczna, I.; Hege, I.; Holzer M.; Adler M. & Fischer, M. R. (2008). Scenarios for the implementation of VPs into the medical curriculum by the example of JUMC's participation in the eViP-Programme; *Proceedings of AMEE 2008 Conference*, pp. 155, Prague

Stevens, A.; Hernandez, J.; Johnsen, K.; Dickerson, R.; Raij, A.; Harrison, C.; DiPietro, M.; Allen, B.; Ferdig, R.; Foti, S.; Jackson, J.; Shin, M.; Cendan, J.; Watson, R.; Duerson, M.; Lok, B.; Cohen, M.; Wagner, P. & Lind, D. S. (2006). The use of virtual patients to teach medical students history taking and communication skills., *Am J Surg*, 191, 6, pp. 806-811

Triola, M.; Feldman, H.; Kalet, A. L.; Zabar, S.; Kachur, E. K.; Gillespie, C.; Anderson, M.; Griesser, C. & Lipkin, M. (2006). A randomized trial of teaching clinical skills using virtual and live standardized patients. *J Gen Intern Med*, 21, 5, pp. 424-429

Valcke, M.; De Wever B. (2006). Information and communication technologies in higher education: evidence-based practices in medical education. *Med Teach*, 28, 1, pp. 40-48

Waldmann, U.; Gulich M. S. & Zeitler H. P. (2008). Virtual patients for assessing medical students-important aspects when considering the introduction of a new assessment format. *Med Teach*, 30, 17-24

Zary, N.; Johnson, G.; Boberg, J. & Fors, U. G. H. (2006). Development, implementation and pilot evaluation of a Web-based Virtual Patient Case Simulation environment-Web-SP. *BMC Med Educ*, 6, 10

Zary N., Hege I., Heid J., Woodham L., Donkers J. & Kononowicz A. A. (2009) Enabling Interoperability, Accessibility and Reusability of Virtual Patients across Europe - Design and Implementation. *Accepted for MIE 2009 Conference*, August 30 - September 2, 2009, Sarajevo

10.1 Web resources

[WWW_01] ADL SCORM http://www.adlnet.gov/Scorm [accessed 30.03.2009]

[WWW_02] CAMPUS-Software http://www.medizinische-fakultaet-hd.uni-heidelberg.de/CAMPUS-Software.109992.0.html?&L=en [accessed 01.04.2009]

[WWW_03] CCLearn http://learn.creativecommons.org/. [Accessed 02.04.2009]

[WWW_04] CLIPP Project http://www.clippcases.org [accessed 30.03.2009]

[WWW_05] Creative Commons http://www. creativecommons.org [accessed 01.04.2009]

[WWW_06] eViP Project, http://www.virtualpatients.eu [accessed 30.03.2009]

[WWW_07] IEEE Standard for Learning Object Metadata, http://ltsc.ieee.org/wg12/ [accessed 30.03.2009]

[WWW_08] IMS Question & Test Interoperability Specification

[WWW_09] MedBiquitous, http://www.medbiq.org/ [accessed 30.03.2009]

[WWW_10]MedBiquitous, Virtual Patient Working Group http://www.medbiq.org/working_groups/virtual_patient/index.html [accessed 30.03.2009]

[WWW_11] Medical Council of Canada. Objectives for the qualifying examination. http://www.med.mun.ca/ugme/docs/Complete_Objectives-e.pdf

[WWW_12] Open Labyrinth http://sourceforge.net/projects/openlabyrinth [accessed 30.03.2009]

[WWW_13] Second Life http://secondlife.com/ [accessed 30.03.2009]

[WWW_14] Shibboleth http://shibboleth.internet2.edu/ [accessed 30.03.2009]

[WWW_15] World Intellectual Property Organization. What is Intellectual Property? http://www.wipo.int/about-ip/en/ [Accessed 02.04.2009]

[WWW_16] WIPO Convention, Art 2, para. Viii, (1967). Available online at: http://www.wipo.int/treaties/en/convention/trtdocs_wo029.html. [Accessed 02.04.2009]

19

Data Warehouse Technology and Application in Data Centre Design for E-government

Xuanzi Hu
Dongguan College
China

1. Introduction

E-government allows governments to service citizens in a more timely, effective, and cost-efficient method. E-Government services focus on four main customers: citizens, the business community, government employees, and government agencies. E-government can provide four types of services, which are Government-to-Citizen (G2C), Government-to-Business (G2B), Government-to-Employee (G2E), and Government-to-Government (G2G). E-government system has already been very popular all over the world, because E-government helps to disseminate information. Further, it aids in the collection of information that helps decision makers serve citizens more effectively. E-Government allows government agencies to centralize decision making.

China have started first E-Government program in the late 1980s, in which the governments both at central and local levels built up office automation (OA) systems and established an intranet, subsequently the Central Government of China had formally launched five Golden Projects (Golden Bridge Project, Golden Customs Project, Golden Card Project, Golden Tax Project and Government online Project) aimed at building E-Government in China ever since 1990s. After realizing five Golden Projects, Chinese government has set ambitious visions in the implementation of E-Government: quicken the pace of change in government functions to suit the requirement of reform, opening up and modernization policies, improve the performance of government operation, introduce new government measures in a scientific manner and more effective mechanisms to monitor the economic activities, place a greater emphasis on central co-ordination and transparency of government work, carry out administrative functions in accordance with law and provide better service for the public. To meet above ambitious visions, the Central Government of China have programmed to establish four governance information resource databases in next five years, governance information resource databases consist of four databases: population basic information database, judicial entity basic information database, natural resource and geography basic information database, and macroscopically economy database.

A data warehouse has been defined as a collection of data in support of management decisions which is: subject oriented, integrated, nonvolatile, time variant. Data warehouse, as a collection of database or data management technologies, emerged in the early 1990s. The data warehouse has now been more generally seen as a strategy to bring heterogeneous data together under a common conceptual and technical umbrella and to make the data available for new operation or decision support application. Three intrinsic features of data warehouse are data integration, data completeness and decision-making support.

Management of government is from top to down, but collecting data of government is from down to top. To support construction of four databases, building data center is becoming an important project for E-government. Nanhai city of Guangdong province is a leading the way of E-government in China, this chapter put forward the design of data center based on data warehouse technology for Nanhai city, this solution not only consider to provide data for high level four databases, but also solve integration, share and exchange of data in various departments of Nanhai city, especially devised application database based on data warehouse technology for better utilizing accumulated data.

The remainder of this chapter is organized as follows. The section 2 provides an introduction to the basic technology of data warehouse for reader to understand explicitly data centre design. In the following sections, data centre design of Nanhai city is depicted. In section 3, we summarize requirement analysis of data centre. In Section 4, we give the architecture of data center based on data warehouse technology. Section 5 gives some pivotal techniques of realizing data center. Finally, Section 6 gives the conclusion.

2. Data warehouse technology

2.1 Definition of Data Warehouse

A data warehouse is a subject oriented, integrated, non-volatile, and time-variant collection of data in support of management decisions. The goal of using a data warehouse is to allow businesses and organizations to make strategic decisions. According to the definition of a data warehouse, a data warehouse generally has following four characteristics.

(a) Subject-Oriented

Subject-Oriented means that the main objective of data warehouse is to facilitate decision process of a company, and within any company data naturally concentrates around subject areas, so information gathering in data warehouse is aiming for a specific subject rather than for the functions of a company.

(b) Integrated

Being integrated means that the data is collected within the data warehouse, that can come from different tables, databases or even servers, but can be combined into one unit that is relevant and logical for convenience of making strategic decision.

(c) Non-volatile

Being the snapshot of operational data on a given specific time, the data in the data warehouses should be stable. The data in the data warehouse usually be added, but it should rarely be deleted.

(d) Time-variant

Time-variant means that all the data within the data warehouse can be found with a given period of time.

2.2 Architecture of Data Warehouse

Data warehouses and their architectures vary depending upon the specifics of an organization's situation. Many architectures of data warehouse exists in the literature, According to study of Thilini Ariyachandra and Hugh J. Watson, Data Warehouse has five architectures: (1) independent data marts, (2) data mart bus architecture with linked dimensional data marts, (3) hub-and-spoke, (4) centralized data warehouse (no dependent data marts), and (5) federated. Other architectures tend to be variations on the five.

(1) Independent data marts

This architecture is common for organizational units to develop their own data marts. These marts are independent of other marts. These marts typically have inconsistent data definitions and use different dimensions and measures, so the architecture is difficult to analyze data across all the marts. Figure 1 shows the architecture for independent data marts.

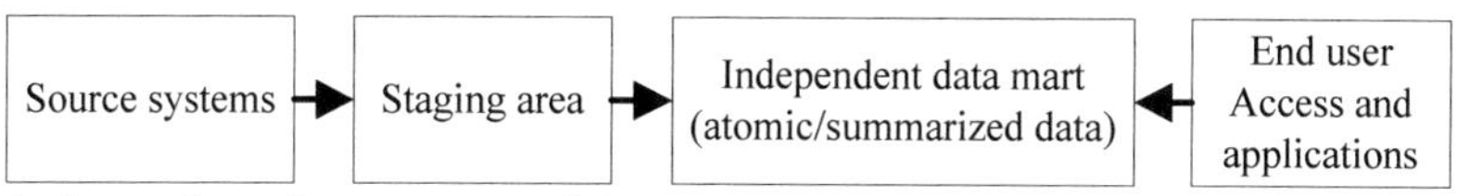

Fig. 1. The independent data marts architecture

(2) Data mart bus architecture with linked dimensional data marts

A business requirements analysis for a specific business process is the foundation for this architecture. The first mart is built for a single business process using dimensions and measures that will be used with other marts. Additional marts are developed using these dimensions and measures, which results in logically integrated marts and an enterprise view of the data. Atomic and summarized data are maintained in the marts and are organized in a star schema to provide a dimensional view of the data. This architecture is illustrated in Figure 2.

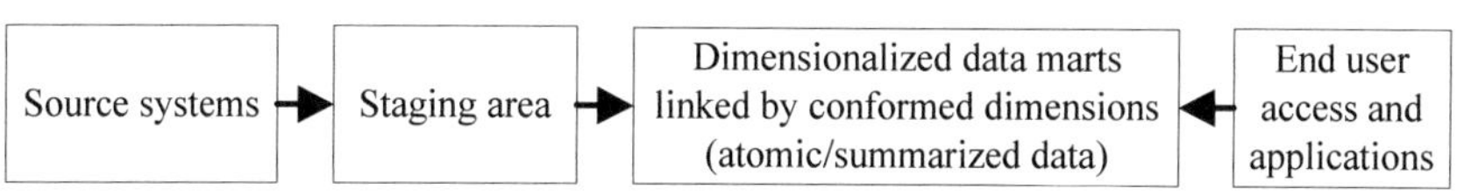

Fig. 2. The data mart bus architecture with linked dimensional data marts

(3) Hub-and-spoke

An extensive enterprise-level analysis of data requirements provides the basis for this architecture. Attention is also focused on building a scalable and maintainable infrastructure. Using the enterprise view of the data, the architecture is developed in an iterative manner, subject area by subject area. Atomic level data is maintained in the warehouse in third normal form. Dependent data marts are created that source data from the warehouse. The dependent data marts may be developed for departmental, functional area, or special purposes and may have normalized, de-normalized, or summarized/atomic dimensional data structures based on user needs. Most users query the dependent data marts. Figure 3 shows this architecture.

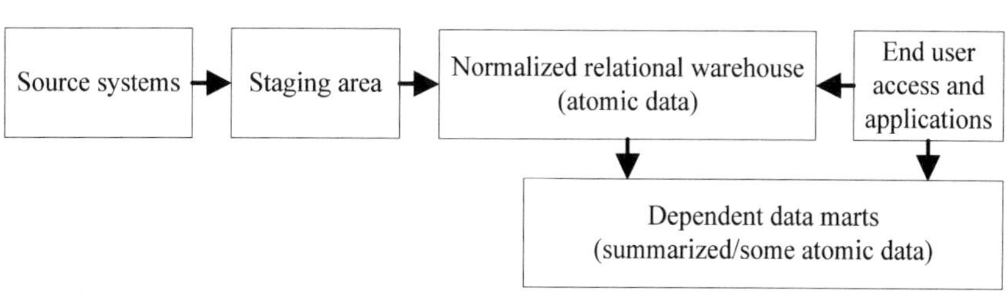

Fig. 3. The hub and spoke architecture

(4) Centralized data warehouse (no dependent data marts)
This architecture is similar to the hub and spoke architecture except that there are no dependent data marts. The warehouse contains atomic level data, some summarized data, and logical dimensional views of the data. Queries and applications access data from both the relational data and the dimensional views. This architecture is typically a logical rather than a physical implementation of the hub and spoke architecture. This architecture is shown in Figure 4.

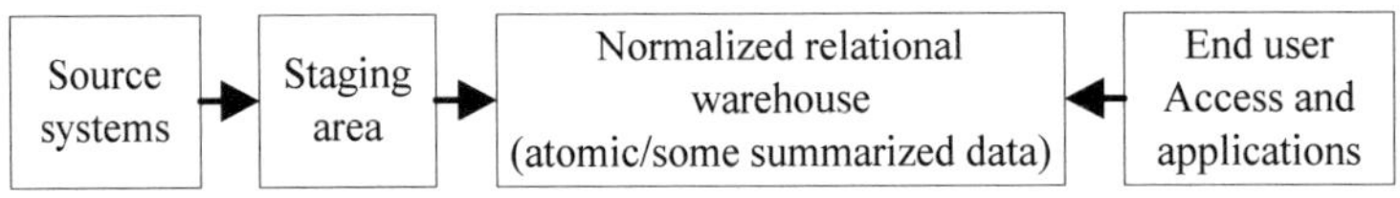

Fig. 4. The centralized data warehouse architecture

(5) Federated
This architecture is advocated as a practical solution for firms that have a pre-existing, complex decision support environment and do not want to rebuild. Based on business requirements, data is accessed from existing data warehouse, data marts, and legacy systems. The data is either logically or physically integrated using shared keys, global metadata, distributed queries or other methods. This architecture is shown in Figure 5.

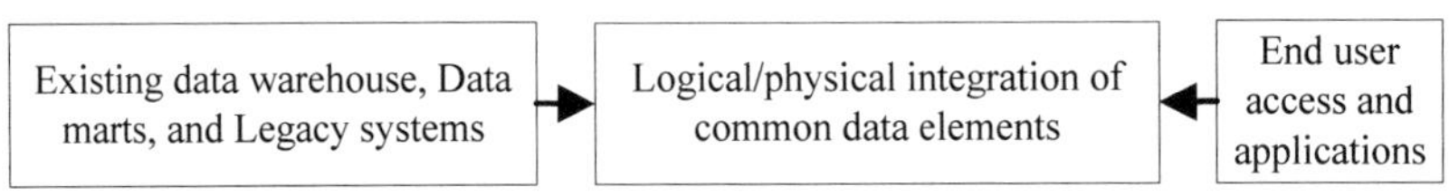

Fig. 5. The Federated Architecture

2.3 Building of data warehouse

Building a data warehouse is only extracting the operational data and entering it into the data warehouse (Inmon, 2007), which sounds simple. However, creating a data warehouse is more than that. Extracting data, analysis data, and presentation result are a complex problem. The major steps of building data warehouse are described.
(a) Data collection
The very first step before you start to build data warehouse, the data source will be identified. You need to figure out what are the data that are required to be put into your data warehouse. The data in the warehouse usually come from a number of source systems. Most of the data have been stored originally in transactional databases. External data may be stored in spreadsheets or personal databases. In some cases, source data may be collected automatically. If new data are required, a suitable system may need to be built to collect them. Otherwise, only minor changes should be needed to existing systems. In all cases, the owners of source data are responsible for maintaining quality, and this may require substantial effort.
(b) Transformation & cleansing
This can be the most time consuming part where you need to grab the data from various data source and store it into the staging database. In this process, data are usually restructured to optimize subsequent use for querying, reporting and analysis. This is often done in stages, in a data staging area. These data feeds need to be run on a regular basis to keep the data warehouse up-to-date. To minimize disruption to other systems, and

warehouse users, this often has to be completed within a tight overnight time window. Task of this stage is very hard and time-consuming, and usually can be done with the help of ETL tools.

(c) Aggregation & analysis

Selected data are taken from the central warehouse using query tools and processed to produce useful results. Often, the most frequently accessed data are first summarized and stored in data marts to improve response times. Additional performance measures are typically derived at the same time. Analytic applications may also be developed to help users get useful information.

(d) Presentation

Presentation is displaying results for end users, usually in the form of reports. Several different report types are normally needed to suit different types of user. The results might appear as text, tables or charts and could be viewed on-line, printed, published on a web server or distributed by email.

2.4 Tools of data warehouse

Developing data warehouse is a very complex and time-consuming task. In the process of building data warehouse, many tools can help developer to build data warehouse. According to purpose, data warehouse tools can be divided into ETL tools, OLAP tools, report tools, data mining tools, and database management systems (DBMS). These tools are introduced as following. Many materials get from official website of products.

(a) ETL tools

IBM WebSphere DataStage delivers three key capabilities necessary for success in enterprise data integration: the most comprehensive connectivity to easily and quickly access any source or target system; advanced development and maintenance tools, which speed implementation and simplify administration; and a scalable platform that can easily handle today's massive volumes of corporate data. WebSphere DataStage is an industry-leading data integration and transformation product that provides advanced development and maintenance capabilities for virtually unsurpassed levels of productivity.

Teradata Parallel Transporter was designed for increased functionality and customer ease of use for faster, easier and deeper integration. The capabilities include: Simplified data transfer between one Teradata Database and another; Ability to load dozens of files using a single script makes development and maintenance of the data warehouse easier; Distribution of workloads across CPUs on the load server eliminates bottlenecks in the data load process.; The open database connectivity (ODBC) operator reads from the ODBC driver, which could pull data from any database; for example, DB2 or Oracle; Accessibility to myriad data sources via open standards is possible.

SAS ETL Studio is a visual design tool for building, implementing and managing ETL and data integration processes from source to destination, regardless of data sources or platforms. In-depth data transformations are provided to efficiently meet enterprise data integration requirements and support business and analytic intelligence. It also improves quality management by providing impact analysis of potential changes made throughout the data management life cycle. SQL Server Integration Services (SSIS) is a component of Microsoft SQL Server. SSIS is only available in the "Standard" and "Enterprise" editions. SSIS provides a platform to build data integration and workflow applications. The primary use for SSIS is data warehousing, as the product features a fast and flexible tool for data extraction, transformation, and loading (ETL). The tool may also be used to automate maintenance of SQL Server databases, update multidimensional cube data, and perform other functions.

Informatica PowerCenter is a single, unified enterprise data integration platform for accessing, discovering, and integrating data from virtually any business system, in any format, and delivering that data throughout the enterprise at any speed.

(b) OLAP tools

Oracle Discoverer is an ad hoc query tool that operates in the Caltech data warehouse environment. Discoverer's desktop-reporting features provide users the ability to generate financial reports and analyze financial information easily and quickly. Discoverer has three main components: User Edition (it provides the graphical interface utilized by users on a day-to-day basis to generate reports and analyze data), Administration Edition (it is the tool used to design and present the hierarchy of financial data) and End User Layer (it shields users from the complexity of the relational database from which Discoverer retrieves data).

SQL Server Analysis Services (SSAS) is a part of the Microsoft SQL Server platform. It adds OLAP and data mining capabilities for SQL Server databases. The OLAP engine supports MOLAP, ROLAP and HOLAP storage modes for data. Analysis Services supports the XML for Analysis standard as the underlying communication protocol. The cube data can be accessed using MDX queries. Data mining specific functionality is exposed via the DMX query language. Analysis Services includes various algorithms - Decision trees, clustering algorithm, Naive Bayes algorithm, time series analysis, sequence clustering algorithm, linear and logistic regression analysis, and neural networks - for use in data mining.

DB2 OLAP Server is a strategic member of IBM's Business Intelligence family. It integrates the powerful OLAP engine and the application programming interfaces of Hyperion Essbase with IBM's DB2® family of relational databases. It provides a fast path to turn user's warehouse data into business insight. It is built for e-business with tools to help you quickly deploy Web-based analytical applications.

SAS OLAP Server is a multidimensional data store designed from the outset to provide quick access to pre-summarized data generated from vast amounts of detailed data. Decision makers need quick access to summarized data so they can make timely decisions based on knowledge instead of gut feelings.

BusinessObjects OLAP Intelligence is an On Line Analytical Processing (OLAP) application for analysis business data. It was previously known as Crystal Analysis Professional, it is part of BusinessObjects Crystal Decisions.

(c) report tools

Cognos ReportNet is the first all-in-one reporting software that lets user create, modify and distribute any report – invoices, statements, weekly sales and inventory reports to list a few. User can standardize all enterprise reports, not simply with one vendor – with one product and architecture.

Crystal Reports Server is software product of SAS. Crystal Reports Server provides a complete report management solution that enables IT professionals to securely share, schedule, and deliver interactive reports over the Web, in e-mail, and in Microsoft Office documents. It empowers business users to view, print and share more compelling reports.

Oracle Reports is Oracle's award-winning, high-fidelity enterprise reporting tool. It enables businesses to give immediate access to information to all levels within and outside of the organization in an unrivaled scalable and secure environment. Oracle Reports consists of Oracle Reports Developer (a component of the Oracle Developer Suite) and Oracle Application Server Reports Services (a component of the Oracle Application Server).

SQL Server Reporting Services is a report generation environment for data gathered from SQL Server databases. It is administered via a web interface. Reporting services features a web services interface to support the development of custom reporting applications. Reports are created as RDL files. Once created, RDL files can be rendered in a variety of formats including Excel, PDF, CSV, XML, TIFF (and other image formats), and HTML Web Archive.

(d) Data mining tools

IBM Intelligent Miner can help user detect fraud, segment your customers, and simplify market basket analysis. IBM's in-database mining capabilities integrate with existing systems to provide scalable, high performing predictive analysis without moving your data into proprietary data mining platforms. Use SQL, Web Services, or Java to access DB2's data mining capabilities from own applications or business intelligence tools from IBM's business partners.

Oracle Data Miner is the graphical user interface for Oracle Data Mining that helps data analysts mine their Oracle data to find valuable hidden information, patterns, and new insights. Data analysts can mine data with Oracle Data Miner's easy-to-use wizards that guide them through the data preparation, data mining, model evaluation, and model scoring process. Oracle Data Miner can automatically generate code needed to transform the data mining steps into an integrated data mining/BI application.

SAS Enterprise Miner streamlines the data mining process to create highly accurate predictive and descriptive models based on analysis of vast amounts of data from across the enterprise. Enterprise Miner Support the entire data mining process with a broad set of tools, for example, association, clustering, decision-tree, neural network, classical regression technology.

Teradata Warehouse Miner provides an array of data profiling and mining functions ranging from data exploration and transformation to analytic model development and deployment that are performed directly in Teradata Database. Teradata warehouse miner allows you to analyze detailed data without data movement, streamlining the data mining process.

(e) Database management systems

Database management systems (DBMS) can be divided into two categories -- desktop databases and server databases. Generally speaking, Data warehouse applications adopt server database, such as Microsoft SQL Server, Oracle and IBM DB2, which offer organizations the ability to manage large amounts of data efficiently and in a manner that enables many users to access and update the data simultaneously.

Microsoft SQL Server is a relational model database server produced by Microsoft. Its primary query languages are T-SQL and ANSI SQL.

Oracle Database (commonly referred to as Oracle) consists of a relational database management system (RDBMS) produced and marketed by Oracle Corporation. Its primary query languages are Plus/SQL and ANSI SQL.

DB2 is a "Relational Database Management System" (RDBMS), DB2 is designed to make the storage and analysis of data easier. All access to and manipulation of data in DB2 is accomplished via SQL.

Sybase IQ is a highly optimized analytics server designed specifically to deliver faster results for mission-critical business intelligence, data warehouse and reporting solutions on any standard hardware and operating systems. It works with diverse data - including unstructured data - and diverse data sources to deliver unsurpassed query performance at the lowest price/performance available.
Teradata Database is a relational model database server produced by Teradata. Its data models are Relational, ANSI SQL Compatible, Full Query Parallelism and Balanced Performance.

3. Requirement analysis of data centre

Nanhai city of Guangdong province is the state-level pilot city for information-based. Consequently Nanhai city is listed as the pilot cities for Model Project of China's E-government Application. Nanhai city has successfully programmed and developed a series of E-government projects, including village management, finance decision-making, education, irrigation management, soil management, police management, etc, which vigorously promoted information-based construction in such fields as governments, rural areas, education, culture. With many system applications in every department, data exchange among departments, data share among departments and data integration application are becoming a big demand for improving greatly management efficiency and service standards. The relations of data provider and user for population data and for judicial entity data are depicted in Figure 6 and Figure 7, respectively.

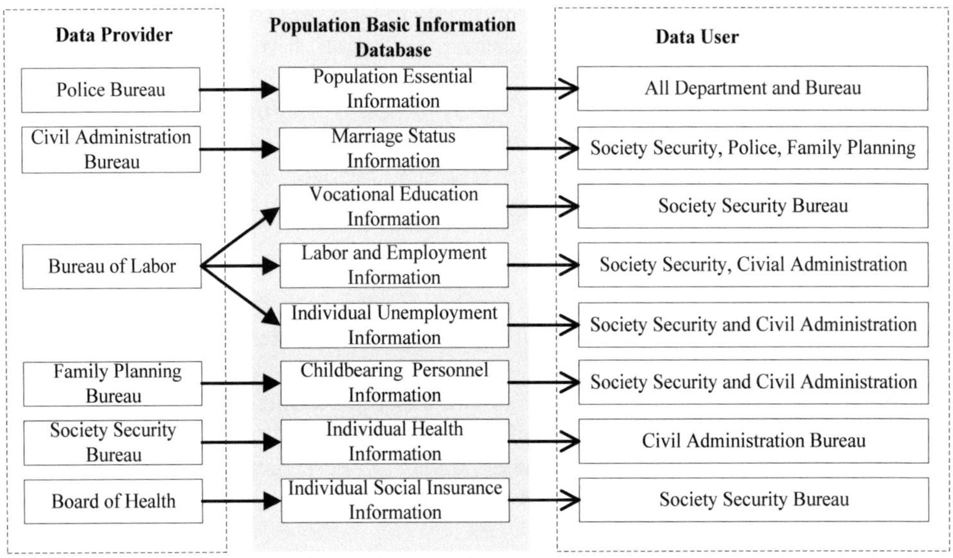

Fig. 6. Relation of provider and user for population data

To solve data share and exchange among departments, establishing data centre is a prime method. Main requirements of data centre are summarized as following:
Realizing data share and exchange in the various departments, supplying data collecting, processing and loading from data sources to data centre, achieving centralized storage of

government information resource, in favour of the higher level construction of four databases, offering integration application service for government, enterprises and citizens, Offering integration management for population information.

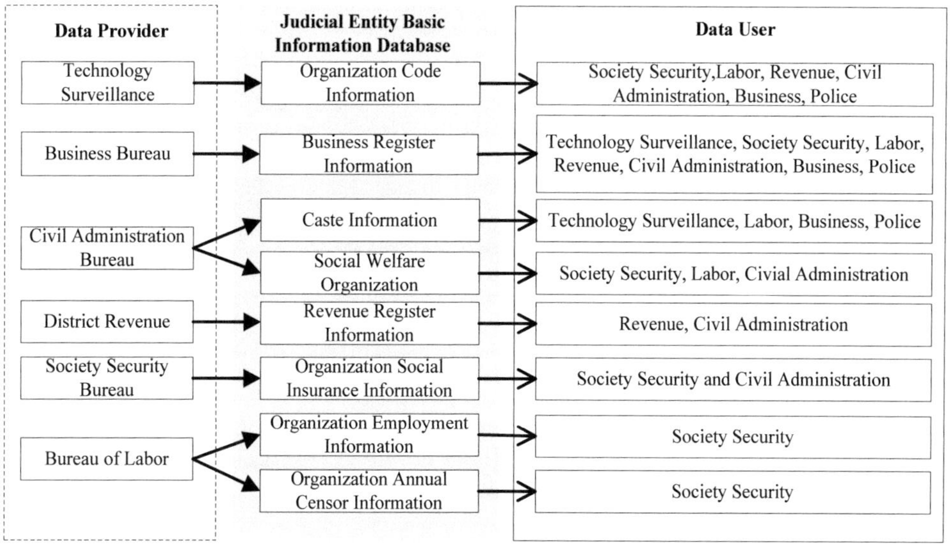

Fig. 7. Relation of provider and user for judicial entity data

4. Architecture of data centre based on data warehouse technology

The architecture of data centre based on data warehouse is presented in Figure 8. Data centre is composed of six main components: data share and exchange platform, kernel database, support application platform, application database, data centre management platform, and data centre security platform.

The very essence of the data warehouse is the flexible and unpredictable access of data. Thus, required is the ability to access data quickly and easily. If data is not efficiently indexed and users cannot access data rapidly, the data warehouse will not succeed. In addition, the data in the data warehouse needs to be able to be monitored at will. The cost of monitoring data cannot be so high and the complexity of monitoring data cannot be so hard that a monitoring program cannot be run whenever necessary. The data warehouse also needs to be able both to receive data from and pass data to the various departments of Nanhai city.

4.1. Data Share and Exchange Platform

Data share and exchange platform is made up of ETL (extraction, transformation and load) and data share agent. ETL is data provider for kernel data, which collects data from data source and load to kernel data. Data share agent deal with dispensing share data stored in kernel database into various departments that need data.

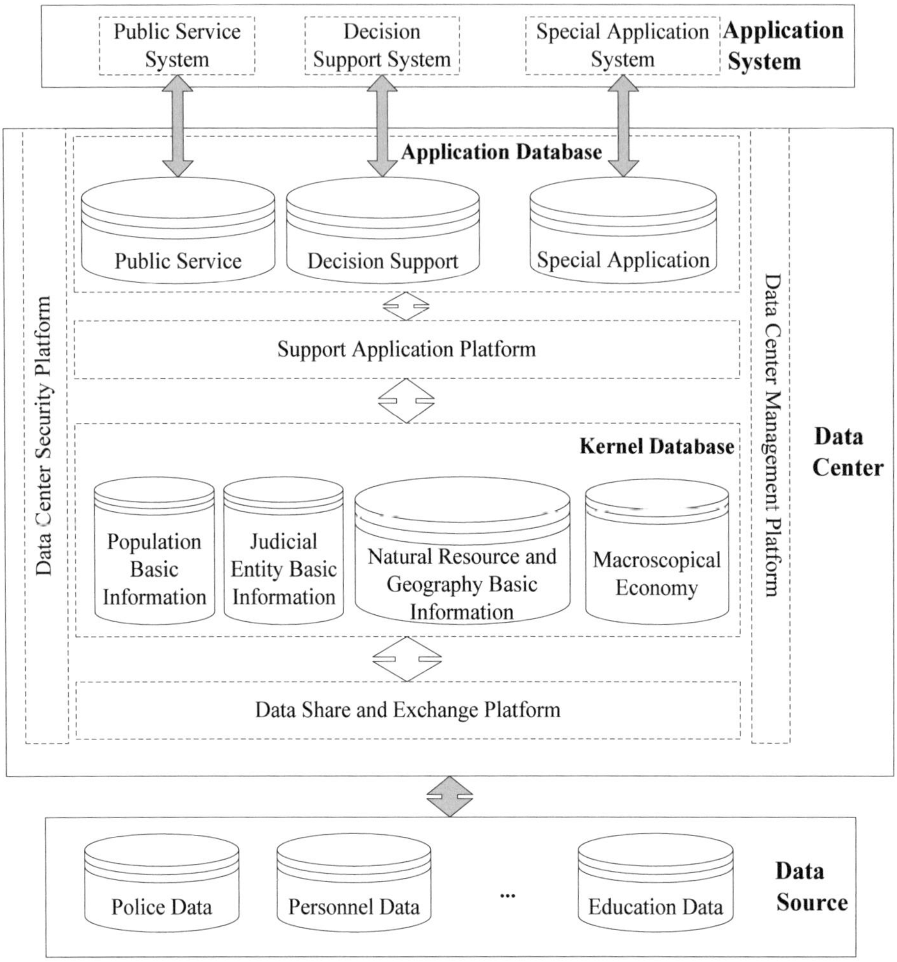

Fig. 8. Architecture of Data Centre

4.2. Kernel Database

Kernel database of data centre is composed of four parts: population basic information database, judicial entity basic information database, natural resource and geography basic information database, and macroscopical economy database, which is organized according to user requirements and is maintained by administrators of data centre.

4.3. Support Application Platform

Support application platform is a secondary development tool possessed by data centre, main function of which is establish special database by extracting data directly from kernel database according requirements of application.

4.4. Application Database

Application database may be treated as data mart, which is composed of three parts: public service database, decision support database and special application database. Data Special application database is provided by kernel database and source database according to application requirement. Application database is organized according to requirements of decision-making, which is maintained by both administrators of data centre and department.

4.5. Data Centre Management Platform

Its main function is to manage and control data centre, including share management, exchange management, run management, log management, authorization management, backup management and recovery management.

4.6. Data Centre Security Platform

To deal with alarming and unpredictable security threats, data centre must consider security. Data centre Security Platform is a base of other platform that monitors and protects data centre.

5. Key techniques of data centre

5.1. ETL Technique

The process of extracting data from data sources and bringing it into the kernel database is commonly called ETL, which stands for extraction, transformation, and loading. During Extraction, the desired data has to be identified and extracted from data sources. Very often, it is not possible to identify the specific subset of interest; therefore more data than necessary has to be extracted, since the identification of the relevant data will be done at a later point in time. The size of the extracted data varies from hundreds of kilobytes to hundreds of gigabytes, depending on the source system and the organization situation. Just as the size of the data extraction may vary widely, the frequency at which the data is extracted may also vary widely: the time span may vary between hours and minutes to near real-time. After extracting (and transporting) the data, the most challenging and time consuming parts of ETL follow: Transformation and Loading into the target system. This may include applying complex filters; validating the incoming data against information which already existing in target database tables; comparing new data to existing data in the data warehouse, to determine whether the new data needs to be inserted or updated; computing aggregations and other derived data based on the new data. Generally there are three kind approaches of ETL: transformation-then-load, load-then-transformation and transformation-while-load.

5.2. Data Storage Technique

Data storage techniques is very important and complicated for realizing goal of data center, to support future decision support system, star schema for the warehouse is adopted to build application databases. Every application database is composed of several fact tables and a set of dimensional tables, the fact table contains a list of all measures and points to the key value of the lowest level of each dimension. Each of these measurements is taken at the intersection of all dimensions. Dimensions are qualifiers that give meaning to measures.

They organize the data based on the what, when, and where components of a organization question. Dimensions are stored in dimension tables made up of dimensional elements and attributes. Each dimension is composed of related items or elements. Dimensions are hierarchies of related elements. Each element represents a different level of summarization. Choosing the appropriate fact measures for the grain in the fact table depends on the organization and analysis purposes. For example, the star schema for the contract data is constructed as shown in Figure 9.

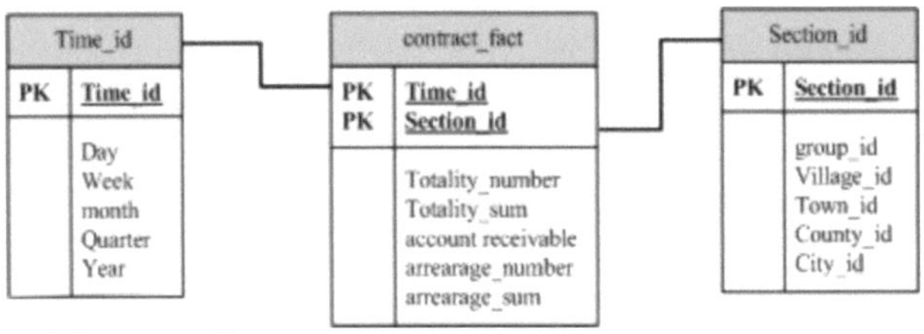

Fig. 9. Star Schema of Contract Data

5.3. Data Share and Exchange Technique

Data exchange is the problem of finding an instance of a target schema, given an instance of a source schema and a specification of the relationship between the source and the target. Such a target instance should correctly represent information from the source instance under the constraints imposed by the target schema, and should allow one to evaluate queries on the target instance in a way that is semantically consistent with the source data. XML stands for extensible markup language. XML was released in the late 90's and received a great amount of application. The XML standard was created by World Wide Web Consortium to provide an easy to use and standardized way to store self-describing data. The main benefit of XML is that you can take data from a platform, convert it into XML, and then share that XML with other platforms. Each of these receiving platforms can then convert the XML into a structure the platform uses normally and you have just communicated between two potentially very different platforms! So XML is adopted to realize data share and exchange. Data stored in the data source is converted into XML file, and then send it to data share and exchange platform, when receive XML file, data share and exchange platform again convert XML to structure data of kernel database, data stored in the kernel database is sent to application department in the same way, therefore, function of data share and exchange is realized easily.

6. Conclusion

In this chapter, definition, architecture, process of building and tools of data warehouse are introduced. Then Nanhai city E-government project is acted as example to illustrate the data warehouse based data centre deign. Relation of provider and user for data in various departments of government is given in detail. On the base of data analysis, the architecture of data center based on data warehouse technology has been presented. In our proposed method, XML technology is used for data share and exchange. The proposed method has already been successfully used in development of data center system for Nanhai city.

7. References

Teh Ying Wah, Ng Hooi Peng, and Ching Sue Hok. Building Data Warehouse. Special Issue of the International Journal of the Computer, the Internet and Management, Vol.15 No. SP4, November, 2007.

Donna Evansa, David C, Yenb. (2006). E-Government: Evolving relationship of citizens and government, domestic, and international development Government Information Quarterly 23, pp. 207-235.

State Information Construction Promotion Office (SICPO) (2001). Report on China's Internet Resources. July 2001. http://www.cei.gov.cn.

Lijuan Zhou, Chi Liu, Chunying Wang. (2006). The Design and Application of Data Warehouse during Modern Enterprises Environment. Data Mining, Intrusion Detection, Information Assurance, and Data Networks Security.

Xiaohua Hu, Nick Cercone. (2004). A Data Warehouse/Online Analytic Processing Framework for Web Usage Mining and Business Intelligence Reporting. International Journal of Intelligent Systems, Vol. 19, pp. 585-606.

Dr.Katherine Jones. (1998). An Introduction to Data Warehousing: What Are the Implications for the Network? International Journal of Network Management, Vol. 8, pp. 42-56.

Keqin Wang, Shurong Tong and et al. (2007). Review on Application of Data Mining in Product Design and Manufacturing, International Conference on Fuzzy Systems and Knowledge Discovery .

Alex A. Freitas, Jon Timmis. (2007). Revisiting the Foundations of Artificial Immune Systems for Data Mining. IEEE Transactions on Evolutionary Computation, Vol.11, No.4, August.

http://www.sap.com/solutions/sapbusinessobjects/sme/reporting/crystalreportsserver/index.epx.

http://www.microsoft.com/Sqlserver/2005/en/us/reporting-services.aspx.

http://www.sas.com/technologies/dw/storage/mddb/index.html.

http://en.wikipedia.org/wiki/Microsoft_SQL_Server.

http://www.terry.uga.edu/~hwatson/DW_Architecture_Report.pdf .

Hu Xuanzi, Wang Kuanfu. Application of Data Warehouse Technology in Data Center Design. 2008 International Conference on Computational Intelligence and Security.

20

The Emergence of the Intelligent Government in the Second Society

Dennis de Kool and Johan van Wamelen
Erasmus University Rotterdam, Center for Public Innovation
The Netherlands

1. Introduction

Modern society is facing two developments that are increasingly being interwoven with each other, namely societal and technological developments and the evolution of a virtual world alongside the physical world. The focal point of these two developments is what we will call the Second Society. New internet applications, which are often grouped under the label 'Web 2.0', play an important role in the Second Society. Well-known examples of Web 2.0 applications are Google, Weblogs, Wikipedia, YouTube, MySpace and Second Life. Web 2.0 is often presented as a revolutionary way of gathering, organizing and sharing of information. Despite the fact that some people embrace Web 2.0, some critical sounds can be heard as well. Critics state that Web 2.0 is an exaggerated hype and raise the question whether the potential of Web 2.0 will be realized in practice. Nevertheless Web 2.0 developments cannot be ignored by the public sector, because they can make governments more intelligent. In this chapter we will discuss the impact of these applications in the emergence of the intelligent government in the Second Society. The research questions to be answered in this chapter are:

* What is the public context in which new web applications can be placed?
* What is the expected impact of new internet applications on the public sector and citizens?
* How can modern internet applications be classified?
* What is the empirical impact of two specific Dutch applications within the public sector?

This chapter is organized as follows. In section 2 we explore the notion of the Second Society and the role of new internet applications. Against this background we present a framework to classify new internet applications. In section 3 we will analyze two modern Dutch internet applications in more detail, namely the website "how safe is my district?" (www.hoeveiligismijnwijk.nl) and the virtual platform against airport hindrance (www.vlieghinder.nl). In section 4 we draw some conclusions and reflect about the emergence of the intelligent government.

2. The Second Society

In recent years one can observe the evolution of a virtual world alongside the physical world. A growing number of activities is taking place within the virtual reality of the internet. More and more (business) services are delivered on line. Nowadays websites can be used for digital banking, shopping, dating, chatting and sharing interests with others. New virtual communities and networks are developing. An example is Second Life. The evolution of a virtual world has impact on the public sector too. An indicator is the number of government services available on-line that is growing steadily in the Netherlands (Ministry of Economic Affairs, 2006). Nowadays the public sector stands with one leg in the physical world and with the other leg in the virtual world. This is no static situation. New technological and societal developments will have impact on a further evolution.

The development of new technology is impressive. Examples are mobile navigation systems (TomTom) and YouTube. All these new technologies have societal implications. They will change the way citizens interact with each other and with governments. New technology can play a crucial role in fixing the problems of modern governments too (Eggers, 2007). An example is the provision of (integrated) services by governments. Some scientific reports speak about a user generated state (Frissen et al., 2008).

At the same time the public sector is facing some societal developments in which technology plays or can play an important role. Examples are individualization, the fragmentation of society, the growing attention for the quality of the provision of services and performance measurement, the active role of citizens in the policy process (co-production), the effects of aging and the discussion about scaling up and down in for example hospitals and schools. Web 2.0 applications make it possible to observe these developments from a different perspective. In the current society personalized forms of integral and tailor-made services are becoming more important.

To summarize: both technological and societal developments will change the position of the public sector in the virtual and physical world. We define the possible evolution of the public sector as the Second Society (Center for Public Innovation, 2007). See figure 1.

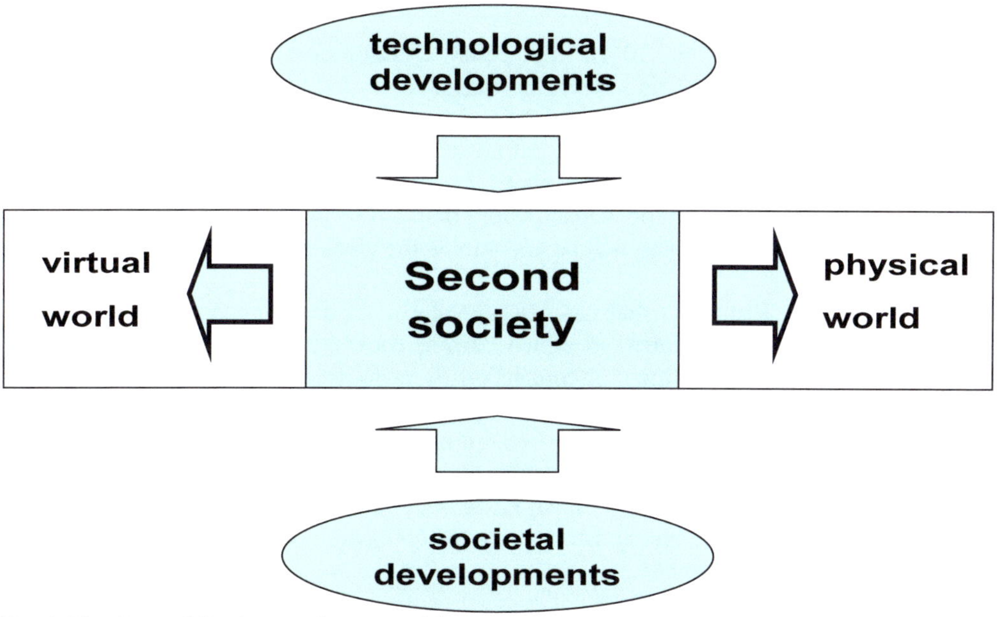

Fig. 1. The Second Society as the central focus point

The Second Society can be approached on a macro level (like a state or global community) and on a micro level (like a district in a city). In this chapter we will explore the implications of Web 2.0 on the local level, because the interaction between the government and citizens (two important actors in the Second Society) are most visible here.

From E-Government to I(ntelligent)-Government?

Under the label of E-Government governments are undertaking different activities that are directly related to the development of the Second Society. In this chapter we explore the implications of local Web 2.0 applications on E-government, because Web 2.0 is expected to have far-reaching impact on (electronic) governments (Frissen et al., 2008). Web 2.0 applications can stimulate the further development of E-government. The notion of E-Government is commonly used within the public sector (Bekkers & Homburg eds., 2005; Heeks, 2006; Hernon et al., 2006). E-Government is also a prominent item on the Dutch and European agenda (Ministry of Economic Affairs, 2006; European Commision, 2007). E-Government can be described as "the use of modern information and communication technologies, especially internet and web technology, by a public organization to support or redefine the existing and/or future (information, communication and transaction) relations with 'stakeholders' in the internal and external environment in order to create added value" (Bekkers & Homburg eds., 2005).

All policy stages within the public sector are currently being influenced by new internet applications, namely policy development, policy implementation, monitoring and management. We state that Electronic government is not a goal in itself but a process in which intelligent Web 2.0 technology is being used to make the policy process more effective and efficient. For this reason it is better to speak about Intelligent Government (I-Government). An indicator for the Intelligent Government in the Second Society is that the application must meet a successful linkage between the problem and solution, both perceived by the actors involved. The implications are as follows:

Intelligent policy making

An example of using Web 2.0 in the policy development process is the website www.wijbouweneenwijk.nl. This website has been launched recently by the municipality of Smallingerland. The goal behind this virtual community is to mobilize 'the wisdom of the crowds' in order to get creative ideas before a new district in Smallingerland will be developed. Some media already speak about the wiki-district. More than 400 ideas and reactions have been placed on the website. More than 14.000 people from 43 countries have visited the website. The next step will be to combine the ideas and suggestions in a plan for a new district.

Another example is Virtuocity that has been developed by the municipality of Helmond. Virtuocity is a 3D GIS-application in which citizens could walk though the inner city of Helmond through their own internet connection by using an avatar. With this avatar one can walk around the neighborhood and see all the new plans the same way as when playing a computer game. Additionally there is a forum on which citizens can communicate with the local government and chat sessions with aldermen are organized. The municipality of Helmond hopes with Virtuocity to inform citizens but also to consult them regarding the future of the city. The municipality also expects the application will make sure that citizens feel more involved with their city.

Intelligent policy implementation

An example of intelligent policy implementation is the launch of the website www.politieonderzoeken.nl some years ago by the Dutch police. The website contains information about serious cases that have not been solved yet. The goal of this website is to solve the cases by activating the 'wisdom of the crowds' (Surowiecki, 2004). The idea behind this this website is that the ideas and suggestions of citizens can be valuable to solve serious crimes.

Another example is the potential of Web 2.0 based technologies in inspection processes. Web 2.0 applications make it more easy to share information and to generate user generated content. Nevertheless, most inspection units, both national and international, are still reserved by making inspection results transparent and activating citizens in inspection proceses (Meijer & Homburg, 2008).

Intelligent policy monitoring and management

Finally, Web 2.0 applications can be applied to make monitoring processes more effective and efficient. An example is the GIS-based Watermonitor developed by the Regional Water Authority Aa en Maas. This internal web application monitors the implementation process of the water policy goals and ambitions of this organization annually (De Kool, 2008). Other examples of GIS-based monitoring are the website www.hoeveiligismijnwijk.nl and the website www.vlieghinder.nl. Both of these websites will be discussed in more detail in the next section.

From Web 1.0 to Web 2.0

Web 2.0 is not a uniform concept, but a generic term or metaphor for new internet technologies and applications. Web 2.0 can be seen as a revival, intensification, renewal or even as a second generation of the internet in which user generated content has a central place. Osimo and Burgelman state that Web 2.0 is about both technology and attitude (Osimo & Burgelman, 2007). Miller describes Web 2.0 as follows: "Web 2.0 is the network as platform, spanning all connected devices; Web 2.0 applications are those that make the most of the intrinsic advantages of that platform: delivering software as a continually-updated service that gets better the more people use it, consuming and remixing data from multiple sources, including individual users, while providing their own data and services in a form that allows remixing by others, creating network effects through an architecture of participation and going beyond the page metaphor of Web 1.0 to deliver rich user experiences" (Miller, 2005). Web 2.0 has also been called the social web, because its content can be more easily generated by users as well as the collective intelligence of users. Users are not the passive consumers of content, but the active co-producers of content. Interaction plays an important role in Web 2.0 in order to create shared information.

It is important to state that Web 2.0 is a new stage in the technical development and no replacement of previous technologies (Boulos & Wheelert, 2007). Woods states that Web 2.0 is best understood as the latest phase in the evolution of the internet and the Web (Woods, 2007). We have to consider too that our actual frames of reference are different from the frames of references we had in the past. Interaction by sending e-mails in the past has for example a different character then interaction in virtual communities in the Web 2.0 era.

New internet applications can be classified in different ways. In the first place we can make a classification based on distinguishable characteristics.

Generic versus specific

Web 2.0 applications can have a general character. An example is Google Earth. At the other hand Web 2.0 applications can have a specific character too, like an interactive website of a specific district within a city. A Dutch example is the website www.ede-west.nl.

Static versus dynamic

Web 2.0 applications can have a static character. An example is YouTube (www.youtube.com). On this website one can watch self made movies created by other users. These movies have to be put on the website first, before they can be viewed by other people. At the other hand Web 2.0 applications can have a dynamic character too. An example is MSN, on which one can have live chats and exchange pictures or documents.

Closed versus open

Web 2.0 applications can be operational in a closed environment (Frissen et al., 2008). An example is Linked-in. On this professional networking community people can block their contacts. At the other hand Web 2.0 applications can be open. An example is Google Maps. This application makes it possible to search for information in specific geographical locations.

Personal versus collective
Web 2.0 applications can be personal. An example are weblogs, on which people can share personal experiences with other interested people. The number of blogs in the public sector is growing at a rapid rate (Wyld, 2007). At the other hand Web 2.0 applications can also serve collective interests. A Dutch example is the website www.vlieghinder.nl that aims to protect the interests of the people who suffer from the noise of airplanes. See figure 2.

Web 1.0 ◄	► **Web 2.0**
General	Specific
Static	Dynamic
Closed	Open
Collective	Personal

Fig. 2. Characteristics of Web 1.0 and Web 2.0

Second, we can classify local Web 2.0 applications based on the functions that these applications fulfill (Van Wamelen & De Kool, 2008).
Sharing of information
Web 2.0 applications can be used as a new way to share and exchange information, like pictures, movies, news and music. Governments can use Web 2.0 applications to inform citizens, for example by means of GIS. Dutch examples are "Almere in maps" (www.almere.nl) and "Rotterdam in maps" (www.rotterdam.nl). Some websites contain (personal) assessments about persons, like teachers (wwww.meinprof.de) or books.
Mobilisation of interests
Web 2.0 applications have mobilizing potential (Eggers, 2007). An example is to make other people aware of some unwelcome situations, for example unsafe locations in cities. People can mark these locations on digital maps by tagging. On the website www.landroof.nl one can mark nature areas that are at risk because of building plans. The government and politicians can also use Web 2.0 applications for their own purposes. An example are the potential American president candidates who tried to reach their voters by movies placed on YouTube.
Social interaction
Web 2.0 applications can be used to meet each other ("virtual platform"). These social activities can be restricted to contacts in virtual worlds only (for example MySpace and Second Life) but also be a starting point for real meetings. These social contacts can be without obligations ("fun"), but can have functional goals as well. For example bringing together of people with shared interests of the same professional background in communities.
Delivery of services
Web 2.0 applications offer new ways of delivering services. Several cities in the Netherlands offer digital maps that contain information about locations of public organizations, like hospitals, libraries, nursery and schools. Some cities (like Nijmegen and Brugge) offer information about the history of houses, building licenses and so on.

Transactions
Web 2.0 applications can offer new ways of doing business ("transactions") by developing new services or by matching supply and demand in innovative ways. An example is eBay. A Dutch example is the website www.marktplaats.nl. On this virtual market everybody can sell and buy goods. Another example is www.lula.com. This website offers the possibility to publish and distribute documents in an active way. The authors can be publisher, printer and/or shopper. See figure 3.

Function	Examples
Sharing of information	• www.youtube.com • www.flickr.com • www.fotoshooter.nl
Mobilisation of interests	• www.upmystreet.com • www.vlieghinder.nl • www.vroegopstap.nl
Social interaction	• www.myspace.com • www.secondlife.com • www.hyves.nl
Delivery of services	• www.askbristol.com • www.hoeveiligismijnwijk.nl • www.voorst.nl
Transactions	• www.eBay.com • www.markplaats.nl • www.fotoshooter.nl

Fig. 3. Functions of new internet applications

Not these functions in itself, but the way these functions are filled in is typical for Web 2.0. In the First World War the carrier pigeon was used to send messages to soldiers. This is an example of sharing information. However, the range of the carrier pigeon was literally limited. Internet has no limitations (time, space and amount of messages) for sharing information. So in the modern knowledge society sharing of information has a different dimension.

3. Empirical findings

In this section we will describe and analyze two cases in more detail, namely the websites www.hoeveiligismijnwijk.nl and www.vlieghinder.nl. The first reason to select these websites is that the first website is a 'top-down' project initiated by the government ('Intelligent Government') and the second website is a bottom-up project initiated by citizens ('Intelligent Citizens'). In the Second Society I-Govenments and I-citizens interact with each other. The second reason to restrict the cases to intelligent policy monitoring is that most of Web 2.0 based activities in the Netherlands in the policy making and policy implementation are still in the pilot stage or have been developed very recently, so it is still too early to draw conclusions about the empirical impact of Web 2.0 in these two policy stages.

3.1 Neighborhood: crimes in the region Haaglanden

In April 2006 the police department Haaglanden launched the website www.hoeveiligismijnwijk.nl. With this website citizens can view eleven of the most frequent crimes committed within the region per neighborhood, namely car theft, intimidation, mugging, theft of mopeds, theft from cars, theft from companies, theft from houses, theft of bikes, ill-treatment, shop-lifting and pick-pocketing. The viewers of the website can select the crimes-categories, the period in which the crimes took place and the municipality, district or neighborhood in which these crimes had been committed. Special software has been developed to show the data on geographical maps. By comparing current numbers with past data it is also possible to get insight in trends in crime. Besides crimes figures the website provides viewers also with information to prevent crimes. The idea behind this is that prevention measures will reduce the number of crimes within the region Haaglanden.

Characteristics of website

The website has a specific focus, namely to deliver data about specific crimes in the region Haaglanden. The content on the website is quite static, although the data on the website is being renewed regularly. The website can be viewed by every citizen, without login-codes. The website has not a personalized but collective focus. The primary focus group are citizens in the region Haaglanden.

Functions of website

The launch of the website is part of a large campaign by the police department 'Haaglanden'. With this campaign the police department hopes to actively inform citizens and societal organizations on the developments regarding criminal facts, unsafety and the achievements of the. With specially designed software the information on reported crimes is made available on geographical maps. The maps contain the numbers on eleven of the most frequent crimes. By using the maps citizens can obtain a complete image of these crimes in their neighbourhood in one blink of an eye. One must keep in mind that the site is based on reported crimes only.

The idea behind this website is that well informed citizens attribute to a safer environment. A safer environment is a common interest of both police offices and citizens. In contrary to the website www.vlieghinder.nl, the mobilisation of interests plays no role at this website. In terms of social interactions the website presents crimes reported by citizens, according to the police department, the website in itself feeds this back to citizens. Citizens were also asked to give their opinion on the website and among those who do prizes can be won. The website does not contain an interactive forum. Still the police departments views the website as an important portal by which citizens can contact the police. The main service offered by the website is to provide citizens which location-based data about crimes in their neighbourhood. Next to crime statistics the website also provides for useful tips for the prevention of crime. Transactions is no relevant function for this website.

Intelligent linkage

In this case we see that the linkage between solution and problem not completely matches. In the area of information provision the linkage proves to be a large success, citizens visit the website and are informed on the safety issues in their neighborhood. The active involvement of citizens in the safety of their neighborhood has, up till now, not been apparent.

3.2 Platform against airport hindrance

On June 24th 2003 the Platform Vlieghinder Regio Castricum (PVRC) (Platform for airport hindrance in the area of Castricum) was established. An important incentive for the start of this initiative by citizens was the use of a new airport runway, the so-called "Polderbaan" by the airport of Schiphol. This, according to citizens had led to a large increase in noise nuisance. An important goal behind this association is to reduce the noise nuisance around the airport of Schiphol by providing the airport authorities and governments with grounded data. This data is real-life gathered by noise-measurement equipment around the airport and shown on a live 'radar' on the website www.vlieghinder.nl.

Characteristics of website

The website has a specific focus, namely to inform or mobilize citizens who want to reduce the noise nuisance around the airport of Schiphol. The content on the website is very dynamic. The PVRC together with the Stichting Geluidsnet (Association Noise net) designed a system in which one can look at the actual flights via Google Earth. According to the starters of the website the combination of GIS, real-time measurements and internet account for one of the key success factors for the website. The website has an open character, because everybody can enter the website without login-codes. The website has not a personalized but collective focus. The primary focus group are citizens in the region of Castricum.

Functions of website

Informing citizens and government is the most important goal of the website, since the PVRC supposes that citizens have a lack of information compared to the airport. The website contains a lot of information among which background information, radar maps and flight routes. With the help of this information the PVRC can base their complaints on noise nuisance. The PVRC on the website voices its opinion that the government will not inform them on the noise nuisance. Because of this the PVRC actively tries to inform citizens themselves. The interest of the PVRC is decreasing the noise nuisance caused by Schiphol airport. The PVRC also feels that legislation has done them wrong. The law claims that there is a norm for the amount of noise allowed for areas next to the airport. But this norm does not apply to the areas of Castricum, Limmen, Heemskerk and parts of Beverwijk because these areas are located too far from the airport. The mission of this group is defending the interests of the citizens living in the area. To reach its goal the PVRC wants to use publicity and that is why they have started their website. On the website interested citizens are urged to register and become a member. A cooperation with 18 citizens groups in the region is also established. According to the starters of the website the possibility for citizens to react is one of the key factors for success of the website. There are also meetings between members. The main service provided on the website is to provide viewers of the website with actual data about the noise of airplanes and relevant policy documents about this theme. Transactions is no relevant function for this website.

Intelligent linkage

For the case of the PVRC the linkage between problem and solution is practically a hundred percent successful. The goal of informing citizens proves to be a success but also being taken seriously in negotiations has been successful.

4. Conclusions and Reflections

A shift can be traced from the so-called Web 1.0 to Web 2.0. Web 2.0 is not a uniform concept, but a generic term for new internet technologies and applications. Important characteristics of Web 2.0 applications are virtual networks, sharing of information, active users that influence the products and the dynamic content of information. Both these technological and societal developments have impact on what we call the Second Society. In this chapter we explored the implications of Web 2.0 applications for the emergence of the intelligent government.

The study has shown that Web 2.0 applications can have different characteristics and functions. For that reason we have tried to classify Web 2.0 applications. We made classifications based on distinguishable characteristics (generic versus specific, dynamic versus static, closed versus open and personal versus collective) and functions (sharing of information, mobilisation of interests, social interaction, delivery of services and transactions) of Web 2.0 applications.

All policy stages within the public sector are currently being influenced by new internet applications, namely policy development, policy implementation, monitoring and management. We state that Electronic government is not a goal in itself but a process in which intelligent Web 2.0 technology is being used to make the policy process more effective and efficient. For this reason it is better to speak about Intelligent Government (I-Government). An indicator for the Intelligent Government in the Second Society is that the application must meet a successful linkage between the problem and solution, both perceived by the actors involved.

In the case of the police department Haaglanden we can conclude it is an initiative by the government aiming to inform citizens about crimes in their neighborhoods in the region of Haaglanden. The linkage between problem and solution is less than optimal, where the linkage is successful in providing information, it is less successful in involving citizens.

In the case of the platform against airport hindrance we can conclude it is an initiative by citizens aiming to mobilize citizens who claim to suffer from airport hindrance in the region of Castricum. The linkage between problem and solution is completely successful. When citizens obtain the possibility to, within ones own problem perception, contribute to a solution, the added value of this solution will be higher.

When we focus on the characteristics of these websites, we can conclude that both websites have a specific and collective focus and open access to all viewers. A difference between the two websites is that the 'governmental' website is more static then the 'citizen' website. When we focus on the function, we can conclude that informing is the most important function, but that, surprisingly, the degree of interaction is quite modest.

A critical key success factor is the influence of citizens on the process. We can conclude that websites in which citizens have a large impact on the problem perception and on the solution for this problem, have a larger degree of success than websites where this is not the case. An intelligent government is a government that mobilize the intelligence of citizens and activate, to speak in Web 2.0 terms, the wisdom of the crowds.

5. References

Bekkers, V.J.J.M. & Homburg, V.M.F. eds. (2005), *The information ecology of E-Government: E-Government as institutional and technological innovation in public administration*, IOS Press, Amsterdam et al.
Boulos, M.N. & Wheelert, S. (2007) "The emerging Web 2.0 social software: an enabling suite of sociable technologies in health and health care education", *Health Information and Libraries Journal* (24), 2007, pp. 2-23.
Center for Public Innovation (2007), *Second Society: over vernieuwing in de straat, de stad en de* staat. Voorstel voor een praktijkgericht onderzoeksprogramma, Rotterdam.
Eggers, W.D. (2007) *Government 2.0: using technology to improve education, cut red tape, reduce gridlock, and enhance democracy*, Rowman & Littlefield Publishers, Lanham et al.
European Commission (2007) *European eGovernment 2005-2007: taking stock of good practice and progress towards implementation of the i2010 eGovernment Action Plan*, DG Information Society and Media, Brussels.
Frissen, V. et al. (2008), *Naar een 'User Generated State'? De impact van nieuwe media voor overheid en openbaar bestuur*, TNO, Delft.
Heeks, R. (2006) *Implementing and managing eGovernment: an international text*, SAGE, London et al.
Hernon, P., Cullen, R. &Relyea, H.C. eds (2006) *Comparative perspectives on E-Government*, The Scarecrow Press, Lanham et al.
Kool. D. de (2008) *Monitoring in kaart: een studie naar de doorwerking van op GIS gebaseerde beleidsinformatie in het leerproces van organisaties die een rol spelen bij de uitvoering van beleid*, Center for Public Innovation: Rotterdam.
Meijer A. & Homburg, V.M.F. (2008) *Op weg naar Toezicht 2.0*, Boom Juridische uitgevers, Den Haag.
Miller, P. (2005) "Web 2.0: building the new library", *Ariadne*, No. 45, October.
Ministry of Economic Affairs (2006), *The Digital Economy*, The Hague.
Osimo, D. & Burgelman, J.C. (2007) "Web 2.0 for eGovernment: why and how", 4th Ministerial eGovernment Conference, Lisbon (presentation).
Surowiecki, J. (2004) *The wisdom of crowds: why the many are smarter then the few and how collective wisdom shapes business, economies, societies, and nations*, Doubleday, New York et al.
Wamelen, J. van & Kool, D. de (2008) "Web 2.0 and the implications for E-Government" In: P. Cunningham and M. Cunningham (eds.) (2008) *Collaboration and the Knowledge Economy: Issues, Applications, Case Studies*, Volume 5, IOS Press: Amsterdam et al., pp. 423-432. Proceedings of eChallenges e2008 Conference and Exhibition, Stockholm, Sweden, 22-24 October 2008.
Woods, E. (2007) "Web 2.0 and the public sector", http://www.silicon.com/publicsector/0,3800010403,39168737,00.htm, 11 October.
Wyld, D.C. (2007) *The blogging revolution: government in the age of Web 2.0*, IBM Center for The Business of Government, Washington (E-Government Series).

A Lightweight SOA-based Collaboration Framework for European Public Sector

Adomas Svirskas[1,2], Jelena Isačenkova[1] and Refik Molva[1]
[1]*EURECOM*
Sophia-Antipolis, France
[2] *Vilnius University*
Vilnius, Lithuania

1. Introduction

E-Business and e-Government solutions are becoming more and more widespread with constantly growing number of users depending on availability, accuracy and security of such e-Services. The users must be able to trust these services, otherwise they will be reluctant to embrace the new opportunities and will not be able to reap the potential benefits. In addition, the end users wish to use the e-services in the simplest way possible and to have them "on tap" 24x7 as other conventional utilities. For this to become possible, a robust interoperability fabric among the involved institutions needs to be established. This means having a lot of collaborative interactions invisible to the end-user (a business or an individual citizen) in order to fulfil the promise of e-Services. Such interactions become more complex when the organizations belong to different countries, act according different laws in different languages. This chapter presents the work among to create an efficient, secure and trusted interoperability framework for public sector agencies of European Union member countries.

In a simplified view, the administrations in Europe as a whole can be seen as a forest. Each tree is one specific administration of one member state (Fig. 1.). Each leaf is one particular service provided by this administration. E-Administration today mostly consists of providing services via IT tools and reducing the paper support via a user-friendly interface to the service. This is what we call "e-Administration in the small".

The real challenge is to enable smooth collaboration between the trees, i.e. between administrations of the same or of different member states. This is "e-Administration in the large" and reflects our understanding of collaborative e-Government systems. The R4eGov project (R4eGov, 2005), aims at providing the basic conceptual and technical framework for the first e-Administration in the large for Europe. R4eGov emphasises the basic control and security principles of:

- Local data ownership: each "leaf" uses data stores, in most cases local, to store its data. For example, civil status data (état civil), which records the birth, marriage, death of French citizens born in France are managed by each city.

- Local information access policies: data access is generally restricted to some personnel of the administration which operates the service. Access to some of the data, certainly not to the entire data stores, must be granted to personnel of other administrations, under controlled conditions. Data stores/bases in their entirety should never be displaced nor copied nor merged to permit e-Administration in the large.
- Local enforcement of organisational control and security policies, according to the local legislative acts

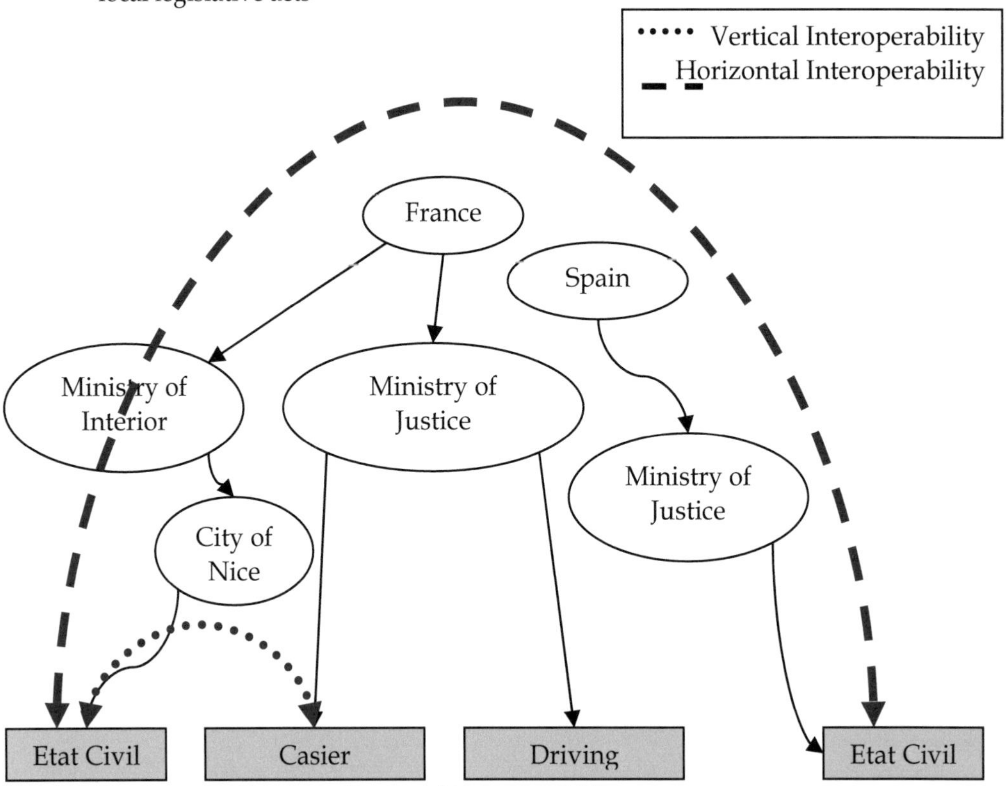

Fig. 1. E-Government Forest and types of interoperability

A stepwise refinement approach focusing on progressive development and seamless deployment of collaborating, cross-organisational collaborative workflows is required as no single process model covering all European administrations will ever be created from scratch. To permit the progressive take-up of government process modelling, the environment must allow for incomplete and not fully formal descriptions, in addition to descriptions being developed separately with little concern for interoperability.
The R4eGov project takes into account the answers provided by existing bodies (eEurope eGovernment Subgroup, IDABC Management Committee , ADAE , etc), which debate on how to best grant access to private data owned by other Member States, while protecting privacy as requested in the constitution of the concerned Member State. To be practical, we address the problems raised by the case studies of the R4eGov project (such as Europol/Eurojust, Austrian government etc). We develop a collaborative interaction model

of the European e-Administration, where the processes, the levels of control, security and timing requirements are described. This will constitute the top level picture of the European e-Government. Boxes at the bottom of Fig. 1 are examples of domains (Etat civil, Casier judiciaire, Driving offences) that have adopted IT and are examples of successful e-Administration applications. Today, exchanges between administrations of one country (such as, for example, between French Etat civil and Casier judiciaire) are being put in place with often little consideration for the need of mutual trust. Exchanges between states are possible but of little practical use. It is urgent to address these issues.

Thus, the three main objectives of the R4eGov project are:

- To gather and elicit the requirements for e-Administration in the large, on basis of which a concrete interoperation of web service enabled legacy public sector applications will be achieved using collaborative interactions.
- To provide the tools and methods for an e-Administration in the large from a technical and sociological perspective.
- To provide the required security and privacy for an e-Administration in the large, defining the appropriate methods and tools for control, security and privacy at the collaborative workflow and application layer.

One of the main results of this project is a reference framework and its proof-of-concept implementations based on several case-studies derived from the business requirements of the public administration organizations participating as partners in R4eGov project, such as Europol, Eurojust etc. The framework, thus, is quite generic and customizable to fit varying business needs.

Interactions among the participants of knowledge-intensive collaborations are often based on the Service Oriented Architecture (SOA) paradigm - the partners use each others' services. Such collaborative on-demand interactions take various forms depending on various factors such as complexity, scope, duration of the interactions, level of formalization and the application domain. Within the scope of our work, the term *collaborative* denotes the type of interactions where the partners are peers, i.e. they do not have direct control over each other and communicate by exchanging mutually understandable messages among themselves.

The notion of peers is well suited to collaboration of the governments and other public service agencies of 27 European Union member countries - these organizations are independent, act according to the law of their respective countries yet have strong needs (and obligations) for interoperable interaction. For example in the Hague Programme (Hague, 2004), the European Council stated: "*The mere fact that information crosses borders should no longer be relevant. With effect from 1 January 2008 the exchange of such information should be governed by conditions (...) with regard to the principle of availability, which means that, throughout the union, a law enforcement officer in one Member State who needs information in order to perform his duties can obtain from this from another Member State (...)*". Currently, in European law enforcement domain work is underway to implement the principle of availability with respect to six categories of data: DNA, fingerprints, ballistics, vehicle registrations, telephone numbers and other communications data, and civil registers.

2. A motivating case study from the European e-Government field

We have motivated our work, to a large extent, with a use case from the Europol (EP)/Eurojust (EJ) collaboration domain. These two agencies have been set up to help the EU member states co-operate in the fight against cross-border organised crime. Co-operation in criminal matters is a subject dealt with in the "third pillar" of the EU (Title VI of the Treaty of the European Union). Eurojust stands for the European Judicial Cooperation Unit whereas Europol refers to the European Police Office. Europol and Eurojust carry out very specific tasks in the context of the dialogue, mutual assistance, joint efforts and co-operation between the police, customs, immigration services and justice departments of the EU member states.

Europol became fully operational in 1999; Eurojust was set up by a Council Decision in 2002. Both agencies are based in The Hague, The Netherlands. Establishing a secure IT connection between Eurojust and Europol has been an objective shared by the two organisations for several years. Europol and Eurojust are two key elements of the European system of international collaboration within the areas of law enforcement and justice. Even though they differ considerably in the way they are organized, on how they operate and on their mandated areas, there is an overarching need to ensure smooth collaboration and effective information exchange between the two organizations.

In spite of the presence of legal basis for collaboration between the two organizations since 2002 (the Eurojust Decision and the Agreement between Eurojust and Europol of 9 June 2004), the complexity of the nature of the exchange (content, channels, sources, recipients, means, etc.), the compliance framework (legal basis, compliance and data protection rules) and the different implementation of policies and procedures in the 27 member states, have all limited the collaboration on cases to a small number.

From the technical point of view, it should be noted that both organisations already manage their information through computerised systems (Europol's Overall Analysis System for Intelligence and Support (OASIS) and Eurojust Case Management System) but these systems are currently separate.

Therefore, a structured approach on how to deal with the barriers to information exchange must be undertaken. While lines of communications at various levels already exist, these channels should be supported by computerised technical devices to allow the secure and swift exchange of information in the framework of the above legal instruments and the applicable data protection rules. In practical terms, it is necessary to follow an appropriate methodology to establish sound solution architecture and obtain/create ready-to-use tools (framework and software) in order to:

- Facilitate collaboration between Europol and Eurojust
- Improve the collaboration of the sources of Europol and Eurojust
- Get the tools and implement a practical viable solution

The creation of a framework (conceptual and practical, including tools) that allows dealing with the multiplicity of instances of technological and business rules, would allow for an identification of the barriers that impede international collaboration and for taking appropriate countermeasures on a technological or business level (including the change in legal framework) where necessary.

In order to illustrate the aforementioned issues, let's take a simple information exchange scenario depicted in the Fig. 1. The scenario involves four parties, each having their own independent administrative and security domains. All the parties should use some kind of

Collaborative Workflow Management System (CWfMS) to better integrate and automate their collaboration processes.
Eurojust uses a Case Management System (CMS) to support the work of its prosecutors, but the CMS is not the only source of information. EJ depends on information provided by EP, which does the main investigation work. Furthermore, as EP is also a centre of collaboration of all member states of the European Union, it can request information on a suspect from a national investigation bureau. This is what happens in the chosen scenario, which, roughly, consists of the following individual collaboration steps:

1) An EJ case is created in the CMS
2) During a meeting at EJ, it is decided that the National Member of state a (NMa) will request data from the Case Analysis bureau of her/his member state (MSCAa)
3) NMa sends the request to the Europol Liaison Officer of her/his state (ELOa)
4) ELOa contacts the Europol National Unit of her/his state (ENUa). ENUa contacts MSCAa and MSCAa sends back data to ENUa, which passes it on to ELOa
5) ELOa retrieves additional data from the InfoEx system
6) ELOa sends back both data sets to NMa.
7) NMa updates the CMS with the data

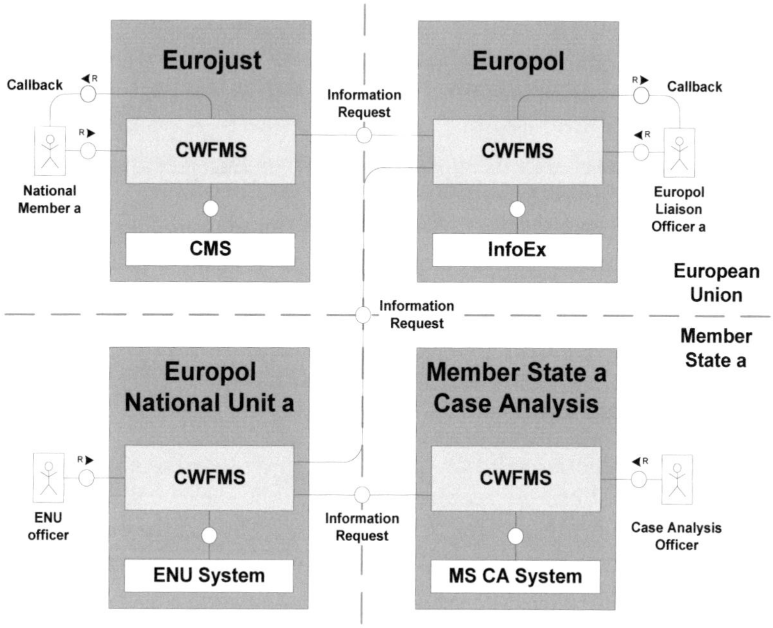

Fig. 2. A sample information exchange scenario from EP/EJ case study

These steps, with some variation, are further depicted in more detailed and complex way in the Fig. 3, which is a real-world example of the issues to be dealt with. Furthermore, this simple scenario is only a very small part of the EP/EJ collaborative interaction needs and, in turn, the EP/EJ case study as whole is just a tiny (however important) bit in the overall European e-Government landscape.

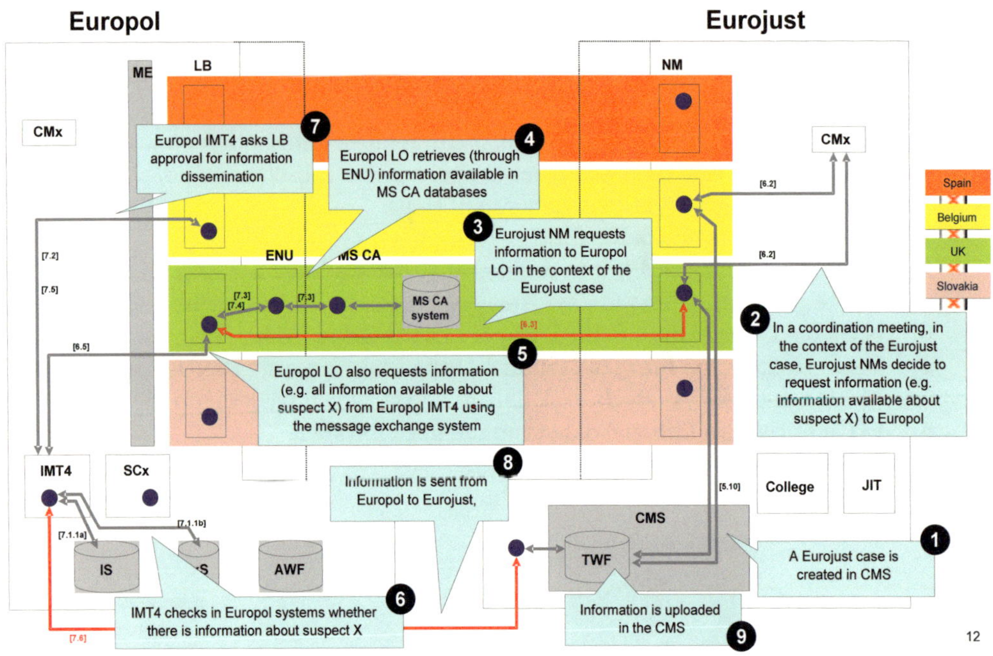

Fig. 3. Interaction Flow - Exchange of information between Eurojust and Europol

It is obvious that the problem of pan-European interoperability among the public administration bodies is a very complex one and, of course, the R4eGov project is not the first effort trying to deal with it. In the following section we will outline the principles, which constitute the basis of our solution architecture and framework.

3. The solution architecture

Before presenting the proposed solution, it is worth to discuss the architectural context in brief. Having studied the business requirements of public sector collaborative interactions (R4eGov case studies, 2007; eGovInterop Case Studies, 2006) and the current state of the art of possible implementation technology, we distinguish a few important factors, which determine the context of our solution architecture:

- A need for the public administration agencies (or their units) of the EU member countries to have *standard* ways for interconnecting and integrating their heterogeneous IS to ensure interoperability at shared information level.
- Independence of each agency and its operation according to the local legislative acts, regulations etc.
- Agencies being very protective of their data with regard to who can have access to it, what kind of "channels" the data can travel, who has seen the data etc.
- Enormous variety of the technical solutions being used by different agencies and countries

- Different countries and agencies are at very different levels of readiness to embrace e-Government collaborative interactions. The differences are found at legal, procedural, conceptual, cultural, technical, human skills levels.

These factors make a good case for using the service oriented (SOA) approach to integration of the information resources, i.e. each data source being exposed via well-defined interface, following the DaaS (data as a service) principle. The concept of data as a service (DaaS) suggests using service-oriented architecture (SOA) for accessing data "where it lives" - the actual platform on which the data resides doesn't make crucial difference for overall collaborative interaction among the partners. Thus, the key issues such as independence of the agencies and their differences become manageable – the agencies expose as much data as they possibly can and are willing to while the access to this data is granted only to the authorised parties.

3.2 The conceptual SOA approach

The architectural approach based on service and data virtualization is a sound practical foundation for implementing the *data as a service* concept in practice. Virtualization also allows uniform access to the software services exposed by the partners of collaborations. Virtualization and uniformity of services, provided by public administrations, are very important in order to have on-demand data aggregation, also referred to as enterprise mash-ups. This relatively new concept of Web 2.0 paradigm has already found its place in e-Government: for example, the U.S. Department of Defense's lead intelligence agency is using wikis, blogs, RSS feeds and enterprise "mashups" to help its analysts collaborate better when sifting through data used to support military operations, (Havenstein, 2007).
In addition to this, the integration framework needs to be lightweight and reasonably simple, taking into account that the level of integration readiness varies greatly from agency to agency in different countries. Simplicity allows the agencies to start small, experience benefits of integration and collaborative interactions, then iteratively add new services, as needed. Such approach will lower the entrance barrier for the less-prepared partners and will increase the chance of successful adoption of the solution.
In our R4eGov solution architecture, service virtualization is implemented using the concept of application-level gateway - each participant of collaboration communicates with the peers via Web services based Interoperability (IOP) Gateway. That is, the real services within an agency participating in the interactions, are accessible by sending a request to well known address of the gateway and specifying what kind of resource is needed. Gateway redirects such request to the internal provider, access control rules permitting. This pattern is not a new concept (Schmidt, 2000; Svirskas, 2007) defines a gateway as a mediator that decouples cooperating peers throughout a network and allows them to interact without having direct dependencies on each other. We have chosen this pattern and the newest SOA-based technologies to implement a lightweight, flexible and efficient interoperability platform, which will be explained below.
Each participant, with rare exceptions, at different points of the interaction can find itself at either the sending or receiving end of the information (SOAP/XML messages). In other words, in this asynchronous mode of interaction each participant is capable to receive requests from outside (other participants) to access its internal resources (data, services) as well as to initiate the requests towards other participants (or respond to their requests).

The latter case means that the internal resources (legacy/back-end systems) of a participant issue requests to the outside of the participant domain. Thus we have requests coming in and the requests/data coming out for each given participant multiple times during an instance (a collaboration scenario or business protocol, choreography) of collaborative interaction.

3.2 Implementation technology

Technically speaking, R4eGov SOA-based solution architecture primarily relies on Web services technology, including both the basic protocols/specifications such as SOAP, WSDL, HTTP/S and the more advanced ones - WS-Addressing, WS-ReliableMessaging, WS-Security, WS-Trust etc. - collectively known as Web services advanced architecture (Web Services, WS Security). Web services are used for both inter-domain communication between the gateways and internal services, which may represent some newly developed functionality or serve as wrappers for legacy systems.

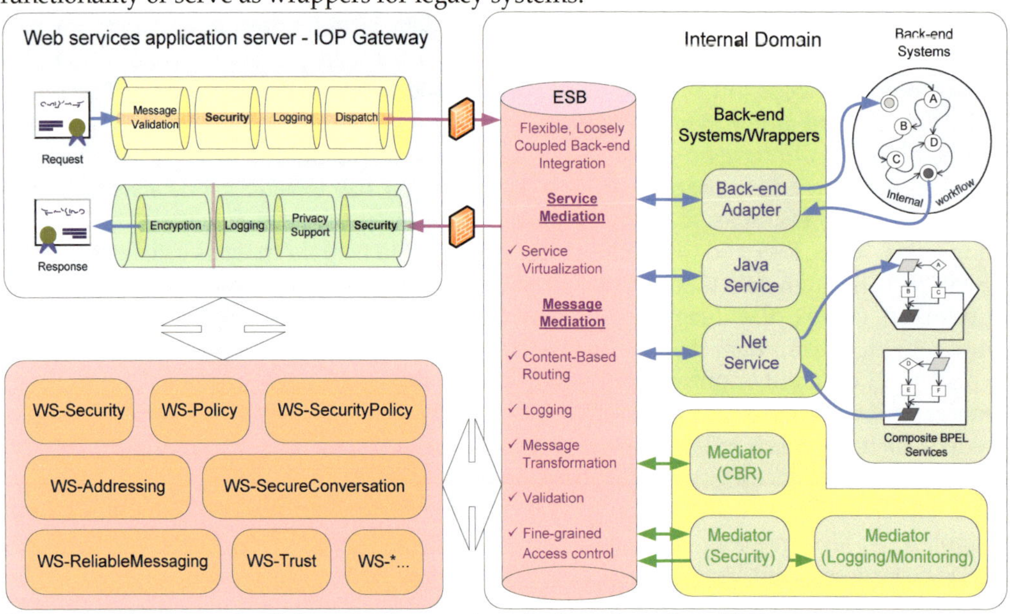

Fig. 4. Architecture of collaborative interaction platform based on IOP gateways

It is quite clear, that implementing the IOP Gateway features, as depicted in Fig. 4., configuring gateway instances for operating in different environments and, in particular, ensuring appropriate security level, is not a trivial task - the gateway needs to map incoming messages to internal operations, support business rules, enact business protocols (choreographies), which govern collaborative interactions, enforce security policies, provide logging, and monitoring, at least .

To ensure manageability, adaptability and flexibility, functionality of the gateway needs to be decomposed and developed/deployed accordingly. Firstly, there is a need for *modularity* - each separate gateway function should be well-defined and of manageable scope. The R4eGov architecture (R4eGov), introduces the notion of *extension module*. Extension module

is a software component that can be plugged into the execution environment and which fulfils a certain non-functional task in the context of collaborative workflows.
In addition, this architecture need to support *pluggability* - the extension modules should be ready for deployment by changing gateway configuration; no extra coding should be involved for registering, un-registering, changing order of invocation and similar administrative tasks. This helps achieving flexibility, as it should be possible to compose modules into flows (pipelines) for sequential message processing, separately for outgoing and incoming messages, specifying necessary order of message processing.
Let's look how these principles are applied in R4eGov IOP Gateway architecture. The main functionality of the gateway – connecting inter-domain collaborative interactions with the internal services is achieved combining modern web services engines (Apache Axis2), which support pluggable message handler architecture, allowing to implement message processing chains in an elegant and efficient way. Furthermore, modern Enterprise Service Bus (ESB)-based mediation frameworks (Apache Synapse) support extensions called mediators, which facilitate such message processing functions as:

- Content-based routing
- Message transformation
- Logging
- Security support
- Message schema validation
- Load balancing and fail-over
- Quality of Service support
- Protocol (e. g. SOAP, REST, JMS) and presentation format (e.g. POX, JSON, XML) conversion

ESB-based mediation framework can act like an intelligent yet lightweight and efficient application level router connecting the internal services providing access to the actual data with the external collaborative interactions. Such framework provides powerful means to define the rules according to which the messages are directed and handled.
As we can see, security-related extension modules can be implemented in two ways, depending on the context - they can be either Web services engine handlers or user-defined mediators in ESB mediation infrastructure. Such combination of Web service message processing handlers and ESB message mediators provides possibilities for composing very flexible chain of actions to be performed on a given message, which is crucial for IOP flexibility and usefulness. The implementations we have chosen, Apache Axis2 and Apache Synapse, packaged as WSO2 protocol stack (WSO2) are designed to work together, have solid developer and user base, which increases the chances of successful practical use.

4. Security features of the R4eGov framework

In a complex and heterogeneous ICT environment like the one R4eGov project faces, security requirements and expectations are often interpreted differently by different organizations and individuals, or simply specified in too-vague terms. For any security architecture related activity it is important to scope the area of security measures precisely, otherwise it is not possible to design and implement security solution in a timely and manageable manner. In short, our security/privacy solution addresses the following security concerns:

- Confidentiality of information items transferred between the IOP Gateways of collaborating organizations - implemented using Web services and XML security specifications (WS-Security, XML Encryption/Digital Signature).
- Authenticity of the information items being transferred between the organizations. This is implemented the same way as confidentiality.
- Role based access control to the resources offered by one organization to another. This is done by the *target* organization, based on the set of *distributed roles*.
- Role and identity based access control to the targets of partner organizations. This is done by the source organization, evaluating for each outgoing request whether the subject is *entitled to be assigned a distributed (external) role in a particular collaboration* and thus have an access right to a *particular resource offered by target organization.*
- Protecting privacy of the subjects in above authorization mechanisms by substituting their identity with pseudonyms. This way, the Personally Identifiable Information (PII) of the subjects remains within the boundaries of their "home" organization.

Apart from these general security concerns one of the frequent questions asked by the collaboration participants is whether their partners will apply adequate security measures to the data handed over to them. In a peer-to-peer collaborative environment, where data is transmitted among multiple partners it may happen, for example , that the transmitting authority applies higher security standards than the receiving authority, which consequently has to apply additional measures (which it does not usually apply to this type of information) in order to guarantee the same protection as the transmitting authority. Alternatively, if we reverse the roles, both parties will simply need to apply their own security measures (and the security measures applied by the recipient of the information will actually be stricter than the ones applied by its owner).

These requirements essentially mean that R4eGov solution will need to provide information *protection policy harmonisation mechanisms*. In our security architecture we address this issue by proposing the collaboration partners to share a common set of distributed roles. Inherently, the access control rights will be transferable across the domain boundaries and harmonisation of the security measures will be quite straightforward. The solution of distributed roles support based on (and extending) XACML (Lee & Luedeman, 2007).

In order for this to happen there must be a level of trust established between the transmitter and the receiver. The former needs to be sure that the latter actually enforces the specified policies. There are several ways to establish such trust, for example implementing access control enforcement using trusted code - components and services. (Djordjevic et al. 2007) describe a method for combining software resource level security features offered by Web services technologies, with the hardware-based security mechanisms offered by Trusted Computing Platform and system virtualisation approaches. They propose a trust-based architecture for protecting the enforcement middleware deployed at the policy enforcement endpoints of web and grid services. Such approach can be used in conjunction with our distributed roles-based access control.

4.1 Organization of security mechanisms

Security mechanisms of such solution are not simple and cannot be implemented in one piece/concentrated in one place. It is commonly (with some variations) acknowledged, that these mechanisms need to be distributed and grouped according to their purpose.
We can distinguish the following main security tiers:

- Protection and threat prevention
- Access enablement: Identity and Access Management - IAM

The security mechanisms are distributed accordingly. In our security architecture the "protection and thread prevention" part spans not only network/transport layer security but also message (e.g. SOAP) layer security, delivery of messages between the gateways according to the confidentiality, authenticity and integrity requirements.
Similar security functionality distribution is also advocated by (Mozes, 2004), he distinguishes between the SOAP intermediaries and security intermediaries in WS-based collaborative security architecture. The authentication (between the IOP gateways) and coarse-grained authorization can be performed at the system boundary (we put these functions into Web services engine message processing handlers), using any one of a variety of authentication mechanisms, such as conventional Web-access management techniques or one of the available federated identity solutions. This ensures that messages must pass a rigorous test before being allowed into the internal network. If service interfaces must be exposed to unauthenticated clients, messages must be subjected to a different test. In this case, schema-validation is a suitable test to prevent XML attacks. In both cases certain attacks remain a problem, e.g. Denial of Service (DoS) attacks. Gruschka & Luttenberger propose a mechanism to address the threats of DoS attacks (Gruschka & Luttenberger, 2006). On the other hand, schema-validation, fine-grained authorization and other aspects of security policy can be enforced close to the application environment. This allocation of security services also supports an appropriate division of responsibilities between network administrators, who are responsible for the integrity of the internal network and who must have the controls necessary to do that, and application administrators, who are responsible for policy enforcement in the applications and who must have the controls necessary to do that. This functionality of our security solution resides in ESB mediators.
Protection and threat prevention part of our solution focuses on data authenticity, integrity and confidentiality, which actually means encryption and digital signatures. In the Web services domain, WS-Security, an OASIS standard, is an open format for signing and encrypting message parts (leveraging XML Digital Signature and XML Encryption protocols), for supplying credentials in the form of security tokens, and for securely passing those tokens in a message. The core standards in this group comprise WS-Security Core (SOAP Message Security) and several token profiles including UserName Token Profile, X.509 Token Profile, Kerberos Token Profile, and SAML Token Profile. The token profiles enable serializing credentials in a consistent manner across platforms, certainly one of the driving forces behind the adoption of WS-Security in the first place.

4.2 Access control mechanisms

One of the central questions in security solutions is that of access control. In a nutshell, access control is the process of mediating every request to data and services maintained by a system and determining whether the request should be granted or denied. Access control is meant to protect resources (i.e., data and services) against unauthorized disclosure (secrecy,

confidentiality) and unauthorized changes (integrity), at the same time ensuring accessibility of the resources by authorized users whenever needed (availability). These aspects sometimes are mutually conflicting and balancing them requires a careful approach.
An important access control implementation principle of our security architecture is well coordinated operation usage of Policy Enforcement Points (PEP) and Policy Decision Point (PDP) - access control decision making is concentrated in a single place (dealing with a vulnerability of having a single point of failure is a separate issue) and accessed from several PEPs:

- Loose standards-based (XACML) coupling of PEP and PDP facilitates flexibility of potential deployment
- Policy management service supports the specification, interpretation and instantiation of different types of policies: access control & obligation (event-condition-action, ECA).
- Policy deployment service supports distribution and deployment of policies for usage by PDP.

One of the apparent virtues of the XACML framework is its modularity. XACML specification explicitly acknowledges that PEPs can be implemented in a variety of ways and use the same PDP, essentially enabling authorization as a service.
For instance, PEP may be part of a remote-access gateway, a part of a Web server or part of an email user-agent, etc. In our architecture we can foresee two types of PEP. Firstly, the *incoming* requests received by the IOP Gateway are processed by a chain of handlers, one of them serving as PEP and providing the initial crude screening of the request. This PEP acts as a "bouncer", performing fast "face control" and protecting the inner workings of the gateway from obviously unwelcome requests. The *outgoing* requests and responses are subject to inspection, outward access control and potential transformations, which are achieved by processing these outgoing messages by a chain of handlers controlling the outgoing flow. Once again, one of these handlers acts as a PEP and ensures enforcement of applicable policies.
Therefore, there is a need for a canonical form of the request and response handled by an XACML PDP. This canonical form is called the *XACML context*. Its syntax is defined in XML schema. The XACML-conformant PEPs may issue requests and receive responses in the form of an XACML context. But, where this is not the case, an intermediate step is required to convert between the request/response format understood by the PEP and the *XACML context* format understood by the PDP, as depicted in Fig . 5.

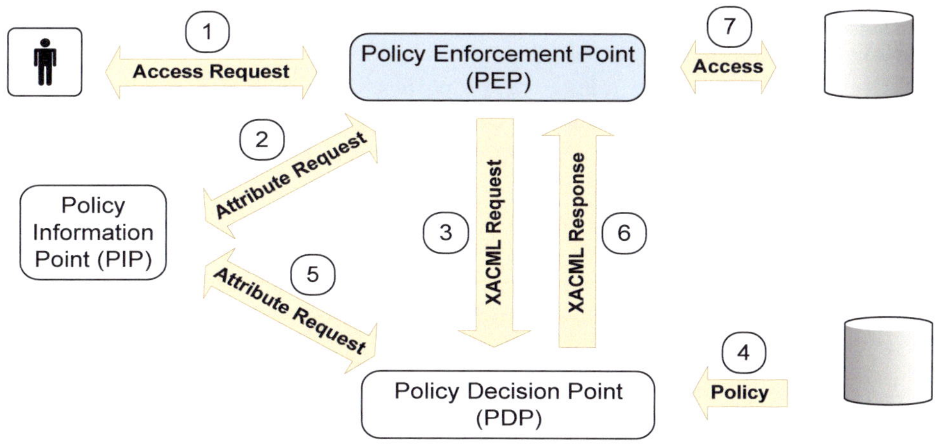

Fig. 5. Typical XACML-based authorization process scheme

Assuming that integration of the IOP Gateway with the back-end systems of the participants of the collaborations is done using Enterprise Service Bus (ESB), certain functionality of modern ESB implementations can be leveraged to further secure the interactions. In particular, the feature of *mediators*, which can be set up to intercept the messages sent via ESB, can be used for installing additional PEPs for finer-grained access control to the resources. There can be additional PEPs implemented as required and installed at some points of the system, which can't be foreseen in advance due to the scale of integration. In addition, there can be legacy PEPs, which will need to enforce new and/or updated policies. Given the variety of PEPs, it is unrealistic to expect that all the PEPs in an enterprise do currently, or will in the future, issue decision requests to a PDP in a common format. Nevertheless, a particular policy may have to be enforced by multiple PEPs. It would be inefficient to force a policy writer to write the same policy several different ways in order to accommodate the format requirements of each sort of PEP.

The benefit of this approach is that policies may be written and analyzed independent of the specific environment in which they are to be enforced. The principle of separating the concerns of policy modelling/management from their enforcement environments/decision request formats is very important, as it allows to have consistent policy definition, verification and reasoning for all the requests/resources. XACML specification provides an abstraction-layer that insulates the policy-writer from the details of the application environment. As mentioned before, the canonical representation of a decision request and an authorization decision is called XACML context. Context handler is an entity, which converts decision requests in the native request format to the XACML canonical form and converts authorization decisions from the XACML canonical form to the native response format.

In multi-party interactions quite often is important to preserve privacy of the subjects (requestors), without compromising appropriate access control. Our contribution aims to solve this issue without a need to explicitly involve a third trusted party into the interactions. Privacy preservation is a complex task, affected by different kind of policies, defined by different parties:

- Access control policies govern access/release of data/services managed by the party (as in traditional access control)
- Release policies govern release of properties/credentials/PII of the party and specify under which conditions they can be disclosed
- Sanitization policies provide filtering functionalities on the response to be returned to the counterpart to avoid release of sensitive information related to the policy itself
- Data processing policies define how the PII will be (or should be) used and processed In our solution we will be using access control policies for fine-grained resource protection on the service provider side and properties/credentials release policies along with the sanitization policies on the requestor side.

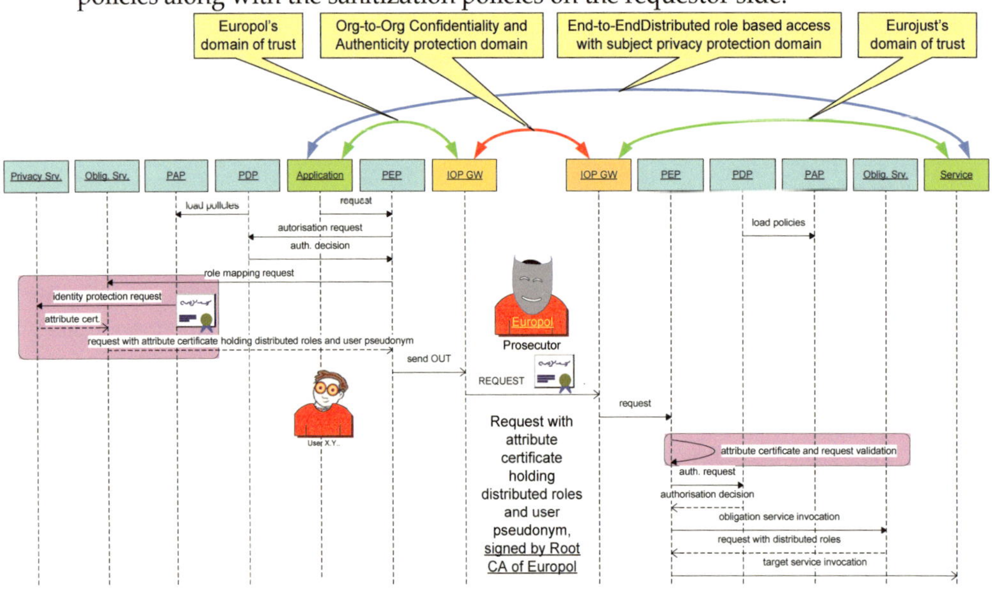

Fig. 6. Typical XACML-based authorization process scheme

The traditional identity-based access control models where subjects and objects are usually identified by unique names are not always suitable due to privacy concerns. It is easy to foresee a need to protect subject's privacy in e-Government interactions, for example in judicial and/or law enforcement domain. Therefore, attributes other than identity are needed to determine the party's rights to access a resource. In this case access restrictions to the data/services should be expressed by policies specifying the attributes a subject has to possess to get access to the data/services. For example, a role or several roles (unless very explicit, such as top management) does not reveal person's PII. This is in line with role-based access control principles. Fig. 6. illustrates privacy-preserving access control protocol of the R4eGov framework.

There are various ways to implement attribute based security tokens, one of them is to use digital certificates. Traditionally, a digital certificate has been mostly used as the identity certificate. An identity certificate is an electronic document used to recognize an individual, a server, or some other entity, and to connect that identity with a public key, thus solving key management issue. Another type of digital certificate is attribute certificate, which can be used in attribute-based access control mechanisms. An attribute certificate has a structure similar to an identity certificate but contains attributes that specify access control information associated with the certificate holder (e.g., group membership, role, security clearance).

5. Conclusions

The number of complex multi-domain/multi-country collaborations is constantly increasing, as the SOA concepts and supporting technologies are maturing. In order to gain acceptance, such solutions must be efficient, easy to use, secure and trusted. The work presented in this chapter aims to leverage the best implementations of standard and interoperable Web services specifications to provide a lightweight and modular framework for inter-organizational collaborative interactions. The concept of application-level gateway is implemented using pluggable extensions of Web services engine and further enhanced by using intelligent message processing based on Enterprise Service Bus and mediation techniques. This kind of virtualization allows achieving needed flexibility and security level providing standards based interoperability, data confidentiality, authenticity, integrity and role/policy based access control. These features, combined with the concept of Data as a Service (DaaS) enable the end users to have more power of creating ad-hoc enterprise data mash-ups, leverage benefits of enterprise social computing and gain additional opportunities when creating and reusing value-added knowledge.

A prototype of the described solution has been implemented using Apache and WSO2 Web services platform, WS-Security family of specifications. This prototype will be used to assess solution performance and suitability before moving towards enhancing choreographed interactions. A good case study for application of such compliance proof mechanism can be collaboration between public administrations of different EU Member States in legal/law enforcement domain (R4eGov case studies, 2007) where efficiency, security and trustworthiness of interaction steps is highly important. Further work is planned on privacy-preserving access control protocol, fine grained specifications of access entitlement and distributed authorization mechanisms.

6. Acknowledgements

The work presented here is partially funded by the European Commission under contract IST-2004-026650 through the project R4eGov (R4eGov). The authors would like to thank members of the organizations involved in R4eGov for their contribution: SAP Research Labs, University of Hamburg, Unisys Belgium, Europol, Eurojust, Austrian Bundes-chancellor office, in particular.

7. References

Apache Axis2, http://ws.apache.org/axis2
Apache Synapse, http://ws.apache.org/synapse
Corporation, (2002). http://www.verisign.com/wss/architectureRoadmap.pdf
eGovInterop Case Studies, 2006, http://www.egovinterop.net

Djordjevic, I.; Nair, K.S. & Dimitrakos, T. (2007). Virtualised Trusted Computing Platform for Adaptive Security Enforcement of Web Services Interactions. ICWS 2007, p.p. 615-622

Gruschka, N. & Luttenberger, N. (2006). Protecting Web Services from DoS Attacks by SOAP Message Validation

Hague Programme: strengthening freedom, security and justice in the European Union, 2004, http://www.libertysecurity.org/IMG/pdf/hague_programme_en.pdf

Havenstein, H. (2007). US Government Agency Embraces Web 2.0, PCWorld, http://www.pcworld.com/article/id,129328-c,internetnetworking/article.html

Lee, H. & Luedeman, H. (2007). A Light-weighted Decentralized Authorization Model for Inter-domain Collaborations, ACM Workshop on Secure Web Services (SWS'07)

Moses, T. (2004). Security in Web services world", Entrust Inc.

R4eGov, R4eGov case studies (2007). EU IST FP6 project, http://www.r4egov.eu

Schmidt, D.C. (2000)."Applying a Pattern Language to Develop Applicationlevel Gateways," in Design Patterns in Communications (L. Rising, ed.), Cambridge University Press

Svirskas, A.; Wilson, M.D.; Roberts, B.; Ignatiadis, I. (2007). Adaptive Support of Inter-Domain Collaborative Protocols using Web Services and Software Agents, eds. O. Vasilecas, J. Eder, A. Caplinskas, Frontiers in Artificial Intelligence and Applications, IOS Press, Amsterdam

Web Services, W3C, (2004). http://www.w3.org/TR/ws-arch/#technology

WSO2 Web services Application Server, http://wso2.org/projects/wsas/java

WS Security: A Proposed Architecture and Roadmap, IBM Corporation & Microsoft

XACML, eXtensible Access Control Markup Language , OASIS Standard

22

Spatial Aided Decision-making System for E-Government

Liang WANG, Rong ZHAO, Bin LI, Jiping LIU and Qingpu ZHANG
Chinese Academy of Surveying and Mapping
China

1 Building background and application status of the system

1.1 basic concepts of Spatial Decision-making System

Geographical Information System (GIS) is a new subject which rose in the 1960s, and is combined with computer science and geographic information science, and is also a technology system, it analyzes and manages geographic data contains spatial information using system engineering and information science theory under the support of software and hardware, and meets the need of planning, management, decision-making and researches. Decision Support System (DSS) generated in the 1970s, it is added to model base and management system based on Management Information System (MIS), is a computer system aiming at doing decision-making, and it provides decision support environment of analysis, model construction, decision-making simulation, decision evaluation for managers. With the development of its support scientific theory, DSS not only absorbs expert systems, fuzzy logic, neural networks, genetic algorithms, rough set techniques, etc, but also uses method base and its management system, knowledge base and management system to support intelligent decision-making.

Spatial Aided Decision-making System consists of spatial decision support, a number of interdependence and interaction elements of spatial databases. It is an organic whole for spatial data processing, analysis and decision-making. It is a really new information system on the basis of the combination of conventional decision support system and geographic information system. It transforms spatial data, extracts facts and relations which hides in the spatial data and expresses these using forms of graphics, tables, character, provide scientific and reasonable decision-making support for all kinds of applications in the real-world finally.

In order to adapt to the needs of information technology and enhance the level of administrative efficiency and decision-making, then realize optimization restructuring for government organizational structure and workflow, establish the government and the public electronic interactive channels, at last to achieve the development of national economic and social information, the government manage administrative departments use modern information technology roundly which is a new mode of management and organization providing quality services to the public, this is so-called e-government. The research and application of domestic and international e-government proved that more than eighty percent of integrated business management and decision support activities in e-government are associated with geo-spatial distribution. Therefore, the geo-spatial information and spatial support decision-making technologies have become an important content of e-government construction and applications, and its main functions are as follows:

(1) E-government is the basis of diverse government information relationship. Almost all government affairs are related to spatial location: in macro view, activates such as resources, environment, economic, social and military all take place in a certain area on Earth. In medium view, environmental protection, traffic, population, commerce, taxation, education, health care, sports, culture and heritage charged by government all have a specific location. In tiny view, social services also take place in specific locations, such as financial-commercial site, tour place, schools, hospitals and public transportation site. So it can be said that the majority of government affairs are related to locations, location is government information's integration basic.

(2) E-government is means of various types of government information visualization. Aiming at characteristics of management information targets, it can realize visualization of multi-dimensional spatial data processing and analysis process, multi-dimensional dynamic expression and process simulation of spatial phenomenon through spatial information visualization technology, which provides technical means for users to understand spatial information location features, the relations of composition and data quality.

(3) E-government is the platform associated with attribute information. By connecting a variety of professional information related to geographic information, comprehensive information applications can be formed through geo-coding technology. Similarly, collaborative information network of sharing data for that professional information based on relational database, which has no spatial orientation, can be also formed.

To sum up, the integration of spatial decision-making technology and e-government technology using GIS and DSS as the core can provide spatial quantitative analysis and scientific decision-making tools for government management.

1.2 Characteristics and key technologies of spatial aided decision-making system

Compared to general decision-making system, spatial aided decision-making system has five main differences:

(1) Different forms of data: spatial data refers to natural, social and cultural economic data which uses earth's surface spatial location as reference. they can have graphics, images, text, tables, and digital form with some attributes such as coordinates, location relationship and properties;

(2) Different ways of gaining information: spatial data have special access of gaining data, they are input to spatial information system through hardware devices such as digitizers, scanners, or image processing system and their corresponding input-driven software;

(3) Different decision-making models: there are many spatial models in Spatial Decision-making System, spatial models sometimes can be transformed into non-spatial

model to compute, and non-spatial model can be transformed into spatial model through implementing the model in each spatial unit.

(4) Different output results of decision-making: most of spatial decision-making system results are graphics, images, forms, etc.

(5) Different system structure: it is added to GIS spatial database and database management systems.

Due to these features, the construction process of spatial decision-making system will involve a number of high technology, such as computer technology, information technology, network communication technology and spatial information technology, in those technologies, new search engine, data mining technology, mass data management, comprehensive application technology of 3S (GIS, RS, GPS) and four-dimensional or three-dimensional virtual reality technology have developed very rapidly, the application foreground becomes explicit gradually.

Regarding to new search engine: collect and find information using a certain strategy in the Internet, understand, extract, organize and process the information, provide retrieval services for users, and realize the purpose of information navigation. New search engine contains the natural language understanding technology, XML extensible markup language and intelligent search engine technology; more accurate search technology is the core of intelligent search engine, which contains intelligent search, personalized search, structured search, vertical search, and localized search.

About Data Mining: With the development of computer and Internet technology, data resources are becoming richer and richer. However, the knowledge which is in data resources is not be fully excavated and used until now, the problem of "rich data but poor knowledge" is serious. The technology of data mining brought a ray of hope to solve the problem in recent years. It can reason the data and extract information from large amount of data to find some new interesting links; it is the extension of new knowledge discovery study in the database system.

In connection with massive data management: mass data storage and Internet are two important factors for database technology, it is already cannot meet the people's need using memory and external memory secondary storage of computer, so we need to use three-level data management. It should adopt different strategies for large database access and management, at the same time there is a big new problem to search and browse data in such a large database, so in some respects we must reconsider or abandon the intrinsic concepts and methods.

About integrated application technology of "3S": spatial information technology will come through a great development period in the next few years, satellites observes the Earth firing continuously provide up-to-date spatial data, and there is no need to translate the map to enter the GIS database, the commercialization of high-resolution satellite imagery will change the strategic position of vector map.

Regarding to technologies of three-dimensional, four-dimensional and virtual reality: from two-dimensional to three-dimensional and until virtual reality, from symbolic system to visualization, naturalizing landscape and even using natural language to interact, this kind of technology enable people to enjoy the results of modern IT technology with natural forms. Time dimension makes GIS change into four-dimensional spatial-time system.

About Decision support system: it finds necessary data from database and produces needed information systems for users applying mathematical models. It is mainly used to solve problems, such as computer organization automatically, the operation of multi-model, so as to achieve a higher level of decision-making capacity.

1.3 Spatial aided decision-making systems pattern and operational mechanisms

The operational pattern of spatial aided decision-making systems and government management business processes are closely related with information flow, In essence, business processes pattern of government is the application and construction operating mode of spatial decision-making systems. In e-government environment, there are three actors which are related to the application and construction of spatial decision-making systems: government agencies, enterprises and the public. In fact, spatial aided decision-making system has four construction and application patterns, which are government-to-government, government-to-government public servants, government-to-business, and government to citizens.

(1) Government-to-government pattern, government-to-government pattern is the basic pattern of e-government, is mainly referring to e-government activities which happen inside the government, among the different levels in government and different regions, different functional departments. It has many expressional forms, such as internal government network office systems, electronic regulations and policies systems, electronic document systems, electronic financial management systems, vertical network management systems, horizontal coordination management systems, network evaluation system, city network management system.

(2) Government-to-government public servant pattern, which refers to e-government between government and government public servant, it is a important form for government agencies to use to achieve internal electronic management through network technology. It is also the basic of government-to-government, government-to-business and government to the public e-government pattern. The key of the pattern is to establish an effective administrative office and staff management system using Intranet to enhance government efficiency and the level of public servant management. The specific contents include daily management of the public service and electronic personnel management.

(3) Government-to- business pattern, which includes the Government e-procurement, e-tax system, the administration of e-business systems, electronic foreign trade management system, small and medium-sized e-services, integrated information service systems.

(4) Government to citizens' pattern, the core of which is the government provides services for citizens through electronic network system. These services include electronic authentication, electronic social security services, e-health services, e-employment services, and e-education and training services.

Diversity, complexity and state administration of E-government provide Chinese support decision-making mechanism possesses the following features:

(1) Government leads unified planning. The construction of spatial support decision-making system is a complex systematic project, involving many departments and subject fields, such as the choice of network platform, the establishment of standards, design and construction of integrated resource database, the building of hardware and software environment, the support of regulations system, the establishment of information-sharing mechanisms, the building of organizational and investment channels, and so on. All these problem need government heads make unified planning and deployment. Without government's unified

leadership, the construction of spatial support decision-making system must be in serious difficulties. In addition, we had better adopt the top-down building strategy considering the data infrastructure, standards, technology infrastructure and talent base, and economic strength and application needs of the actual situation. That is, from the construction and application of general office of the state council, general office of the province government and department of the state council, through a typical demonstration, can sum up experience, improve inadequate, and then extends to geotropism government agencies. This mode of construction and operation can save time and has fast results.

(2) Unified network platform building. Unified government affair network platform is one of the cores of e-government construction, and its quality and efficiency affect the e-government construction. The network platform of spatial aided decision-making support system and e-government is consistent. Considering China's national conditions, outside administrative network and inside administrative network constitute e-government network platform, implement physical isolation between outside administrative network and inside administrative network, and implement logic isolation between outside administrative network and internet; In addition, we should build central government unified network gradually, integrated online information resources and services, and make the public get government information and services quickly and expediently and propose advice to government in time, and achieve interactive exchange of information among government, companies(enterprise) and residents step by step.

(3) Uniform norms and standards. As a unified platform or cross-platform structure, spatial aided decision-making support system requires standardization of guideline. Norms and standards include: application technology standardization, administrative information and public information production standardization, administrative processes standardization, spatial decision-making system criterion, database standards, government public network name standards, and interfaces standardization.

(4) Coordinated service is the basic operation mechanism. Coordinated service is the basic operation mechanism of spatial decision-making system, the so-called coordinated service can realize maximum commutative information resources sharing and application inside government agencies, between central government and local governments, between government agencies and relevant government agencies, between government agencies and companies(enterprise), and between government agencies and the public under the support of unified network platform, unified standard, unified geo-spatial information basis framework and unified information security system, and give priority to provide information services for government leadership agencies.

1.4 Application results of China's spatial aided decision-making system

The construction of China's spatial aided decision-making system commences since 1990s, the main representative is the project of GIS implemented by Surveying and Mapping administration and general office Secretary department of the state council in February 1992. From now on, it has lasted more than 16 years. The project followed our country's construction objectives and development strategy, insist the combination of technology and business, applicant it and at the same time, develop it. The project makes GIS become the powerful tool that provides information service for government's macro-management and decision-making and have great application the results:

(1) Establish basic spatial databases aiming at government macro-management which can provide basic spatial information and orientation framework for government spatial aided decision-making system.
(2) Develop special GIS application platform whose name is"Geo-Windows" fully by self aiming at government spatial information, expand it to become e-government spatial decision-making support software platform according to the government operation and finally become spatial information service tool which is easy-to-use for government department.
(3) Establish special spatial database support government spatial decision-making application. Through data processing, integrate special spatial database from professional sector base on national spatial database. Data include comprehensive national conditions, natural disasters, resource ecological environment, government information resources, western region, and economic cooperation with foreign countries.
(4) Establish multi-sectored coordination services operating environment, form an effective multi-sectored coordination service and integrated spatial information application pattern.
(5) Establish application service system which services the general office of the state council and local government.

2. Spatial information integration and database construction

2.1 The characteristics of E-Government data

The contents of E-Government involve many-sided government affairs such as geographical environment, national economy, social development, disaster prevention and mitigation, resources, conditions, population, corporate body, international economy, diplomacy and etc. So E-Government data represent the following characteristics: the variety of data types, the complexity of relationships and the multi-level.
(1) The variety of data types. The E-Government data mainly include foundational spatial data and thematic data with various proportional scales, remote sensing images which have characteristic of multi-platform, multi-spectral and multi-temporal, various statistics, large surveying records and other data such as text, images and video information. After digital processing, the display type of all above data can be divided into vector data, image data, raster data, relational databases, multimedia data and etc.
(2) Multi-levels. Because the geographical information system needs to meet the people orderly and gradually understanding on the geographical phenomenon, systems usually are demanded to provide multi-level magnification ratio data to different users. But it's difficult to build a geographical information system, which can integrate information fully and automatically through modern technologies. However, a method, to build multi-scale database, can resolve this question and can be realized easily.
(3) Complex relationships. In addition to topological relations between spatial data and hierarchy network crossing relations of data itself, there exist pivotal relations, the spatial location matching between different types of graphics and images, in the comprehensive utilization of spatial data, especially the relations of multiple entities in the region established by breaking the map-sheet limit when spatial database are being queried.
(4) More data origin. The government management covers all aspects. So, production, maintenance and updating of data need different departments. These make data come from

different origins and difficultly maintain and update.
In response to these characteristics, the system needs an appropriate model on the data organization. With the popularity of spatial data, the system needs distributed maintenance for different data, particularly the non-spatial data, and requires the data separation and data integration between spatial data and non-spatial data.

2.2 Database design and construction

The latest trend of GIS technology is to use the relational database or the object-relational database to manage spatial data and to establish GIS data server. It can take full advantage of the data management of RDBMS, of the data operation of the SQL langue and, at the same time, of management on massive data, transaction processing, record locking, concurrency control, warehouse and so on. These can integrate spatial data and non-spatial data, and then realize the Client / Server and Browser / Server structure veritably. In this project, we use the large-scale relational database system to manage data so that ensure the integration of spatial and non-spatial data.

2.2 .1 Whole design of database

From the view of application, the system adopts the following method, described as Figure 1, which designs an open, easy to reconstruct and well-suited decision-making database through taking advantage of the features of the GIS and the DSS.
According to the storage feature, the system data can be divided into spatial data and non-spatial data including the national economic statistics, text, images and multimedia. According to the data life cycle, the spatial data and non-spatial data can be both separated into static data and dynamic data. Static data has long update cycle and is maintained and updated by the professional maintenance tool of the system. Dynamic data is updated automatically through the clearinghouse and load to the spatial database and non-spatial database according to the type of data.

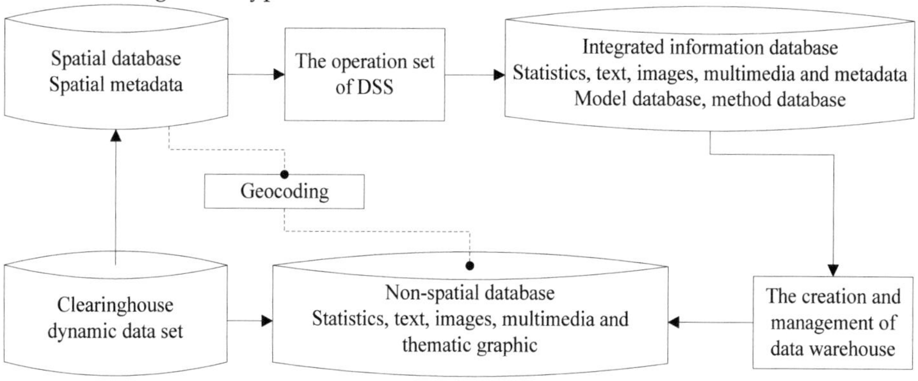

Fig. 1. The whole design of database

Spatial database stores the location-related data including vector graphics data, digital elevation model(DEM) data, thematic raster data, remote sensing image, spatial metadata and the basic attribute of spatial features. Non-spatial database store the original economic statistics, text, images, multimedia data and part of the non-spatial data contained geo-coding information, such as administrative divisions' codes and the road code. Based on non-spatial database, model database and method database, the integrated information warehouse can be established to face decision-making services. The multi-level connectivity of spatial elements can be realized through the DSS set, geo-coding technology and information stored in integrated information database, such as information-level object, foundational data tables, intermediate results and display results. The whole database adopts a unified database management tools to manage.

2.2 .2 Logical design of spatial database

Based on large-scale mature commercialization management system, such as Oracle, the spatial database uses an entire relationship storage model, which supports the multi-scale, multi-type and seamless massive spatial data management in logic. The specific logic model is like the Figure 2.

Organizations of various types' spatial data are as follows. Map-sheet is the collective set of point, line, polygon and annotation features belonging to the same logic region. Vector features in one map-sheet may include polygon features, line features, point features, annotation features and combination features of above basic features. Entity is the integrated and continuous complexity object aggregated by simple features, such as line and polygon feature, and is not subject to the restriction of map-sheet. Layer is a set of map-sheets, which have the same reference system, the same logical content and continuous distribution of spatial location. Database is a set of various types' data not only including vector layers, raster layers and image layers but also attributes data and ancillary data corresponded the vector data, and without any internal structure. The maps of database, usually refers to all spatial information of a region, may use different projection type and data type.

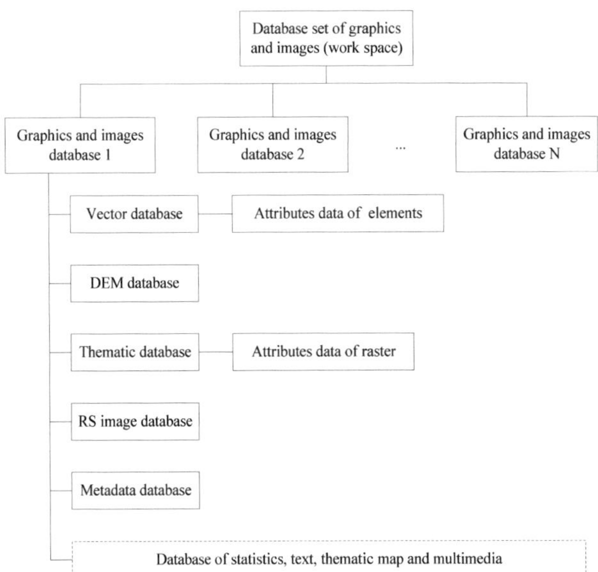

Fig. 2. The logic design of the spatial database

Spatial data are described by database sets, one work space, and are true of the geographic region which studied in one application. Database sets are composed of a series of graphics and images database. In this design, database is regarded as logic cell and it has various types but the same or similar expression of spatial resolution and the same mathematical basis. Data set stored in spatial database has characteristics of geographic location and spatial relationship, and can be separated into different spatial blocks and layers according to space and features' attributes. Spatial features can interconnect with non-spatial data in the data warehouse, such as statistics, text, image and multimedia, through geo-coding.

2.2 .3 Logical design of non-spatial database

Non-spatial database includes social economic statistics, text, images, multimedia, thematic graphics and other professional databases, which provide the data source for integrated information warehouse. Non-spatial database uses physical relational table to store non-spatial data, establish the tree structure information index relying on the theme and supports the use of geo-coding.

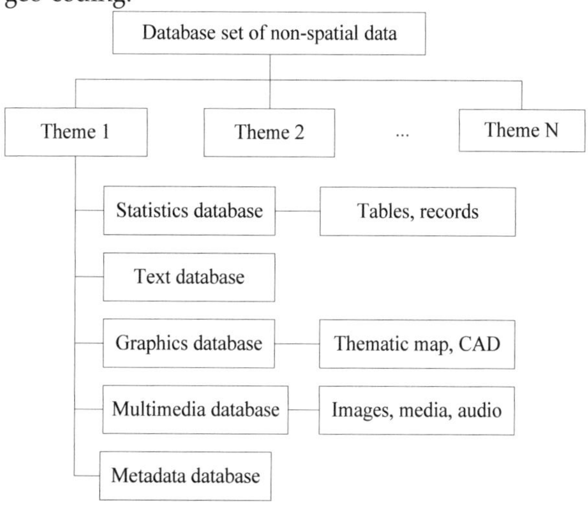

Fig. 3. The logic design of the non-spatial database

2.2 .4 Main flow of spatial database's establishment

The establishment of spatial database includes format conversion, projection transformation, data cropping, storage and symbolic expression. Each process has a batch tools to be completed quickly. Vector data supports the shape, E00 and SDE database format. Raster data supports the exchange format of ArcInfo grid and SDE database. Image data supports Geotiff, img, bmp, tiff and SDE database.

The establishment process of vector data includes projection conversion, format conversion, data storage, symbolic expression, annotation distillation and edition. The establishment process of raster data includes projection conversion, format conversion, data cropping, data storage, image creation and pyramid creation.

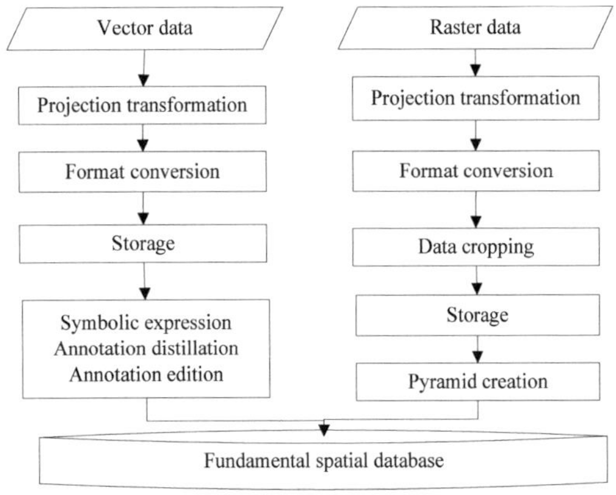

Fig. 4. The establishment process of spatial database

2.2 .5 Main flow of non-spatial database's establishment

Non-spatial data usually include a variety of tables, text, images and multimedia data. The core of non-spatial data management is the unified organization and storage of various discrete data, the logic relation between the different data based on its entity and the description information of data. So the system can provide standardized thematic dataset for applications. The steps of non-spatial database establishment include the following parts.
(1) Storage of various types' data
The system formats various types' data, such as tables, text and multimedia, into a unified relational database, uses alterable field to store its body paragraphs and creates entity code, type, storage time and other information for each non-spatial entity.
(2) Subject-oriented organization
In order to facilitate the data selection in the future, the system needs to establish a tree-view, and included subjection and parallel relations, using the entity geo-coding according to the theme.
(3) The establishment of logical relationship between spatial data and non-spatial data
The system defines a few of special field as the bridge to connect the no-spatial data with the spatial data.

2.3 The integration based on spatial framework for government information

2.3 .1 Integration technology of various types' data

Because administrative data have more sources and complex structure, there exist semantic differences and discontinuity between foundational spatial data and non-spatial data. It is difficult to integrate and share non-spatial data directly. The system uses geo-coding technology to realize the spatial data correlation and integration, uses geographical ontology technology to solve the semantic integration, uses dynamic projection to resolve rapid superposition of different projection data, uses data mining technology to achieve the integration of spatial data and text and uses the expression technology of economic statistics grid to integrate statistics and spatial data.

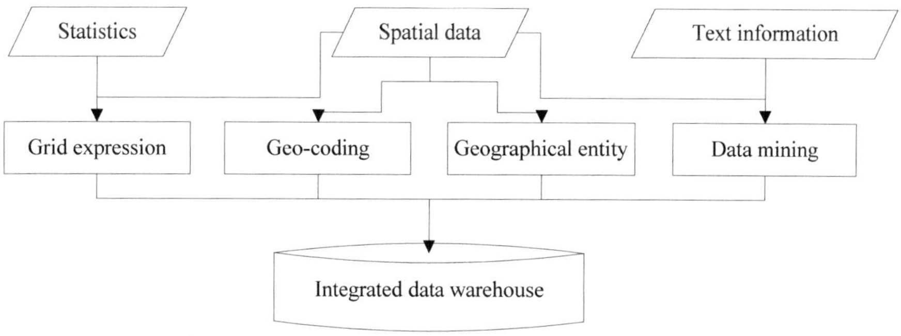

Fig. 5. Integration and fusion process of massive multi-source information

2.3 .2 Spatial data integration model

Administrative data involve civil affairs, land, water conservancy, agriculture, earthquake, environmental protection, marine, forestry, military and other departments. In order to ensure the integration services of the system and ensure that various types' spatial data can be displayed, queried and integrated analysis, the system must integrate the foundational spatial data and thematic data together. Department thematic spatial data involve various types' data, which can be divided into static and dynamic data. The static data are department data which have small change frequency, long change cycle and hugeness of data volume, whose management are off-line. The dynamic data are department data which have quick change frequency and very short change cycle, whose management are realized by real-time exchange and integration. Thematic data belong to different departments, most of which have established a respective classification indicator. For the departments with larger covers and more professional application, it is very difficult to provide a unified format for professional exchange in a short period of time. So those departments can provide a special data interface and resolve the question through a special conversion platform. Responding to changes in the thematic data, data integration can be completed in the foreground and background of the system to solve the integration of static data and dynamic data.

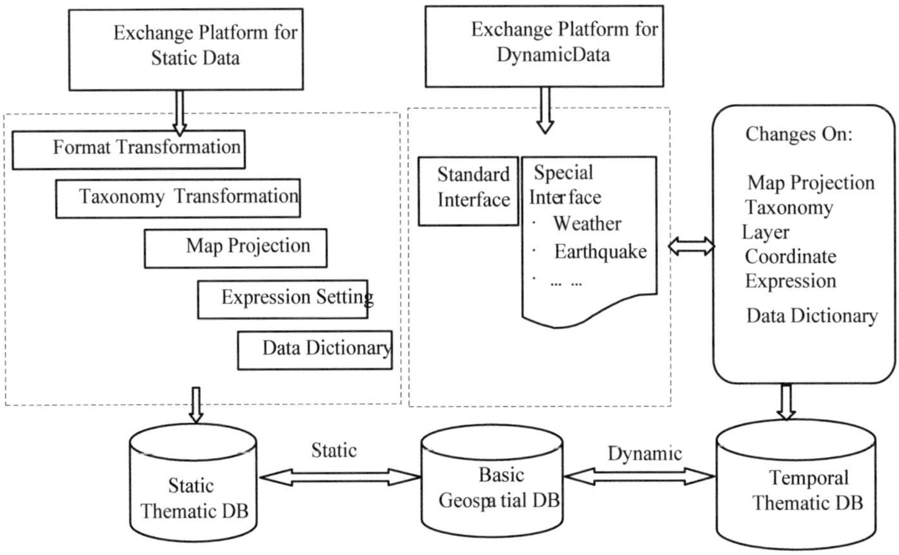

Fig. 6. Schema of data exchange and integration

3. Spatial aided decision-making software platform development

GIS is one of construction technology for E-government, and is also an aided tool to carry out management and macro analysis for all levels governments. It has an effect on national economy management, disaster prevention and governmental affairs management. But GIS and DSS usually independently work, the interactive relation between them is unsubstantial, so that application of e-government in GIS is inconvenient and inefficient.

Under the actual situation, we need to construct software platform of the spatial aided decision support system in the network environment, and to tightly integrate DSS technique with GIS technique, so that we can supply comprehensive information and decision-making service for the governments.

3.1 Design method of the platform based on GIS and DSS integration

3.1.1 The integration target of software platform

According to macro construction target of the e-government in China and system management requirement, the platform adopts uniform system structure design, database structure design, module and function design and component development, and takes the foundational spatial database as a framework to integrate a thematic spatial information, national economy statistics information, government affair information and multi-media information, and establishes spatial database with comprehensive information warehouse, and implements GIS, DSS and close integration and vivid function call according to the safe electron governmental affairs platform, and sets up an uniform spatial decision software platform for the E-government application.

The following principles are used in making the general design of the software platform: to meet the overall requirements of electronic government affairs and digital China construction, to conform to the national standard and specification and principle of information share and multi-protocols, to apply the integrated application pattern of C/S and B/S systems, to support information management structure of multi-subjects and multi-levels standardization and personality application, to realize the distributed management and maintenance.

3.1.2. The uniform database design

The work points of the database design are to accomplish the following works:

(1) Confirm design principle. Based on large relational database characteristics, we establishes some principle of database design, and at the same time, gives attention to request of GIS and DSS integration, request of application function.

(2) Choose database contents. According to application and characteristics of the spatial system the data contents of the platform are chosen such as the thematic data, spatial data, attribute data, document and multimedia data , etc.

(3) Design database. The concept/logic design of the database, physical design of the database and setting up the demonstration test of the database will be carried out in prescriptive method.

3.1.3. Uniform data management and scheduling

The implement of uniform storage and management for spatial data and non-spatial data are different from pure relational data management, also is different from file management. The important point is to resolve management efficiency of spatial data within relational database and concretely involved technique is described as following:

(1) The establishment of spatial data query mechanism. The key of spatial data organization is index and the good or bad performance of the spatial data index directly influences the whole performance of spatial database and GIS platform.

(2) Data compression. Regular GIS manages amount of data, high or low system performance have very great relation to transmission speed of network. In order to reduce load on network, we consumedly lower the transmission network quantity using data compression of spatial data, so the performance of the system has got higher.

(3) Making use of large relational database technique. The query of the great capacity for spatial data may return to a very big result to gather and attain several 100, 000 even million records. So we can put the records to database buffer in server.

3.1.4. The uniform software development

In order to exert respective characteristics of GIS and DSS in the application, attain the close integration of their function, the platform adopts component to accomplish function integration of GIS and DSS. The component can define a general call method for software serve, it can cross over a link library, application program, system software even network, the component can still provide valid path to separate software block, each block provides respectively service, the developer can use an object-oriented method to design and develop program, simplified complicated system.

For implement method of the software function, because system includes spatial data and relational data or statistic data, for the attribute data of spatial data adoption relational model are suitable and using SQL statement to carry out query is efficient. But object oriented method with abstraction, packaging, encapsulation; polymorphism is feasible to handle spatial data. Therefore, mixing object oriented with relational model is suitable for implement integral management of spatial data and attributes data.

3.2. The architecture of the platform

Application service structure of the platform adopts B/S, and the system maintenance adopts C/S structure, such as figure 7.

The software platform can be divided into three parts: application integration tools, application server and client module. The tools can deal with spatial data, such as input, processes, edit, and application theme integration/modify in server side. Application server runs in server side which receives and analyzes client's request, then, gets spatial and non-spatial data from database and send them to client. For complicated spatial operation, which could not be performed in client side, such as spatial analysis, the application server will call component in server side to perform the operation. Client side module is consisted of display and user interface.

Through uniform system structure design, database design, modularized function design and component development method we can implement close GIS and DSS integration and vivid function calling, set up uniform spatial decision software platform.

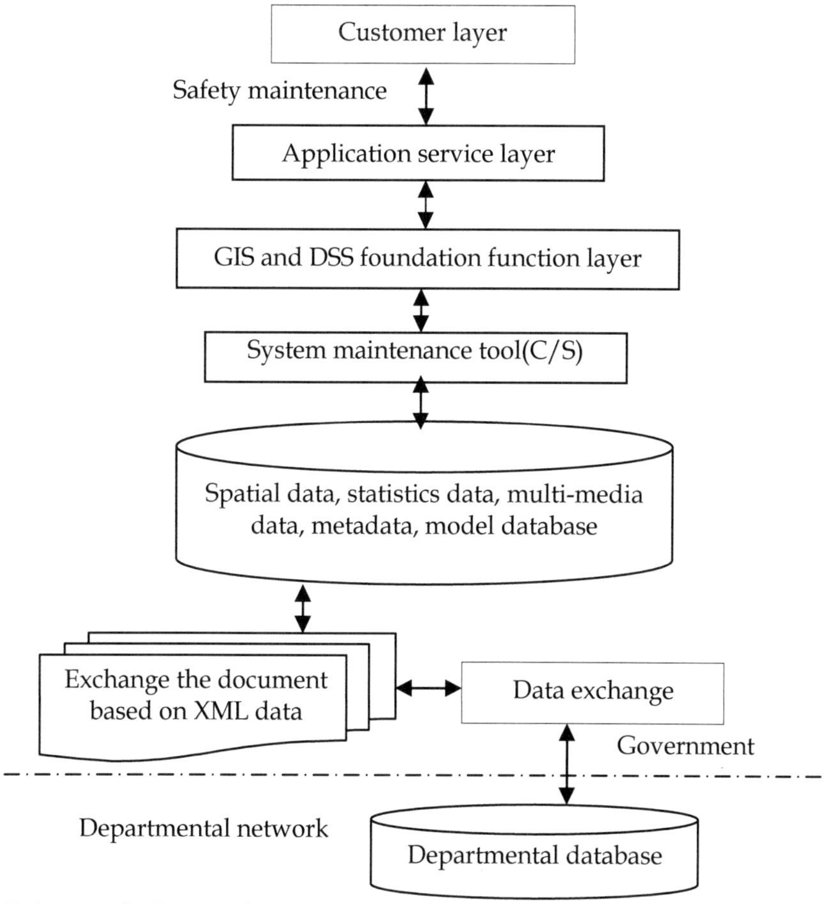

Fig. 7. Software platform architecture

3.3 The running software and hardware environment of the platform

Hardware environment: that includes high efficiency PC server, microcomputer client and wire network whose speed is above 2M.
Software environment: that includes the Windows operation system in server and client side, data management by Oracle 9i.

3.4 Integrated design and development of the software platform functions

To take GIS as a foundation framework and to use function calling to implement the close integration with DSS, the integration of their function are exhibited on three levels: data layer, maintenance layer and application service layer. Integration method is shown in figure 8.

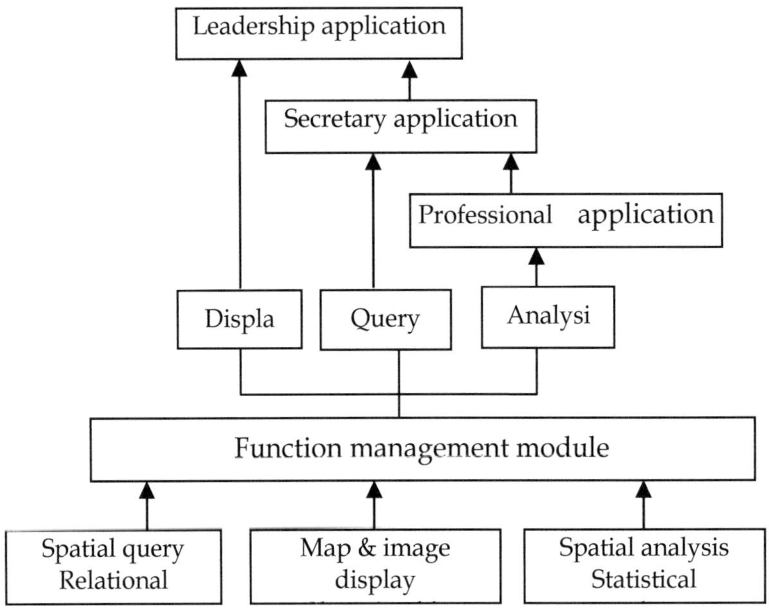

Fig. 8. GIS and DSS function integration

3.4.1 The integration function design of data maintenance layers

Using C/S system structure, the system administrator with professional GIS background can carry out management and support of the spatial database, comprehensive information database, operation process and the user interface.

(1) Geography spatial database support tools. It includes data import module, spatial database creation module, meta database maintenance module, database management module and data automatic exchange module.

(2) The non-spatial database support tools. It includes data import module, non-spatial data index creation module, database management module, data automatic exchange module.

(3) The comprehensive information data warehouse support tools. It includes relational database basic management component:, data interface component and data description metadata management component etc.

(4) The thematic database management tools. User interface consists of series of application thematic term and these themes are organized and spread by tree form. The system provides uniform maintenance tool of the thematic information to implement an user interface establishment and to make custom operation, on the thematic information tree each node can link with a series of spatial data, non-spatial data and correspond an operating command, create theme object entity, is used for description thematic spatial place, attribute information and operating command.

By providing uniform maintenance tool of the thematic information the system can complete a thematic tree creation, register, the increment, delete, copy, modify, operation for node, and at thematic tree node we can add spatial information (extent, entity), non-spatial information (table, text, thematic graphics, multimedia) and spatial query, spatial analysis and comprehensive information data warehouse analysis, etc.

3.4 .2 The function design and implementation of the application service layer

With adoption of uniform component standard method to integrate GIS and DSS function of being different hierarchy in serve, the application server takes GIS as a calling framework, GIS call the component function provided by DSS, and supports function of gentle assemble each other.

(1) Foundational function design. To complete the design of basic function of the system floor and corresponding correlation, reasonable grain dimension of the partitioning function, implement the united data access, data query, data operation.

Map display class: Show several data, vector map layer data, map library data, event.

The vector data query class: Provide map query, attribute query, metadata query, result conservancy.

The report prints class: Print the data (library, table, memory), record print and the sort print and the report make to order.

The vector quantity edits class: Edition setup, point, line, polygon and annotation edition, the map connecting side, metadata update.

The spatial analysis class: Overlaying analysis, buffer analysis, network analysis, the spatial statistic operation.

The terrain analyzes class: According to DEM, the system implements profile and factor creation output.

The spatial data processing class: Projection change, projection alteration, linear transformation, polynomial transformation, cut to slice, concatenation and attribute concatenation.

Statistics graphic class: Statistics cartographic model and statistics, the map decoration, thematic mapping, map keeping.

The intelligent graph component: To use artificial intelligence (AI) technique, applying rule knowledge processing thought, give the data information format according to the data list processing tool, national economy statistics information table and statistical charts automatically are expressed.

Combine time sequence model: Include model data processing component, the model creation component, settle information processing, model application analysis component.

The population simulation of spatial distribution model: Include model data processing component, the model creation component, settle information processing, the model application analysis component, census taking and spatial distribution analysis component etc.

(2) Application service function design. Through the function component of the assemble foundational function and custom development the system can provide more integrated information, text, multimedia and assistance the geography spatial information for application system.

Query function: Vector and raster data blending query, condition query, spatial relation query, Topology query, the spatial factor gather, sort and statistics, text data browsing, table data browsing, the intelligence make graph, information incident query etc.

The DSS function server can be run by the operation of defining command (usage operation coding start service) in advance, also query operation with GIS to combine an operation.

Analyze a function: The spatial topology overlay, buffering analysis, shortest path analysis, the best path analysis, resource allocation, DEM analysis, evaluation analytical, and region national economy decision analytical model.

Display function: Multi-dimensions map displays, remote sensing image the multistage show with roaming, data table, text, statistical charts.
The web serve. Provide a united user management, command request and respond to a function.
(3) User layer function design. Providing the system information service according to the WEB environment, the user can establish thematic information tree getting into an operation interface in advance.
Thematic tree: Show current theme name, we can click it to carry out a theme selecting.
Operate: Showing the information that includes current theme and its related operation is the main entry point of thematic tree.

3.4.3 Design of data layer integration and implementation methods

The spatial data and non-spatial data adopt large relational database such as Oracle to storage.
Provide uniform information framework to implement geographic spatial data, non-spatial data with comprehensive information warehouse based on the GIS platform.
Comprehensively adopt relational database to storage through geography code by making the spatial data linked with non-spatial data.
Implement the data integration of the exterior dynamic state through XML file from data switch center. In memory, GIS and DSS and use XML file as a medium to realize data exchange.

4. Spatial aided decision-making applications

With the development of the application of GIS and DSS facing Government management, it has been basically completed the application system of spatial aided decision-making services which support s the government management and decision-making. The mode of government services is from a single sector to multi-sector collaboration to support services. The application software is upgraded to the online version information systems from stand-alone version. The application fields from the simple electronic map to the information services whose business is associated closely. It has formed standardized services technical specifications and operating mechanism. Its application become more and more abroad.

4.1 Application fields

According to related statistics, more than 80% of the information that is supported to government agencies to carry out macroeconomic analysis and aided decision-making is related to spatial location information. Therefore, spatial decision-making system has a deep and broad application in government agencies. The main areas include:
(1) Integrated business management and macro-aided decision-making of the central government agencies
The spatial aided decision-making applications system, which is based on the organic integration of multi-scale, multi-temporal, multi-types geospatial data and a variety of non-spatial data, can provide comprehensive national information service to the leader,

including querying, tracking and understanding of the geographical environment throughout the country, economic and social development, disaster prevention and mitigation, emergency, infrastructure, and so on.

(2) Integrated business management and macro-aided decision-making of the government department

The application fields of spatial aided decision-making are broader in the government department, the example as follows:

i) Urban planning and management

ii) Land planning, management and use

iii) Population management

iv) Agriculture, forestry and meteorology

v) Environmental Protection

vi) Transportation

4.2 Work mode

Spatial aided decision-making system based on DSS and GIS mainly uses the mode of collaborative application of WAN and LAN as well as remote information service. It also uses construction methods of collaborative service based on the unified technology architecture and data standard and oriented the Chief of macro-and micro-level. It has completed collaborative work with many departments and can automatically load and integrate the related thematic information, such as meteorological, hydrological, remote sensing, disaster, and statistical information. The system achieves a continuous operation every day, and ultimately provides aided decision-making services of relevant information for the leaders.

Spatial decision-making services technology for e-government, based on functional synergy, adapts from the structure of E-Government which simplify the work of information services. Without changing the current computing environment of e-government, it accomplished the collaboration of a variety of spatial information between service and browser through a service agreement. It avoided the original spatial data transmission through the transmission to calculation results, so it improved the operating efficiency.

Spatial aided decision-making system based on DSS and GIS is a highly technical and complex project. It relates many aspects. Its effective application is not only dependent on technology, but also other factors, such as: data acquisition, data processing, data distribution, data sharing and so on. Under some conditions, the factors that affect the system success are not a lack of data or technical ability, but the practicality of the data. We have to be provided the most appropriate data to make the system work together.

4.3 Society benefit and roles

Now, spatial aided decision-making system has a considerable role and effectiveness in the social, economic, disaster prevention and mitigation, planning and construction of major projects and emergency. As follows:

(1) Providing decision-making services for leaders of government agents and improving efficiency and quality of government decision-making.

(2) Accelerating the development of domestic self-copyright software technology about

e-government, raising the level of application effectively, and promoting the development of e-government market.

(3) Through integration of e-government information resources database, it speeds up and promotes the process of the information sharing, integration and standardization and e-government development in China.

(4) It broadens the application field of geospatial data and promotes its application in government departments to a new level of the distributed network of government. Furthermore, because of the applications running in the government network, it provided services not only for the central departments and the four western provinces, but also for all the 1 local government and relevant departments. The application has a strong demonstration effect. This method may be popularized in building e-governance for government agencies.

4.4 Typical demonstration application

Under the support of the central and local government departments, Chinese Academy of Surveying and Mapping has developed spatial aided decision-making software platform based on DSS and GIS. It has used construction methods of collaborative service based on the unified technology architecture and data standard. It has built a series of application systems using business management and macro-spatial decision support, which include disaster prevention and mitigation, analysis of economic development, development of the western region and China electronic map. The system covers the applications of government comprehensive departments and professional departments in the government's macro-management, earthquake resistance and disaster relief, environmental protection and facilities planning. In addition, it has built e-government resource database including geography, economy, social development, disaster prevention and mitigation, resource and environment, conditions, population, corporate, international economic and foreign relations. The data is from the authority departments. The integration of spatial data and non-spatial statistical data, text data, multimedia data is achieved. It has established basically the update mechanism and technology system for thematic data.

4.4.1 Application systems running in the special network of the central government departments

(1) Information service subsystem of disaster prevention and mitigation

On the basis of geo-spatial data, through jointing the departments of State Council in charge of natural disasters and their command centers, and integration of the relevant important information, it provides the geographical location, socio-economic background, disaster live information and disaster-regional economic statistics and analysis when the disaster occurs. The main contents include the flood information, meteorological information, remote sensing information, earthquake disaster information, geological disaster information and so on. As shown in Figure 9 - Figure 12.

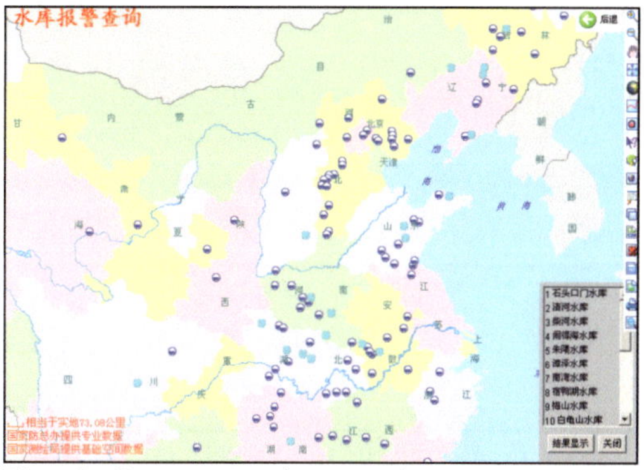

Fig. 9. Reservoir alarm information

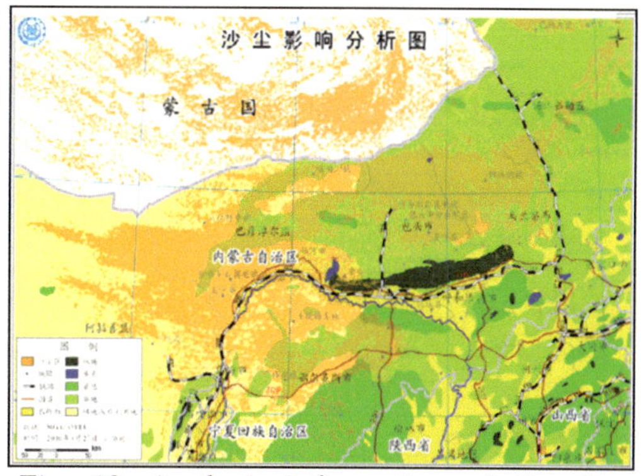

Fig. 10. Analysis information of the dust distribution and impact

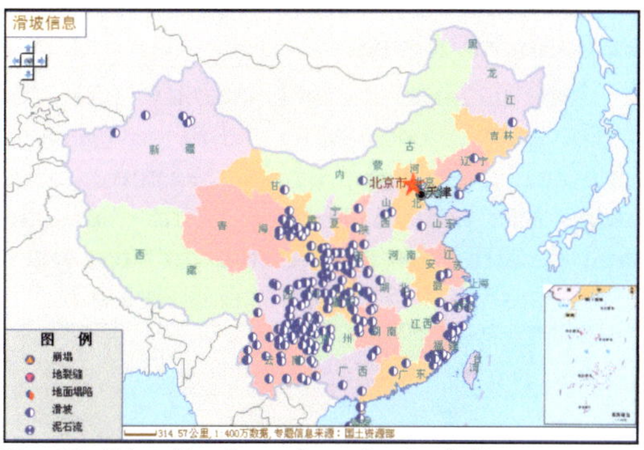

Fig. 11. Distribution of geological disasters and statistical information

Fig. 12. Hailstorm disaster information

(2) Information service subsystem of the western region development

It provides the management information of western region's economic development strategy, including the latest reports of the western development strategy and planning which are published by relevant national authorities each year, the basic information with a large number of national information about western region and the comparison of Middle, East, West, as well as the condition of western infrastructure and key projects. The system can connect with the related application system of western provinces to integrate services. As shown in Figure 13.

(3) Economic development and analysis subsystem

Through the function integration of GIS and DSS, it provides economic statistics about the world and China's economic development trend and the latest research and statistical analysis results of national and international authorities. This subsystem includes: the world economy, international trade, international investment, regional integration arrangements, the main indicators of China's economy, the main indicators of the world economy. As shown in Figure 14.

Fig.13 Distribution information of the surface morphology

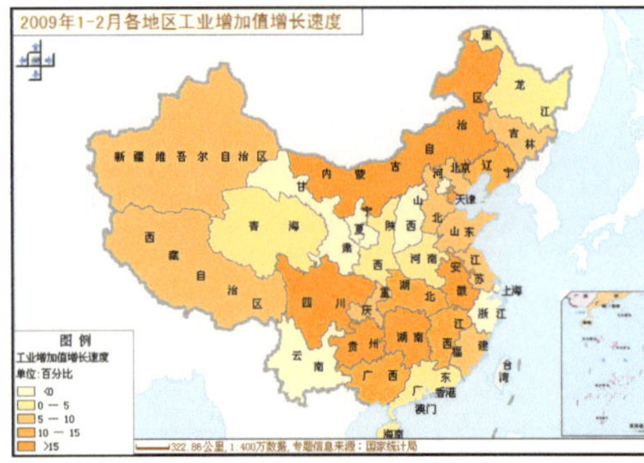

Fig.14 Economic development and statistical information

(4) National resources and environmental monitoring subsystem

China is a drought, water shortage and desertification-affected country and the development trend is more and more serious. The sub-system mainly makes government departments get the monitor and analyze information timely and provides decision-making support. It contains two topics on desertification and water resources. It integrates the monitoring and analysis information of national desertification since 2002 and the water resources of Beijing and its surrounding since 1999. As shown in Figure 15 and Figure 16.

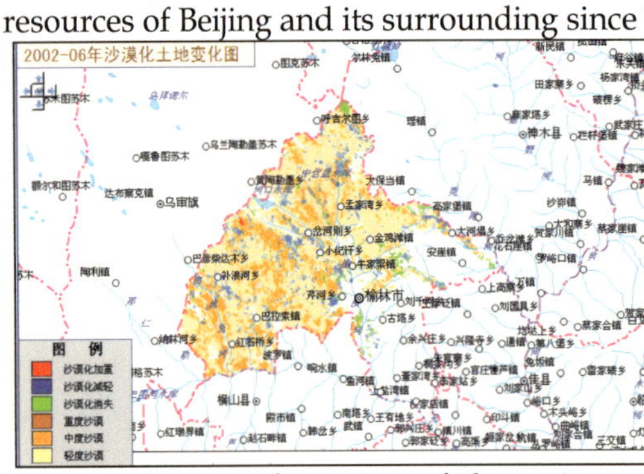

Fig. 15. Change information of desert in Yulin City, 2002-06

Fig. 16. Dynamic monitoring information on Miyun Reservoir

(5) Urban development and comparison subsystem on 30 years of reform and opening-up

Making Multi-spectral remote sensing data of "Beijing-1" satellite as the data source, combining with 70's US Land Satellite MSS data, it monitors the central built-up area expansion of 131 cities (including Lhasa) on China's mainland whose population is over 500,000. Combining with general classification system of national land use and using uniform standards and technical processes, it carries out research of resources and environment monitoring. As shown in Figure 17, Figure 18.

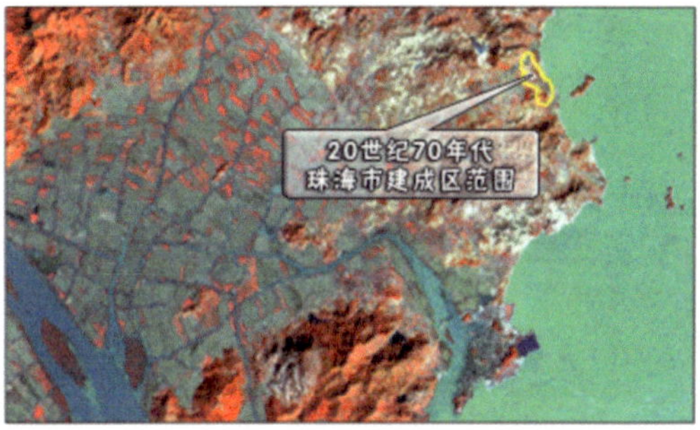

Fig. 17. Urban area of Zhuhai in 70's of the 20th Century

Fig. 18. Urban area of Zhuhai in 2007

(6) Major disaster service subsystem

The system integrates statistical analysis information and images of disaster of the Wenchuan earthquake and freezing disaster early in 2008 in more details, including the geographical location of the earthquake disaster, disaster information, as well as statistics and analysis of economic losses in disasters regional. It contains two topics: Wenchuan earthquake disaster and freezing disaster. As shown in Figure 19, Figure 20.

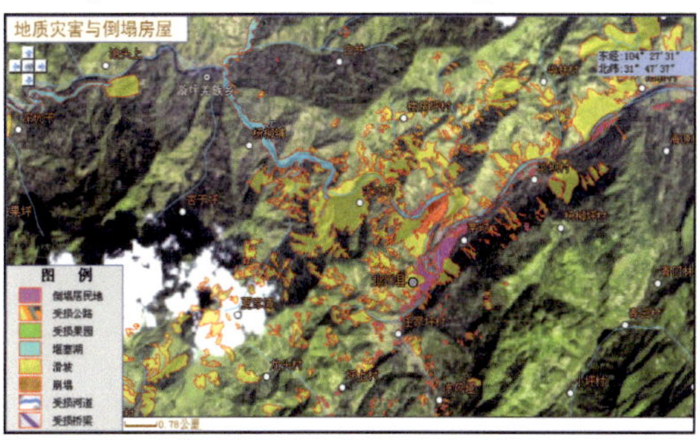

Fig.19 Distribution and statistics information of Wenchuan Earthquake

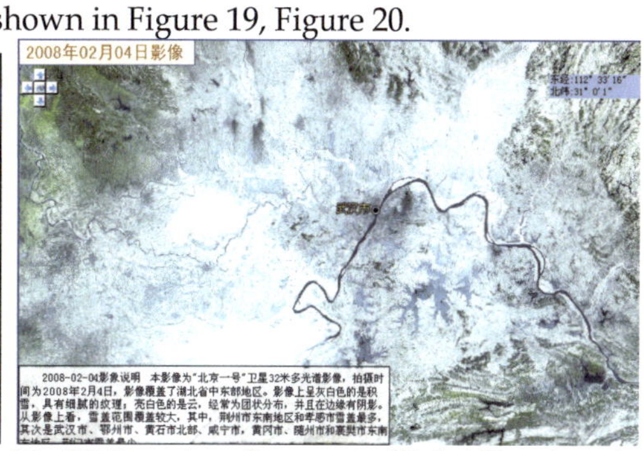

Fig.20 Freezing disaster in Hubei Province in 2008

(7) Strategic resource subsystem

It mainly provides the statistical and analytical information of the strategic resources from domestic and international authority, such as geographical distribution, supply and demand, production of the world's energy, forest resource and important mineral resource. As shown in figure 21.

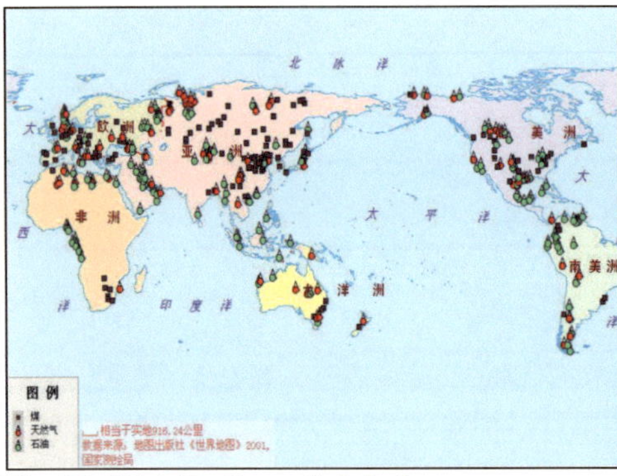

Fig. 21. Distribution of global energy

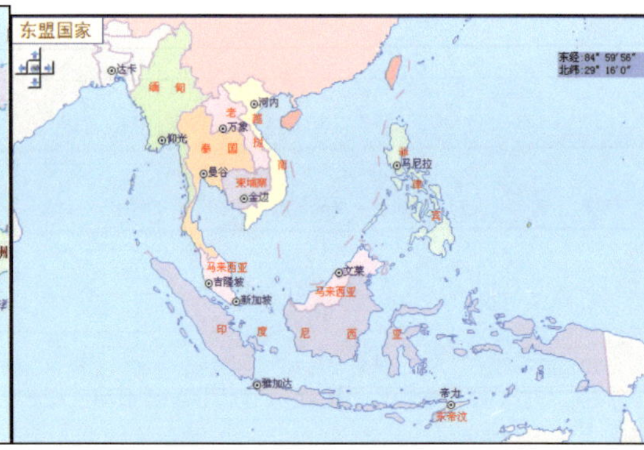

Fig. 22. Distribution of ASEAN countries

(8) Integration arrangements subsystem

It mainly provides the information of regional economic cooperation and economic globalization. It focuses on the basic situation, run profiles, macro-policy options and statistics and analysis of economic and trade. They involve China-ASEAN Free Trade Area, Association of Southeast Asian Nations, the European Union, North American Free Trade Area. As shown in Figure 22.

(9) China electronic map subsystem

The system is mainly to facilitate the function of "mobile office" for leaders. According to affiliation of the national administrative divisions, it combines the basic geo-spatial data and attribute information to provide the latest national information of the county administrative. The national electronic map is multi-scales, rich and powerful. As shown in Figure 23.

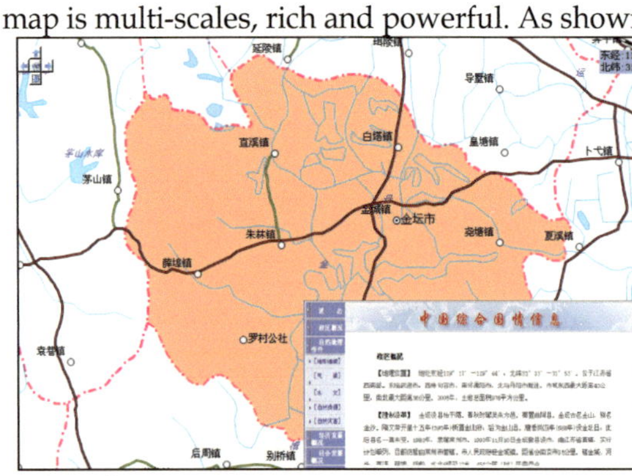

Fig. 23. The basic information of a county

4.4.2 Application systems of the provincial government agencies

In addition to the central departments, the application of spatial aided decision-making system also set Chongqing, Guizhou, Gansu, Yunnan, Henan, Xinjiang, and other provincial government departments as models, which are being widely used and founded corresponding application systems. As described below.

Chongqing City Economic and Social Development Aided Decision-making System

The system integrates population database, corporation database and basic spatial database to establish the Chongqing Municipality level of urbanization evaluation model. And by using government network and software platform provided by e-government spatial aided decision-making demonstration projects, it builds e-government spatial aided decision-making system, which consists of spatial data center, attribute data center and government information and resources service platform. It forms the working mechanism of coordinate services. As shown in Figure 24.

Guizhou Province Resource and Environment Application System

It builts the resources and environment database, which integrates provincial and county levels basic geographic data and resources, ecology, environmental data. And it establishes Zunyi County and Guizhou Province resources and environment information systems to provide information services for leader. It integrates many results of Land and Resources Office about land, resources, environment, ecology and accomplishes the information integration of the resources, ecology, environment. As shown in figure 25.

Gansu Province Returning Farmland to Forest and Grassland Application System

The system is established based on Zhuanglang County as an experimental unit according to the demands of 'detailed to the village to monitor the land, corresponds to the farmers'. Remote sensing monitoring images contrast in the latest and before returning can be made to monitor the effectiveness of farmland in the interior departments to complete check and acceptance work in the manner of combining with the traditional method. As shown in Figure 26.

Yunnan - ASEAN Free Trade Area Application System

The system has finished the construction work of macro-scale geo-spatial data framework in Yunnan Province and ASEAN. This system can integrate social, economic information resources based on B/S structure and reflect the geographical distribution of ASEAN countries, Yunnan's regional advantages in China-ASEAN Free Trade Area as well as construction information of international channels to connect Southeast Asia. As shown in Figure 27.

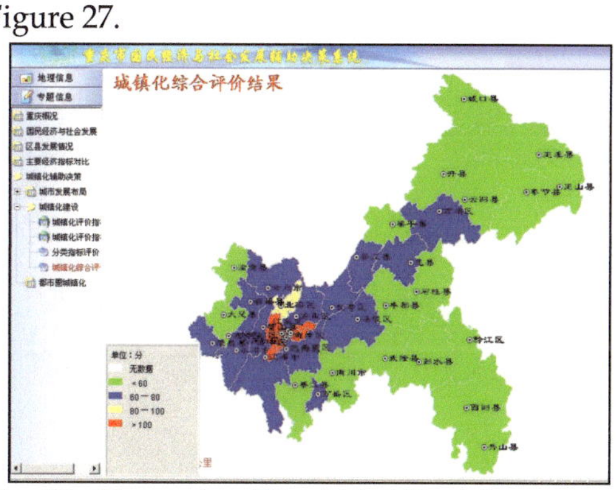

Fig. 24. Chongqing City Aided Decision-making Application System

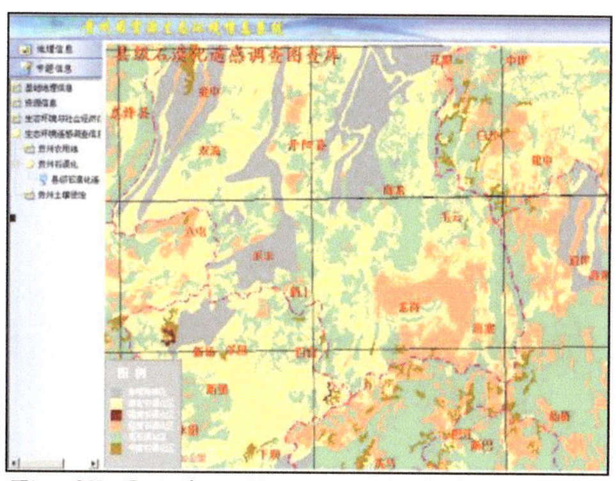

Fig. 25. Guizhou Province Aided Decision-making Application

Fig. 26. Yunnan Province Aided Decision-making Application System

Fig. 27. Gansu Province Aided Decision-making Application System

(5) Spatial Information Service System of Xinjiang E-Government

The system builds the three-level topics architecture and database of autonomous regions, autonomous prefectures (regions, cities), counties (cities). And it establishes thematic information of national economic development, tourism, mining, transportation and so on. It reflects the development of the autonomous region and provides decision-making information for the leaders. As shown in figure 28.

(6) Spatial Information Service System of Henan E-Government

On the basis of "Central China city groups", it can load and integrate e-government information of different industries and sectors in e-government aided decision-making platform. The system can provide information, such as province's economic, social development and urbanization development, to provide aided decision-making for related departments. As shown in Figure 29.

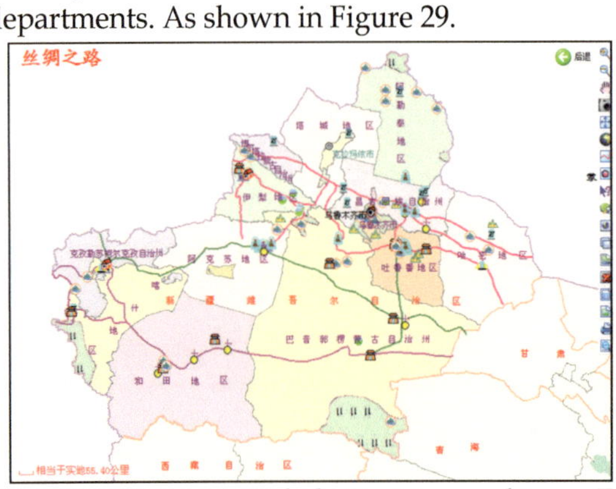

Fig. 28. Xinjiang Aided Decision-making Application System

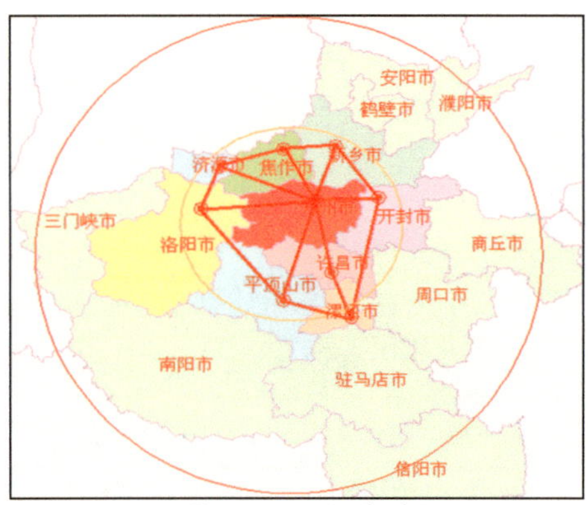

Fig. 29. Henan Province Aided Decision-making Application System

4.5 Development trends of application

With the rapid development of modern science and technology, GIS and DSS technology are being improved continuously. At the same time, with a series of e-government approach, regulations and policies being put forward, applications of e-government spatial aided decision-making system have new trends under the new situation.

(1) The end-user of e-government spatial aided decision-making system should not be limited to government departments. Information resources with no secret or being relatively low can open to the public after taking some safety measures.

(2) E-government spatial aided decision-making system becomes more and more demand-driven, application-oriented and data-centric.

(3) E-government spatial aided decision-making system takes more and more characteristics of human nature and makes the public as the core.

5. References

Guo Zhendan. (2007). Humanity t is the essence of e-governmen.http://www.chinabyte .com

Liu Yankai. (2004). Relying on GIS to achieve the integration of basic data, Informatization Construction

Liu Jiping. (2005). Application of spatial information technology in management and decision-making of government agencies. E-government spatial aided decision-making system report

Liu Jiping. etc. (2005). Study and Application of Comprehensive Data management for Spatial Decision-Making for E-government, Science of Surveying and Mapping, Beijing China

Li Bin, etc. (2005). Analysis and applications of e-government spatial aided decision-making system based on GIS and DSS. Geomatics World

Li Bin, etc. (2006). The practice of disaster management system based on GIS and RS. Survey and Mapping Sciences

Wang Liang, etc. (2005). Design and Development of Software Platform of Spatial Aided Decision-Making Based on GIS and DSS. Science of Surveying and Mapping, Beijing China

Wang Liang. (2008). GIS as a management tool for government. Computer World

Zhang Qingpu, Liu Jiping. (2003). Government Geographic Information System, Science Publisher, Beijing China

Evaluating Local E-Government: A Comparative Study of Greek Prefecture Websites

Prodromos Yannas and Georgios Lappas
Technological Educational Institution of Western Macedonia
Greece

1. Introduction

This chapter explores the use of the internet by Greek local government. Prefectures may use the internet for delivering services to citizens efficiently. A four-stage evaluation scheme is developed to investigate the quality and sophistication of prefecture websites. The study adopts a comparative focus enabling us to analyze prefecture websites before and after the 2006 local elections and to draw conclusions on the sophistication and the upgrading of websites regarding information provision, interactivity, transactions, and citizen-oriented services.

Compared to politics at a national scale, politics at the local level is much closer to the concerns and lives of citizens. Issues are more linked to the everyday lives of citizens (ie., environment, sanitation, traffic congestion, local development projects, etc) and the use of information and communication technologies (ICTs) transforms the interface of local politicians and officials with citizens by rendering local administration more efficient and local politicians more accountable to citizens' concerns and demands. Local government in Greece is comprised of two levels. The first level consists of municipalities (cities and smaller village communities) and the second deals with prefectures. In performing their local administration duties, elected mayors and prefects are assisted by elected representatives that make up the municipal and prefectural councils as well as the staff comprising the local bureaucracy.

Following the 'Capodistrias Reform Program' and the enactment of Law 2539/1998 aimed at municipal amalgamations, there exist currently in Greece 51 prefectures, 900 municipalities and 133 village communities. In the case of prefectures, the prefecture of Attica is further split into four prefecture units of Athens, Piraeus, Western Attica and Eastern Attica. Greek policy makers have been talking for some time for a further major reduction of the total number of prefectures from 54 to 16-18.

E-government has made very few inroads in Greek local government. There are at least three major reasons for the slow-pace embracement of the ICTs by local government in Greece. First, internet penetration in Greece throughout the first decade of 2000 is maintained at low levels, whereas in 2002 households with internet access were close 18% (Flash Eurobarometer, 2002) the figure rose only by 4% to 22% in 2008 (Special Eurobarometer, 2008). The Greek figures lag considerably behind the 2002 average of 43%

(Flash Eurobarometer, 2002) for the 15 EU-member-states as well as the 2008 average of 49% for the 27 EU member-states (Special Eurobarometer, 2008). Additional support for the low internet penetration in Greece is provided by United Nations (UN) data. In UN reports related to E-government rankings Greece falls from 35th place in 2005 (UNPAN, 2005) to 44th place in 2008 (UNPAN, 2008) on the global e-government readiness index.

This low level of internet penetration maybe related to the expensive rates internet providers charge for connecting households to the world wide web. Second, Greek prefectures are not autonomous from central government and they are financially dependent on transfers from the Greek state. It is estimated that local governments of the United Kingdom, the Netherlands and Greece are the most dependent and those of France, Denmark and Sweden the least dependent on financial transfers from central governments (Lalenis, 2003). The economic dependence is coupled by the partisan dependence of local leaders on political parties for electoral nomination and continuous support. Third, people residing in local communities all over Greece, with the exception of the metropolitan cities in greater Athens and Thessaloniki areas, prefer to engage in face-to-face communication with their elected representatives rather than interact over the internet.

This last observation is corroborated by previous studies of Greek e-political campaigning at both the national and local levels which demonstrate that a) according to Pippa Norris' classification of campaigns into pre-modern, modern and post-modern (Norris 2000: 137-179) campaign communication in the Greek periphery resembles characteristics of pre-modern campaigns with an emphasis on interpersonal communication whereas political campaigns in Athens and Thessaloniki exhibit definite modern traits (Doulkeri and Panagiotou, 2005); b) interpersonal candidate-voters relationships figure prominently in local press coverage of electoral contests (Demertzis and Armenakis, 2002: 220); and c) the web is more widespread, probably due to population size and time constraints, as a political marketing tool among politicians in metropolitan areas than those in the periphery of Greece (Yannas and Lappas, 2005: 39-40).

In this chapter a four stage scheme for evaluating local government websites is proposed and an attempt is made to assess the performance of Greek prefecture websites against this scheme. Prefecture websites are evaluated in two different periods separated by the 2006 local elections. Local elections can be considered as a watershed event, offering us a comparative lens for discerning continuities and patterns in the performance of Greek prefecture websites.

2. E-Government Sophistication Levels

E-government aims at the administrative coordination of government units for more efficient and less costly provision of services to clients. According to the Danish Ministry of Finance, "e-government is the use of ICT to improve and make the handling of public management tasks more efficient for the benefit of citizens, companies and the public sector" (Torpe, 2003). Proponents of e-government adopt a one-way managerial discourse geared to improving government performance with citizens taking a backstage role.

Government organizations go through stages in delivering services to citizens. The stages an organization goes through usually begins from a simple informational website and reaches the climax of using the web as an important medium to offer services to citizens and internal services to various levels of employees and departments and other groups related to the organization. The e-government dimension of an institution is usually implemented gradually. Public demand, cost reduction, familiarization with the medium or organizational strategic plans can be driving forces for going through the stages.

A number of e-Government models, ranging from three to six stages, have been proposed in the literature (Irani, et al 2006). All models start with an informational stage and having a number of different intermediate stages end to a final stage. Most models seem to have in common the four stages of (Chandler & Emanuels, 2002) amounting to information provision, interaction, transaction and integration.

The first stage referred to as information stage (Chandler & Emanuels, 2002) or publishing stage (Howard, 2001) or emerging stage (United Nations, 2002), describes the online presence of an organization enabling one-way government to-citizen communication without enabling interaction with the public.

The second stage, a step up from the first, includes the feature of interactivity in the government agency to citizen relationship (G2C).

The third stage called the transaction stage incorporates various levels of complete and secure transactions between government agents and citizens.

The final stage referred to as integration stage (Chandler & Emanuels, 2002), or horizontal integration (Layne & Lee, 2001), or otherwise known as fully integrated stage (United Nations, 2002), is related to the highest level of integration of government services from a single point, which usually requires transformation of the organization.

The integration of government services provides internal services across administrative and departmental lines and provides for the security of all personal data. The transformation of the organization also involves training employees to get familiarized with the integration of the government electronic services and hiring or assigning more employees to support the services and become familiar with computer technology. It should, however, be mentioned that there exist no clear lines demarcating the stages, rendering the task of identifying the stage at which an organization is operating rather difficult. It is expected that as the sophistication of the site and the required technology increases, there is a corresponding increase in the benefits that accrue to citizens from service provision.

3. A Proposed E-Government Evaluation Scheme

The evaluation of prefecture websites follows the four-stage model of Chandler & Emanuels (2002). Our study goes a step further by proposing an evaluation scheme to accompany the four-stage model. The evaluation scheme is composed of 11 overall sub-stages and 154 overall indices. It uses a weighted ranking scheme totaling 1000 points with each stage assigned 250 points as maximum score. Each sub-stage is evaluated according to criteria that best describe the stage category, with the accompanied scores being assigned in parenthesis (see Appendix A).

In Stage I (Information Provision Stage), the prefecture decides to go online and provides information to site visitors. The information is directed from the local government to citizens and is similar to a brochure or a leaflet. The stage is subdivided into 5 sub-stages that follow a marketing plan procedure. Beginning with the query whether the site can be easily located, the evaluation scheme proceeds to examine users' perceptions regarding the attractiveness of the site, the ease of navigation, the richness of content, and the frequency of providing new information as an inducement for revisiting the site.

In Stage II (Interaction Stage), the prefecture incorporates various forms of interaction with citizens, (i.e. email, newsletters, forums etc.). The stage is subdivided into four sub-stages indicating the type of interaction: passive government to citizen (G2C) and citizen to government interaction (C2G), as well as real time G2C and C2G interactions.
In Stage III (Transaction Stage), the prefecture offers citizens the service to perform a number of transactions online, such as requesting documents, accessing payments, downloading official documents or programs etc.
In Stage IV (Integration Stage), the prefecture undergoes through a transformation at the organizational level to maximize citizen satisfaction. The transformation is reflected in the way the web is used by officials and employees to carry out functional duties. A website will have attained the transformation stage if different levels of access are assigned to different groups of people and if menu and content categories are suited to the interests of different groups of people (employees, citizens, tourists, members of the prefecture council, other governmental officials, authorities, etc). Web site personalization to meet citizen preferences is also included at this stage. Therefore this stage is subdivided into two sub-stages: Prefecture Transformation and Site Personalization.

4. Application of the E-Government Evaluation Scheme to Greek Local Government

To demonstrate the relevance and value of the proposed e-government evaluation scheme a quantitative content analysis of the 54 Greek Prefectures was carried out in two different periods separated by the local elections of 2006: a) the period March to October 2006, and b) the period October to December 2008. The local 2006 elections were considered an important point of reference leading us to expect that new administrations would embark upon fresh initiatives in a number of areas including improved e-government performances. Prefecture website addresses were drawn from the listings of the websites of the Greek Ministry of the Interior (www.ypes.gr) and the Association of the Greek Prefectures (www.enae.gr). The sample for the first period numbered 48 prefectures with active websites, whereas the sample of the second period consisted of all 54 prefectures. A coding form was developed specifically suited to conform to the four stages e-government scheme. Previous e-government studies (Stowers, 2002; UNPAN, 2005; Zhang, 2005) were used as a basis for developing the coding form of Appendix A.
Pre-testing of the coding scheme was undertaken in a study conducted during the period June to July 2005 (Yannas & Lappas, 2006). To assure validity of the coding scheme three trained coders reached agreement on the overall structure and content of the coding form.
Table 1 lists the top prefectures across the various stage and sub-stage categories. None of the top prefectures in 2006 maintained the leading position in a category after two years. A quick look at Table 1 demonstrates that there is a great deal of fluctuation among prefectures in capturing leadership positions. Regarding period 2006, the prefecture of Kozani appears four times in the list of top prefectures, followed by Thessaloniki, Evia and Viotia that appear three times, while several prefectures appear only one time. The four times that Kozani appeared on the top prefecture lists in 2006 coupled with the fact that it topples the list in indices of more sophisticated stages make this prefecture the most comprehensive and sophisticated of all Greek prefectures in the use of ICTs for 2006. The drop out of Kozani from leadership positions in 2008, is more likely to be attributed to

changes in leadership positions as a result of the 2006 elections. In period 2008 the prefecture of Kastoria appears three times as one of the top prefectures, followed by the prefectures of Chania, Corfu, Lasithi, Serres and Western Attika, each appearing two times as top prefectures. As there was no leadership change in administration due to 2006 election in Thessaloniki and Kastoria, it is evident that the dropping of Thessaloniki from leadership positions of 2008 and the ascendancy of Kastoria among the top prefectures in 2008 was due to policy changes.

Stages	Sub-stage	Best Prefecture 2006	Best Prefecture 2008
Stage I	Site Locating	25 Prefectures	31 Prefectures
Stage I	Attractiveness	Drama	Pellas, Fokida
Stage I	Navigability	Thessaloniki, Leykada	Kefallinia
Stage I	Content	Magnesia	Western Attica
Stage I	Update Frequency	Thessaloniki	Chania, Corfu
Stage I	*Overall Performance*	*Thessaloniki*	*Western Attica*
Stage II	Passive G2C	Thessaloniki, Viotia, Xanthi	Kastoria, Corfu
Stage II	Passive C2G	Viotia, Evia	Kastoria, Chania
Stage II	Real Time G2C	Kozani, Serres	Evia, Heraklion
Stage II	Real Time C2G	Kozani Corfu, Evia	4 Prefectures
Stage II	*Overall Performance*	*Viotia*	*Kastoria*
Stage III	*Online Transactions*	*17 Prefectures*	*Kozani, Lasithi, Serres*
Stage IV	*Overall Performance*	*Kozani, Evia*	*Lasithi*
All Stages	*Total Performance*	*Kozani*	*Serres*

Table 1. List of the top prefectures at the two periods under examination.

From an e-government perspective the average performance of Greek prefectures and the best scores are presented in Table 2. The data of the first period (before the elections of 2006) reveal that the average performance scores of Greek prefectures, as recorded in our evaluation scheme, are: 120.4 (48.2%) in information provision; 36.3 (14.5%) in interactivity; 17.7 (7.1%) in online transactions; 24.4 (9.8%) in integration stage; and finally 198.8 (19.9%) for overall. Clearly prefectures at that period performed satisfactorily only in the first stage, using the internet more as an information provision portal to citizens than a service facility. A closer look at the 84 indices that makeup the content category indicates that prefecture websites adopt a promotional-commercial character of information. Prefectures seem not to differentiate between offering "services to citizen" and "Tourist Information Provision" as both indices are close to 50%. Citizen engagement seem to be a low priority category for prefectures as the average performance scores regarding transparency in decision-making are considerably low 1.8 (9%).

The data of the second period (two years following the elections of 2006) reveal that the average performance scores of Greek prefectures, as recorded in our evaluation scheme, are: 130.5 (52.2%) in information provision; 39.9 (15.9%) in interactivity; 28.7 (11.5%) in online transactions; and 20.9 (8.4%) in integration stage; and finally 220 (22%) for overall. A common finding for both periods is that the majority of prefectures engage in e-government services that are limited to information provision only. The second period is much alike the previous period. However, the second period registers a marked improvement over the first on the following:

a) A clear increase in the final best score of prefectures from 2006 (383) to 2008 (506). However this has not been followed by a similar increase in the final averages as the figures

198.3 and 220 are close enough. The prefectures of Serres and Lasithi , which have attained a best score of 506 and 425 respectively have over a two year time made genuine efforts to achieve high e-government performance. Their websites have sophisticated features and both offer comprehensive e-services to citizens;
b) The increase in the average performance of prefectures from 17.7 in 2006 to 28.7 in 2008 concerning the transaction stage demonstrates the willingness of prefectures to offer quality e-services to citizens;
c) A limited progress in interactivity is documented by a look at two indices: i) the best score in the overall performance of interactivity (from 88 to 100) and ii) the small increase of the average prefecture score in the overall performance in interactivity (from 36.3 to 39.9). This finding may indicate a policy direction of prefectures to start engaging more in interactive services;
d) The rise in the score of the sub-content category "transparency in decision making" from 1.8 (9%) in 2006 to 4.6 (23%) in 2008 indicates willingness on the part of prefectures to experiment with e-democracy characteristics in their websites.

Stages	Sub-stage	No of Variables	Max Score	Best Score 2006	Best Score 2008	Average Score 2006 N=48	Average Score 2008 N=54
Stage I	Site Locating	2	30	30	30	26.0	26.6
Stage I	Attractiveness	17	28	24	22	14.3	13.9
Stage I	Navigability	10	30	30	30	17.9	20.7
Stage I	Content	84	130	94	96	49.9	55.4
Stage I	Update Frequency	8	32	28	24	11.9	13.9
Stage I	*Overall Performance*	*120*	*250*	*180*	*172*	*120*	*130.5*
Stage II	Passive G2C	7	60	48	60	27.7	27.9
Stage II	Passive C2G	7	70	40	40	6.9	10.0
Stage II	Real Time G2C	5	60	12	12	0.5	0.4
Stage II	Real Time C2G	3	60	20	20	1.3	1.5
Stage II	*Overall Performance*	*12*	*250*	*88*	*100*	*36.3*	*39.9*
Stage III	*Online Transactions*	*5*	*250*	*50*	*200*	*17.7*	*28.7*
Stage IV	*Overall Performance*	*7*	*250*	*120*	*90*	*24.4*	*20.9*
Total	All Stages	155	1000	383	506	198.3	220

Table 2. Evaluation of Greek Prefectures

Figure 1 depicts schematically the comparison between the two periods along the four stages and the overall performance. A figure of this kind may be used to accommodate longitudinal and cross-national comparisons. We could envisage in the future a figure depicting the performances of many local government entities from many countries facilitating in this way the purpose of a cross-national comparison regarding local e-government.
The findings from the first to the second period follow the national trend in internet household penetration (Flash Eurobarometer, 2002; Special Eurobarometer, 2008) and the national e-government readiness indices of UN studies (UNPAN, 2005; UNPAN, 2008). This observation did not confirm our initial expectation that changes due to elections would result within a two year time frame in improved e-government performance.

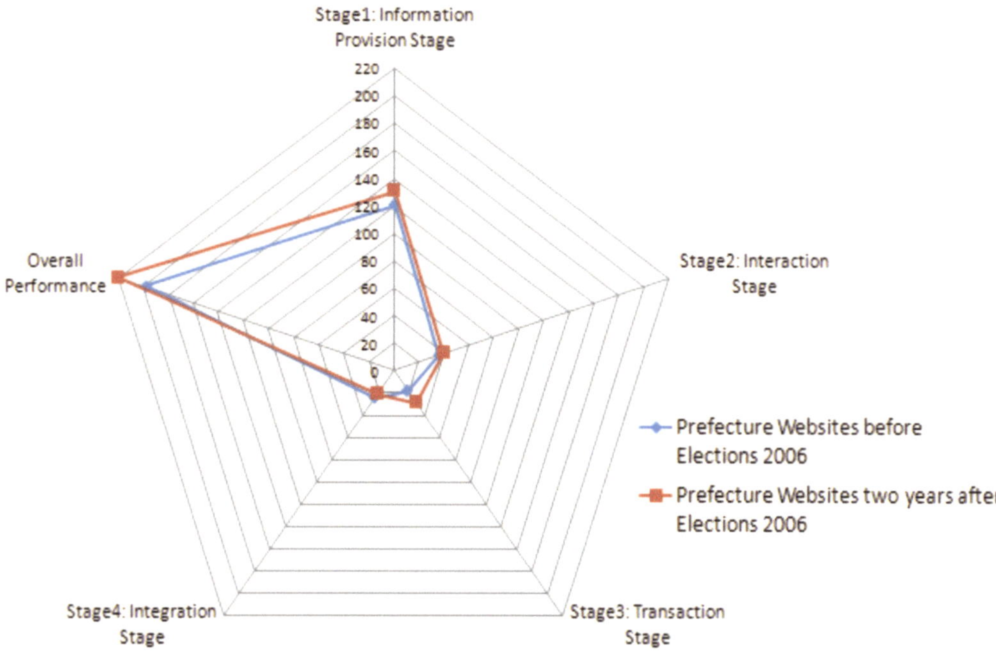

Fig. 1. Comparison of Prefecture Websites before and after 2006 elections.

5. Conclusion

This chapter is a comparative study of e-government provision by local Greek administration over two periods of time. A new evaluation scheme is proposed to identify various levels of e-government services. The novelty of the evaluation scheme lies with its comprehensiveness given that 154 indices are recorded. The findings of this work clearly demonstrate that the internet has not taken root among local government authorities. A number of prefectures are engaged with e-government features in an attempt to supply basic information to residents and tourism-relevant information to visitors. The fact that prefectures on average fulfilled only 48% of the maximum score they could potentially achieve (120 out of 250) for 2006 and 52% (130 out of 250) for 2008, indicates that most of the prefectures still have a long way to go in information provision. The picture appears to be bleaker in indices that measure stages II to IV. However, some prefectures (Serres, Lasithi) seem to be experimenting with more sophisticated e-government services.

Between the two periods under examination there is a noticeable trend among prefectures to experiment more in the transaction stage offering e-services to citizens. Surely, the fact that some prefectures are willing in the second period to experiment with more interactive and e-democracy features is an encouraging sign.

Our proposed scheme contributes toward the ongoing discussion for the development of a worldwide evaluation scheme that would measure the quality and sophistication of e-government websites. It would be interesting to compare the local Greek e-government performance with that of other countries using the same evaluation scheme. Such a comparison would not only provide a better picture of the Greek e-government landscape in local administration but would also validate the proposed scheme cross-nationally.

6. References

Chandler, S. & Emanuels, S. (2002). Transformation Not Automation, Proceedings of 2nd European Conference on E-Government, pp. 91-102, Oxford, UK, 2002.

Demertzis, N. & Armenakis, A. (2002). The Parliamentary Elections of 1996 and 2000 in the Greek Local Press, In Political Communication in Greece, Demertzis, N. (Ed.), pp. 211-232, Papazzisis Publishers, Athens

Doulkeri, T. & Panagiotou, N. (2005). Political Advertising in Greek Municipal and Prefecture Elections of 2002: The Cases of Thessaloniki and Kastoria. Journal of Political Marketing, 4 (1), pp. 17-31.

Flash Eurobarometer (2002). Internet and the Public at Large, No 135, November 2002.

Howard, M. (2001). E-Government Across the Globe: How Will 'e' Change Government. Government Finance Review, 17 (4), pp. 6-9.

Irani, Z.; Al-Sebie, M. & Elliman, T. (2006). Transaction Stage of e-Government Systems: Identification of its Location & Importance, Proceedings of the 39th Hawaii International Conference on System Sciences, Hawai, USA.

Lalenis K. (2003). The Evolution of Local Administration in Greece: How Using Transplants from France became a Historical Tradition, University of Thessaly Discussion Paper Series, vol. 9(14), pp. 293-312.

Layne, K. & Lee, J. (2001). Developing Fully Functional E-government: A Four Stage Model. Government Information Quarterly, vol. 18, pp. 122-136.

Norris P (2000). A Virtuous Circle: Political Communications in Postindustrial Societies, Cambridge University Press, Cambridge.

Stowers, G.N. L.(2002). The State of Federal Websites: The Pursuit of Excellence, Arlington, The PricewaterhouseCoopers Endowment for the Business of Government, VA.

Special Eurobarometer (2008). E-Communication Household Survey, Report 293, European Union.

Torpe, L. (2003). The Internet and Local Communities, Copenhagen, Denmark: Center for Media and Democracy in the Network Society, Available at http://www.hum.ku.dk/modinet/ [accessed May 13, 2004]

United Nations (2002). Benchmarking E-Government: A Global Perspective, Available at http://pti.nw.dc.us/links/docs/ASPA_UN_egov_ survey.pdf [accessed March 14, 2006]

UNPAN (2005). UN Global E-Government Readiness Report 2005: From E-Government to E-Inclusion. United Nations, New York.

UNPAN (2008). UN E-Government Survey 2008: From E-Government to Connected Governance, United Nations, New York.

Yannas, P. & Lappas, G. (2005). Web Campaign in the 2002 Greek Municipal Elections. Journal of Political Marketing, 4 (1), pp. 33-50.

Yannas, P. & Lappas, G. (2006). E-Government and E-Democracy in Local Greek Government, Paper presented at 3rd Int. Political Marketing Conference, April 2006, Nicosia, Cyprus.

Zhang, L.(2005). Good Governance Through E-Governance? Assessing China's E-Government Strategy. Journal of E-Government, vol. 2(4), pp. 39-71.

APPENDIX A

Stage	Sub Category	Evaluation Indices
I-a Site Locating		Prefecture's name figures in the top-10 listings of Google search engine (15); Friendly, easy to figure out URL, like www.prefecture-name-or-abbreviation-name.country-initials. (15)
I-b Attractive ness		Dynamic media are portrayed in Introductory video before entering main page (2); video files (2); speech files (2); music in the site (2); animating text (2); animating graphics (2); photos (2); cliparts (2); banners (2); avoiding annoying pop-up advertisements (2); and 3d simulation (2) like a panoramic view of the area by using mouse clicks. The characteristics of design sophistication are portrayed in layout consistency (1), proper use of italics (1), proper use of bold (1), proper background (1), the use of no more than three main colors (1), proper editorial appearance (1) avoiding classes between colors, letters etc.
I-c Navigabili ty		Site maps (3); Return at home page option (3); No dead links or no "under construction pages" (3); Tags and labeling hypertexts (3); Labeling hypermedia and avoiding using hyperlinks in graphics that usually are missed by users (3); Appropriate number of lines that allows minimum page scroll (3); Search this site feature (3); Fast download (3); Recognizable new sections (3); Proper names in the various menus (3).
I-d Content	Services to Prefecture Citizens	Access to Official Documents (4) , Job Announcements (4), Staff Members (4), Contact Information for Staff Members (4), Organization Departments (4), Required Application Documents (4), Information for Citizen Service Centers (4).
I-d Content	Transpare ncy in Decision Making	Dates of the Next Council Meeting (4), Agenda of the Next Council Meeting (4), Invitation to the Council Meetings (4), Council Decisions (4), Archives of Previous Council Decisions (4)
I-d Content	Services to Tourists	Transportation to reach us (1); Transportation Schedules for reaching us (1), Sightseeing's (1), Museums (1), Operating Hours (1), How to reach various places (1); Interactive Map of Interesting Places (1); Map of the Area (1); Accommodation (1); Restaurants and Food Services(1); Entertainment (1); Local Events (1); Local Products (1); Local Transportation (1); Activities around the area (1).
I-d Content	Prefecture Achieveme nts	Description of the Action Plan (projects) used in Election Campaign (2); Completed Projects so far (2); Technical and Financial Details of Projects (2); Photos from completed

		Projects Action Plan (2); Multimedia usage for promoting projects (2); Description of next projects (2); current state of projects (2); Financial Information of New Projects (2); Call for Project Participation (2); Project Reports (2)
I-d Content	Leader Information	Leader CV (1); Details of Studies (1); Political Achievements (1); Professional Achievements (1); Achievements in Prefecture (1); Family Details (1); Personal Photo (1); Political Photos (1); Professional Photos (1); Family Photos (1); Photos of action plan (1); Photos from Local Events (1); Multimedia Usage for promoting the leader (1);
I-d Content	Members of the Council	List of names (1); Duties of Members (1); Photos of members (1); Members CV's (1); Multimedia usage for promoting members (1); Contact details of Members (1)
I-d Content	Promotion of Prefecture Area	Sightseeing Photos (1); Museum Photos(1); Local Events Photos(1); Local Products Photos (1); Multimedia usage for Sightseeing's (1); Multimedia usage for Museums (1); Multimedia usage for Local Events (1); Multimedia usage for Local Products (1); Weather Forecast (1)
I-d Content	Local Enterprises, NGO's etc	Prefecture and Municipality Organizations (1); Local Public Agencies (1); Local Professional Organizations and Associations (1); Local Cultural Organizations (1); Local Athletic Organization and Clubs (1); Local Business Enterprises (1); Local Media (1)
I-d Content	Links to Local Enterprises, NGO's etc	Link to Prefecture and Municipality Organizations (1); Link to Local Public Agencies (1); Link to Local Professional Organizations and Associations (1); Link to Local Cultural Organizations (1); Link to Local Athletic Organization and Clubs (1); Link to Local Business Enterprises (1); Link to Local Media (1)
I-d Content	Other Information etc	Calendar (1); Anniversaries (1); Change Language (1); Local Elections (1); Other(1)
I-d Update Frequency		Date Updated (4); Press Releases (4); Archives of Press Releases (4); Content Update (daily 4, weekly 2, monthly 1); News (daily 4, weekly 2, monthly 1); Newsletters (Weekly 4, Monthly 3, 3-months 2, semester 1); Site Statistics (4);
II-a Passive G2C		Contact Address (4); Telephones (4); Fax Number (4); Contact Emails(12); Contact Form (12); Registration to Newsletter (12); Registration to Newsgroup (12).
II-b Passive C2G		E-polls (10); Online Surveys (10); Send your Opinion (10); Guestbook (10); Send this site/file (10); E-cards (10); Sign for E-petitions (10).
II-c Real Time G2C		Video Conferences (12); Netmeetings(12); Online Reviews and Debates (12); Online Radio (12); Online Interactive Games (12)

II-c Real Time C2G		Discussion Forums (20); Chat Rooms (20); Bi-directional Newsgroups (20)
III Transactio n Stage		Online Official Forms Completion and Submital (50); Online Access to Public Databases (50); Online Payments (50); Online Certification Requesting and Issuing (50); Download Official Documents and Programs (50)
IV-a Prefecture Integratio n		Different level of confidentiality access (40), Inter-department functional operations or traditional administrative operations appearing on the web (40); Group-oriented access menus (40);
IV-b Site Personaliz ation		Allow users to personalize the content of the site (40); Subscription services for parts of the site (40); Use of cookies/logs to segment users and expose them to site versions that suit their personal style (50)